£25·95

ENVIRONMENTAL ECONOMICS

AN INTRODUCTION

Barry C. Field

Department of Resource Economics
University of Massachusetts at Amherst

McGRAW-HILL, INC.

New York   St. Louis   San Francisco   Auckland   Bogotá   Caracas
Lisbon   London   Madrid   Mexico City   Milan   Montreal
New Delhi   San Juan   Singapore   Sydney   Tokyo   Toronto

This book was set in Palatino by ComCom, Inc.
The editors were Scott D. Stratford and Ira C. Roberts;
the production supervisor was Denise L. Puryear.
The cover was designed by Carol Couch.
R. R. Donnelley & Sons Company was printer and binder.

ENVIRONMENTAL ECONOMICS

An Introduction

This book is printed on acid-free paper.

567890 DOC/DOC 998765

ISBN 0-07-020797-6

Library of Congress Cataloging-in-Publication Data

Field, Barry C.
    Environmental economics: an introduction / Barry C. Field.
        p.   cm.
    Includes bibliographical references and index.
    ISBN 0-07-020797-6 (alk. paper)
    1. Environmental policy—Economic aspects.   2. Economic
development—Environmental aspects.   I. Title.
HC79.E5F47   1994
658.4'08—dc20   93-14507

ABOUT
THE AUTHOR

BARRY C. FIELD is Professor of Resource Economics at the University of Massachusetts in Amherst. Previously he taught at the University of Miami and The George Washington University. He received his B.S. and M.S. degrees from Cornell University, and his Ph.D. from the University of California at Berkeley.

At the University of Massachusetts he has devoted many years to teaching environmental economics to students at all levels, and has worked to develop an undergraduate major in environmental and resource economics.

Professor Field is the author of numerous articles on resource and environmental economics.

To Tory

CONTENTS

PREFACE

When our descendants look back at the last part of the twentieth century, we want them to be able to say: "That's when they began to take the degradation of the natural environment, with its threats to human life and the life of the planet, seriously." And we would like them to be able to see that around this time we took serious steps to halt and reverse this process. This book is an introduction to environmental economics, one way of approaching the steps that need to be taken. It's about the way human decisions affect the quality of the environment, how human values and institutions shape our demands for improvement in the quality of that environment, and, most especially, about how to design effective public policies to bring about these improvements.

Problems of environmental quality are not something new; in fact, history is filled with bleak examples of environmental degradation, from deforestation by ancient peoples to mountains of horse manure in urban areas in the days before automobiles. But today's world is different. For one thing, many people in economically developed countries, having reached high levels of material well-being, are beginning to ask questions: What good is great material wealth if it comes at the cost of large-scale disruptions of the ecosystem by which we are nourished? More fundamental, perhaps, is the fact that with contemporary economic, demographic, and technological developments around the world, the associated environmental repercussions are becoming much more widespread and lethal. What once were localized environmental impacts, easily rectified, have now become widespread effects that may very well turn out to be irreversible. Indeed some of our most worrisome concerns today are about global environmental impacts.

It is no wonder, then, that the quality of the natural environment has become a major focus of public concern. As we would expect, people have responded in many ways. Environmental interest groups and advocates have become vocal at every political level, especially in those countries with open political systems. Politicians have taken environmental issues into their agendas; some have sought to become environmental statespersons. Environmental law has burgeoned, becoming a specialty in many law schools. Thousands of environmental agencies have appeared in the public sector, from local conservation commissions to environmental agencies at the United Nations. At the scientific level environmental problems have become a focus for chemists, biologists, engineers, and many others. And within economics a new focus of study has appeared: *environmental economics*, the subject of this book.

Environmental economics focuses on all the different facets of the connection between environmental quality and the economic behavior of individuals and groups of people. There is the fundamental question of how the economic system shapes economic incentives in ways that lead to environmental degradation as well as improvement. There are major problems in measuring the benefits and costs of environmental quality changes, especially intangible ones. There is a set of complicated macroeconomic questions; for example, the connection between economic growth and environmental impacts and the feedback effects of environmental laws on growth. And there are the critical issues of designing environmental policies that are both effective and equitable.

The strength of environmental economics lies in the fact that it is analytical and deals with concepts like efficiency, trade-offs, costs, and benefits. Many believe strongly that the times call for more direct political action, more consciousness-raising, more political organizing, and, especially, more representation and influence of environmental interests on the political scene. Nobody can doubt this. We live in a complicated world, however, where human problems abound; domestically we have health care, drugs, education, violence, and other critical issues, all competing for attention and public resources. Throughout the world, vast numbers of people struggle to alter their political and economic institutions, develop their economies, and raise their material standards of living.

In these settings, just raising the political heat for environmental issues is necessary but not sufficient. We have to get hard scientific results on how people value environmental quality and how they are hurt when this quality is degraded. We also have to put together environmental policy initiatives that get the maximum impact for the economic and political resources spent. This is where environmental economics comes in. It is a way of examining the difficult trade-off types of questions that all environmental issues entail; it is also a valuable means of inquiring why people behave as they do toward the natural environment, and how we might restructure the current system to rectify harmful practices.

In fact, the subject is important enough to deserve to be widely available to the nonspecialist. Economics is a discipline that has developed a sophisticated body of theory and applied knowledge. Courses in economics now follow a hierarchy of introductory and intermediate-level principles that are designed to lead students along and prepare them for the more advanced applications courses. But these run the risk of closing off the subject, making it inaccessible to those who do not want to become specialists. This book is intended, instead, for people who have not necessarily had any economics courses, at least not yet. I wrote it on the assumption that it's possible to present the major principles of economics in a fairly commonsensical, though rigorous, way and then apply them to questions of environmental quality.

The first section of the book is an introduction, beginning with a chapter on what environmental economics is about, followed by one on the basic relationships between the economy and the environment. The next section is devoted to studying the "tools" of analysis, the principles of demand and cost, and the elements of economic efficiency both in market and nonmarket activities. These chapters are not meant to be completely thorough treatments of these theoretical topics. However, given the objective of the book, the introductory chapters are essential. Even those who have had a course in microeconomic principles might find them valuable for purposes of review. Section II also contains a chapter in which these economic principles are applied to a simple model of environmental pollution control. In these chapters, as well as the others, I have tried to leaven the presentation with examples taken from current sources, such as newspapers.

Section III is on environmental analysis. Here we look closely at some of the techniques that have been developed by environmental economists to answer some of the fundamental value questions that underlie environmental decision making. We focus especially on the principles of benefit–cost analysis. After this we move to Section IV, on the principles of environmental policy design. It begins with a short chapter dealing with the criteria we might use to evaluate policies, then moves on to chapters on the main approaches to environmental quality management.

Sections V and VI contain policy chapters, where we examine current developments in environmental policy with the analytical tools developed earlier. Section V is devoted to environmental policy in the U.S., covering federal policy on water, air, and toxic materials. It also contains a chapter on environmental issues at the state and local levels. Finally, the last section looks at international issues, such as environmental policy developments in other countries, global environmental issues, and the economics of international environmental agreements.

This book is an introduction to the basic principles of environmental economics as they have been developed in the past and as they continue to evolve. The real world, certainly the real world of environmental policy, is much more complicated than these principles would often seem to imply. The examples discussed represent only a sample of the full range of issues that actually exists. If and when you confront that real world of environmental politics and policy, you will find it necessary to adapt these principles to all the details and nuances of reality. Unfortunately, there is not enough space in one book to look at all the ways that environmental economists have found to make the basic concepts and models more specific and relevant to concrete environmental issues. So we stick to the basic ideas and hope they excite your interest enough to make you want to pursue the refinements and adaptations of these ideas as they relate to a subject of growing relevance and importance.

ACKNOWLEDGMENTS

This text is the result of teaching the subject for many years in the classroom, so I must first thank all those students through the years who have listened, asked questions, and provided the feedback that shaped the book. Special thanks go to Stephen Fazio for his assistance in tracking down tons of material in the library, to Bill Thompson and the staff of the government documents section of the library at the University of Massachusetts, and to the reference librarians and interlibrary loan staff who helped me locate background material. Sincere thanks also to the following economists who reviewed portions of the manuscript: Roger Bolton, Williams College; John Braden, University of Illinois; Richard Bryant, University of Missouri–Rolla; Dallas Burtraw, Resources for the Future; Donald J. Epp, Pennsylvania State University; Jeffrey Krantkraemer, Washington State University; Henry McCarl, University of Alabama–Birmingham; Lars Olson, University of California–Riverside; J. Barkley Rosser, James Madison University; and John Stranlund, University of Massachusetts–Amherst.

Very special thanks go to Darleen Slysz. Without her wizardry and diligence on the word processor, this book would never have seen the light of day. Thanks also to Eileen Keegan for the fine graphics.

I owe a special debt to Scott Stratford, Michael Fried, and Iness Snider at McGraw-Hill, who showed such enthusiasm for the book and so effectively held my hand during its completion.

Finally, enormous gratitude, and love, for Martha, for reading, giving solid advice, and keeping the spirits fresh as the book progressed.

Barry C. Field

INTRODUCTORY

This first section contains two introductory chapters. The first is a brief, nontechnical review of some of the main topics and ideas within environmental economics. In the second we develop a general view of the interactions between the economy and the environment, and introduce some fundamental concepts and definitions which we will use throughout the book.

CHAPTER 1

WHAT IS ENVIRONMENTAL ECONOMICS?

Environmental economics is the study of environmental problems with the perspective and analytical ideas of economics. You may have thought that economics is mostly about business decisions and how to make profits in a capitalist system. This is not the case. Economics is, rather, the study of how and why "people," whether they are consumers, firms, nonprofit organizations, or government agencies, make decisions about the use of valuable resources. It is divided into microeconomics, the study of the behavior of individuals or small groups, and macroeconomics, the study of the economic performance of economies as a whole. Environmental economics draws from both sides, but more from microeconomics than from macroeconomics. It focuses primarily on how and why people make decisions that have environmental consequences. And it focuses on how we can change economic institutions and policies to bring those environmental impacts more into balance with human desires and the needs of the ecosystem itself.

One of our first jobs, therefore, will be to get acquainted with some of the basic ideas and analytical tools of microeconomics. But we do not want to jump directly into the study of these principles because that would suggest we are more interested in the tools than in what we can do with them. We are not interested in these ideas for themselves, but for the understanding they can give us about why the natural environment gets degraded, what the consequences are, and what can be done effectively to reduce the degradation. So this first chapter will be devoted to sketching out, in reasonably commonsense terms, the types of questions environmental economists ask and the types of answers they seek. To do this we first consider briefly what we mean by the "economic approach," and then give a series of examples of the types of environmental problems on which economists have worked. Then in the second chapter we will take a look at the broad linkages existing between economy and environment. After that we will be ready to study the economic principles we will need.

THE ECONOMIC APPROACH

Why do people behave in ways that cause environmental destruction? There are several types of answers to this question. One goes like this: Environmental degradation comes about from human behavior that is unethical or immoral. Thus, for example, the reason people pollute is because they lack the moral and ethical strength to refrain from the type of behavior that causes environmental degradation. If this is true, then the way to get people to stop polluting is somehow to increase the general level of environmental morality in the society. In fact, the environmental movement has led a great many people to focus on questions of environmental ethics, exploring the moral dimensions of human impacts on the natural environment. These moral questions are obviously of fundamental concern to any civilized society. Certainly one of the main reasons environmental issues have been put on the front burner of social concern is the sense of moral responsibility that has led people to take their concerns into the political arena.

But there are problems with relying on moral reawakening as our main approach to combatting pollution. People don't necessarily have readily available moral buttons to push, and environmental problems are too important to wait for a long process of moral rebuilding. Nor does a sense of moral outrage, by itself, help us make decisions about all the other social goals that also have ethical dimensions: housing, health care, education, crime, etc. In a world of competing objectives we have to worry about very practical questions: Are we targeting the right environmental objectives, can we really enforce certain policies, are we getting the most impact for the money, and so on. But the biggest problem with basing our approach to pollution control strictly on the moral argument is the basic assumption that people pollute because they are somehow morally underdeveloped. It is not moral underdevelopment that leads to environmental destruction; rather, it is the way we have arranged the economic system within which people go about the job of making their livings.

So a second way of approaching the question of why people pollute is to look at the way the economy and its institutions are set up, and how they lead people to make decisions that result in environmental destruction. People pollute because it's the cheapest way they have of solving a certain very practical problem. That problem is the disposal of the waste products remaining after consumers have finished using something, or after business firms have finished producing something. People make these decisions on production, consumption, and disposal within a certain set of economic and social institutions;[1] these institutions structure the *incentives* that lead people to make decisions in one direction and not in another. What we have to study is how this incentive process works and, especially, how we might restructure it so that people will be led to make

---

[1] By "institutions" we mean the fundamental set of public and private organizations, laws, and practices that a society uses to structure its economic activity. Markets are an economic institution, for example, as are corporations, a body of commercial law, public agencies, and so on.

decisions and develop life styles that have more benign environmental implications.

One simplistic incentive-type statement that you often hear is that pollution is a result of the profit motive. According to this view, in private enterprise economies like the Western industrialized nations people are rewarded for maximizing profits, the difference between the value of what is produced and the value of what is used up in the production process. Furthermore, the thinking goes, the profits that entrepreneurs try to maximize are strictly monetary profits. In this headlong pursuit of monetary profits, entrepreneurs give no thought to the environmental impacts of their actions because it "doesn't pay." Thus, in this uncontrolled striving for monetary profits, the only way to reduce environmental pollution is to weaken the strength of the profit motive.

But this proposition doesn't stand up to analysis. It is not only "profit-motivated" corporations that cause pollution; individual consumers are also guilty when they do things like pour paint thinner down the drain or let their cars get seriously out of tune. Since individuals don't keep profit-and-loss statements, it can't be profits per se that lead people to pollute. The same can be said of government agencies, which have sometimes been serious polluters even though they are not profit motivated. But the most persuasive argument against the view that the search for profits causes pollution comes from recent political events in Eastern Europe and the former USSR. With the collapse of these ex-Communist regimes, we have become aware of the enormous environmental destruction that has occurred in some of these regions—heavily polluted air and water resources in many areas, with major impacts on human health and ecological systems. Many of these problems exceed some of the worst cases of environmental pollution experienced in market-driven countries. But they have happened in an economic system where the profit motive has been entirely lacking. Which means, quite simply, that the profit motive, in itself, is not the main cause of environmental destruction.

In the sections and chapters that follow we will place great stress on the importance of incentives in the functioning of an economic system. *Any* system will produce destructive environmental impacts if the incentives within the system are not structured to avoid them. We have to look more deeply into any economic system to understand how its incentive systems work and how they may be changed so that we can have a reasonably progressive economy without disastrous environmental side effects.

INCENTIVES: A SIMPLE HOUSEHOLD EXAMPLE

An "incentive" is something that attracts or repels people and leads them to modify their behavior in some way. An "economic incentive" is something in the economic world that leads people to channel their efforts at economic production and consumption in certain directions. We often think of economic incentives as consisting of payoffs in terms of material wealth; people have an incentive to behave in ways that provide them with increased wealth. But there

---

EXHIBIT 1-1

TOWNS ADOPT PAY-AS-YOU-THROW GARBAGE

By Robert Hanley
Special to The New York Times

CHESTER TOWNSHIP, N.J., July 9—Steve and Cally Frysinger and their four children have almost eliminated the need for the family garbage can.

Wizards at recycling and composting, they have cut the amount of trash they put out for curbside pickup each month to one 30-pound container—a minuscule amount for a household of six.

To cart that off, the Frysingers pay the town's garbage hauler, Waste Management of North Jersey, $1.90 a month.

Mr. Frysinger is an architect and a devotee of a billing system that is slowly taking root in the New York region and other parts of the country and revolutionizing trash disposal.

The new system requires residents to pay a fixed price for each bag or can of garbage they generate, much as they pay on the basis of usage for electricity, water and long-distance telephone service. In most localities, the per-bag or per-container system re-places or reduces flat fees all residents paid garbage haulers directly or through their property taxes.

Proponents say billing by the bag gives a big boost to recycling, thus reducing garbage costs and the expanding need for landfills and multimillion dollar incinerators. And, they argue, the shift of garbage expenses out of the property tax structure promotes fairness. No longer, they say, will small families that produce little garbage underwrite large families that fill several cans a week.

Until Chester Township changed its system in July 1990, each family paid $30 monthly or $360 a year for trash removal. Now residents pay Water Management $1.90 for each 30-pound can they set out, plus a monthly charge that varies with a home's assessment but averages $9.50, said Mr. Frysinger, who is on the town council. The fee covers the weekly collection of trash and recycling materials.

A resident with the average collection fee

---

are also nonmaterial incentives that lead people to modify their economic behavior; for example, self-esteem, the desire to preserve a beautiful visual environment, or the desire to set a good example for others.

For a simple first look at the importance of changing incentives to get improvements in environmental quality, consider the newspaper story shown in Exhibit 1-1. It is about new ways of paying for trash disposal, focusing on the experience of a New Jersey town. Before the program, people in the town paid a flat annual fee to have their trash collected. This is common practice in most communities. The problem with this approach is that there is simply no incentive for any individual family to limit its trash production, since they will pay the same annual trash-collection fee no matter how much, or little, they produce. This might not be a problem if there were ample landfill space and if there was no danger that the landfill would contaminate the surrounding environment, such as a nearby groundwater system. But for most communities these conditions don't hold any more, if they ever did. The New Jersey community in the story was in fact paying a stiff price for shipping its solid waste out of town. It faced the problem of how to get a significant reduction in the quantity of solid waste handled by the town.

and one 30-pound can of garbage a week pays $17.10 a month or $205.20 a year, $154.80 less than the flat $360 fee of two years ago.

Weight limits are enforced informally; Waste Management says its workers can sense when a can is excessively over 30 pounds and will leave it uncollected. Some people weigh their trash and themselves on the bathroom scale to make sure they do not exceed the limit.

The Frysinger family's devotion to recycling has meant a saving of $223 a year, Mr. Frysinger said.

"Basically," Mr. Frysinger said, "it's possible for a large family to recycle 80 percent of its garbage."

The family uses no paper towels in the kitchen, only sponges and towels, and buys nothing "excessively packaged," like wrapped fresh fruit or hardware in boxes with plastic or cellophane windows.

Since Chester Township began billing by the container, it has increased the amount of trash It recycles from 540 tons in 1989 to 1,158 tons in 1991, said Sara Noll, the town's recycling coordinator.

The details of the per-container system vary from town to town. Chester Township uses circular stickers that residents buy in sheets of 10 for $19, or $1.90 each. One sticker is attached to the top bag in the 30-pound container each collection day.

Other communities, especially in Columbia County, N.Y., use special bags instead of stickers because stickers are sometimes blown off or stolen and reused by thieves.

Perhaps the largest, oldest and most studied per-container billing system in the country is Seattle's, which started in 1981. Since then, Seattle has increased from 5 to 42 percent the proportion of its trash that is recycled, ...

The main criticism of billing by the bag or can is that the system encourages illegal dumping. Mr. Pealy said a few Seattle homeowners have probably left garbage in apartment-house Dumpsters. Some companies that use privately owned Dumpsters have started padlocking them, he said. The most flagrant illegal dumping, he said, involves construction debris.

Source: New York Times, July 14, 1992. Copyright © 1992 by the New York Times. Reprinted by permission.

The response in this case was to introduce a system that gives people an incentive to search for ways to reduce the amount of solid waste they produce. This was done by charging people for each bag of trash they put out on the curb. There is also a small monthly fee. What this does is to give families the incentive to reduce the number of bags of trash they set out. They can do this by recycling, by switching to products that have less waste, by putting food scraps in a compost pile, etc. These have led, according to the story, to a large increase in the amount of trash recycled. It probably also induced a reduction in the total amount of trash, although the story does not detail this. The article notes many other communities around the country where this system has been adopted. Of course, no system is perfect. Increases in illegal dumping and difficulties with applying the plan to apartment houses are problems. Nevertheless, the new approach does illustrate in a very clear way the effects of a shift from a system where there were no incentives for people to reduce their solid waste to one where there are such incentives. [2]

---

[2] The technical name for this approach is "unit pricing." See: U.S. Environmental Protection Agency, *Unit Pricing* (EPA/530-SW-91-005), Washington, D.C., February 1991.

INCENTIVES: A BUSINESS EXAMPLE

Incentives are also critically important in reducing industrial pollution. All industrial firms work within a given set of incentives: to increase profits if they are firms in market economies, to fulfill the annual production plan if they are Socialist firms. Firms have an incentive to take advantage of whatever factors are available to better their performance in terms of these criteria. One way they have been able to do this historically is to use the services of the environment for waste disposal services. The motivation for this is that these services have essentially been free, and by using free inputs as much as possible a firm obviously can increase its profits or better meet its production targets. It's this state of affairs that has contributed to the excessive levels of pollution we have today.

One policy approach is to pass and then try to enforce laws making pollution illegal. A more effective technique frequently will be to design a system that takes advantage of firms' normal monetary incentives in such a way as to lead them to pollute less. The newspaper article in Exhibit 1-2 illustrates a case in which the state of Louisiana seeks to give firms a direct financial incentive to reduce their polluting behavior. It does this by linking a firm's property taxes to its environmental performance. Specifically, each firm is rated on a scale ". . . according to the number of environmental violations it has received, the amount of chemicals it releases into the environment and other factors." The worse the firm's rating on the scale, the smaller its property tax exemption and, thus, the higher its tax payments. With this system firms would presumably have a direct incentive to do whatever they could to increase their environmental ratings—provided, of course, that the tax saving was sufficiently large to be attractive.

There are a lot of questions about how this system might work, especially on what firms have to do to avoid environmental citations, how closely the ranking score reflects actual emissions of polluting substances, and so on. But the important point is that authorities have apparently recognized the importance of changing the incentive structures of polluting firms in order to motivate them to search for ways of reducing their emissions. In recent years more emphasis is being put on incorporating economic incentive approaches into environmental policies at federal and local levels. The essence of this approach is to restructure the incentives facing firms and consumers in such a way that it mobilizes their own energy and ingenuity to find ways of reducing their impacts on the environment.

INCENTIVES IN THE POLLUTION-CONTROL INDUSTRY

Another critical focal point where incentives are vital, and where environmental economics plays an analytical important role, is in the growth and performance of the pollution-control industry. This is the industry that develops waste recycling techniques, new pollution-control equipment, and new pollution-monitoring technology. It sometimes handles and treats waste products, and is often involved in managing waste disposal sites. It also includes firms that develop

---

EXHIBIT 1-2

USING TAXES TO DISCOURAGE POLLUTION

By Keith Schneider
Special to The New York Times

NEW ORLEANS, Feb. 24—After taking a hard look at the financial and ecological toll from industrial development, Louisiana has enacted a new tax rule that ties the amount of business property taxes a company pays to its environmental record.

Established in December, the new policy was imposed after officials determined that some corporations were benefiting from tax exemptions while being liable for thousands of dollars in pollution fines in a state with some of the worst chemical contamination in the country.

Gov. Buddy Roemer and two state agencies took the action to reduce pollution while trying to collect millions of dollars in industrial property taxes from which the same polluters had been exempted.

The new policy, which has already come under challenge in state court, is considered the most innovative step taken by any state to specifically link its tax policy with the dual goals of reducing pollution and gaining greater compliance with environmental law.

Pattern of Exemptions

For 65 years, an important facet of Louisiana's policy for attracting industry was to exempt from local business property taxes all new equipment and other capital expenditures for 10 years. Exemptions came up for renewal half-way through the 10-year period.

Under the new policy, each company applying for an exemption or seeking renewal is rated on a scale according to the number of environmental violations it has received, the amount of chemicals it releases into the environment and other factors. The worse a company's record, the lower the score and the smaller its tax exemption.

"We weren't trying to be the first state to do this," said Vicki Arroyo, director of policy and planning at the state Department of Environmental Quality. "But in looking to other states for guidance about how to link a company's environmental record to economic incentives, we couldn't find any other program."

Ms. Arroyo added: "We found, on one hand, that we had companies with serious environmental problems liable for hundreds of thousands of dollars in fines, and on the other hand, they were getting millions of dollars of tax exemptions. That is not the message we wanted to send to industry."

In recent years, states have sought to use tax policy to achieve environmental goals. Minnesota exempts some land from property taxes to preserve marshy areas, and New York and New Hampshire reduce property taxes for wetlands that are protected from development. North Carolina charges a fee for personalized license plates to pay for acquiring undeveloped lands and Maryland has a similar program to finance environmental research on Chesapeake Bay.

Missouri designates a portion of its sales tax for environmental programs. Washington State applies part of its cigarette sales tax for curtailing pollution in Puget Sound. And many states exempt pollution control equipment from business property taxes.

Source: New York Times, February 27, 1991. Copyright © 1991 by the New York Times. Reprinted by permission.

---

new environmentally friendly products like low-phosphate detergents and recyclable paper products. A lively and progressive pollution-control industry is obviously needed if we are to come to grips effectively with all of our present and prospective environmental problems. Thus, one of the major things environmental economists must study is the incentives facing this industry—what causes it to grow or decline, how quickly or slowly it responds to new needs, and so on.

A good example of this is illustrated in the news clipping of Exhibit 1-3. It discusses the opportunities for U.S. firms to supply pollution-control equipment and know-how to localities in Europe that are feeling the effects of new environmental regulations instituted by the European Community (EC). The reason the U.S. companies are in a position to do this is because the more demanding environmental policy climate in the U.S. has created greater incentives for the pollution-control industry to innovate and develop improved means of handling residuals. This incentive effect of environmental laws is often overlooked, but it is a critically important facet of the long-run effort to reduce the environmental impacts of modern economies. Throughout the book we will have much to say about this particular incentive.

THE DESIGN OF ENVIRONMENTAL POLICY

Environmental economics has a major role to play in the design of public policies for environmental quality improvement. There is an enormous range and variety of public programs and policies devoted to environmental matters, at all levels of government: local, state, regional, federal, and international. They vary greatly in their efficiency and effectiveness. Some have been well designed and will no doubt have beneficial impacts. Others, perhaps the majority, are not well designed. Not being cost-effective, they will end up costing lots of money and having much smaller impacts on environmental quality than they might have had with better design.

The problem of designing efficient environmental policies is often not given the emphasis it deserves. It is easy to fall into the trap of thinking that any programs or policies that flow out of the rough and tumble of the environmental political process is likely to be of some help, or that they certainly will be better than nothing. But history is full of cases where policymakers and public administrators have pursued policies that don't work; the public is frequently led to believe a policy will be effective even when any reasonable analysis could predict that it will not. All of which means that it is critically important to study how to design environmental policies that are effective and efficient.

The Environmental Protection Agency (EPA) estimated that in 1990 the U.S. devoted about 2 percent of the total cost of goods and services in the country to pollution control and environmental cleanup. They expect this percentage to rise to around 2.8 percent by the end of the 1990s. These are very large sums of money, even though the percentage probably should be higher. But it is important not to get totally fixated on the percentage, whether it is high or low, whether it compares favorably with other countries, etc. Of equal or greater importance is whether we are getting the most improvement possible in environmental quality for the money spent. EPA Director Reilly is quoted as saying: ". . . at this level of expenditure, there's a very large obligation to get it right." By "getting it right"

EXHIBIT 1-3

CLEANING UP ON CLEANING UP IN THE EUROPEAN COMMUNITY

The Green Rush Over There May Benefit U.S. Firms.

By Patrick Oster
Special to The Washington Post

BRUSSELS—Earlier this year, a large chemical company in northern Europe contacted Pall Corp. of East Hills, N.Y., a leading maker of emission filters.

The chemical company, which asked not to be identified, was discharging heavy metals into the atmosphere through its plastics manufacturing process. With the 12-nation European Community about to pass a new hazardous waste law regulating such metals, it wanted Pall to come up with a filter that would enable the chemical company's emissions to comply with the regulations.

"Our filters cost more, but we've been doing this for some time now and have an edge in design know-how," says Adrian Fox, senior vice president for marketing for Pall's European operations, explaining why the European firm turned to a U.S. company to comply with a European law.

A handful of European countries have had strict environmental controls for years, but now similar calls are being made to experienced U.S. environmental firms by European companies that face a spate of recently enacted environmental laws and a growing list of pending ones.

After 20 years of dithering, the EC is suddenly passing environmental legislation with a frenzy, and American companies, which have been responding to similar U.S. laws for two decades, are well positioned to take advantage of the opportunity.

At stake is a market for environmental services that is expected to triple to $171 billion in Western Europe alone by the year 2000. The enormous environmental calamity left behind by Communist regimes to the east will only add to this market.

Arvin Industries Inc. of Columbus, Ind., a leading maker of catalytic converters, is already grabbing a chunk of the market for environmental products and services.

The new, EC-wide rules will force automakers early next year to install catalytic converters on all new cars to comply with U.S.-style emissions limits. The converters were required in the United States in 1975.

That means about 10 million converters will be needed. Analysts estimate Arvin will sell $400 million worth and either it or Tenneco Inc., another U.S. catalytic-converter maker, should emerge as market leader in a close European race.

The new Europe-wide environmental laws are partly a response to the growing importance of "green issues" in European politics, themselves a response to environmental conditions that have gotten so bad that the EC can't afford to wait any longer.

Such laws also are sailing through because a recent EC court decision now allows a simpler approval process.

"U.S. environmental legislation is about five to 10 years ahead of EC legislation, especially in the enforcement area," says David Owen, who is the head of research for Ecofin, a London-based environmental financial services firm. "There's quite a lot of pious talk here, but many laws are just lying around."

"American firms have benefited from being exposed to a more robust enforcement regime," says Owen. "They understand about liability. Europe is still naive about it."

Helping European firms cope with existing and proposed waste legislation is expected to provide the largest revenue for U.S. companies, especially those laws likely to create liabilities regarding cross-border transportation, incineration and disposal of hazardous wastes.

Source: Washington Post Weekly Edition, June 22–28, 1992. Reprinted with permission.

he means having programs that get the maximum improvement in environmental quality for the resources spent. Everybody has an interest in this: environmentalists, for obvious reasons; public regulators, because they are tapping a limited supply of taxpayer resources and consumer tolerance; and the regulated polluters themselves, because matters of efficiency are critical to business success.

To see what "getting it right" might entail, consider the recent (1990) Clean Air Act. It contains hundreds of provisions aimed primarily at three air pollution problems: urban smog, emissions of sulfur dioxide from power plants, and toxic chemical emissions. The law includes all kinds of things: tailpipe standards, new technology for gasoline nozzles, production of a variety of super-clean cars, new standards for toxic emissions, emission trading among power plants in the South and Midwest, and so on. And it goes into enormous detail; for example, it requires that fleet cars (taxis and the like) meet stricter tailpipe standards by 1998, but it exempts fleet cars that are parked at private homes at night! On a quick reading this looks like a serious law, that it will have an impact across a broad range of air-quality problems. But how can we be reasonably sure this great collection of bits and pieces represents anything like a cost-effective way of attacking these problems? How can we be sure that we have the right mix of techniques, that we don't have just a grab bag of items that have been pushed by a variety of interest groups on one side or another of this issue?

Thus one of the primary jobs for environmental economists is to examine different approaches to pollution control, to cut through all the political hoopla and look carefully at the impacts of different policy approaches. We need to know if these policies are cost-effective, in terms of getting the most pollution reduction possible for the money spent, and whether they are efficient, in terms of appropriately balancing the benefits and the costs of environmental improvements. Thus, policy design and analysis is a major part of environmental economics, and we will spend a great deal of this book on this subject.

MACROECONOMIC QUESTIONS: ENVIRONMENT AND GROWTH

The incentive issues discussed above are microeconomic problems; they deal with the behavior of individuals or small groups of consumers, polluting firms, and firms in the pollution-control industry. The macroeconomy, on the other hand, refers to the economic structure and performance of an entire country taken as a single unit. When we study topics like changes in gross domestic product (GDP), rates of inflation, and the unemployment rate, we are focusing on the performance of the country as a whole, that is to say, we are doing macroeconomics.

There are a number of important questions about the relationship between environmental issues and the behavior of the macroeconomy. One is the relationship between environmental pollution-control measures and the rate of unemployment and economic growth: Will stricter policies tend to retard growth and increase unemployment and if so, how much? What impact will environmental regulations have, if any, on the rate of inflation? There is a reverse side to these macroeconomic questions. It's the subject of the newspaper article shown in Exhibit 1-4: the impacts of economic growth on environmental quality. Do higher rates of growth, that is, increases in our traditional measures like GDP, imply greater environmental degradation or might the opposite be true? The article cites the work of two environmental economists who studied the relationship between growth and the environment. Their conclusion is that some ". . . pollution increases during the early stages of a country's development and then begins to diminish as countries gain adequate resources to tackle pollution problems." This happens because at low incomes people tend to value development over environmental quality, but as they achieve greater wealth they are willing to devote greater resources to environmental quality improvements. This is clearly a matter of great importance for developing countries, and we will come back to it in Chapter 19. In developed countries also, macroeconomic problems— growth, recession, inflation, unemployment—are constant topics of national concern. So it's important to pursue studies of the relationships between these phenomena and questions of environmental quality.

COST-EFFECTIVENESS ANALYSIS

Several types of environmental analysis are common in environmental economics. One is called "cost-effectiveness" analysis. This is simply an analysis where we look for the least expensive way of achieving a given environmental quality target or, to put it in different but equivalent terms, where we look for the way of achieving the greatest improvement in some environmental target for a given expenditure of resources.

Exhibit 1-5 shows a news clip that focuses on this concept of cost-effectiveness: in this case, of technical alternatives to reduce energy consumption. The overall objective is to reduce the output of carbon dioxide, the primary gas responsible for the "greenhouse effect." What is at issue is the cost of different technical options—efficiency standards for lights, electric motors, office buildings, providing incentives for renewable energy, etc.—and their effectiveness in terms of lowering the output of CO_2. Studies of this sort require close coordination of scientific and engineering analysis to determine realistic technical parameters, and economic analysis to determine the values associated with these parameters.

BENEFIT–COST ANALYSIS

In cost-effective analysis, economists are concerned only with the costs of achieving some stated environmental goal. In benefit–cost analysis, both costs *and* benefits of a policy or program are measured and expressed in comparable terms. Benefit–cost analysis is the main analytical tool used by economists to evaluate environmental decisions. It was first used in this country early in the twentieth century to evaluate water-development projects of the U.S. Army Corps of Engineers. Today it is used throughout the public sector. Sometimes it is used as

EXHIBIT 1-4

LOWER POLLUTION TIED TO PROSPERITY

By Keith Bradsher
Special to The New York Times

WASHINGTON, OCT. 27—A study correlating economic development and air pollution by two Princeton University professors has concluded that pollution tends to diminish as a country's economy grows beyond a certain level of prosperity.

The study, which taps international pollution data not readily known to economists, also finds that patterns of United States investment in Mexico do not indicate an effort by companies to avoid American pollution controls.

The research tends to support the Bush Administration's position that a free-trade agreement with Mexico would not be environmentally destructive. And it suggests that some environmentalists' predictions that economic growth and free trade in the developing world may ravage the world's environment are overstated.

The study was done by Gene M. Grossman and Alan B. Krueger, economics professors at Princeton's Woodrow Wilson School of Public and International Affairs, and was presented at a conference at Brown University on Oct. 18. Mexico's Ministry of Commerce and Industry sponsored the conference and indirectly helped to finance the research, although the authors said the Mexican Government took no part in their work.

The study compared national economic output figures with air-pollution studies conducted in several dozen cities worldwide over the last 14 years by the United Nations Environment Program and the World Health Organization. It found that air pollution was most severe for countries with an economic output of $4,000 to $5,000 a person and less severe for considerably poorer and considerably richer countries.

Vinod Thomas, the World Bank's chief economist for Asia, said the study was the first to confirm many experts' suspicions that pollution increases during the early stages of a country's development and then begins to diminish as countries gain adequate resources to tackle pollution problems.

Jagdish Bhagwati, the Columbia University professor of economics who is overseeing a report on trade and the environment for the General Agreement on Tariffs and Trade, said, "There's been no systematic work" until now. He added that the GATT report would include a separate discussion of the new findings.

Justin R. Ward, a senior resource specialist and trade expert at the Natural Resources Defense Council, a New York-based environmental group, said that while the Princeton study's results were encouraging, specific environmental safeguards should be written into the agreement to insure that Mexico did not prove an exception.

To examine the role of pollution regulations in trade and investment with Mexico, the Princeton professor used Census Bureau data on pollution control spending as a percentage of total costs in each of many different industries. Savings on labor costs dwarfed pollution control savings, they found, and American industries with the highest pollution-control costs have lost an almost imperceptibly larger portion of their markets to imports than industries with average pollution control costs.

EXHIBIT 1-5

COST-EFFECTIVE TECHNOLOGIES MAY REDUCE US EMISSIONS

Even without a "carbon tax" to make people pay a fee for greenhouse-gas emissions, investments in energy efficiency make good economic sense, experts say.

"It would be very easy to . . . reduce emissions" below 1990 levels with strong leadership on the issue in Washington, says Nicholas Lenssen of the Worldwatch Institute.

The Union of Concerned Scientists says aggressive policies to promote energy efficiency could save the United States $5 trillion in electricity and fuel bills over the next 40 years. The program—using technologies that are on the market or in labs today—would cost $2.7 trillion, yielding a net savings of $2.3 trillion.

Studies by Congress's Office of Technology Assessment and the National Academy of Sciences also suggest that maintaining or cutting greenhouse-gas levels can be achieved using cost-effective technologies.

But if that is true, economists ask, why aren't businesses and consumers investing more?

William Cline, an economist with the Institute for International Economics, says one explanation is that "there is a certain amount of lethargy in any economic system" that blocks sweeping change. Publicity and promotion by government could help get the process moving, he suggests.

But W. David Montgomery, an economist with the consulting firm Charles River Associates, says the answer may be that these technologies aren't as cost-effective as the studies imply.

The money that a homeowner or a businessman gives up today to invest in an efficient appliance could be used for other purposes, perhaps with a higher rate of return, he notes.

Government is moving on several fronts to stimulate investment in energy efficiency.

Some 15 states have "demand-side management" programs in place, whereby electric utilities work to cut demand for power. The utilities give rebates to customers who install efficient light bulbs, and refrigerators.

In addition, the energy bill nearing completion in Congress is likely to:

- Set efficiency standards for lights, electric motors, commercial heating and air conditioning systems, and shower heads.
- Set efficiency standards for federal buildings, and encourage similar standards for the private sector.
- Reject a plan to tax utility rebates that reduce demand for power.
- Provide incentives for renewable energy.

Congress decided not to boost fuel-economy requirements for automobiles, a move sought by environmentalists but opposed by carmakers.

an aid in selecting efficient policies, sometimes an agency uses it to justify what it wants to do, and sometimes officials use it to try and stop new regulations or weaken old ones. It is such an important and widely used approach that we will devote several chapters to it later in the book (Chapters 6, 7, and 8). In this type of analysis, as the name implies, the benefits of some proposed action are estimated and compared with the total costs that society would bear if that action were undertaken. If it is a proposal for a public park, for example, the benefits in

EXHIBIT 1-6

THE NEW ECO-NOMICS

After Years of Pooh-Poohing Cost-Benefit Analyses and Economic Impact Studies, Environmental Activists Have Finally Copied a Page from the Enemy's Playbook. Now They're Fighting Industry's Numbers with Numbers of Their Own.

By Margaret E. Kriz

The way Lester R. Brown, the president of the Worldwatch Institute, sees it, environmental activists are changing the art of economics—and perhaps vice versa.

After years of protesting the government's use of cost-benefit analyses to shape environmental policy, environmentalists are taking a different page out of the same book to argue for tough controls on global warming gases.

Where the cost-benefit analyses of the past measured obvious industrial costs (installing smokestack pollution controls, for example), the new studies are based partly on such less traditional approaches as quantifying the long-term benefits of cleaner air or biological diversity, for example, and predicting quick public adoption of energy-efficient technologies.

"It's not just the cost of manufacturing and income from sales that counts today in public policy making," Brown said. "These externalities are beginning to work their way onto the table, and I see that as an exciting development."

Brown was particularly enthusiastic about a global warming study by William R. Cline, a senior fellow at the Institute for International Economics. Cline's analysis concluded that by taking action to curb global warming, the United States could avoid $350 billion in economic damages over the next 300 years. Among the projected savings toted up in the report is $4 billion for endangered species protection—a rough number Cline said he developed by figuring out how much it costs to protect the northern spotted owl and multiplying that number by 25.

Cline, in releasing the study, defended his inclusion of such nontraditional calculations. "This issue is a hybrid of science, economics and human behavior," he said. "You can ignore the great bulk of this problem, but you do so at great risk to society."

The environmental community has em-braced economics out of necessity, not choice. After years of arguing that environmental protection was morally right at any cost, environmental activists realized that they had to fight economics with economics, particularly during a recession, when industry groups charged that new global warming emission controls would eliminate thousands of jobs.

There's a realization that you cannot afford to cede to the other side the whole economic waterfront," said Alden Meyer, the director of the climate change and energy policy program of the Union of Concerned Scientists. "Policy makers and the public clearly do care what happens to the economy, what happens to job creation. If you don't address the economic issues, you're leaving yourself open to be defeated on the policy front."

Last October, for example, Meyer's group and three other environmental organizations released a study that concluded that the United States could, by cutting its global warming gas emissions, save consumers $2.3 trillion by 2030.

Just a decade earlier, however, cost-benefit analyses were fighting words to environmental activists. Rather than issuing their own economic studies, environmental groups were busy criticizing the Reagan Administration's policy of banning pollution controls if it decided that their cost outstripped their likely environmental benefits.

Such strict economic reasoning was anathema to environmentalists. They pointed out that although industry could easily estimate the cost to it of new pollution control equipment, scientists had a far more difficult time calculating the potential long-term health and environmental benefits of regulation.

16

terms of recreational experiences provided by the park are compared with the expected costs of building the park and of using the land in this way rather than some other way. Or a proposal to build a solid-waste incinerator would compare the costs of building and operating the incinerator, including the costs of disposing of the remaining ash and the costs of possible air-borne emissions, with benefits, such as reducing the use of landfills for the solid waste.

The benefit–cost approach implies that we need to consider both the benefits and the costs of environmental programs and policies. This often puts benefit–cost studies squarely in the middle of political controversy on many environmental issues. In the political struggles that characterize many environmental problems, groups on one side consist of people whose major concern is with the benefits, while groups on the other side are primarily concerned with costs. Environmental groups typically stress the benefits; business groups usually focus on the costs. Look at the news story excerpted in Exhibit 1-6. It discusses some of the recent efforts to estimate the benefits and costs of CO_2 emission reduction, aimed at forestalling the "greenhouse effect." It describes how many environmental groups, historically somewhat doubtful of the usefulness of benefit–cost analysis, have now accepted the approach, realizing that more careful analysis of environmental programs can be a better way of defending them than an attempt simply to avoid any analysis whatever. The ultimate long-run acceptance of programs to protect the environment depends on people coming to realize that they are worth the cost. The benefit–cost, tradeoff type of approach is the best way to accomplish this.[3]

INTERNATIONAL ISSUES

Not all environmental problems are pollution related, and not all are contained within individual countries. In recent years international issues have become increasingly important. The news clipping in Exhibit 1-7 tells about the globally important question of species diversity. Because of disruptions in habitats, such as housing developments in developed countries and deforestation in many developing economies, the rate of extinction among plant and animal species has been increased greatly above its natural level. The clipping tells of some of the maneuvering leading up to the Earth Summit of 1992, and indicates some of the economic issues involved. These include the question of the most cost-effective ways to reduce the rate of species extinctions, the issue of whether national property rights ought to be exercised over species, the problem of international technology transfers, and the very thorny problem of how the costs of preserving species diversity are to be divided among rich and poor countries.

---

[3]A brief comment is appropriate about this newspaper article. The writer makes it sound as if benefit–cost analysis has been used historically only by those who have been opposed to environmental programs. This is not true. Environmental economists, most of them passionate advocates of the environment, have been using benefit–cost analysis for decades.

EXHIBIT 1-7

TALKS SEEK TO PREVENT HUGE LOSS OF SPECIES

Nations Work Toward a Pact, Preserving Biological Diversity.

By William K. Stevens

As the world approaches the day of decision on a treaty to deal with the threat of global warming, separate negotiations on another overarching environmental question, maintaining biological diversity, are moving toward their own denouement.

The object of these less prominent but nevertheless high-stakes talks is to forge a binding agreement among the world's nations to slow or halt a steady loss of plant, animal and microbial species that many biologists fear will result in a mass extinction of epic proportions in mere decades.

The basic question involves actions that nations should be required to take in conserving species, habitats and ecosystems. Despite a patchwork of international agreements like the Convention on International Trade in Endangered Species, there is no legally binding treaty that directly and comprehensively addresses the overall problem of preserving biological diversity.

Some countries have developed national action plans to identify, conserve and manage biological resources. But most, including many tropical countries that are richest in species, have not. These are precisely the main countries where economic and development pressures are destroying habitats at a rate that alarms many scientists and conservation biologists.

The negotiators have agreed that such programs should be the primary line of defense, with seed banks, gene banks and zoos secondary.

Issues other than the central question of conservation measures are posing greater difficulty. One of these involves the ownership of genetic materials. Historically, seeds, germ plasm and specimens of individual species have been considered to be in the public domain. Anyone who found them could exploit them without compensating the country of origin. Now developing countries are seeking to claim control over these resources and to share in their economic benefits.

Argument also attends the issue of the terms on which the industrialized countries should transfer conservation technology and know-how to developing countries. But the biggest point of contention is the one between North and South over money.

To many developing countries, conservation is clearly secondary to the day-to-day struggle to support their surging populations. "Seeing it from where you are or I am, the environment might look very important," said Fiona McConnell, the head of the British delegation. "But if your concern is survival, you might need some persuading."

Money is the persuader, and some developing countries are proposing that the North not only bear the costs of putting new conservation measures into effect but also compensate the South for foregoing the economic benefits of cutting down forests to expand commercial agriculture or timbering, for example. But other developing countries believe that if the forests are preserved and properly exploited for medicine and renewable products, they are worth more than if they are cut down.

The United States opened a possible wedge into the financial issue last week when it reversed position and pledged unilaterally to contribute $75 million to developing countries' costs of coping with global warming.

Of that sum, $50 million would be paid into the Global Environmental Facility, a pilot program established last year by the World Bank, the United Nations Environment Program and the United Nations Development program to channel environmental money from North to South. Developing countries welcomed the reversal with reservations. Many fear that the Global Environment Facility, which is controlled by developed countries, will shut them out of a say in administering the funds.

ECONOMICS AND POLITICS

Finally, we need to discuss briefly the question of how to achieve effective environmental policy in a highly political policy environment. Environmental policies not only affect the natural environment, they also affect people. This means that environmental policy decisions come out of the political process, a process where, at least in democratic systems, people and groups come together and contend for influence and control, where interests collide, coalitions shift, and biases intrude. Policies that come out of a process like this may bear little relationship to what we might think of as efficient approaches to particular environmental problems. Many people have questioned the very idea that a democratic political process could or should strive to produce policies that are efficient in some technical economic sense.

So where does that leave the environmental economist? Why spend so much time and energy on questions of efficiency and cost-effectiveness when the political process most likely is going to override these considerations and go its own way? Why worry about economic incentives and economic efficiency when "everything is political," as the saying goes? The answer is that although we know that the real world is one of compromise and power, the best way for scientists and economists to serve that process is to produce studies that are as clear and as objective as possible. It is the politician's job to compromise or seek advantage; it is the scientist's job to provide the best information he or she can. For economists, in fact, this means studies in which economic efficiency is a central role, but it means more than this. Since the policy process is one where "who gets what" is a dominant theme, environmental economics must also deal with the distribution question, on how environmental problems and policies affect different groups within society. It is also the role of scientists and economists to provide information to policymakers on alternative courses of action. Although we will focus in later chapters on what appear to be "the" most efficient policies or "the" least-cost courses of action, we need to recognize that in the give-and-take of the political world in which policy is actually made, choosing among alternatives is always the order of the day.

But economists have no right these days to bemoan their fate in the environmental policy process. If anything these are the days of the rising influence of economists. Benefit–cost procedures and results have become more widely accepted, in public policy arenas and in law courts hearing environmental cases. New pollution-control initiatives incorporating economic incentive principles are being adopted at both federal and state levels in the U.S. All the more reason, then, to study and understand the basic economics of environmental analysis and policy.

SUMMARY

The purpose of this brief chapter was to whet your appetite for the subject of environmental economics by indicating some of the main topics that the field encompasses, showing very briefly the approach that economists take in studying them. It's also to give you something to remember. When we get involved in some of the conceptual and theoretical issues that underlie the topic, it is easy to lose sight of what we are trying to accomplish. We are trying to develop these principles so that we can actually use them to address real-world problems like those discussed in this chapter. Although the principles may appear abstract and odd at first, remember the objective: to achieve a cleaner, healthier, and more beautiful natural environment.

SELECTED READINGS

Council on Environmental Quality: *United States of America National Report* (to the U.N. Conference on Environment and Development), Washington, D.C., 1992.

El-Hinnawi, Essam, and Manzur H. Hashmi: *The State of the Environment*, United Nations Environment Program, Butterworth, London, 1987.

Magat, Wesley A. (ed.): *Reform of Environmental Regulation*, Ballinger Publishing Company, Cambridge, Mass., 1982.

Miller, Alan S.: *Gaia Connections: An Introduction to Ecology, Ecoethics, and Economics*, Rowman and Allenheld, Lanham, Md., 1991.

Repetto, Robert C.: *World Enough and Time: Successful Strategies for Resource Management*, Yale University Press, New Haven, Conn., 1986.

Vig, Norman J., and Michael E. Kraft: *Environmental Policy in the 1990's*, Congressional Quarterly Press, Washington, D.C., 1990.

Yandle, Bruce: *The Political Limits of Environmental Regulation: Tracking the Unicorn*, Quorum Books, New York, 1989.

CHAPTER 2

THE ECONOMY AND THE ENVIRONMENT

The economy is a collection of technological, legal, and social arrangements through which a group of people seek to augment their material and spiritual standards of life. In any economic system, the elementary functions of production, distribution, and consumption take place within an all-encompassing natural world. One role the natural world plays is that of provider of raw materials and energy inputs, without which production and consumption would be impossible. Thus, one type of impact that an economic system has on nature is by drawing upon raw materials to keep the system functioning. Production and consumption activities also produce leftover waste products, called "residuals," and sooner or later these must find their way back into the natural world. Depending on how they are handled, these residuals may lead to pollution or the degradation of the natural environment. We can illustrate these fundamental relationships with a simple schematic:

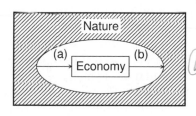

Environmental Economics
(a) Nature + fuels
*   Economics   wood*
* — raw material coal*
*   Production   energy*
*   Consumption   inputs*
(b) Impact of economic
*   activity on Natural*
*   environment.*

The link marked (a) represents raw materials flowing into production and consumption. The study of nature in its role as provider of raw materials is called *natural resource economics*. The link labeled (b) shows the impact of economic activity on the quality of the natural environment. The study of this residuals flow and its resultant impacts in the natural world comes under the heading of *environmental economics*. While pollution control is the major topic within environmental economics, it is not the only one. Human beings impact on the environment in many ways that are not pollution related in the traditional sense. Habitat disruption from housing developments and scenic degradation from any

21

number of human activities are examples of environmental impacts that are not related to the discharge of specific pollutants.

The topic of this book is environmental economics. We will study the management of waste flows and the impacts of human activity on environmental resources. But in a real sense many of these problems originate back in the initial, raw material phase of the nature–economy interaction. So before proceeding we will consider briefly the major dimensions of natural resource economics.

NATURAL RESOURCE ECONOMICS

In modern societies it is sometimes easy to overlook the fact that economic activity makes use of a great variety of natural resource inputs. In recent years events have reminded us of the importance of energy resources, especially the fossil-based ones such as coal, petroleum, and natural gas. The massive petrochemical industry is also based on these resources. The vast number of materials used in industrial societies, and even in the so-called "information society," come from various minerals and forest resources. Water is an essential input in many production processes as well as directly in household consumption. Food production depends on the natural resource base, either for direct harvesting, as in fisheries, or to provide the essential inputs for plant and animal growth. Air is an essential input in virtually all economic production processes.

To sort out this variety of natural resources the most common distinction is between *renewable* and *nonrenewable resources*. The living resources, like fisheries and timber, are renewable; they grow in time according to biological processes. Some nonliving resources are also renewable, the classic example being the sun's energy that reaches the earth. Nonrenewable resources are those for which there are no processes of replenishment—once used they are gone forever. Classic examples are petroleum reservoirs and nonenergy mineral deposits. Certain resources, such as many groundwater aquifers, have replenishment rates that are so low that they are in effect nonrenewable.

A resource that has only recently impressed itself upon us is one that resides not in any one substance but in a collection of elements: biological diversity. Biologists estimate that there may be as many as 30 million different species of living organisms in the world today. These represent a vast and important source of genetic information, useful for the development of medicines, natural pesticides, resistant varieties of plants and animals, and so on. Human activities have substantially increased the rate of species extinctions, so habitat conservation and species preservation have become important contemporary resource problems.

One of the distinguishing features of most natural resource issues is that they are heavily "time dependent." This means that their use is normally spread out over time, so rates of use in one period affect availabilities and use rates in later periods. In the case of nonrenewable resources this is relatively easy to see. How much petroleum should be pumped from a deposit this year, realizing that the more we pump now the less there will be available in future years? But these trade-offs between present and future also exist for many renewable resources.

What should today's salmon harvesting rate be, considering that the size of the remaining stock will affect its availability in later years? Should we cut the timber this year, or is its growth rate high enough to justify waiting until some future year?

These are issues with a strong *intertemporal* dimension; they involve trade-offs between today and the future. Certain environmental problems are also like this, especially when dealing with pollutants that accumulate, or pollutants that require a long time to dissipate. What is in fact being depleted here is the earth's "assimilative capacity," the ability of the natural system to accept certain pollutants and render them benign or inoffensive. Some of the theoretical ideas about the depletion of natural resources are also useful in understanding environmental pollution. In this sense "assimilative capacity" is a natural resource akin to traditional resources like oil deposits and forests.

One feature of the modern world is that the dividing line between natural resources and environmental resources is blurring in many cases. Many resource extraction processes, such as timber cutting and strip mining, have direct repercussions on environmental quality. And there are plenty of instances where environmental pollution or disruption impacts resource extraction processes. Estuarine water pollution that interferes with the replenishment of fish stocks is an example, as is air pollution that reduces agricultural yields. And certain things, like wildlife, may be considered both natural resources and attributes of the environment. Despite these blurred edges, however, the distinction that economists have made between these two services of the natural world—as raw materials and as environment—is sufficiently strong and well developed that it makes sense for us to proceed with a book that focuses primarily on the latter. We will begin by considering a somewhat more complicated version of the simple diagram depicted above.

THE FUNDAMENTAL BALANCE

In this book you will find a lot of simple analytical "models" of situations that in reality are somewhat complex. A model is a way of trying to show the essential structure and relationships in something, without going into all of its details, much as a caricature of a person accentuates distinguishing features at the cost of all the details.

Figure 2-1 is a more complex rendering of the relationships shown at the beginning of the chapter. The elements within the circle are parts of the economic system, the whole of which is basically encapsulated within the natural environment. The economy has been divided into two broad segments, producers and consumers. The "producers" category includes all the firms that take inputs and convert them to useful outputs, but it also includes units like public agencies, nonprofit organizations, and firms producing services, such as transportation; in short, all economic entities in the system up to the consumers themselves. The primary inputs from the natural environment to the producing sector are materials, in the form of fuels, minerals, and wood, fluids like water and petroleum,

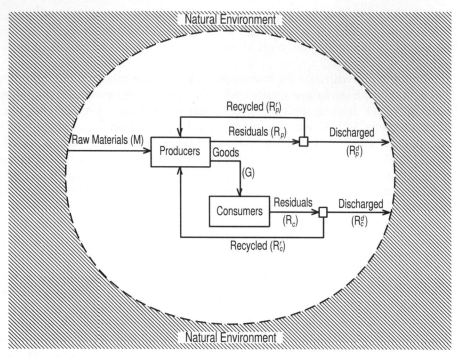

FIGURE 2-1
The Environment and the Economy.

and gases of various types, like natural gas and oxygen. All goods and services are derived from materials with the application of energy inputs. The produced goods and services, embodying a portion of these materials and energy, then flow to consumers. One could argue that consumers utilize materials inputs directly from nature themselves without the intermediary of producers. Thus, we have water pumped from domestic wells or, in many countries, fuel wood harvested directly by householders. But in the interest of keeping it simple, these functions are not directly drawn into the figure. In these cases we can consider producers and consumers as being the same people. Of course, in an even wider sense we need to keep in mind that "producers" and "households" actually consist of people, and in fact the same people in each case. The "us versus them" attitude that characterizes many environmental disputes is in fact an internal disagreement within a single group. Society as a whole is essentially in the same position as a single household that pumps water from its own well and discharges wastes into its own septic system, which happens to be near the well.

Production and consumption create "residuals," which is another way of saying leftovers. It includes all types of materials residuals that may be emitted into the air or water or disposed of on land. The list is incredibly long: sulfur dioxide, volatile organic compounds, toxic solvents, animal manure, pesticides, particulate matter of all types, waste building materials, heavy metals, and so on and on. Waste energy in the form of heat and noise, and radioactivity, which has characteristics of both material and energy, are also important production residuals. Consumers are also responsible for enormous quantities of residuals, chief among which are domestic sewage and automobile emissions. All materials in consumer goods must eventually end up as leftovers, even though they may be recycled along the way. These are the source of large quantities of solid waste as well as hazardous materials like toxic chemicals and used oil.

Let us first consider the question of production and consumption residuals from a strictly physical standpoint. Figure 2-1 shows materials and energy being extracted from the natural environment and residuals being discharged back into the environment. The first law of thermodynamics, the famous law on the conservation of matter, assures us that, in the long run, these two flows must be equal. In terms of the symbols of Figure 2-1:[1]

$$M = R_p^d + R_c^d$$

We must say "in the long run" for several reasons. If the system is growing, it can retain some proportion of the natural inputs, which go toward increasing the size of the system, through a growing population, the accumulation of capital equipment, etc. These would be disposed of if and when the system ceases to grow. Also, recycling can obviously delay the disposal of residuals. But recycling can never be perfect, each cycle must lose some proportion of the recycled material. Thus, the fundamental materials balance equation must hold in the long run. This shows us something very fundamental: If we wish to reduce the mass of residuals disposed of in the natural environment, we must reduce the quantity of raw materials taken into the system.[2] We can look more closely at the options before us if we substitute for M. According to the flow diagram,

$$R_p^d + R_c^d = M = G + R_p - R_p^r - R_c^r$$

which says that the quantity of raw materials (M) is equal to output (G) plus production residuals (R_n), minus the amounts that are recycled from producers (R_p^r) and consumers (R_c^r). There are essentially three ways of reducing M and, therefore, residuals discharged into the natural environment.

Reduce G   Assuming the other flows stay the same, we can reduce residuals discharged by reducing the quantity of goods and services produced in the economy. Some people have fastened on this as the best long-run answer to environmental degradation; reducing output, or at least stopping its rate of growth, would allow a similar change in the quantity of residuals discharged.

---

[1] To make these direct comparisons all flows must be expressed in terms of mass.
[2] Note that G $= R_v$, i.e., everything that flows to the consumption sector eventually ends up as a residual from that sector.

Some have sought to reach this goal by advocating "zero population growth" (ZPG).[3] A slowly growing or stationary population can make it easier to control environmental impacts, but does not in any way ensure this control, for two reasons. First, a stationary population can grow economically, thus increasing its demand for raw materials. Second, environmental impacts can be long run and cumulative, so that even a stationary population can gradually degrade the environment in which it finds itself. But it is certainly true that population growth will often exacerbate the environmental impacts of a particular economy. In the U.S. economy, for example, although the emissions of pollutants per car has dramatically decreased over the last few decades through better emissions-control technology, the sheer growth in the number of cars on the highways has led to an increase in the total quantity of automobile emissions in many regions.

Reduce R_p   Another way of reducing M, and therefore residuals discharged, is to reduce R_p. Assuming the other flows are held constant, this means essentially changing the amounts of production residuals produced for a given quantity of output produced. There are basically just two ways of doing this. We can invent and adopt new production technologies and practices that produce smaller amounts of residuals per unit of output produced. We can call this reducing the "residuals intensity" of production. When we discuss the global issue of CO_2 emissions and atmospheric warming, for example, we will see that there is much that could be done to reduce the CO_2 intensity of energy production, especially by shifting to different fuels but also by reducing (actually by continuing to reduce) energy inputs required to produce a dollar's worth of final output.

The other way of reducing R_p is to shift the internal composition of output. Output G actually consists of a large number of different goods and services, with great differences among them in terms of the residuals left after they are produced. So another way to reduce the total quantity of residuals is to shift the composition of G away from high- and toward low-residuals items, while leaving the total intact. The shift from primarily a manufacturing economy toward services is a step in this direction. Most developed, "industrial" economies have experienced relatively fast rates of growth in their service sectors over the last half century or so. The rise of the so-called "information sectors" is another example. It is not that these new sectors produce no significant residuals; indeed, some of them may produce harsher leftovers than we have known before. The computer industry, for example, uses a variety of chemical solvents for cleaning purposes. But on the whole these sectors probably have a smaller waste disposal problem than the traditional industries they have replaced.

Increase $(R_p^r + R_c^r)$ The third possibility is to increase recycling. Instead of discharging production and consumption residuals into the environment, we can recycle them back into the production process. What this shows is that the

---

[3] For example, see Herman E. Daly, *Steady State Economics, Second Edition with New Essays,* Island Press, Washington, D.C., 1991.

central role of recycling is to replace a portion of the original flow of virgin materials (M). By substituting recycled materials for virgin materials, we can reduce the quantity of residuals discharged while maintaining the rate of output of goods and services (G). In modern economics recycling offers great opportunities to reduce waste flows. But we have to remember that recycling can never be perfect, even if we were to devote enormous resources to the task. Production processes usually transform the physical structure of materials inputs, making them difficult to use again. The conversion of energy materials makes materials recovery impossible. And recycling processes themselves can create residuals. But materials research will continue to progress and discover new ways of recycling. For a long time, automobile tires could not be recycled because the original production process changed the physical structure of the rubber. But recently a way has been found to overcome this problem, opening up the possibility that vast stockpiles of used tires with nowhere to go will no longer blight the landscape.[4]

These fundamental relationships are very important. We must remember, however, that our ultimate goal is to reduce the damages caused by the discharge of production and consumption residuals. Reducing the total quantity of these residuals is one major way of doing this, and the relationships discussed indicate the basic ways that may be done. But we can also reduce damages by working directly on the stream of residuals. We will look at this aspect of the problem, after a short pause to clarify terminology.

TERMINOLOGY

Throughout the chapters that follow we will be using the following terms:

- Ambient quality: "Ambient" refers to the surrounding environment, so ambient quality refers to the quantity of pollutants in the environment, e.g., the concentration of SO_2 in the air over a city or the concentration of a particular chemical in the waters of a lake.
- Environmental quality: A term used to refer broadly to the state of the natural environment. This includes the notion of ambient quality, and also such things as the visual and aesthetic quality of the environment.
- Residuals: Material that is left over after something has been produced; a plant takes in a variety of raw materials and converts these into some product; materials and energy left after the product has been produced are *production residuals. Consumption residuals* are what is left over after consumers have finished using the products that contained or otherwise used these materials.
- Emissions: That portion of production or consumption residuals that are placed in the environment, sometimes directly, sometimes after treatment.
- Recycling: The process of returning some or all of the production or consumption residuals to be used again in production or consumption.

---

[4] "A Scrappy Stretch of Road: It's Made of a Mixture of Asphalt and Rubber from Recycled Tires." *Los Angeles Times,* June 8, 1992, p. B1.

- Pollutant: A substance, energy form, or action that, when introduced into the natural environment, results in a lowering of the ambient quality level. We want to think of this as including not only the traditional things like oil spilled into oceans or chemicals placed in the air, but also activities, like certain building developments, that result in "visual pollution."
- Effluent: Sometimes "effluent" is used to talk about water pollutants, and emissions to refer to air pollutants, but in this book these two words will be used interchangeably.
- Pollution: Pollution is actually a tricky word to define. Some people might say that pollution results when any amount, no matter how small, of a residual has been introduced into the environment. Others hold that pollution is something that happens only when the ambient quality of the environment has been degraded enough to cause some damage.
- Damages: The negative impacts produced by environmental pollution; on people in the form of health effects, visual degradation, etc.; on elements of the ecosystem through disruption of ecological linkages, species extinctions, etc.
- Environmental medium: Broad dimensions of the natural world which collectively constitute the environment, usually classified as land, water, and air.
- Source: The location at which emissions occur, such as a factory, an automobile, or a leaking landfill.

EMISSIONS, AMBIENT QUALITY, AND DAMAGES

Let us now focus on what happens at the end of those two discharge arrows at the right side of Figure 2-1. Very simply, emissions produce changes in ambient levels of environmental quality, which in turn cause damages to humans and nonhumans. Figure 2-2 shows one way of sketching out this relationship. It shows two sources of emissions; they might be private firms, government agencies, or consumers. Sources take in various inputs and goods and use different types of technologies in production and consumption. In the process they produce residuals. How these residuals are handled then has a critical effect on subsequent stages. Some may be recovered and recycled back into production or consumption. Many can be put through treatment processes (residuals handling) that can render them more benign when emitted. Some of these processes are strictly physical (mufflers on cars and trucks, settling ponds at wastewater treatment plants, catalytic converters); others involve chemical transformations of various types (advanced treatment of domestic wastewater).

All emissions must necessarily go into one or more of the different environmental media, and there is an important relationship among them. There is a natural tendency in policy deliberations to keep these different media in separate compartments, dealing with air pollution separately from water pollution, and so on. But they are obviously interconnected; once residuals are produced, all that are not recycled must end up being discharged into one or more of the different media. Thus, for a given quantity of total residuals, if we reduce the

FIGURE 2-2
Emissions, Ambient Quality, and Damages. (*Inspired by John B. Braden and Kathleen Segerson, "Information Problems in the Design of Non-point Source Pollution Policy," in Association of Environmental and Resource Economics (AERE) Workshop Papers,* The Management of Non-point Source Pollution, Lexington. June 6-7, 1991.)

amounts going into one medium, we must necessarily increase the amounts going into the others. When we remove sulfur dioxide (SO_2) from the stack gases of power plants, for example, we have not destroyed the sulfur compounds. Instead, we end up with a sulfurous sludge that must be disposed of some other way, perhaps by land burial. If we incinerate this material, we are in fact emitting some into the air, but we still end up with certain quantities of solid residuals that must be disposed of elsewhere.

The streams of emissions come from the two different sources, but once emitted they merge into a single flow. In the real world this mixing may be complete; for example, the effluent from two pulp mills located at the same point on a river may mix so thoroughly that a few miles downstream it is impossible to differentiate one source's effluent from the other's. When there are a million or so cars moving about an urban area, the emissions from all become uniformly mixed together. In other cases the mixing is less than complete. If one power plant is just outside the city and another is 20 miles upwind, the closest plant will normally bear a greater responsibility for deteriorating air quality in the city than the other.

This mixing of emissions is a more significant problem than might first appear. With just a single source, the line of responsibility is clear, and to get an improvement in ambient quality we know exactly whose emissions we have to control. But with multiple sources, responsibilities become less clear. We may know how much we want to cut back total emissions, but we still face the problem of distributing this total reduction among the different sources. Each source then has an incentive to get the others to bear a larger share of the burden of reducing emissions. With every source thinking along the same lines, pollution control programs face a real problem of design and enforcement. We will run into this problem many times in the chapters to come.

Once a given quantity and quality of residuals has been introduced into a particular environmental medium, it is the physical, chemical, biological, meteorological, etc., processes of the natural system that determine how the residuals translate into particular ambient quality levels. For example, wind and temperature conditions will affect whether and how residuals emitted into the air affect nearby neighborhoods, as well as people living farther downwind. And since these meteorological conditions vary from day to day, the same level of emissions can produce different ambient quality levels at different times. Acid rain is produced through chemical processes acting primarily on sulfur dioxide emissions emitted far upwind; smog is also the result of complex chemical reactions involving sunlight and quantities of various pollutants. Underground hydrological processes affect the transportation of materials disposed of in landfills. And so on. Thus, to know how particular emissions will affect ambient quality levels we must have a good understanding of the physical and chemical workings of the environment itself. This is where the natural and physical sciences come in, to study the full range of environmental phenomena, from small, localized models of groundwater flow in a particular aquifer, to complex models of large lakes and river basins, to studies of interregional wind patterns, to global climate models. The fundamental goal is to determine how particular patterns of emissions are translated into corresponding patterns of ambient quality levels.

Finally, we have damages. A given set of ambient conditions translates into particular exposure patterns for living and nonliving systems. Of course, these exposures are a function not only of the physical processes involved, but also of the human choices that are made about where and how to live, and of the susceptibilities of living and nonliving systems to varying environmental conditions. Lastly, damages are related to human values. Human beings do not have amorphous preferences over all possible outcomes of the economic/environmental interaction; they prefer some outcomes over others. A major part of environmental economics is trying to determine the relative values that people place on these different environmental outcomes, a subject to which we will turn in later chapters on benefit–cost analysis.

TYPES OF POLLUTANTS

Physically, the residuals identified in Figure 2-2 consist of a vast assortment of materials and energy flowing into the three environmental media. We will want to distinguish among broad types of emissions according to factors that critically affect their economic status.

Cumulative vs. Noncumulative Pollutants

One simple and important dimension of environmental pollutants is whether they accumulate over time or tend to dissipate soon after being emitted. The classic case of a noncumulative pollutant is noise; as long as the source operates, noise is emitted into the surrounding air, but as soon as the source is shut down, the noise stops. At the other end of the spectrum we have pollutants that cumulate in the environment in nearly the same amounts as they are emitted. Radioactive waste, for example, decays over time but at such a slow rate in relation to human life spans that for all intents and purposes it will be with us permanently; it is a strictly cumulative type of pollutant. Another cumulative pollutant is plastics. The search for a degradable plastic has been going on for decades, but so far plastic is a substance that decays very slowly by human standards; thus, what we dispose of will be in the environment permanently. Many chemicals are cumulative pollutants; once emitted they are basically with us forever.

Between these two ends of the spectrum there are many types of effluent that are to some extent, but not completely, cumulative. The classic case is organic matter emitted into water bodies; for example, the wastes, treated or not, emitted from municipal waste treatment plants. Once emitted the wastes are subject to natural chemical processes that tend to break down the organic materials into their constituent elements, thus rendering them much more benign. The water, in other words, has a natural assimilative capacity that allows it to accept organic substances and render them less harmful. As long as this assimilative capacity has not been exceeded in any particular case, we can shut off the source of the effluent, and in a few days or weeks or months the water quality will return to normal. Of course the fact that nature has some assimilative capacity doesn't automatically mean that we have a strictly noncumulative pollutant. Once our emissions exceed the assimilative capacity we would move into a cumulative process. For example, the atmosphere of the earth has a given capacity to absorb CO_2 emitted by human activity, as long as this capacity is not exceeded. CO_2 is a noncumulative pollutant. But if the earth's assimilative capacity for CO_2 is exceeded, as it seems to be at the present time, we are in a situation where emissions are in fact accumulating over time.

Whether a pollutant is cumulative or noncumulative we still have essentially the same basic problem: trying to figure out the environmental damages and relating these back to the costs of reducing emissions. But this job is much more difficult for cumulative than for noncumulative pollutants. Consider the graphs in Figure 2-3. Panel (a) represents a noncumulative pollutant, while panel (b) depicts one that is cumulative. In panel (a) the graph begins at the origin, implying that current ambient concentrations are proportional to current emissions. Ambient concentrations are strictly a function of current emissions—reducing these emissions to zero would lead to zero ambient concentrations. But with cumulative pollutants the relationship is more complex. Today's emissions, since they accumulate and add to the stock of pollutant already existing, will cause damages not only today but also in the future, perhaps in the distant future. It also means that the current ambient quantity of an accumulating pollutant may be only weakly related to current emissions. The graph in panel (b) begins well up the vertical axis from the origin and has a flatter slope than the other. Thus a cutback in today's emissions has only a modest effect on current ambient concentrations. Even if today's emissions were cut to zero, ambient quality would still be impaired because of the cumulative effect of past emissions. The fact that a pollutant cumulates over time in the environment has the effect of breaking the direct connection between current emissions and current damages. This has a number of implications. For one thing it makes the science more difficult. The cause-and-effect relationships become harder to isolate when there

FIGURE 2-3
Relationship Between Current Emissions and Ambient Pollution Concentration.

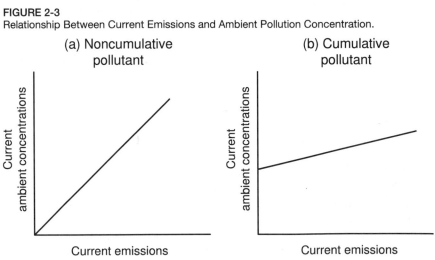

is a lot of time intervening between them. It also may make it more difficult to get people to focus on damages from today's emissions, again because there may only be a weak connection between today's emissions and today's ambient quality levels. Furthermore, cumulative pollutants by definition lead to future damages, and human beings have shown a depressing readiness to discount future events and avoid coming to grips with them in the present.

Local vs. Regional and Global Pollutants

Some emissions have an impact only in restricted, localized regions, while others have an impact over wider regions, perhaps on the global environment. Noise pollution and the degradation of the visual environment are local in their impacts; the damages from any particular source are usually limited to relatively small groups of people in a circumscribed region. Note that this is a statement about how widespread the effects are from any particular pollution source, not about how important the overall problem is throughout a country or the world. Some pollutants, on the other hand, have widespread impacts, over a large region or perhaps over the global environment. Acid rain is a regional problem; emissions in one region of the U.S. (and of Europe) affect people in other parts of the country or region. The ozone-depleting effects of chlorofluorocarbon emissions from various countries work through chemical changes in the earth's stratosphere, which means that the impacts are truly global.

Other things being equal, local environmental problems ought to be easier to deal with than regional or national problems, which in turn ought to be easier to manage than global problems. If I smoke out my neighbor with my wood stove, we may be able to arrange a solution among ourselves, or we can call on local political institutions to do it. But if my behavior causes more distant pollution, solutions may be more difficult. If we are within the same political system, we can call on these institutions to arrange solutions. In recent years, however, we have been encountering a growing number of international and global environmental issues. Here we are far from having effective means of responding, both because the exact nature of the physical impacts is difficult to describe and because the requisite international political institutions are only beginning to appear.

Point-Source vs. Nonpoint Source Pollutants

Pollution sources differ in terms of the ease with which actual points of discharge may be identified. The points at which sulfer dioxide emissions leave a large power plant are easy to identify; they come out the end of the smokestacks associated with each plant. Municipal waste treatment plants normally have a single outfall from which all of the wastewater is discharged. These are called *point-source pollutants*. On the other hand there are many pollutants for which there are no well-defined points of discharge. Agricultural chemicals, for example, usually run off the land in a dispersed or defused pattern, and even though they may pollute specific streams or underground aquifers, there is no single pipe or stack from which these chemicals are emitted. This is a *nonpoint source* type of pollutant. Urban storm water runoff is also an important nonpoint source problem.

As one would expect, point-source pollutants are likely to be easier to come to grips with than nonpoint source pollutants. They will probably be easier to measure and monitor and easier to study in terms of the connections between emissions and impacts. This means that it will ordinarily be easier to develop and administer control policies for point-source pollutants. As we will see, not all pollutants fit neatly into one or another of these categories.

Continuous vs. Episodic Emissions

Emissions from electric power plants or municipal waste treatment plants are more or less continuous. The plants are designed to be in operation continuously, though the operating rate may vary somewhat over the day, week, or season. Thus the emissions from these operations are more or less continuous, and the policy problem is to manage the rate of these discharges. We can make immediate comparisons between control programs and rates of emissions. The fact that emissions are continuous does not mean that damages are also continuous, however. Meteorological and hydrological events can turn continuous emissions into uncertain damages. But control programs are often easier to carry out when emissions are not subject to large-scale fluctuations.

Many pollutants are emitted on an episodic basis, however. The classic example is accidental oil or chemical spills. The policy problem here is to design and manage a system so that the probability of accidental discharges is reduced. But with an episodic effluent there may be nothing to measure, at least in the short run. Even though there have been no large-scale radiation releases from U.S. nuclear power plants, for example, we could still have a "pollution" problem if they are being managed in such a way as to increase the *probability* of an accidental release in the future. To measure the probabilities of episodic emissions we have to have data on actual occurrences over a long time period, or we have to estimate them from engineering data and similar information. We then have to determine how much insurance we wish to have against these episodic events.

Environmental Damages Not Related to Emissions

So far the discussion has focused on the characteristics of different types of environmental pollutants as they relate to the discharge of residual materials or energy. But there are many important instances of deteriorating environmental quality that are not traceable to residuals discharges. The conversion of land to housing and commercial areas destroys the environmental value of that land, whether it be its ecosystem value, such as habitat or wetland, or its scenic value. Other land uses, such as logging or strip mining, can also have important impacts. In cases like these our job is still to understand the incentives of people whose decisions create these impacts, and to change these incentives when appropriate. Although there are no physical emissions to monitor and control, there are nevertheless outcomes that can be described, evaluated, and managed with appropriate policies.

SHORT-RUN AND LONG-RUN CHOICES

Most of the discussion so far has focused on the physical connections among inputs, residuals, emissions, and ambient quality levels. These relationships are of prime interest to the physical and natural scientists working on environmental issues. We can move the discussion more toward the economist's bailiwick by examining the trade-offs inherent in the relationship between market output and environmental quality. This will give us a way also of considering the differences between short-run and long-run environmental decisions.

The basic relationship is shown in Figure 2-4. This depicts several *production possibility curves* (PPCs) between marketed output and environmental quality. A PPC is a way of depicting diagrammatically the choice faced by a group of people between two desirable outcomes. Consider for the moment panel (a) of Figure 2-4. The vertical axis has an index of the aggregate economic output of an economy, that is, the total market value of conventional economic goods traded in the economy in a year. The horizontal axis has an index of environmental quality, derived from data on different dimensions of the ambient environment, e.g., airborne SO_2 concentrations, urban noise levels, and water quality data. The curved relationship shows the different combinations of these two outcomes—marketed output and environmental quality—that are avail-

FIGURE 2-4
Production Possibility Curves for Current and Future Generations.

| (a) | (b) |
| PPC today | PPC in 60 years |

able to a group of people who have a fixed endowment of resources with which to work.[5]

The production possibility curve is determined by the technical capacities in the economy together with the ecological facts—meteorology, hydrology, etc.—of the natural system in which the country is situated. It says, for example, that if the current level of economic output is c_1, we can obtain an increase to c_2 only at the cost of a decrease in environmental quality from e_1 to e_2. But while the PPC itself is a technical constraint, where a society chooses to locate itself on its PPC is a matter of *social choice*. And this depends on the relative values that people in that society place on conventional economic output and environmental quality.

The current year production possibility curve depicts a competitive relationship between environmental quality and marketed output. More of one implies less of the other. But if our concern is what happens over a relatively long period of time, the single PPC can be misleading. This is because in the long run, environmental quality may be less substitutive than complementary with conventional economic outputs. In the long run the natural environment plays the role of environmental capital input into the production system, and a significant drawing down of that environmental capital may have serious negative effects on the ability of the economic system to sustain itself. A production possibility curve depicts the trade-offs facing today's generation. But what about future generations? One way to think of this is to consider the impacts of our decisions today on the production possibility curves facing *future* generations. Consider panel (b) of Figure 2-4. It shows the production possibilities curve for people in, say, 60 to 80 years, the generation consisting of your great grandchildren. According to today's PPC we could choose combinations (c_1, e_1), or (c_2, e_2), or any others on the curve. But the future is not independent of the choice we make today. It's conceivable, for example, that degrading the environment too much today will affect future possibilities—for example by depleting certain important resources, or by pollution that is so high it causes irreversible damage, or simply by a pollutant that is very long-lived and affects future generations. In effect this could shift the future PPC back from where it otherwise would be. This is depicted in panel (b) of the diagram. Your grandchildren will be confronted with a reduced set of possibilities as compared to the choices we face today. The future generation, finding itself on the inner production possibilities curve, can still have the same level of marketed output we have today (c_2), but only at a lower level of environmental quality (e_3) than we have today. Alternatively, it could enjoy the same level of environmental quality, but only with a reduced level of marketed output (c_3).

We have to recognize, of course, that the influence of today's decisions on future production possibilities is much more complicated than this discussion

---

[5] At the extremes I have drawn the PPCs with dashed lines. It's not clear what an outcome would be with "zero" environmental quality, nor what one would be with "zero" economic output. Thus, these extreme points are essentially undefined, and we will concentrate on points in the interior of the diagrams.

might suggest. It's not only environmental degradation that affects future conditions, but also technical developments and changes in human capacities. Thus, today's decisions could shift the future PPC either in or out, depending on a great many dynamic factors that are hard to predict. But we need to be particularly alert to avoid decisions today that would have the effect of shifting the future PPC to the left. This is the essence of recent discussions about *sustainability*. Sustainability means simply that future production possibility curves are not adversely affected by what we do today. It does not mean that we must maximize environmental quality today, since that implies zero output of goods and services. It means simply that we reduce our environmental impacts enough today to avoid shifting future production possibilities curves back in comparison to today's production possibilities. We will meet the idea of sustainability at several points throughout this book.

POLLUTION CONTROL IN THE U.S. ECONOMY

We will close this chapter by taking a general look at the U.S. economy and the role within it of pollution control. In 1990 the U.S. gross national product (GNP) was $5,463,000,000,000. Since the estimated population of the country in that year was 250,390,000, the GNP per capita was about $21,800. The U.S. Environmental Protection Agency (EPA) has estimated that in 1990 total expenditures on pollution control in the U.S. were $115,000,000,000.[6] This amounts to 2.1 percent of GNP, about $460 per capita. This cost includes all the private costs of complying with pollution control laws, that is, all the costs of purchasing, installing, operating, and maintaining pollution-control technology that firms need to be in compliance with these laws. It also includes the costs of changing internal operating procedures to meet pollution control laws. It includes household and local government costs of such programs as trash collection and disposal. Lastly, it includes all the public costs, at federal, state, and local levels, of administering and enforcing these pollution control laws and regulations.[7]

Is the price high or low? It's impossible to answer that in an absolute sense, but we might be able to give it more meaning by making some comparisons. The following tabulation shows costs of certain categories of expenditures made by U.S. citizens in 1987 as a proportion of GNP in that year.[8]

Clothing and shoes	4.2
Medical care	7.0
Food	11.7
National defense	6.9

[6] U.S. Environmental Protection Agency, *Environmental Investments: The Costs of a Clean Environment, A Summary* (EPA-230-12-90-084), Washington, D.C., 1990, p. 2-1.

[7] It does not include nonpollution-control environmental costs, however, like wildlife protection.

[8] U.S. EPA, *Environmental Investments*, p. 4-4. These and the following numbers are based on GNP (Gross National Product), which has been superseded in U.S. national income accounting by GDP (Gross Domestic Product). Ratios based on GDP are not yet available, but they would not be very different from the ones cited here.

Housing	9.3
Pollution control	1.7

Pollution control falls below such things as medical care and housing, and well below such public expenditures as national defense. Although pollution-control costs are expected to take a bigger share of GNP in future years, they will probably never get as large as the expenditures in basic consumer categories like clothing, housing, and food.

Another interesting comparison is between the U.S. and other industrialized countries. The following tabulation shows pollution-control costs as a percentage of GNP in several countries for 1985:[9]

United States	1.67
Finland	1.32
France	1.10
West Germany	1.52
Netherlands	1.26
Norway	.82
United Kingdom	1.25

These proportions range from .82 to 1.67 percent, with the U.S. comparing quite favorably because it has the highest expenditure share of this group of countries. We can't infer directly that people in the U.S. are enjoying a cleaner environment—less air pollution, cleaner water, and so on. Nothing is said here about the effectiveness with which pollution-control resources are being made in the different countries. It might be, for example, that although Norway spends less as a percentage of GNP on pollution control, it spends it more effectively than the resources spent in other countries. Another factor that is not taken into account in simple comparisons is the severity of the pollution problems in different countries. Because of differences in industrial structure and differences in environmental resources (like meteorological patterns, for example), it may cost more to reduce pollution to acceptable levels in one country than in another.[10] But the numbers are nevertheless interesting; it may be slightly surprising that most of these percentages are between 1.0 and 1.5.

Finally, Table 2-1 shows a breakdown of total U.S. pollution-control costs among the different environmental programs, and how the EPA projects these costs to increase over the decade of the 1990s. It shows that total costs are expected to be about 500 percent higher in 2000 than they were in 1972. You can see that the rate of increase in the near future is expected to be lower: The change from $26.5 billion in 1972 to $58 billion in 1980 was a 120 percent increase, while total costs are expected to increase about 60 percent in the 1990s. Whether this will happen depends on how briskly old laws are enforced and new ones are added to the books. The effort accounting for the greatest share of control costs

[9] U.S. EPA, *Environmental Investments,* p. 4-7.
[10] We will discuss this question at greater length in Chapter 18.

TABLE 2-1
TOTAL CONTROL COSTS,* ASSUMING FULL IMPLEMENTATION OF CURRENT POLICY
(Millions of 1986 Dollars)

	1972	1980	1990	2000
Total Costs	26,481	57,969	100,167	160,416
Percentage of GNP	.88	1.58	2.14	2.83
Percentage of Total Costs				
Air and radiation	30.1	30.7	28.0	28.0
Water	37.4	42.7	42.3	40.0
Land	31.8	23.5	26.5	28.8
Chemicals	.3	1.6	1.6	1.8
Multimedia	.4	1.5	1.6	1.4

*Includes compliance costs plus regulatory costs.

Source: U.S. Environmental Protection Agency, *Environmental Investments: The Costs of a Clean Environment* (EPA-230-12-90-084), Washington, D.C., 1990, pp. 2-2 to 2-3.

is water pollution control, approximately 42 percent of the total in 1990. Air pollution control and land programs, chiefly solid waste disposal, are of similar magnitude, around 26–28 percent of total costs. Special programs to control chemical pollution account for less than 2 percent of total control costs in 1990, but these are projected to increase in the 1990s.

One can take almost any position one wants on cost figures like these. Total pollution-control costs are many billions of dollars each year, but they are not enormous in comparison to many other types of expenditures. Certainly they are large enough that we should be sensitive to the need for getting the most pollution-control impact for the money we are spending. A large part of what follows in this book is about designing efficient and effective pollution-control policy, as well as trying to measure some of the environmental values involved in this policy.

SUMMARY

The purpose of this chapter was to explore some basic linkages between the economy and the environment. We differentiated between the role of the natural system as a supplier of raw material inputs for the economy and as a receptor for production and consumption residuals. The first of these is normally called natural resource economics and the second environmental economics. After a very brief review of natural resource economics, we introduced the fundamental balance phenomenon, which says that in the long run all materials taken by human beings out of the natural system must eventually end up back in that system. This means that to reduce residuals flows into the environment we must reduce materials taken from the ecosystem, and we discussed the three fundamental ways that this can be done.

We then focused more directly on the flow of residuals back into the environment, making a distinction among emissions, ambient environmental quality, and damages. The environmental damages from a given quantity of emissions can be very substantially altered by handling these emissions in different ways. Our next step was to provide a brief catalogue of the different types of emissions and pollutants, as well as nonpollution types of environmental impacts such as aesthetic effects. We then covered some ideas about how environmental quality and the output of conventional economic goods are related in the short and long run. Finally, we discussed some results showing pollution-control expenditures in the U.S., comparing them to other cost categories as well as to expenditures in other developed countries. Our conclusion here was that although pollution-control expenditures are not large in comparison to other expenditure categories, they are large enough that we should be concerned about getting the greatest results possible in terms of improvements in environmental policy.

QUESTIONS FOR FURTHER DISCUSSION

1 How does population growth affect the balance of flows shown in Figure 2-1?
2 If all goods could be changed overnight so that they lasted twice as long as before, how would this change the flows of Figure 2-1 in the short and long runs?
3 A given quantity of a residual, discharged at one time and place, can be a pollutant; while if it is discharged at another time or place it may not constitute a pollutant. Why is this true?
4 Why are long-lived, cumulative pollutants so much harder to manage than short-lived, noncumulative pollutants?
5 Consider the visual pollution that is produced when an ugly factory is built in a scenic area; is that a cumulative or noncumulative pollutant? How about the scarred landscape of strip-mined land? Urban trash?
6 What considerations come into play when considering whether the U.S. or any other political entity is spending the "right" amount for environmental quality improvements?

SELECTED READINGS

Ayres, Robert U.: *Resources, Environment and Economics, Applications of the Materials/Energy Balance Principle*, John Wiley and Sons, New York, 1978.
Baumol, William, and Wallace Oates: *Economics, Environmental Policy and the Quality of Life*, Prentice-Hall, Englewood Cliffs, N.J., 1979.
Council on Environmental Quality: *Environmental Quality*, Washington, D.C., published annually.
Enthoven, Alain C., and A. Myrick Freeman III (eds.): *Pollution, Resources and the Environment*, Norton, New York, 1973.
Kneese, Allen V.: *Economics of the Environment*, Penguin Books, New York, 1977.
Kneese, Allen V., and Blair T. Bower: *Environmental Quality and Residuals Management*, Johns Hopkins Press for Resources for the Future, Baltimore, Md., 1979.
Krutilla, John V.: "Conservation Reconsidered," *American Economic Review*, 57(4), September 1967, pp. 777–786.
McKee, David L.: *Energy, the Environment, and Public Policy: Issues for the 1990s*, Praeger, New York, 1991.

Ophuls, William: *Ecology and the Politics of Scarcity*, W. H. Freeman, San Francisco, 1977.
Organization for Economic Cooperation and Development: *The State of the Environment*, Paris, 1991.
Pearce, David, Anil Markandya, and Edward B. Barbier: *Blueprint for a Green Economy*, Earthscan Publications, London, 1989.
Wilson, Edmund O.: "Biodiversity, Prosperity and Value," in F. Herbert Bormann and Stephen R. Kellert (eds.), *Ecology, Economics, Ethics: The Broken Circle*, Yale University Press, New Haven, Conn., 1991, pp. 3–25.

ANALYTICAL TOOLS

Scientific analysis consists of giving coherent explanations of relevant events and of showing how other outcomes might have occurred if conditions had been different. It is to show connections among variables and to detail the ways in which they are interrelated. To do this, a science must develop a specialized vocabulary and conceptual structure with which to focus on its chosen subject matter. In this section we cover some of the basic ideas of economics and of their application to environmental matters. Those of you who have already been introduced to microeconomics can treat the next few chapters as a review. For those who are seeing this material for the first time, remember that the purpose is to develop a set of "analytical tools" which we can then use to focus on issues of environmental quality.

CHAPTER 3

BENEFITS AND COSTS, SUPPLY AND DEMAND

In this and the next chapter we cover certain basic tools of microeconomics. They are not meant to turn you into an economist, but they are aimed at giving you enough of an understanding of fundamental concepts that we can use them later in analyzing environmental impacts and policies. The present chapter is about benefits and costs. The juxtaposition of these two words indicates that we are going to approach things in a trade-off, or balancing, mode. Economic actions, including environmental actions, have two sides: On the one side they create value and on the other side they encounter costs. Thus, we must have basic concepts that deal with these two parts of the problem. We look first at the question of value, later at costs.

We must mention at the very outset that microeconomic theory is "abstract." This means that it normally proceeds with simplified models that try to capture the essence of a problem without all the details that one observes in the real world. The reason for this is that we want to reveal basic connections and relationships among the important elements of a problem, relationships that are difficult to see if we just observe the surface richness of the real world. There are dangers in this, of course; we can inadvertently overlook details that do have an important impact in reality. For example, in the past many environmental models have been developed without considering the costs of actually enforcing environmental laws. But in the real world enforcement costs are more than a detail; they can have a great impact on realized outcomes. Thus, we need to be careful that our abstractions truly serve to reveal basic connections and do not cover up important dimensions of problems we are trying to understand.

WILLINGNESS TO PAY

The value side of our analysis is based on the fundamental notion that individuals have preferences for goods and services; given a choice they can express preferences for one good over another, or one bundle of goods over another bundle. How can we make visible this abstract notion of preference? First we need to simplify the discussion; in a modern economy there are thousands of different goods and services available, so let us focus on just one of them. We now can present the following fundamental concept: The value of this good to a person is what the person is willing and able to sacrifice for it. Sacrifice what? It could be anything, but it makes most sense to talk about sacrificing generalized purchasing power. Thus, the value of a good to somebody is what that person is willing to pay for it. What determines how much a person is willing to pay to obtain some good or service, or some environmental asset? It's partly a question of individual values. Some people are willing to sacrifice a lot to visit the Grand Canyon; others are not. Some people are willing to pay a lot for a quiet living environment; others are not. Some people place a high value on trying to preserve the habitat of unique animal and plant species; others do not. It is obvious also that a person's wealth affects the willingness to sacrifice; the wealthier a person is, the better that person can afford to pay for various goods and services. Willingness to pay, in other words, also reflects ability to pay.

Let's consider the willingness to pay of a person for a particular good. We want to build a picture of this willingness to pay for various amounts of this good. Assume that the person has none of the good to begin with. We ask her, or perhaps deduce from watching her spend her money, how much she would be willing to pay for a single unit of a good rather than go without. Suppose this is some number, like $38 pictured in the top of Figure 3-1. We then ask, assuming she already has one unit of this good, how much she would be willing to pay for a second unit. According to Figure 3-1 her answer is $26. In similar fashion, her willingness to pay for each additional unit is shown by the height of the rectangle above that unit: $17 for unit 3, $12 for unit 4, and so on. These numbers depict a fundamental relationship of economics: the notion of diminishing willingness to pay. As the number of units consumed increases, the willingness to pay for additional units of that good normally goes down.

It is not very convenient to work with diagrams that are step-shaped as in the top of Figure 3-1. So we now change things a bit by assuming that people can consume fractions of items in addition to integer values (as in, e.g., the number of pounds of potatoes consumed per week). What this does is give us a smoothly shaped willingness-to-pay curve, like the one pictured in the bottom of Figure 3-1. In effect the steps in the willingness-to-pay curve have become too small to see, giving us a smooth curve to work with. On this smooth function we have singled out one quantity for illustrative purposes. It shows that the marginal willingness to pay for the third unit is $17.

We need to make a distinction here between *total* and *marginal*, since this is something we will be running into constantly in later chapters. Suppose a person is already consuming two units of this good; according to the willingness-to-pay curve, that person would be willing to pay $17 for a third unit. This is the *marginal* willingness to pay— in this case, for the third unit. Marginal is thus a word that describes the *additional* willingness to pay of a person for one more unit. So the

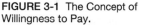

FIGURE 3-1 The Concept of Willingness to Pay.

height of the rectangles in the top of Figure 3-1 or of the height of the curve in the bottom graph shows the marginal willingness to pay for this good.

The *total* willingness to pay for a given consumption level refers to the total amount a person would be willing to pay to attain that consumption level rather than go without the good entirely. Suppose the person is consuming at a level of three units; her total willingness to pay for consuming this quantity is $81, which is in fact the sum of the heights of the demand rectangles between the origin and the consumption level in question ($38 for the first plus $26 for the second plus $17 for the third). This corresponds in the smooth version of the willingness-to-pay function in the bottom to the whole area under the willingness-to-pay curve from the origin up to the quantity in question. For three units of consumption, the total willingness to pay is equal to an amount represented by the combined areas *a* and *b*.

Demand

There is another way of looking at these marginal willingness-to-pay relation-ships. They are more familiarly known as *demand curves*. An individual demand curve shows the quantity of a good or service that the individual in question would demand (i.e., purchase and consume) at any particular price. For example, suppose a person whose marginal willingness-to-pay/demand curve is shown in the bottom part of Figure 3-1 is able to purchase this item at a unit price of $17. The quantity he would demand at this price is three units. The reason is that his marginal willingness to pay for each of the first three units exceeds the purchase price. He would not push his consumption higher than this, since his marginal willingness to pay for additional quantities would be less than the purchase price.

An individual's demand/marginal willingness-to-pay curve for a good or service is a way of summarizing his personal consumption attitudes and capa-bilities for that good. Thus we would normally expect these relationships to differ somewhat among individuals, because individual tastes and preferences vary. Some people are willing to pay more for a given item than other people. Figure 3-2 displays a number of different demand curves. Panel (a) shows two demand curves, one steeper than the other. The steeper one shows a situation in which marginal willingness to pay drops off fairly rapidly as the quantity consumed increases; with the other one marginal willingness to pay, though lower to begin with, goes down less rapidly as quantity increases. What could account for this difference? One possibility is that the two demand curves apply to two different people but the same product; the demand curves are essentially telling us that these two people have different tastes and preferences for this good. Or they might picture the case of one person but two different goods.

Panel (b) of Figure 3-2 also has two demand curves; they have the same general shape, but one is situated well to the right of the other. The demand curve lying above and to the right shows a good for which the marginal

FIGURE 3-2
Typical Demand/Marginal Willingness-to-Pay Curves.

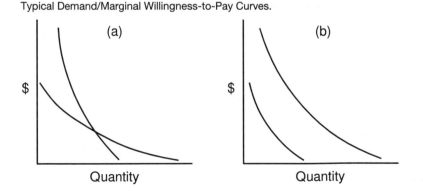

willingness to pay is substantially higher than it is for the same quantity of the other good. What could account for the difference? They might be the demand curves of two different people for the same good. But there are other possibilities. How much a person is willing to pay for something obviously depends on how much money she has; more than likely the higher her income, the more she is willing to pay. So the two demand curves in panel (b) could apply to the same individual and the same good, but at two different points in time, the one to the right being her willingness to pay after she has had a substantial increase in her income.

There is another way of looking at the two demand curves of panel (b), one that may be very important for the application of these ideas to environmental assets. Peoples' tastes depend on a lot of factors of a psychological and historical kind that are hard to pin down and describe but are nevertheless real. They will depend in part on the experiences that people have and the information they gather over time about the qualities of different goods and how they feel about them. So, for example, the demand curve to the right could be the same consumer's demand curve for a good for which his appreciation has increased over time. For example, these might be his demand curves for outdoor wilderness experiences, the one to the left applying before he knew much about this type of activity and the one to the right applying after he had some wilderness experiences and learned to like them. Other factors are information and psychology; the demand curve on the right might be a person's demand for a food item before an announcement of the presence in it of pesticide residues, the curve on the left being the demand curve after the announcement.

Note that the demand curves are in fact curvilinear, rather than straight lines. A straight-line demand relationship would imply a uniform change in the quantity demanded as its price changes. For most goods, however, this is unlikely to be true. Consider water, for example. At low prices and high rates of consumption, studies have shown that relatively small increases in price will lead to substantial reductions in quantity demanded. At high prices and low quantity demanded, however, price increases have a much smaller effect, they produce much smaller reductions in quantity demanded. This gives us a demand relationship that is convex to the origin, i.e., relatively flat at low prices and steep at higher prices.

Economics is sometimes misunderstood as assuming that people are driven only by thoughts of their own welfare, that they are complete egoists. Since these are individual demand curves, they do indeed summarize the attitudes of single individuals, but this does not imply that individuals make decisions with only themselves in mind. Some people may indeed act this way, but for most there are many other powerful motives that affect their demands for different goods, including altruism toward friends and relatives, feelings of civic virtue toward their communities, a sense of social responsibility toward fellow citizens, and so on. Individual tastes and preferences spring from these factors as well as from more narrow considerations of personal likes and dislikes.

AGGREGATE DEMAND/WILLINGNESS TO PAY

When we examine real-world issues of environmental quality and pollution-control policy, we normally focus our attention on the behavior of groups of people rather than single individuals. Our interest is in the total, or aggregate, demand/marginal willingness to pay of defined groups of people.

An aggregate demand curve is the summation of a number of individual demand curves. What individuals are involved depends on which particular aggregation we want to look at: the demand of people living in the city of New York for brussels sprouts; the demand of people living in New Orleans for clean water in the Mississippi; the demand of people living in the entire country for public parks, and so on. An aggregate demand curve is simply the summation of the demand curves of all the people in the group of interest.

Figure 3-3 depicts a very simple aggregate demand curve, one in which the "group" consists of only three people. At a price of $8, Person A demands 10 units of this good, while at the same price Person B demands six units and Person C demands eight units of the good. Thus, the aggregate demand curve, pictured to the far right, shows an aggregate demand of 24 units for the price of $8. Note that we are summing these individual demand curves horizontally. Looked at in the other direction we note that when Person A is consuming 10 units his marginal willingness to pay is $8, while when Persons B and C consume, respectively, at six units and eight units, their marginal willingnesses to pay are also $8. Therefore, on the aggregate level, the marginal willingness to pay is $8. If we make one more unit available to this aggregate, it must be distributed to Person A, Person B, or Person C, each of whom has a marginal willingness to pay of $8; thus, the aggregate marginal willingness to pay is also $8.

BENEFITS

We now come to the idea of "benefits." Benefit is one of those ordinary words to which economists have given a technical meaning. When we clean up the

FIGURE 3-3
Aggregate Demand/Marginal Willingness-to-Pay Curves.

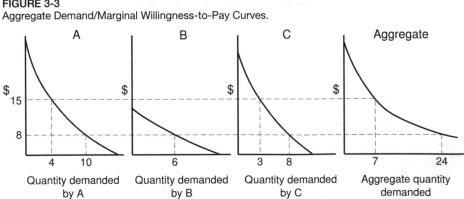

environment, we provide benefits to people, and when we all ment to deteriorate in quality, we are taking benefits away from effect causing them damage. We need some way of conceptua uring this notion of benefits.

The word "benefits" clearly implies being made better off; if someone is benefited by something, her position is improved; she is better off. Conversely, if she is worse off, it must be because benefits were somehow taken away from her. How do we confer benefits on somebody? By giving him something he values. How do we know that he values something? By the fact that he is willing to sacrifice, or willing to pay, for it. According to this logic, then, the benefits that people get from something are equal to the amount they are willing to pay for it.

The logic behind this definition of "benefits" is quite strong. It means we can use ordinary demand curves to determine the benefits of making various things available to people. For example, Figure 3-4 shows two demand curves, and on the horizontal axis two quantity levels are indicated. Suppose we wish to estimate the total benefits to the two groups of people whose aggregate demand curves these are, of increasing the availability of this item from quantity q_1 to quantity q_2. According to our previous thinking, benefits are measured by willingness to pay, and we know that total willingness to pay is measured by areas under the demand curve, in this case the area under the demand curves between quantity q_1 and quantity q_2. So for the lower demand curve the benefits of such an increase in availability are equal to an amount shown by area b, while benefits in the case of the higher demand curve are equal to the total area $a + b$.

This apparently is as it should be. The people with the higher demand curve must place a greater value on this item; whatever it is, they are willing to pay

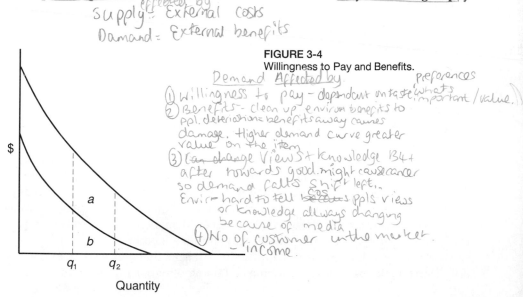

FIGURE 3-4
Willingness to Pay and Benefits.

...ore for it than the people whose demand curve is the lower function. This is in agreement with common sense. The more people value something the more they are benefited by having more of that something made available, or, to say the same thing, you can't damage people by taking away from them something that they don't value.

This is the fundamental logic underlying much of environmental economics. It underlies, for example, questions of how we place a value on the damage done to people when the natural environment surrounding them is degraded. It underlies the question of how we evaluate the impacts of environmental programs and policies undertaken by local, state, and federal governments. This is its strength, the fact that it is based on a clear notion of the value that people place on different things.

But we must also recognize its shortcomings. For one thing demand, and therefore benefits, are often very hard to measure when it concerns environmental questions, as we will see in later chapters. For another, we have to remember that demand curves are critically affected by the ability to pay for something as well as the sheer willingness to pay for it. In Figure 3-4, for example, the lower demand curve could represent a group of people with lower incomes than those with the higher demand curve. The logic of our argument would lead us to conclude that the increase in quantity of $q_2 - q_1$ would produce fewer benefits among lower income people than among higher income people. This may not be a very equitable conclusion, depending on the circumstances. Thus, although the logic of the concept is clear, we have to be careful in using it, especially when we are dealing with groups of people with diverse income levels. The main step in doing this is to find out as clearly as possible how the various environmental policies and programs, present or proposed, affect people at different income levels. We will discuss this at greater length in later chapters.

One other possible problem exists in using conventional demand curves to measure benefits. An individual's demand for something is clearly affected by how much she knows about it; a person would not be willing to pay for a good if, for example, she was ignorant of its very existence. In Figure 3-4, the higher demand curve might be the demand for a good before it is found out that it contains a carcinogenic substance, and the lower demand curve shows demand after this fact becomes known. There is nothing especially surprising about this; people do after all become more knowledgeable about things over time as a matter of course. But in today's world this could be a complication, especially with regard to the environment. We don't fully understand many of the effects of environmental degradation; furthermore, peoples' views about the importance of many of these effects are blown back and forth almost from day to day, by the media, by the scientific press, and so on. In some of these cases, we may want to be a little careful about taking peoples' demand curves of the moment, influenced as they are by all kinds of real and imagined factors, as true expressions of the benefits of environmental actions. It's not that they are irrelevant, it's only that they have to be taken with a certain amount of caution.

COST

We now switch to the other side of the picture and consider costs. Although some things in life are free—an idea, for example—it is generally true that goods and services cannot be produced out of thin air; they require the expenditure of productive resources, or inputs, in the process. The more we want of something the more resources we will have to devote to its production. We need a way of describing and talking about the costs of producing useful things, whether these are normal consumer goods like cars or hot-water bottles, or services like transportation or insurance, or environmental quality through the treatment of waste residuals, recycling, or land-use controls.

Imagine a simple production process. Suppose, for example, we are producing a certain line of cardboard boxes. To produce boxes we require a variety of productive inputs—labor, machinery of various descriptions, energy, raw materials, waste handling equipment, and so on. The first thing we need is a way of valuing these productive resources. If we are a private firm operating in a market economy, we would have little problem: We would value them according to what they cost to procure in the markets. Our profit-and-loss statement at the end of the year would reflect the monetary "out-of-pocket" costs of the inputs we used in the production operation. But we will use a broader concept of cost. From this wider perspective the costs of these cardboard boxes is what could have been produced with these productive inputs had they not been used in box production. The name for this is *opportunity cost*.

Opportunity Cost

The *opportunity cost* of producing something consists of the maximum value of other outputs we could and would have produced had we not used the resources to produce the item in question. The word "maximum" is in there for a reason. The productive inputs we used to produce our cardboard boxes could have been used to produce a variety of other things, perhaps automobiles, or books, or pollution-control equipment. The opportunity cost of the boxes consists of the maximum value of the alternative output we could have obtained had we used these resources differently.

Opportunity costs include out-of-pocket costs but are wider than this. Some inputs that are actually used in production may not get registered as cash costs. For example, the husband of the cardboard box plant operator works as an unpaid assistant in the front office. This may not register as an out-of-pocket cost, but he certainly has an opportunity cost because he could have been working somewhere else if he weren't working here. Even more importantly for our purposes, the cardboard box manufacturing process may produce waste products that are pumped into a nearby stream. Downstream these production residuals produce environmental damage, which are real opportunity costs of producing cardboard boxes, even though they do not show up as costs in the plant's profit-and-loss statement.

In this example we have a private firm producing boxes, but the opportunity cost idea is relevant in any situation in which a decision must be made about using productive resources for one purpose rather than another. For a public agency with a given budget, the opportunity costs of a particular policy are the value of alternative policies it might have pursued. For a consumer, the opportunity cost of spending time searching for a particular item is the value of the next most valuable thing to which the consumer could have devoted time.

How do we measure opportunity cost? It's not very useful to measure it in terms of the number of other physical items that could have been produced. Nor do we have enough information in most cases to be able to measure the value of the next best output that was forgone. In practice, therefore, we measure opportunity costs by the value of inputs used up in production. For this to work, we have to take care that the inputs have been correctly valued. The office labor must be valued at the going rate even though it is not paid in practice. The effects on downstream water quality must be evaluated and included. Once all inputs have been accounted for, their total value may be taken as the true opportunity costs of production.

Cost Curves

We need some way to summarize cost information, just as we did in the case of willingness to pay. We will do this with cost curves, which are geometric representations of production costs. And, just as in the case of willingness to pay, we will differentiate between *marginal costs* and *total costs*. Consider the cost curves in Figure 3-5. They are meant to apply to a single producing organization, a firm, or perhaps a public agency, that is producing some good or service. The graph is laid out, the same as earlier, with quantity on the horizontal axis and a monetary index on the vertical axis. The top panel shows marginal costs in terms of a step-shaped relationship. It shows that it costs $5 to produce the first unit of output. If the firm wants to increase output to two units it must spend an added $7. The addition of a third unit would add $10 to total costs, and so on. Marginal cost is a symmetrical measure; it is the added costs, the amount by which total costs increase, when output is increased by one unit. It is also the cost savings if production were to decrease by one unit. Thus, the reduction in output from four to three units would reduce total costs by $15, the marginal cost of the fourth unit.

It is inconvenient to work with step-shaped curves, so we make the assumption that the firm can produce intermediate quantities as well as integer values. This gives us a smooth marginal cost curve, as shown in the bottom panel of Figure 3-5. This curve now tells us the marginal cost—the added cost of one more unit of output—for any level of output. For example, at an output level of 4.5 units, marginal cost is $19.

We can use marginal cost curves to determine *total production costs*. On the stepped marginal cost curve of Figure 3-5, suppose we wish to know the total cost of producing five units of this item. This is equal to the cost of the first unit

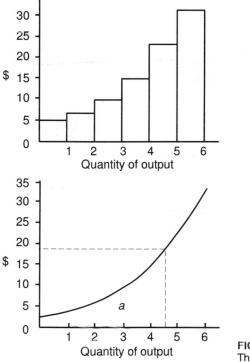

FIGURE 3-5
The Concept of Marginal Cost.

($5), plus that of the second ($7), plus that of the third ($10), and so on. This total is $60; geometrically we can see that it is equal to the total area of the rectangles above the first five units of output. Analogously, in the smoothly shaped marginal cost function in the bottom of the diagram, the total cost of producing a given quantity is the dollar amount equal to the area under the marginal cost curve between the origin and the quantity in question. The total cost of producing 4.5 units of output is thus given by the area marked *a* in the figure.

The Shapes of Cost Curves

The height and shape of the marginal cost curve for any production process will differ from one situation to another. A key determining factor is the technology utilized in production, and we will discuss this concept below. The price of inputs is also an important factor influencing the heights of marginal cost curves. In general, if input prices increase to a firm or group of firms, their marginal cost curves will shift upward. Another important element is *time*, specifically the amount of time that a firm has to adjust to changes in its rate of output. We can understand these factors better by looking at some actual marginal cost curves.

Figure 3-6 shows several marginal cost curves. Panel (a) shows a very typical marginal cost curve; initially it declines as output increases but then eventually it increases as output gets larger. The initial decline comes about because of basic efficiencies achievable with larger quantities at this level. Suppose our "output" refers to the quantity of wastewater handled in a municipal treatment plant. At very low levels of output the plant is not being fully utilized; thus output increases in this range are accompanied by less than proportionate increases in production cost, given marginal costs that diminish. But as output increases, the capacity of the plant is approached. Machinery must be worked longer, additional people must be hired, etc. Thus, marginal cost begins to increase. As the capacity of the operation is neared, these problems become more acute. To continue to increase output, more extraordinary measures are required, which can only be done at a high cost; thus, marginal cost increases even more. A point may come at which it becomes almost impossible to increase output further, which is the same as saying that the marginal costs of production at this point increase without limit. This limit is indicated by the vertical dashed line in panel (a) of Figure 3-6.

This marginal cost curve depicts an important generic characteristic of all marginal cost curves, namely, that although they may initially decline, they will always increase, eventually, as output becomes large enough. These increases are related to certain underlying factors such as increased plant utilization, the need to reach farther away for raw materials, and the inevitable higher management costs that accompany larger operations. Virtually all economic studies of particular operations and industries demonstrate increasing marginal production costs, and this fact will be an important shaping element in our later discussions specifically related to environmental quality management.

Panel (b) of Figure 3-6 shows a marginal cost curve similar in general shape to the one in panel (a), but with less pronounced curvature. In particular, although this marginal cost curve eventually increases, it does so less steeply

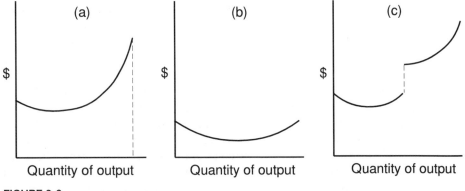

FIGURE 3-6
Typical Marginal Cost Curves.

than the earlier one. This is more typical of a long-run marginal cost curve, i.e., one where enough time is given for operators of firms to adapt fully to an increase in the rate of output. In the short run, our wastewater treatment plant had a certain capacity that was basically fixed. But in the long run, there is time to build a larger treatment plant with higher capacities. For larger outputs, the marginal costs of this larger plant will be lower than those of the smaller plant. But even in these long-run situations marginal costs will eventually increase, as is depicted in panel (b). *In our subsequent discussions we will assume that we are working with long-run marginal cost curves, unless we specify otherwise.*

Panel (c) of Figure 3-6 represents a more complicated case where there is a discontinuity in the marginal cost curve. After a short downward section the marginal costs generally trend upward, and at one point they jump upward by some amount. This might represent a "lumpy" investment in new types of technology at a certain point as output increases.

TECHNOLOGY

The most important factor affecting the shapes of marginal cost functions is the technology of the production process. By technology we mean the inherent productive capabilities of the methods and machines being employed. Any modern production requires capital goods (machinery and equipment) of various types and capacities, labor inputs, operating procedures, raw materials, and so on. The quantity of output a firm can get from a given set of inputs depends on the technical and human capabilities inherent in these inputs. The marginal cost curves pictured in Figure 3-6 could relate to different industries, because the marginal cost curves are so different. But even within the same industry marginal cost curves can differ among firms. Some firms will be older than others; they may be working with older equipment that has different cost characteristics. Even firms of the same age may have different production techniques; past managerial decisions may have put them in different positions in terms of marginal production costs today.

This concept of technology is vitally important in environmental economics because we rely heavily on technological change to find ways to produce goods and services with fewer environmental side effects and also to handle better the quantities of production residuals that remain. In our simple cost model, technical advancement has the effect of shifting marginal cost curves downward. Technological progress makes it possible to produce a given increase in output at a lower marginal cost. It also reduces total production cost. Consider Figure 3-7. MC_1 is the firm's marginal cost curve before a technical improvement; MC_2 is the marginal cost curve after some technical improvement has been put into effect. The technical change, in other words, shifts the marginal cost curve downward. We can determine how much total production costs are reduced as a result of technological change. Consider output level q^*. With MC_1 the total cost of producing an output of q^* is represented by the area $a + b$, while after the reduction in the marginal cost curve to MC_2 the total cost of producing q^* is equal

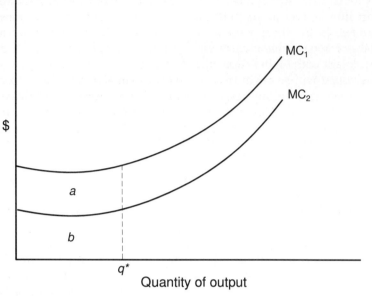

FIGURE 3-7
Technological Improvement.

to area *b*. Thus, the reduction in total cost made possible by the technological change is equal to area *a*.

Technological change does not normally happen without effort; it normally requires research and development (R&D). R&D in environmental industries is obviously an important activity to promote, and one of the criteria we will want to use to evaluate environmental policies is whether the policies create incentives for individuals, firms, and industries to engage in vigorous R&D programs. In very simple terms, the incentive to engage in R&D is the cost savings that results from the new techniques, materials, procedures, etc., that are discovered in the effort. The cost savings shown in Figure 3-7 (area *a*) shows part of this incentive. This is the cost savings that would result each year, and the accumulation of these annual cost savings represents the full R&D incentive.

THE EQUIMARGINAL PRINCIPLE

We come now to the discussion of a simple but important economic principle, one that we will use repeatedly in chapters to come. It's called the "equimarginal" principle. To understand it, assume that we have a firm producing a certain product, and that the firm's operation is divided between two different plants. For example, suppose there is a single power company that owns two different generating plants. Each plant produces the same item, so that the total output of the firm is the sum of what it produces in the two plants. But let us assume that the plants were built at different times and make use of different technology. The old one, Plant A in Figure 3-8, has older technology; this gives a marginal cost curve that starts relatively low but rises steeply as production increases. The new plant, Plant B in Figure 3-8, uses newer technology; it has a higher marginal cost at low output levels, but marginal costs do not rise as steeply as production increases.

Consider now a situation in which this two-plant firm wants to produce a total output of, say, 100 units. How many units should it produce in each plant, in order to produce the 100 units at the *least total cost*? Would it be best to produce 50 units in each plant? This is depicted in Figure 3-8; at an output of 50, Plant A has a marginal cost of $12 while Plant B has a marginal cost of $8. Total production costs are the sum of total costs at each plant, or $(a + b + c) + d$. But here is the important point: We can lower the total cost of our 100 units by reallocating production. Reduce production in Plant A by one unit; costs will fall by $12. Then increase the production in Plant B by one unit; costs there will rise by $8. We are still producing the 100 units as we have specified, but we have saved $12 - $8 = $4. Thus, our total cost, the sum of the costs in the two plants, has gone down.

As long as the marginal costs in the two plants differ from one another, we can continue to reallocate production—away from the high marginal cost plant and toward the low marginal cost plant —and get a reduction in total cost. In fact, our total costs of producing the 100 units in the two plants will be at a minimum only when the marginal costs of the two plants are equal—hence the "equimarginal principle." In the figure, this happens when the output in Plant A is 38 units and the output in Plant B is 62 units. Total costs in geometric terms are now $a + (d + e)$.

The equimarginal principle, therefore, says the following: If you have multiple sources to produce a given product or achieve a given goal, and you want to

FIGURE 3-8
The Equimarginal Principle.

minimize the total cost of producing a given quantity of that output, distribute production in such a way as to equalize the marginal costs between the production sources. There is another way of saying it that may look different but actually isn't: If you have a given amount of resources and you want to maximize the total amount produced, distribute total production among the sources in such a way as to equalize marginal costs. This principle will be very valuable when we take up the issue of getting maximum emissions reductions from given amounts of resources.

MARGINAL COST AND SUPPLY

We will have many occasions to question whether private profit-seeking firms (as well as public, politically minded agencies) will produce the correct quantities of output from the standpoint of society as a whole, not only for conventional items like cardboard boxes but also for less conventional things like the amounts of environmental quality. To address this question we must understand how firms normally determine the quantities they will produce. The marginal cost of production is a key factor in determining the supply behavior of firms in competitive circumstances. In fact, the marginal cost curve of a firm acts essentially as a supply curve, showing the quantity of the good the firm would supply at different prices. Consider Figure 3-9. Assume that the firm with the indicated marginal cost curve

FIGURE 3-9
Marginal Cost and Supply.

Quantity of output

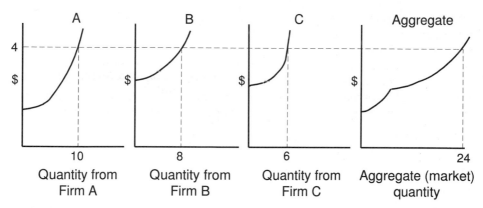

FIGURE 3-10
Derivation of Aggregate (Market) Supply from Individual Firm Supply Curves.

is able to sell its output at a price of p^*. The firm will maximize its profits by producing that quantity of output where marginal cost is equal to p^*; that level is designated q^*. At any output level less than this, $MC < p^*$, so a firm could increase its profits by increasing output. At any output level above this, $p^* < MC$, so a firm is actually producing items the marginal cost of which is higher than price; in this case, the firm should reduce output if it wishes to maximize its profits.

We are often interested in the supply performance of industries composed of many firms rather than that of individual firms. In this case, the marginal cost/supply curve refers to a collection of firms all producing the same output. This is the concept of *aggregate supply*, analogous to the concept of aggregate demand we had in the previous chapter. The aggregate supply curve of a group of firms is the sum of the individual supply curves of all the firms in the group. This is depicted in Figure 3-10. There are three firms, A, B, and C, with marginal cost curves as depicted in the first three panels of the figure. At a common price, say $4, Firm A supplies 10 units, Firm B supplies eight units, and Firm C supplies six units. Thus, the aggregate supply at that price is 24 units, as depicted in the far right panel of Figure 3-10.

SUMMARY

In this chapter we have covered briefly some of the basic tools of microeconomics. The concepts covered were the following:

- Individual willingness to pay, marginal and total
- Individual demand
- Individual benefits, marginal and total
- Aggregate willingness to pay, demand, and benefits
- Opportunity costs
- Marginal and total production costs

- The equimarginal principle
- Supply
- Technological change.

We are going to be relying heavily on these ideas in the chapters to come, especially on the equimarginal principle and on graphs, where we will want to jump back and forth between marginal and total measures. When we begin to look at real-world problems of environmental analysis and policy design, it is easy to get pulled so far into the countless details that basic economic ideas get lost. It's the fundamental economic building blocks, such as those in this chapter, that allow us to identify the primary economic characteristics of these problems and proceed to develop solutions to them.

QUESTIONS FOR FURTHER DISCUSSION

1 What would happen to a demand curve showing aggregate quantity demanded per month of some good or service if it became widely expected that the price of this item was going to be very high next year?
2 The logic of equating benefits with willingness to pay could lead us to the conclusion that cleaning the air to which low-income people are exposed would probably create fewer benefits than if it were done for high-income people. Does this undermine the idea of defining benefits as equal to willingness to pay?
3 Figure 3-10 illustrates the derivation of an industry supply curve under competitive conditions where each firm receives the same price for its output. What is the relationship of this procedure to the equimarginal principle discussed earlier in the chapter?
4 How do you think the shape of the long-run marginal cost curve for the production of electricity might differ from that of lawn-mowing services? From that of wastewater treatment plants?
5 For the marginal cost curves in Figure 3-6, draw the *total* cost curve, i.e., the cost curve showing the level of total cost at different rates of output.
6 Suppose that for a certain production process it is technically impossible to increase output beyond a level of 1,000 units per month. What would the marginal cost curve look like if all inputs were free?

SELECTED READINGS

The subjects treated in this chapter—demand, supply, willingness to pay, costs, etc.—are treated in most introductory microeconomic texts. The best way to proceed, in order to get a somewhat deeper explanation of these concepts, or a slightly different perspective, is to consult the appropriate chapters of one of these books. Some of the more popular texts are the following:

Baumol, William J., and Alan S. Blinder: *Microeconomics, Principles and Policy*, 5th ed., Harcourt, Brace, Jovanovich, Dallas, Tex., 1991, Chapters 5, 7, 8.
Byrns, Ralph T., and Gerald W. Stone: *Microeconomics*, 5th ed., Harper-Collins, New York, 1992, Chapters 5, 6, 7, 8.
Heilbroner, Robert L., James K. Galbraith, and Thomas Beveridge: *The Economic Problem*, 9th ed., Prentice-Hall, Englewood Cliffs, N.J., 1990, Chapter 8.

Lipsey, Richard G., Peter O. Steiner, and Douglas D. Purvis: *Economics*, 8th ed., Harper-Collins, New York, 1987, Chapter 4.

McConnell, Campbell R., and Stanley L. Brue: *Economics*, 12th ed., McGraw-Hill, New York, 1993, Chapters 23, 24.

Parkin, Michael: *Economics*, Addison-Wesley, Reading, Mass., 1990, Chapters 7, 10.

Samuelson, Paul A., and William D. Nordhaus: *Economics*, 14th ed., McGraw-Hill, New York, Chapters 6, 8.

Schiller, Bradley R.: *The Microeconomy Today*, 6th ed., McGraw-Hill, New York, 1994, Chapter 2.

Waud, Roger N.: *Microeconomics*, 5th ed., Harper-Collins, New York, 1992, Chapters 4, 5.

ECONOMIC EFFICIENCY
AND MARKETS

In this chapter we do two things. We first develop the notion of economic efficiency, as an index for examining how an economy functions and as a criterion for judging whether it is performing as well as it might. We also discuss the relationship between economic efficiency and economic equity. We then ask whether a market system, left to itself, can produce results that are economically efficient. Economic efficiency is a simple idea but one that has much to recommend it as a criterion for evaluating the performance of an economic system or a part of that system. But it has to be used with care. A single firm or group of firms may be judged very efficient in their own limited way as long as they are keeping costs low and making a profit. But if we want to evaluate the *social* performance of these firms, we must use the idea of economic efficiency in a wider sense. To do this we must include all the social values and consequences of economic decisions, in particular environmental consequences. We will see that there are cases in which a system of private markets will not normally be able to bring about results that are efficient in this wider sense. This will lead into the next chapter, where we will examine the policy question; i.e., if the economy is not operating the way we want it to, especially in matters of environmental quality, what kind of public policy might we use to correct the situation?

Economic efficiency is a criterion that can be applied at several levels: to input usage and to the determination of output levels. We are going to concentrate in this chapter on the second of these because ultimately we want to apply the concept to the "output" of environmental quality. There are two questions of interest: (1) What quantity ought to be produced and (2) what quantity is produced in fact? The first question deals with the notion of efficiency, the second with the way markets normally function.

ECONOMIC EFFICIENCY

In the preceding chapter we looked at two relationships, that between the quantity of output and willingness to pay, and that between output and marginal production costs. Neither of these two relationships can, by itself, tell us what the most desirable level of output is from society's standpoint. To identify this output level, we must bring these two elements together. The central idea of *economic efficiency* is that there should be a balance between the value of what is produced and the value of what is used up to produce it. In our terminology, there should be a balance between willingness to pay and the marginal costs of production.

Efficiency is a notion that has to have a reference point. We must ask: efficient from the standpoint of whom? What is "efficient" for one person, in the sense of balancing costs and benefits, may not be "efficient" for somebody else. We want to have a concept of efficiency that is applicable to the economy as a whole. This means that when we refer to marginal costs, we must include *all* the costs of producing the particular item in question, no matter to whom they accrue. When we talk about marginal willingness to pay, we must insist that this represents accurately *all* of the value that people in the society place on the item. This does not necessarily mean that all people will place a value on all goods; it means only that there are no missing sources of value.

How do we identify the rate of output that is socially efficient? Suppose we focus on a particular type of output; in practice it could be refrigerators, or automobiles, or college educations, or a certain type of pollution-control equipment. Suppose that our item is currently being produced at a particular rate, and that we wish to know whether it would make sense for us, that is, society, to increase this output level by a small amount. To answer this we must compare the marginal willingness to pay for that extra output with the marginal opportunity costs of the output; if the former exceeds the latter, we would presumably want the extra output to be produced; otherwise we would not.

We can look at this by bringing together the two relationships discussed in the last chapter. In Figure 4-1, we picture the aggregate marginal willingness-to-pay curve (labeled MWTP) and the aggregate marginal cost curve (MC), for the good in question. The efficient level of production for this item is the quantity identified by the intersection of the two curves, labeled q^e in the figure. At this output level the costs of producing one more unit of this good are just exactly equal to the marginal value of it, as expressed by the marginal willingness-to-pay curve. This common value is p^e.

The equality of marginal willingness to pay and marginal production cost is the test for determining if output is at the socially efficient level. There is another way of looking at this notion of efficiency. When a rate of output is at the socially efficient level, the net value, defined as total willingness to pay minus total costs, is as large as possible. In fact, we can measure this net value on the diagram. At q^e we know that the total willingness to pay is equal to an amount corresponding to the area under the marginal willingness-to-pay curve from the origin up to q^e; this area consists of the sum of the three subareas: $a + b + c$. Total cost, on the other hand, consists of the area under the marginal cost curve, or area c. Thus, the surplus is $(a + b + c) - c = a + b$, which is the triangular area enclosed by the marginal willingness-to-pay curve and the marginal cost curve. At any other

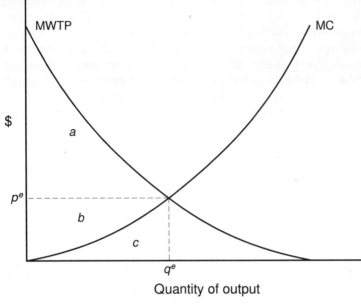

FIGURE 4-1
The Socially Efficient Rate of Output.

quantity the corresponding value of total willingness to pay minus total production costs will be less than this area $a + b$.

Let's be clear on what this graph is telling us. We noted above that the marginal willingness-to-pay curve is assumed to represent accurately all the benefits that people in our economy actually experience when the good becomes available. The marginal production cost curve is assumed to contain all the true opportunity costs that are required to produce this good—no hidden or overlooked costs have been left out. Thus, the quantity q^e is "efficient" because it produces a balance between the two sides—between the marginal worth of a good, as indicated by consumers' willingness to pay for it, and what it costs society to produce it, as measured by marginal costs.

EFFICIENCY AND EQUITY

From the standpoint of society at large, production is at an efficient level when marginal benefits equal marginal production costs, i.e., when net benefits are maximized, *no matter to whom those net benefits accrue.* Efficiency doesn't distinguish among people. A dollar of net benefits to one person is considered to be worth a dollar to anybody else. One hundred dollars of benefits to one person is considered to be worth the same as one dollar of benefits to each of one hundred people. In the real world, an outcome that benefits very rich people at the expense of poor people would be regarded by most people as inequitable. Which is simply another way of saying that an outcome that is efficient in the above sense need not necessarily be equitable.

Equity is tied closely to the distribution of wealth in a society. If this distribution is regarded as essentially fair, then judgments about alternative output levels may justifiably be made using only the efficiency criterion. But if wealth is distributed unfairly, the efficiency criterion by itself may be too narrow. Having said this, however, we have to recognize that in judging economic outcomes, the relative emphasis to be put on efficiency and equity is a matter of controversy. It is controversial in the political arena; it is controversial among economists themselves.

We will have much to say about distributional issues and equity throughout the book. In Chapter 6 we will develop terminology for describing the distributional impacts of environmental policies. And in Chapter 9 we will discuss the role of economic equity as a criterion for evaluating environmental policies.

MARKETS

Having specified what we mean by economic efficiency, we next ask whether a market system, a system in which the major economic decisions about how much to produce are made by the more or less unhindered interaction of buyers and sellers, gives us results that are socially efficient. In other words, if we rely entirely on the market to determine how much of this item gets produced, will it settle on q^e?

Why worry about this question? Why not simply jump to the question of public policy? Doesn't this question imply that, at bottom, we are committed to the market system, and isn't this the system that, from an environmental point of view, has gotten us into trouble in the first place? If the market doesn't do the job, maybe we should just ignore whatever the market does and proceed through political/administrative means to bring about the desired rate of output.

The short answer to this is that as a nation we are in fact committed to a market-based economy. For all its faults, a market system will normally give us better economic results, overall, than any other system. Those who doubt this need only look at the environmental horror stories being uncovered in the countries of Eastern Europe following the Communist era. Of course, we have to remember that although our system is "market based," we do not necessarily have to accept whatever results it gives us. The results are acceptable only if they are reasonably efficient and equitable. We will find that in the case of environmental quality, market institutions are not likely to give us results that are socially efficient.

The slightly longer answer to the question is that the market system contains within it certain incentive structures that in many cases can be harnessed toward the objective of improved environmental quality. One of these is the cost-minimizing incentive that stems from the competitive process. Another is the incentive provided through the rewards that may be reaped through initiative in finding better, i.e., less expensive, technical and organizational means of production. It will be far more effective in many cases to take advantage of these incentives than to try to do away with them. By altering them so that they take environmental values into account, we can often get more effective results than if we tried to jettison the whole system and adopt a different set of institutions.

A market is an institution in which buyers and sellers—of consumer goods, of factors of production, etc.—carry out mutually agreed-upon exchanges. We normally expect that people, when they buy or sell on a market, are looking for the best terms they can get. Presumably buyers would like to pay a low price while sellers would prefer high prices. What brings all these conflicting objectives into balance is the adjustment of prices on the market. We picture in Figure 4-2 a simple market model. Buyers' desires are represented by the demand curve labeled D; it shows the quantity of the good that buyers would buy at different prices. It has the typical downward slope; the higher the price, the lower the quantity demanded, and vice versa. Underlying the demand curve are such factors as consumer tastes and preferences, the number of potential consumers in the market, and their income levels.

The curve labeled S is the supply curve showing the quantity of the good that suppliers would willingly make available at different prices. It is upward sloping; higher prices represent greater incentives for suppliers and, therefore, larger quantities are supplied, and vice versa. The main factors affecting the height and shape of the supply curve are production costs; these, in turn, are related to the

FIGURE 4-2
The Market Model.

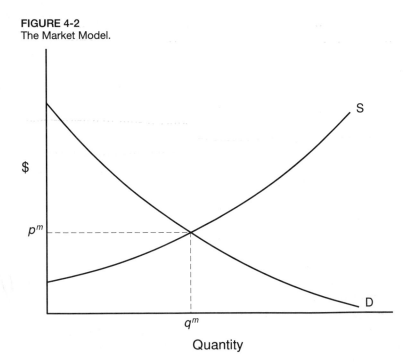

prices of inputs used in the production of this item and the level of technology inherent in the production process.

It is important to keep in mind that the demand and supply curves represent possibilities, or alternatives. During any particular time only one quantity of a good can change hands, and sellers and buyers can be on only one point of their supply and demand curves, respectively. It is easy to see that there is only one price at which the quantity demanded by buyers is consistent with the quantity that sellers will make available. That is the price where the two curves intersect, marked p^m. Similarly, the total quantity that buyers and sellers will exchange at this price is labeled q^m.

For the market to work effectively there must be competition among sellers and among buyers. None can be large enough that their own performance affects market prices, or powerful enough that they can control how the market performs. Price must be allowed to adjust freely, so that it can "discover" the quantities that bring buyers and sellers into balance. At prices higher than p^m sellers will attempt to supply more than buyers want. In a surplus situation like this, competition forces prices downward. If prices are temporarily lower than p^m, a shortage develops and competition will force the price to adjust upward. At the equilibrium, quantity demanded equals quantity supplied. It is important to look at it also from the other direction. At the quantity q^m there is an equality between the marginal willingness to pay by consumers for an additional unit of the item and the marginal costs of producing the item. These are equal at the value of p^m. If price and quantity are allowed to adjust freely and competition does in fact exist, an equality will arise through the normal interaction of buyers and sellers, between the marginal valuation that consumers have for a good (their marginal willingness to pay) and the costs of making available another unit of the good (the marginal costs of production).

MARKETS AND SOCIAL EFFICIENCY

The next question is whether markets ordinarily produce results that are efficient from the standpoint of society. Compare Figures 4-1 and 4-2. They look the same, but there is actually a big difference. The first shows a socially efficient rate of output for a particular item; the second shows the rate of output and price that would prevail on a competitive market for that item. Are these two rates of output, labeled q^e and q^m, likely to be the same in the real world? The answer is yes *if*, and it's a big if, the market demand and supply curves, as pictured in Figure 4-2, are the same as the marginal cost and willingness-to-pay curves shown in Figure 4-1. And here is the nub of the problem: When environmental values are concerned, there are likely to be very substantial differences between market values and social values. This is called *market failure*, and it will often call for public intervention, either to override the markets directly or to rearrange things so that they will work more effectively.

In the rest of this chapter we will discuss the performance of markets when matters of environmental quality are involved. There are two phenomena to account for, one on the supply side and the other on the demand side. Environmental effects can drive a wedge between normal market supply curves and true marginal social cost curves. On the other side of the market, environmental effects can create a difference between market demands and true social marginal willingness to pay. On the supply side the problem is "external costs," while on the demand side the problem is "external benefits."   production

EXTERNAL COSTS

When entrepreneurs in a market economy make decisions about what and how much to produce, they normally take into account the price of what they will produce and the cost of items for which they will have to pay: labor, raw materials, machinery, energy, and so on. We call these the *private* costs of the firm; they are the costs that show up in the profit-and-loss statement at the end of the year. Any firm, assuming it has the objective of maximizing its profits, will try to keep its production costs as low as possible. This is a worthwhile outcome for both the firm and society because inputs always have opportunity costs; they could have been used to produce something else. Furthermore, firms will be alert to ways of reducing costs when the relative prices of inputs change. For example, we know that during the U.S. energy "crisis" of the 1970s, when energy inputs became much more expensive, firms found ways of reducing energy inputs by using more energy-efficient machinery, changing operating procedures, and so on.

But in many production operations there is another type of cost that, while representing a true cost to society, does not show up in the firm's profit-and-loss statement. It is the *external costs*. They are called "external" because, although they are real costs to some members of society, firms do not normally take them into account when they go about making their decisions about output rates. Another way of saying this is that there are costs that are external to firms but internal to society as a whole.[1]

One of the major types of external cost is the cost inflicted on people through environmental degradation. An example is the easiest way to see this. Suppose a paper mill is located somewhere on the upstream reaches of a river and that, in the course of its operation, it discharges a large amount of wastewater into the river. The wastewater is full of organic matter that arises from the process of converting wood to paper. This waste material gradually is converted to more benign materials by the natural assimilative capacity of the river water but, before that happens, a number of people downstream are affected by the lower quality of water in the river. Perhaps the water-borne residuals reduce the number of fish in the river, affecting downstream fishers. The river may also be

---

[1] External costs are sometimes called "third-party" costs. The first two parties are, respectively, the producer and the consumer. So a third-party cost is one that is inflicted on people who are not directly involved in the economic transactions between buyers and sellers. It is also sometimes called a "spillover" effect.

less attractive to look at, affecting people who would like to swim or sail on it. Worse, the river water perhaps is used downstream as a source of water for a public water supply system, and the degraded water quality means that the town has to engage in more costly treatment processes before the water can be sent through the water mains. All of these downstream costs are real costs associated with producing paper, just as much as the raw materials, labor, energy, etc., used internally by the plant. But from the mill's standpoint these downstream costs are *external costs*. They are costs that are borne by someone other than the people who make decisions about operating the paper mill. At the end of the year the profit-and-loss statement of the paper mill will contain no reference whatever to these real downstream external costs.

If we are to have rates of output that are socially efficient, decisions about resource use must take into account both types of costs—the private costs of producing paper plus whatever external costs arise from adverse environmental impacts. In terms of full social cost accounting:

Social costs = Private costs + External (Environmental) costs.

This is pictured in Figure 4-3. The top panel shows the relationship between the rate of paper production and the occurrence of these downstream external costs. It shows that the marginal external costs increase as paper production increases. The bottom panel shows several things. It shows the demand curve for paper and the marginal private costs of producing paper. The intersection of these occurs at a price of p^m and a quantity of q^m. This is the price and quantity that would arise in a competitive market where producers pay no attention to external costs. But marginal social costs are in fact higher, as shown, since they contain both the marginal private costs and the marginal external costs. Thus, the full socially efficient rate of output is q^*, and the associated price is p^*.

Compare the two rates of output and the two prices. The market output is too high compared to the socially efficient rate of output. And the market price is too low compared to the socially efficient price. It's not hard to understand the reason for this. In considering just its private costs the firm is essentially using a productive input it is not paying for. What is this unpaid input? The services of the river, which provides the firm with a cheap way to dispose of its production residuals. But while it may be cheap for the firm to do this, it may not be cheap to society; in fact, in this case we have costs being inflicted on downstream users that are being overlooked by the paper mill. So the private market system in this case produces too much paper at too low a price compared to socially efficient results.

Most of the cases of environmental destruction involve external costs of one type or another. Electricity-generating plants emit airborne residuals that affect the health of people living downwind. Users of chemicals emit toxic fumes that affect people living in the vicinity. Developers build on land without taking into account the degradation of the visual environment of local inhabitants, and so on. Nor are businesses the only ones responsible for external environmental

FIGURE 4-3
External Costs and Market
Outcomes.

costs. When individuals drive their automobiles, exhaust gases add to air pollution, and when they dispose of solid waste materials (like old cans), they may affect the quality of the local environment.

There are many different types of environmental externalities. Most, but not all, are expressed through physical linkages among parties involved, polluter and people damaged. The simplest is where there are just two parties involved—one polluter and one person suffering damages. An upstream pulp mill and a downstream firm that uses the river water in its production operations is an example. There are cases of single polluters and multiple damaged parties, such as a power plant that emits SO_2 affecting a group of community residents living downwind. Other cases involve multiple polluters but only one damaged party; e.g., the runoff from many farms that affects a local water supply system. And finally there are many cases where both polluters and parties damaged are many in number; for example, urban air pollution stemming from automobile emissions: Each driver is both a producer and a recipient of the externality. The same is true of global phenomena, such as the greenhouse effect.

Some externalities do not involve physical linkages. Degradation of the scenic environment through thoughtless land development is an example. And some externalities involve neither physical linkages nor close proximity. People in one part of a country, for example, may feel loss when those in another region cause damage to an important environmental resource; for example, a unique species of animal or plant. This brings up a problem that we will state but not solve. What is the limit, if any, to be placed on external damage that people may legitimately claim? I suffer damages when someone in my vicinity plays her stereo too loudly, but can I legitimately claim that I suffer damages if, for example, she adopts a life style with which I don't agree? If people in Boston pollute the waters of Boston harbor, may residents in California claim that they have been damaged? If residents of New Jersey thin out the suburban deer population in order to save their flower gardens, may people in Chicago justifiably claim that they have been damaged?

Exhibit 4-1 shows a news clip that centers on this issue. It concerns the legal doctrine of "standing." In order for a person to bring suit on environmental cases, he must have standing; i.e., he must be able to show that he is in fact being damaged by the activity in question. This case, having to do with the application of the U.S. Endangered Species Act abroad, hinged on whether members of the U.S. group bringing the lawsuit (Defenders of Wildlife) could legitimately claim they were being damaged by development projects in Egypt and Sri Lanka which would put pressure on several endangered species. The U.S. Supreme Court ruled in this case that they did not have standing.

Open-Access Resources

One source of external costs has been widely studied by environmental economists (as well as natural resource economists): open-access resources. An open-access resource is a resource or facility that is open to uncontrolled access by individuals who find it profitable or useful in some way to use the resource. A classic example is an ocean fishery, where anyone willing to buy a boat and take up fishing is free to do so. Other examples are a pasture that is open to anyone to graze animals, or a forest where anyone may go and cut wood.

In these situations we have, in effect, problems in property rights—their definition, distribution, and/or enforcement. Suppose there are four similar firms situated on a lake. The firms use the water of the lake in producing their output and discharge emissions back into the lake. Because of the emissions, each firm must treat the water taken from the lake before it uses the water in production. The treatment costs of each firm depend on the ambient quality of the lake, which of course depends on the total emissions of the four firms. Suppose that the cost of intake water treatment is currently $40,000 per year for each firm. A new firm is contemplating starting operations on the lake. If it adds

EXHIBIT 4-1

COURT LIMITS LEGAL STANDING IN SUITS

By Linda Greenhouse
Special to The New York Times

WASHINGTON, June 12 — The Supreme Court today dismissed a challenge to the Interior Department's interpretation of the Endangered Species Act, ruling that the environmental group that brought the challenge was not sufficiently injured by the policy to be entitled to file a lawsuit.

In limiting its decision to the issue of legal standing to sue, the Court did not take a position on the substantive question in the case: the validity of a regulation issued during the Reagan Administration that limits the reach of an important provision of the Endangered Species Act to within the United States.

The regulation, which the Bush Administration supports, rejects the original interpretation by the Carter Administration, which required all Federal agencies to insure that no endangered or threatened species would be harmed by Federal activities overseas.

Applies to Other Policies

The Court's decision on standing, supported by a 6-to-3 vote, applies to suits against Government policies generally and is not limited to the environmental area. But the long-running legal debate over standing has been particularly vigorous in the field of environmental regulation.

The environmental policies adopted during the Reagan and Bush Administrations have spawned many lawsuits, and those bringing the challenges often lack the direct economic interests that would automatically confer standing to sue. Obstacles to standing on the part of those who can claim little more than a general aesthetic or scientific concern could have the effect of making Administration policies of this sort unreviewable by Federal courts.

The Supreme Court has been cutting back on standing in environmental cases, and today's decision was a continuation of that trend. The majority's tone was notably hostile in its rejection of the concept of standing based on "procedural injury," an idea accepted by the lower court in this case to permit lawsuits by those who had not themselves suffered any concrete harm from the Government policy they were challenging.

Justice Scalia said that even if Congress opens the door to lawsuits of this sort through the inclusion of "citizen suit" provisions, such as a provision in the 1973 Endangered Species Act, the Federal courts would be barred from hearing such cases under Article III of the Constitution, which limits the jurisdiction of the Federal courts to concrete "cases" and "controversies."

"One More Nail in the Coffin"

Both the standing issue in the case and the underlying dispute about the Endangered Species Act had attracted widespread interest in the environmental community. Lawyers for environmental groups predicted today that the challenge to the regulation was likely to be renewed in a lawsuit designed to overcome the hurdles that the Court established today. But they said that given the Court's mood and the Bush Administration's willingness to press the standing issue, the long-term outlook was unfavorable.

"This is one more nail in the coffin of citizen standing," said Robert Houseman, a lawyer for the Center for International Environmental Law, which filed a brief in the case.

Defenders of Wildlife supported its claim to standing with affidavits of two members, who had visited areas in Egypt and Sri Lanka where Federal funds were being used for large public works projects. The two members said the projects posed threats to the habitats of several endangered species. They said they planned to return to the areas at some time in the future and would be injured by not being able to see the animals.

In his majority opinion, Justice Scalia said: "Such 'some day' intentions — without any description of concrete plans, or indeed even any specification of when the some day will be — do not support a finding of the 'actual or imminent' injury that our cases require."

its untreated emissions to those of the current four, it will make ambient water quality worse and drive the cost of water treatment for each firm up to $60,000 per year. When the fifth firm makes its location and production decisions, it will take into account its various operating costs, which will include the $60,000 per year of water treatment costs. But the total social water-related costs of the firm's decisions are higher. There are also external costs inflicted on the other four firms, amounting to $20,000 each of added water treatment costs if the fifth firm locates on the lake. The social marginal costs of water supply when the new firm locates on the lake are $140,000, consisting of $60,000 internal costs of the new firm plus $80,000 ($20,000 × 4) of external costs inflicted on firms already on the lake. These are often called open-access externalities, because they result from the fact that the firms have uncontrolled access to the lake.

We have focused on the externalities flowing from the fifth firm's decisions, but everything is symmetrical, in the sense that we could say exactly the same thing about each of the other firms. Each firm will make its decisions without regard to the external costs inflicted on other firms. It is this reciprocal nature of these externalities that distinguishes them from the type we talked about before (e.g., the pulp mill upstream inflicting external costs on people downstream). But the effect is the same: When externalities are involved, market supply curves will understate social marginal production costs. If someone owns a pasture or a forest, he or she will presumably keep out encroachers, or perhaps charge them for use of the resource or otherwise control their rate of access. But when a resource or facility is open to unrestricted access there is no way of ensuring that its rate of use is kept to the level that will maximize its overall value.[2]

Let us demonstrate the logic of this in a simple way by using the example of a road that is open to access by anyone desiring to use it. A road is not a natural resource, but a person-made facility. But the essence of the uncontrolled access problem is identical, and it perhaps is easier to understand with this particular example. It uses very simplifying assumptions so that we can highlight the basic issues. There is a road connecting two points; call them Point A and Point B. The figures in Table 4-1 show the average travel time it takes to get from Point A to Point B along this road, as a function of the number of motorists using the road. Thus, for example, if there is just one traveler on the road, it takes 10 minutes to get from A to B (we assume a speed limit that is enforced). Likewise, when there are either two or three motorists on the road the average travel time is still 10 minutes. But when the traffic increases to four travelers, the average travel time increases to 11 minutes. This is because of congestion; cars begin to get in each other's way and average speeds drop. As the number of motorists continues to increase, the congestion increases, thus driving up travel times even more.

Now suppose you are considering using this road to go from A to B, and that there are already five cars using it. Suppose, furthermore, that you have an

[2] This is what is involved in the "tragedy of the commons," as it was popularly termed by Garrett Hardin in "Tragedy of the Commons," *Science*, Vol. 162, December 13, 1968, pp. 1243–1248. His example was an open-access pasture on which all farmers had the right to pasture their sheep.

TABLE 4-1
TRAVEL TIMES RELATED TO THE NUMBER
OF CARS ON THE ROAD

Number of cars	Average travel time between A and B
1	10
2	10
3	10
4	11
5	12
6	14
7	18
8	24

alternative route that will take you 18 minutes. We assume you know the state of the traffic and the resulting travel times. Since taking the given road will save you 4 minutes over the alternative, your individual decision would be to use the road. But from the standpoint of "society," in this case consisting of you plus all the other motorists on the road, this is not efficient. When you enter the highway on which there are already five cars, the added congestion causes an increase in average travel times of 2 minutes to the people already using the road. Thus, your 4-minute individual saving is offset by added travel costs of 10 minutes (five cars times 2 minutes per car) on the part of the other motorists, meaning that if we treat all minutes as equally valuable, there is a net social loss of 6 minutes when you decide to use the road.

The problem arises because there is uncontrolled access to the road, and in using it people may inflict external costs on others, in the form of added congestion and higher travel times. The same kind of effect holds when a fisher enters a fishery; in catching a portion of the stock he leaves fewer to be caught by other fishers. When one farmer puts animals on a common pasture, he or she reduces the forage available to other herds on that pasture. When one person cuts wood from a communal forest, she leaves fewer trees for other users and makes it more difficult for them to supply themselves with wood. We can see that this is related to the notion of external costs. The added costs that one user of a common-property resource inflicts on other users of that resource are in fact costs that are external to that user, but internal to the whole group of users. When a single individual is making a decision about whether and how much to utilize a common-property resource, she takes into account the costs and benefits that impinge directly on her. Some people might also altruistically take into account the common-property externalities they inflict on others, but most will not. And the result will be, as it was with the road example, a rate of use that is higher than what is called for on grounds of social efficiency.

Thus, when external costs are present, private markets will not normally produce quantities of output that are socially efficient. This market failure may justify public policy to help move the economy toward efficiency. This may be done sometimes by changing rules, such as property rights rules, so that the market will function efficiently. Other cases may call for more direct public intervention. We will take up these matters again in Section IV. We must now move to the demand side of the market and consider another important source of market failure, that of external *benefits*.

EXTERNAL BENEFITS

An external benefit is a benefit that accrues to somebody who is outside, or external, to the decision about consuming or using the good or resource that causes the externality. When the use of an item leads to an external benefit, the market willingness to pay for that item will understate the social willingness to pay. Suppose a quieter lawn mower would provide $50 a year of extra benefits to me if I were to buy it. This is therefore the maximum that I would be willing to pay for this machine. But suppose my use of the new lawn mower would create $20 of added benefits to my neighbor because of reduced noise levels in the course of the year. These $20 of benefits to the neighbor are external benefits for me. I make my purchasing decision on the basis of benefits accruing only to me. Thus, my marginal willingness to pay for a quieter lawn mower is $50, whereas the social marginal benefits (where "society" in this case includes just me and my neighbor) is $70 (my $50 and her $20).

As another example of an external benefit, consider a farmer whose land is on the outskirts of an urban area. The farmer cultivates the land and sells his produce to people in the city. Of course, the farmer's main concern is the income he can derive from the operation, and he makes decisions about inputs and outputs according to their effect on that income. But the land kept in agriculture produces several other benefits, including a habitat for birds and other small animals, and scenic values for passers-by. These benefits, while internal from the standpoint of society, are external from the standpoint of the farmer. They don't appear anywhere in his profit-and-loss position; they are external benefits of his farming decisions. In this case the agricultural value of the land to the farmer understates the social willingness to pay to have the land in agriculture.

Many goods do not involve external benefits. Indeed, when economists discuss the rudiments of supply and demand, we usually use as examples very simple goods that do not create this complication. Farmers produce and supply so many thousand cantaloupes, individual and market demand curves for cantaloupes are easy to comprehend. If we want to know the total number of cantaloupes bought, we can simply add up the number bought by each person in the market. Each person's consumption affects no one else. In this case the market demand curve will represent accurately the aggregate marginal willingness to pay of consumers for cantaloupes. But in cases involving external benefits, this no longer holds. We can perhaps best see this by considering a type of good that inherently involves large-scale external benefits, what economists have come to call "public goods."

Public Goods

Consider a lighthouse. This is a service provided to mariners at sea so that they can locate themselves and avoid running aground at night. But the lighthouse has an interesting technical characteristic: If its services are made available to one mariner at sea, they immediately become available to all others in the vicinity. Once the services are made available to one person, others cannot be excluded from making use of the same services. This is the distinguishing characteristic of a *public good*. It is a good which, if made available to one person, automatically becomes available to others.

Another example of a public good is a radio signal. Once a radio station broadcasts a signal, it is available to anybody who has a receiver. Each individual can listen to the broadcast without diminishing its availability to all other people within range of the station. Note carefully that it is not the ownership of the supplying organization that makes a public good public. Lighthouses are usually publicly owned, but radio stations, at least in the U.S., are typically privately owned. A public good is distinguished by the technical nature of the good, not by the type of organization making it available.

We are interested in public goods because environmental quality is essentially a public good. If we clean up the air for one person in an urban area, we automatically clean it up for everybody else in that community. The benefits, in other words, accrue to everyone in the community. Private markets are likely to undersupply public goods, relative to efficient levels. To see why, let's take another very simple example: a small freshwater lake the shores of which have three occupied homes. The people living in the houses use the lake for recreational purposes but, unfortunately, the water quality of the lake has been contaminated by an old industrial plant that has since closed. The contaminant is measured in parts per million (ppm). At present the lake contains 5 ppm of this contaminant. It is possible to clean the water by using a fairly expensive treatment process. Each of the surrounding homeowners is willing to pay a certain amount to have the water quality improved. Table 4-2 shows these individual marginal willingnesses to pay for integer values of water quality. It also shows the total marginal willingness to pay, which is the sum of the individual values.

TABLE 4-2
INDIVIDUAL AND AGGREGATE DEMAND FOR LOWERING LAKE POLLUTION

Level of contaminant (ppm)	Marginal willingness to pay ($ per year)				Marginal cost of cleanup
	Homeowner A	Homeowner B	Homeowner C	Total	
4	110	60	30	200	50
3	85	35	20	140	65
2	70	10	15	95	95
1	55	0	10	65	150
0	45	0	5	50	240

The table also shows the marginal cost of cleaning up the lake, again just for integer values of water quality. Note that we have increasing marginal cost, as the lake becomes cleaner the marginal cost of continued improvement increases. Marginal cost and aggregate marginal willingness to pay are equal at a water quality of 2 ppm. At levels less than this (higher ppm), aggregate marginal willingness to pay for a cleaner lake exceeds the marginal cost of achieving it. Hence from the standpoint of these three homeowners together, improved water quality is desirable, but at quality levels better than 2 ppm, total willingness to pay falls below marginal costs. Thus 2 ppm is the socially efficient level of water quality in the lake.

This is depicted graphically in Figure 4-4. The three top panels show the marginal willingness to pay by each of the three homeowners. When we summed individual demand curves for private goods, we could add together the individual quantities demanded at each price to get the aggregate quantity demanded. But with a public good people are, in effect, consuming the same units, so we must add together the individual marginal willingnesses to pay at each quantity to get the aggregate demand function, as shown in Figure 4-4. At a water-quality level of 3 ppm, for example, the marginal willingnesses to pay are, respectively, $85, $30, and $20 for individuals A, B, and C. Thus the total marginal willingness to pay at this level of water quality is $135. The bottom panel of the graph shows the aggregate marginal willingness-to-pay/demand function labeled D, the marginal cost function (MC), and the efficient level of water quality.

Having identified the efficient level of water quality, could we rely on a competitive market system, where entrepreneurs are on the alert for new profit opportunities, to get the contaminant in the lake reduced to that level? Suppose a private firm attempts to sell its services to the three homeowners. The firm goes to person A and tries to collect an amount equal to that person's true willingness to pay. But that person will presumably realize that once the lake is cleaned up, it's cleaned up for everybody no matter how much each homeowner actually contributed. And so A may have the incentive to underpay, relative to his true willingness to pay, in the hopes that the other homeowners will contribute enough to cover the costs of the cleanup. But, of course, the others may react in the same way. When a public good is involved, each person may have an incentive to "free ride" on the efforts of others. A free rider is a person who pays less for a good than her or his true marginal willingness to pay, a person who underpays, that is, relative to the benefits he receives.

Free riding is a ubiquitous phenomenon in the world of public goods, or in fact any good the consumption of which produces external benefits. Because of the free-riding impulse, private, profit-motivated firms will have difficulty covering their costs if they go into the business of supplying public goods.[3]

---

[3] This sentence emphasizes the point made earlier: It is the technical nature of the good that makes it a public or private good, not whether the organization providing it is public or private. A lighthouse (a public good) might be built and operated by a private firm; insurance (a private good) might be provided by a public agency.

FIGURE 4-4
Aggregate Willingness to Pay for a Public Good.

Because of these reduced revenues, private firms will norm
goods and services of this type. Environmental quality ir
essentially public goods. Since we cannot rely on the market sy
efficient quantities of "goods" of this type, we must fall back on some ty
nonmarket institution involving collective action of one type or another. In the
lake example, the homeowners may be able to act collectively, perhaps through
a homeowner association, to secure contributions for cleaning up the lake. Of
course, the free-rider problem will still exist even for the homeowners' association, but if there are not too many of them, personal acquaintance and the
operation of moral pressure may be strong enough to overcome the problem.
When there are many thousands or millions of people, however, as there
usually are in most environmental issues, the free-rider problem may be
handled effectively only with more direct collective action through a govern-
mental body that has taxing power. It is not that we wish completely to replace
market processes in these cases. What we want to do is add sufficient public
oversight to the market system that we do finally end up with efficient levels
of environmental quality that are equitably distributed. We will take a closer
look at these questions in the next chapter.

SUMMARY

Our main goal in this chapter was to discuss the operation of private markets
and then apply the market model to situations in which environmental quality
is an issue. Markets are places where buyers and sellers interact over the quantities and prices of particular goods or services. Buyers' desires are represented
by the aggregate demand curve, which shows the quantities demanded at
alternative prices. Sellers supply capabilities are represented by supply curves,
which ultimately are based on underlying production costs, and show quantities
that would be made available at alternative prices. The intersection of supply
and demand curves shows the unique quantity and price that can simultaneously satisfy both buyers and sellers. This we called the "efficient" level of
output, since it is the only output level where marginal willingness to pay is equal
to marginal costs of production.

We then discussed two main reasons, when environmental quality issues are
involved, market prices and quantities will not be fully efficient from a social
standpoint. The primary reason, on a conceptual level, is the existence of external
costs and external benefits. In matters of the environment, external costs are the
damages that people experience from environmental impacts that are not taken
into account by the firms, public agencies, or consumers whose decisions produce them. A classic case is water pollution from an upstream pulp mill that
damages people using the water downstream. Another important case is the
external costs that users of an open-access resource inflict upon one another
through uncontrolled use of the resource. External benefits are benefits accruing
to people other than the direct buyers or recipients of a good. The classic case of

external benefits is what are called public goods; these are goods or services which, when they are made available to one person, automatically become available to others.   *farmer selling goods but beneficial to habits*

Faced with external costs and benefits, public goods, and common-property resources, markets cannot be relied upon to supply efficient levels of environmental quality. Public environmental policies are called upon to rectify these market failures.

QUESTIONS FOR FURTHER DISCUSSION

1 Below are portions of the demand curves of three individuals for air quality in their neighborhood. Air quality (integer values only) is measured in terms of $\mu g/m^3$ (micrograms of SO_2 per cubic meter of air). If the marginal cost of reducing ambient SO_2 is \$40 per $\mu g/m^3$, what is the socially efficient level of air quality, assuming that "society" in this case consists of just these three people?

Cost of sulfur removal (dollars per $\mu g/m^3$)	Quantity demanded			Price of orange juice (cents per oz.)
	A	B	C	
60	1400	1200	1500	0
50	1300	1100	1400	10
40	1200	1000	1300	20
30	1100	900	1200	30
20	1000	800	1100	40
10	900	700	1000	50
0	800	600	900	60

2 Suppose that Question 1 referred not to air quality but to ounces of orange juice demanded per year by the three individuals. In this case the price (shown on the right) refers to cents per ounce. Suppose the marginal cost of orange juice production is 40¢. What is the efficient aggregate level of orange juice production for these three people?

3 Considering the definition of public goods given in the chapter, are movie theaters public goods? Public telephones? Ski hills? Food stamps?

4 It is easy to see why pulp mill emissions may produce external costs, but what about loud radio music played by your neighbor? Your neighbor painting her house a color you can't stand? Your neighbor watching a film that offends your values?

5 In the discussion of equity considerations we talked about wealth distributions as being fair or unfair, whereas one often hears such discussions carried out in terms of distributions that are equal or unequal. What is the difference?

6 What is the relationship between public goods and open-access resources?

7 Consider the example of the three homeowners around the lake. Suppose the lake was cleaned up to the efficient level, and that the total costs of the cleanup were shared equally among the homeowners (stick to integer values here). Will all three homeowners be better off? What problems does this bring up about sharing the costs of public goods?

SELECTED READINGS

The same comment is relevant here as appeared in the bibliography of the last chapter: Consult the appropriate chapters of one of the popular microeconomics texts. In the present case you want to look specifically for "efficiency" and market failures in the face of externalities, public goods, and common-property resources. The best-known texts are:

Baumol, William J., and Alan S. Blinder: *Microeconomics, Principles and Policy*, 5th ed., Harcourt, Brace, Jovanovich, Dallas, Tex., 1991, Chapters 4, 13.

Byrns, Ralph T., and Gerald W. Stone: *Microeconomics*, 5th ed., Harper-Collins, New York, 1992, Chapters 9, 20.

Heilbroner, Robert L., James K. Galbraith, and Thomas Beveridge: *The Economic Problem*, 9th ed., Prentice-Hall, Englewood Cliffs, N.J., 1990, Chapter 27.

Lipsey, Richard G., Peter O. Steiner, and Douglas D. Purvis: *Economics*, 8th ed., Harper-Collins, New York, 1987, Chapter 22.

McConnell, Campbell R., and Stanley L. Brue: *Economics*, 12th ed., McGraw-Hill, New York, 1993, Chapter 25.

Parkin, Michael: *Economics*, Addison-Wesley, Reading, Mass., 1990, Chapter 4.

Samuelson, Paul A., and William D. Nordhaus: *Economics*, 14th ed., McGraw-Hill, New York, Chapter 6.

Schiller, Bradley R.: *The Microeconomy Today*, 6th ed., McGraw-Hill, New York, 1994, Chapters 3, 12.

Waud, Roger N.: *Microeconomics*, 5th ed., Harper-Collins, New York, 1992, Chapter 4.

CHAPTER 5

THE ECONOMICS OF
ENVIRONMENTAL QUALITY

In the preceding chapter we concluded that the market system, left to itself, is likely to malfunction to some extent when matters of environmental pollution are involved. That is to say, it will not normally produce results that are socially efficient. That was a question in *positive economics*, the study of how events actually occur in the real world; how various outcomes come to pass. The quantity of output that actually appears in a market and its price are matters of positive eonomics. This also includes questions like how much sulfur dioxide (SO_2) is produced by a group of power plants, how these are related to the fuel choices made by the utilities, and so on. We now move to the public policy question: If we don't like the fact that certain results occur in the economic real world, how should we change them? This is a matter of *normative economics*; if, for example, our objective is to reduce the amount of SO_2 in the air, how should we go about doing so?

There are several closely related policy problems to address. First is that of identifying the most appropriate level of environmental quality we ought to try to achieve. The second question is how to divide up the task of meeting environmental quality goals. If we have many polluters, how should we seek to allocate among them an overall reduction in emissions? Third, we need to address the question of how the benefits and costs of environmental programs are distributed across society and whether this distribution is appropriate. In this chapter we take up these issues on a conceptual basis; in subsequent chapters we will look at specific policy alternatives.

Before developing our simple policy model we should stress again that effective public policy depends on good information on how economic and environmental systems actually work. We might call this the scientific basis of environmental policy: the study of how firms and consumers normally make decisions in the market economy, how residuals are emitted into the natural environment, and the ways in which these residuals behave in that environment to produce human and nonhuman damages. Thousands of scientists have worked and continue to work on these issues to clarify these diverse linkages.

Great effort will continue to be needed to expand the scientific base on which to develop environmental policy.

POLLUTION CONTROL—A GENERAL MODEL

Diverse types of environmental pollutants obviously call for diverse types of public policy, but in order to build up the required policy analyses we must start with a very simple model that lays out the fundamentals of the policy situation. The essence of the model consists of a simple trade-off situation that characterizes all pollution-control activities. On the one hand, reducing emissions reduces the damages that people suffer from environmental pollution; on the other hand, reducing emissions takes resources that could have been used in some other way.

To depict this trade-off consider a simple situation where a firm (e.g., a pulp mill) is emitting production residuals into a river. As these residuals are carried downstream, they tend to be transformed into less damaging chemical constituents, but before that process is completed the river passes by a large metropolitan area. The people of the area use the waters of the river for various purposes, including recreation (boating, fishing) and as a source for the municipal water supply system. When the river becomes polluted with industrial waste, the people downstream are damaged by the disruption of these and other services provided by the river. One side of the trade-off, then, is the damages that people experience when the environment is degraded.

Upstream, the offending pulp mill could reduce the amount of effluent put in the river by treating its wastes before discharge, as well as by recycling certain materials that currently just run out of the discharge pipe. This act of reducing, or abating, some portion of its wastes will require resources of some amount, the costs of which will affect the price of the paper it produces.[1] These abatement costs are the other side of the basic pollution-control trade-off.

Pollution Damages

By "damages" we mean all the negative impacts that users of the environment experience as a result of the degradation of that environment. These negative impacts are of many types and will of course vary from one environmental asset to another. In the river pollution example damages were to recreators, who could no longer use the river or who suffered a higher chance of picking up waterborne diseases, and to all the city dwellers who had to pay more to treat the water before they could put it into the public water mains. Air pollution produces damage through its impacts on human health. Excess deaths from diseases such as lung cancer, chronic bronchitis, and emphysema are related to elevated levels of

---

[1] The word "resources" has a double meaning in economics. On the one hand it is a shorthand way of referring to "natural resources." More generally, it sometimes is used to refer to the inputs that are utilized to produce outputs.

various pollutants, such as sulfur dioxide, asbestos fibers, and radon emissions. Air pollution can cause damages through the degradation of materials (all of the important outdoor sculpture from Renaissance Florence has had to be put inside to protect it from air pollution), and the deterioration of the visual environment. Besides damage to human beings, environmental destruction can have important impacts on various elements of the nonhuman ecosystem. Some of these, such as the destruction of genetic information in plant and animal species driven to extinction, will ultimately have important implications for humans. Estimating environmental damages is one of the primary tasks facing environmental scientists and economists, and we will devote Chapter 7 to a discussion of this problem.

In general, the greater the pollution, the greater the damages it produces. To describe the relationship between pollution and damage, we will use the idea of a *damage function*. A damage function shows the relationship between the quantity of a residual and the damage that residual causes. We can distinguish *emission damage functions*, which show the relationship between the quantity of a residual emitted from a particular source or sources and the resulting damages, and *ambient damage functions*, which show how damages are related to the concentration of a residual contained in the ambient environment. Our primary graphical approach will be the *marginal damage function*, which shows the change in damages stemming from a unit change in emissions or ambient concentration. We can also use these to discuss total damages, since we know that, geometrically, the area under the marginal damage function is equal to total damages.

Several marginal damage functions are depicted in Figure 5-1. The top two are marginal emission damage functions; the horizontal axes measure the quantity of an effluent emitted into the environment during some specified period of time. The exact units (pounds, tons, etc.) in any particular case depend on the specific pollutant involved. The vertical axes measure environmental damages. In physical terms, environmental damage can include many types of impacts: miles of coastline polluted, numbers of people contracting lung disease, numbers of animals wiped out, quantities of water contaminated, and so on. Every case of environmental pollution normally involves multiple types of impacts, the nature of which will depend on the pollutant involved and the time and place it is emitted. To consider these impacts comprehensively we need to be able to aggregate them into a single dimension. For this purpose we use a monetary scale. It is sometimes easy to express damage in monetary units; for example, the "defensive" expenditures that people make to protect themselves against pollution (e.g., heavier insulation to protect against noise). But usually it is very difficult, as we will see below.

The marginal emission damage function in panel (a) of Figure 5-1 shows marginal damages increasing only modestly at the beginning but more rapidly as emissions get larger and larger. Work by environmental scientists and economists seems to suggest that this is a typical shape for many types of pollutants, though probably not for all of them. At low levels of emissions marginal damages may be comparatively small; ambient concentrations are so modest that only the

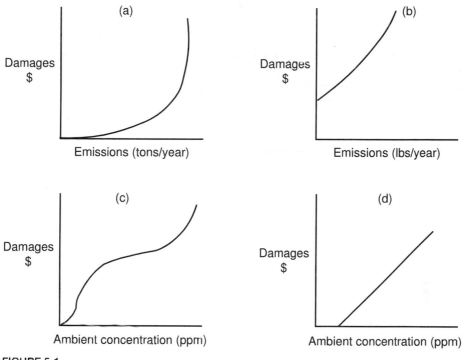

FIGURE 5-1
Representative Marginal Damage Functions.

most sensitive people in the population are affected. But when emission levels go higher, damages mount, and at still higher levels of emissions, marginal damages become very elevated as environmental impacts become widespread and intense.

Panel (b) shows a marginal (emission) damage function that has the same general shape as panel (a) (i.e., it shows increasing marginal damage), but it begins much higher on the vertical axis and rises more sharply. It might represent a toxic substance that has a deadly effect even at very low levels of emission.

The two bottom relationships in Figure 5-1 are marginal ambient damage functions. While the vertical axes have a monetary index of damages, the horizontal axes have an index of ambient concentration, such as parts per million (ppm). Panel (c) shows a complicated function that increases at low concentrations, then tends to level off until much higher concentrations are reached, after which damages increase rapidly. This might apply, for example, to an air pollutant that causes marked damages among particularly sensitive members of society at relatively low concentrations, and among all people at very high concentrations, while in the middle ranges marginal damages do not increase rapidly. Panel (d) demonstrates an ambient marginal damage function that begins to the right of the origin and then increases linearly with ambient concentration.

Panels (a) and (d) show a characteristic that is in fact quite controversial. They have *thresholds*, that is, values of emissions or ambient concentrations below which marginal damages are zero. Thus, the pollutant can increase to these threshold levels without causing any increase in damages. As we will see in chapters to come, the assumed existence or nonexistence of a threshold in the damage functions for particular pollutants has had important impacts on real-world environmental control policies. There have been long, vigorous arguments about whether the damage functions of certain types of pollutants do or do not have thresholds.

We need to look more deeply into the concept of the damage function because we will want to use it to express and analyze a variety of different types of pollution problems and public policy approaches. The analysis in the remainder of the chapter could be done with either ambient functions or emissions functions. I have chosen emissions relationships because I think it is easier to use these when we come to pollution control from particular sources of emissions. Accordingly, Figure 5-2 shows two marginal emissions damage functions. It is important to remember that, like the demand and supply curves we discussed earlier, these are time specific; they show the emissions and the marginal damages for a particular period of time. There are a couple of ways of thinking about this. One is to assume, for purposes of simplicity, that we

FIGURE 5-2
Anatomy of a Marginal Damage Function.

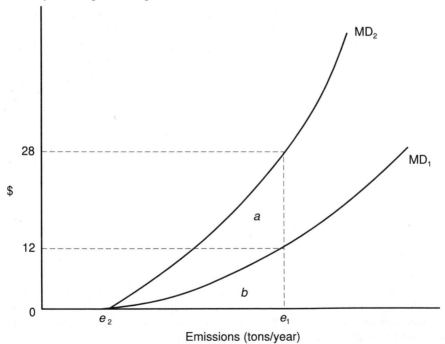

have a strictly noncumulative pollutant. Thus, all damages occur in the same period as emissions. A somewhat more complicated assumption is that for a pollutant that cumulates over time, the damage function shows the total value that people place on current and future damages. In Chapter 6 we will discuss this concept more fully.

Consider first just one of the marginal damage functions—say, the lower one labeled MD_1. In previous chapters we discussed the relationship between marginal and total quantities; for example, the relationship between marginal and total costs. We have the same relationship here. The height of the marginal damage curve shows how much total damages would change with a small change in the quantity of emissions. When the effluent level is at the point marked e_1, for example, marginal damages are $12. That is to say, if emissions were to increase by 1 ton from point e_1, the damages experienced by people exposed to those emissions would increase by $12; by the same token, if emissions decreased by a small amount at point e_1, total damages would be reduced by $12. Since the height of the curve, as measured on the y-axis, shows marginal damages, the area under the curve between the point where it is zero and some other point, like the one labeled e_1, shows the total damages associated with that level of emissions. In the case of marginal damage function MD_1 and point e_1, total damages are equal to the monetary amount expressed by the triangular area bounded by the x-axis, the curve MD_1, and the effluent quantity e_1. That is area b in Figure 5-2. At this emission level the total damages that would occur if the damage function were MD_2 would be a sum equal to the area under MD_2—in this case, $(a + b)$.

What factors might account for the difference between MD_1 and MD_2 in Figure 5-2? Let us assume that they apply to the same pollutant. We note that the one labeled MD_2 lies above MD_1; thus, for any given level of emissions, marginal damages are higher for MD_2 than for MD_1. At emission level e_1, for example, a small increase in effluent would increase damages by $12 if the marginal damage function were MD_1 but by $28 if it were MD_2. Remember that any damage function shows the impacts of emitting a particular effluent in a particular time and place, so one possible explanation might be that MD_2 refers to a situation in which many people are impacted by a pollutant, like a large urban area, while MD_1 refers to a more sparsely populated rural area; fewer people, smaller damage. One major factor that moves damage functions upward, in other words, is an increase in the number of people exposed to a particular pollutant.

Another possibility that might offer an explanation of why one marginal damage function lies above another is that although they apply to the same group of people, they refer to different time periods. Damage results from ambient pollution, while what we have on the horizontal axis is quantity of emissions. The functioning of the environment is what connects these two factors. Suppose the pollutant in question is some sort of material emitted into the air by industrial firms located near an urban area and that the damage functions refer to impacts felt by people living in that area. Marginal damage function MD_2 might occur when there is a temperature inversion that traps the pollutant over the city and produces relatively high ambient concentrations. MD_1 would be the damage function, on the other hand, when normal wind patterns prevail so that most of the effluent is blown downwind and out of the area. Thus the same emission levels at two different times could yield substantially different damage levels owing to the workings of the natural environment.

Having considered the concept of damages we must now look at the other side of the trade-off relationship mentioned above. It is tempting not to do this, to conclude instead that the damage functions themselves give us all the information we need to make decisions about pollution control. One might be tempted to say, for example, that society ought to strive for emission levels around point e_1, where marginal damages are zero, or perhaps even the origin, corresponding to a point at which emissions are zero. There may be certain pollutants and situations where the efficient level of emissions is indeed zero. But to determine this we have to look at the other side of the problem: abatement costs.

Abatement Costs

Abatement costs are the costs of reducing the quantity of residuals being emitted into the environment, or of lowering ambient concentrations. Think of the pulp mill located upstream. In its normal course of operation it produces a large quantity of organic wastes. On the assumption that it has free access to the river, the cheapest way to get rid of these wastes is simply to pump them into the river. But the firm normally has technological and managerial means to reduce these emissions. The costs of engaging in these activities are called "abatement costs" because they are the costs of abating, or reducing, the quantity of residuals put in the river. These costs will differ from one type of effluent to another. The costs of reducing emissions of SO_2 from electric power plants will obviously be different from the costs of reducing, say, toxic fumes from chemical plants. Even for sources producing the same type of effluent the costs of abatement are likely to be different because of differences in the technological features of the operation. One source may be relatively new, using modern production technology, while another may be an old one using more highly polluting technology. In the discussion that follows keep in mind that "abatement" is used with the widest possible connotation and includes all the many ways there are of reducing emissions: changes in production technology, input switching, residuals recycling, treatment, abandonment of a site, etc.

As is our habit, we will represent this idea graphically. As usual also, it is more convenient to work with marginal abatement costs than with total abatement costs. The units on the axes are the same as before: quantities of pollutants on the horizontal axis and monetary value on the vertical axis. Marginal emission abatement costs show the added costs of achieving a one-unit decrease in emission level, or alternatively the costs saved if emissions are increased by a unit. On the horizontal axis, marginal abatement cost curves originate at the uncontrolled emission levels; that is, emission levels prior to undertaking any

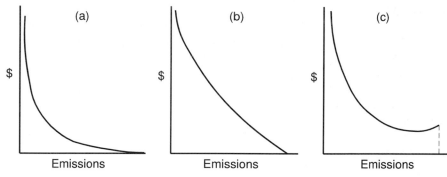

FIGURE 5-3
Representative Marginal Abatement Cost Functions.

abatement activities. In general they slope upward to the left, depicting rising marginal abatement costs.[2]

Figure 5-3 shows three alternative marginal abatement cost functions. The one in panel (a) depicts marginal abatement costs rising very modestly as emissions are first reduced, but then rising very rapidly as emissions become relatively small. Panel (b) shows marginal abatement costs that rise rapidly from the beginning. Panel (c) shows a marginal abatement cost curve that has an initial declining phase, followed by increasing values. This might characterize a situation in which small reductions can only be handled by technical means that require a substantial initial investment. For somewhat larger reductions the marginal costs may actually decline as it becomes possible to utilize these techniques more fully. Ultimately, however, marginal abatement costs increase. We have to keep in mind that in dealing with abatement costs we are dealing with a cost concept similar to that discussed in Chapter 3. The level of costs encountered when carrying out any particular task depends on the technology available to do the task and also on the managerial skills that are applied to the job. It is quite possible to suffer extremely high abatement costs if the wrong technology is used or if what is available is used incorrectly.

To investigate more deeply the concept of marginal abatement cost, consider Figure 5-4, which shows two marginal abatement cost curves. For the moment we focus on the higher one, labeled MAC_2. It begins at an effluent level, marked $\bar{e}$, the uncontrolled emission level. From there it slopes upward to the left. Beginning at the uncontrolled level, the first units of emission reduction can be achieved with a relatively low marginal cost. Think again of the pulp mill. This first small decrease might be obtained with the addition of a modest settling pond. But as emission levels are reduced further the marginal cost of achieving additional reductions increases. For example, to get a 30–40 percent reduction the pulp mill may have to invest in new technology that is more efficient in terms

---

[2] In Chapter 3, we showed marginal cost curves sloping upward to the right. The graph goes in the opposite direction because here we are producing *reductions* in emissions.

FIGURE 5-4
Anatomy of a Marginal Abatement Cost Curve.

of water use. A 60–70 percent reduction in effluent might require substantial new treatment technology in addition to all the steps taken previously, while a 90–95 percent reduction might take very costly equipment for recycling virtually all of the production residuals produced in the plant. Thus the larger the reduction in emissions, the greater the marginal costs of producing further reductions. This yields a marginal abatement cost function which gets steeper in slope as emissions are reduced.

Of course, there is an upper limit on these abatement costs. The extreme option for a single plant or pollution source is to cease operations, thereby achieving a zero level of emissions. The costs of doing this depend on circumstances. If the source is just one small plant within a large industry consisting of many such plants, the costs of closing it down may not be that great. In fact it may have very little impact on, say, the price to consumers of whatever is being produced (paper in the pulp mill example), though the local impact on jobs and community welfare may be substantial. But if we are talking about the marginal abatement costs for an entire industry—electric power production in the midwestern U.S., for example—the "shutdown" option, as a way of achieving zero emissions, would have enormous costs.

As with any marginal graph, we can depict not only marginal but also total values. If emissions are currently at e tons per year, the value on the vertical axis shows the marginal cost of achieving one more unit of emission reduction. The area under the marginal abatement cost curve, between its origin at point $\bar{e}$ and any particular emission level, is equal to the total costs of abating emissions to that level. For example, with the curve labeled MAC_2, the total abatement cost of achieving an emission level of e tons per year is equal to the area under the curve between e and $\bar{e}$, the area $a + b$; remember we are reading the graph from right to left.

Consider now the other marginal abatement cost curve shown in Figure 5-4, labeled MAC_1. Its main feature is that it lies below MAC_2, meaning that it corresponds to a situation where the marginal abatement costs for any level of emissions are lower for MAC_2. At e tons per year of emissions, for example, the marginal costs of abating an extra ton are only c_2 in the case of MAC_1, which are substantially lower than the marginal abatement costs of MAC_2 at this point. What could account for the difference? Let us assume that we are dealing with the same pollutant in each case. One possibility is that these apply to different sources—say, a plant that was built many years ago and another that was built more recently and uses different production technology. The newer plant lends itself to less costly emissions reduction.

Another possibility is that MAC_1 and MAC_2 relate to the same pollutant and the same source, but at different times. The lower one represents the situation after a new pollution-control technology has been developed, while the upper one applies before the change. Technological change, in other words, results in a lowering of the marginal abatement cost curve for a given pollutant. We can measure the annual cost that this source would save if it emitted at a rate e before and after the change. Before the firm adopted the new technology, its total abatement cost of achieving effluent level e was equal to $(a + b)$ per year, while after the change the total abatement costs are b per year. The annual cost savings from the technological change is thus a. This type of analysis will be important when we examine different types of pollution-control policies, because one of the criteria we will want to use to evaluate these policies is how much cost-saving incentive they offer to firms to engage in research and development to produce new pollution-control technologies.

Aggregate Marginal Abatement Costs

Our discussion of the last few pages has treated the marginal abatement cost function as something applying to a single firm; for example, a single pulp mill on a river. Suppose, however, we want to talk about the marginal abatement cost of a group of firms, perhaps a group of firms in the same industry or a group of firms all located in the same region. Most environmental policies, especially at state or federal levels, are aimed at controlling emissions from groups of pollution sources, not just single polluters. Suppose, furthermore, that the individual marginal abatement cost functions differ among the various firms. If we were trying to control organic pollutants in Boston Harbor or San Francisco Bay, for example, we would be faced with a large variety of different sources in different industries with different production technologies, and therefore with very different individual marginal abatement cost functions. In this case we would have to construct the aggregate, or overall, marginal abatement cost function for the collection of firms by adding together the individual marginal abatement cost curves.

While this sounds simple, and it basically is, it nevertheless will lead us into one of the more important concepts underlying the design of effective environmental policy. We have to keep in mind the central idea of the abatement cost function. It is a function that shows the *least costly* way of achieving reductions in emissions for an individual firm if we are looking at an individual marginal abatement cost function, or for a group of polluting sources if we are interested in the aggregate marginal abatement cost function.

Figure 5-5 shows, on the left, two individual marginal abatement cost functions, labeled Source A and Source B. We note that they are not the same (although remember that the scales are the same; i.e., we are dealing with the same pollutant). MAC_A starts at 20 tons/week and rises rather rapidly as emissions are reduced. MAC_B also begins at the uncontrolled discharge level of 20 tons/week, but rises much less rapidly. Why the difference? Perhaps Source B is a newer plant with more flexible technological alternatives for pollution control. Or perhaps the two sources, although producing the same type of effluent, are manufacturing different consumer goods, using different production techniques. For whatever reason, they have different marginal abatement cost curves.

The aggregate marginal abatement cost curve is a summation, or aggregation, of these two individual relationships. But since the individual curves are different, it makes a great deal of difference how we add them together. The problem is that when we have two (or any other number greater than one) sources with different abatement costs, the total cost will depend on how we allocate the total emissions among the different sources. The principle we want to follow is to add together the two individual functions in such a way as to yield the lowest possible

FIGURE 5-5
Aggregate Abatement Costs.

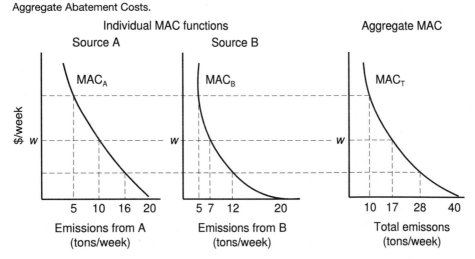

Individual MAC functions

Source A   Source B   Aggregate MAC

Emissions from A   Emissions from B   Total emissons
(tons/week)   (tons/week)   (tons/week)

aggregate marginal abatement costs. The way to do this is to add them horizontally. Select a particular level of marginal abatement cost—for example, the one marked w in Figure 5-5. This level of marginal abatement cost is associated with an effluent level of 10 tons/week from Source A, and an effluent level of about 7 tons/week from Source B. On the aggregate curve, thus, a marginal abatement cost of w would be associated with an effluent level of 10 tons + 7 tons = 17 tons/week. All the other points on the aggregate marginal abatement cost are found the same way, by summing across horizontally on the individual marginal abatement cost curves.

In effect what we have done here is to invoke the important equimarginal principle, an idea that we introduced earlier in Chapter 4. If we are going to have the minimum aggregate marginal abatement cost curve, the aggregate level of emissions must be distributed among the different sources in such a way that they will all have the same marginal abatement costs. Start at the 10 tons/week point on the aggregate curve. Obviously, this 10-ton total could be distributed among the two sources in any number of ways: 5 tons from each source, 8 tons from one and 2 from the other, etc. But only one allocation will give the lowest aggregate marginal abatement costs; this is the allocation that leads the different sources to the point at which they have exactly the same marginal abatement costs. At the end of this chapter we will come back to this equimarginal principle, illustrating it with a simple numerical example.

The Efficient Level of Emissions

Having considered separately the marginal damage function and the marginal abatement cost function related to a particular pollutant being released at a particular place and time, we have now to bring these two relationships together to see what they tell us. This we do in Figure 5-6. This depicts a set of conventionally shaped marginal damage and marginal abatement cost curves labeled, respectively, MD and MAC. Marginal damages have a threshold at emission level $\hat{e}$, while the uncontrolled emission level is e'.

The "efficient" level of emissions is defined as that level at which marginal damages are equal to marginal abatement costs. What is the justification for this? We note the trade-off that is inherent in the pollution phenomenon: higher emissions expose society, or some part of it, to greater costs stemming from environmental damages. Lower emissions involve society in greater costs in the form of resources devoted to abatement activities. The efficient level of effluent is thus the level at which these two types of costs exactly offset one another; that is, where marginal abatement costs equal marginal damage costs. This is emission level e^* in Figure 5-6. Marginal damages and marginal abatement costs are equal to each other and to the value w at this level of emissions.

We can also look at this outcome in terms of total values, since we know that the totals are the areas under the marginal curves. Thus the triangular area marked a (bounded by points $\hat{e}$, e^* and the marginal damage function) depicts the total damages existing when emissions are at level e^*, while the triangular

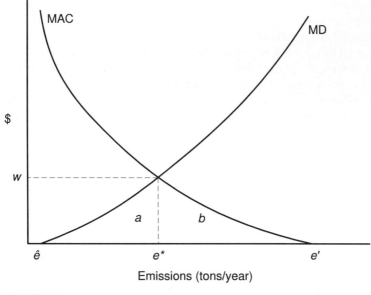

FIGURE 5-6
The Efficient Level of Emissions.

area b shows the total abatement costs at this level of emissions. The sum of these two areas $(a + b)$ is a measure of the total social costs from e^* tons per year of this particular pollutant. The point e^* is the unique point at which this sum is minimized. Note that area a need not equal area b.

You might get the impression, on the basis of where point e^* is located on the x-axis, that this analysis has led us to the conclusion that the "efficient" level of emissions is always one that involves a relatively large quantity of emissions and substantial environmental damages. This is not the case. What we are developing, rather, is a conceptual way of looking at a trade-off. In the real world every pollution problem is different. This analysis gives us a generalized way of framing the problem that obviously has to be adapted to the specifics of any particular case of environmental pollution. In Figure 5-7, for example, we have depicted three different situations that might characterize particular environmental pollutants. In each case e^* depicts the efficient level of emissions and w shows marginal damages and marginal abatement costs at that quantity of emissions. In panel (a) we have a pollutant for which e^* is well to the right of zero (of course since the horizontal axis has no units it's not clear exactly what "well to the right" actually means here). But marginal damages at this point are quite small; so are total damages and abatement costs, as shown by the small size of the triangles corresponding to these values. The reason is that we have a pollutant where both marginal abatement costs and marginal damages increase at first only very slowly.

Panel (b) shows a situation where the marginal abatement function rises

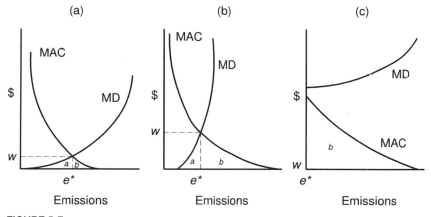

FIGURE 5-7
Efficient Emission Levels for Different Pollutants.

moderately, then rapidly, while the marginal damage function rises very rapidly from the beginning. In this case e^* is well to the right of zero, and w lies well above what it was in the first diagram (assuming the vertical axis of these diagrams all have the same scale). Note, however, that at e^* total abatement costs are substantially higher than total damages, as is indicated by the relative sizes of the triangles that measure these total values (a and b). What this emphasizes is that it is not the equality of total abatement costs and total damages that defines the efficient level of effluent, but the equality of the *marginal* abatement costs and marginal damages.

In panel (c) of Figure 5-7 the efficient level of emissions is zero. There is no point of intersection of the two functions in the graph; area a does not even appear on the graph. The only way we could conceivably get them to intersect is if we could somehow extend them to the left of the vertical axis, but this would imply that emissions could actually be negative, which is an oddity that we will avoid. What makes $e^* = 0$ is that the marginal damage function doesn't begin at zero, but rather well up on the abscissa, implying that even the first small amount of this pollutant placed in the environment causes great damage (perhaps this diagram applies to some extremely toxic material). Relative to this the marginal costs of abatement are low, giving an efficient emission level of zero.

The real world is a dynamic place, and this is especially true of environmental pollution control. For our purposes this implies, for example, that the level of emissions that was efficient last year, or last decade, is not necessarily the level that is efficient today, or that is likely to be in the future. We know the factors that lie behind the marginal damage and marginal abatement cost functions, and thus we realize that when any of these underlying factors change, the functions themselves will shift and e^*, the efficient level of emissions, will also change.

Before we take a look at this we need to remind ourselves of what we are doing. Remember the distinction we made earlier between positive and normative

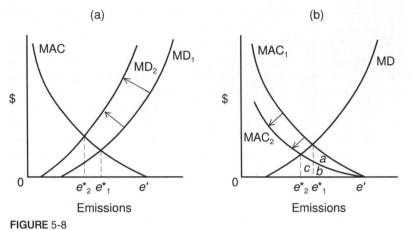

FIGURE 5-8
Changes in e^*, the Efficient Level of Emissions.

economics, between the economics of *what is* and the economics of *what ought to be*. The idea of the efficient level of emissions comes firmly under normative economics, under the idea of what ought to be. We are presenting emission level e^*, the level that balances abatement costs and damage costs, as a desirable target for public policy. We must not get this confused with the actual level of emissions; if the world worked so that the actual level of emissions was always equal to, or close to, the efficient level, we presumably would have no need to worry about intervening with environmental policy of one type or another. Of course it doesn't, which is why we must turn to public policy.

In Figure 5-8 we analyze several ways in which e^* might change when underlying factors change. Panel (a) shows the results of a shift upward in the marginal damage function, from MD_1 to MD_2. One of the ways this could happen is through population growth. MD_1 might apply to a municipality in 1950, and MD_2 to the same municipality in 1990 after its population has grown. More people means that a given amount of effluent will cause more damage.[3] This leads us to a conclusion that is intuitively straightforward: The efficient level of emissions drops from e_1^* to e_2^*. With a higher marginal damage function, the logic of the efficiency trade-off would lead us to devote more resources to pollution control.

Panel (b) of Figure 5-8 shows the case of a shift in the marginal abatement cost function, from MAC_1 to MAC_2. What could have caused this? The most obvious, perhaps, is a change in the technology of pollution control. We noted above that abatement costs depend critically on the technology available for reducing

---

[3] This diagram could also apply, of course, to a different situation. MD_1 could be the damage function pertaining to a relatively sparsely settled rural region; MD_2 could be the marginal damage function pertaining to a more populous urban area. Everything we say about the relationship between e_1^* and e_2^* applies also to cases like this where we are comparing two different places at the same time, in addition to the above comparison of the same place at two different times.

effluent streams: treatment technology, recycling technology, alternative fuel technology, etc. New techniques normally arise because resources, talents, and energy have been devoted to research and development. So the shift downward in marginal abatement costs depicted in Figure 5-8 might be the result of the development of new treatment or recycling technologies that make it less costly to reduce the effluent stream of this particular pollutant. It should not be too surprising that this leads to a reduction in the efficient level of emissions, as indicated by the change from e_1^* to e_2^*. We might note that this could lead to either an increase or a decrease in the total cost of abating emissions. Before the change, total abatement costs were an amount equal to the area $(a + b)$; that is, the area under MAC_1 between the uncontrolled level e' and the amount e_1^*. After the change total abatement costs are equal to area $(b + c)$, and the question of whether total abatement costs at the efficient level of emissions have increased or decreased hinges on the relative sizes of the two areas a and c. This in turn depends on the shapes of the curves and the extent to which the marginal abatement cost curve has shifted; the more it has shifted the more likely it is that the efficient level of total abatement costs after the change will exceed the costs before the change.[4]

Enforcement Costs

So far we have considered only the private costs of reducing emissions. But emission reductions do not happen unless resources are devoted to enforcement. To include all sources of cost we need to add the marginal enforcement costs to the analysis. Some of these are private, such as added recordkeeping by polluters. But the bulk are public costs related to various components of the enforcement process. Figure 5-9 shows a simple model of pollution control with enforcement costs added. To the normal marginal abatement cost function has been added the marginal costs of enforcement, giving a total marginal cost function labeled MAC + E. The vertical distance between the two marginal cost curves equals marginal enforcement costs. The assumption drawn into the graph is that marginal enforcement costs, the added costs of enforcement that it takes to get emissions reduced by a unit, increase as emissions decrease. In other words, the more polluters cut back emissions the more costly it is to enforce further cutbacks. We will have more to say about enforcement and its costs in later parts of the book.

In effect, the addition of enforcement costs moves the efficient level of emissions to the right of where it would be if they were zero. And this shows the vital importance of having good enforcement technology, because lower marginal

---

[4] These diagrams can also be used to examine some of the implications of making mistakes. For example, suppose we (i.e., the public control authorities) think that the real marginal abatement cost was MAC_1, but that, in fact, because there is a cheaper way of reducing this effluent that we don't know about, marginal abatement costs are actually MAC_2. Then we would conclude that the efficient level of effluent is e_1^* whereas it is actually e_2^*. We might be shooting at a target that involves excessive emissions.

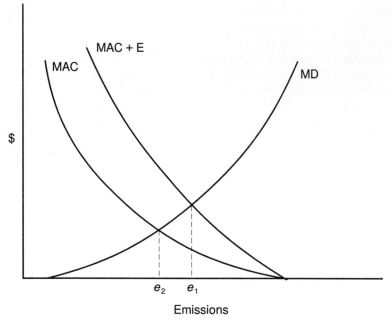

FIGURE 5-9
Enforcement Costs.

enforcement costs would move MAC + E closer to MAC, decreasing the efficient emission level. In fact, technical change in enforcement has exactly the same effect on the efficient level of emissions as technical change in emissions abatement itself.

THE EQUIMARGINAL PRINCIPLE APPLIED TO EMISSION REDUCTIONS

Before going on we want to take a last, very explicit look at the equimarginal principle. One of its implications is that if a pollutant has multiple sources and we wish to reduce the overall level of emissions in the least costly way, we must reduce the emissions from each source in accordance with the equimarginal principle. Achieving the lowest abatement costs or, alternatively, achieving the greatest emissions cutback for a given total cost requires that we satisfy the equimarginal principle.

To illustrate this look at the numbers in Table 5-1. This shows explicitly the marginal abatement costs of each of two firms emitting a particular residual into the environment. If neither source makes any effort to control emissions, they will each emit 12 tons/week. If Plant A reduces its emissions by 1 ton, to 11 tons/week, it will cost $1,000/week; if it reduces effluent further to 10 tons/week, its abatement costs will increase by $2,000/week, and so on. Note

TABLE 5-1
THE EQUIMARGINAL PRINCIPLE

Emissions (tons/week)	Marginal abatement costs ($1,000/week)	
	Source A	Source B
12	0	0
11	1	2
10	2	4
9	3	6
8	4	10
7	5	14
6	6	20
5	8	25
4	10	31
3	14	38
2	24	58
1	38	94
0	70	160

that the marginal abatement cost relationships of the two sources are different: that of Source B increases faster than that of Source A.

Suppose that initially each plant is emitting at the uncontrolled level; total emissions would then be 24 tons/week. Now let us assume that we want to reduce overall emissions to half the present level, or a total of 12 tons/week. One way to do this would be to have *equiproportionate* cutbacks; since we want a total reduction of 50 percent, we require each source to reduce by 50 percent. If Source A were cut 50 percent to 6 tons/week, its marginal abatement costs at this level would be $6,000/week, while at this level of emissions the marginal abatement costs of Source B would be $20,000/week. Total abatement costs of the 12-ton total can be found by adding up the marginal abatement costs; these are $21,000/week for Source A ($1,000 + $2,000 + $3,000 + $4,000 + $5,000 + $6,000) and $56,000/week for Source B ($2,000 + $4,000 + $6,000 + $10,000 + $14,000 + $20,000), or a grand total of $77,000/week.

But we can achieve the overall reduction to 12 tons/week with a substantially lower total cost. We know this because with the equiproportionate reduction we are violating the equimarginal principle; marginal abatement costs are not equalized when each source reduces its effluent to 6 tons/week. What we seek are different emission rates for the two sources, where, simultaneously, they will emit no more than 12 tons of effluent and have the same marginal abatement costs. This condition is satisfied if Source A emits 4 tons and Source B emits 8 tons. These rates add up to 12 tons total and give each source a marginal abatement cost of $10,000/week. Calculating total abatement costs at these emission levels gives $39,000/week for Source A ($1,000+$2,000+$3,000+$4,000

+ $5,000 + $6,000 + $8,000 + $10,000) plus $22,000/week for Source B ($2,000 + $4,000 + $6,000 + $10,000), or a grand total of $61,000/week. We have, by following the equimarginal principle, obtained our desired reduction in total emissions with a savings of $16,000/week over the case of an equiproportionate reduction.

Thus, we see that an emission reduction plan that follows the equimarginal rule gives emission reduction at minimum cost. Another way of saying this is that for any particular amount of money devoted to effluent reduction, we can get the maximum quantitative reduction in total effluent if we follow the equimarginal principle. The importance of this principle cannot be overstated. When we defined the efficient level of emissions, we were going on the assumption that we were working with the lowest possible marginal abatement cost function. The only way we can achieve this is if we are controlling individual sources in accordance with the equimarginal rule. If we are designing public policy under the rule of equiproportionate reductions at the various sources, we will be working with a marginal abatement cost function that is higher than it should be. And one of the results of this is that we will define an "efficient" emission level that is higher than it should be, or, to say the same thing, we will seek smaller reductions in emissions than are socially efficient.

LONG-RUN SUSTAINABILITY

The model we have discussed in this chapter hinges on the idea of efficiency, where decisions are made by comparing costs and benefits—in the case of pollution control comparing marginal abatement costs and marginal damages. A question arises over whether this approach is consistent with the notion of long-run sustainability, as discussed in Chapter 2. In comparing costs and benefits like this, are we not giving undue primacy to the people who are in the better position to have their values counted—namely, present generations? Are we perhaps not giving enough consideration to future generations? They are not here to be heard from directly, so the only way they can be factored in is through the bequest motive of present generations, which may not be strong enough.

This would not be a problem if all environmental resources were renewable and all pollutants noncumulative. But these conditions don't hold. Species extinctions are forever. And certain long-lasting pollutants can accumulate to become legacies from the present generation to those of the future. In the history of the human race very long-run negative environmental impacts have often eventually undermined the productivity of a society's resource base.[5] Most of these have been regional or local in scope; for example, the salting of soils in the Tigris–Euphrates lowlands (1900–1600 B.C.).[6] Today these local and regional

[5] Eric P. Eckholm, *Losing Ground: Environmental Stress and World Food Prospects*, W. W. Norton, New York, 1976.

[6] B. L. Turner II, ed., *The Earth as Transformed by Human Action*, Cambridge University Press, Cambridge, England, 1990, pp. 27–30.

situations continue, and we are also concerned about long-run global sustainability.

The easy answer is to say that the marginal abatement cost and (especially) the marginal damage functions of our basic model must be interpreted as containing all impacts, both short and long run, insofar as we can predict them. Conceptually, this is correct, but in practice it may be difficult to do. It is much easier to estimate short-run costs and damages than costs and damages occurring well off in the future. The great uncertainty about future impacts often means that more weight is put on the better-known short-run impacts. The other problem is how to compare present and future effects. Should we treat a dollar's worth of damage that will occur 100 years from now as equivalent to a dollar's worth of damages incurred today?

Some have suggested that we might be able to identify an upper limit on damages strictly on physical grounds. Whatever the short-run trade-off we wish to make to achieve efficiency, we may be able to identify emission levels which, if exceeded, would diminish significantly the long-run physical status of particular environmental resources. For certain renewable resources, like animal and plant species, we could perhaps identify this point with some level below which extinction would result. But for most environmental resources, a physical limit is not definable. All decisions, even when long-run impacts are involved, must incorporate human judgments to some extent. And where judgments are involved, trade-offs automatically become relevant.

SUMMARY

In this chapter we have looked at a simple model of pollution control. It is based on the notion of a trade-off of environmental damages and pollution abatement costs. We introduced the notion of a marginal damage function, showing the marginal social damages resulting from varying levels of residual emissions or ambient pollutant levels. Then we looked at marginal abatement cost relationships, first for an individual pollution source and then for a group of such sources. By bringing together these two types of relationships we then defined an efficient level of emissions: that level at which marginal damages and marginal abatement costs are equal. At this level of emissions total social costs, the total of abatement costs and damages, are minimized.

The efficient level of emissions is subject to change as underlying factors shift. Population growth and the results of scientific studies can shift marginal damage functions, technological changes can cause marginal abatement cost functions to shift. One sometimes hears statements to the effect that "the optimal level of pollution can never be zero." While this may be true when considering all pollutants in the aggregate, it is most definitely not true when considering individual pollutants. We illustrated one case in which the efficient level of a particular pollutant is zero. Finally, we reviewed the equimarginal principle as it applies to pollution control. That principle states that with multiple sources having different marginal abatement cost functions, we achieve a given total emission reduction at least total cost only if we distribute the emission reduction among the various sources in such a way as to equalize their marginal abatement costs.

A word of caution is appropriate. The model presented in this chapter is very general and risks giving an overly simplistic impression of pollution problems in the real world. In fact, there are very few actual instances of environmental pollution where we know the marginal damage and marginal abatement functions with certainty. The natural world is too complex, and human and nonhuman responses are too difficult to identify with complete clarity. Furthermore, polluters come in all types and sizes and economic circumstances, and it takes enormous resources to learn even simple things about the costs of pollution abatement in concrete instances. Pollution control technology is changing rapidly, so what is efficient today will not necessarily be so tomorrow. Nevertheless, the simple model is useful for thinking about the basic problem of pollution control, and it will be useful in our later chapters on the various approaches to environmental policy. Before discussing complicated policy issues, it is appropriate to study the ways economists have tried to measure and make visible marginal abatement costs and marginal damages in specific cases of environmental quality changes.

QUESTIONS FOR FURTHER DISCUSSION

1 Prove (graphically) that the point labeled e^* in Figure 5-6 is indeed the point that minimizes total social costs, the sum of abatement and damage costs. (Do this by showing that at any other point, this total cost will be higher.)
2 Consider a large harbor through which many oil tankers pass on their way to and from an oil refinery. How would the efficient level of oil pollution in the waters of the harbor be affected by: (1) the invention of better equipment for recovering spilled oil, (2) the redevelopment of the harborside to make it more attractive to tourists, (3) the opening of a new refinery next to the existing one?
3 Suppose a new law is put into effect requiring oil tankers to use certain types of navigation rules in coastal waters of the U.S. Suppose that the very next year there is a large tanker accident and oil spill in these waters. Does this mean that the law has had no effect?
4 In establishing the efficient level of emissions of any pollutant, what are the important roles to be played by physical scientists, natural scientists, economists, and policymakers?
5 Environmental economics is sometimes criticized because it seems to lead to the conclusion that the efficient level of all pollutants can never be zero. Comment on this.
6 How might equity considerations make the most "socially desirable" level of emissions different from the socially efficient level?

SELECTED READINGS

Freeman, A. Myrick, III, Robert H. Haveman, and Allen V. Kneese: *The Economics of Environmental Policy*, John Wiley, New York, 1973.

Hite, James C., et al.: *The Economics of Environmental Quality*, American Enterprise Institute, Washington, D.C., 1972.

Kneese, Allen V., and Charles L. Schultze: *Pollution, Prices, and Public Policy*, The Brookings Institution, Washington, D.C., 1975.

Magat, Wesley A.: *Reform of Environmental Regulation*, Ballinger Publishing Company, Cambridge, Mass., 1982.

Mills, Edwin S., and Philip E. Graves: *The Economics of Environmental Quality*, 2nd ed., Norton, New York, 1986.

Pearce, David W., and R. Kerry Turner: *Economics of Natural Resources and the Environment*, Johns Hopkins Press, Baltimore, Md., 1990.

Portney, Paul R.: "The Evolution of Federal Regulation," in Paul R. Portney (ed.), *Public Policies for Environmental Protection*, Resources for the Future, Washington, D.C., 1990, pp. 7–25.

ENVIRONMENTAL ANALYSIS

In the last few chapters we have used the concepts of "abatement costs" and "damages" without worrying too much about how we might measure their magnitudes in particular situations. In the next three chapters we will rectify this. Several types of analysis have been developed over the years to provide environmental, economic, and social information to the policy process. In the next chapter we will deal with these at the framework level. From the standpoint of economics, benefit–cost analysis is the primary analytical tool, and we will spend much of the chapter discussing its major elements. Then in the following two chapters we will look more closely at the methods available for estimating benefits and costs relevant to environmental policy decisions.

CHAPTER 6

FRAMEWORKS OF ANALYSIS

Policy decisions require information and, although the availability of good information doesn't automatically mean that decisions also will be good, its *un*availability will almost always contribute to bad decisions. There are a variety of alternative frameworks for generating and presenting information useful to policymakers, calling for different skills and research procedures. We briefly review the most important of these, before focusing on benefit–cost analysis.

IMPACT ANALYSIS

"Impact" is a very general word, meaning the effects of any actual or proposed policy. Since there are many types of effects, there are many different types of impact analysis. We focus here on two of these: environmental impacts and economic impacts.

Environmental Impact Analysis

An Environmental Impact Analysis (EIA) is essentially an identification and study of all significant environmental repercussions stemming from a course of action. For the most part these focus on impacts that are expected to flow from a proposed decision, though retrospective EIAs are of great value also, especially when they are done to see if earlier predictions were accurate. EIAs can be carried out for any social action, public or private, industrial or domestic, local or national. They are largely the work of natural scientists, who focus on tracing out and describing the physical impacts of projects or programs, especially following through the complex linkages that spread these impacts through the ecosystem. They do not address directly the issue of placing social values on these impacts.

Many countries have laws requiring environmental impact studies when substantial public programs and projects are under consideration, as well as private projects in some cases. The one in the U.S. stems from the National Environmental Policy Act of 1970 (NEPA). This law requires that agencies of the federal government conduct environmental impact assessments of proposed legislation and "other major federal actions significantly affecting the quality of the human environment." Over the years this has been extended to include any actions funded in part or regulated by the federal government, even though they are carried out by private parties.[1] The result of the assessment is an Environmental Impact Statement (EIS). EISs are to contain information on the following topics:

- "a description of the environmental impact of the proposed action,"
- "any adverse environmental effects that cannot be avoided should the proposal be implemented,"
- "alternatives to the proposed action,"
- "the relationship between short-term uses of man's environment and the maintenance and enhancement of long-term productivity," and
- "any irreversible and irretrievable commitments of resources that would be involved in the proposed action should it be implemented."[2]

NEPA also created the Council on Environmental Quality, an executive agency whose job is to manage the EIS process and publish an annual report on the state of the environment.

Although EISs are primarily the work of natural scientists, economics has a distinct role to play as well. It is not only ecological linkages through which environmental impacts spread; they spread also through economic linkages. Suppose, for example, it is proposed to build a dam that will flood a certain river valley, while providing new flat-water recreation possibilities. A substantial part of the environmental impact will stem from the inundation itself and the resulting losses in animals and plants, wild-river recreation, farmland, etc. But much also could come from changes in patterns of behavior among people affected by the project. Recreators traveling into and out of the region could affect air pollution and traffic congestion. New housing or commercial development spurred by the recreation opportunities could have negative environmental effects. Thus, to study the full range of environmental impacts from the dam, it is necessary to include not just the physical effects of the dam and its water impoundment, but also the ways people will react and adapt to this new facility.

Economic Impact Analysis

When interest centers on how some action—a new law, a new technological breakthrough, a new source of imports—will affect an economic system, in whole or in terms of its various parts, we can speak of economic impact analysis. In most countries, especially developing ones, there is usually wide interest in the impact of environmental regulations on economic growth rates. Sometimes

---

[1] Many of the individual states also have laws requiring environmental impact statements for state-funded actions.

[2] Council on Environmental Quality, *Environmental Quality 1984*, Washington, D.C., 1985, p. 513.

the focus will be on tracing out the ramifications of a public program for certain economic variables that are considered particularly important. One might be especially interested, for example, in the impact of an environmental regulation on employment, the impact of import restrictions on the rate of technological change in an industry, the effects of an environmental law on the growth of the pollution-control industry, the response of the food industry to new packaging regulations, and so on.

A good example of an impact analysis is a recent study by two Dutch environmental economists.[3] In the Netherlands there is an important problem with soil acidification, resulting in part from industrial emissions of sulfur dioxide (SO_2) and nitrogen oxides (NO_x), but also in part from agricultural practices in animal feeding and manure disposal. Various proposals have been made to reduce agricultural emissions of ammonia (NH_3). The objective of the researchers was to trace out the impacts of these proposed regulations on the agricultural sector. They concluded that the control program would lead to a decrease in net farm revenues of 35 percent over the period 1985–2010, a decline in the number of dairy cows, increases in yields per cow, declines in numbers of other animals, and a substantial reduction in the amounts of ammonia coming from the agricultural sector.

Economic impact analyses can be focused at any level. Local environmental groups might be interested in the impact of a wetlands law on the rate of population growth and tax base in their community. Regional groups might be interested in the impacts of a national regulation on their particular economic circumstances. At the global level, an important question is how efforts to control CO_2 emissions might impact the relative growth rates of rich and poor countries. Whatever the level, economic impact analysis requires a basic understanding of how economies function, and how their various parts fit together.

COST-EFFECTIVENESS ANALYSIS

Suppose a community determined that its current water supply was contaminated with some chemical, and that it had to switch to some alternative supply. Suppose it had several possibilities: It could drill new wells into an uncontaminated aquifer, it could build a connector to the water supply system of a neighboring town, or it could build its own surface reservoir. A cost-effectiveness analysis would estimate the costs of these different alternatives with the aim of showing how they compared in terms of, say, the costs per million gallons of delivered water into the town system. Cost-effectiveness analysis, in other words, essentially takes the objective as given, then costs out various alternative ways of attaining that objective. One might think of it as one-half of a benefit–cost analysis where costs, but not benefits, are estimated in monetary terms.

---

[3] Paul J. J. Veenendaal and Hoor M. Brouwer, "Consequences of Ammonia Emission Abatement Policies for Agricultural Practices in the Netherlands," in Frank J. Dietz et al. (eds.), *Environmental Policy and the Economy*, North-Holland, Amsterdam, 1991, chapter 12, pp. 241–279.

Table 6-1 shows some of the results of a cost-effectiveness analysis done by the U.S. Office of Technology Assessment. The study looked at different ways of reducing mobile-source emissions of volatile organic compounds (VOCs), which produce smog. The results show the estimated reduction in tons of VOC emissions per $1,000 dollars of cost for each of the different technological approaches listed. These cost-effectiveness coefficients range from .03 to 1.96. Thus, it would appear, for example, that $1 million put into making gas less volatile will reduce VOC emissions about 75 times more than the same amount put into the development of alternative fuels. But we have to interpret these cost coefficients with care. Although the fuel volatility option has the highest tons of VOC reduced per dollar, we can't conclude from this that the best way to clean up smog in this region is to concentrate solely on this one approach. Each of the technologies has limits as to the total amount of VOC it is capable of reducing, so, depending on what the desired total reduction is, different combinations of these techniques will have to be utilized.

TABLE 6-1
COST-EFFECTIVENESS OF DIFFERENT MEASURES FOR THE CONTROL OF VOLATILE ORGANIC COMPOUNDS (VOCs) IN NONATTAINMENT CITIES

Strategy	Tons of VOC reduced per $1,000
RACT	0.20
New CTGs	0.16
Federal controls	0.59
On-board controls	0.83
Stage II	1.00
Stage II and on-board controls	0.83
Enhanced I&M[*]	0.26
Fuel volatility[†]	1.96
New highway vehicle standards[*]	0.42
Methanol fuels	0.03

[*]Estimates reflect costs associated with VOC control only. Enhanced I&M controls also apply to NO_x and carbon monoxide emissions; new highway vehicle standards also apply to NO_x emissions.
[†]Estimates reflect cost-effectiveness during the 5-month summertime period when controls are required.

Strategy Descriptions
RACT is the reasonable available control technology on all existing stationary sources that emit more than 25 tons per year of VOC; new CTGs are new control technique guidelines for existing stationary sources that emit more than 25 tons per year of VOC; federal controls are on selected small stationary sources of VOC (consumer and commercial solvents, and architectural surface coatings); on-board controls are on motor vehicles to capture gasoline vapor during refueling; stage II control devices are on gas pumps to capture gasoline vapor during motor vehicle refueling; fuel volatility controls limit the rate of gasoline evaporation; enhanced inspection and maintenance (I&M) programs are for cars and light-duty trucks; new highway vehicle emission standards are for passenger cars and light-duty gasoline trucks; methanol fuels are a substitute for gasoline as a motor vehicle fuel.

Source: Adapted from: Office of Technology Assessment, *Urban Ozone and the Clean Air Act*, Washington, D.C., 1988, p. 108.

You may have noticed that cost-effectiveness analysis can be used along with the equimarginal principle, in this case as applied to comparisons across different emission-abatement technologies. In putting together an effective control program, authorities would want to choose techniques that have the lowest marginal abatement costs, and combine them in a way that satisfies the equimarginal principle. Of course, this leaves out the important prior question. In this example, how much VOC reduction is efficient, in the light of damages done by these emissions? But you can see that the efficiency question is intertwined with the issue of cost-effectiveness. We can't answer the efficiency question until we know what emission reduction costs are going to be, but these costs depend on the cost-effectiveness of the particular techniques chosen to reduce emissions.

It may make good sense to do a cost-effectiveness analysis even before there is a strong public commitment to the objective you are costing out. In many cases people may not know exactly how much they value a given objective. Once a cost-effectiveness analysis is done, they may be able to tell, at least in relative terms, whether any of the different alternatives would be desirable. They may be able to say something like: "We don't know exactly how much benefits are in monetary terms, but we feel that they are more than the costs of several of the alternatives that have been costed out, so we will go ahead with one or both of them."

BENEFIT–COST ANALYSIS

Benefit–cost analysis is for the public sector what a profit-and-loss analysis is for a business firm. If an automobile company contemplated introducing a new car, it would want to get some idea of how its profitability would be affected. On the one hand, it would estimate costs of production and distribution: labor, raw materials, energy, emission control equipment, transportation, etc.[4] On the other hand, it would estimate revenues through market analysis. Then it would compare expected revenues with anticipated costs. Benefit–cost analysis is an analogous exercise for programs in the public sector. This means there are two critical differences between benefit–cost analysis and the car example: It is a tool for helping to make public decisions, done from the standpoint of society in general rather than from that of a single profit-making firm; and it usually is done for policies and programs that have *unmarketed* types of outputs like, for example, improvements in environmental quality.

Benefit–cost analysis has led two intertwined lives. The first is among its practitioners, economists inside and outside public agencies who have developed the techniques, tried to produce better data, and extended the scope of the analysis. The second is among the politicians and administrators who have set

---

[4] Of course, it probably would not factor in the costs of air pollution damage inflicted on people breathing the emissions of the new cars; if it did this without being required to, we probably wouldn't be here studying this topic.

the rules and procedures governing the use of benefit–cost analysis for public decision making. In the U.S., benefit–cost analysis was first used in conjunction with the United States Flood Control Act of 1936. That act specified that federal participation in projects to control flooding on major rivers of the country would be justifiable ". . . *if the benefits to whomever they accrue are in excess of the estimated costs. . . .*" In order to determine if this criterion was satisfied for any proposed flood-control dam or large levee project, procedures had to be developed to measure these benefits and costs.

These procedures have been altered from time to time as benefit–cost analysis has evolved and matured. The status and role of benefit–cost analysis in public natural resource and environmental decision making have been the subject of continuing discussions as well as political and administrative conflicts. Public agencies have often been taken to task by outsiders for trying to use benefit–cost analysis in ways that would help them justify ever-larger budgets. Some observers have taken the position that benefit–cost analysis is really an attempt to short-circuit the process of political discussion and decision that should take place around prospective public projects and programs. And in the 1980s the conservative administration in Washington sought to use benefit–cost analysis as an extra hurdle for program approval, in order to reduce the scope of public programs.

Despite its up and down history, however, benefit–cost analysis is now the major tool for the economic evaluation of public programs in natural resource management, such as flood control, irrigation, hydropower, harbor improvements, and alternative energy supply projects. It is an integral part of the Environmental Impact Analysis process, meant to evaluate the impacts of public and private developments on environmental resources. Its use in evaluating programs of environmental pollution control is less widespread. The United States Environmental Protection Agency (EPA) does not routinely do benefit–cost analyses of all its regulatory programs. This is partly because the laws don't call for it, and probably because benefit measurement is so difficult. Some programs have been evaluated from a benefit–cost perspective, however; for example, the plan for phasing out leaded gasoline, disposing of sludge from wastewater treatment plants, and establishing rules for municipal solid waste landfills. In addition, the EPA as well as other federal agencies have sought to develop better methods for estimating the benefits and costs of environmental programs.

The Basic Framework

As the name implies, a benefit–cost analysis involves measuring, adding up, and comparing all the benefits and all the costs of a particular public project or program. There are essentially four steps in a benefit–cost analysis:

1 Specify clearly the project or program.
2 Describe quantitatively the inputs and outputs of the program.

3 Estimate the social costs and benefits of these inputs and outputs.
4 Compare these benefits and costs.

Each of these steps incorporates a number of component steps. In doing a benefit–cost analysis, the very first step is to decide on the *perspective* from which the study is to be done. Benefit–cost analysis is a tool of public analysis, but there are actually many publics. If you were doing a benefit–cost study for a national agency, the "public" normally would be all the people living in the particular country. But if you were employed by a city or regional planning agency to do a benefit–cost analysis of a local environmental program, you would undoubt-edly focus on benefits and costs accruing to people living in those areas. At the other extreme, the rise of global environmental issues has forced us to undertake some benefit–cost analyses from a worldwide perspective.

When we have decided on the perspective from which to do a study, step 1 also includes a complete specification of the main elements of the project or program: location, timing, groups involved, connections with other programs, etc. We can distinguish between the two primary types of public environmental programs for which benefit–cost analyses are done:

1 *Physical projects* that involve direct public production: public waste treatment plants, beach restoration projects, hazardous-waste incinerators, habitat im-provement projects, land purchase for preservation, and so on.
2 *Regulatory programs* that are aimed at enforcing environmental laws and regulations, such as pollution-control standards, technological choices, waste disposal practices, restrictions on land development, and so on.

When we have specified the basic project or program the next step is to determine the relevant flows of inputs and outputs. For some projects this is reasonably easy. If we are planning a wastewater treatment facility, the engineer-ing staff will be able to provide a full physical specification of the plant, together with the inputs required to build it and keep it running. For other types of programs it is much harder. A restriction on development in a particular region, for example, can be expected to deflect development elsewhere into surrounding areas. These must be predicted with tolerable accuracy. It is in this step that we first have to recognize the great importance of time. Environmentally related projects or programs do not usually last for a single year, but are spread out over long periods of time. So the job of specifying inputs and outputs involves predictions of future events, often quite remote in time. This puts a premium on having a good understanding of things like future growth patterns and future rates of technological change and possible changes in consumers' preferences.

The next step is to put values on input and output flows; that is, to measure costs and benefits. We could do this in any units we wish, but normally we try to measure benefits and costs in monetary terms. This does not mean in market-value terms, because in many cases we will be dealing with effects, especially on the benefit side, that are not directly registered on markets. Nor does it imply that only monetary values count in some fundamental manner. It means that we need a single metric into which we can try to translate all of the impacts of a project or program, in order to make them comparable among themselves as well as with other types of public activities. Ultimately, certain environmental impacts of a program may be irreducible to monetary terms because we cannot find a way of measuring how much people value these impacts. In this case we must supplement the monetary results of the benefit–cost analysis with estimates of these intangible impacts.

Finally, we must compare benefits and costs. To understand what is involved in very general terms consider the numbers in Table 6-2. They are meant to illustrate the estimated benefits and costs of a regulatory program to control various airborne and waterborne pollutants coming from a group of pulp mills. These emissions reduce downstream water quality in the river on which they are located and contribute to serious air pollution in the vicinity of the plants. The numbers pertain to the totals of the various cost and benefit categories over the life of the program. Compliance costs in the industry consist of $580 million of capital equipment costs and $560 million of operating costs. Public-sector monitoring and enforcement required to achieve an acceptable level of compliance total $96 million. There are three major benefit categories. Downstream recreators (fishers and boaters) are benefited from the improved water quality: The value of these benefits is $1,892 million. Agricultural operators in the vicinity of the plants are expected to suffer $382 million loss in damages to crops and livestock because of reduced airborne emissions. Finally, there are intangible benefits which we have found no way of measuring in monetary terms. These are shown simply as some quantity "A."

We can compare total benefits and costs in several ways. One way is to subtract the total costs from total benefits to get "*net benefits.*" In Table 6-2 the net benefits

TABLE 6-2
ILLUSTRATIVE RESULTS FROM A BENEFIT–COST ANALYSIS OF A PROPOSED EMISSION REDUCTION PROGRAM FOR A GROUP OF PULP MILLS

	Totals over life of the program
	($1,000,000)
Costs	
Private compliance	
Capital equipment	580
Operating	560
Public monitoring and enforcement	96
Total	1,236
Benefits	
Increased benefits to recreators from improved water quality	1,896
Reduced damages to agricultural crops and livestock	382
Intangible	A
Total	2,278 + A
Net benefits: $1,042 + A	
Benefit–cost ratio: 1.8 + a	

are shown as $1,042 million ($2,278 − $1,236), together with an indeterminate allowance for intangible benefits. Another criterion is the *benefit–cost ratio*, found by taking the ratio of benefits and costs. This shows the benefits the project will produce for each dollar of costs; in Table 6-2 the benefit–cost ratio is 1.8 (2,278 ÷ 1,236), together with an indeterminate adjustment (indicated as "a") for the intangible benefits.

Scope of the Project

This example, simple as it is, illustrates a number of problems in benefit–cost analysis. One important one is deciding on the scope of the project or program. How can we be sure that this one is the appropriate size—that a somewhat more restrictive or, alternatively, less restrictive program might not be better? The basic problem here is reconciling the fact that in reality it is always possible to vary the scope of a program—to make it larger or smaller by any amount, whereas in doing a benefit–cost analysis we have to focus on a program of a specific size.

To explore this issue consider Figure 6-1. It shows our standard emission control model as developed in the last chapter, with marginal damage (MD) and marginal abatement cost (MAC) functions. Let us assume that the current level of emissions is e_1, that is, emissions are essentially uncontrolled. A control program is proposed that would lower emissions to e_2. For this program, total

FIGURE 6-1
Establishing the Size of a Public Program.

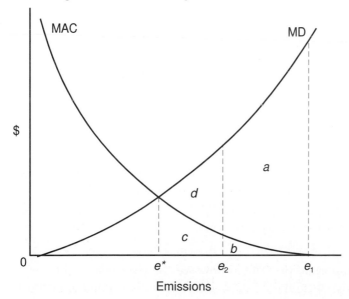

benefits (total damages reduced) are equal to $(a + b)$ while total abatement costs are equal to b. Net benefits are therefore equal to area a.

For an emission reduction program to give maximum net benefits, however, it would have to reduce emissions to e^*, the level at which MD = MAC. Here, net benefits would equal $(d + a)$. The problem is, when we do a benefit–cost analysis of a specific proposal, how can we be sure that we are dealing with one such as e^* in the figure, and not one such as e_2? For example, how can we be sure that the program analyzed in Table 6-2 represents one that is close to efficient size?

The general procedure here is to carry out *sensitivity analyses* on these results. This means recalculating benefits and costs for programs somewhat larger and somewhat smaller than the one shown in the table. We would analyze a program that has somewhat more restrictive emission reductions, with appropriate enforcement resources, and one that is somewhat less restrictive. If our chosen program is indeed appropriately scaled, each of the variations will produce lower net benefits.

The benefit–cost ratio is often used in public debates in describing environmental projects or programs. But the efficient program size is not the one that gives the maximum benefit–cost ratio. At emission level e^* the benefit–cost ratio is equal to $(a + b + c + d) \div (b + c)$. At emission level e_2, the benefit–cost ratio is $(a + b) \div b$, which is higher than that at e^*. The benefit–cost ratio may be used to make sure that, at the very least, benefits exceed cost, but beyond this it is a misleading indicator in planning the appropriate scope of public programs.

Under some circumstances, there may be grounds for sizing programs at less than that which maximizes net benefits. Suppose you are a regional public agency in charge of enforcing air-pollution laws in two medium-sized urban areas. Suppose further that you have a fixed and predetermined budget of $1 million to spend. You have two possibilities: (1) Put it all in one enforcement program in one of the cities or (2) divide it between two programs, one in each city. Suppose the numbers are as follows:

	Costs	Benefits	Net benefits	Benefit/Cost ratio
One-city program	$1,000,000	$2,000,000	$1,000,000	2.0
Two-city program				
City A	500,000	1,200,000	700,000	2.4
City B	500,000	1,200,000	700,000	2.4

In this case we do better with our fixed budget by putting it into two half-sized programs rather than just one. In this case what we want to do is allocate our resources so that the net benefits produced by the total budget are maximized.

Discounting

We turn now to the important problem of how we compare costs and benefits that occur at very different points in time. If we institute a pollution-control policy, how do we weigh the high initial-year capital costs of abatement equipment and the long-run costs of maintaining it? In the global warming problem, how do we compare the very high costs today of controlling CO_2 emissions with the benefits that won't really start accruing for several decades? Suppose we have two programs, one with relatively high net benefits that materialize well into the future, and another with smaller net benefits that occur in the near future. How do we compare these two options? The standard way to address problems like these is through *discounting*, a technique employed to add and compare costs and benefits that occur at different points in time. Discounting has two facets: first, the mechanics of doing it; then, the reasoning behind the choice of discount rates to be used in specific cases. We take these up in turn.

A cost that will occur 10 years from now does not have the same significance as a cost that occurs today. Suppose, for example, that I have incurred a cost of $1,000 that I must pay today. To do that I must have $1,000 in the bank, or my pocket, with which to pay the obligation. On the other hand, suppose I have a commitment to pay $1,000, not today, but 10 years from now. If the rate of interest I can get in a bank is 5 percent, and I expect it to stay at that level, I can deposit $613.90 in the bank today and it will compound up to $1,000 in 10 years, exactly when I need it. The formula for compounding this sum is:

$$\$613.90(1 + .05)^{10} = \$1,000$$

We can now turn this around and ask: What is the *present value* to me of this $1,000 obligation 10 years from now? Its present value is what I would have to put in the bank today to have exactly what I need in 10 years, and we get this by rearranging the above expression:

$$\text{Present value} = \frac{\$1,000}{(1 + .05)^{10}} = \$613.90$$

The present value is found by discounting the future cost back over the 10-year period at the interest rate, now called the discount rate, of 5 percent.[5] If it were higher—say, 8 percent—the present value would be lower—$463.20. The higher the discount rate, the lower the present value of any future cost.

The same goes for a benefit. Suppose you expect someone to give you a gift of $100, but only at the end of 6 years. This would not have the same value to you today (i.e., the same present value) as $100 given to you today. If the applicable discount rate is 4 percent, the present value of that future gift would be:

$$\frac{\$100}{(1 + .04)^6} = \$79.30$$

Discounting is used extensively in benefit–cost analyses. Its main role is to help in aggregating a series of costs or benefits that are strung out over the life

---

[5] In general, the discount formula is $PV = m/(1 + r)^t$, where m is the future value, r is the discount rate, and t is the number of years involved.

of a project or program. Consider the following illustrative numbers, showing benefits for two different programs over their short lives:

	Benefits ($) in year:			
	1	2	3	4
Project A	20	20	20	20
Project B	50	10	10	10

If we simply add these benefits across the four years for each project, they have the same total: $80. But Project A has a series of equal annual benefits, while B has substantial benefits in the first period and lower annual benefits thereafter. To compare the total benefits of the two projects, we must calculate the present value of total benefits for each program. For illustrative purposes we used a discount rate of 6 percent.

$$PV_A = \$20 + \frac{\$20}{1 + .06} + \frac{\$20}{(1 + .06)^2} + \frac{\$20}{(1 + .06)^3} = \$73.45$$

$$PV_B = \$50 + \frac{\$10}{1 + .06} + \frac{\$10}{(1 + .06)^2} + \frac{\$10}{(1 + .06)^3} = \$76.73$$

Note first of all that both present values are less than the undiscounted sums of benefits. This will always be true when a portion of a program's benefits accrues in future years. Note also that the present value of benefits for B exceeds that of A, which is what we would expect because more of B's benefits are concentrated early in the life of the program. That is to say, the time profile of B's benefits is more heavily concentrated in earlier years than the time profile of A's benefits.

Similar calculations are made for costs if we wish to know the present value of the stream of annual costs of a program. And the same reasoning applies; discounting reduces the present value of a dollar of cost more the farther out in the future that cost will be incurred. The present value of the stream of benefits minus the present value of costs gives the present value of net benefits. Alternatively, we could calculate for each year of the life of a project its *net benefits*, then calculate the present value of this stream of net benefits in the same way, by summing their discounted values.

Since discounting is a way of aggregating a series of future net benefits into an estimate of present value, the outcome depends importantly on which particular discount rate we use. If we were to use a very low rate, we would essentially be treating a dollar in one year as very similar in value to a dollar in any other year. If we use a very high rate, we are saying that a dollar in the near term is much more valuable to us than one later on. Thus, the higher the discount rate, the more we would be encouraged to put our resources into programs that have relatively high payoffs (i.e., high benefits and/or low costs) in the short run.

The lower the discount rate, on the contrary, the more we would be led to select programs that have high net benefits in the more distant future.

Choice of the Discount Rate

The choice of a discount rate has been a controversial topic through the years, and we can only summarize some of the arguments here. Firstly, we have to keep in mind the difference between *real* and *nominal* interest rates. Nominal rates are what you actually see on the market. If you take a nominal rate and adjust it for inflation, you get a real interest rate. Suppose you deposited $100 in a bank at an interest rate of 8 percent. In 10 years your deposit would have grown to $216. But this is in monetary terms. Suppose over that 10-year period prices increase 3 percent per year on average. Then the real value of your accumulated deposit would be less; in fact, the real interest rate at which your deposit would accumulate would only be 5 percent (8 percent – 3 percent), so in real terms your deposit would be worth only $161 after the 10 years.[6] So we have to be careful about the interest rate we use for discounting. If the cost estimates we are using are expected real costs, i.e., adjusted for expected inflation, we want to use a real interest rate for discounting purposes. If our cost estimates are nominal figures, then we use a nominal interest rate in the discounting analysis.

The discount rate reflects the current generation's views about the relative weight to be given to benefits and costs occurring in different years. But even a brief look will show that there are dozens of different interest rates in use at any one time—rates on normal savings accounts, certificates of deposit, bank loans, government bonds, etc. Which rate should we use? There are essentially two schools of thought on this question. The first is that the discount rate should reflect the way people themselves think about time. Any person normally will prefer a dollar today to a dollar in 10 years; in the language of economics, they have a positive rate of time preference. We see people making savings decisions by putting money in bank accounts that pay certain rates of interest. These savings account rates show what interest the banks have to offer in order to get people to forgo current consumption. We might, therefore, take the average bank savings account rate as reflecting the average person's rate of time preference.

The problem with this is that there are other ways of determining peoples' rates of time preference, and they don't necessarily give the same answer. Economists at Resources for the Future[7] recently completed a large survey in which they asked individuals to choose between receiving $10,000 today and larger amounts in 5 or 10 years. The responses yielded implied rates of discount

---

[6] These are slight approximations. The deposit would actually be worth $160.64 and the real rate of accumulation would be 4.89 percent.

[7] Resources for the Future (RFF) is a well-known Washington organization that specializes in natural resource and environmental economics research. It publishes a quarterly newsletter discussing its work. This information comes from RFF, *Resources*, No. 108, Summer 1992, p. 3.

of 20 percent for a 5-year time horizon and 10 percent for a 10-year horizon. These were substantially higher than bank savings rates at the time of the survey.

The second approach to determining the "correct" rate of discount is based on the notion of investment productivity. When investments are made in productive enterprises, people anticipate that the value of future returns will offset today's investment costs; otherwise, these investments would not be made. The thinking here is that when resources are used in the public sector for natural resource and environmental programs, they ought to yield, on average, rates of return to society equivalent to what they could have earned in the private sector. Private-sector productivity is reflected in the rates of interest banks charge their business borrowers. Thus, by this reasoning, we should use, as our discount rate, a rate reflecting the interest rates that private firms pay when they borrow money for investment purposes. These are typically higher than savings account interest rates.

With the multiplicity of interest rates the real world offers, and these different arguments for choosing a discount rate, it is no wonder that practices differ among agencies in the public sector. In 1990, for example, the Office of Management and Budget, the major executive branch spending oversight agency, used a discount of 10 percent. The Congressional Budget Office, an oversight agency for the U.S. Congress, used a rate of 2 percent. The U.S. Environmental Protection Agency uses several discount rates for evaluating environmental programs. Some agencies also require sensitivity analysis, showing how program net benefits are affected when calculated with slightly higher or lower discount rates. We can conclude that although discounting is widely accepted, the rate controversy is far from being resolved.

Discounting and Future Generations

The logic of a discount rate, even a very small one, is inexorable. A billion dollars, discounted back over a century at 5 percent, has a present value of only slightly over $7.6 million. The present generation, considering the length of its own expected life, may not be interested in programs having very high, but long-run, payoffs like this.

The logic is even more compelling if we consider a future cost. One of the reasons that environmentalists have looked askance at discounting is that it can have the effect of downgrading future damages that result from today's economic activity. Suppose today's generation is considering a course of action that has certain short-run benefits of $10,000 per year for 50 years, but which, starting 50 years from now, will cost $1 million a year *forever*. This may not be too unlike the choice faced by current generations on nuclear power, or on global warming. To people alive today the present value of that perpetual stream of future cost discounted at 10 percent is only $85,000. These costs may not weigh particularly heavily on decisions made by the current generation. The present value of the benefits ($10,000 a year for 50 years at 10 percent, or $99,148) exceeds the present value of the future costs. From the standpoint of today, therefore, this might look like a good choice, despite the perpetual cost burden placed on all future generations.

The problems associated with using positive discount rates for environmental programs with long-run impacts are difficult to resolve. Exhibit 6-1, on the following page, is a news clip illustrating some of the differences on this point among economists. Many take the view that for long-run environmental projects the appropriate discount rate is zero. But we have to be very careful here. A great deal of harm has been done to natural and environmental resources by using very low discount rates to evaluate development projects. With low discount rates, it's often possible to justify very disruptive public infrastructure projects because enough distant and uncertain benefits can be accumulated to outweigh the tremendous near-term costs.

One factor that comes into play, and that is hard to pin down, is the extent to which the current generation is sensitive to the needs of future generations as it makes its decisions. Clearly it has, to some extent, through regard for future family members, the desire to leave something for descendants, and generally a social conscience that leads people to care about the distant future. But are these motives strong enough to be sure that future generations are adequately represented today?

Given these uncertainties about discounting when looking at very long-run environmental impacts, we may want to fall back on additional criteria to help us in making current decisions. One of these might be the concept of *sustainability*, an idea that has become very popular in recent years. Sustainability connotes the idea that we should avoid courses of action that reduce the long-run productive capabilities of our natural and environmental resource base. In practice the concept is very difficult to pin down, and we will have much more to say about it in a later chapter on environment and economic development.

Distributional Issues

The relation of total benefits and total costs is a question of economic efficiency. Distribution is a matter of who gets the benefits and who pays the costs. In public sector programs, distributional matters must be considered along with efficiency issues, which implies that benefit–cost analyses must incorporate studies of how net benefits are distributed among different groups in society. In this section we introduce some of the main concepts of distribution analysis.

The distribution of benefits and costs is primarily a matter of equity, or fairness. There are two main types of equity: horizontal and vertical. Horizontal equity is a case of treating similarly situated people the same way. An environmental program that has the same impact on an urban dweller with $20,000 of income as on a rural dweller with the same income is horizontally equitable. Consider the following numbers; they refer to the annual values of a particular program accruing to three different individuals who, we assume, all have the same income. Abatement costs show the costs of the program to each individual; these may be higher prices on some products, more time spent on recycling

---

EXHIBIT 6-1

WHAT A DIFFERENCE A DISCOUNT MAKES

By Bruce Stokes

In 1808, when Thomas Jefferson planted the stately tulip poplars that grace the west front lawn at Monticello, he did so knowing full well that he would never benefit from their shade on a muggy Virginia summer afternoon. By the time the poplars' boughs spread their leafy canopy over Monticello's lawn, Jefferson would long be dead.

For his investment of time and money, the immediate return he received was nil. Yet, by all accounts, Jefferson never once considered not planting the poplars.

Jefferson's paradox—investments in the environment often cannot be justified on purely economic grounds—is at the heart of today's debate between environmentalists and economists over what to do about global warming.

In assessing the costs and benefits of building a factory, erecting a bridge or putting a scrubber on a smokestack, it is standard practice for economists to compare the benefits to be gained from the investment with the potential return that might be gener-

ated if the money were used in some other way. That estimated rate of return is called the discount rate. Corporations frequently use a 15 percent discount rate to weigh new investments. The World Bank uses double-digit rates, and the U.S. government often relies on rates of more than 10 percent.

The choice of a discount rate can make or break the case for investing in the environment. Suppose, for example, that scientists agree that a particular pollutant will cause $100 million in damage in the year 2092. Society has two economic choices: invest now in pollution abatement technology to avoid the damage, or channel the investment elsewhere on the assumption that a century from now, the economy will be richer as a result and thus will be better able to absorb the costs of any damage to the environment.

In weighing this decision, if policy makers assume that for every $1 they invest now, they can get $1.10 next year (applying, in essence, a 10 percent discount rate), it would

---

matters, higher taxes, or other factors. The reduced damages are measures of the value of the improvements in environmental quality accruing to each person.

	Person A	Person B	Person C
Reduced environmental damages ($/year)	60	80	120
Abatement costs ($/year)	40	60	80
Difference	20	20	40

Costs and reduced damages are different for individuals A and B, but the difference between them ($20/year) is the same; hence the difference as a proportion of their income is the same. With respect to these two people, therefore, the program is horizontally equitable. It is not, however, for individual C, because this person experiences a net difference of $40/year. Since Person C be fiscally irresponsible to spend more than $7,305 on pollution control now to avoid $100 million in cleanup costs 100 years from now. If the current pollution control costs are even a dollar higher, economists conclude that it would be better to invest the money in roads or education (which have a higher return) and compensate the victims of pollution down the road.

The assessment of the proposed pollution abatement action changes radically, however, if a 2 percent discount rate is used. At that assumed rate of return, nearly $14 million in expenditures for pollution control are economically justifiable today to avoid $100 million in costs a century from now.

"This illustrates," said William R. Cline, a senior fellow at the Institute for International Economics, "that those who prefer discount rates of 10 percent can, for all practical purposes, dismiss global warming 100 years from now, because however catastrophic it might be, it is worth only a few dollars today to try to avert it."

In his recent book, *Global Warming: The Economic Stakes* (Institute for International Economics, 1992), Cline suggests using a 2 percent discount rate—a figure based on the expected future growth in per capita income, plus an allowance for the cost of capital—to

justify an aggressive and expensive effort to slow global warming.

Nobel prize-winning economist James Tobin, a professor emeritus at Yale University, concurred with Cline's choice of a discount rate. "For long-run things, one should not use interest rates set in the market," Tobin said. The use of current interest rates to assess the economics of environmental projects only "reflects the impatience of those on the globe who would like their goodies now," he added.

Lawrence H. Summers, the chief economist at the World Bank, disagrees. He argued that the compelling needs of the poor and the uncertainty over future climate changes justify using the same discount rate for global warming projects as is applied to sanitation or education projects in the Third World.

"Do I sacrifice to help those in the future or help the one billion extremely poor people who share the planet Earth with me today?" Summers said. "I hold no greater grief for people who will die 100 years from now from global warming than for people who will die tomorrow from bad water."

is assumed to have the same income as the other two people, they are clearly better off as a result of this program; horizontal equity in this case has not been achieved.

Vertical equity refers to how a policy impinges on people who are in different circumstances, in particular on people who have different income levels. Consider the numbers in Table 6-3. These show the impacts, expressed in monetary values, of three different environmental quality programs on three people with, respectively, a low income, a medium income, and a high income. In parentheses next to each number is shown the percentage that number is of the person's income level. Note, for example, the "difference" row of Program 1; it shows the difference between how much the person benefits from the program (in terms of reduced environmental damages impinging on him) and how much it will cost him (in terms of the extent to which he will bear a part of the abatement costs of the program). Note that this net difference represents 1 percent of the income of each person. This is a *proportional impact*; i.e., it affects the people of each income level in the same proportion.

TABLE 6-3
VERTICAL EQUITY*

	Person A		Person B		Person C	
Income	5,000		20,000		50,000	
Program 1						
Reduced damages	150	(3.0)	300	(1.5)	600	(1.2)
Abatement costs	100	(2.0)	100	(0.5)	100	(0.2)
Difference	50	(1.0)	200	(1.0)	500	(1.0)
Program 2						
Reduced damages	150	(3.0)	1,400	(7.0)	5,500	(11.0)
Abatement costs	100	(2.0)	800	(4.0)	3,000	(6.0)
Difference	50	(1.0)	600	(3.0)	2,500	(5.0)
Program 3						
Reduced damages	700	(14.0)	2,200	(11.0)	3,000	(6.0)
Abatement costs	200	(4.0)	1,000	(5.0)	1,500	(3.0)
Difference	500	(10.0)	1,200	(6.0)	1,500	(3.0)

*Figures in the table show annual monetary values. Numbers in parentheses show the percentage of income these numbers represent.

Program 2, on the other hand, is *regressive*; it provides higher proportional net benefits to high-income people than to low-income people. Program 3 has a *progressive* impact because net benefits represent a higher proportion of the lower-income person's income than it does of the rich person's income. Thus an environmental program (or any program for that matter) is proportional, progressive, or regressive, according to whether the net effect of that policy has proportionally the same, greater, or less effect on low-income people as on high-income people.

We need to note also that although the net effects of a program may be distributed in one way, the individual components need not be distributed in the same way. For example, although the overall effects of Program 2 are regressive, the abatement costs of that program are in fact distributed progressively (i.e., the cost burden is proportionately greater for high-income people). In this case damage reduction is distributed so regressively that the overall program is regressive. So also in Program 3; although the overall program is progressive, abatement costs are distributed regressively.

These definitions of distributional impacts can be misleading. A program that is technically regressive could actually distribute the bulk of its net benefits to poor people. Suppose a policy raised the net income of one rich person by 10 percent, but raised each of the net incomes of 1,000 poor people by 5 percent. This policy is technically regressive although more than likely the majority of its aggregate net benefits go to poor people.

It is normally very difficult to estimate the distributional impacts of environmental programs, individually or in total. To do so requires very specific data showing impacts by income groups, race, or other factors. In general, environmental and health data have not been routinely collected by income and race. Thus, data on environmentally related diseases don't typically allow the comparison of differences across socioeconomic and racial groups. Nor is it easy to estimate how program costs are distributed among these groups, because these depend on complex factors related to tax collections, consumption patterns, the availability of alternatives, and so on. Despite the difficulties, however, benefit–cost analyses should try to look as closely as possible at the way in which the aggregates are distributed through the population. We will meet up with distributional issues throughout the later chapters of the book.

Uncertainty

In applications of benefit–cost analysis to natural and environmental resources we are projecting events well off into the future, and when we do this we run squarely into the fact that we have no way of knowing the future with certainty. Our uncertainty can arise from many sources. We may not be able to predict the preferences of future consumers, who may feel very differently than we do about matters of environmental quality. For studies of the long-run impacts of global warming, future population growth rates are important, and it is impossible to know these with certainty. Uncertainty may arise from technological change. Technical advancement in pollution-control equipment or in the chemistry of materials recycling could markedly shift future costs of achieving various levels of emission control. Nature itself is a source of uncertainty. Meteorological events can affect the outcomes of pollution-control programs; for example, in some cases we are still uncertain of the exact way human activities impact natural phenomena.

How should we address the fact that future benefits and costs are uncertain; that is, that future outcomes are "probabilistic"? If we know something about how these future probabilities manifest themselves, we may be able to estimate the "most likely" or "expected" levels of benefits and costs. Consider the problem of predicting the effect of certain policy changes on oil spills. In any given year we may have no tanker accidents, or one, or several; the exact number is uncertain. But we want a way to talk about the annual number of spills we could anticipate under different types of oil-spill control policies. One way of doing this is to estimate the *expected value* of oil spills we would anticipate in a year's time. Where would we get the information for this? If we have been collecting data over a long period of time, we might know something about actual long-run averages. If we don't have information like this, we might have to fall back on estimates provided by engineers, scientists, or people familiar with the problem. Assuming we can get information of this type, we could develop a *probability distribution* of the number of oil tanker accidents, as shown in Table 6-4. This shows the probabilities of having different numbers of tanker accidents in a year.[8] For example, the probability is .77 that we will have no tanker accidents,

---

[8] These are illustrative numbers only.

TABLE 6-4
CALCULATING THE EXPECTED NUMBER OF "LARGE" OIL SPILLS

Number of spills	Probability	Expected value of the number of oil spills
0	.77	$0 \times .77 = 0$
1	.12	$1 \times .12 = .12$
2	.07	$2 \times .07 = .14$
3	.03	$3 \times .03 = .09$
4	.01	$4 \times .01 = .04$
Over 4	—	—
		Expected value: .39

.12 that we will have one accident, .07 that we will have two accidents, and so on. Having obtained probabilities, we can then calculate the *expected value* of oil spills in a year's time. In effect this is the average number of oil spills we would experience each year over a period of time many years long. This is done by calculating a weighted average, as shown in Table 6-4. According to this calculation, the expected number of tanker accidents is .39 per year. We could then go on and estimate the expected quantity of oil that will be spilled and, perhaps, the expected value of damages. Thus, in this case of uncertainty, we are able to proceed by estimating expected values of probabilistic events, in particular the expected values of benefits and costs.

This approach is appropriate if we have reliable estimates of the probabilities of future events. But in many cases these may not be available, because we have not had enough experience with similar events to be able to know the future probabilities of different outcomes with any degree of confidence. One possibility here, made possible by the modern computer, is to carry out a *scenario analysis*. Suppose we are trying to predict the long-run costs of reducing CO_2 emissions as a step toward lessening the greenhouse effect. These costs depend critically on the future pace of technological developments affecting the energy efficiency of production. We have little experience with predicting technical change over long periods of time, so it is unrealistic to try to estimate the probabilities that technical change will occur at different rates. Instead, we run our analysis several times, each time making a different assumption about the rate at which technical change will occur. Thus, our results might consist of three scenarios, with different results based on whether future technical change is "slow," "moderate," or "fast."

There is another difficulty that you should be aware of in using expected values on which to base decisions. These are appropriate if we are analyzing a relatively large number of recurrent situations, where good results in some will outweigh bad results in others. In the oil-spill case, we expect the annual number of spills to approach its expected value. But for unique events that will occur only once, we may want to look beyond expected values decisions. Consider the following numbers:

Program A		Program B	
Net benefits	Probability	Net benefits	Probability
$500,000	.475	$500,000	.99
$300,000	.525	−$10,000,000	.01
Expected value:	$395,000	Expected value:	$395,000

These two programs have exactly the same expected value. But suppose we had only a one-time choice between the two; perhaps it relates to the choice of a nuclear versus a conventional power plant to generate electricity. With A the net benefits are uncertain, but the outcomes are not extremely different and the probabilities are similar—it's very nearly a 50–50 proposition. Program B, on the other hand, has a very different profile. The probability is very high that the net benefits will be $500,000, but there is a small probability of a disaster, where there would be large negative net benefits. If we were making decisions strictly on the basis of expected values, we would treat these projects as the same; we could flip a coin to decide which one to choose. If we did this, we would be displaying *risk*-neutral behavior—making decisions strictly on the basis of expected values. On the other hand, if this is a one-shot decision, we might decide that the low probability of a large loss in the case of project B represents a risk to which we do not wish to expose ourselves. In this case, we might be *risk averse*, preferring Project A over B.

There are many cases in environmental pollution control where risk aversion is undoubtedly the best policy. The rise of planetary-scale atmospheric change opens up the possibility of catastrophic human dislocations in the future. The potential scale of these impacts argues for a conservative, risk-averse approach to current decisions. Risk-averse decisions are also called for in the case of species extinction; a series of incremental and seemingly small decisions today may bring about a catastrophic decline in genetic resources in the future, with potentially drastic impacts on human welfare. Global issues are not the only ones where it may be prudent to avoid low risks of outcomes that would have large negative net benefits. The contamination of an important groundwater aquifer is a possibility faced by many local communities. And in any activity where risk to human life is involved, the average person is likely to be risk averse.

RISK ANALYSIS

The importance of risk in environmental management has led in recent years to modes of analyses specifically directed at this dimension of the problem. *Risk analysis* essentially covers two types of activities: *risk assessment* and *risk management*.

Consider the case of a hazardous waste dump into which a hazardous chemical has been dumped over the years. Suppose also that the people of a nearby community rely on a groundwater aquifer for their water supply. In a situation like this a risk assessment can be carried out to determine the size and significance of the risk the site poses to people in the community. One part of this is to determine the risks that the chemical might end up contaminating the aquifer. This requires engineers, hydrologists, etc., who can study the physical aspects of the landfill and surrounding area. A second element is to study the likely impacts on the health of community residents if the aquifer is contaminated. This involves taking the predicted chemical levels to which people in the community would be exposed if contamination occurred, and estimating the resulting health effects, such as, for example, the expected number of increased cases of cancer. This would call on *dose-response* relationships that scientists have developed in analyzing this particular substance. Often this type of information will come from laboratory studies with animals, the results of which are then extrapolated to human beings.

Economics comes into risk assessment in determining how much people value alternative situations involving differing risk levels. In our terminology, this is the estimation of peoples' willingness to pay for changes in levels of risk to which they are exposed. Experience has shown that the scientific results of relative risks stemming from different sources may not agree very well with how people actually feel about different types of risk. For example, people may be willing to pay substantial sums to have a chemical taken out of their water supply even though the health risk is relatively low; whereas they may not be willing to pay much for improved seat belts, which would reduce their overall risk by a great deal.

Risk management refers to public policies that have as their objective the reduction of risks to which humans are exposed. In the landfill example, after the levels and significance of the risk have been established, the problem becomes one of considering different policy options for managing the landfill and the water supply system. This could call upon *comparative risk analysis*, the investigation of different policy options and the levels of risk each would produce.

Risk management also calls on *risk–benefit analysis*. Suppose an administrative agency, such as the EPA, is considering whether a particular pesticide should be allowed on the market. It might do a study comparing the benefits farmers and consumers would gain, in the form of production cost savings, when the pesticide is used, to the increased health risks to farm workers, who must handle it, and possibly to consumers if there are pesticide residues on the marketed crop. In essence this is a benefit–cost analysis in which the cost side is treated more explicitly in terms of risk.

SUMMARY

In previous chapters we put the issue of environmental improvement in a trade-off type of format, where we have willingness to pay (benefits) on one side and abatement costs on the other. In this chapter we started to focus on the problem of measuring these benefits and costs. To do this researchers have to use some underlying analytical framework to account for these benefits and costs. We considered several types of frameworks (impact analysis and cost-effectiveness analysis), then settled on the primary approach used in resource and environmental economics: benefit–cost analysis. The rest of the chapter was devoted to a discussion of the main conceptual issues involved in benefit–cost analysis. These are:

- The basic analytical steps involved,
- Determining the appropriate size of a project or program,
- The difference between net benefits and the benefit–cost ratio as a decision criterion,
- Discounting,
- Distributional issues, and
- Uncertainty.

Having discussed the basic structure of benefit–cost analysis, we will turn now to problems of actually measuring the benefits and costs of specific environmental programs.

QUESTIONS FOR FURTHER DISCUSSION

1 In the section on choosing the current size of a project or program we mentioned the problem of a regional planning agency allocating its budget among several programs in different cities. What is the relevance here of the equimarginal principle?
2 When setting public policy on environmental risks, should we base it on the levels of risk to which people think they are exposed or on the risk levels scientists have determined them to be in fact?
3 Suppose we are comparing two ways of protecting ourselves against mobile-source air pollution: putting additional controls on the internal combustion engine or developing an entirely different type of engine that is cleaner. How would changes in the discount rate be likely to affect the comparison between these two options?

SELECTED READINGS

Abelson, Peter: *Cost-Benefit Analysis and Environmental Problems*, Saxon House, Farnborough, England, 1979.

Coker, Annabel, and Cathy Richards: *Valuing the Environment, Economic Approaches to Environmental Evaluation*, Belhaven Press, London and Boca Raton, Fl., 1992.

Dasgupta, Ajit K., and D. W. Pearce: *Cost-Benefit Analysis: Theory and Practice*, Barnes and Noble, New York, 1972.

Freeman, A. Myrick, III: *Air and Water Pollution Control: A Benefit–Cost Assessment*, John Wiley, New York, 1982.

Kneese, Allen, and Blair Bower: *Environmental Quality Analysis*, Johns Hopkins Press, Baltimore, Md., 1972.

Lave, Lester B.: *The Strategy of Social Regulation: Decision Frameworks for Policy*, The Brookings Institution, Washington, D.C., 1981.

Lind, Robert C.: "Reassessing the Government's Discount Policy in Light of New Theory and Data in a World Economy with a High Degree of Capital Mobility," *Journal of Environmental Economics and Management*, 18(2), March 1990, pp. S-29 to S-50.

Russell, Clifford S., and V. Kerry Smith: "Demands for Data and Analysis Induced by Environmental Policy," in Ernst R. Berndt and Jack E. Triplett (eds.), *Fifty Years of Economic Measurement*, National Bureau of Economic Research, Studies in Income and Wealth, University of Chicago Press, Chicago, 1990, pp. 299–340.

Sugden, Robert, and Alan Williams: *The Principles of Practical Benefit–Cost Analysis*, Oxford University Press, Oxford, England, 1978.

Tolley, George S., Philip F. Graves, and Glenn C. Blomquist: *Environmental Policy, Elements of Environmental Analysis*, Vol. I, Ballinger Publishing Company, Cambridge, Mass., 1981.

U.S. Environmental Protection Agency: *Costs and Benefits of Reducing Lead in Gasoline*, EPA-230-03-84-005, Washington, D.C., 1984.

BENEFIT–COST ANALYSIS: BENEFITS

We have already made the connection between benefits and willingness to pay. The benefits of something are equal to what people are willing to pay for it, remembering the provisos about the distribution of income and the availability of information. If we want to estimate peoples' willingness to pay for potatoes, we can go and observe them buying potatoes—so many potatoes at such-and-such prices—and develop a good idea of the value people place on this item. But we can't do this when valuing changes in environmental quality. There are no markets where people buy and sell units of environmental quality, so we can't measure consumer benefits directly the way we can with potatoes. Instead, we have to fall back on indirect means. As one environmental economist has put it: ". . . benefit estimation often involves a kind of detective work for piecing together the clues about the values individuals place on [environmental services] as they respond to other economic signals."[1]

The measurement of benefits is an activity pursued on many levels. For an analyst working in an environmental agency, it can turn into a plug-in-the-numbers exercise. So many acres of clambed destroyed (information provided by a marine biologist) times the going price of clams (provided by a quick trip to the local fish market) equals damages of water pollution in the "X" estuary. At the other extreme, for an environmental economist whose interest is in extending the technique, it can be an excursion into sophisticated means of squeezing subtle information from new sets of data. Our path in this chapter will lie between these extremes. We will review the main techniques environmental economists have developed to measure the benefits of improvements in environmental quality. We will try to understand the economic logic lying behind these techniques, without getting bogged down in all the theoretical niceties and statistical details.[2]

[1] A. Myrick Freeman III, "Benefits of Pollution Control," in U.S. Environmental Protection Agency, *Critical Review of Estimating Benefits of Air and Water Pollution Control*, Washington, D.C., EPA 600/5-78-014, 1978, p. II-16.

[2] There are a number of recent books reviewing the current state of environmental benefits measurement. These are listed in the bibliography at the end of the chapter.

MEASURING DAMAGES DIRECTLY

When environmental degradation occurs, it produces damages; our emissions control model of Chapter 5 is based in part on the relationship between emissions and marginal damages. So in a very direct sense the benefits of improved environmental quality come about because of reduced damages. To measure a complete emissions damage function, it is necessary to go through the following steps:

1 Measure emissions,
2 Determine the resulting ambient quality,
3 Estimate human exposure,
4 Measure impacts (health, aesthetic, recreation, etc.),
5 Estimate the values of these impacts.

The first three of the steps are largely the work of physical scientists. Models that show the relation between emissions and ambient levels are often called *diffusion models*. Step 4 involves economists to some extent, but also biological scientists and epidemiologists. The linkage of Steps 3 and 4 is often called a *dose-response* function. This means estimating the response in terms, for example, of human mortality and morbidity to varying exposure levels to environmental pollutants. Step 5 is where economics comes strongly into play, in estimating the values associated with different impacts as identified in the previous step. It might appear easy to measure benefits by measuring damages directly, but this will turn out not to be the case. To understand this let us look at several approaches that have been made in the past to measuring damages directly.

Health Damages

Some of the most important damages caused by environmental pollution are those related to human health. Air pollution, especially, has long been thought to increase mortality and morbidity among people exposed to it, certainly in the episodic releases of toxic pollutants, but also from long-run exposure to such pollutants as SO_2 and particulate matter. Diseases such as bronchitis, emphysema, and lung cancer are thought to be traceable in part to polluted air. Estimates of the health costs of air pollution suggest that many billions of dollars are lost each year. Water pollution also produces health damages, primarily through contaminated drinking water supplies. So the measurement of the human health damages of environmental pollution is a critical task for environmental economists.

Fundamental to this work is the underlying dose-response relationship showing the relationship between human health and exposure to environmental pollution of various types. Many factors affect human health—life styles, diet, genetic factors, age, etc.—besides ambient pollution levels. To separate out the effects of pollution, one has to account for all the other factors or else run the risk of attributing to pollution effects that are actually caused by something else. This calls for large amounts of accurate data on health factors as well as the numerous suspected causal factors. Some of this—air or water quality, mortality statistics, etc.—may be available from published sources, but these may be too highly aggregated to give accurate results. Similarly, although published data may give us information on, e.g., average air pollution levels in certain areas of a city, it doesn't give completely accurate exposure data because that depends on how long individuals have lived in that environment. In a mobile society it's hard to develop accurate exposure data for people, since they may have lived in a variety of places throughout their lives. Epidemiologists have developed extensive experience with panel data, information developed through in-depth interviews with people about their life styles, consumption habits, locational history, etc.

The first major study of air pollution and human health in the U.S. was done by Lave and Seskin in the 1970s.[3] The data were for 1969 and refer to published information on standard metropolitan statistical areas (SMSAs). They concluded that, in general, a 1 percent reduction in air pollution produces a .12 percent reduction in death rates. Since that study, researchers have examined these and other data on health and pollution to improve the statistical procedures and add new explanatory variables. One conclusion is that the results one gets are very sensitive to the data used and the way they are handled, which means we are still very uncertain about the exact links between air pollution and human mortality rates.

The same conclusion holds for the dose-response function with respect to human morbidity. Morbidity refers to the incidence of disease, so it can be expressed in different ways. One study looks at the relationship between air pollutants and morbidity expressed in two ways: (1) days absent from work and (2) days affected by ill health.[4] The author found no connection between these variables and sulfur pollution but did find an effect for total suspended particulates. Other morbidity studies have been carried out on air pollution and water pollution, but there is certainly no consensus yet on the underlying relationships. Much more work remains to be done.

The main work of economists comes after the dose-response research, in putting values on the various health impacts. How should we approach placing a value on a life prematurely shortened or on a debilitating illness suffered as a result of exposure to environmental pollutants? Your first reaction may be that it's a dubious moral exercise to try and attach a monetary value to a human life. Isn't life "priceless"? In a sense it is. If you stop a person in the street and ask her how much her life is worth, you may not get an answer because the question seems to violate a common moral standard. Nevertheless, society as a whole— that is, all of us acting collectively—doesn't behave that way. In fact, through our collective decisions and behavior, we implicitly assign values to human lives. The clearest place to see this is in traffic control. Each year approximately 40,000

[3] Lester B. Lave and Eugene P. Seskin, *Air Pollution and Human Health*, Johns Hopkins Press, Baltimore, Md., 1977.

[4] Bart D. Ostro, "Air Pollution and Morbidity Revisited: A Specification Test," *Journal of Environmental Economics and Management*, 14(1), March 1987, pp. 87–98.

people are killed on the nation's highways. Yet we do not see a massive outpouring of funds to redesign highways, slow traffic, make substantially safer cars, etc. This is because we are making an implicit trade-off between traffic deaths and other travel-related impacts, especially the benefits of reasonably fast and convenient travel. The same may be said of other risky technologies and practices of which modern life is replete. Thus, despite the moral prescriptions about the ultimate values of human life, it makes sense to examine the values that society actually places on lives and human health in the everyday course of its operation.

For some years it was standard procedure to estimate health damages by looking at such things as increased monetary expenditures on health care and reductions in worker productivity accompanying deteriorated health and shortened lives. For example, we might try to measure the value of a human life by looking at the economic contribution that society forgoes when that life is stopped. Over their working lives people contribute to the production of useful goods and services enjoyed by others in society. When they die, this productivity ceases; thus, we might estimate the cumulative value of production that they would have produced had they lived. Lost productivity would vary among individuals, as a function of their age, skills, employment history, etc., so we might take averages for people in different categories. Using the same logic, we might estimate the value of reduced morbidity by measuring the value of increased production this would make possible.

Another direct approach at measuring health damages is to look at medical expenditures. As health is affected by increasing pollution we would expect increased medical expenditures, on hospitals, doctors, rehabilitation, etc. Reducing pollution would, therefore, lead to a reduction in medical expenditures, which can be counted as a benefit of the environmental change.

Other Types of Damages

Some types of air pollution have been implicated in damages of agricultural crops. One way of measuring these might be to take the dose-response information developed by physical and natural sciences and use it to predict the increased yields resulting from the amelioration of a particular case of air pollution. These increased yields would then be multiplied by the market price of the item to get a measure of the benefits of the improved air quality.

Another type of direct damage estimation might be applied to materials damage. Air pollution in urban areas has been shown to lead to deterioration in exposed materials, from buildings to outdoor sculpture. These damages might be measured by looking at the increased maintenance costs required to keep these materials from deteriorating.

Problems with Direct Damage Approaches

The basic problem with direct damage estimates like this is that they are almost always seriously incomplete. Consider the case of measuring health damages by lost productivity and medical expenditures. We note, first, that these are market measures. They measure the value of marketed goods and services a person might, on average, produce. So the many nonmarket contributions people make, both inside and outside the home, don't get counted. This method would also assign a zero value to a handicapped person unable to work, or a retiree. There is also the question of whether a person's consumption should be subtracted from his production to measure his actual net contribution. This might seem reasonable but, if we do this, we would be forced into awkward conclusions, such as that the premature death of a welfare recipient would be a benefit to society. There are numerous monetary, as well as psychic, benefits received by others—friends and relatives, for example—that the productivity measure does not account for. Nor does it account for the pain and suffering of illness. Thus, although the productivity approach may be useful in some circumstances, it can give misleading results in others. The same may be said of using medical expenditures to estimate damages from reduced environmental quality. Suppose we estimate the damages to me of getting a head cold. We come up with an estimate of $1.27, the cost of the aspirin I will consume to reduce the discomfort. This probably would be a serious understatement of the true damages of the cold. If I were asked how much I would be willing to pay to avoid the cold, the answer is likely to be substantially more than the cost of the aspirin. This is perhaps an unfair example because major medical expenditures for a person suffering from air pollution–induced lung cancer are much more significant than a bottle of aspirin. Nevertheless, because of problems like these we must turn back to our fundamental concept for determining value: willingness to pay.

WILLINGNESS TO PAY

The problem with the direct approach to damage estimation discussed above is that it is usually incomplete. This is a difficulty with measurement, not with the concept. A marginal damage function shows the changes in damages suffered by people or other elements of the ecosystem when exposed to pollution or environmental alteration. We must think of "damages" in the broad sense; it includes what we would think of as direct physical damage, such as health impacts, but also such impacts as degradation of the aesthetic quality of the environment (e.g., lowered visibility or psychic damage). In other words, "damages" include all the negative effects of the airborne emissions. Looked at from a different perspective, the marginal damage function for increases in emissions is the same as the demand/willingness-to-pay function for decreases in emissions. If a small increase in emissions causes me $10 in increased damages, the maximum I would be willing to pay to decrease emissions by that small amount would presumably be $10. We want to focus, therefore, on willingness to pay for environmental improvements.

There are essentially three ways of trying to find out how much people are willing to pay for improvements in environmental quality. We can illustrate them by considering a case of noise pollution. One feature of the modern world is high-speed roadways (expressways, freeways, and turnpikes), and a major characteristic of these roads is that the traffic on them creates noise. Thus, the people who live nearby suffer damages from this traffic noise. Suppose we would like to estimate the willingness to pay of people living near expressways to reduce traffic noise. How might we do this?

1 The homeowners themselves may have made expenditures to reduce the noise levels inside their homes. For example, they may have installed additional insulation in the walls of their homes or put double-thick glass in the windows. When people make expenditures like this, they reveal something about their willingness to pay for a quieter environment. In general, then, if we can find cases where market goods are purchased in order to affect a consumer's exposure to the ambient environment, we may be able to analyze these purchases for what they say about the value people place on changes in that ambient environment.

2 The noise in the vicinity of the road may have affected the prices that people have paid for the houses there. If two houses have exactly the same characteristics in all respects but the level of exterior noise, we would expect the one in the noisier environment to be less valuable to prospective buyers than the one in the quieter environment. If the housing market is competitive, the price of the noisier house would be lower than the other one. Thus, by looking at the difference in house prices we can estimate the value people place on reduced noise pollution. In general, therefore, any time the price of some good or service varies in accordance with its environmental characteristics, we may be able to analyze these price variations to determine people's willingness to pay for these characteristics.

3 Both of the foregoing techniques are indirect, in the sense that they look for ways of analyzing market data to find out what they imply about the willingness to pay of people for closely associated environmental characteristics. The third way is deceptively direct. We could conduct a survey among homeowners and ask them how much they would be willing to pay for reductions in noise levels around and inside their homes. This direct survey approach has received a lot of attention from environmental economists in recent years, primarily because of its flexibility. Virtually any feature of the natural environment that can be described accurately to people can be studied by this method.

In the remainder of the chapter we will examine some of the ways these approaches have been applied to estimate the benefits of improvements in environmental quality.

WILLINGNESS TO PAY: INDIRECT METHODS

The thought behind these indirect approaches is that when people make market choices among certain items that have different characteristics related to the environment, they will reveal the value they place on these environmental factors. Perhaps the most important is what they reveal about the values of health and human life.

The Value of Human Health as Expressed in "Averting" Costs

Air and water pollution can produce a variety of adverse health conditions, ranging from slight chest discomfort or headaches all the way to acute episodes requiring hospital care. People often make expenditures to try to avoid, or avert, these conditions, and these averting costs are an expression of their willingness to pay to avoid them. A number of studies have been done in which these averting expenditures have been analyzed for what they tell about willingness to pay.[5] One study was done of a sample of people in the Los Angeles area in 1986 looking at expenditures they made to avoid a variety of respiratory symptoms. Expenditures included such things as cooking with electricity rather than gas, operating a home air conditioner, and driving an air-conditioned car. Their estimates of the willingness to pay to avoid various respiratory symptoms ranged from $0.97 for shortness of breath to $23.87 for chest tightness.

The Value of Human Life as Expressed in Wage Rates

Diminished air quality and contaminated water can lead to deteriorated health and death. How are these impacts to be valued? It is tempting to say "human life is beyond measure," but that is not the way people behave in the real world. We can see by casual observation that individuals do not, in fact, behave as if prolonged life, or the warding off of disease, is in some sense an ultimate end to which all their resources must be devoted. We see people engaging in risky activity; in some sense trading off risk for the benefits received. Almost everybody drives a car, some people smoke, some rock climb, many strive to get tans, and so on. We also see people allocating portions of their income to reducing risk; buying locks, installing smoke alarms, staying away from dark places at night. And we observe people making differential judgments of their own worth; parents with children buying more life insurance than single people, and so on. All of which suggests that people treat the risk of death in a reasonably rational manner, and that we could use willingness to pay as a way of evaluating the benefits of reducing the risk of death or illness.

But we must be clear on exactly what is involved. There is a joke about the stingy millionaire, walking down a street, who gets held up. The robber points a gun at her and says, "Your money or your life," and the victim replies: "Ah, let me think about that." Estimating the willingness-to-pay value of a human life does not involve this kind of situation. We do not ask people to express their

---

[5] These are reviewed in Maureen L. Cropper and A. Myrick Freeman III, "Environmental Health Effects," in John B. Braden and Charles D. Kolstad (eds.), *Measuring the Demand for Environmental Quality*, North-Holland, Amsterdam, 1991, pp. 200–202.

willingness to pay to save their own lives. Under some circumstances a person presumably will be willing to give everything he owns. But these are not the kinds of situations people normally face. When I express a willingness to pay for reducing air pollution, the relevant concept is the value of the *statistical life*, not the life of some particular individual. This does not imply that people are assumed to care only about the average, or random, person, and not certain specific people. People obviously feel closer to their relatives, friends, and neighbors than to strangers. What is involved is the value of rearranging the living conditions of a large group of people by, e.g., reducing their exposure to environmental pollutants, in order to lower the probability that some randomly determined individual from the group will suffer illness or premature death. Suppose, for example, that the average person in a group of 100,000 people would be willing to pay $5 to lower the probability of a random death among members of that group from 7 in 100,000 to 6 in 100,000. Then the total willingness to pay is $5(100,000) = $500,000, which is the value of a statistical life based on willingness to pay.[6]

Using willingness to pay to measure health benefits has the virtue of being consistent with other types of economic demand studies, and it recognizes that even with something as important as health care, it is peoples' evaluations of its worth that should count. But we need to use the concept with care. In any real-world situation, willingness to pay implies ability to pay; one cannot express a willingness to pay for something if one lacks the necessary income or wealth. So we must be sensitive to the income levels of people whose demand we are trying to measure. If, in our analysis, we have included a substantial number of people with low incomes, the measured willingness to pay we obtain may be lower than justified. We may not want to lower the estimated health benefits of an environmental program simply because the target population has lower than average incomes.

Another feature about health care as a normal economic good is that people may be willing to pay for the health of others. I do not care if my daughter eats meat; her own willingness to pay is a good expression of her demand for meat. But I do care about her health and, to her own willingness to pay for good health, I would be willing to add a substantial sum of my own. Thus, strictly individualistic measures of willingness to pay for health improvements may underestimate the true benefits of programs that increase health.

The most fully developed approach to measuring the willingness to pay for reducing risk to life is through *industrial wage rate studies*. In work situations, whether industrial, agricultural, mining, or marine, pollutants are often present in concentrated form because of seriously diminished ambient conditions in the vicinity of the production process, because production requires workers to handle relatively large amounts of potentially harmful substances, or because accidents can lead to high-level exposure of workers to pollutants of various types. Many pollutants that pose few threats when dispersed throughout the

---

[6] This example comes from Freeman, *The Benefits of Environmental Improvement*, p. 168.

general population may have substantial impacts in the concentrated amounts in which they occur in the workplace. Many cases of workplace exposure and damage have come to light in recent decades. "Black lung" from working in mines, "brown lung" from working in cotton mills, and severe lung damage from working with asbestos are examples. Agricultural workers handling pesticides are at risk from exposure to these toxic chemicals.

If we study wage rates among different jobs that expose workers to different pollution-exposure risk, we may be able to measure the value people put on these reduced health risks. It's hard to get good data on workplace exposure to various pollutants. Where wage rate studies have been used more effectively is in measuring the value of reducing the risk of premature death. They have been used, in other words, to get at the problem of the value of a statistical life. Suppose there are two jobs similar in all respects except that in one, because of the type of machinery used, the risk of death is somewhat higher than in the other. Suppose that initially the wage rates in the two industries were the same. In this case it would obviously be preferable to work in the safer industry—same wage, lower risk. Workers would then seek to move from the dangerous to the safer industry. This would tend to drive down the wage in the safer industry and increase the wage in the other, as firms sought to keep workers from leaving that industry. Thus, a wage differential would evolve between the two industries; the amount of that differential would show how workers valued the differences between them in terms of risk of death. By analyzing wage differences like this, we can get a measure of the benefits people would get from reducing pollution-related premature deaths.

Table 7-1 summarizes some of the recent results of wage-rate studies aimed at estimating the value of a statistical life. Note that the estimates for the U.S. vary widely, from a low of $400,000 to a high of $11,000,000. What accounts for these differences? Different data and statistical techniques probably account for most of them. These studies are difficult because there are many other factors that have to be taken into account and because it is hard to get exactly the right data. For example, most worker accident and wage data apply to industry groupings, and within these groups there may be substantial variation among individual firms, not only because of technological differences among them but also because some firms may have done a lot more than others to make the workplace safer. It's also the case that wage-rate studies like this are predicated on the reasonably efficient working of the labor market, and this may not be the case in some industries. Union agreements, collusion among firm managers, and lack of information can upset the competitive wage-making process in some industries. These problems do not mean that these studies are not useful, only that we have not yet reached a point where they are giving us a consistent story.

The Value of Environmental Quality as Expressed in House Prices

The wage-rate studies we just looked at estimate the willingness to pay to be exposed to lower risk of death; i.e.; the willingness to pay for a specific conse-

TABLE 7-1
VALUE OF LIFE IN OCCUPATIONAL RISK STUDIES: THE UNITED STATES AND THE
UNITED KINGDOM

Study	Best estimate of value of a statistical life (U.S. = $ mil; UK = £ mil; 1982 prices)
United States	
Arnould/Nichols (1983)	0.64
Dillingham (1979)	0.40
Olson (1981)	7.10
Smith, R. (1976)	3.30
Thaler/Rosen (1975)	0.57
Viscusi (1978)	2.90–3.90
United Kingdom	
Marin/Psacharopoulos (1982)	1.64
Veljanovski (1981)	3.39–4.59
Needleman (1979)	0.13–0.72

Sources: Richard Arnould and Len Nichols, "Wage Risk Premiums and Workers' Compensation: A Refinement of Estimates of Compensating Wage Differential," *Journal of Political Economy*, 91(2), April 1983, pp. 332–340; A. Dillingham, "The Injury Risk Structure of Occupations and Wages," Ph.D. dissertation, Cornell University, 1979; Alan Marin and George Psacharopoulos, "The Reward for Risk in the Labor Market: Evidence from the United Kingdom and a Reconciliation with Other Studies," *Journal of Political Ecomony*, 90(4), August 1982, pp. 827–853; L. Needleman, "The Valuation of Changes in the Risk of Death by Those at Risk," Working Paper 103, University of Waterloo, 1979; Craig Olson, "An Analysis of Wage Differentials Received by Workers on Dangerous Jobs," *Journal of Human Resources*, 16(2), Spring 1981, pp. 167–185; Robert Smith, "The Feasibility of an Injury Tax Approach to Occupational Safety," *Law and Contemporary Problems*, 38(4), 1974, pp. 730–744; Richard Thaler and Sherwin Rosen, "The Value of Saving a Life: Evidence from the Labor Market," in Nester Terleckyj (ed.), *Household Production and Consumption*, Columbia University Press, New York, 1976, pp. 265–297; C. Veljanovski, "Regulating Industrial Accidents: An Economic Analysis of Market and Legal Responses," Ph.D. thesis, University of York, 1981; W. Kip Viscusi, "Health Effects and Earnings Premiums for Job Hazards," *Review of Economics and Statistics*, 60(3), August 1978, pp. 408–416.

quence of being exposed to higher levels of environmental pollution. But there are wider benefits to a cleaner environment than simply health benefits. A more inclusive approach to take is to examine peoples' willingness to pay to live in a less polluted environment. This would include the health effects but also other dimensions such as aesthetic impacts.

Suppose you had two houses that were exactly the same in terms of all their physical characteristics—number of rooms, floor area, age, etc.—as well as in locational factors—distance to neighbors, distance to shopping facilities, etc. But assume one house is located in an area of substantial air pollution, while the other is located in an area with relatively clean air. We would expect the market prices of these two houses to differ because of the air quality difference. This conclusion generalizes to a large housing market involving many properties. The surrounding air quality is essentially a feature of the location of a house so, as houses are bought and sold in the house market, air quality differences would tend to get "capitalized" into the market prices of the houses.[7] Of course, homes differ in

---

[7] By "capitalized" we mean that house prices adjust to reflect the present value of the stream of future damages to which homeowners would be exposed if they lived in the various houses.

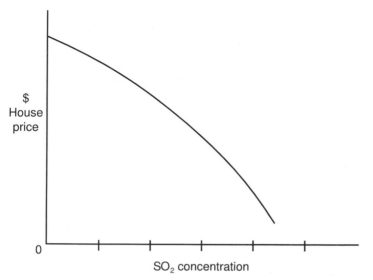

FIGURE 7-1
Relationship of Ambient SO₂ Concentration and House Prices.

many respects, not just in terms of air quality. So we must collect large amounts of data on many properties, then use statistical techniques to identify the role played by air pollution, as well as of other factors.[8]

Assuming we had collected enough data and conducted the appropriate statistical analyses, we might end up with a relationship like that shown in Figure 7-1. This shows that as the ambient SO₂ concentration increases house prices decrease, *everything else being equal*. This is not a demand function, though it may look like one. It shows total house prices as they are affected by SO₂ and a demand curve would show the impacts of SO₂ on the marginal value of houses. Further statistical manipulation of the data shown in Figure 7-1 may be able to give us a bona fide demand curve for reductions in ambient SO₂ concentrations.

Table 7-2 shows results from a number of studies in which economists have looked for impacts of air pollution on property values. The results are given in terms of elasticities, i.e., percentage change in house prices for a 1 percent change in air pollution. Note that there have been numerous types of air pollutants studied, with similar results for different ones. They show that for sulfur pollution a 1 percent increase in ambient concentration is associated with a change in house prices of between .06 and .12 percent. For particulates the sizes of the elasticities are quite similar.

The same kind of approach might be used with some cases of water pollution. In Chapter 4 we used lake pollution to introduce the concept of a public good.

---

[8] The technical name for this type of approach is "hedonic" analysis. When the price of something is related to the many characteristics it possesses, we can study patterns of price differences to deduce the value people place on one of those characteristics.

TABLE 7-2
HOME PRICES AND AIR POLLUTION

City	Year	Pollutant	Results[*]
St. Louis	1960	Sulfation[†]	.06–.10
	1963	Particulates	.12–.14
Chicago	1964–1967	Particulates and sulfation	.20–.50
Washington	1970	Particulates	.05–.12
	1967–1968	Oxidants	.01–.02
Toronto	1961	Sulfation	.06–.12
Philadelphia	1960	Sulfation	.10
	1969	Particulates	.12
Pittsburgh	1970	Dustfall and sulfation	.09–.15
Los Angeles	1977–1978	Particulates and oxidants	.22

[*]Percentage reduction in value of house per 1 percent increase in ambient concentration of pollutant.
[†]A measure of SO_2 using the lead peroxide candle method.

Sources: A. Myrick Freeman III, The Benefits of Environmental Improvement: Theory and Practice, Johns Hopkins Press for Resources for the Future, 1979, pp. 156–160; David S. Brookshire, Mark A. Thayer, William D. Schulze, and Ralph C. D'Arge, "Valuing Public Goods: A Comparison of Survey and Hedonic Approaches," American Economic Review, 72(1), March 1982, pp. 165–171; David W. Pearce and Anil Markandya, Environmental Policy Benefits: Monetary Valuation, Organization for Economic Cooperation and Development, 1989, p. 31.

Suppose a lake is surrounded by a number of residences. The market price of these homes will be affected by many things—their age, size, condition, etc. They will also be affected by the water quality of the lake. If this water quality degrades over time, we would expect the market values of the surrounding properties to go down. The deteriorating water quality means that homeowners will obtain less utility from living in that vicinity, other things remaining equal, and this will get capitalized into the values of the houses. One way we might approach measuring the benefits of cleaning up the lake is to estimate the overall increase in property values among the homes in the vicinity of the lake. We have to remember, however, that this is likely to be only a partial estimate of total benefits. If nonresidents have access to the lake or park, they would also be gaining benefits, but these would not show up in property value changes. Property value changes to measure benefits from pollution reduction can also be used in other situations; for example, in valuing the damage from noise around airports and major highways and in measuring the benefits flowing from urban parks.

The Value of Environmental Quality and Intercity Wage Differentials

We talked about using wage rate differences among jobs to measure the value of reducing health risks from pollution. Wage rate studies have also been used to estimate the value of living in a cleaner environment. Suppose there were two cities, alike in every respect, but one has higher air pollution than the other. Suppose that initially wage rates in the two cities were equal. Since everything else is exactly the same, it would be more desirable to work in the less polluted city—same wage but less air pollution. Workers would, therefore, migrate to the cleaner city. In order to keep a labor force in the dirty city, one of two things must happen: The air must be cleaned up or a higher wage must be offered to offset the damages of living in more polluted air. So we could study wage rate differentials among cities with different degrees of, say, air pollution to measure the value that people place on cleaner air. And this would give us a way of estimating the benefits of cleaning up the air in the more polluted cities.

The Effects of Pollution on Production Costs

Air pollution can reduce crop yields on exposed farms; it can also reduce the growth rates of commercially valuable timber. Water pollution can adversely affect firms and municipalities that use the water for production purposes or for domestic use. Diminished water quality can also have a negative impact on commercial fishing industries. Soil contamination can have serious impacts on agricultural production. Pollution in the workplace can reduce the effectiveness of workers and can often increase the rate at which machinery and buildings deteriorate. In these cases the effects of pollution are felt on the production of goods and services. The damage caused by the pollution comes about because it interferes in some way with these production processes, in effect making it more costly to produce these outputs than it would be in a less polluted world.

How we actually measure production-related benefits of reducing pollution depends on circumstances. Suppose we are looking at a small group of agricultural producers living in a certain region who will be affected by reduced airborne emissions coming from an upwind factory. Pollutants from the factory have depressed yields, so reducing emissions will cause yields to increase. The crop being produced is sold in a national market, and its price will be unaffected by the output changes in this one region. This situation is depicted in Figure 7-2. In this diagram, S_1 is the supply curve for this group of farms before the improved air quality; S_2 is the supply curve after the improvement.[9] Price of the output is p_1. Before the change, these farmers produce at an output level of q_1, while after the improvement their output increases to q_2.

One way of approximating the benefits of this environmental improvement is to measure the value of increased output produced by this group of farms. The increased output is simply multiplied by the price of the crop. This gives an estimate corresponding to the area $(d + e)$ in Figure 7-2.

A number of studies have been done along these lines.[10] Moskowitz et al.[11]

---

[9] See Chapters 3 and 4 for a discussion of supply curves.

[10] These are reviewed in Gardner M. Brown, Jr., and Mark L. Plummer, "Market Measures of User Benefits," in *Acid Deposition: State of Science and Technology*, Report 27, Methods for Valuing Acidic Deposition and Air Pollution Effects, National Acid Precipitation Assessment Program, Washington, D.C., U.S. Superintendent of Documents, 1990, pp. 27-35 to 27-73.

[11] Paul D. Moskowitz et al., "Oxidant Air Pollution: A Model for Estimating Effects on U.S. Vegetation," *Journal of Air Pollution Control Association*, 32(2), February 1982, pp. 155–160.

FIGURE 7-2
Benefits from Reduced Production Costs.

studied the effects of air pollution on alfalfa in the U.S. They measured the quantity of production lost because of air pollution and valued this loss at the going price of alfalfa. They found that air pollution was responsible for a loss in 1974 of between $24 million and $210 million. The difference between these figures comes about because of uncertainties over the actual pollution dose the alfalfa received in that year. Another study was done by Page et al.[12] to measure crop-related air pollution losses in a six-state area. They estimated annual losses in the production of soybeans, wheat, and corn and then aggregated these to see what the present value of total losses would be over the period 1976–2000. They came up with an estimate of about $7 billion.

A more refined approach to this problem is possible. The problem with taking just the value of the increased output is that production costs may also have changed. When air pollution diminishes, farmers may actually increase their use of certain inputs and farm this land more intensively. How do we account for this possibility? Note that we can analyze the full change in the following way, using net incomes of the farmers (total value of output minus total production costs).

¹² Walter P. Page et al., "Estimation of Economic Losses to the Agricultural Sector from Airborne Residuals in the Ohio River Basin," *Journal of Air Pollution Control Association*, 32(2), February 1982, pp. 151–154.

Situation before the change:

Total value of output: $a + b + c$
Total costs: $b + c$
Net income: a

Situation after the change:

Total value of output: $a + b + c + d + e$
Total costs: $c + e$
Net income: $a + b + d$

Thus, the improvement in net incomes is $(a + b + d) - a$, or an amount equal to area $b + d$ in the diagram.

How we measure this amount depends on how much information we are able to get. If we have studied these farms and know their supply curves before and after the change, we can measure the increased net income directly. If we don't know the supply curves, another possibility might be to look at the increased values of agricultural land in the area. In many cases, added net incomes of this type will get capitalized into land values, and we can use the increased land values to estimate the benefits of the environmental improvements.

Materials Damage

Air pollutants cause damage to exposed surfaces, metal surfaces of machinery, stone surfaces of buildings and statuary, and painted surfaces of all types of items. The most heavily implicated pollutants are the sulfur compounds, particulate matter, oxidants, and nitrogen oxides. For the most part, the damage is from increased deterioration that must be offset by increased maintenance and earlier replacement. In the case of outdoor sculpture, the damage is to the aesthetic qualities of the objects.

In this case the dose-response relationship shows the extent of deterioration associated with exposure to varying amounts of air pollutants. The basic physical relationships may be investigated in the laboratory, but in application to any particular area one must have data on the various amounts of exposed materials that actually exist in the study region. Then it is possible to estimate the total amount of materials deterioration that would occur in an average year of exposure to the air of the region with its "normal" loading of various pollutants. One must then put a value on this deterioration. Taking a strict damage-function approach, we could estimate the increased cost of maintenance (labor, paint, etc.) made necessary by this deterioration.[13] But this would be an underestimate of the true

---

[13] This approach is taken from R. L. Horst et al., "A Damage Function Assessment of Building Materials: The Impact of Acid Deposition," Washington, D.C., U.S. Environmental Protection Agency, 1986.

damages from a willingness-to-pay perspective. Part of the damages would be aesthetic, the reduced visual values of less sightly buildings and painted surfaces. We might get at these values through contingent valuation methods, discussed below. The maintenance cost approach would not be complete also if pollution causes builders to switch to other materials to reduce damages.

The Value of Environmental Amenities as Expressed in Travel Costs

One of the first approaches that environmental economists use to estimate the demand for environmental amenities is a method that takes travel costs as a proxy for price. Although we don't observe people buying units of environmental quality directly, we do observe them traveling to enjoy, for example, recreation experiences in national and state parks, swimming and fishing experiences in lakes and streams, and so on. Travel is costly; it takes time as well as out-of-pocket travel expenses. By treating these travel costs as a price that people must pay to experience the environmental amenity, we can under some circumstances estimate a demand function for those amenities.

By getting travel cost data for a large number of people, we can build up estimates of the aggregate willingness to pay for particular environmental amenities. Of course, we must get information on more than just their travel costs. Families will differ in terms of many factors, not just in terms of their travel costs to this park. They will have different income levels, they will differ in terms of the presence of alternative parks and other recreational experiences available to them, and so on. So surveys have to collect large amounts of data on many visitors in order to be able statistically to sort out all these various influences on park visitation rates.

We can use this approach to estimate the benefits of improving the quality of the environment at the visitation site; for example, by improving the water quality at a recreation lake so that fishing is better. To do this we must collect information not only on the travel costs of recreators to a single recreation site, but on the travel costs to many different sites with differing natural characteristics. Then we can parse out the effects on visitation of various qualitative aspects of different sites. From this we can then determine their willingness to pay for improvements in these qualitative changes.

WILLINGNESS TO PAY: DIRECT METHODS

We come now to the direct approach to estimating willingness to pay, called the "contingent valuation" method. Contingent valuation (CV) is based on the simple idea that if you would like to know the willingness to pay of people for some characteristic of their environment, you can simply ask them. The word "simply" is a little extreme because it turns out not to be so simple, even though the basic idea seems straightforward. The method is called "contingent" valuation because it tries to get people to say how they would act if they were placed in certain contingent situations. Going back to our potatoes example, when we want to measure peoples' willingness to pay for potatoes, we can actually station ourselves at stores and see them choosing in real situations. But when there are no real markets for something, like an environmental quality characteristic, we can only ask them to tell us how they would choose *if* they were placed in certain situations; that is, *if* they were faced with a market for these characteristics.

Contingent value studies have been done to date for a long list of environmental factors: air quality, the value of view-related amenities, the recreational quality of beaches, preservation of wildlife species, congestion in wilderness areas, hunting and fishing experiences, toxic waste disposal, preservation of wild rivers, and others.[14] In fact, CV methods have spread into nonenvironmental areas; e.g., the value of programs for reducing the risks of heart attacks, the value of supermarket price information, and the value of a seniors companion program. Over time the method has been developed and refined to give what we think are reasonably reliable measures of the benefits of a variety of public goods, especially environmental quality.

The steps in a CV analysis are the following:

1 Identification and description of the environmental quality characteristic to be evaluated.
2 Identification of respondents to be approached, including sampling procedures used to select respondents.
3 Design and application of a survey questionnaire through personal, phone, or mail interviews (in recent years, focus groups have sometimes been used).
4 Analysis of results and aggregation of individual responses to estimate values for the group affected by the environmental change.

We can best appreciate the nature of CV analysis by looking more closely at the questionnaire design phase.

The Questionnaire

The questionnaire is designed to get people to think about and reveal their maximum willingness to pay for some feature of the environment. It has three essential components:

1 A clear statement of exactly what the environmental feature or amenity is that people are being asked to evaluate.
2 A set of questions that will describe the respondent in economically relevant ways, e.g., income, residential location, age, and use of related goods.

---

[14] For a review of many of these studies and of the general problems of CV analysis, see Paul Cameron Mitchell and Richard T. Carson, *Using Surveys to Value Public Goods: The Contingent Valuation Method*, Washington, D.C., Resources for the Future, 1989, and Ronald G. Cummings, David S. Brookshire, and William D. Schulze, *Valuing Environmental Goods: An Assessment of the Contingent Valuation Method*, Rowland and Allanheld Publishers, Totowa, N.J., 1986.

3 A question, or set of questions, designed to elicit willingness-to-pay responses from the respondent.

The central purpose of the questionnaire is to elicit from respondents their estimate of what the environmental feature is worth to them. In economic terms this means getting them to reveal the maximum amount they would be willing to pay rather than go without the amenity in question. A number of techniques have been used to get at this response. The most obvious is to ask people outright to provide the number with no prompting or probing on the part of the inter-viewer. Other approaches include using a bidding game, where the interviewer starts with a bid at a low level and progressively increases the value until the user indicates that the limit has been reached. Alternatively, the interviewer could start with a high figure and lower it to find where the respondent's threshold value is located. Another method is to give the respondents printed response cards with a range of values, then ask the respondents to check off their maximum willingness to pay. Exhibit 7-1 presents some examples of questions used in several contingent valuation studies.

Some Results

One great advantage of contingent valuation is that it is flexible and applicable to a wide range of environmental amenities, not just those that can somehow be measured in conjunction with some marketable good. Virtually anything that can be made comprehensible to respondents can be studied with this technique.

CV was first used in 1963 by Bob Davis to estimate the benefits of outdoor recreation opportunities in the Maine backwoods. He found that the modal willingness to pay per family for the use of a wilderness recreation area was between $1.00 and $2.00 per day.[15]

A number of researchers have used the approach to estimate willingness to pay to avoid ill health. For example, Chestnut et al. asked respondents how much they would be willing to pay to reduce by half the number of bad asthma days experienced each year.[16] The mean response per asthma day was $10.

Several CV studies have been done to measure the willingness to pay for increased visibility of the air in urban areas of the U.S. The results that researchers have obtained vary a lot; for a 10 percent increase in visual range, estimates of the annual willingness to pay per household (in the early to mid-1980s) vary from $7 to $101, although most of the results are in the $20 to $40 range.[17] Schulze and

[15] Robert K. Davis, "The Value of Big Game Hunting in a Private Forest," in *Transactions of the Twenty-ninth North American Wildlife Conference*, Wildlife Management Institute, Washington, D.C., 1964.

[16] Lauraine G. Chestnut et al., *Heart Disease Patient's Averting Behavior, Cost of Illness and Willingness to Pay to Avoid Angina Episodes*, U.S. Environmental Protection Agency, EPA/230/10-88/042, Washington, D.C., 1988.

[17] Gardner M. Brown, Jr., and J. M. Callaway, *Acid Deposition: State of the Science and Technology*, National Acid Precipitation Assessment Program, Report 27, Washington, D.C., U.S. Government Printing Office, 1990, pp. 27–164.

EXHIBIT 7-1

SAMPLE OF QUESTIONS USED IN SEVERAL CONTINGENT VALUATION STUDIES

Study to Estimate Benefits of National Freshwater Quality Improvements

1. How many people in this household are under 18 years of age?

2. During the last 12 months, did you or any member of your household boat, fish, swim, wade or water-ski in a freshwater river, lake, pond, or stream?

   Here are the national water pollution goals:

   > Goal C — 99 percent of freshwater is at least boatable,
   > Goal B — 99 percent of freshwater is at least fishable,
   > Goal A — 99 percent of freshwater is at least swimmable.

3. What is the highest amount you would be willing to pay each year:

   a. To achieve Goal C?
   b. To achieve Goal B?
   c. To achieve Goal A?

4. Considering the income classes listed in the accompanying card, what category best describes the total income that you and all the members of the household earned in 19__?

Study to Estimate the Value of Salmon Restoration

Suppose that all funding to restore Atlantic salmon in New England is stopped. Without this funding, there will be no organized effort to restore or preserve Atlantic salmon in New England and Atlantic salmon will be extinct in most New England rivers. Now suppose an independent private foundation is formed to restore Atlantic salmon in New England. The foundation's activities will include maintaining and restoring Atlantic salmon habitats and reintroducing infant salmon into selected waters. Please assume that the foundation will be able to restore the Atlantic salmon to all New England's major river systems in the next five years providing they receive adequate funds.

The foundation will be funded by private donations over the next five years. All contributors will be provided with information, at no cost, on how the Atlantic salmon are doing in New England, which rivers provide opportunities to see Atlantic salmon, and where in New England Atlantic salmon may be fished for.

Would you contribute $___ per year for the next 5 years, to help restore Atlantic salmon in New England? (Please circle the number of your choice.)

1. YES—I WOULD CONTRIBUTE THIS AMOUNT. IN FACT, I WOULD DONATE UP TO $____ PER YEAR OVER THE NEXT 5 YEARS. (Write in the highest dollar amount you would pay.)
2. NO—I WOULD NOT CONTRIBUTE THIS AMOUNT. IF NOT, WHY NOT?

   a. THE AMOUNT IS TOO HIGH, BUT I WOULD DONATE $____ PER YEAR OVER THE NEXT 5 YEARS. (Please write in the highest amount you would pay.)

Sources: Water quality: Robert Cameron Mitchell and Richard T. Carson, *Using Surveys to Value Public Goods: The Contingent Valuation Method*, Resources for the Future, Washington, D.C., 1989. Salmon restoration: Tim Hager, Tom Stevens, and Cleve Willis, *Economic Benefits of Salmon Restoration in Massachusetts*, Massachusetts Agricultural Experiment Station, Research Bulletin No. 726, December 1989.

his coworkers did a CV study to see how much people would be willing to pay for an increase in air visibility in the Grand Canyon. The average willingness to pay among their respondents was $9.20 for an iterative bidding approach and $5.69 for a payment card approach.[18]

Desvouges, Smith, and McGivney used CV to estimate the value of water quality improvements for water-based recreational purposes. They found that users of the recreation sites they sampled would on average be willing to pay $12.30 per person to increase the water quality from "boatable" to "fishable" and $29.60 per person to go from "boatable" to "swimmable" water.[19] Brookshire et al. used CV to measure the benefits of improving air quality. For the people in their study they found a mean willingness to pay of $14.50 per month to go from "poor" to "fair" quality air and $20.30 per month to go from "fair" to "good" quality air.[20]

Boyle and Bishop used CV methods to investigate the benefits of undertaking steps to preserve the bald eagle. Their results varied from $11.84 to $75.31 per person, depending on whether they had ever traveled to view bald eagles and whether they had ever contributed to Wisconsin's Endangered Resources Donation program.[21]

Randall and his associates used CV to estimate the benefits people would get from reducing the environmental damages stemming from large power plants in the four-corners area of the U.S. These were amenity damages from reduced visibility and the visual aspects of transmission lines. Respondents were shown pictures representing a situation of no control, one of moderate control, and one representing high levels of control for airborne emissions and location of transmission lines. For moderate levels of control the aggregate willingness to pay was $11,250,000, while for high levels of control it was $19,310,000.[22]

Brookshire and Coursey did a CV study to determine people's willingness to pay for a change in tree density in an urban park from 200 to 250 trees per acre. The median willingness to pay among their respondents was $9.30. In eliciting these responses researchers showed respondents pictures of the park with different tree densities.[23]

[18] William D. Schulze et al., "The Economic Benefits of Preserving Visibility in the National Parks of the Southwest," *Natural Resources Journal*, 23(1), January 1983, pp. 149–173.

[19] William H. Desvouges, V. Kerry Smith, and Matthew P. McGivney, "A Comparison of Alternative Approaches for Estimating Recreation and Related Benefits of Water Quality Improvements," Environmental Protection Agency, EPA/230/05-83/001, Washington, D.C., 1983.

[20] David Brookshire, Mark A. Thayer, William D. Schulze, and Ralph C. D'Arge, "Valuing Public Goods: A Comparison of Survey and Hedonic Approaches," *American Economic Review*, 72(1), March 1982, pp. 165–171.

[21] Kevin J. Boyle and Richard C. Bishop, "Valuing Wildlife in Benefit–Cost Analysis: A Case Study Involving Endangered Species," *Water Resources Research*, 23(5), May 1987, pp. 943–950.

[22] Alan Randall, Berry Ives, and Clyde Eastman, "Bidding Games for Valuation of Aesthetic Environmental Improvements," *Journal of Environmental Economics and Management*, 1(2), August 1974, pp. 132–149.

[23] David S. Brookshire and Don L. Coursey, "Measuring the Value of Public Goods: An Empirical Comparison of Elicitation Procedures," *American Economic Review*, 77(4), September 1987, pp. 554–566.

These are just a few of the hundreds of contingent valuation studies that have been done in the U.S. and other countries for the purpose of measuring the benefits of environmental improvements. The technique is still evolving and will undoubtedly lead to more accurate estimates of the values people place on environmental assets of all types.

Problems of CV Analysis

The most problematic aspect of contingent valuation is its hypothetical character. When people buy potatoes, to go back to our example, they have to "put their money where their mouth is," as the saying goes. It's a real situation and if the wrong choices are made, people suffer real consequences. But in a CV question- naire the same real-world implications are not present. People face a hypothetical situation, to which they may give hypothetical responses, not governed by the discipline of a real marketplace. In thinking about this, two types of questions come up: First, will people know enough about their real preferences to be able to give valid responses and, second, even if they know their preferences, will they have incentives to misrepresent them to the investigator?

Everyone develops experience buying some things, but not others, on the market. In seventeenth-century New England, people were used to buying and selling pews in the church. In some countries official papers from public officials require standard monetary bribes. In contemporary society there are going prices for cantaloupes and blood. When people face market prices for a good or service over a period of time, they have time to learn about their values, adjust their purchases, and settle on a willingness to pay that accurately represents their preferences. But when asked to place a monetary value on something that does not normally carry a price, it may be much more difficult to state one's true willingness to pay. What would you be willing to pay for 10 more beautiful sunsets per year? People also develop ideas over time about the appropriate extent of the market in allocating certain goods and services; when asked to put a value on something that is currently beyond the market, their answers may reflect not just the value of a particular item, but something about what kind of an economic system they want to live in, which is a much broader question.

The other question is whether respondents could normally be expected to have incentives to misstate their true willingness to pay. Environmental quality characteristics are public goods, as we saw in Chapter 4. People can be expected to understate their preferences for these kinds of goods when they expect that their answers will be used to establish payment schedules for the goods. But in CV studies, there is no threat that responses could be used, for example, to set taxes to pay for the item being evaluated. So, perhaps, this source of bias is unlikely. The opposite bias may be more likely. People may be led to give an inflated estimate of their willingness to pay hoping, perhaps, that others will do the same thing, realizing that their share of the cost of making the item available will, in any case, be very small.

PROBLEMS IN BENEFIT ESTIMATION

Many problems remain in estimating the benefits of improved environmental quality. Good data are always hard to come by. Better techniques are always useful to separate out the effects of other factors and isolate the true environmental impacts. More thought has to be given to the conceptual problems that remain. We will very briefly indicate some of the latter.

Discounting

One of the most important is the matter of *discounting*. Should we discount future benefits, as we talked about in the last chapter about discounting costs and, if so, what discount rate should we use? When we discount the future value of something, we reduce its present value, and the further into the future we go the lower the present value. So in discounting future benefits we tend to decrease the relative value of programs that produce benefits far in the future and increase those that produce benefits in the next few years. This might make sense when we talk about certain types of benefits. People today presumably would put more value on reducing environmentally related premature deaths next year than they would on premature deaths 50 years from now. But there are some significant environmental issues, like global warming, where substantial impacts are expected to occur in the distant future, and in this case discounting tends to reduce substantially the importance of programs addressing this problem.

There is no easy answer to this problem. We cannot simply reject discounting altogether; even future generations would be unlikely to agree with that if they could make their wishes known. But in ordinary affairs the present generation is undoubtedly too oriented to the short run; too much reliance is placed on recent history and not enough on future possibilities. For society as a whole a longer-run perspective is appropriate. As we mentioned in the last chapter, perhaps the best approach is to combine discounting with the idea of sustainability. Discounting is appropriate as long as it does not lead to a reduction in the long-run environmental capital of the society.

Willingness to Pay vs. Willingness to Accept

We have used throughout the notion of willingness to pay as a measure of benefits. Willingness to pay, besides reflecting a person's tastes and preferences, also reflects her income level. Another way of approaching the problem of valuing environmental improvements is to ask people how much they would be willing to accept to give up some environmental amenity. To value better air quality we could ask either how much people would be willing to pay for a small improvement or how much they would have to receive to compensate them for a small reduction in air quality. Suppose public authorities are contemplating locating a hazardous waste incinerator in a particular community. As a measure of the damages suffered by the community, we could take the amount of money required to get the community willingly to accept the incinerator (rather than, in other words, the amount they would be willing to pay to keep it out).

Clearly, willingness to accept is not constrained by one's income, as is willingness to pay. So it may be no surprise that when people are asked willingness-to-accept questions, their answers are usually higher than their willingness-to-pay responses for the same item. To some extent it may depend on what they are asked. For a small change we would expect the two measures to be close. Suppose what is involved is a single cantaloupe. If I am willing to pay $1.49 for one more cantaloupe, that is also probably close to what it would take to compensate for my loss of a single cantaloupe. But for large changes (what are called "nonmarginal" changes) this may not be the case. If we are talking, for example, of large changes in air pollution in my neighborhood that will substantially change my welfare, the two measures may be quite different.

Economists have taken several approaches to resolving this problem. One is to look closely at the questionnaire and the way questions are asked of respondents. Experience has shown that responses will differ according to how questions are phrased, so one possibility is that the differences between willingness to pay and willingness to accept are traceable primarily to the way questions are being framed. The other approach is to replace the standard economic principles, which imply that there should be no difference between these two measures, with new concepts that can explain the difference. This is a matter of current controversy.

Nonuse Values

When people buy potatoes, we assume that they do so because they expect to eat them; the value of potatoes to people lies in their *use* value. This reasoning extends also to environmental assets, but in this case there may be more. When people voluntarily donate money for the preservation of unique environmental assets that they may never even see, except perhaps in photographs, something other than use value must be involved. Peoples' willingness to pay for these environmental characteristics must also involve certain nonuse values. One possibility is that although perhaps not currently in a position to experience directly a particular environmental asset, people often want to preserve the option to do so in the future. *Option value* is the amount a person would be willing to pay to preserve the option of being able to experience a particular environmental amenity in the future. People may even be willing to pay to preserve something they will in all likelihood never see—African wildlife, for example. In this case, we may measure an *existence value*, a willingness to pay simply to help preserve the existence of some environmental amenity. Such altruistic values may be focused to some extent on future generations, in which case they might be called *bequest values*. Lastly, we might add a *stewardship value*, that is, a value not related necessarily to human use of the environment, but rather to maintaining the health of the environment for the continued use of all living organisms. One of the reasons contingent valuation studies have become more common is that questions can be phrased so as to get at these nonuse values.

NATURAL RESOURCE DAMAGES

The Comprehensive Environmental Response, Compensation and Liability Act (CERCLA) of 1980, as amended in 1986,[24] provides that parties who injure public natural resources through releases of oil or other hazardous substances may be required to make compensatory payments equal to the damages caused by these releases. The payments are to be used by states or the federal government to restore, replace, or acquire the equivalent of the damaged resources. The U.S. Department of Interior (DOI) was assigned the job of determining how "damages" are to be measured in these cases.

The conclusions of the DOI were that damages should be equal to the lesser of: (1) the lost resources use value, as measured by willingness to pay, or (2) the value of restoring the resource to its former state. Consider the following figures, representing willingness to pay and restoration values, for several cases:

	A	B
Willingness to pay	$1.2 million	$1.6 million
Restoration cost	$.6 million	$3.8 million

For case A, willingness to pay to avoid the oil or hazardous waste release is $1.2 million, but the cost of restoring the resource to its former state is only $.6 million, so the latter is taken as the true measure of damages. In case B, willingness to pay, at $1.6 million, is substantially less than restoration costs, so the former would be used to assess damages.

On the surface it might seem easier to measure restoration costs than willingness to pay for damaged environmental resources. Restoration appears to involve primarily engineering actions based on knowledge from physical and biological sciences. But "restoration" is in fact a rather complicated idea. In some cases restoration may be technically impossible, e.g., when there is some element of uniqueness in the destroyed resource. Restoration of the physical values of a resource (e.g., soil pH, water temperature, amount of tree cover) may not restore all of its ecological characteristics. Experience with this law and its legal clarification is just beginning to develop.[25] As it does, it will be necessary to come to grips with the fact that it is impossible to discuss restoration in physical terms without considering its monetary costs.

---

[24] These laws are discussed in Chapter 16.

[25] See, for example, Ellen Louderbough, "The Role of Science in Valuing Natural Resources after State of Ohio vs. Department of Interior, 880F. 2nd 432 (D.C. Cir. 1989)," *Natural Resources Journal,* 32(1), Winter 1992, pp. 137–148.

SUMMARY

Benefit measurement is a major focus of study within environmental economics. New techniques are being developed to uncover values that previously were hidden from view. From legislatures and courts a brisk demand has arisen for benefits information on which to base laws and legal settlements. Public environmental agencies have devoted considerable time and effort to generating benefits estimates in order to justify their policy rulings. After reviewing briefly what we mean by "benefits," we discussed some of the main techniques environmental economists use to measure these benefits. Health impacts, previously assessed by direct damage estimation, are now more frequently pursued through willingness-to-pay procedures, especially wage rate studies showing how people value risks to health. We also covered house-price studies, production cost studies, and travel cost studies. Finally, we reviewed the recently popular technique of contingent valuation. This technique allows us to measure the benefits of a much wider range of environmental phenomena than traditional techniques permitted. Indeed, contingent valuation techniques allow us to push beyond traditional "use values" and explore some of the less tangible, but no less real, sources of environmental benefits, like "option value," "existence value," and "stewardship value."

QUESTIONS FOR FURTHER DISCUSSION

1 Suppose you were hired by the homeowners located around a lake to determine the benefits of improving the water quality in the lake. How might you go about doing it?
2 Suppose the city council in a particular city votes to spend $5 million to improve air quality in the city. Is this a useful measure of the benefits of cleaner air in that city?
3 When the "average" person considers how much she or he is willing to pay to have environmental pollution reduced, do you think that person considers the views of unborn future generations?
4 Suppose you want to find out what value people place on increasing the expected human life span by one year. What ways can you think of to accomplish this?
5 Suppose you want to determine the aggregate willingness to pay among students at your school for reducing litter on the school grounds. How might you do this?
6 Many people object to trying to estimate the "value" of a human life, on the grounds that life is "priceless." What are the strengths and weaknesses of that viewpoint?

SELECTED READINGS

Bentkover, Judith D., Vincent T. Covello, and Jeryl Mumpower (eds.): *Benefits Assessment: The State of the Art*, D. Reidel Publishing Company, Dordrecht, Holland, 1986.

Braden, John B., and Charles D. Kolstad (eds.): *Measuring the Demand for Environmental Quality*, North-Holland, Amsterdam, 1991.

Desaiques, Brigitte, and Patrick Point: *Economie du Patrimoine Naturel, La Valorisation des Bénéfices de Protection de L'environnement*, Economica, Paris, 1993.

Dixon, John A., and Paul B. Sherman: *Economics of Protected Areas, A New Look at Benefits and Costs*, Island Press, Washington, D.C., 1990.

Freeman, A. Myrick, III: *The Benefits of Environmental Improvement: Theory and Practice*, Johns Hopkins Press for Resources for the Future, Baltimore, Md., 1979.

Hall, Jane V., Arthur M. Winer, Michael T. Kleinman, Frederick W. Lurmann, Victor Brajer, and Steven D. Colome: "Valuing the Health Benefits of Clean Air," *Science*, 255, February 14, 1992, pp. 812–817.

Kneese, Allen V.: *Measuring the Benefits of Clean Air and Water*, Resources for the Future, Washington, D.C., 1984.

Krutilla, John V., and Anthony C. Fisher: *The Economics of Natural Environments*, Johns Hopkins Press for Resources for the Future, Baltimore, Md., 1975.

Mitchell, Robert Cameron, and Richard T. Carson: *Using Surveys to Value Public Goods: The Contingent Valuation Method*, Resources for the Future, Washington, D.C., 1989.

Organization for Economic Cooperation and Development: *Benefits, Estimates and Environmental Decision Making*, Paris, 1992.

Pearce, David W., and Anil Markandya: *Environmental Policy Benefits: Monetary Valuation*, Organization for Economic Cooperation and Development, Paris, 1989.

Rowe, Robert D., and Lauraine G. Chestnut: *The Value of Visibility: Theory and Application*, Abt Books, Cambridge, Mass., 1982.

Schelling, Thomas: "The Life You Save May Be Your Own," in Samuel Chase (ed.), *Problems of Public Expenditure Analysis*, Brookings Institution, Washington, D.C., 1968, pp. 127–158.

Smith, V. Kerry, and William H. Desvouges: *Measuring Water Quality Benefits*, Kluwer-Nijhoff Publishing, Boston, Mass., 1986.

U.S. Environmental Protection Agency: *The Economics of Improved Estuarine Water Quality: An NEP Manual for Measuring Benefits*, Washington, D.C., EPA 503/5-90-001, September 1990.

CHAPTER 8

BENEFIT–COST ANALYSIS: COSTS

In this chapter we look at the cost side of benefit–cost analysis. The importance of accurate cost measurement has often been underestimated. It is a full half of the analysis, the results of which can as easily be affected by, e.g., overestimating costs as by underestimating benefits. In developing countries, where people place a high priority on economic growth, it is critically important to know how environmental programs will affect that growth rate and how costs are distributed among different social groups. In industrialized countries opposition to environmental policies frequently centers on their estimated costs, which means that those doing benefit–cost analyses of these programs are well advised to get the cost estimates right. In this chapter we will first take up some general considerations about costs, then look at some specific issues and examples of cost estimation.

THE COST PERSPECTIVE

Cost analysis can be done on many levels. At its simplest, it focuses on the costs to a single community or firm of an environmental program, or of a single environmental project like a wastewater treatment plant, incinerator, or beach restoration project. The reason for calling these the simplest is that they usually proceed by costing out a definite engineering specification that has clear boundaries, and for which the "rest of the world" can rightly be assumed to be constant. At the next level we have costs to an industry, or perhaps to a region, of meeting environmental regulations or of adopting certain technologies. Here we can no longer rely on simple engineering assumptions; we must do things like predict with reasonable accuracy how groups of polluting firms will respond to changes in laws on emissions or how they will respond to changes in recycling regulations. Problems will arise because not all firms will be alike—some small, some large, some old, some new, etc.—and each of them will usually have multiple possibilities for reacting to regulations. At a still higher level, our concern may be with the costs to an entire economy of achieving stated environmental goals.

Estimating costs at the national level calls for an entirely different approach. Here everything is connected to everything else; when pollution-control regulations are imposed, adjustments will reverberate throughout the economy. To trace them out we must deal with macroeconomic data and usually fairly sophisticated aggregate models. In the following pages we will deal with cost estimation at these different levels.

OPPORTUNITY COSTS

In economics the most fundamental concept of costs is *opportunity costs*. The opportunity cost of using resources[1] in a certain way is the highest valued alternative use to which those resources might have been put and which society has to forgo when the resources are used in the specified fashion. Note the word "society." Costs are incurred by all types of firms, agencies, industries, groups, etc. Each has its own perspective, which will focus on those costs that impinge directly on them. Suppose a community is contemplating building a bicycle path to relieve congestion and air pollution downtown. Its primary concern is what the town will have to pay to build the path. Suppose it will take $1 million to build it, but 50 percent of this will come from the state or federal government. From the town's perspective the cost of the bike path will be a half million dollars, but from the standpoint of society the full opportunity costs of the path are $1 million.

The trouble is that when most people think of cost they usually think of money expenditure. Often the monetary cost of something is a good measure of its opportunity costs, but frequently it is not. Suppose the bike path is going to be put on an old railroad right-of-way that has absolutely no alternative use, and suppose the town must pay the railroad $100,000 for this right-of-way. This money is definitely an expenditure the town must make, but it is not truly a part of the opportunity costs of building the path, because society gives up nothing in devoting the old right-of-way to the new use.

Environmental Costs

It may seem paradoxical to think that environmental protection control programs might have environmental costs, but this is in fact the case. Most of our specific emissions-reduction programs are media based; i.e., they are aimed at reducing emissions into one particular environmental medium like air or water. So when emissions into one medium are reduced, they may increase into another. Reducing untreated domestic waste outflow into rivers or coastal oceans leaves quantities of solid waste that must then be disposed of—perhaps through land spreading or incineration. Reducing airborne SO_2 emissions from power plants

---

[1] Remember that "resources" is a word that can have two meanings: It can be a short way of saying "natural resources" or a general reference analogous to the word "inputs." Here we are using it in the second sense.

by stack-gas scrubbing also leaves a highly concentrated sludge that must be disposed of in some way. Incinerating domestic solid waste creates airborne emissions.

Media switches are not the only source of environmental impacts stemming from environmental improvement programs. There can be direct effects; e.g., sediment runoff from construction sites for new treatment plants or sewer lines. There can also be unforeseen impacts when firms or consumers adjust to new programs. Gasoline producers reduced the amounts of lead in their product but, since consumers still insisted on high-powered performance, they added other compounds, which ended up having environmental impacts in their own right. With the beginning of community programs to charge consumers for solid waste disposal, some have been faced with substantial increases in "midnight dumping," i.e., illegal dumping along the sides of roads or in remote areas.

Some of the potential environmental impacts from these public projects or programs can be *mitigated*; that is, steps can be taken to reduce or avoid them. More enforcement resources can help control midnight dumping, extra steps can be taken to reduce construction-site impacts, special techniques may be available to reduce incinerator residuals, and so on. These mitigation costs must be included as part of the total costs of any project or program. Beyond this, any remaining environmental costs must be set against the overall reduction in environmental damages to which the program is primarily aimed.

No-Cost Improvements in Environmental Quality

Sometimes environmental improvements can be obtained at zero social cost, except the political cost of making the required changes in public laws or regulations. In virtually any type of political system, usually some laws and administrative practices are instituted primarily to benefit certain groups within society for political reasons, rather than to move toward economically efficient resource use or achieve deserving income redistributions. These regulations, besides transferring income to the favored groups, often have negative environmental effects.

Consider, for example, coastal zone flood insurance in the U.S. Commercial insurance for property constructed in the coastal zone would normally have such high premiums—because of the expected losses from floods—that few coastal homeowners could afford it. The U.S. government, therefore, subsidizes coastal zone insurance, so that people building in these areas can get insurance at substantially less than commercial rates. The effects of this have been to reduce the private monetary costs of building and maintaining houses in the coastal zone, so substantial development has occurred there, with attendant environmental impacts. A reduction in these public subsidies to coastal homeowners would not only work to reduce these environmental impacts but would also lead to an increase in national income. Of course, coastal homeowners would suffer losses.

There are many other examples like this. Agricultural subsidies in many developed countries have provided the incentive to develop intensive, chemical-based production methods, which has resulted both in increased agricultural output and in the nonpoint source water and air pollution to which these methods lead. Reducing these agricultural subsidies would increase national income and reduce the environmental impacts, though of course many farmers would be worse off.

Enforcement Costs

Environmental regulations are not self-enforcing. Resources must be devoted to monitoring the behavior of firms, agencies, and individuals subject to the regulations, and to sanctioning violators. Public environmental facilities, such as wastewater treatment plants and incinerators, must be monitored to be sure they are being operated correctly.

There is an important application of the opportunity idea in the enforcement phenomenon. Many environmental laws are enforced by agencies whose enforcement budgets are not strictly tailored to the enforcement responsibilities they are given. Thus, budgets can be stable, or even declining, at the same time that new environmental laws are passed. Enforcing the new laws may require shifting agency resources away from the enforcement of other laws. In this case the opportunity costs of new enforcement must include the lower levels of compliance in areas that now are subject to less enforcement.

COSTS OF SINGLE FACILITIES

Perhaps the easiest type of cost analysis to visualize is that for a single, engineered project of some type. There are many types of environmental quality programs that involve publicly supported construction of physical facilities (although the analysis would be the same whatever the ownership), such as public wastewater treatment plants, of which hundreds of millions of dollars worth have been built over the last few decades. Other examples include flood control projects, solid-waste handling facilities, hazardous-waste incinerators, beach-restoration projects, public parks, wildlife refuges, and the like.

Facility-type projects like this are individualized and substantially unique, though of course they have objectives and use technology that is similar to that used for many other projects. To estimate their costs, primary reliance is placed on engineering and technical specifications, developed largely through experience with similar types of facilities. Consider the simple example shown in Table 8-1. It gives the estimated costs of a new wastewater treatment plant for a small community. The plant is expected to use standard technology, as specified in the engineering plans for the treatment plant, collector lines, and other essential parts of the system. It will be built by a private firm but owned and operated by the town.

TABLE 8-1
PROJECTED COSTS OF A SMALL WASTEWATER TREATMENT PLANT ($1,000)

	Construction Costs			
	Initial cost	Life (years)	Replacement costs	Salvage value
Treatment plant				
Mechanical	1,104	20	125	—
Structural	1,296	40	—	544
Engineering (15%)	360	—	—	—
Contingencies (10%)	240	—	—	—
Total	3,000	60	125	544
Conveyances				
Pumping station	245	15	245	164
Metering station	40	40	—	7
Piping	1,028	40	—	480
Engineering (15%)	195	—	—	—
Contingencies (10%)	131	—	—	—
Total	1,639	95	245	651
Sludge disposal works (land spreading)				
Site work	254	40	—	—
Piping	228	40	—	95
Land purchase	350	40	—	—
Other	150	40	—	—
Total	982	—	—	95
Mitigation of construction-related environmental costs	24	40	—	—

Annual Costs

Operation and maintenance (O&M)			Environmental costs	
Pumping station	21		Mitigation costs	8
Treatment plant			Unmitigated environmental costs	46
Labor	60			
Electric power	45			
Parts and supplies	13			
Chemicals	6			
Other	7			
Sludge disposal	4			
Total	156			

Present Values

Cost item	Total	Present value (@8%)
Construction	5,645	5,645
Replacement	370	107
Salvage values	-1,290	-320
Annual O&M	156	1,860
Annual environmental	54	644
Total		7,936

Source: Adapted from U.S. Environmental Protection Agency and Wisconsin Department of Natural Resources, *Environmental Impact Statement, Wastewater Treatment Facilities at Genwa Lake Area, Walworth County, Wisconsin,* Washington, D.C., June 1984.

There are three types of construction costs: the treatment plant proper, conveyances, and sludge-disposal works. The latter refers to disposal of the solid waste produced at the plant. The waste materials extracted from the wastewater stream don't just disappear, these heavily treated substances must be disposed of in some fashion. There are various ways of doing this (composting, land spreading, incineration). In the case of land spreading, the costs involve buying a large area of land on which the sludge will be spread and allowed to decompose and mix with the soil. The assumed life of the plant is 40 years. Some portions of the plant—for example, certain pieces of equipment—will wear out and have to be replaced during this period. The costs of this are listed under "replacement costs." Additionally, certain parts of the plant and conveyance system are expected to have a salvage value at the end of the 40 years; these are shown in the last column. Note that allowances have been made for engineering work and construction contingencies. An estimate has also been included of the initial costs of some environmental mitigation activities.

Annual costs are divided into operation and maintenance (O&M) of the treatment plant, O&M of the pumping station, sludge disposal operation, and environmental costs. The latter includes certain mitigation costs, together with some remaining, or unmitigated, environmental costs. The latter might refer, for example, to odor problems at the plant and on the sludge disposal lands. These are, in fact, environmental damages, which might be estimated, for example, with contingent valuation techniques.

The last section of Table 8-1 includes the present values of the costs, evaluated with a discount rate of 8 percent. Replacement costs are discounted to the present from the year in which they are expected to be required. Salvage values are discounted back from the end of the project's life, in this case 40 years. These appear with negative signs because they act to lower the total cost of the project. The present value of annual environmental costs is also included.

With the exception of unmitigated environmental costs, these items are all expenditure figures, and only close inspection can tell if they represent true social opportunity costs. Suppose, for example, that in the construction phase a number of local unemployed people are hired. Although the construction costs include their wages, their opportunity costs would be zero because society had to give up nothing when they went to work on the plant. It might be that the land on which the plant is to be placed is town land that is to be donated. In this case there will be no specific cost entry for land, but there will be an opportunity cost related to the value the land could have had in its next best use. Suppose that the construction firm, because it is working on a public project, is able to get subsidized loans from local banks (i.e., borrow money at lower than market rates). Then the true opportunity costs of construction will be higher than the monetary costs indicated. There are no specific rules for making these adjustments; only a knowledge of the specific situations can reveal when it is important enough to make them and where sufficient data are available to do the job.

COSTS OF A LOCAL REGULATION

Environmental regulations are frequently enacted at the local level and impact on local firms. In fact, in the political economy of pollution control, it is often the fear of these local impacts that deters communities from enacting the regulations. Fears of lost payrolls and the secondary losses to other firms from shrinking local markets loom large at the local level; from a national perspective the opportunity costs are less severe.

Suppose in a particular small town there is a large apple orchard that provides substantial local employment. Suppose further that presently the orchard managers use relatively large applications of chemicals to control apple pests and diseases, and that the chemical runoff from this activity threatens local water supplies. Assume the community enacts an ordinance requiring the orchard to practice "integrated pest management" (IPM), a lower level of chemical use coupled with other means to compensate for this reduction. Assume further, for purposes of illustration, that the IPM practices increase the costs of raising apples in this orchard.[2] What are the costs of this regulation?

If the orchard raises and sells the same number of apples it previously did, the true social opportunity costs of the regulation are the increased production costs. If local consumers are willing to pay somewhat higher prices for locally grown apples, some of this cost gets passed on to these consumers. But suppose competitive conditions make it impossible for the orchard to sell its apples for any higher price than pertained before. In this case the higher production costs must be reflected in lower incomes of either the apple orchard owners themselves, or perhaps orchard workers, if they will accept lower wages.

But suppose the orchard was just breaking even before the local IPM ordinance, and that the statute leads to such cost increases that production is substantially curtailed; in fact, assume for purposes of argument that the orchard goes out of business. Clearly there will be local costs: lost payrolls of orchard workers, lost income to the local orchard owners, lost income to local merchants because their markets shrink. But these lost incomes are not likely to be social opportunity costs in their entirety, unless the workers become permanently unemployed. Assuming they transfer to other job opportunities (this requires obviously that the economy be operating at full employment), their new incomes will offset, at least partly, the lost incomes they had been earning previously. There may be certain valid opportunity costs in the form of adjustment costs, as workers and owners have to move to new places of employment.

What about the value of the apples no longer produced in this orchard? If we assume that there are many other orchards in neighboring towns and other regions to take up the slack with essentially no cost increases, then this lost production is offset by others, consumer prices are stable, and the social opportunity costs of this marginal rearrangement of apple production are basically nil.

To summarize, when we are dealing with a single local ordinance affecting

---

[2] In fact, various authorities and scientific studies suggest that IPM practices can actually lower costs relative to chemical-intensive growing techniques.

one firm and the economy is at or near full employment, ensuing resource adjustments ensure that social opportunity costs are small, limited to the costs of actually carrying out the adjustments. From the standpoint of the affected community, of course, costs will seem high, because of lost local incomes brought about by the increased apple production costs.

COSTS OF REGULATING AN INDUSTRY

These conclusions do not follow when we impose an environmental regulation on an entire industry. Higher production costs for the industry are true social opportunity costs, because they require added resources that could have been used elsewhere. But when we deal with whole industries, we can't make the assumption, like we did with the one apple orchard, that its production could easily be picked up by the others. For an industry we may have to make many adjustments in order to get from higher production costs to social opportunity costs.

We will consider first the standard approach to estimating increased industry production costs, which is to measure the added expenditures that an industry would have to make to come into compliance with an environmental regulation. Cost estimation in this case requires the analyst to predict how polluters will respond to environmental regulations, and then to estimate the costs of this response. If the regulation is very specific, requiring for example that manufacturing firms install a certain piece of pollution-control equipment or that farmers adopt certain cultivation practices to avoid soil runoff, the cost estimation may be fairly straightforward. But if the regulation leaves the polluters considerable latitude in making their response, it may be hard to predict exactly what they will do and, therefore, what their costs will be.

Suppose, for example, a group of pulp mills are required to reduce their emissions by some percentage, and that we (a public agency) wish to estimate the impact of this on the production costs of the firms in the industry. In effect, we want to estimate the aggregate marginal abatement cost function for this group of firms. To do this with reasonable accuracy, we have to know enough about the pulp business to be able to predict how the firms will respond, what treatment techniques they will use, how they might change their internal production processes, and so on. Or suppose we wanted to estimate the costs among farmers of a ban on a certain type of pest control chemical. We would need to know what alternatives farmers had available to replace this chemical, what impacts this would have on yields, how much additional labor and other inputs they would use, and so on.

An Example

The metal finishing industry provides services to major industries like aircraft, automotive, jewelry, and hardware. Products from these industries are provided with metal surfaces that enhance their durability, corrosion resistance, conductivity, and appearance. In the early 1970s the EPA was charged with estimating the costs to firms in the metal finishing industry of meeting proposed emission-reduction goals. As is true of most studies of regulatory impacts, there were too many firms in the industry to do a technical study of each one. A common way of addressing this problem is to estimate costs for the "average" or "representative" or "model" plant, one that corresponds to typical operating conditions in the industry but not to any particular plant. But in this case, as in most cases, the size and technical heterogeneity of plants in the industry made it necessary to specify a number of representative plants, each of which corresponded to one portion of the firms in the industry. Abatement costs are shown in Table 8-2 for four different plant sizes, where "size" is given by the number of employees working in the plant. The first row shows the estimated number of plants in each size class. Note that most of these plants are quite small; in fact, the metal finishing industry in the U.S. consists of a large number of relatively small firms.

The first section in the table shows investment costs needed to install the new equipment that will allow the firms to reduce their emissions flows. These are the "up-front" investment costs of new buildings, equipment, and the land to put them on. The second part of the table shows annualized costs. These include the conventional items like energy, labor, etc., and also the annualized invest-

TABLE 8-2
ESTIMATED COSTS ($1,000) OF COMPLYING WITH ENVIRONMENTAL REGULATIONS, METAL FINISHING INDUSTRY (ANODIZING PROCESS)

	Size of plant (number of employees)			
	1–9	10–19	20–49	50+
Number of plants in size class	137	65	70	26
Investment costs				
Equipment	46	57	72	264
Building and land	11	17	22	47
Equipment installation	9	12	14	53
Total	66	86	108	364
Annual costs				
Capital costs[*]	3.3	4.3	5.4	18.2
Depreciation[†]	6.6	8.6	10.8	36.4
Labor	12.2	24.1	32.9	105.1
Energy	3.1	5.2	7.4	14.1
Other costs	8.7	12.3	19.8	28.3
Total	33.9	54.5	76.3	202.1

[*]10% of *average* investment costs. Annual investment each year of the project is equal to original investment minus depreciation. Average investment is the mean of these annual investments. Since depreciation is 10-year straight-line, average investment is actually equal to one-half of the original investment.
    [†]Straight-line depreciation—10-year life.

    Source: Adapted from U.S. Environmental Protection Agency, *Economic Analysis of Effluent Guidelines, The Metal Finishing Industry*, EPA 230/1-74/032, Washington, D.C., September 1974.

ment costs. In the waste-treatment plant example above, we aggregated discounted annual operating costs and added these to initial investment costs to get the present value of total costs. The other way of adding initial investment costs and annual operating costs is to "annualize" the investment costs, that is, spread them out over the years of life that the investments are assumed to have. This is done in Table 8-2. Annualized investment costs consist of two parts: the opportunity costs of the capital, and depreciation. The former is the forgone return that one could earn if the investment were made in some other industry. Depreciation is the cost associated with the progressive using up of the equipment and buildings over their useful life.

Total annual costs are shown for each of the representative plants. If we wanted to have an estimate of the total costs of meeting the emission standard for the entire industry, we could calculate a weighted total:

Size of firm (No. of employees)	Costs ($1,000)	No. of firms	Total costs ($1,000)
1–9	33.9	137	4,644.3
10–19	54.5	65	3,542.5
20–49	76.3	70	534.1
50+	202.1	26	5,254.6
Total			13,975.5

Thus, the anticipated total annual cost of this industry to meet the emission reduction standards is $13,975,500. We might note that these costs are incomplete in at least one sense. In regulatory programs of any type, public enforcement resources are required if we expect to get large-scale compliance by the regulated firms. Table 8-2 contains nothing about these costs, but in a full social benefit–cost analysis, they would obviously have to be included.

Where does one get the cost data necessary to construct these representative firms? Many of the basic data are generated through *cost surveys* of existing firms. In effect, questionnaires are sent out to these firms, asking them to supply information on number of employees, processes used, costs of energy and materials, etc. With a sufficiently detailed questionnaire and a reasonably high response rate by firms, researchers can get a good idea of basic cost conditions in the industry and how they might be affected by environmental regulations.

One problem with cost surveys is that they are usually better at getting information on past cost data than on future costs under new regulations. Firms can probably report past cost data with more reliability than they can estimate future costs of meeting environmental constraints. Historical data may not be a good guide to the future, especially since environmental regulations almost by definition confront firms with novel situations. In these cases it is common to supplement survey data with technical engineering data that can be better adapted to costing out the new techniques and procedures that firms may adopt. Surveys are also problematic because they rely on accurate responses. If firms know that the results of the survey are to be used in developing an environmental control program, they may have a strong incentive to overstate their costs. Or they may substantially understate their current emissions, which would lead administrators to overestimate the costs of achieving particular emission standards.

The "representative firm" approach, while dictated by the large number of firms in an industry, has its own problems, especially when those firms are substantially heterogeneous among themselves. In following this procedure, for example, the EPA runs into the problem of whether costs of the real plants in the industry, each of which is to some degree unique, can be accurately represented by a composite cost estimate. In this case "accurately" means close enough that individual firms will not be inclined to take the agency to court on grounds that their own unique cost situations are misrepresented by the figures for the "representative" firm. Many legal resources have been used up fighting court battles over this issue.

Actual vs. Minimum Pollution Control Costs

The costs shown in Table 8-2 show the estimated costs of the metal finishing industry meeting the environmental standards imposed by law. There is an important question of whether these costs are the *least* costs necessary to achieve the emission reductions sought in the law. This is an important point because, as we saw in Chapter 5, the efficient level of emissions or ambient quality is defined by the trade-off of emission abatement costs and environmental damages. If abatement costs used to define the efficient level are higher than they need to be, the point so defined will be only a pseudo-efficient outcome.

When there is a single facility involved, we must rely on engineering judgment to ensure that the technical proposal represents the least costly way of achieving the objectives. When what is involved is an entire industry, both technical and economic factors come into play. We saw earlier that in order for the overall costs of a given emission reduction to be achieved at minimum cost, the equimarginal principle has to be fulfilled. Frequently, environmental regulations work against this by dictating that different sources adopt essentially the same levels of emission reductions or install the same general types of pollution-control technology. As we will see in later chapters, many environmental laws are based on administratively specified operating decisions that firms are required to make. These decisions may not lead, or allow, firms to achieve emission abatement at least cost. Thus, industry costs such as those depicted in Table 8-2 may not represent minimum abatement costs.

There is no easy way out of this dilemma. If one is called on to do a benefit–cost analysis of a particular environmental regulation, one presumably is committed to evaluating the regulation as given. But in cases like this it would no doubt be good policy for the analyst to point out that there are less costly ways of achieving the benefits.

The With/Without Principle

There is an important principle that has to be kept in mind in this work. In doing a benefit–cost analysis of how firms will respond to new laws, we want to use the "with/without" approach and not the "before/after" approach. We want to estimate the differences in costs that polluters would have with the new law, *compared to what their costs would have been in the absence of the law*. This is not the same as the difference between their new costs and what their costs used to be before the law. Consider the following illustrative numbers, applying to a manufacturing firm for which a pollution-control regulation has been proposed:

Estimated production costs:

Before the regulation: $100
In the future without the regulation: $120
In the future with the regulation: $150

It would be a mistake to conclude that the added costs of the pollution-control regulation will be $50 (future costs with the regulation minus costs before the law). This is an application of the before/after principle and does not accurately reflect the true costs of the law. This is so because in the absence of any new law, production costs are expected to increase (for example, because of increased fuel costs, unrelated to environmental regulations). Thus, the true cost of the regulation is found by applying the with/without principle. Here these costs are $30 (costs in the future with the regulation minus future costs without the regulation). Of course this makes the whole job of cost estimation harder because we want to know not historical costs of a firm or an industry but what its future costs would be if it were to continue operating without the new environmental laws.

Output Adjustments

The increase in abatement expenditures may not be an accurate measure of opportunity costs when an entire industry is involved. This is because market adjustments are likely to alter the role and performance of the industry in the wider economy. For example, when the costs of a competitive industry increase, the price of its output increases, normally causing a reduction in quantity demanded. This is pictured in Figure 8-1, which shows supply and demand curves for two industries. For convenience the supply curves have been drawn horizontally, representing marginal production costs that do not vary with output. Consider first panel (a). The initial supply function is C_1, so the initial quantity produced is q_1. The pollution-control law causes production costs to rise, represented by a shift upward in supply from curve C_1 to C_2. Suppose we calculate the increased cost of producing the initial rate of output. This would be an amount equal to the area $(a + b + c)$. The comparable cost in panel (b) is $(d + e + f)$. But this approach to measuring costs will overstate the true cost increase because when costs and prices go up, quantity demanded and output will decline.

FIGURE 8-1
Output Adjustments in
Industries Subject to
Pollution-Control Regulations.

How much output declines is a matter of the steepness of the demand curve. In panel (a), output declines only from q_1 to q_2. But in panel (b), with the flatter demand curve, output will decline from r_1 to r_2, a much larger amount. The correct measure of the cost to society is $(a + b)$ in panel (a) and $(d + e)$ in panel (b). Note that the original approach to cost estimation, calculating the increased cost of current output, is a much better approximation to the true burden on society in panel (a) than in panel (b). This is because the output adjustment is much larger in the latter. The lesson here is that if increased expenditures are to be taken as true opportunity costs, they must be calculated taking into account price and output adjustments that occur in the industries affected by the environmental regulations.

The graphs in Figure 8-1 can help us understand something about the *incidence* of pollution-control costs. By incidence we mean who actually ends up paying the costs. Firms in the affected industries bear these costs in the beginning, but the final burden depends on how the cost increase is passed forward to consumers or backward to workers and stockholders. We note that in both panels (a) and (b) the market prices of the goods increased by the amount of the cost increase. But the response is quite different. In panel (a) consumers continue buying close to what they did before, little adjustment is called for in terms of output shrinkage in the industry. Thus, workers and shareholders in this industry will be little affected, in relative terms. In panel (b) the same price increase leads to a large drop in output. Consumers have good substitutes to which they can switch when the price of this output goes up; in effect, they can escape the full burden of the price increase. On the other hand, the industry adjustment is large. Resources, particularly workers, will have to flow out of the industry and try to find employment elsewhere. If they can, the costs may be only temporary adjustment costs; if not, the costs will be much longer run.

Long-Run Adjustments

In the foregoing example cost estimation required that we predict the effect of emission-control regulations on a group of existing firms, most of which were expected to continue operating in the future. But in many cases environmental regulations can have long-run affects on the very structure of an industry, that is, on the number and size of firms. In this case, long-run prediction requires that we be able to predict these "structural" changes with some accuracy.

Consider the case illustrated in Exhibit 8-1. It applies not to long-run structural changes in a manufacturing industry but to changes in the structure of the landfill industry, which is actually a complex mixture of public agencies and private firms. The EPA has established regulations for construction of landfills to reduce the risk of leakage and contamination of nearby surface or groundwater resources. These regulations require new technology and procedures, like plastic liners, sophisticated construction techniques, and monitoring of dumped material. The effect of these regulations is substantially to increase the cost of landfills. To determine the total cost of these regulations to the people of a particular state, for example, it would not be correct to estimate the effects of the new regulations at all of the existing town landfills. This is because the regulations are going to lead to substantial changes in the very structure of the landfill industry.

In particular, the new regulations will create conditions in which many individual towns will abandon their own landfills and join large regional operations, many of which will be privately owned. Thus, in order to estimate the full long-run costs of these EPA regulations, we would want to know more than just the different technologies of landfill operations; we would also want to study the economics of the industry, or potential industry, that will develop in response to the regulations.

Another very important long-run impact is on technological change in the industry affected by pollution-control requirements. When firms are subject to

---

EXHIBIT 8-1

EPA ISSUES RULES ON TRASH LANDFILLS

Guidelines Tighten Regulations, Call for Fewer and Larger Dumps.

WASHINGTON — The Environmental Protection Agency set national standards for garbage landfills yesterday, issuing rules that could speed a trend toward replacing town dumps with large regional facilities.

The regulations, to be phased in from 1993 through 1996, will require monitoring for leaks of dangerous chemicals at nearly all sites. New landfills will have to meet more stringent conditions, including protective liners to prevent pollutants from seeping through the soil.

Environmentalists said that many states already have tougher rules and that the EPA's program would leave too many loopholes for landfills in states with looser regulations.

Many of the nation's nearly 6,000 landfills "are simply not environmentally acceptable," William K. Reilly, the EPA administrator, said at a news conference.

Ten years ago, the United States had 16,000 landfills; the number is expected to shrink to about 3,000 within five years.

"We will see fewer landfills and larger landfills," Reilly said. He said the new rules may accelerate some closings, and other agency officials said their estimate of how may closures would be forced by the new rules ranged from none to 600.

Reilly said the nationwide standards would "ensure against the creation of a whole new generation" of hazardous waste sites. About 200 of the 1,200 sites on the Superfind priority cleanup list are former landfills.

Robert Peters, the director of technical programs for the Solid Waste Association of North America, said new landfills will probably have to cover at least 50 acres to collect enough revenue to cover the costs of the tougher standards.

"I think there will be additional impetus for regionalization," Peters said.

The EPA estimated the cost of complying with the regulations at $330 million, which it said worked out to $4 per household nationwide.

Don Clay, the agency's assistant administrator for solid waste, said an original estimate of $600 million to $1 billion was reduced because many states already have landfill standards at least as strict as the new federal rules.

Source: Boston Globe, September 12, 1991. Copyright 1991 by the Associated Press. Reprinted by permission.

---

emission reduction requirements, they have an incentive to engage in research and development (R&D) to find better emissions abatement technology. There is some evidence that in reality this may draw resources away from output-increasing R&D efforts, thereby affecting the firm's ability to reduce costs in the long run. On the other hand, there is evidence also that environmental regulations have led to unanticipated, marketable products or processes stemming from their research. And some studies have even shown that after investing in pollution-control R&D some firms have reduced their long-run production costs. In cases like this the short-run cost increases arising from pollution-control regulations are not accurate estimates of the long-run opportunity costs of these regulations.

COSTS AT THE NATIONAL LEVEL

We finally come to the most aggregative level for which cost studies are normally pursued, the level of the national economy. The usual question of interest is the extent of the macroeconomic cost burden of the environmental regulations a country imposes, or might be planning to impose, in a given period of time. Sometimes interest centers on the totality of the regulations put in place. Sometimes the focus is on specific regulations which will nevertheless impact broadly on a national economy, such as a program of CO_2 emissions reduction.

Considered as a single aggregate, an economy at any point in time has available to it a certain number of inputs—labor, capital, equipment, energy, materials, etc.—which it converts to marketed output. Suppose the firms in the economy are subject to a variety of environmental regulations requiring them, or inducing them, to devote a portion of the total inputs to reductions in emissions. Marketed output must go down (assuming full employment) because of the input diversion. By how much will it drop? There are two answers to this, one applicable to the short run and the other to the long run.

In the short run marketed output must drop because a portion of total resources is devoted to pollution control rather than to the production of marketed output. But if we simply add up the pollution-control expenditures made by all the industries subject to environmental controls, we may not get an accurate picture of how these controls are affecting the national economy. Expenditures for plant, equipment, labor, and other inputs for reducing emissions can affect other economic sectors not directly covered by environmental regulations, and macroeconomic interactions of this type need to be accounted for to get the complete picture. An industry subject to environmental controls and trying to lower its emissions puts increasing demand on the pollution-control industry, which expands output and puts increasing demands on other sectors—for example, the construction sector—which responds by increasing output.

Another economy-wide adjustment is through prices. Increased pollution-control expenditures lead to increased prices for some items, which leads to reductions in quantity demanded, which leads to lower outputs in these sectors and thus to lower production costs. Total employment will also be affected by pollution-control expenditures. On the one hand, diverting production to pollution control will lower employment needs in the sector producing marketed output. On the other, it will increase employment in the pollution-control industry. So the net result cannot be predicted in the absence of relatively sophisticated macroeconomic modeling.

In the long run more complicated macroeconomic interactions are at work. Long-run economic change—growth or decline—is a matter of the accumulation of capital: human capital and inanimate capital. It also depends on technical change, getting larger amounts of output from a given quantity of inputs. So an important question is how environmental laws will affect the accumulation of capital and the rate of technical innovation. Diverting inputs from conventional sectors to pollution-control activities lowers the rate of capital accumulation in those conventional sectors. This can be expected to reduce the rate of growth of productivity (output per unit of input) in the production of conventional output and thus slow overall growth rates. The impacts on the rate of technical innovation in the economy are perhaps more ambiguous, as mentioned above. If attempts to innovate in pollution control reduce the efforts to do so in market production, the impact on future growth could be negative. But some people think that efforts to reduce emissions can have a positive impact on the overall rate of technical innovation, which would have a positive impact. Needless to say, the last word on the matter has not yet been spoken.

The standard way to proceed in working out these relationships is through macroeconomic modeling. Mathematical models are constructed using the various macroeconomic variables of interest, such as total output, perhaps broken down into several economic subsectors, employment, capital investment, prices, pollution-control costs, etc. The model is then run using historical data, which show how various underlying factors have contributed to the overall rate of growth in the economy. Then the model is rerun under the assumption that the pollution-control expenditures were in fact not made. This comes out with new results in terms of aggregate output growth, employment, and so on, which can be compared with the first run. The differences are attributed to the pollution-control expenditures.

Table 8-3 shows a few results of a recent review study done by the Organization for Economic Cooperation and Development (OECD) pertaining to the macroeconomic costs of environmental expenditures in a number of developed countries. They show the percentage difference in gross domestic product (GDP) with environmental regulations compared to what it would have been without the regulations. Two things stand out. One is that in several countries GDP was actually higher in the year indicated under environmental controls than it would have been without them. This is attributed to the fact that these

TABLE 8-3
EFFECT OF ENVIRONMENTAL REGULATIONS ON GROSS
DOMESTIC PRODUCT, SELECTED OECD COUNTRIES

	Percentage difference of GDP with environmental regulations compared to without
Austria (1985)	−.2
Finland (1982)	.6
France (1974)	.1
Netherlands (1985)	−.6
U.S. (1987)	−.7

Source: Organization for Economic Cooperation and Development, *The Macro-Economic Impact of Environmental Expenditures*, Paris, 1985, p. 27.

years were relatively early in the life of the environmental programs, when the stimulating effect of pollution-control expenditures were still somewhat dominant. The other conclusion is that for countries whose GDP was lower as a result of the environmental programs, the effect was quite small. These results confirm what others have found—that environmental regulations have lowered the growth rates of the countries applying them, but only by relatively small amounts.

SUMMARY

In this chapter we reviewed some of the ways that costs are estimated in benefit–cost studies. We began with a discussion of the fundamental concept of opportunity costs, differentiating this from the notion of cost as expenditure. We then looked at cost estimation as it applied to different levels of economic activity. The first was a cost analysis of a single facility, as represented by the estimated costs of a wastewater treatment facility. We then considered the costs of an environmental regulation undertaken by a single community, distinguishing between costs to the community and opportunity costs to the whole society.

We then shifted focus to cost estimation for an entire industry. We put special attention on the difference between short-run and long-run costs and the problem of achieving minimum costs. We finally expanded our perspective to the national economy as a whole, where cost means the loss in value of marketed output resulting from environmental regulations.

QUESTIONS FOR FURTHER DISCUSSION

1 Suppose that in the example of the waste treatment plant depicted in Table 8-1, the town donated the sludge-disposal land to the operators of the plant at no financial cost. Does this mean that the total opportunity costs of this project would now be $350,000 lower?

2 Suppose that in the local apple orchard problem, the cessation of production by the orchard led to much more land being put on the local market, producing a drop in local land prices. Is this reduction in the value of land in the community a part of the social opportunity cost of the IPM regulation?

3 "The EPA has estimated that a certain pesticide used by farmers leads to an average of 2.1 excess deaths per year among farm workers. This means that banning the pesticide could be expected to lower farm worker deaths by 2.1 per year." Comment.

4 Suppose that a certain environmental regulation results in the closing down of many firms in an industry, leaving just two or three dominant firms. How might this affect the long-run costs of the regulation?

5 A wastewater treatment plant is built for a community thereby improving the water quality in a nearby river. But the plant is a scenic disaster. How might we measure the costs of the plant in terms of losses in scenic quality?

6 "The costs of achieving emission reductions in the future will depend importantly on the types of policies used to reduce emissions today." Explain.

SELECTED READINGS

Babcock, Lyndon R.: "Costs of Pollution Abatement," in George S. Tolley, Philip E. Graves, and Glenn C. Blomquist (eds.), *Environmental Policy, Volume I,* Ballinger, Cambridge, Mass., 1981, pp. 75–91.

Christiansen, G. B., and T. H. Tietenberg: "Distributional and Macroeconomic Aspects of Environmental Policy," in Allen V. Kneese and James L. Sweeney (eds.), *Handbook of Natural Resource and Energy Economics,* Vol. 1, North-Holland, Amsterdam, 1985, pp. 345–393.

Kneese, Allen V.: "Costs of Water Quality Improvement, Transfer Functions and Public Policy," in Henry M. Peskin and Eugene P. Seskin (eds.), *Cost Benefit Analysis and Water Pollution Policy,* The Urban Institute, Washington, D.C., 1975, pp. 175–206.

Palmer, Karen L., and Alan J. Krupnick: "Environmental Costing and Electric Utilities' Planning and Investment," *Resources,* 105, Resources for the Future, Washington, D.C., Fall 1991.

ENVIRONMENTAL POLICY ANALYSIS

The public policy problem arises when there is a discrepancy between the actual level of environmental quality and the preferred level. How to change this state of affairs? Something has to be done to change the way people behave on both the production and consumption sides of the system. The available public policy approaches for doing this are as follows:

Liability laws
Property rights
Moral suasion
Standards
Incentive-based policies
  Taxes and subsidies
  Transferable discharge permits.

In the chapters of this section we will discuss each of these policy approaches. But before that we must address briefly a prior question: What criteria do we use to evaluate alternative policies and identify the one best suited to any particular environmental problem? We consider a number of these criteria in the next chapter, then analyze in depth the specific policy approaches listed above.

CHAPTER 9

CRITERIA FOR EVALUATING ENVIRONMENTAL POLICIES

One way of thinking of different environmental policies is along a centralized/decentralized continuum. A centralized policy requires that some central administrative agency take the lead in determining what is to be done and how. A decentralized policy derives results from the interaction of many individual decision makers, each of whom is essentially making her own assessment of the situation. The classic case of a centralized system is that of environmental *standards*, established and enforced by central authorities. At the other end of the spectrum are *property-rights approaches*; once the basic laws and enforcement machinery have been put in place, individual decisions determine how these rights will be distributed and what the effect will be on environmental quality. The significance of this difference will come out more as we discuss the specific criteria for evaluating policy, which are:

- Their ability to achieve efficient and cost-effective reductions in pollution.
- Their fairness.
- The incentives they offer to people to search for better solutions.
- Their enforceability.
- The extent to which they agree with certain moral precepts.

EFFICIENCY

By "efficiency" we mean the balance between abatement costs and damages. An efficient policy is one that moves us to, or near, the point (either of emissions or of ambient quality) where marginal abatement costs and marginal damages are equal. To discover where this point is we must know both costs and damages. In a centralized policy approach the burden is usually on an administrative agency to make this determination. In policies that rely on decentralized decisions information about costs and damages arises out of the interactions of the people involved.

It is often the case that we cannot effectively measure damages produced by environmental degradation. This pushes us back to the use of cost-effectiveness as a primary policy criterion. A policy is cost-effective if it produces the maximum environmental improvement possible for the resources being expended or, equivalently, it achieves a given amount of environmental improvement at the least possible cost. For a policy to be efficient it must be cost-effective, but not necessarily vice versa. A policy might be cost-effective even if it were aimed at the wrong target. Suppose we decided to clean up New York harbor, regardless of what the benefits are. We would still be interested in finding policies that did the job cost-effectively. But for a policy to be socially efficient, it must not only be cost-effective, it must also balance costs with benefits. To be efficient, the harbor-cleaning project must balance marginal benefits with marginal cleanup costs.

The capability of a policy to achieve cost-effective emission reductions, besides yielding the maximum improvement for the resources spent, is also important for another reason. If programs are not cost-effective, the policymakers and administrators will be making decisions using an aggregate abatement cost function that is higher than it needs to be, leading them to set less restrictive targets in terms of desired amounts of emission reductions. This is shown in Figure 9-1, for a case of SO_2 emissions. With a cost-*in*effective policy the perceived marginal abatement cost is the higher one, labeled MAC_1, whereas with a cost-effective approach marginal abatement costs would be MAC_2. Thus, with the MD function as shown, the emissions level a_1 appears to be the efficient level of pollution, whereas with a cost-effective program the efficient level would be a_2. The real problem with having costs higher than they need to be is that we will

FIGURE 9-1
Mistaking the Efficient Emissions Level When Abatement Technologies Are
Not Cost-Effective.

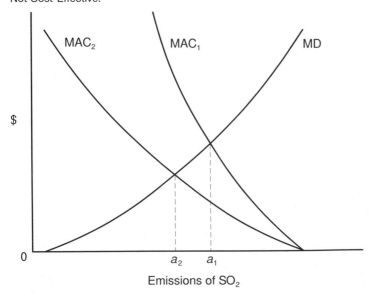

Emissions of SO_2

be inclined to set our objectives too low in terms of the amount of emission reduction we seek.

Efficiency and cost-effectiveness are important because, although preserving environmental resources is critically important, it is only one of the many desirable things that people seek. Advocates are usually convinced that their objectives are automatically worth the cost, but success depends on persuading large numbers of other people that environmental policies are efficiently designed. Thus, the resources devoted to environmental quality improvement ought to be spent in ways that will have the greatest impact. This is especially important in less-developed economies, where people have fewer resources to put in environmental programs and can ill-afford policies that are not cost-effective and efficient. Cost-effectiveness also becomes an important issue in industrialized countries during times of recession or economic stagnation.

FAIRNESS

Fairness, or equity, is another important criterion for evaluating environmental policy (or any policy, for that matter). Equity is a matter of morality and the regard that relatively well-off people have for those less fortunate. In a sense it is also a concern for policy effectiveness, because policies may not be supported as enthusiastically in the political arena if they are thought to be inequitable. Having said this, however, we have to recognize that there is no agreement on how much weight we should put on the two objectives: efficiency and distribution. Consider the following hypothetical numbers, which might relate, for example, to the costs and benefits of several alternative approaches to air pollution control in a given region.

Program	Total costs	Total benefits	Net benefits	Distribution of net benefits	
				Low income	High income
A	50	100	50	25	25
B	50	100	50	30	20
C	50	140	90	20	70
D	50	140	90	40	50

The first three columns show total costs, total benefits, and net benefits, respectively. Programs A and B have the same net benefits, but these are distributed more progressively in B than in A. We might agree that B is preferable to A because it has the same net benefits and "better" distributional effects. But compare Programs B and C. The net benefits of Program C are much higher than in B. Unfortunately, they are not distributed as progressively as those of B; in fact, they are distributed more toward higher-income people. If we had to choose between B and C, which should we pick? Some might argue that we should take B for distributional reasons, others might argue for C on overall efficiency grounds. Or compare Programs B and D. In this case, D has the advantage in overall efficiency, although, as in the case of C, more of the net benefits go to higher-income people. But here we also see that low-income people would be better off in absolute terms, though not relatively, with D than with B. On these grounds we might prefer D.

It is an open question how much emphasis we should put on the distributional impacts of environmental policy compared to their other characteristics. On one side is the argument that environmental degradation is so pervasive that we should focus primarily on policies that are the most efficient, that give us the most impact for the resources spent. On the other is the position that we should avoid policies, even efficient ones, that have a (strongly?) regressive impact. Whatever one feels about these distributional impacts, and it does depend on personal values to a great extent, we need to keep in mind that distributional considerations should have some weight in the selection of environmental policies.

Equity considerations also loom large in the making of international environmental policy. As we will discuss later in chapters on global and international environmental problems, countries at different stages of development have different views on how the burdens of international pollution-control programs should be distributed. These views are driven by considerations of what seems fair in the light of the wide economic disparities around the globe.

It is usually very difficult to determine the ultimate distributional impacts of any environmental policy. Take, for example, the regulations of airborne emissions from electric power plants. These regulations will increase the costs of electricity, and it may not be too hard to estimate the effect on different income groups because we have pretty good data on electricity consumption by these groups (but suppose the item is something like apples, about which very little relative consumption information is available?). Of course, even here we would run into some difficulty, because consumers will engage in some amount of energy conservation to escape the effects of the higher price. On the benefit side, we have to know how much the regulation will change ambient conditions for people in different income groups, and this kind of information is very difficult to obtain.

The relative scarcity of information on the distributional impacts of environmental policies argues for putting more effort into finding out what they are. Recently the U.S. Environmental Protection Agency has moved in this direction, though it has not yet become part of official policy. To the normal benefit–cost analyses of environmental regulations, it has suggested adding a "population distribution analysis" where appropriate.[1] This means an analysis that shows how the total benefits and costs of a regulation are distributed among various income, ethnic, and racial groups within society. If this effort is pursued with

---

[1] U.S. Environmental Protection Agency, *Environmental Equity, Reducing Risk for All Communities*, EPA 230-R-92-008, Washington, D.C., June 1992, p. 28.

vigor, we should be able over time to build up a body of results about efficiency–equity trade-offs in environmental policies.

INCENTIVES FOR IMPROVEMENTS

In studying environmental policy much of the focus normally gets cast on the performance of public officials, since they appear to be the source of that policy. We need to keep clearly in mind, however, that it is private parties, firms, and consumers whose decisions actually determine the range and extent of environmental impacts,[2] and the incentives facing these private parties determine how and where these impacts will be reduced. Thus, a critically important criterion that must be used to evaluate any environmental policy is whether that policy provides a strong incentive for individuals and groups to find new, innovative ways of reducing their impacts on the ambient environment. Does the policy place all the initiative and burden on public agencies, or does it provide incentives for private parties to devote their energies and creativities to finding new ways of reducing environmental impacts?

We can miss the importance of this sometimes when we concentrate on the abatement cost and damage functions in our standard analysis. These show the efficient level of emissions according to the current functions, but over the longer run it is important that we try to shift the functions. It's especially important to try to shift downward the marginal abatement cost function, to make it cheaper to secure reductions in emissions, because this will justify higher levels of environmental quality. Technological change, flowing from programs of research and development (R&D), shifts the marginal abatement cost function downward. So do education and training, which allow people to work and solve problems more efficiently. So ultimately we want to know whether, and how much, a particular environmental policy contains incentives for polluters to seek better ways of reducing pollution. The greater these incentives, the better the policy, at least by this one criterion.

ENFORCEABILITY

There perhaps is a natural tendency among people to think that enacting a law automatically leads to the rectification of the problem to which it is addressed. Among the environmental community this tendency is depressingly strong. It extends even among environmental economists, who have often implicitly assumed in their policy discussions that polluters will more or less automatically comply with whatever laws are enacted. A moment's reflection should convince us that this isn't so, even in countries that have relatively strong legal traditions and institutions. Enforcement requires energy and resources, just like any other

---

[2] Though we must keep in mind that many serious cases of environmental destruction have been caused by public agencies.

activity, and there will always be other calls on these resources. Furthermore, there will always be people whose interests lie in not having environmental policies enforced. Thus, enforcement is unlikely to happen automatically.

It's difficult to get good information on enforcement and compliance behavior. The few studies that have been done show that there is cause for concern. In a 1983 study the General Accounting Office (GAO) surveyed a large number of major wastewater dischargers in the country to determine if they were complying with existing laws. They found that a substantial fraction (more than one-third) of the sources were not in compliance.[3] Other studies of enforcement activities by the states, which are often relied upon to enforce both state and federal environmental laws, show that enforcement activity is far less energetic than we might hope, certainly far less than would be required to ensure a high rate of compliance. The reason, of course, is that enforcement is costly.

Environmental economists at Resources for the Future (RFF) recently surveyed a large number of state enforcement agencies to determine common practices and costs associated with enforcing pollution-control regulations.[4] A very widespread practice is for agencies to require self-reporting of emissions by firms, with the public authorities carrying out periodic audits of these records and perhaps also periodic testing of emissions. Table 9-1 shows some of the results of the RFF survey. The number of sources for which enforcing agencies were responsible varied enormously, with an average of 4,550 for air pollution sources and 1,770 for sources of water pollution. The costs per audit visit depended on whether the visit included the measurement of emissions along with the investigation of the firm's own records. The costs per visit averaged $155 and $301 for, respectively, air and water sources, when there was no emission

---

[3] U.S. General Accounting Office, *Wastewater Discharges Are Not Complying with EPA Pollution Control Permits*, Washington, D.C., 1983.

[4] Clifford Russell, Winston Harrington, and William J. Vaughn, *Enforcing Pollution Control Laws*, Resources for the Future, Washington, D.C., 1986.

TABLE 9-1
SURVEY INFORMATION ON STATE ENFORCEMENT AGENCIES, 1982

| Type of source | Number of sources for which agency was responsible | | Costs per audit visit | |
	Average	Range	When no discharges were measured	When discharges were measured
Air	4,550	40–8,140	$155 ($129)[*]	$1,725 ($1,042)
Water	1,770	220–3,900	$301 ($324)	$ 955 ($932)

[*]Numbers in parentheses are standard deviations.

Source: Clifford S. Russell, Winston Harrington, and William J. Vaughn, *Enforcing Pollution Control Laws*, Resources for the Future, Washington, D.C., 1986, pp. 50–57.

monitoring. But these jumped to $1,725 for air and $955 for water sources when emission measurement was also carried out. There was an enormous variation in these costs among agencies, however.

These results show that enforcement costs are an important segment of environmental quality programs. Public agencies virtually everywhere face budget stringencies, but also responsibilities which are large and continually growing. Thus, the costs of enforcement, though perhaps not as large as overall compliance costs in most cases, are critical to the success of environmental quality programs and ought to be treated explicitly in evaluating the overall social costs of these programs.

The reason for pursuing this is that policies differ in terms of how easy it is to enforce them. Some may require sophisticated technical measures to get reasonable enforcement, others may be enforceable at much lower cost. There is no sense in attempting a dazzling new policy approach if it is essentially impossible, or very costly, to enforce. We may be better off settling for a less perfect policy that is more easily enforceable. There are two main steps in enforcement: *monitoring* and *sanctioning*. Monitoring refers to measuring the performance of polluters in comparison to whatever requirements are set out in the relevant law. Sanctioning refers to the task of bringing to justice those whom monitoring has shown to be in violation of the law. The objective of enforcement is to get people to comply with an applicable law. Thus, some amount of monitoring is normally essential; the only policy for which this does not hold is that of moral suasion. Monitoring polluting behavior is far more complicated than, say, keeping track of the temperature. Nature doesn't really care, and so it won't willfully try to outwit and confound the monitoring process. But polluters, who are intelligent human beings and who may stand to lose money if environmental laws are vigorously enforced, can usually find many ways of frustrating the monitoring process. And the more sophisticated and complicated that process, the easier it may be for polluters to find ways of evading it.

The other main part of enforcement is sanctioning polluters who are in violation of the law. This may sound like a simple step; if violators are found, we simply take them to court and levy the penalties specified in the relevant law. But things are much more complicated than this. Court cases take time and energy and resources. With many laws and many more violators, the burden on the legal system of trying to bring all violators to justice may be overwhelming. Violators are also reluctant participants; they may devote many resources to fighting the sanctions, turning the procedure into long, drawn-out, costly court battles. In many cases the data underlying the sanctions will be imperfect, leading to challenges and costly conflicts. To create a demonstration effect it may be desirable for authorities to sanction only a few of the most egregious violations, but this opens up the problem of trying to determine just which violators to single out. It is perhaps no wonder that in the real world many violators, especially first-time violators, are not sanctioned with the full penalties allowed by the law. Very often authorities try to achieve voluntary compliance and encourage violators to remedy the situation without penalty.

There is a paradox built into the sanctioning process. One might think that the greater the potential sanctions—higher fines, long jail terms for violators, etc.—the more the law would deter violators. But the other side of the coin is that the higher the penalties the more reluctant courts may be to apply them. The threat to close down violators, or even to levy stiff financial penalties, can in turn threaten the economic livelihoods of large numbers of people. Courts are usually reluctant to throw a large number of people out of work, and so may opt for less drastic penalties than allowed by the law. So the sanctioning process can become much more complicated than the simple model implies.

MORAL CONSIDERATIONS

We earlier discussed questions of income distribution and the impacts of different environmental policies on people with different levels of wealth. These are ethical issues on which different people will feel differently, but they are important to discuss when deciding on alternative public policies. But moral considerations extend beyond these distributional questions. The innate feelings that people have about what is right and wrong undoubtedly affect the way they look at different environmental policies. These have to be weighed in the balance along with the more technical criteria we have discussed above.

Take, for example, the question of choosing between effluent taxes and effluent subsidies. Both are economic incentive-type policies, and both might have roughly the same effect in given cases of pollution control. From the standpoint of effectiveness, one might argue that subsidies would be better. Polluters might very well respond quicker and with greater willingness to a subsidy program than to one that is likely to cost them a lot of money. Strictly from the standpoint of getting the environment cleaned up as soon as possible, subsidies might be the most effective. But this may run counter to the ethical notion that people who are causing a problem ought not to be "rewarded" for stopping, which is how subsidies are sometimes viewed.

Some people would take this idea further, arguing that, since we should regard polluting behavior as essentially immoral to begin with, we should adopt policies that tend to recognize it as such.[5] By this criterion, policies that declare outright that certain types of polluting behavior are illegal are to be preferred to policies that do not. Another idea grounded in morality is that those who cause a problem ought to bear the major burden of alleviating it. We see this, for example, in discussions of global environmental issues. The industrial nations, especially the most economically developed among them, are largely responsible for the atmospheric buildup of CO_2, and the deterioration of the protective ozone layer. Many people take the view that these countries ought to bear the major burden in rectifying the situation.

With these criteria in hand, we are now ready to launch into a study of

[5] Steven Kelman, *What Price Incentives? Economists and the Environment*, Auburn House, Boston, 1981.

different types of environmental policies. We begin with several traditional decentralized approaches, after which we investigate the use of environmental standards, the approach most frequently resorted to in the past. Finally, we look at what are called economic-incentive types of policies.

QUESTIONS FOR FURTHER DISCUSSION

1 "Efficiency implies cost-effectiveness but cost-effectiveness does not imply efficiency." Explain this statement.
2 If the net benefits of a particular environmental program were found to be regressively distributed among different income groups, would this be sufficient grounds to oppose the program?
3 Besides having different impacts on people at different income levels, environmental policies could also have varying impacts in different regions of a country. How might a federal policy, applied uniformly across a country, have different impacts in different regions?
4 Some people have stressed that "political feasibility" ought to be a criterion in designing environmental policies. Discuss this.
5 Ultimately, it is the policy process itself that must determine the weight to be put on different policy criteria. What is the role of the policy analyst in facilitating this decision?

SELECTED READINGS

Bernstein, Janis: "Alternative Approaches to Pollution Control and Waste Management: Regulatory and Economic Instruments," World Bank, Infrastructure and Urban Development Department, Washington, D.C., Discussion Paper INU 79, May 1991.

Bohm, Peter, and Clifford S. Russell: "Comparative Analysis of Alternative Policy Instruments," in Allen V. Kneese and James L. Sweeney (eds.), *Handbook of Natural Resources and Energy Economics*, Vol. 1, North-Holland, Amsterdam, 1985, pp. 395–460.

Congressional Research Service: "Summaries of Environmental Laws Administered by the Environmental Protection Agency," Washington, D.C., Library of Congress, March 27, 1989.

Dewees, Donald N.: "Instrument Choice in Environmental Policy," *Economic Inquiry*, 21(1), January 1983, pp. 53–71.

Eskeland, Gunnar, and Emanuel Jimenez: "Choosing Among Policy Instruments in Pollution Control: A Review," World Bank, Country Economics Department, June 20, 1990.

Organization for Economic Cooperation and Development: *Environmental Policies for Cities in the 1990s*, Paris, 1990.

Ruff, Larry E.: "The Economic Common Sense of Pollution," *The Public Interest*, No. 19, Spring 1970, pp. 69–85.

CHAPTER 10

DECENTRALIZED POLICIES: LIABILITY LAWS, PROPERTY RIGHTS, MORAL SUASION

By "decentralized" policies we mean policies which essentially allow the individuals involved in a case of environmental pollution to work it out themselves. Think back to the example we used in previous chapters of water quality in a lake. Suppose there are several industrial plants around the lake. One is a food processing plant, and the water of the lake is an important input in its operation. The other is an industrial operation that uses the lake for waste disposal. How can we balance the pollution damage suffered by the first firm with the abatement costs of the second? A decentralized approach to finding the efficient level of ambient water quality in the lake is simply to let the two plants work it out between themselves. They might do this either through informal negotiations or through more formal interaction in a local court of law. Decentralized approaches like this have the advantage that the people directly involved are the ones who may know the most about damages and abatement costs, and therefore can presumably find the right balance between them. Sometimes decentralized approaches can be very effective. But not always.

LIABILITY LAWS

Almost everybody has an intuitive notion of liability and compensation. To be liable for some behavior is to be held responsible for whatever untoward consequences result from that behavior. Questions of liability are usually worked out in the courts. The party claiming damage proceeds against the party it believes to be responsible, and judges and juries decide according to whatever provisions of common and statutory law are applicable.

One approach to environmental issues, therefore, is to rely on liability laws. This would work simply by making polluters liable for the damages they cause. The purpose of the laws is not simply to compensate people after they have been injured, though that is important. The real purpose is to get would-be polluters to make careful decisions. Knowing that they will be held liable for environmental damages in effect internalizes what would otherwise be ignored external effects.

Consider Figure 10-1. It's our familiar model of environmental pollution showing marginal abatement costs and marginal damages, both related to the rate at which some production residual is emitted. Suppose that the actual emission rate is initially at e_1, substantially above the efficient rate e^*. Suppose further that we now invoke a liability law that requires polluters to compensate those damaged in an amount equal to the damages caused. The effect of the law is to internalize the environmental damages that were external before the law. They now become costs that polluters will have to pay, and so will want to take into account when deciding on their emission rate. At e_1 the total damages, and hence the amount of the compensation payment, would be a monetary amount equal to the area $b + c + d$. This polluter could reduce its compensation payments by reducing emissions. As it does that, of course, its marginal abatement costs increase. But as long as the marginal abatement costs are less than marginal damages, it would have an incentive to move to the left; i.e., to reduce its rate of emissions. In theory, then, a liability system could automatically lead this polluter to emission level e^*. We say "automatically" because it would not require any centralized control authorities to intervene and mandate emission reductions. It requires rather a system of decentralized courts and liability laws that would permit those damaged by pollution to seek compensation for damages suffered.

Theoretically, this approach appears to address the incentive question—getting people to take into account the environmental damages they may cause—as well as the question of compensating those who are damaged. It also appears to

FIGURE 10-1
Policy Options: Liability and Property-Rights Approaches.

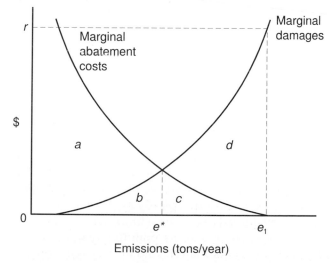

solve the problem of determining just where e^* is along the emission axis. This would be discovered as a result of the interactions in court of polluters and those damaged. Both sides would present evidence and claims which, assuming the court is impartial, would lead to something approaching the efficient level of emissions.

The requirement that polluters be held liable for damages may be part of a country's basic legal code, or it could be provided through special statutory enactments. In common-law countries such as the U.S. and the United Kingdom, doctrines of nuisance and liability have been developed through the evolution of court decisions. This law now recognizes the difference between *strict liability*, which holds people responsible for damages regardless of circumstances, and *negligence*, which holds them responsible only if they did not take appropriate steps to avoid damage. A firm disposing of hazardous materials might be held strictly liable for damages done by these wastes. Thus, any damages that resulted, regardless of how careful the firm had been in disposing of the waste, would require compensation. On the other hand, negligence would hold it responsible only if it failed to take appropriate steps to ensure that the materials did not escape into the surrounding environment.

In civil-law countries liability requirements may be written into the appropriate parts of the code. And in any country environmental laws may specify conditions under which polluters may be held liable for damages. We will talk in Chapter 18 about the pollution-liability laws of Japan and the Netherlands. Many countries, individually and in international agreements, have sought to use liability policy to address the problem of maritime oil spills. Several international conventions have been devoted to specifying the liability requirements of companies whose tankers release, accidentally or not, large quantities of oil into the sea. And many countries have individually enacted laws specifying liability of their oil companies for damages from spills in coastal waters. One particularity of oil tanker spills is that it is very difficult to monitor the behavior of the polluters in this case. It is an episodic emission, so there is no continuous flow to measure, and spill probabilities depend on many practices (navigation, tanker maintenance, etc.) that are difficult for public authorities to monitor continuously. When polluter behavior is extremely difficult to monitor, we nevertheless would like to know that the polluters have undertaken all appropriate steps to reduce the probability of accidents. To provide the incentive for this, the most appropriate response may be to rely on a system of strict liability.

But a number of factors work against a wholesale reliance on liability to solve environmental problems. The critical factors in a liability system are where the burden of proof lies and what standards have to be met in order to establish that proof. In the U.S., those who believe they may have been injured by pollution must file an action within a specified time period, typically 2 or 3 years, and then in court must establish a direct causal link between the pollution and the damage. This involves two major steps: first to show that the polluting material was a direct cause of their damage, and then that the material did in fact come from the specific defendant that appears in court. Both steps are difficult because the standards of proof required by the courts may be more than current science can supply. Most chemicals, for example, are implicated in increased disease only on a *probabilistic* basis; i.e., exposure to the substance involves an increased probability of disease, not certainty. Even though we "know" that smoking "causes" lung cancer, for example, this causal link remains probabilistic; an increased number of people will get lung cancer if they smoke, but we can't tell exactly which ones. In Woburn, Massachusetts, contamination of well water was estimated by some epidemiologists to have probably caused 6 of the 12 excess cases of leukemia in the town. But under traditional standards of proof, a plaintiff could not conclusively prove that a *specific* cancer was caused by the water contamination. In other words, without being able to show explicitly how the polluting material operated in a particular body to produce cancer, the plaintiff cannot meet the standard of proof historically required in U.S. courts.[1]

The other link in the causal chain is to show that the material to which one was exposed came from a particular source. This won't be difficult in some cases; the oil on the Alaskan shoreline definitely came from the Exxon Valdez wreck, the hazy atmosphere over the Grand Canyon definitely comes from the power plant, etc. But in many cases this direct linkage is unknown. For an urban dweller in New York or Los Angeles, which specific industrial plant produced the SO_2 molecules that a particular person may have breathed? For the people living in towns of the Connecticut Valley, which specific tobacco farms were responsible for the chemicals that showed up in their water supply? Without being able to trace a polluting substance to specific defendants, those who have been damaged by it may be unable to obtain compensation.

Another major point to make about liability systems can best be understood by introducing the concept of *transactions costs*. In general terms transactions costs are the costs of reaching and enforcing agreements. The concept was first introduced in economics to apply to the costs that buyers and sellers encounter in making a successful transaction—costs of searching out information, costs of bargaining over terms, and costs of making sure an agreement is actually carried out. But the transactions costs also apply to liability systems where plaintiffs and defendants are competing in a court of law to determine the question of liability and the appropriate amounts of compensation. In this case transactions costs are all the legal costs associated with gathering evidence, presenting a case, challenging opponents, awarding and collecting damages, etc.

If we are dealing with simple cases, with one party on each side and a reasonably clear case of damage, the liability system may function, with a minimum of transactions costs, to give something approaching the efficient level of emissions. In the case of the two small factories on a small lake, the two can

---

[1] In some cases the law is beginning to change to recognize the special characteristics of pollution-caused damage. For example, statutes of limitation are being changed to count from the time the disease first becomes apparent, in recognition of the fact that many pollution-caused diseases may not show up for many years after exposure. Some courts are also beginning to allow statistical cause-and-effect linkages.

go to court and argue about the economic values to each of them of using the lake for their purposes. And since these values are comparable, it presumably would not be too difficult for a judge to determine the extent of the damages that the one firm is inflicting on the other. But things are very different when large numbers of people are involved on one or both sides of an issue. In the case of the Exxon Valdez oil spill, for example, probably tens of thousands of people regard themselves as having been directly damaged, hundreds of lawyers represent all the different sides, and numerous environmental groups, government organizations, and business groups are involved, as Exhibit 10-1 makes clear. At the end of a very long series of court battles some compensation will be paid. But the transactions costs will be enormous, and at the end of the process the compensation probably won't accurately reflect real damages. This is no doubt why the major parties tried to settle this case with a lump-sum agreement relatively early in the process, although continuing lawsuits are not ruled out.

We may rely on private liability arrangements to identify efficient pollution levels when relatively few people are involved, causal linkages are clear, and damages are easy to measure. These conditions may be met in some localized cases of pollution, but for most cases of environmental externalities they are not, and so we must consider other means of arranging relationships between polluters and the people they affect.

PROPERTY RIGHTS

In the previous section we discussed the case of a small lake which one firm used for waste disposal and another for a water supply. On deeper thought we are led to a more fundamental question: Which one of the firms is really causing damage and which firm is the one suffering damages? This may sound counterintuitive because you might naturally think that the waste-disposing firm is of course the one causing the damage. But we might argue just as well that the presence of the food-processing firm inflicts damages on the waste-disposing firm because its presence makes it necessary for the latter to take special efforts to control its emissions. (Assume for purposes of argument that there are no other people, like homeowners or recreators, using the lake.) The problem may come about simply because it is not clear who has the initial right to use the services of the lake; that is, who effectively owns the property rights to the lake. When someone owns a resource, she has a strong incentive to see to it that it is managed in a way that gives it the maximum value. To solve the problem of lake pollution, therefore, it may be sufficient simply to specify clearly who has the rights of ownership to the lake.

Private property rights are, of course, the dominant institutional arrangement in most developed economies of the West. Developing countries also are moving in that direction, as are even the ex-Socialist countries. So we are familiar with the operation of that institutional system when it comes to person-made assets such as machines, buildings, and consumer goods. Private property in land is also a familiar arrangement. If somebody owns a piece of land, he has an

EXHIBIT 10-1

EXXON VALDEZ'S SEA OF LITIGATION

Bickering among Lawyers Has Added to the Tension.

By Barnaby J. Feder

Can a bartender in Anchorage claim damages for tips he might have received from fishermen thrown out of work as a result of the Exxon Valdez spill?

What about California drivers who had to pay sharply higher gasoline prices after the Valdez grounding temporarily closed the port of Valdez and interrupted the flow of North Slope oil to California refineries?

And how about citizens of other states who have no plans to ever visit Alaska, but who, because of the spill, no longer have the knowledge that they could visit an unsullied region. What of the "bequest value" such knowledge would bring to future generations?

These are just a few of the legal questions stemming from the grounding of the Valdez in Prince William Sound on March 24 and the disgorgement of 11 million gallons of Alaskan crude oil into its pristine waters. The lawsuits began proliferating within days of the spill as lawyers from across the nation rushed to the scene.

"One of the mayors up there told me that the only thing worse than the oil hitting the shore was the wave of gray-flanneled lawyers that came next," said T. Barry Kingham, a lawyer with the New York firm of Curtis, Mallet-Prevost, Colt and Mosie. Mr. Kingham is not involved with the Exxon litigation but is one of the many lawyers who expects it to drag on into the next century. And he is in a better position than most to know why. He represents the French fishermen and villagers suing Amoco in the still unsettled litigation in the United States District Court in Chicago that began 11 years ago when the Amoco Cadiz ran aground off the Brittany coast.

The Amoco Cadiz case involved a spill seven times larger than the one in Alaska, but the latter may well involve more extensive environmental damage and more complicated interactions between state and Federal law. Already, it involves far more types of plaintiffs and byzantine negotiations among high-powered law firms from all over the country over how to share both the work and control over litigation strategy. "You have to ask whether the legal system is set up to cope with something like this," Mr. Kingham said.

"It will be a fun case, a chance to do some good for the public, but I don't think it's going to be very remunerative for plaintiffs' lawyers," said Stephen D. Susman, a Houston lawyer who was an early leader among the class-action plaintiffs' lawyers but was forced to drop out because of a conflict.

"Alaska is a funny place — they love the environment but they also love the oil industry and they won't want to punish it too badly," Mr. Susman said. "Spill cases tend to have their maximum value in the early days when there are dead birds on television. There's going to be real questions in this case on how you measure damages."

That issue alone may drag out the case, and delay the day when lawyers are paid. One solution, according to Mr. Gerry, may be to treat the spill as a running nuisance case in which damages are re-examined and new payments made every few years. "It would be unfair to both Exxon and plaintiffs to try to settle some things quickly because it would be sheer guesswork," said Mr. Gerry.

Whatever the complications, many lawyers believe the Valdez case is unlikely to set any lasting standard for how much it costs the legal system to sort out liabilities after environmental disasters. "Look at Chernobyl," said Professor Schoenbaum, referring to the devastation caused by the 1987 failure of a Soviet nuclear reactor. "It is hard to imagine the legal impact of something like that if it occurred in the United States. We haven't scratched the surface."

Source: New York Times, November 19, 1989. Copyright © 1989 by the New York Times. Reprinted by permission.

incentive to see to it that the land is managed in ways that maximize its value. If somebody comes along and threatens to dump something onto the land, the owner may call upon the law to prevent it if he wants to. By this diagnosis, the problem of the misuse of many environmental assets comes about because of imperfectly specified property rights in those assets.

Consider again the case of the lake and the two firms. Apparently we have two choices for vesting ownership of the lake. It could be owned either by the polluting firm or by the firm using it for a water supply. How does this choice affect the level of pollution in the lake? Would it not lead to zero emissions if owned by the one firm, and uncontrolled emissions if owned by the other? Not if we allow owners and nonowners to negotiate. Of course, this is the very essence of a property rights system. The owner decides how the asset is to be used, and may stop any unauthorized use, but may also negotiate with anybody else who wants access to that asset.

Look again at Figure 10-1. Suppose the marginal damage function refers to all the damages suffered by the brewery—call this Firm A. Assume the marginal abatement cost curve applies to the firm emitting effluent into the lake—call this one Firm B. We have to make some assumption about who owns the lake, Firm A or Firm B. We will see that, *theoretically*, we will get the same quantity of emissions in either case, provided that the two firms can come together and strike a bargain about how the lake is to be used.

In the first case, suppose we assume that Firm B owns the lake. For the moment we need not worry about how this came about, only that this is the way it is. Firm B may use the lake any way it wishes. We can suppose that emissions initially would be at e_1. Firm B is initially devoting no resources at all to emissions abatement. But is this where matters will remain? At this point marginal damages are r, while marginal abatement costs are nil. The straightforward thing for Firm A to do, therefore, is to offer Firm B some amount of money to reduce its effluent stream; for the first ton any amount agreed upon between 0 and r would make both parties better off. In fact, they could continue to bargain over the marginal unit as long as marginal damages exceeded marginal abatement costs. Firm B would be better off by reducing its emissions for any payment in excess of its marginal abatement costs, while any payment less than the marginal damages would make Firm A better off. In this way, bargaining between the owners of the lake (here Firm B) and the people who are damaged by pollution would result in a reduction in effluent to e^*, the point at which marginal abatement costs and marginal damages are equal.

Suppose, on the other hand, that ownership of the lake is vested in Firm A, the firm that is damaged by pollution. In this case we might assume that the owners would allow no infringement of their property; i.e., that the emission level would be zero or close to it. Is this where it would remain? Not if, again, we allow bargaining between owners and others who would like to use the lake. In this case Firm B would have to buy permission from Firm A to place its wastes in the lake. Any price for this lower than marginal abatement costs but higher than marginal damages would make both parties better off. And so, by a similar process of bargaining with, of course, payments now going in the opposite direction, the emissions level into the lake would be adjusted from the low level where it started toward the efficient level e^*. At this point any further adjustment would stop because marginal abatement costs, the maximum the polluters would pay for the right to emit one more ton of effluent, are equal to marginal damages, the minimum Firm A would take in order to allow Firm B to emit this added ton.

So, as we have seen in this little example, if we clearly define who has the property right over the environmental asset and then allow bargaining among owners and prospective users, we will arrive at the efficient level of effluent irrespective of who was initially given the property right. In fact, this is a famous theorem, called the "Coase theorem," after the economist who invented it.[2] The wider implication is that by defining private property rights (not necessarily individual property rights because private *groups* of people could have these rights), we can establish the conditions under which decentralized bargaining can produce efficient levels of environmental quality. This has some appeal. The good part of it is that the people doing the bargaining may know more about the relative values involved—abatement costs and damages—than anybody else, so there is some hope that the true efficiency point will be arrived at. And since it would be a decentralized system, we would not need to have some central bureaucratic organization making decisions that are based mostly on political considerations instead of the true economic values involved. Ideas like this have led some people to recommend widespread conversion of natural and environmental resources to private ownership as a means of achieving their efficient use.

How well is this property rights approach likely to work in practice? As we saw with liability laws, something that looks good in theory may not work well when faced with the complexities of the real world. In order for a property rights approach to work right—i.e., to give us something approaching the efficient level of environmental pollution—essentially three main conditions have to be met:

1 Property rights must be well defined, enforceable, and transferable.
2 There must be a reasonably efficient and competitive system for interested parties to come together and negotiate about how these environmental property rights will be used.
3 There must be a complete set of markets so that private owners may capture all social values associated with the use of an environmental asset.

If Firm A cannot keep Firm B from doing whatever the latter wishes, of course a property rights approach will not work. In other words, owners must be physically and legally able to stop others from encroaching on their property. Owners must be able to sell their property to any would-be buyer. This is especially important in environmental assets. If owners cannot sell the property, this will weaken their incentives to preserve its long-run productivity. This is because any use that does draw down its long-run environmental productivity

[2] See the references at the end of the chapter.

cannot be punished through the reduced market value of the asset. Many economists have argued that this is a particularly strong problem in developing countries; since ownership rights are often "attenuated" (i.e., they do not have all the required characteristics specified above), people do not have strong incentives to see that long-run productivity is maintained.

We saw above that the efficient use of the lake depended on negotiations and agreement between the two interested firms. Negotiating costs, together with the costs of policing the agreement, could be expected to be fairly modest. What we are referring to here is transactions costs, the idea that we introduced in the preceding section. In the simple lake case, transactions costs would probably be low enough that the firms would be able to negotiate on the efficient level of emissions. But suppose we replace Firm A, the firm using the lake as a water supply source, with a community of 50,000 people who use it not only for a water supply, but also for recreational purposes. Now the negotiations must take place between a single polluting firm on one side and 50,000 people, or their representatives, on the other side. For each of these individuals the value of improved water quality is small relative to the value to the firm of polluting the lake. Moreover, the level of water quality in the lake is a public good for these individuals. This seriously increases the transactions costs of negotiating an agreement among different users.

To make matters worse, suppose we replace the one polluting firm with 1,000 polluting firms, together with a few thousand homeowners who are not yet hooked into the public sewer system and so are using septic tanks on the shores of the lake. Here the possibilities of vesting the ownership of the lake in one person, and expecting negotiations between that person and prospective users to find the efficient levels of use, essentially vanish. This is another way of saying that in large and complex cases of environmental degradation, where free-rider problems abound, very high transactions costs will seriously reduce the potential of the private property approach to identify the efficient level of emissions.

For private property institutions to ensure that an environmental asset is put to its best use, the process must also work in such a way that the owner is able to capture the full social value of the resource in that use. Suppose you own a small island in the Florida Keys. There are two possible uses: Develop a resort hotel or devote it to a wildlife refuge. If you build the hotel, you get a direct flow of monetary wealth because the tourism market is well developed in that part of the world and you can expect customers to find your hotel and pay the going rate for your services. But there is no comparable "market" for wildlife refuge services. The value of the island as refuge may well be much higher than its value as resort, in terms of the actual aggregate willingness to pay of all the people in the country and the world. But there is no good way for them to be able to express that value; there is no ready market like the one in the tourism market where they can in effect bid against the tourists who would visit the island. You might think that a nature conservancy could buy up the island if its value as refuge really is higher than its value as hotel. But the nature conservancy runs on the basis of voluntary contributions, and islands and other lands are in effect public goods. We saw earlier that when public goods are involved, voluntary contributions to make something available are likely to be a lot less than its true value, because of free-riding behavior. The upshot is that, while you as an owner could certainly expect to reap the full monetary value of the island as resort, you would not be able to realize its full social value if you held it as a preserve.

Exhibit 10-2 shows a real-world example of this problem. It is about a person in Kansas who owns a piece of land that was one of the largest remaining stretches of virgin land in the country. An 80-acre piece, it had never known the plow. As such it probably had important ecological as well as historical value. But these values, though we all recognize their validity and importance, cannot very well be captured by a private landowner. The basic problem is that there is no way for the full ecological values to be made apparent and expressed in a direct way. Although a private group bid for the land,[3] without success, its budget was limited by its voluntary character and the free-rider problems inherent in preserving what are in effect public goods. But development values are real and immediate. Thus, the private landowner opted for development, in spite of the ecological and historical value of the property.

This example is actually a local version of a larger problem that has global significance. Much attention has been focused in recent years on biological diversity and the stock of unique genetic material contained in the millions of animal and plant species worldwide. A disproportionately large share of these species is located in developing countries. But these are countries also where development pressures have led to high rates of land clearance and habitat destruction. When landholders in these countries are considering their options, they weigh the value of the land in different uses. Unfortunately, there is no way at present that they can capture the value of the land left as species habitat. No ready economic markets exist where these services can be sold; if they did, landholders could reap private benefits from keeping land undeveloped or using land in ways that are consistent with the preservation of species.

One role for public authorities in this situation might be to create the demand side for such a market. This could be done by offering to pay the landowners an amount equal to the wider ecological value of the land, provided these ecological values were not impaired by the landholders' use of the land. Of course, this would involve enormous difficulties in measuring these ecological values with some degree of accuracy, as well as in finding sources of funds to pay for these services. But without these kinds of market or marketlike institutions, private property rights institutions are unable to give society the fully efficient amounts of preservation and environmental quality.[4]

---

[3] The group is the Nature Conservancy, which seeks to protect sensitive resources from damage by buying them outright. Over the last few decades it has acquired more than 5.5 million acres of land in the U.S. and Canada; some has been transferred to other public and private conservation groups; the rest still belongs to the Nature Conservancy.

[4] Recently a private U.S. drug company agreed to pay the government of a Latin American country certain sums of money for plant species useful in drug development. We will discuss this in Chapter 20.

EXHIBIT 10-2

IGNORING PLEAS OF ENVIRONMENTALISTS, KANSAS MAN DIGS UP VIRGIN PRAIRIE

Special to The New York Times

LAWRENCE, Kan., Nov. 22 — The largest remaining stretch of virgin prairie in northeast Kansas disappeared under the plow this week after futile attempts by the Nature Conservancy and local environmentalists to buy it.

The plowing of the 80-acre Elkins Prairie was first noticed soon after sunrise on Sunday, and the news quickly spread to a community group that had worked for two years to preserve the land, one of the few remaining unspoiled pieces of the 200 million acres of tall grass prairie that once covered North America.

Environmentalists hurried to the site and pleaded with the landowner to stop his tractor. The Douglas County Commission called an emergency meeting and after negotiating half the night offered to pay the landowner $6,000 an acre within six months, the equivalent of what developers had recently paid for nearby land.

But the owner, Jack Graham, rejected the offer and resumed plowing. By late Monday, only a small strip of virgin prairie remained.

Home to 150 Plant Species

It's heart-wrenching," said Joyce Wolf, leader of a group that had hoped to buy the land for an environmental education area. "He has stolen a resource from a community."

Mr. Graham, a 39-year-old businessman who bought the land five years ago, declined to comment on his action. His lawyer, Thomas Murray, said Mr. Graham and his family "simply wanted to make their property more productive," but he would not elaborate.

Only about 2 percent of the original tallgrass prairie in North America remains, and Craig Freeman, coordinator of the state's Natural Heritage Program, said the Elkins stretch, about a mile outside this booming college town, was a particularly fine example of the complex prairie ecosystem. It was home to 150 species of plants, including two threatened species, Mead's milkweed and the western prairie fringed orchid.

Federal plant protection laws do not apply to private property that receives no Federal money.

Last year the Nature Conservancy, a national land preservation organization, offered to buy the Elkins Prairie for $3,500 an acre within a year, Ms. Wolf said, a bid that had unintended consequences. The organization's failure to offer a higher price, Mr. Murray said, convinced the Grahams that the land was not as environmentally important as many Lawrence residents believed.

The Kansas director of the conservancy, Alan Pollom, defended the offer, saying it was based on an appraisal. "We can't unjustifiably enrich someone using the funds of a nonprofit organization," he said.

In the past few years Lawrence residents have tried to balance urban growth and preservation of the environment. Home to the University of Kansas, Lawrence has grown 23 percent to nearly 65,000 people since 1980, but development has been tempered by strong community support for preservation.

Philosophy on the Highway

Throughout the day on Monday, people gathered on a corner across the busy two-lane highway from the Elkins Prairie, talking as they watched the tractor work its way back and forth across the land.

"I question the wisdom of plowing up good prairie, but I would defend his right to do it," said Larry Warren, a farmer and neighbor. "It's his land; it's his prerogative."

But Buzz Hoagland, a biology professor at the University of Kansas, argued that individuals have a responsibility to preserve the environment, even at the expense of their own profits.

"It took a couple of million years for this land to evolve to the state it is in today, and it took 48 hours to destroy it," Dr. Hoagland said.

MORAL SUASION

By "moral suasion" we mean programs of persuasion that appeal to a person's sense of moral values or civic duty, to get him to refrain voluntarily from doing things that degrade the environment. The classic case of this is the Smokey the Bear effort of the National Forest Service, a publicity campaign aimed at getting people to be more sensitive about littering in the woods and about avoiding things that would raise the risk of forest fires. While there are fines and penalties for doing these things, the campaign was not based on threats of penalties as much as it was on appealing to people's sense of civic morality. "Don't Be a Litterbug" campaigns are essentially the same type of approach.

In the early days of recycling, communities often mounted voluntary efforts, where appeals were made on the basis of civic virtue. In some cases these efforts were successful; in others they fell flat. Today we are moving in the direction of more mandatory recycling programs, though it is true that they still must rely heavily on moral suasion to get high rates of compliance. Other situations clearly exist where appeals to civic morality may be effective public policy. This is especially the case with "emissions" like litter, where violators are normally scattered throughout a population in a way that makes it impractical to monitor them and detect violations as they occur.

The good thing about moral suasion is that it may have widespread spillover effects. Whereas an effluent tax on a single type of effluent will have no impact on emissions of other types of waste products, appeals to civic virtue for one problem may produce side effects on other situations. People who, through a special publicity campaign, are brought to feel a greater sense of civic virtue when they refrain from littering in cases where they clearly could get away with it may find themselves having the same feelings when they, for example, refrain from sneaking used motor oil into their household waste, or keep the pollution-control systems on their cars in a higher state of repair.

There are problems, however, with relying on moral suasion as a primary policy approach. Not all people are equally responsible from an ethical stand-point. Some people will respond to moral arguments; others will not. The burden of this policy will fall, therefore, on the part of the population that is morally more sensitive; those who respond less to moral arguments will be free riding on the others, enjoying the benefits of others' moral restraint but escaping their rightful share of the burden. What is especially bad about this is the long-run demonstration value. If those who would be responsive to moral arguments are confronted with the sight of widespread moral free riding, this may in the long run tend to erode the general level of civic and moral responsibility. Thus, appeals to the moral responsiveness of people, although perhaps effective in the short run, could actually have the opposite effect in the long run. This is similar to the cynicism that people often feel when new environmental laws are continu-ally put on the books but never enforced.

While moral virtue is its own reward, it is even better if other people know about it. Moral suasion will be more effective in deterring pollution if informa-

---

EXHIBIT 10-3

JOAN BAVARIA'S CRUSADE FOR THE ENVIRONMENT

Social Activist Is Driving Force Behind the Valdez Principles, a Corporate Code of Conduct.

By Stan Hinden

When the Exxon Valdez tanker plowed into a reef in March 1989 and spilled millions of gallons of crude oil into the pristine waters of Prince William Sound, the massive damage to the Alaskan environment set off angry cries across America.

One of the anguished voices belonged to an idealistic Boston money manager named Joan Bavaria, who has spent a decade on the front line of social investing, searching out companies that make safe products and pursue worthy social goals.

Within months of the Valdez spill, as the cries of anger turned to cries for action, the 47-year-old social activist emerged as the driving force behind a new and potent alliance of investors and environmentalists that was formed to force corporations to accept more responsibility for their environmental conduct. The members of the coalition, called Ceres, hold millions of shares of stock in major corporations.

Out of their alliance came the Valdez Principles—a tough 10-point code of conduct that asks corporations to disclose their environmental problems and act decisively to remedy them.

"We are trying, in a very fundamental way, to change the way corporations look at the environment and at their practices around the environment," said Bavaria, whose coalition controls $150 billion in pension and mutual funds and represents environmental groups with some 10 million members.

The stringent standards of the Valdez Principles, the heightened public concern about pollution and new federal cleanup laws have all combined to put environmental issues on the front burner in the board rooms of America.

In the coming year, more than 50 major corporations will get shareholder resolutions from environmental and church groups, asking the companies to sign the Valdez Princi-

---

tion is readily available about emission levels and changes in them.[5] Thus, as a counterpart to campaigns of moral suasion, efforts to measure and publicize emission levels and efforts people take to reduce these emissions are an important adjunct. These factors lie behind the recent attempt by environmental groups in the U.S. to develop an antipollution code of conduct to which companies could voluntarily subscribe. As indicated in the news clipping of Exhibit 10-3, these "Valdez Principles" involve voluntary disclosure of operations that might cause harm to the environment.[6]

It is easy to be cynical about moral suasion as a tool for environmental improvement. In this era of increasing mass society and heightened environmental destruction, tough-minded policymakers are naturally drawn toward

---

[5] Much like the United Way uses the large red thermometer to show the progress of community fund drives.

[6] There may be more than moral suasion involved here; the article mentions the possibility of such things as boycotts and shareholder actions, which have more direct economic implications for targeted companies.

ples. Boiled down, they ask corporations to end air and water pollution, conserve energy, market safe products, pay for damages to the environment and make public reports on their progress.

That is more than many corporations are willing to promise—primarily because they fear they might open themselves to legal problems.

But the principles fit neatly with Bavaria's vision of the future, which is that U.S. corporations will learn to live with tough environmental standards—just as they now live with tough accounting standards.

Bavaria's battle to make the Valdez Principles the standard for corporate behavior will be opposed by many in the corporate world. But few companies and industries will ignore the steadily growing public concern about global warming, acid rain and toxic waste.

Many corporate officials share the view of Harvey Alter, manager for resources policy at the U.S. Chamber of Commerce who said the Valdez Principles showed that Ceres was "naive" about the way companies operate and that companies could achieve the same environmental goals on their own.

"Ceres," he said, "has put up a litmus test in which a company has to say 'yes' or 'no.' It's not that easy."

Up to this point, Bavaria and her colleagues at Ceres (short for Coalition for Environmentally Responsible Economies) have been using persuasion and the threat of shareholder action to gain signers for the Valdez Principles. Bavaria said any thoughts of boycotts would be far in the future.

In the coming year, each of the Fortune 500 companies will be asked by Ceres to fill out a 37-page questionnaire about their environmental problems and policies.

Among the environmental groups that belong to Ceres are the Sierra Club, Friends of the Earth, the National Audubon Society, the National Wildlife Federation and the Wilderness Society.

One of the most powerful demands for corporations to sign the Valdez Principles has come from the $16.4 billion New York City Employees Retirement System fund. The fund has asked the Exxon Corp., Occidental Petroleum Corp. and Champion International Corp. to sign the Valdez Principles.

environmental policies that have more teeth in them. This would probably be a mistake. It perhaps is true that we cannot rely very heavily on moral suasion to produce, e.g., a significant reduction in air pollution in the Los Angeles basin or substantial drops in the use of groundwater-contaminating farm chemicals. But in our search for new effective, concrete, public policy devices to address specific pollution problems, we perhaps underestimate the contribution of the overall climate of public morality and civic virtue. A strong climate in this sense makes it possible to institute new policies and makes it easier to administer and enforce them. From which we can also deduce the importance of politicians and policy-makers in doing things that replenish this moral climate rather than erode it.

SUMMARY

In this chapter we began our exploration of different types of public policies that might be used to combat environmental pollution. We began the chapter with a brief discussion of the criteria we might use to evaluate the effectiveness of alternative environmental policies. While the most important may be the ability of policies to attain efficient levels of emissions, there are other important criteria such as equity considerations, the ability to create incentives for future changes, and enforceability.

In the chapter we discussed two main decentralized types of approaches to environmental quality improvement. The first was to rely on liability rules, which require polluters to compensate those they have damaged. In theory, the threat of liability can lead potential polluters to internalize what would ordinarily be external costs. By weighing relative compensation and abatement costs, polluters would be brought to efficient emission levels. While liability doctrines may work well in simple cases of pollution where few people are involved and cause-and-effect linkages are clear, they are unlikely to work reliably in the large-scale, technically complicated environmental problems of contemporary societies.

The second major approach we discussed was reliance on the institution of private property rights. Looked at from this perspective, environmental externalities are problems only because ownership of environmental assets is often not clearly defined. By establishing clear property rights, owners and others who would like to use environmental assets for various purposes can negotiate agreements that balance the relative costs of different alternatives. Thus, negotiations among parties could theoretically bring about efficient emission rates. But problems of transactions costs, especially related to the public goods aspects of environmental quality, and lack of markets for environmental services work against relying primarily on traditional property rights institutions in environmental quality issues. We will see in a subsequent chapter, however, that some new types of property rights approaches may hold greater promise.

Finally, we mentioned the idea of moral suasion, which may be useful when it is impossible to measure the emissions stemming from particular sources. The problem of moral free riding was discussed, as was the problem of public disclosure as a means of encouraging ethical behavior in environmental matters.

QUESTIONS FOR FURTHER DISCUSSION

1 Neighbors could, relatively easily, negotiate with one another to settle questions of externalities, such as excessive noise or incompatible property development. So why do most communities rely on local laws and regulations to manage these externalities?

2 In the case of a pollutant which has an uncertain effect on people, the courts could put the burden of proof either on the people damaged to show that they indeed were injured or on the polluters to show that the pollutant is not harmful. What difference would this make to the working of the liability system?

3 Suppose a community weighed each resident's solid waste disposal when it was picked up and published the individual totals each year in the local newspaper. Do you think this would lead to a reduction in the total quantity of solid waste disposed of in the community?

4 In the negotiations among property owners and potential users, how are future generations taken into account?

5 Accidents with trucks carrying hazardous wastes have become fairly common. Suppose the perpetrators of any accident of this type are held liable for a sum equal to the average damages done in all such accidents. Would this lead trucking companies to take the efficient amount of precautions against such accidents?[7]

SELECTED READINGS

Anderson, Terry L.: "The Market Process and Environmental Amenities," in Walter E. Block (ed.), *Economics and the Environment: A Reconciliation*, The Fraser Institute, 1990, pp. 137–157.

Anderson, Terry L., and Donald R. Leal: *Free Market Environmentalism*, Pacific Research Institute, San Francisco, 1991.

Coase, Ronald H.: "The Problem of Social Cost," *Journal of Law and Economics*, Vol. 3, October 1960, pp. 1–44.

Dales, J. H.: *Pollution, Property and Prices*, University of Toronto Press, Toronto, 1968.

Hoffman, W. Michael, Robert Frederick, and Edward S. Petry, Jr. (eds.): *The Corporation, Ethics, and the Environment*, Quorum Books, New York, 1990.

Kneese, Allen V., and William D. Schulze: "Ethics and Environmental Economics," in Allen V. Kneese and James L. Sweeney (eds.), *Handbook of Natural Resource and Energy Economics*, Vol. 1, North-Holland, Amsterdam, 1985, pp. 191–220.

Rothbard, Murray N.: "Law, Property Rights, and Air Pollution," in Walter E. Block (ed.), *Economics and the Environment: A Reconciliation*, The Fraser Institute, 1990, pp. 233–279.

Singer, Steven T.: "An Analysis of Common Law and Statutory Remedies for Hazardous Waste Injuries," *Rutgers Law Journal*, 12, Fall 1980, pp. 117–150.

[7] This question is based on a similar one in Tom Tietenberg, *Environmental and Natural Resource Economics*, 3rd ed., Harper Collins, New York, 1992, p. 71.

CHAPTER 11

COMMAND-AND-CONTROL STRATEGIES: THE CASE OF STANDARDS

A "command-and-control" (CAC) approach to public policy is one where, in order to bring about behavior thought to be socially desirable, political authorities simply mandate the behavior in law, then use whatever enforcement machinery—courts, police, fines, etc.—are necessary to get people to obey the law. In the case of environmental policy, the command-and-control approach consists of relying on *standards* of various types to bring about improvements in environmental quality. In general, a standard is simply a mandated level of performance that is enforced in law. A speed limit is a classic type of standard; it sets maximum rates that drivers may legally travel. An emission standard is a maximum rate of emissions that is legally allowed. The spirit of a standard is, if you want people not to do something, simply pass a law that makes it illegal, then send out the authorities to enforce the law.

Figure 11-1 is our familiar graph showing marginal abatement costs and marginal damages related to the rate at which some production residual is emitted into the environment. Suppose that initially the actual level of effluent is at e_1, a rate substantially above the efficient rate of e^*. To achieve e^* the authorities set an emission standard at that level; e^* becomes a mandated upper limit for the emissions of this firm. To enforce this standard we would then send out various enforcement authorities to measure and detect any possible violations of the standard. If infractions are found, the source is fined or subject to some other penalty. Assuming the firm reduces emissions in accordance with the standard, it would be paying an amount equivalent to area *a* per year in total abatement costs. These total abatement costs can be called the *compliance costs* of meeting the standard.

Standards are popular for a number of reasons. They appear to be simple and direct. They apparently set clearly specified targets. They appeal, therefore, to the sense that everybody has of wanting to come directly to grips with environmental pollution and get it reduced. Standards also appear to be congenial to our ethical sense that pollution is bad and ought to be declared illegal. The legal system is geared to operate by defining and stopping illegal behavior, and the standards approach conforms to this mindset. We will see, however, that the

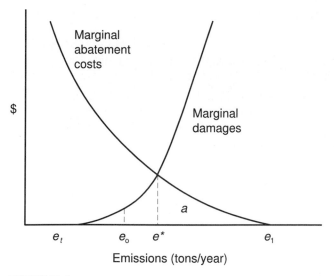

FIGURE 11-1
Emission Standards.

standards approach is a lot more complex than might first appear. In fact, a very
practical reason for the popularity of standards is that they may permit far more
flexibility in enforcement than might be apparent. What appears to be the
directness and unambiguousness of standards becomes a lot more problematic
when we look below the surface.

TYPES OF STANDARDS

Any action you can think of could be the subject of a standard, but in environmental matters there are three main types of standards: ambient, emission, and
technology.

Ambient Standards

Ambient environmental quality refers to the qualitative dimensions of the surrounding environment; it could be the ambient quality of the air over a particular
city, or the ambient quality of the water in a particular river. So an *ambient
standard* is a never-exceed level for some pollutant in the ambient environment.
For example, an ambient standard for dissolved oxygen in a particular river may
be set at 3 parts per million (ppm), meaning that this is the lowest level of
dissolved oxygen that is to be allowed in the river. Ambient standards cannot be
enforced directly, of course. What can be enforced are the various emissions that
lead to ambient quality levels. To ensure that dissolved oxygen never falls below
3 ppm in the river, we must know how the emissions of the various sources on

the river contribute to changes in this measure, then introduce some means of controlling these sources.

Ambient standards are normally expressed in terms of average concentration levels over some period of time. For example, the current national primary ambient air quality standard for sulfur dioxide (SO_2) is 80 $\mu g/m^3$ on the basis of an annual arithmetic mean and 365 $\mu g/m^3$ on a 24-hour average basis.[1] The standard, in other words, has two criteria: a maximum annual average of 80 $\mu g/m^3$ and a maximum 24-hour average of 365 $\mu g/m^3$. The reason for taking averages is to recognize that there are seasonal and daily variations in meteorological conditions, as well as in the emissions that produce variations in ambient quality. Averaging means that short-term ambient quality levels may be worse than the standard, so long as this does not persist for too long and so long as it is balanced by periods when the air quality is better than the standard.

Emission Standards

Emission standards are never-exceed levels applied directly to the quantities of emissions coming from pollution sources. Emission (or effluent) standards are normally expressed in terms of quantity of material per some unit of time; e.g., grams per minute or tons per week. Continuous emissions streams may be subject to standards on "instantaneous" rates of flow; e.g., upper limits on the quantity of residuals flow per minute or on the average residuals flow over some time period.

It is important to keep in mind the distinction between ambient standards and emission standards. Setting emission standards at a certain level does not necessarily entail meeting a set of ambient standards. Between emissions and ambient quality stands nature, in particular the meteorological and hydrological phenomena that link the two. The environment usually transports the emissions from point of discharge to other locations, often diluting and dispersing them along the way. Chemical processes occur in all environmental media that often change the physical character of the pollutant. In some cases this may render the emitted substance more benign. Organic wastes put in rivers and streams will normally be subject to natural degradation processes, which will break them down into constituent elements. Thus, the ambient quality of the water at various points downstream depends on the quantity of emissions as well as the hydrology of the river—its rate of flow, temperature, natural reaeration conditions, and so on.

Sometimes the environment will convert a certain type of pollutant into something more damaging. Research to link emission levels and ambient quality levels is a major part of environmental science.

The link between emissions and ambient quality can also be vitally affected by human decisions. A classic case is automobiles. As part of the mobile-source air-pollution program, we establish emission standards for new cars in terms of emissions per mile of operation. But since we have no way of controlling either

---

[1] $\mu g/m^3$ stands for micrograms per cubic meter.

the number of cars on the roads or the total number of hours each is driven, the aggregate quantity of pollutants in the air and, thus, ambient air quality, is not directly controlled.

Emission standards can be set on a wide variety of different bases; for example:

1 Emission rate (e.g., pounds per hour),
2 Emission concentration (e.g., parts per million of biochemical oxygen demand, or BOD, in wastewater),
3 Total quantity of residuals (rate of discharge times concentration times duration),
4 Residuals produced per unit of output (e.g., SO_2 emissions per kilowatt-hour of electricity produced),
5 Residuals content per unit of input (e.g., sulfur content of coal used in power generation),
6 Percentage removal of pollutant (e.g., 60 percent removal of waste material before discharge).

In the language of regulation, emission standards are a type of *performance standard*, because they refer to end results that are meant to be achieved by the polluters who are regulated. There are many other types of performance standards; for example, workplace standards set in terms of maximum numbers of accidents or levels of risk to which workers are exposed. A requirement that farmers reduce their use of a particular pesticide below some level is also a performance standard, as is a highway speed limit

Technology Standards

There are numerous standards that don't actually specify some end result, but rather the technologies, techniques, or practices that potential polluters must adopt. We lump these together under the heading of "technology standards." The requirement that cars be equipped with catalytic converters, or seat belts, is a technology standard. If all electric utilities were required to install stack-gas scrubbers to reduce SO_2 emissions,[2] these would be in effect technology standards, since a particular type of technology is being specified by central authorities. This type of standard also includes what are often called "design standards" or "engineering standards." There are also a variety of product standards specifying characteristics that goods must have, and input standards that require potential polluters to use inputs meeting specific conditions.

At the edges the difference between a performance standard and a technology standard may become blurred. The basic point of differentiation is that a performance standard, such as an emission standard, sets a constraint on some performance criterion and then allows people to choose the best means of

---

[2] A "scrubber" is a device that treats the exhaust gas stream so as to remove a substantial proportion of the target substance from that stream. The recovered material must then be disposed of elsewhere.

achieving it. A technology standard actually dictates certain decisions and techniques to be used, such as particular equipment or operating practices to be used by polluters. For illustrative purposes, Exhibit 11-1 shows a list of federal standards applicable to retail dealers of agricultural chemicals. Some are emis-

---

EXHIBIT 11-1

STANDARDS APPLICABLE TO RETAIL CHEMICAL HANDLERS, 1992

FIFRA '88 STORAGE, DISPOSAL[a]
(Requires dealer to build dikes, rinse pads, fireproof warehouses, etc.)

PESTICIDE RECORD KEEPING
(Requires dealer to keep detailed records of pesticides sold and applied. The 1990 Farm Bill increases this requirement.)

CERTIFICATION AND TRAINING REQUIRE-MENTS
(Requires dealer and employees to obtain training in various areas of pesticide application.)

OTHER FIFRA REGULATIONS
(Special state laws and EPA policy requirements.)

FARM WORKER PROTECTION
(Requires dealer to train applicators.)

SARA TITLE III COMMUNITY RIGHT-TO-KNOW[b]
(Requires dealers of chemicals to report quantities of all chemicals held on site.)

OSHA REGULATIONS[c]
(Requires training of employees and safety equipment.)

DOT HAZARDOUS MATERIALS REGULA-TIONS[d]
(Requires 24-hour hotline, manifest placarding of hazardous material being shipped.)

COMMERCIAL DRIVERS' LICENSES
(Requires drivers to obtain CDL and drug testing.)

STORM WATER PERMITTING
(Requires dealers to hire consultants to perform engineering and testing of storm water runoff at individual facilities.)

EFFLUENT GUIDELINES
(Requires dealers to build pesticide waste-water treatment systems.)

PESTICIDE WASTE REMOVAL
(Required under CWA, CERCLA, and RCRA.[e])

PESTICIDE FEES (PER YEAR)
(State fee for licensing and environmental programs.)

ENDANGERED SPECIES ACT
(Requires reduction or elimination of pesticide application in some areas.)

PESTICIDE ILLNESS REPORTING
(Requires dealers to report illness related to pesticide exposure in some states.)

GROUNDWATER
(Requires dealers to reduce or eliminate pesticide and fertilizer application in some areas under the Clean Water Act, special USDA programs, and the 1990 Farm Bill.)

[a]FIFRA: Federal Insecticide, Fungicide and Rodenticide Act.
[b]SARA: Superfund Amendments and Reauthorization Act of 1986.
[c]OSHA: Occupational Safety and Health Administration.
[d]DOT: Department of Transportation.
[e]CWA: Clean Water Act; CERCLA: Comprehensive Environmental Response, Compensation and Liability Act; RCRA: Resource Conservation and Recovery Act.

Source: Statement of Chris Myrick, National AgriChemicals Retailers Association, in *Water Pollution Prevention and Control Act of 1991*, Hearings before the Subcommittee on Environmental Protection of the Committee on Environment and Public Works, U.S. Senate, 102nd Congress, 1st Session, Washington, D.C., 1991, p. 623. Reprinted by permission.

sion standards (reducing pesticide and fertilizer application), but most are technology standards of various types.

THE ECONOMICS OF STANDARDS   ⌐ $\mathcal{I}^{m}\mathcal{P}$

It would seem to be a simple and straightforward thing to achieve better environmental quality by applying standards of various types. But standards turn out to be more complicated than they first appear. In the rest of this chapter we will discuss some of these complications, which we will encounter directly when we get to the chapters on specific pollution-control policies.

Setting the Level of the Standard

Perhaps the first perplexing problem is where to set the standard. We saw in the case of the decentralized approaches to pollution control—liability laws and property rights regimes—that there was, at least, the theoretical possibility that the interactions of people involved would lead to efficient outcomes. But with standards we obviously can't presume this; standards get set through some sort of authoritative political/administrative process that may be affected by all kinds of considerations.

The most fundamental question is whether, in setting standards, we should take into account only damages or both damages and abatement costs. Look again at Figure 11-1, particularly at the marginal damage function. One approach in standard setting has been to try and set ambient or emission standards by reference only to the damage function. Thus, one looks at the damage function to find significant points that might suggest themselves. One approach has been to set the standard at a "zero-risk" level, i.e., at the level that would protect everyone, no matter how sensitive, from damage. This would imply setting a threshold level, labeled e_t in Figure 11-1. This concept is fine as long as there is a threshold. Recent work by toxicologists and other scientists, however, seems to indicate that there may be no threshold for many environmental pollutants; that in fact marginal damage functions are positive right from the origin. The accompanying news clip in Exhibit 11-2 discusses new findings on the impacts of ground-level ozone. What were once considered "safe" levels of ozone may not be because of the effect of this substance, at very low levels, on asthma sufferers. This has suggested to many people that the ozone standard ought to be lower. In fact, if we followed a "zero-risk" approach, we would have to set all standards at zero. This may be appropriate for some substances—certain highly toxic chemicals, for example. But it would be essentially impossible to achieve for all pollutants.

We might decide, therefore, that we could accept some "reasonably small" damages, in which case we might set it at a place like e_0, the point where the marginal damage function begins to increase very rapidly. Here again, however, we would be setting the standard without regard to abatement costs. A different logic might suggest that in setting the standard we ought to "balance" damages

EXHIBIT 11-2

LINK BETWEEN ASTHMA AND 'SAFE' OZONE LEVELS IS STUDIED

Sensitivities Double to Some Allergens, a New Report Says.

A new study suggests that ozone pollution at levels generally considered safe can double a person's sensitivity to allergens that cause asthma attacks.

The research, reported in the July 27 issue of the British journal Lancet, is the most recent in a string of studies suggesting that ozone pollution at currently acceptable levels is a threat to human health.

If confirmed in additional studies, the results might help explain the recent rise in hospital admissions and deaths from the breathing disorder, which affects at least 10 million Americans and is a mounting public health concern.

Ozone pollution is formed at ground level when hydrocarbons from motor vehicle exhaust and nitrogen oxides from industrial emissions react chemically in sunlight. The pollutant is distinct from ozone in the upper atmosphere, which is formed naturally and shields the Earth from harmful ultraviolet radiation from the Sun.

The frequency with which people in this country were discharged from a hospital with the diagnosis of asthma has nearly tripled since 1970. For children under 15, the rate rose 43 percent from 1979 to 1987. While better diagnosis could explain a small part of the increase, scientists have been unable to account for the rest.

Previous studies have shown that admissions for asthma are more prevalent in the summer months. That is when high ozone levels coincide with the peak season for airborne allergens, but the new study is the first to suggest a link between the two.

The study was conducted by scientists at the University of Toronto. They studied seven patients who had seasonal symptoms of asthma triggered by an allergic reaction to ragweed or grass.

They found that when patients inhaled air with 0.12 parts per million of ozone, the health standard set by the Environmental Protection Agency, they became twice as sensitive to ragweed or grass as they did when they inhaled clean air.

Stricter Standards Sought

In the Lancet study, the scientists report a peak ozone level in Toronto of 0.15 parts per million in 1988. In comparison, New York City reached a high of 0.18 parts per million.

Previous studies have shown that ozone affects the airways, but most of them involved people who were exercising and breathing much higher concentrations of the pollutant.

Last month the American Lung Association said that stricter Federal standards were needed to protect human health and announced that it would sue the E.P.A. unless the agency moved to set lower limits for ozone pollution within 60 days.

The association cited studies done by researchers at the E.P.A. and elsewhere finding an increase in wheezing, coughing, chest pain, respiratory inflammation and loss of lung function at levels below the current 0.12 standard. One study found temporary lung impairment in young men exercising while breathing as little as 0.08 parts per million of ozone over a six-hour period.

The Environmental Defense Fund, the Natural Resources Defense Council and the states of Connecticut, Maine, Massachusetts, New York and Rhode Island joined in the lung association's actions.

While the lung association did not recommend a specific ozone standard, it said that new studies suggest that levels as low as 0.08 parts per million could cause health problems. Smog concentrations in 182 metropolitan areas exceed that level in summer months, it said.

Source: New York Times, July 6, 1991. Copyright © 1991 by the New York Times. Reprinted by permission.

and abatement costs. This would put us squarely within the logic we used in discussing the notion of economic efficiency and, in this way, lead us to set the standard at e^*, the efficient emission level.

You should note that there is, in effect, a certain amount of "balancing" going on when standards are set on the basis of an average over some time period. In this case short-run periods, when ambient quality is relatively low, are considered acceptable as long as they do not last "too" long. A judgment is being made, in effect, that it is not necessary to install enough abatement technology to hold ambient quality within the standard under all conceivable natural conditions. In other words, an implicit trade-off is being made between the damages that will result from the temporary deterioration of ambient quality below the standard and the high costs that would be necessary to keep ambient quality within the standard under all conditions.

Perhaps the most fundamental aspect of standards is their all-or-nothing quality. Either the standard is being met or it isn't. If it isn't, the implication is that it should be, regardless of the cost of doing so. If it is being met, the implication is that it is not necessary to do any better, even though the cost of doing so may be quite low.

Uniformity of Standards

A very practical problem in standard setting is whether it should be applied uniformly to all situations or varied according to circumstances. We can illustrate this using the problem of the spatial uniformity of standards. The ambient air-quality standards in the U.S., for example, are essentially national. The problem with this is that regions may differ greatly in terms of the factors affecting damage and abatement cost relationships, so that one set of standards, uniformly applied across these local variations, may have serious efficiency implications.

Consider Figure 11-2. It shows two marginal damage functions, one of which (labeled MD_u) is assumed to characterize an urban area, while the other (labeled MD_r) applies to a rural area. MD_u lies above MD_r because there are many more people living in the urban area, so the same quantity of emissions will affect the health of more people there than in the rural region. We assume that marginal abatement costs (labeled MAC) are the same in the two regions. We might suppose, for example, that we are analyzing a production process that also produces emissions of benzene, a carcinogenic substance. The marginal costs of reducing emissions are the same in each area. Since the marginal damages are much higher in the urban than in the rural area, the efficient level of ambient benzene is much lower in the former than in the latter region; the efficient level is e_r in the rural region and e_u in the urban area. Thus a single, uniform standard cannot be efficient simultaneously in the two regions. If it is set at e_u, it will be overly stringent for the rural area, and if it is set at e_r, it will not be tight enough for the urban region. The only way to avoid this would be to set different standards in the two areas. Of course, this confronts us with one of the great

FIGURE 11-2
Regional Variation in Efficiency Levels.

policy trade-offs: The more we try to tailor a policy so that it applies to different and heterogeneous situations, the more efficient it will be in terms of its impacts, but also the more costly it will be in terms of getting the information needed to set the diverse standards and enforcing them once they have been established. The curves in Figure 11-2 could be used to represent other heterogeneous situations as well as differences in geographical regions. For example, MD_u might represent marginal damages in a particular region under some meteorological conditions, or in one season of the year, while MD_r could represent the marginal damage function for the same area but under different meteorological conditions or at a different time of year. Now a single standard, enforced throughout the year, cannot be efficient at all points in time; if it is efficient at one time, it won't be at the other.

Standards and the Equimarginal Principle

Having discussed the issue of setting the standard at the efficient level of emissions, we must remember that the efficient level itself is defined by the minimum marginal abatement cost function. And where there are multiple emissions sources producing the same effluent,[3] the equimarginal principle must hold. The principle states that in order to get this outcome, the different sources of emissions must be controlled in such a way that they have the same marginal abatement costs. This means that different sources of a pollutant would normally be controlled to different degrees, depending on the shape of the marginal

[3] That is, in cases of "uniformly mixed" emissions.

abatement cost curve at each source. A major problem with standards is that there is almost always an overwhelming tendency for authorities to apply the same standards to all sources. It makes their regulatory lives much simpler, and it gives the impression of being fair to everyone, since all are apparently being treated alike. But identical standards will be cost-effective only in the unlikely event that all polluters have the same marginal abatement costs.

Consider Figure 11-3, showing the marginal abatement cost relationships for two different sources, each emitting the same waste material. Note that the marginal abatement cost functions differ; for Firm A they increase much less rapidly as emissions are reduced than they do for Firm B. Why the difference? They may be producing different outputs with different technologies. One firm might be older than the other, and older technology may be less flexible, making it more costly to reduce emissions than at the plant with the newer equipment. One plant may be designed to use a different type of raw material input than the other. This, in fact, mirrors the situation in the real world. Normally one can expect considerable heterogeneity in abatement costs among groups of firms even though they are emitting the same type of residual.

Assume that emissions are currently uncontrolled. Thus, they are 20

FIGURE 11-3
Marginal Abatement Costs for Two Sources.

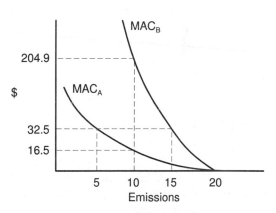

Emission level (tons/month)	Marginal abatement costs ($) A	B
20	0.00	0.00
19	1.00	2.10
18	2.10	4.60
17	3.30	9.40
16	4.60	19.30
15	6.00	32.50
14	7.60	54.90
13	9.40	82.90
12	11.50	116.90
11	13.90	156.90
10	16.50	204.90
9	19.30	264.90
8	22.30	332.90
7	25.50	406.90
6	28.90	487.00
5	32.50	577.00
4	36.30	677.20
3	40.50	787.20
2	44.90	907.20
1	49.70	1037.20
0	54.90	1187.20

tons/month at each firm, or a total of 40 tons/month. Let us assume now that authorities wish to reduce total emissions to 20 tons/month by setting emission standards. How should the standards be set? The procedure that may seem most obvious—it certainly has to most environmental regulators—is to apply the same standard to each source; in this case, 10 tons/month. This has the superficial appearance of being fair, of treating these sources alike, since each would be reduced in the same proportion from their current levels. Of course, the problem is that the sources are economically *unlike* in that they have significantly different marginal abatement costs. By applying uniform standards to dissimilar sources we violate the equimarginal principle and end up getting far less total emission reduction than we might for the costs involved. At emission levels of 10 tons/month Source A has marginal abatement costs of $16.50/ton while Source B has marginal abatement costs of $204.90/ton. Remembering that total costs are the sums of the marginal costs, we calculate total compliance costs as $75.90 for A and $684.40 for B, or a grand total of $760.30.

How much higher is this than the costs that would result from a program satisfying the equimarginal principle? A look at Figure 11-3 shows that we can achieve the total reduction we want and satisfy that principle by having Firm A cut its emissions to 5 tons/month and Firm B to 15 tons/month. At these levels their marginal abatement costs would be the same ($32.50/ton) and the total cost of the cutback would be $272.30 ($204.40 for A and $67.90 for B), a 64 percent reduction in total costs from the equal-standards case. To put it perhaps more dramatically, for the $760.30 cost of the equal-standards case, we could achieve a much larger reduction in total emissions if we cut back in accordance with the equimarginal principle. In fact, cutting Firm A back to zero emissions (total cost: $430.70) and Firm B back to emissions of 12 tons/month (total cost: $322.60) would give total compliance costs about the same as the equal-standards case but with substantially lower total emissions (12 tons/month rather than 20 tons/month).

To summarize: Standards are usually designed to be applied uniformly across emission sources. This practice is almost inherent in the basic philosophy of the standards approach, and to many people this strikes them as an equitable way to proceed. But if marginal abatement costs in the real world vary across sources, as they usually do, the equal-standards approach will produce less reduction in total emissions for the total compliance costs of the program than would be achieved with an approach that satisfied the equimarginal principle. The greater the differences in marginal abatement costs among sources, the worse will be the performance of the equal-standards approach. We will see in the chapters ahead that this difference can be very large indeed.

Could standards be set in accordance with the equimarginal principle? Unless the applicable law required some sort of equiproportional cutback there may be nothing to stop the authorities from setting different standards for the individual sources. To get an overall reduction to 20 tons/month in the example above, they could require Source A to reduce to 5 tons/month and Source B to cut back to 15 tons/month. The difficult part of this, however, is that, to accomplish this, the authorities must know what the marginal abatement costs are for the different sources. We need to stress this strongly. For almost any real-world pollution problem there will normally be multiple sources. For a public agency to set individual standards in accordance with the equimarginal principle *it would have to know the marginal abatement cost relationship for each of these sources*. It would take a prodigious effort for any agency to get high-quality information on marginal abatement costs for many different sources, each perhaps producing different outputs using different production technology and methods. The primary source of data would have to be the polluters themselves, and there is no reason to believe they would willingly share this information. In fact, if they realize, as they certainly would, that the information would be used to establish individual source standards, they would have every incentive to provide the administering agency with data showing that their marginal abatement costs rise very steeply with emission reductions. Thus, there are real problems with authorities attempting to establish source-specific emission standards. *Nevertheless*, a considerable amount of this is done informally, through the interactions of local pollution-control authorities, charged with enforcing common standards, and local sources, each of whom is in somewhat different circumstances. We will come back to this below when we discuss issues of enforcement.

Standards and the Incentives for Further Improvements

One of our criteria for evaluating alternative types of environmental policies is the strength of the incentives they produce for discovering and adopting better technical and managerial means for controlling pollution. The management of production and consumption residuals is not a static pursuit; it is subject to change and improvement through human energy and creativity. But improvements don't just happen randomly; they appear when the appropriate incentives exist.

It is easy to deal with the case of technology standards. Here the incentives to find cheaper ways (considering all costs) of reducing emissions are effectively zero. If control authorities dictate in detail the specific technology and practices that polluters may legally use to reduce emissions, there are no rewards to finding better approaches. In fact, they may be motivated to avoid other techniques in order to protect themselves against charges of noncompliance, even if these other approaches showed considerable promise. Better to play it safe, adopt the technology specified by the standard, and let the public control authorities themselves be saddled with the job of defending the correctness of the choice. Rather than leave firms free to use their own creativity in devising the technological means to achieve a goal, a technology standard instead places the burden on the public authority to make the correct technology decisions.

Now consider emission standards. Figure 11-4 shows marginal abatement costs of a firm in two situations: MAC_1 refers to such costs before a given technological improvement; MAC_2 is the marginal abatement cost curve the firm could expect to have after investing some large amount of resources in an R&D

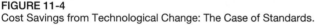

FIGURE 11-4
Cost Savings from Technological Change: The Case of Standards.

effort to develop better treatment or recycling technology. Without any pollu-tion-control program at all there is absolutely no incentive to spend the money on the R&D. But suppose the firm is now faced with having to meet emission standards of e_2 tons/year. With the original marginal abatement costs the total annual cost of compliance for this firm is $(a + b)$ per year. If the R&D program is successful, its compliance costs would be only b/year. The difference, a/year, is the amount by which compliance costs would be reduced and represents, in fact, the incentive for engaging in the R&D effort. We will see in the next chapter that this is a weaker effect than is provided by economic-incentive types of programs. Nevertheless, it is an incentive, which is more than we could say for technology standards.

Nevertheless, the complete logic of standard setting may do much to under-mine this incentive. Suppose authorities are making every effort to set the standard at something approaching the efficient level of emissions. In Figure 11-4, e_2 is their view of the efficient level before the technical change. But the new technology lowers the marginal abatement cost curve, and we know from Chapter 5 that this will reduce the efficient level of emissions. Suppose the authorities estimate that, given their view of marginal damages, the new tech-nology shifts the efficient emission level to e_3 in Figure 11-4, and that they now change the standard to reflect this. Now the firm's compliance cost will be $(b + c)$ per year. The difference is now $(a - c)$. So the firm's cost savings will be substantially less than when the standard was unchanged; in fact, compliance costs may actually be higher than before the R&D program. In other words, the firm could suppose that because of the way regulators may tighten the standards, they would be worse off with the new technology than with the old methods.

The standard-setting procedure in this case has completely undermined the incentive to produce new pollution-control technology.

If emission standards create incentives for technological change, is it not desirable to establish very stringent standards so as to increase that incentive? If, in Figure 11-4, the standard is set at e_3 right at the beginning, this would mean cost savings of $(a + d + e)$ with the new technology rather than just a as it would be with the standard set at e_2. This type of approach goes under the heading of "technology forcing." The principle of technology forcing is to set standards that are unrealistic with today's technology in the hope that it will motivate the pollution-control industry to invent ways of meeting the standard at reasonable cost. By "unrealistic with today's technology," we mean simply so costly that it would lead to widespread economic hardship.

But stricter standards also create another incentive, the incentive for polluters to seek relief from public authorities through delaying the date when they become applicable. In an open political system, firms may take some of the resources that might have gone for pollution-control R&D and devote them instead to influencing political authorities to delay the onset of strict standards. The stricter and more near-term the standards, the more of this activity there is likely to be. Thus, technology forcing is another one of those strategies where the effectiveness of moderate amounts does not imply that more will be even more effective.

We have to remember also that to a significant extent new R&D for pollution control is carried out by a pollution-control industry rather than the polluting industries themselves. Thus, to draw conclusions about the incentives of pollution-control policy for technological change means to predict how these policies will contribute to the growth and productivity of the pollution-control industry. Technology standards are stultifying on these grounds because they substantially drain off the incentives for entrepreneurs in the pollution-control industry to develop new ideas. Emission standards are better in this respect, as we have seen. The evidence for this is the fact that representatives of the pollution-control industry usually take the side politically of stricter environmental standards; in fact, they see the fortunes of their industry tied almost directly to the degree of stringency in the emissions standards set by public authorities.

THE ECONOMICS OF ENFORCEMENT

The typical pollution-control law incorporates standards calling for some degree of emissions reduction from current levels, or the adoption of specified pollution-control technologies. When we evaluate these policies ex ante we often assume implicitly that the penalties written into the law will be sufficient to produce complete compliance. But this is in fact never the case. Pollution-control laws, like any others, require enforcement, and this takes resources. Since public enforcement agencies always work under limited budgets, it is not a forgone conclusion that enough resources will ever be devoted to enforcement to achieve acceptable levels of compliance. In fact, the notion of "acceptable" is itself subject to debate.

To appreciate the importance of enforcement consider the material in Exhibit 11-3. These are excerpts from a presentation made by an official of the General

---

EXHIBIT 11-3

ENFORCEMENT PROBLEMS IN THE MUNICIPAL WASTEWATER TREATMENT FACILITY PERMIT PROGRAM

"Past GAO evaluations have revealed a long-standing pattern of noncompliance with the requirements of EPA's water quality programs. Violations have been numerous and in many cases, serious and long standing:

- Our 1983 report on the NPDES program estimated that over 80 percent of the 531 municipal and industrial facilities we reviewed exceeded the monthly average limits of their permits at least once during an 18-month period, and many exceeded the permit limits for more than 6 months. More importantly, over 30 percent of the violators exceeded permit limits by 50 percent or more in at least 4 consecutive months.
- Our 1988 report on Federal facilities' compliance with NPDES permits also documented widespread significant noncompliance. On average, 15 percent of the 150 major Federal facilities were in significant noncompliance and an additional 5 percent were under enforcement orders during any given quarter in fiscal years 1986 and 1987. Furthermore, over 40 percent of all violating Federal facilities were in noncompliance for a year or longer.
- Our 1989 report on the pretreatment program estimated that over 40 percent of 18,000 industrial users of treatment plants exceeded one or more of their discharge limits over a 12-month period. These violations led to a variety of problems, including (1) untreated pollutants passing through treatment plants to receiving waters, (2) interference with the treatment process, and

(3) health and safety problems for workers.

Some recent reviews conducted by EPA's Office of Inspector General and EPA itself have also found widespread compliance problems:

EPA's Office of Water Enforcement and Permits 1989 midyear evaluation of the NPDES program found that 14 percent of the nation's major municipal facilities, 6 percent of industrial facilities, and 18 percent of Federal facilities were in significant noncompliance. The evaluation noted that "the Federal facility rate is still out of line and needs to be addressed."

A 1990 Inspector General report on the NPDES program found that 18 percent of major treatment plants in the three regions reviewed did not meet the Clean Water Act's requirement to achieve treatment levels necessary to protect water quality. According to the report, "these facilities continue to discharge in violation of their NPDES permits to the detriment of the environment."

Taken together, these evaluations show that there has been widespread and continuing noncompliance with the Clean Water Act. Further, the evaluations identified a lack of strong, consistent enforcement against violators as a major reason for this continuing noncompliance.

Source: Statement of Mr. Richard L. Hembra, General Accounting Office, in *Water Pollution Prevention and Control Act of 1991*, Hearing before the Subcommittee on Environmental Protection of the Committee on Environmental and Public Works, 102nd Congress, 1st Session, Washington, D.C., 1991, p. 791.

Accounting Office (GAO) to a committee of the U.S. Senate, which was considering new water pollution-control legislation at the time. The statement is about the control of discharges from municipal wastewater treatment facilities. Each of these facilities is required to have a permit to discharge treated water; the permit states the conditions and limits that the discharge must meet. The GAO study results show very clearly that just promulgating standards is not enough; that resources must be devoted to enforcement.

Like lots of other problems in economics and the allocation of resources, enforcement involves a trade-off, here between the resources used for this activity, which have opportunity costs, and benefits in the form of greater degrees of compliance. We picture this trade-off in Figure 11-5. MD is the relevant marginal damage curve for this case, while MAC is the conventional marginal abatement cost function, showing the marginal costs required by sources to reduce emissions. The curves labeled C_1 and C_2 are curves that combine marginal abatement costs and marginal enforcement costs. Note that these begin at e_0, which is somewhat to the left of the uncontrolled emission rate e. When an emission standard is set at e^*, some degree of voluntary compliance may be expected to occur—in this case from e to e_0. But to get emission reductions beyond e_0 requires explicit enforcement resources. Curves C_1 and C_2 correspond to different technologies of enforcement. We have normally thought of e^* as the efficient level of emissions, but when enforcement costs are present this is no longer the case. With relatively high enforcement costs (curve C_1), the socially efficient rate of emissions is e_1. At this point total emission reduction costs are equal to $(a+b)$ of enforcement costs and $(c+d)$ of abatement costs. The technology

FIGURE 11-5
The Economics of Enforcement.

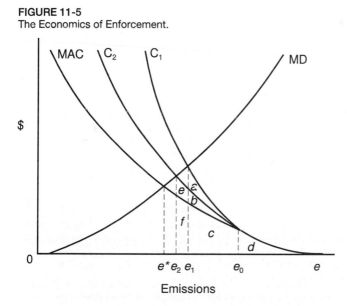

of enforcement includes many things: the monitoring of equipment, the expertise of personnel, the operation of the court system, etc. When changes occur in any of these factors, the effect is to shift the combined cost curve; in Figure 11-5 it shifts to C_2. This leads to a change in the efficient level of emissions to e_2; at this point, total emission reduction costs would be made up of $(e + b)$ of enforcement costs plus $(f + c + d)$ of abatement costs.

When enforcement costs are included in the analysis, it brings up the question of whether standards should be set, at least in part, with enforcement costs in mind. Stricter standards may involve larger enforcement costs because they require larger operating changes on the part of sources. Less strict standards may be achievable with fewer enforcement resources, for the opposite reason. Public environmental agencies are usually faced with budget stringencies. In some cases, greater overall reductions in emissions may be obtained by using less strict standards that can be easily enforced than by stricter standards involving higher enforcement costs.

However, it needs to be stressed that the "strictness" of the standard is not the only factor affecting enforcement costs. A critical element in enforcement is the size of the sanction written into the laws. Most pollution-control statutes contain provisions on the size of the fine (or jail term) that may be levied against violators, if and when they are caught and found guilty. In many cases, fines have been set too low, lower than the abatement costs required to meet the standards.[4] In these situations firms can actually save money by dragging their feet on compliance. With low sanctions like this, enforcement is therefore likely to be much more difficult and costly than if sanctions are higher. Sources faced with the possibility of having to pay substantially higher fines would presumably have a stronger incentive to come into compliance. We need to keep in mind, however, the paradoxical effect mentioned earlier: If laws attempt to set fines that are extremely high, this could actually dissuade local administrators and courts from pursuing violators vigorously, because of the economic dislocation that would result.

Stringency in enforcement budgets helps explain the attractiveness of public authorities to policies of standards. The essential characteristic of most standards approaches is that they do not require, nor automatically commit, a public agency to a costly enforcement process, especially a costly monitoring program. It is true that the more resources devoted to enforcement the more likely it is that the standards will be met. But standards programs can be put on the books while still leaving open the question of how much money and effort will be put into enforcement. Consider an emission standard that specifies an upper limit on the daily or hourly emission rate. To enforce this perfectly one would have to monitor the emission rate continuously. For a public agency charged with monitoring thousands of sources, this would be totally impossible. In the U.S.,

[4] U.S. Environmental Protection Agency, *Consolidated Report on the National Pollution Discharge Elimination System Permit Enforcement Program* (EPA/IG E1H28-01-0200-0100154), Washington, D.C., 1990.

this has led to a system of self-monitoring, where sources themselves keep the books on emissions flows over time. This permits the agencies to visit periodically to audit the records at each source. Agencies can also make random checks to measure emissions. The rate of auditing and random visits can be varied according to agency budgets. Needless to say, the rate of compliance would worsen as fewer resources are devoted to monitoring, but tolerable levels of compliance may still be attainable with fairly modest efforts at monitoring. A cynic, or a political realist, might conclude that standards approaches are favored because of the very fact that in the real world of tight public agency budgets, they permit partial or incomplete compliance.

One very common feature of environmental standards is that they are usually set and enforced by different groups of people. Standards are often set by national authorities; enforcement is usually done by local authorities. For example, the air quality standards established under the Clean Air Act are set at the federal level, but enforcement is mostly carried out by state-level agencies. This has a number of important implications. One is that standards are often set without much thought to costs of enforcement; it is more or less assumed that local authorities will find the necessary enforcement resources. Of course, this is not the case in practice. With limited enforcement budgets, local authorities may react to new programs by reducing resources devoted to other programs. Another implication is that, in practice, environmental policies incorporating standards end up having a lot more flexibility than might at first appear. Laws written at national levels are specific and apparently applicable everywhere. But at the local level, "where the rubber meets the road," as they say, it's a matter of local pollution-control authorities applying the law to local sources, and in this process there can be a great deal of informal give-and-take between the authorities and local plant managers, with participation by local environmental groups as well.

Technology standards allow the same flexibility in enforcement. Here we have to distinguish between *initial compliance* and *continued compliance*. Initial compliance is where a polluter charged with meeting a particular technology standard installs the appropriate equipment. To monitor initial compliance it is necessary to have inspectors visit the site, check to see that the equipment is installed, and make sure it will operate in accordance with the conditions of the standard. Having ascertained this, the administering agency can then give the firm the necessary operating permit. But this does not ensure that the equipment will continue to be operated in the future in accordance with the terms of the permit. It may deteriorate through normal use, it may not be maintained properly, future operating personnel may not be properly trained, etc. Without some amount of monitoring, therefore, there is no assurance that the source will continue to be in compliance. But here again the administering agency has great flexibility in setting up a monitoring program. It can vary from very infrequent visits to randomly selected sites all the way up to permanent observers stationed at each source. While more monitoring will undoubtedly lead to higher rates of compliance, the standards approach essentially leaves open the question of the amount of time, effort, and money to be put into enforcement. It is clearly one of the advantages (some might say disadvantages) of the standards approach that it permits this flexibility in monitoring and enforcement.

SUMMARY

The most popular approach to environmental pollution control historically has been the setting of standards. This has been called the "command-and-control" approach because it consists of public authorities announcing certain limits on polluters, then enforcing these limits with appropriate enforcement institutions. We specified three primary types of standards: ambient, emission, and technology. Initial discussion centered on the level at which standards should be set and the regional uniformity of standards.

A leading problem with standard setting is the question of cost-effectiveness and the equimarginal principle. In most standards programs the administrative bias is to apply the same standards to all sources of a particular pollutant. But pollution control can be cost-effective only when marginal abatement costs are equalized across sources. When marginal abatement costs differ among sources, as they almost always do, uniform standards cannot be cost-effective. In practice, differences among sources in their marginal abatement costs are often recognized informally by local administrators in applying a uniform national standard.

We dealt at length also with the question of the long-run impact of standards through their effects on the incentives to look for better ways of reducing emissions. Technology standards completely undermine these incentives. Emission standards do create positive incentives for R&D in pollution control, though we will see that these are weaker than those of economic-incentive types of pollution-control policies, the subject of the next two chapters. Finally, we discussed the all-important question of enforcement.

QUESTIONS FOR FURTHER DISCUSSION

1 Environmental protection programs are frequently designed to require all polluters to cut back emissions by a certain percentage. What are the perverse incentives built into this type of program?

2 Would it be better to set less restrictive standards and enforce them vigorously, or tighter standards and enforce them more loosely? What are the important factors bearing on this question?

3 What are the factors determining how stringent emission standards should be set in order to have the right degree of "technology forcing"?

4 If emission standards are ruled out because of, e.g., the impossibility of measuring emissions (as in nonpoint source emissions), what alternative types of standards might be used instead?

5 In Figure 11-2, show the social cost of setting a uniform national standard, applicable to both rural and urban areas (to do this you can assume that the national standard is set at either e_u or e_r).

6 Consider the example of Figure 11-3. Suppose we define as "fair" a cutback in which the two sources have the same total costs. Would an equiproportionate reduction be fair in this sense? A reduction meeting the equimarginal principle? Is this a reasonable definition of "fair"?

7 Numerous people have suggested that the most equitable way to resolve the trade and environment problem would be for all countries to adopt the same emission standards. What are the pros and cons of this from an economic standpoint?

SELECTED READINGS

Crandall, Robert W.: *Controlling Industrial Pollution*, The Brookings Institution, Washington, D.C., 1983.

Hawkins, Keith: *Environment and Enforcement*, Clarendon Press, Oxford, England, 1984.

McKean, Roland N.:"Enforcement Costs in Environmental and Safety Regulation," *Policy Analysis*, 6(3), Summer 1980, pp. 269–289.

Richardson, Genevra, with Anthony Orgus and Paul Burrows: *Policing Pollution*, Oxford University Press, Oxford, England, 1983.

Russell, Clifford S.: "Monitoring and Enforcement," in Paul Portney (ed.), *Public Policies for Environmental Protection*, Resources for the Future, Washington, D.C., 1990, pp. 243–274.

Russell, Clifford S., Winston Harrington, and William J. Vaughan: *Enforcing Pollution Control Laws*, Resources for the Future, Washington, D.C., 1986.

Viscusi, W. Kip: *Risks by Choice: Regulating Health and Safety in the Workplace*, Harvard University Press, Cambridge, Mass., 1983.

CHAPTER 12

INCENTIVE-BASED STRATEGIES: EMISSION TAXES AND SUBSIDIES

If we wanted to build a house, we would have to buy some building materials; nobody is likely to give them to us free. If we want to have architects and carpenters work on the house, we will have to hire them; they won't ordinarily work for nothing. In other words, in order to use the services of these inputs, we have to pay for them. We are used to doing this because they are bought and sold in well-developed markets. The fact that we have to pay for them gives us an incentive to use the inputs as sparingly and efficiently as possible. The economic incentive approach to environmental policy works in much the same way. Until recently people have been able to use the waste-disposal services of the environment virtually without cost, so there has been little incentive for them to think about the environmental consequences of their actions and to economize on the use of these environmental resources. The incentive approach seeks to change this situation.

There are basically two types of incentive policies: (1) taxes and subsidies and (2) transferable discharge permits. The first is a centralized system; it requires some administering agency to put the program into effect and to deal directly and continuously with polluters. The second is a decentralized approach; once the system has been established and basic rules set, it is designed to work more or less automatically through the interactions among polluters themselves, or between polluters and other interested parties. In recent years U.S. environmental laws have begun to incorporate many types of transferable discharge permit systems. In other countries, particularly those of Europe, greater reliance is being put on programs of emission taxes. In the present chapter we will examine the economics of emission charges and subsidies. In the next chapter we will consider the technique of transferable discharge permits.

Environmental economists have long favored the idea of incorporating incentive-based policies more thoroughly into environmental policies. These can serve to put more teeth into environmental policies in many cases and substantially improve the cost-effectiveness of these policies. But keep in mind something we said before: No single type of policy is likely to be the best in all circumstances. Incentive-based policies are no exception. They have strengths and they have weaknesses. The strengths are sufficiently strong to encourage greater reliance on them in many circumstances. But there are many types of environmental problems where they may not be as useful as other approaches.

EMISSION TAXES

The most straightforward incentive-based approach to controlling emissions of a particular residual is to have a public agency offer a financial incentive to change those emissions. This can be done in two ways: by taxing each unit of emissions or by giving a subsidy for each unit of emissions that the source cuts back.

We deal first with emission taxes, sometimes also called "emission charges." In a tax system we say to polluters: "You may discharge any amount of residuals you wish, but your emissions will be measured and you will be required to pay a certain tax for every unit (e.g., ton) of effluent you discharge." For example, one of the first emission taxes proposed in the U.S. was in 1970, when President Nixon recommended a tax of 15 cents per pound on sulfur emissions from large power plants. It was never adopted. When an emission tax is put into effect, firms responsible for emissions must essentially pay for the services of the environment—transportation, dilution, chemical decomposition, etc.—just as they must pay for all other inputs used in their operations. And just as they have always had an incentive to conserve on scarce labor and other conventional production inputs, they will now have an incentive to conserve on their use of environmental services. How do they do this? Any way they wish (within reason). This may sound flippant but in fact it represents the main advantage of this technique. By leaving polluters free to determine how best to reduce emissions, we call into play their own energy and creativity and their desire to minimize costs, to find the least-cost way of reducing emissions. It could be any combination of treatment, internal process changes, changes in inputs, recycling, shifts to less polluting outputs, etc. The essence of the tax approach is to provide an incentive for the polluters themselves to find the best way to reduce emissions, rather than having a central authority determine how it should be done.

The Basic Economics

The essential mechanics of an emission tax are depicted in Figure 12-1. The numbers refer to a single source of a particular pollutant. The top panel shows the analysis numerically, while the bottom shows essentially the same information graphically. The tax has been set at $120/ton/month. The second column shows the firm's marginal abatement costs and the third column total abatement costs. The last two columns show the total monthly tax bill the firm would pay at different emission levels, and the total cost, consisting of the sum of abatement costs and the tax bill. We see that the minimum total cost of $850 occurs at an emission rate of 4 tons/month. Let's pursue the logic of this by considering marginal abatement costs. Suppose the firm is initially emitting 10 tons/month;

Emissions (tons/month)	Marginal abatement cost	Total abatement cost	Total tax bill at $120/ton	Total costs
10	0	0	1,200	1,200
9	15	15	1,080	1,095
8	30	45	960	1,005
7	50	95	840	935
6	70	165	720	885
5	90	255	600	855
4	115	370	480	850
3	135	505	360	865
2	175	680	240	920
1	230	910	120	1,030
0	290	1,200	0	1,200

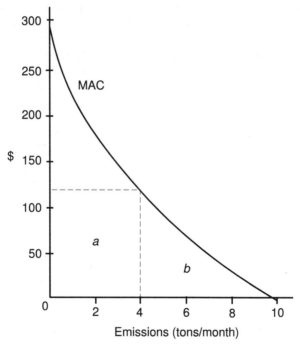

FIGURE 12-1
An Emissions Tax.

if it were to cut emissions to 9 tons, it would cost $15 in abatement costs, but on the other hand it would save $120 in taxes, clearly a good move. Following this logic, it could improve its bottom line by continuing to reduce emissions as long as the tax rate is above marginal abatement costs. The rule for the firm to follow is, thus: Reduce emissions until marginal abatement costs are equal to the emissions tax rate. This is shown diagrammatically in the bottom part of Figure

12-1. With a continuous marginal abatement cost function it's possible to talk about fractions of tons of emissions, something we could not do in the upper panel. So the graph is drawn to agree with the integer values above; i.e., the tax of $120 leads the firm to reduce emissions to exactly 4 tons/month.

After the firm has reduced its emissions to 4 tons/month, its total (monthly) tax bill will be $480. Its monthly abatement costs will be $370. Graphically, total abatement costs correspond to the area under the marginal abatement cost function, labeled b in the figure. The total tax bill is equal to emissions times tax rate, or the rectangle labeled a. Under a tax system of this type, a firm's total cost equals its abatement costs plus the tax payments to the taxing authority.

Why wouldn't the firm simply disregard the tax, continue to pollute as it has been doing, and just pass the tax on to consumers in the form of higher prices? If the firm stayed at 10 tons of emissions, its total outlay would be $1,200/month, consisting entirely of tax payment. This is much higher than the $850 it can achieve by cutting back to 4 tons/month. The assumption in an emissions tax program is that *competitive pressures* will lead firms to do whatever they can to minimize their costs. Thus, when there is competition in the industry subject to the emission tax, it will lead firms to reduce emissions in response to the tax. By the same token, however, we must recognize that if competition is weak, firms may not respond in this way. Electric power plants, for example, are usually operated by regulated monopolies subject to oversight by public utility commissions. They may not respond to taxes on SO_2 emissions in the same way as firms that operate in more competitive economic climates.

For competitive firms, the amount of the response will depend on several factors. The higher the tax, the greater the reduction, and vice versa. In the example of Figure 12-1, a tax of $50 would have led the source to reduce emissions only to 7 tons/month, while a tax of $180 would have produced a cutback to 2 tons/month, etc. Also, the steeper the marginal abatement cost function, the less emissions will be reduced in response to a tax. We will come back to this below.

Compare the tax approach with an emission standard. With the tax the firm's total outlay is $850. Suppose that, instead, the authorities had relied on an emission standard to get the firm to reduce emissions to 4 tons/month. In that case the firm's total outlay would be only the $370 of abatement costs. Thus, the tax system ends up costing the firm more than the standards approach. With a standard the firm has the same total abatement costs as in the tax system, but it is still essentially getting the services of the environment free, while with a tax system it has to pay for those services. But while polluting firms would thus prefer standards to emission taxes, there are good reasons, as we shall see, society would often prefer taxes over standards.

The Level of the Tax

In competitive situations, higher taxes will bring about greater reductions in emissions, but just how high should the tax be set? If we know the marginal

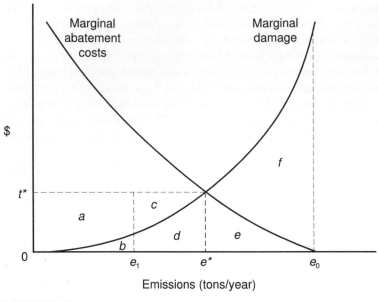

FIGURE 12-2
An Efficient Emission Tax.

damage function, the answer presumably would be to set the tax so as to produce the efficient level of emissions, as in Figure 12-2. At a tax rate of t^*, emissions are e^*, and marginal damages equal marginal abatement costs. The firm's total costs of emission control are divided into two types: total abatement costs (compliance costs) of e and total tax payments of $(a + b + c + d)$. The former are the costs of whatever techniques the firm has chosen to reduce emissions from e_0 to e^*, while the latter are payments to the control agency covering the tax on the remaining emissions. From the standpoint of the firm, of course, these are both real costs that will have to be covered out of revenues. From the standpoint of *society*, however, the tax payments are different from the abatement costs. While the latter involve real resources and therefore real social costs, the taxes are actually *transfer payments*, payments made by the firms (ultimately by people who buy the firms' output) to the public sector and eventually to those in society who are benefited by the resulting public expenditures. When a firm considers its costs, it will include both abatement costs and tax payments; when we are considering the social costs of a tax program, we must exclude transfer payments.

The reduction of emissions from e_0 to e^* has eliminated damages of $(e + f)$. Remaining damages are $(b + d)$, an amount less than the firm pays in taxes. This underscores the idea that the emission tax is based on the right to use environmental resources, not on the notion of compensation. But a "flat tax" like this (one tax rate for all emissions) has been criticized because it would often lead to situations where the total tax payments of firms would substantially exceed remaining damages. A way around this is to institute a *two-part emission tax*. We allow some initial quantity of emission to go untaxed, applying the tax only to emissions in excess of this threshold. For example, in Figure 12-2 we might allow the firm e_1 units of emissions free of tax, and apply the tax rate of t^* to anything over this. In this way the firm would still have the incentive to reduce emissions to e^*, but its total tax payments would be only $(c + d)$. Total abatement costs, and total damages caused by the e^* units of emissions, would still be the same.

How might we set the tax if we did not know the marginal damage function? We know that emissions are connected to ambient quality; the lower the emissions the lower the ambient concentration of the pollutant, in general. So one strategy might be to set a tax and then watch carefully to see what this did in terms of improving ambient quality levels. We would have to wait long enough to give firms time to respond to the tax. If ambient quality did not improve as much as desired, increase the tax; if ambient quality improved more than was thought appropriate, lower the tax. This is a successive approximation process of finding the correct long-run emissions tax. It is not at all clear whether this approach would be practicable in the real world. In responding to a tax, polluters would invest in a variety of pollution-control devices and practices, many of which would have relatively high up-front costs. This investment process could be substantially upset if, shortly afterward, the authorities shift to a new tax rate. Any agency trying to use this method to find the efficient tax rate would undoubtedly find itself embroiled in a brisk political battle over the matter. Rather than planning to make successive adjustments in the tax rate, there would be a strong incentive for policymakers to determine the correct tax rate at the beginning. This would put a premium on prior study to get some idea of the shapes of the aggregate abatement and damage cost curves.

Emission Taxes and Efficiency

Perhaps the strongest case for a policy of effluent taxes is to be made on grounds of their efficiency effects, especially in controlling multiple sources of emissions in a way that satisfies the equimarginal principle. If we apply the same tax rate to different sources with different marginal abatement cost functions and each source reduces its emissions until its marginal abatement costs equal the tax, then marginal abatement costs will automatically be equalized across all the sources.

This is depicted in Figure 12-3.[1] We assume here that there are two sources of a particular type of emission, labeled Source A and Source B. We also assume that these emissions, after they leave the respective sources, are uniformly mixed together, so that the emissions of the two plants are equally damaging in the downstream, or downwind, impact area. The marginal abatement costs for the two sources are the same as those we used in the last chapter. They are shown in graphical form at the bottom of Figure 12-3. The marginal abatement costs of

---

[1] We have seen a graph like this several times before, e.g., in Figures 11-3 and 5-5.

| Emission level | Marginal abatement costs | |
(tons/month)	Source A	Source B
20	0.0	0.0
19	1.0	2.1
18	2.1	4.6
17	3.3	9.4
16	4.6	19.3
15	6.0	32.5
14	7.6	54.9
13	9.4	82.9
12	11.5	116.9
11	13.9	156.9
10	16.5	204.9
9	19.3	264.9
8	22.3	332.9
7	25.5	406.9
6	28.9	487.0
5	32.5	577.0
4	36.3	677.2
3	40.5	787.2
2	44.9	907.2
1	49.7	1,037.2
0	54.9	1,187.2

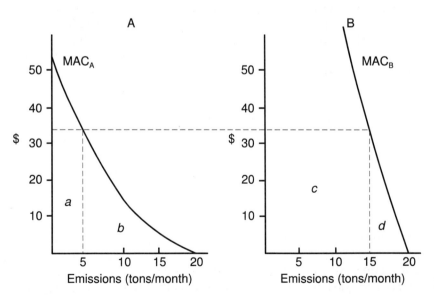

FIGURE 12-3
Emission Taxes and the Equimarginal Rule.

Source A increase much less rapidly with reductions in emissions than do those of Source B. In the real world, differences like this are normally related to the fact that the firms are using different production technologies. They may be producing different outputs (e.g., a pulp mill and a food-canning firm), or they may be plants in the same industry but using different production techniques (e.g., coal-fired and oil-fired electric power plants). According to the graphs, the production technology used by Source B makes emission reduction more costly than it is at Source A. If we impose an effluent tax of $33/ton on each source, the operators of Source A will reduce their emissions to 5 tons/month; those at Source B will cut back to 15 tons/month (dealing only with integer values). After these reductions, the two sources will have the same marginal abatement costs. The total reduction has been 20 tons per month, which the effluent tax has automatically distributed between the two firms in accordance with the equimarginal principle.

Note very carefully that the emission tax has led Source A to reduce its emissions by 75 percent, while Source B has reduced its emissions by only 25 percent. The emissions tax leads to larger proportionate emission reductions from firms with lower marginal abatement costs. Conversely, firms having steeper marginal abatement costs will reduce emissions less, in proportionate terms. Suppose that instead of the tax the authorities had instituted a *proportionate* cutback, on the grounds that "everybody should be treated alike," so they require each source to reduce emissions by 50 percent. Our two sources in Figure 12-3 both reduce emissions to 10 tons/month. At this point their marginal abatement costs would be different. Furthermore, we can calculate total abatement costs, by remembering that total cost is the sum of marginal costs. Thus, e.g., for Source A the total costs of 10 tons of emissions would be $(1.0 + 2.1 + \ldots + 16.5 = 75.9)$.

The following tabulation compares the compliance costs of the equiproportionate reduction and the effluent tax.

	Total compliance costs ($/month)	
	Equiproportionate reduction	Effluent tax
Source A	75.9	204.4
Source B	684.4	67.9
Total	760.3	272.3

Note how much the totals differ. The total compliance cost of an equiproportionate cutback is about 2.8 times the total cost of an emission tax. The simple reason is that the equiproportionate cutback violates the equimarginal principle; it requires the same proportionate cutback regardless of the height and shape of a firm's marginal abatement costs. The difference in total costs between these two approaches is quite large with these illustrative numbers. We will see in later chapters that in the real world of pollution control these differences are often much larger.

The higher the tax rate the more emissions will be reduced. In fact, if the tax rate were increased to something over \$55/ton, Firm A would stop emitting this residual entirely. The marginal abatement cost function for Firm B increases so rapidly, however, that an extremely high tax (more than \$1,187/ton) would be required to get this source to reduce emissions to zero. A single effluent tax, when applied to several firms, will induce a greater reduction by firms whose marginal abatement costs increase less rapidly with emission reductions than from firms whose marginal abatement costs increase more rapidly. Since the firms are paying the same tax rate, they will have different total abatement costs and different tax bills. In Figure 12-3 the total abatement costs are equal to area *b* for Source A and area *d* for Source B. On the other hand, the monthly tax bill sent to Source A would be only *a*, compared to a bill of *c* sent to Source B. Thus, the less steeply the marginal abatement cost of a firm increases, the larger that firm's emission reduction will be and the smaller its tax bill.

We need to emphasize that the efficiency results of the emission tax approach (i.e., that it satisfies the equimarginal principle) are achievable *even though the administering agency knows nothing about the marginal abatement costs of any of the sources*. This is in clear contrast with the standards approach, where the public agency has to know exactly what these marginal abatement costs are for each firm in order to have a fully efficient program. In a tax approach the only requirement is that firms pay the same tax and that they are cost minimizers. After each one has adjusted its emissions in accordance with its marginal abatement costs (which we can expect them to know themselves), they will all be emitting at the appropriate rates to satisfy the equimarginal principle.

Emission Taxes and Nonuniform Emissions

So far we have proceeded under the assumption that the emissions of all sources are uniformly mixed together; i.e., the emissions from one source have the same marginal impact on ambient quality levels as those from other sources. In the real world this is not always the case. Very often the situation is something like, though of course more complicated than, that depicted in Figure 12-4. Here we have two sources. Source A, however, is about twice as far away from the center of population as Source B. This means that emissions from Source A do not produce as much damage in the urban area as emissions from Source B. If the two sources are emitting some material into a river that flows toward the city, the emissions of Source A have a longer time in the water to be broken down and rendered less harmful than do the emissions from Source B. Or if it is an air pollution problem, Source A is much farther upwind than Source B, so there is more time for its emissions to be spread out and diluted than there is for the emissions from Source B. There could be other reasons than location differences for the different impacts; for example, they may emit residuals at different times of the year when wind patterns are different. Studying the

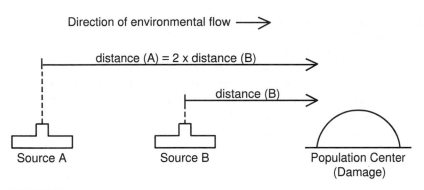

FIGURE 12-4
Nonuniform Emissions.

location problem will allow us to examine the general problem of nonuniform emissions.

In this case a single emission tax applied to both sources would not be fully efficient. A single tax addresses only the problem of differences in marginal abatement costs, not differences in damages caused by the emissions from different sources. In Figure 12-4 a one-unit reduction in emissions from Plant B would improve environmental quality (reduce damages) in the urban area more than a one-unit reduction in emissions from Plant A, and this fact must be taken into account in setting emission tax rates. Suppose emission reductions at Source B are twice as effective at reducing damages as reductions in emissions at Source A. This means, in effect, that the effluent tax paid by Source B must be twice as high as the effluent charge paid by Source A.[2] Thus, after adjusting to these tax levels the marginal abatement cost of Source B would be twice the marginal abatement cost of Source A. But the damage reduction *per dollar spent in reducing emissions* would be equalized across the two sources.

The logic of the preceding discussion would seem to lead us to the conclusion that in these cases we would have to charge different emission taxes to each source. To do this we would have to know the relative importance of the emissions from each source in affecting ambient quality. But finding out exactly what these relative differences are would be a difficult job, as would the administrative task of charging a different tax rate to each firm. The best response here might be to institute what is called a *zoned emission tax*. Here the administering agency would divide a territory into separate zones; the actual number of zones would depend on the circumstances of the case. Within each zone the agency

[2] The technical concept here is called a "transfer coefficient." A transfer coefficient is a number that tells how the emissions from any particular source affect ambient quality at some other point. In the simple example above, suppose 1 ton of SO_2 emitted by B would increase SO_2 concentration over the urban area by .1 ppm. Then a ton emitted from Source A would increase the ambient concentration by .05 (assuming an effect that is strictly proportional to distance). If the transfer coefficient for Source B is 1, that for Source A is .5, so the tax at A has to be half the tax at B.

would charge the same emission tax to all sources, while it would charge different taxes in different zones.

Naturally the zones would be identified by grouping together sources whose emissions have similar effects on ambient quality levels. Figure 12-5, for example, shows the schematic of a river with a dozen different sources of emissions and one urban area where water quality is measured and water quality targets are established. The 10 upstream sources are strung along the river at increasing distances from the urban area. Thus each has a different impact on measured water quality at the monitoring station, and a fully cost-effective program of emissions reductions would have to account for this fact, *in addition to* their different marginal abatement costs. But it would be administratively very costly to apply a different emissions tax to each source. We might, in this case, fall back on a zoned emission tax.

We first define different zones along the river, then apply the same tax to all sources within the same zone, but different taxes to sources in different zones. Each zone would contain sources whose emissions have roughly the same impact on measured water quality. In Figure 12-5, for example, four upstream zones along the river are sketched out. The three sources in Zone 1 would get the same tax, as would the four sources in Zone 2, etc. Sources 11 and 12 are downstream from the urban area and may not get taxed at all. Of course, this is a simplified diagram to show the basic idea; in the real world, there would also very likely be downstream damages. By using a zone system we can achieve a certain amount of administrative simplification while recognizing differences in the locations of different groups of sources.

Emissions Taxes and Materials Balance

It's important at this point to remind ourselves about the fundamental materials balance aspects of residuals. Given a certain quantity of residuals, if we reduce the flow going into one environmental medium, we have to increase the flow going to others. If we forget this, we might run into situations in which, for

FIGURE 12-5
Zoned Emissions Tax.

Key: ☐ Emission sources

⊗ Water-quality monitoring station

example, firms respond to a tax on a certain waterborne residual by adopting a relatively cheap (from their standpoint) method of incineration that substantially increases airborne emissions. This implies that if taxes are put on residuals going into one environmental medium, we have to have some means of coordinating this with discharges of these emissions to other media. This could be done in several ways. We might simply put the same tax on a residual no matter which medium it was discharged into. But if the marginal damages of the residual were different across media, we would want to charge different taxes for different media if we had enough information to determine what they should be. If the administering agency couldn't do this, it might fall back on simply proscribing certain courses of action; it might, for example, simply rule out any increases in airborne emissions from sources subject to a tax on waterborne emissions of the same residual. This should alert us to the problems of coordination implied by the materials-balance principle.

Emissions Taxes and Uncertainty

Pollution-control policies have to be carried out in a world of uncertainty. We don't know exactly what damages stem from diminished ambient water quality. Administrating agencies often do not know exactly what emissions are being produced by each source nor exactly what the human and ecosystem impacts are. Another source of uncertainty is the shape of the marginal abatement cost curve of the sources subject to control; these may be known reasonably well by the polluters themselves but administrators will usually be very unsure of how high they are, how steep they are, how much they differ from source to source, and so on. It is one of the advantages of emissions taxes that they can bring about cost-effective results even within that state of uncertainty.

Nevertheless, when administrators set taxes at certain levels, they will normally be uncertain about how much emission reduction will ensue, for that depends on how sources respond to the tax. This is one of the drawbacks of emission taxes. We can't predict exactly how much total emissions will decrease because we don't know the exact marginal abatement cost relationships. Observe Figure 12-6. It shows two different marginal abatement cost functions, a steep one (MAC_1) and one that is much less steep (MAC_2). They cross at a tax rate of t/pound. Consider MAC_1. If we set a tax at the relatively high rate of t_h, this source would reduce emissions to e_3, while if we had set it at the low rate of t_l, it would adjust emissions to e_2. These two emission rates are relatively close together. In other words, whether the tax is high or low the emissions rate of this source would not vary much; we could count on having an emissions rate of something around e_1.

But for the firm with the less steep marginal abatement costs (MAC_2) things are much more unstable. If the tax were set low, it would change emissions to e_4, while with a high tax emissions would go all the way down to e_5. In other words, for given changes in the tax rate, this firm would respond with much larger changes in emission rates than would the source with the steeper MAC curve.

FIGURE 12-6
Emissions Taxes and Uncertainty.

The upshot of this discussion is that if most firms in a particular pollution problem have relatively flat MAC functions, we may have trouble finding the tax rate that will give us just the amount of reduction in total emissions we want. Since we don't know exactly where the MAC functions really are, we don't know exactly how high to set the tax. If we set it a little high or a little low, these firms will respond with large changes in their emissions. This is one of the main reasons administrators opt for standards: They seem to offer a definite control on quantities of emissions produced. In the next chapter, we will discuss an incentive approach that addresses this problem.

Emission Taxes and the Incentives to Innovate

In a dynamic world, it is critical that we adopt environmental policies that encourage technological change in pollution control. One of the main advantages of emission taxes is that they provide strong incentives for this. This is shown in Figure 12-7, which shows two marginal abatement cost curves for a single firm. MAC_1 represents the current condition. It shows the costs the firm would experience in cutting back its emissions with the particular technology it presently uses. MAC_2, on the other hand, refers to abatement costs that the firm would experience after engaging in a relatively expensive R&D program to develop a new method of reducing emissions. We assume the firm has a reasonably good idea of what the results of the R&D will be, though of course nothing is ever a sure thing. We can use it to measure the strength of the incentives for this firm to put money into the R&D program.

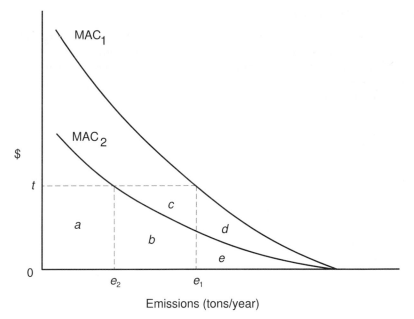

FIGURE 12-7
Emission Taxes and the Incentive for R&D.

Suppose the firm is subject to an effluent tax of t/ton of emissions. Initially it will reduce emissions to e_1; at this point its total pollution-related costs will consist of $(d + e)$ worth of abatement costs and a tax bill of $(a + b + c)$. If it can lower its marginal abatement cost curve to MAC_2 through the R&D activities, it would then reduce its emissions to e_2. At this point it would pay $(b + e)$ in abatement costs and a in taxes. The reduction in total costs has been $(c + d)$. If the firm had instead been faced with an emissions standard of e_1, its cost savings with the new technology would have been only d, as we saw in the last chapter. Also, as we saw in the last chapter, if public authorities shift the standard to e_2 when the new technology becomes available (giving the same emissions reduction as the tax would have), the firm could actually experience an *increase* in costs because of its R&D efforts.

Thus, the firm's R&D efforts will lead to a bigger reduction in its pollution-control–related costs (abatement costs plus tax payments) under a policy of emission taxes than under a standards approach. *Additionally, under the tax system the firm would automatically reduce its emissions as it found ways to shift its marginal abatement cost function downward, whereas under the standard no such automatic process would result.* The difference is that under a tax approach, polluters must pay for emissions as well as for abatement costs, while with standards they need pay only abatement costs. So their potential cost savings from new pollution-control techniques are much larger under the tax program.

Emission Taxes and Enforcement Costs

Taxes pose a different type of enforcement problem than standards. Any tax system requires accurate information on the item to be taxed. If emissions are to be taxed, they must be measurable at reasonable cost. This means that residuals flowing from a source must be concentrated in a small enough number of identifiable streams that monitoring is possible. This rules out most nonpoint source emissions because they are spread thinly over a wide area in a way that makes them impossible to measure. It would normally be impossible to tax the pollutants in agricultural runoff because the diffuse nature of the "emissions" makes them impossible to measure. This may also rule out certain toxic chemical emissions which, in addition to being nonpoint source, often involve such small quantities that their flow rates are difficult to measure.

With emission taxes the taxing authorities would be sending a tax bill to the polluting firms at the end of each month or year, based on their total quantity of emissions during that period. So the agency would require information on cumulative emissions from each source. This is more involved than just information on rate of discharge, because cumulative discharge is rate times duration. There are several ways of getting this information. Perhaps the most ideal would be to have permanent monitoring equipment that measures emissions continuously over the time period in question. Lacking such technology, one could fall back on periodic checking of the rate of emissions, with an estimate of the duration based on normal business considerations or perhaps self-reporting by firms. Alternatively, engineering studies might be carried out to determine prospective emission quantities under specified conditions of operation, inputs used, etc.

It is probably fair to say that the monitoring requirements of an emissions tax policy are more stringent than those for the typical standards program. Polluters, of course, have incentives to find ways, legal and otherwise, to get their tax bills reduced. One way to do this is to influence the monitoring process enough so that reported emissions are smaller. Once they do get their tax bills, recipients will have every incentive to contest them if they appear to be based on uncertain data or have other technical weaknesses. The lack of high-quality monitoring and reporting procedures has undoubtedly contributed to the unpopularity of effluent charge policies for environmental quality control.

Other Types of Taxes

So far we have discussed only one type of tax, an effluent or emissions tax. Since it is the emission of residuals that leads directly to environmental pollution, taxes on emissions presumably have the greatest leverage in terms of altering the incentives of polluters. But it is often impossible or impractical to levy taxes directly on emissions. In cases where we can't measure and monitor emissions at reasonable cost, taxes, if they are to be used, would obviously have to be applied to something else. A good case of this is the problem of water pollution from fertilizer runoff in agriculture. It is impossible to tax the pounds of nitrogen in the runoff because it is a nonpoint source pollutant and thus not directly measurable. The same problem applies to agricultural pesticides. What may be feasible instead is to put taxes on these materials as they are bought by farmers; i.e., a tax per ton of fertilizer or per 100 pounds of pesticide purchased. The tax is to reflect the fact that a certain proportion of these materials ends up in nearby streams and lakes. Because they are paying higher prices for these items, farmers would have the incentive to use them in smaller quantities. Higher prices also create an incentive to use the fertilizer in ways that involve less wastage; for example, by reducing the amounts that run off.

Placing a tax on something other than emissions is usually a "second-best" course of action made necessary because direct emissions can't be closely monitored. In cases like this we have to watch out for distortions that can come about as people respond to the tax, distortions that can substantially alleviate the effects of the tax or can sometimes make related problems worse. We mentioned in Chapter 1 the move by many U.S. communities to tax household trash. One technique is to sell stickers to the residents and require each bag of trash have a sticker on it. The rate of tax is determined by the price of the stickers, and it is relatively easy to monitor and enforce the system through the curb-side pickup operations. But the per bag tax will produce an incentive to pack more into each bag, so the reduction in total quantity of trash may be less than the reduction in the number of bags collected.

Another example. Suppose we put a tax on new cars on the basis of their emissions of residuals like nitrogen oxides and hydrocarbons. The tax on any car is determined by the quantity of emissions per mile that car produces, as determined by testing at the plant. Our objective is to raise the price of heavily polluting cars relative to less-polluting ones, thus giving people more incentive to shift to the latter when they make their new-car purchases. The tax is linked to the quantity of residuals emitted during a typical mile traveled. But the factor we really wish to control is the total quantity of residuals emitted. We have the following relationship:

$$(\text{Total emissions per year}) = (\text{Emissions per mile}) \times (\text{Number of miles driven per year}).$$

In fact, the number of miles driven is as important a factor in determining annual emissions as is the emissions rate of the car. Although consumers might shift to cars that have lower emission rates, they will have absolutely no incentive to look around for ways of driving fewer miles each year such as, taking fewer trips or living closer to work. So total emissions may go down very little despite the tax on new-car emissions. The point is that this tax is being put on something other than what we want to control, so it will have less "leverage" and produce smaller results than if it had been put directly on total emissions.

Distributional Impacts of Emission Taxes

There are two primary impacts of effluent taxes on the distribution of income and wealth: impacts on prices and output and the effects of the expenditures made from the tax revenues. Businesses subject to a tax will experience an increase in costs, because of both abatement costs and the tax payments. From the firm's standpoint these constitute increases in production cost, which they will presumably pass on to consumers like any cost of production. Whether and how much they can do this depends on competitive conditions and the conditions of demand. If the tax is applied to a single firm or small group of firms within a competitive industry, it will not be able to push its price up above the industry price, and so will have to absorb the cost increase. In this case the impacts will be felt entirely by owners of the firm and the people who work there. Many firms fear —or pretend to fear— being in precisely this situation, and base their public objections to taxes on this outcome. If the tax is applied to an entire industry, prices will go up and consumers will bear part of the burden. How much prices go up depends on demand conditions.[3] Price increases are often thought of as regressive because, for any given item, an increase in its price would affect poor people proportionately more than higher-income people. For something that both poor and well-off people consume, like electricity, this conclusion is straightforward. For price increases in goods consumed disproportionately by more well-to-do people (e.g., airline travel), however, the burden would be mostly on them.

The burden on workers is tied closely to what happens to the rate of output of the affected firms. Here again, the extent of the output effect depends on competitive conditions and the nature of the demand for the good. If the emission tax program is applied to a single firm in a competitive industry or if the demand for the output of an industry is very responsive to price, output adjustments will be relatively large and workers could be displaced. The long-run burden is then a matter of whether good alternative sources of employment are available.

While burdens because of price and output changes may be real, we have to remember that, on the other side, the tax program is creating substantial benefits in the form of reduced environmental damages. To know how a program affects any particular group we would have to account also for how these benefits are distributed.

Effluent taxes also could involve substantial sums running from consumers of the goods produced by the taxed industry to the beneficiaries, whoever they may be, of the funds collected by the taxing authorities. These funds could be used for any number of purposes; how they are used would determine their impacts. They might, for example, be distributed to lower-income people to offset the effects of price increases. They might even be returned in part to the firms paying the effluent taxes. This is done in some European countries to help

---

[3] This was discussed in greater detail in Chapter 8.

finance the purchase of pollution-control technology. As long as the return payments do not make the marginal emissions tax rate effectively lower, the incentive effects of the tax are not affected. Alternatively, they might be used to pay for other environmental initiatives in places where direct public action is called for. They might even be used to reduce overall budget deficits, with benefits flowing to general taxpayers.

One final note on tax revenues. The emission taxes we have talked about in this section are designed to induce polluters to use environmental resources more sparingly. The taxes essentially correct the distorted pattern of resource use that results when environmental resources may be used as free inputs. The other feature of emission taxes that ought to be stressed is as a revenue source. This suggests the possibility that is open to governments of replacing certain other taxes, which have distorting effects on the economy, with emission taxes, which are designed to reduce resource-use distortions. For example, many countries have payroll taxes, levied on firms and workers to provide revenues for a variety of purposes, such as social insurance. These taxes have the effect of making labor more expensive, and so cause a reduction in the quantity of labor hired—a reduction in jobs. If this were replaced in whole or in part by an emissions tax, there would be desirable effects both in the labor market and in the reduction of environmental externalities.

ABATEMENT SUBSIDIES

An emission tax works by placing a price on the environmental asset into which emissions are occurring. Essentially the same incentive effects would result if, instead of a tax, we instituted a subsidy on emission reductions. Here a public authority would pay a polluter a certain amount per ton of emissions for every ton it reduced, starting from some benchmark level. The subsidy acts as a reward for reducing emissions. More formally, it acts as an opportunity cost; when a polluter chooses to emit a unit of effluent, it is in effect forgoing the subsidy payment it could have had if it had chosen to withhold that unit of effluent instead. Table 12-1 shows how this works in principle, using the same numbers as in the preceding discussion on emission taxes. The firm's base level is set at its current emissions rate: 10 tons/month. It receives $120 per ton for every ton it cuts back from this base. The third column shows its total subsidy revenues, and the last column shows total subsidies minus total abatement costs. This net revenue peaks at 4 tons/month, the same emissions level the firm would choose with the $120 tax. In other words, the incentive for the firm is the same as for the tax.

Many of the points we made earlier about emission taxes also apply to abatement subsidies. The job of monitoring emissions would be essentially the same. There would undoubtedly be great difficulties in establishing the original base levels from which reductions are to be measured. Each source would wish to have this base level set as high as possible. Perverse incentives might be present

TABLE 12-1
AN ABATEMENT SUBSIDY

Emissions (tons/month)	Marginal abatement cost	Total abatement cost	Total subsidy at $120/ton	Total subsidy minus total abatement costs
10	0	0	0	0
9	15	15	120	105
8	30	45	240	195
7	50	95	360	265
6	70	165	480	315
5	90	255	600	345
4	115	370	720	350
3	130	500	840	340
2	180	680	960	280
1	230	910	1,080	170
0	290	1,200	1,200	0

in the planning stages because sources might try to increase their emissions in the hopes of increasing their base.

Although an abatement subsidy like this would have the same incentive for each individual source, however, total emissions may actually increase. To understand why, note the difference in the financial position of this firm when it emits 4 tons of pollutant under the two programs: with the tax it has total costs of $850 while with the subsidy it has a total *revenue* of $350. Thus, the financial position of the firm is much different. In effect, it will be earning higher profits after the imposition of the subsidy, and this can have the effect of making this industry more attractive for potential new firms. We have the possibility, in other words, of having the emissions per firm go down but the number of firms in the industry, and therefore total emissions, increase. This feature is a major draw-back of simple subsidies like this.

Deposit-Refund Systems

One place where subsidies may be more practical is in deposit-refund systems. A deposit-refund system is essentially the combination of a tax and a subsidy. For example, a subsidy is paid to consumers when they return an item to a designated collection point. The purpose of the subsidy is to provide the incentive for people to refrain from disposing of these items in environmentally damaging ways. The funds for paying the subsidy are raised by levying taxes on these items when they are purchased. In this case, the purpose of the tax is not necessarily so much to get people to reduce the consumption of the item, but to raise money to pay the subsidy. Of course, the tax is called a deposit and the subsidy a refund, but the principle is clear.

Deposit-refund systems are particularly well suited to situations where a product is widely dispersed when purchased and used, and where disposal is difficult or impossible for authorities to monitor. In the U.S. a number of individual states[4] have enacted deposit-refund systems for beverage containers, both to reduce litter and to encourage recycling. This approach has also been widely used in Europe. But many other products could be handled effectively with this type of system.

In the late 1960s, Germany instituted a deposit-refund on waste lubricating oil. Each year very large quantities of waste oil are disposed of improperly, putting many air, water, and land resources under threat. In the German system, new lubricating oil is subject to a tax (a deposit), the proceeds of which go into a special fund. This fund is then used to subsidize (the refund side) a waste oil recovery and reprocessing system. The terms of the subsidy are set so as to encourage competition in the recovery/reprocessing system and to provide an incentive for users to reduce the extent to which oil is contaminated during use.[5]

In Sweden and Norway deposit-refund systems have been instituted for cars. New-car buyers pay a deposit at time of purchase, which will be refunded when and if the car is turned over to an authorized junk dealer. Experience with these systems shows that success depends on more than just the size of the deposit-refund. For example, it is essential that the collection system be designed to be reasonably convenient for consumers.

Other items for which deposit-refund systems might be appropriate are consumer products containing hazardous substances, such as batteries containing cadmium and car batteries. Automobile tires might also be handled this way. The deposit-refund system might also be adaptable to conventional industrial pollutants. For example, users of fossil fuels might pay deposits on the quantities of sulfur contained in the fuels they purchase; they would then get refunds on the sulfur recovered from the exhaust gas. Thus, they would lose their deposit only on the sulfur that went up the stacks.

SUMMARY

Emission taxes attack the pollution problem at its source, by putting a price on something that has been free and, therefore, overused. The main advantage of emission taxes is their efficiency aspects: If all sources are subject to the same tax, they will adjust their emission rates so that the equimarginal rule is satisfied. Administrators do not have to know the individual source marginal abatement cost functions for this to happen; it is enough that firms are faced with the tax and then left free to make their own adjustments. A second major advantage of

---

[4] As of 1990 these were Connecticut, Delaware, Iowa, Maine, Massachusetts, Michigan, New York, Oregon, and Vermont.

[5] Peter Bohm, *Deposit-Refund Systems*, Johns Hopkins Press for Resources for the Future, Baltimore, Md., 1981, pp. 116–120.

emission taxes is that they produce a strong incentive to innovate, to discover cheaper ways of reducing emissions.

The apparent indirect character of emission taxes may tend to work against their acceptance by policymakers. Standards have the appearance of placing direct control on the thing that is at issue, namely emissions. Emission taxes, on the other hand, place no direct restrictions on emissions but rely on the self-interested behavior of firms to adjust their own emission rates in response to the tax. This may make some policymakers uneasy because firms apparently are still allowed to control their own emission rates. It may seem paradoxical that this "indirect" character of effluent taxes can sometimes provide a stronger inducement to emission reductions than seemingly more direct approaches.

But emission taxes require effective monitoring. They cannot be enforced simply by checking to see if sources have installed certain types of pollution-control equipment. If emission taxes are to have the appropriate incentive effects, they must be based closely on *cumulative emissions*. Thus, point sources where emissions can be effectively measured are the likely candidates for pollution control via emissions taxes.

An advantage of emission taxes is that they provide a source of revenue for public authorities. Many have recommended that tax systems be changed, relying less on taxes that have distorting economic effects and more on emissions taxes. This requires that authorities be able to predict with accuracy the effects of particular emissions taxes on rates of emissions.

Emissions subsidies would have the same incentive effect on individual polluters, but they could lead to increases in total emission levels. One place where subsidies have been used effectively is in deposit-refund systems, which are essentially tax and subsidy systems in combination.

QUESTIONS FOR FURTHER DISCUSSION

1 In order to carry out a program of subsidizing emission reductions it would be necessary to start from some baseline level of emissions. What problems are presented in establishing these baselines for different sources?

2 What are the problems and potential of using a deposit-refund system to address the problem of newspaper disposal?

3 How might we design an emission charge program for the control of automobile emissions?

4 Suppose that we institute an emission charge on a particular pollutant, and we use the proceeds of the tax to help subsidize the short-term capital costs of firms in the same industry for installing emission-reduction equipment. Will this approach upset the incentive effects of the emission tax?

5 Opponents of emission charges often say that polluters will simply pay the taxes and pass the cost on to consumers without reducing emissions. Is this correct?

6 Emission charges are sometimes seen as creating a "double burden": Firms must pay the costs of reducing emissions and also pay the government for polluting discharges. How might a charge system be designed to reduce this "double burden"?

7 In the early 1970s the Nixon administration proposed a tax on SO_2 emissions. The tax was to have been levied on the sulfur emitted by utilities and other industries. But in cases where firms had no way of measuring the SO_2 content of exhaust gases, the tax was to be levied on the sulfur content of the fuel. What do you think the effect would have been of this system?

SELECTED READINGS

Ackerman, Bruce A., and Richard B. Stewart: "Reforming Environmental Law: The Democratic Case for Market Incentives," *Columbia Journal of Environmental Law*, 13, 1988, pp. 171–199.

Anderson, Frederick R., et al.: *Environmental Improvements Through Economic Incentives*, Johns Hopkins University Press, Baltimore, Md., 1978.

Anderson, Robert C., Lisa A. Hofmann, and Michael Rusin: *The Use of Economic Incentive Mechanisms in Environmental Management*, American Petroleum Institute, Washington, D.C., June 1990.

Bohm, Peter: *Deposit-Refund Systems: Theory and Application to Environmental, Conservation and Consumer Policy*, Johns Hopkins Press for Resource for the Future, Baltimore, Md., 1981.

Breger, Marshall J., et al.: "Market-Oriented Regulation of Environmental Problems in the Netherlands," *Law and Policy*, 11(2), April 1989, pp. 215–239.

Brown, Gardner M., Jr., and Ralph Johnson: "Pollution Control by Effluent Charges: It Works in the Federal Republic of Germany, Why Not in the U.S.?," *Natural Resources Journal*, 24(4), October 1984, pp. 929–966.

Costanza, Robert, and Charles Perrings: "A Flexible Assurance Bonding System for Improved Environmental Management," *Ecological Economics*, 2(1), February 1990, pp. 57–75.

Hahn, Robert W., and Robert N. Stavins: "Incentive-Based Environmental Regulation: A New Era for an Old Idea?," *Ecology Law Quarterly*, 18(1), 1991, pp. 1–42.

James, D. E., H. M. A. Jansen, and J. B. Opschoor: *Economic Approaches to Environmental Problems: Techniques and Results of Empirical Analysis*, Elsevier Scientific Publications, Amsterdam, 1978.

Moore, John L., Larry Parker, John E. Blodgett, James E. McCarthy, and David E. Gushee: *Using Incentives for Environmental Protection: An Overview*, U.S. Congressional Research Service, Washington, D.C., June 1989.

Nichols, Albert L.: *Targeting Economic Incentives for Environmental Protection*, MIT Press, Cambridge, Mass., 1984.

Organization for Economic Cooperation and Development: *Economic Instruments for Environmental Protection*, Paris, 1989.

Schelling, Thomas C. (ed.): *Incentives for Environmental Protection*, MIT Press, Cambridge, Mass., 1983.

Tietenberg, Tom H.: "Economic Instruments for Environmental Regulation," *Oxford Review of Economic Policy*, 6(1), Spring 1990, pp. 17–33.

U.S. Environmental Protection Agency: *Economic Disincentives for Pollution Control: Legal, Political and Administrative Dimensions*, EPA, Washington, D.C. (EPA-600/5-74-026), 1974.

U.S. Environmental Protection Agency: *Economic Incentives, Options for Environmental Protection*, Washington, D.C. (21P-2001), March 1991.

CHAPTER 13

INCENTIVE-BASED STRATEGIES: TRANSFERABLE DISCHARGE PERMITS

An effluent tax requires that some central public authority establish a tax rate, monitor the performance of each polluter, and then collect the tax bills. It is essentially an interaction between polluters and public authorities in which we might expect the same type of adversarial relationship we get in any tax system. In this chapter we will take a look at a policy approach which, while incorporating economic incentives, is designed to work in a more decentralized fashion. Rather than leaving everything to a centralized public agency, it works through the decentralized market interactions of polluters themselves. It's called the system of "transferable discharge permits."

GENERAL PRINCIPLES

In a transferable discharge permit (TDP) system a new type of property right is created. This property right consists of a permit to emit pollutants. Each permit entitles its holder to emit one unit (pound, ton, however the permit is calibrated) of the waste material specified in the right. Rights holders would ordinarily have a number of such permits at any point in time. If a discharger owned 100 permits, for example, it would be entitled to emit, during some specified period of time, a maximum of 100 units of the designated type of effluent. Thus, the total number of permits held by all sources puts an upper limit on the total quantity of emissions. These discharge permits are *transferable*; they can be bought and sold among anybody allowed to participate in the permit market, at whatever price is agreed upon by the participants themselves.

A TDP program begins by a centralized decision on the total number of discharge permits to be put into circulation. These permits are then distributed among the sources responsible for the emissions. Some formula must be used to determine how many permits each source will receive; we will come back to this problem below. Assuming that the total number of permits is less than current total emissions, some or all emitters will receive fewer permits than their current emissions.

Suppose, for example, that we have a TDP program to reduce the amount of sulfur emitted by a group of power plants. Current total emissions are, say, 150,000 tons of sulfur per year, and policymakers have decided that this must be reduced to 100,000 tons per year. Let's focus on the situation of one of the power plants, which we suppose to be emitting 7,000 tons of sulfur currently. This plant is initially given 5,000 discharge permits. The plant manager now has three choices. The first is simply to reduce the emissions to the level covered by the number of permits the plant was initially given, or 5,000 tons/year. The second is to buy additional permits and emit at higher levels; e.g., it might *buy* an additional 1,000 permits, giving it a total of 6,000 permits. In this case it would reduce its emissions from 7,000 tons to 6,000 tons/year. The third option is to reduce its emissions below the 5,000 tons for which it has permits and then *sell* the permits it doesn't need. For example, if it reduced its emissions to 4,000 tons, 1,000 of its original allocation would not be needed; these could be sold.

It may not be obvious that the buying and selling of permits among polluters (and perhaps others) would lead to the distribution of total emissions among polluters in a way that satisfies the equimarginal principle. We can examine this with the help of Figure 13-1. Here we have pictured two polluters whose emissions are uniformly mixed together (we will treat the case of nonuniform emissions below). They have different marginal abatement costs; costs go up much more rapidly for B than for A as emissions are reduced. Assume that initially neither firm is controlling any of its emissions, so total emissions are 210 tons per year, 120 tons from A and 90 tons from B. Suppose we now wish to reduce total emissions by 50 percent, to 105 tons per year. We create 105 transferable discharge permits, each one of which entitles its possessor to emit 1 ton/year. We distribute these permits to the two sources, using some agreed-upon allocation rule. Let's assume that each is allocated permits in proportion to its current emission rates. Thus, A gets 60 permits and B gets 45 permits in the original distribution.

Firm A will have to cut back to 60 tons/year and Firm B will have to reduce

FIGURE 13-1
How Transferable Discharge Permits Work.

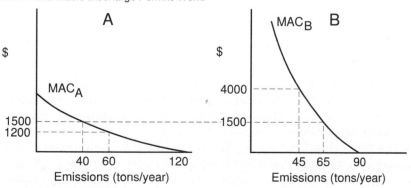

to 45 tons per year, unless they can agree to redistribute the permits among themselves through buying and selling. Suppose Firm B were to cut back to 45 tons; at this point its marginal abatement costs would be $4,000/ton. If it could buy an extra discharge permit for some price less than $4,000, it would be better off because this would allow it to save the difference in abatement costs. Firm A's marginal abatement cost, on the other hand, would be $1,200 per ton if it reduces emissions in accordance with its original holding of 60 permits. If A could sell a permit for some price above $1,200, it would be better off because the revenue from the sale would more than cover the added abatement costs required to reduce its emissions by that unit. Thus, A would be willing to sell a permit for anything above $1,200 and B would be willing to buy a permit for anything below $4,000. Each would obviously be better off by trading the permit, at whatever price they could agree upon between these two extremes. A way of saying this is that there are "gains from trade" for these two polluters in trading a permit from A to B.

After this trade, A will be emitting 1 ton less, or 59 tons per year; and B will be emitting 1 ton more, or 46 tons. But in this situation their marginal abatement costs will still be different. As long as this is true, there will continue to be gains from trade for each of them through trading additional permits. Gains from trade would continue to exist and permits would continue to be traded until marginal abatement costs are equalized. This occurs at emission levels of 40 tons for A and 65 tons for B. At this point Source A has reduced its holdings of discharge permits to 40 (the 60 permits it was initially awarded minus the 20 sold to B), while B has increased its holdings to 65 permits (45 from the original allocation plus the 20 bought from A). Note, however, that as long as the *total* number of permits in circulation is constant, *total* emissions will be constant. Of course, in the bargaining process between A and B it is unlikely that they would have proceeded just one permit at a time. More than likely they would have some idea of the prices for which permits could be bought and sold and the level of their marginal abatement costs, so they could trade blocks of permits for agreed-upon prices. But the essential point is that as long as marginal abatement costs are unequal between these sources, they can both become better off by trading permits at some price between these marginal abatement costs. Thus, in the trading of permits and the adjusting of emissions in accordance with their permit holdings, these sources would be led to an outcome that satisfies the equimarginal principle.

When a large number of firms is involved, the TDP system works in the same way, but trading patterns, of course, will be more complicated. The initial distribution of emission rights will now include many firms, with many potential buyers and sellers. Exhibit 13-1 shows a news clip about proposed transferable discharge permit systems, covering emissions of hydrocarbons and nitrogen oxides, in the Los Angeles area. About 2,000 sources are expected in the hydrocarbon market, and 700 sources in the NO_x market. The expectation is that these markets can achieve emission-reduction goals at substantial savings in costs over traditional programs; the article mentions an estimated saving of $427 million in

EXHIBIT 13-1

AQMD OFFICIALS PROPOSE POLLUTION RIGHTS MARKET

Smog: Incentive Concept Would Let Emitters Direct Own Cleanup Efforts and, If Successful, Sell Excess Shares.

By Judy Pasternak, Times Staff Writer

After two years of studying the pros and cons, the staff of the South Coast Air Quality Management District on Wednesday recommended establishing a revolutionary "smog exchange" that would replace many of the agency's traditional stringent regulations with a trading market in pollution rights.

The prospect previously has generated dire warnings from environmentalists about gambling with public health and excited talk by industry about new freedom and economic relief for recession-weary businesses.

The AQMD staff believes a market would provide incentives to clean the air faster than under the current regulatory system, while saving industry hundreds of millions of dollars. The AQMD board must approve the concept for it to move forward. But if the go-ahead is given as expected in March, trading by 2,000 polluters could begin in 1994.

It would be by far the nation's largest experiment ever in using financial incentives to cut pollution. The progress of the market would be watched closely across the country.

The big question now is what form the "smog exchange" will take, and at a meeting of an AQMD advisory group Wednesday, the staff revealed its blueprint.

About 2,000 facilities that emit hydrocarbons and 700 that emit nitrogen oxides would be eligible to trade under the plan. Some facilities emit both pollutants.

In all, about 24,000 facilities send smog-forming pollutants into the region's air. About 17,000 are regulated by the AQMD. The staff proposal suggests exemptions beyond those for polluters that emit less than four tons of hydrocarbons or nitrogen oxides.

Although the hydrocarbon and nitrogen oxides markets would be separate, they would work in essentially the same way: Polluters would be issued an initial number of shares, based on past emissions. Each share would be worth a pound of pollutant per month or per quarter—a detail yet to be decided.

Over the first 10 years, the value of each share would decline by 5.8% annually for hydrocarbons and by 8% for nitrogen oxides—in theory, forcing cleanup.

In exchange for their participation in the market, businesses would no longer be subject to about 40 existing or proposed AQMD rules that specify certain equipment or methods to reduce pollutants. They could meet their emissions targets however they chose, giving them the flexibility they say they need.

Some businesses would benefit more from a market than others, according to an analysis by the AQMD staff. The analysis found that refineries, for example, would spend $253 million less in 1994 under a market than under the regulatory structure. But the furniture industry, which has complained bitterly about the cost of complying with regulations, would spend about $92 million more in a market than in the current system. Under regulations now in place, furniture makers are allowed an escape hatch if cleaner wood coatings are not developed. The market would require continued emissions reductions regardless of available technology.

Regionwide, the agency predicts, compliance costs under a market system would fall by $427 million in 1994 alone.

Although environmentalists did not object to the nitrogen oxides market, they suggested postponing the market for hydrocarbons for two to three more years, saying it is too difficult to track those emissions.

1994 alone. It also mentions concerns that some observers have about how effectively the markets will operate, especially considering the problems of monitoring emissions. We will discuss this below.

In order for the equimarginal principle eventually to be satisfied in this case it is obviously necessary that all permit buyers and sellers be trading permits at the same price. What this requires is a single overall market for permits where suppliers and demanders may interact openly and where knowledge of transactions prices is publicly available to all participants. We can then expect that the normal forces of competition would bring about a single price for permits. The permits would in general flow from sources with relatively high to those with low marginal abatement costs. Although the example above shows how two sources would redistribute permits among themselves, we would expect that in markets with many sources participating, trading would continue in the future, because of the built-in incentive for polluters to look for better ways of reducing emissions and because of natural changes in a growing economy. We would also anticipate the development of standard market institutions—permit brokers and bankers, permit trading on stock exchanges, etc.—that develop on any market dealing with rights like this, giving us a fully developed market in traded discharge permits, as pictured in Figure 13-2. The demanders in this market would be new firms that wish to begin operations in the trading area or existing

FIGURE 13-2
A Market for Discharge Permits.

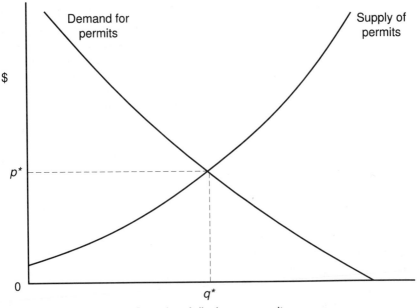

Quantity of discharge permits

sources that wish to expand their operations and require more permits to cover expected increases in emissions. Supplies of permits would include firms leaving the area or going out of business, and most especially firms who have invested in better abatement techniques and now have excess permits to sell. In any particular year there would be a tendency for a market price to establish itself, such as p^* in Figure 13-2, and for a certain number of permits to change hands, such as q^* in the figure.

In recent years the idea of transferable discharge permits has become quite popular among some environmental policy advocates, as well as among policy-makers themselves. Unlike effluent tax approaches, which basically make people pay for something they were once getting free, TDP programs begin by creating and distributing a new type of property right. These property rights will have a market value as long as the total number of permits created is limited. From a political standpoint it is perhaps easier for people to agree on a pollution-control policy that begins by distributing valuable new property rights than by notifying people they will be subject to a new tax. Of course, like any pollution-control policy, TDP programs have their own set of problems that have to be overcome if they are going to work effectively. What looks in theory like a neat way of using market forces to achieve efficient pollution reduction must be adapted to the complexities of the real world.

The Initial Rights Allocation

The success of the TDP approach in controlling pollution depends critically on limiting the number of rights in circulation. Since individual polluters will no doubt want as many as they can get in the first distribution, the very first step of the program is one of potentially great controversy: what formula to use to make the original distribution of emission rights. Almost any rule will appear to have some inequities. We might contemplate distributing them equally among all existing sources of a particular effluent. But this would encounter the problem that firms vary a lot in size. Some pulp mills are larger than others, for example, and the average size of pulp mills, in terms of value of output, may be different from the average size of, say, soda bottling plants. So giving each polluter the same number of permits may not be fair at all.

We might allocate permits in accordance with the existing emissions of a source. For example, each source might get permits amounting to 50 percent of its current emissions. This may sound equitable but, in fact, it has built-in incentive difficulties. A rule like this does not recognize the fact that some firms may already have worked hard to reduce their emissions. One could easily argue that those firms who have already, out of a good conscience, or for any reason, invested in emission reduction, should not now be penalized, in effect, by receiving emission permits in proportion to these lower emission levels.[1] This

---

[1] When we study (in Chapter 15) the Clean Air Act of 1990, we will see that this was the source of great conflict when the details of the SO_2 trading program were being hammered out.

tends to reward firms who have dragged their feet in the past.[2] It could go even further. If polluters believe that permits will soon be allocated in this way, they may have the incentive to *increase* today's emission rate because this would give them a larger base for the initial allocation of permits.

Each allocation formula has its problems, and policymakers must find some workable compromise if the approach is to be widely accepted. Closely related to this issue is the question of whether the rights should be given away or perhaps sold or auctioned. In principle it doesn't matter as long as the permits get distributed fairly widely. Subsequent market transactions will redistribute them in accordance with the relative marginal abatement costs of polluters whatever the original distribution may have been. What a sale or auction would do, however, is transfer some of the original value of the rights into the hands of the auctioning agency. This might be a good way for public agencies to raise funds for worthy projects, but it has to be recognized that a plan like this would create political objections. A hybrid system would be to distribute a certain number of permits free, and then auction some number of additional permits. Or a small surcharge might be put on permits in the original distribution.

Establishing Trading Rules

For any market to work effectively, clear rules must exist covering who may trade and the trading procedures that must be followed. Furthermore, the rules should not be so burdensome that they make it impossible for market participants to gauge accurately the implications to them of buying or selling at specific prices. This implies a "hands-off" stance by public agencies after the initial distribution of the rights. Working against this is the normal tendency for environmental agencies to want to monitor the market closely and perhaps try to influence its performance. The supervising agency, for example, may want to have final right of approval over all trades, so as to be able to stop any trades it considers undesirable in some way. The problem with this is that it is likely to increase the uncertainty among potential traders, increase the general level of transactions costs in the market, and interfere with the efficient flow of permits. The general rule for the public agency should be: set simple and clear rules and then allow trading to proceed.

One basic rule that would have to be established is who may participate in the market. Is this to be limited to polluters, or may anyone trade? For example, may environmental advocacy groups buy permits and retire them as a way of reducing total emissions? One's first reaction is to say that such groups ought to be permitted to buy permits, because that is evidence that society's willingness to pay for lower total emission levels exceeds the price of the permits, which should

---

[2] This is just another example of the perverse incentives built into any program that asks everybody to cut their consumption by x percent from their current rate. It favors those who have consumed at high rates in the past and hurts those who have tried hard to live frugally.

be the same as marginal abatement costs. This conclusion is probably valid if we are dealing with a local or regional environmental group whose membership is roughly coincidental with the trading area, and which has raised money specifically to buy discharge permits in that region. It is probably not valid if large, national advocacy groups were to use their resources to buy permits on a regional market, because the amount they were willing to pay for permits might have no close relationship to underlying true social willingness to pay.

These and other trading rules will have to be worked out for particular programs in particular circumstances. A body of common law governing discharge permit transactions will also develop over time. For the rest of this chapter we will deal with some of the important economic dimensions of these trading institutions.

Nonuniform Emissions

Suppose we are trying to design a TDP program to control total airborne SO_2 emissions in a region where there are numerous different sources, power plants, industrial plants, etc., scattered rather widely around the area. A schematic of this situation is depicted in Figure 13-3. All the emission points are not equally situated relative to the prevailing wind or to the area of highest population density. Some sources are upwind, others are downwind, of the populated area. We assume they are not all equal in terms of marginal abatement costs, but neither are they equal in terms of the impact of their emissions on ambient SO_2 levels over the populated area. In technical terms, they have different transfer

FIGURE 13-3
Nonuniform Emissions and TDP Programs.

Key: ☒ Locations of each emission point

☐ Highest population density

‑ ‑ ‑ Zones for permit trading

coefficients linking their own emissions with damages in the urban area. Having distributed discharge permits we now allow them to be traded. As long as the number of permits in circulation is held constant, we have effectively controlled total SO_2 emissions. But if we allow straight trading, unit for unit, of permits among all sources, the damage caused by that total could change. For example, if a downwind firm sold permits to an upwind firm, the total number of permits would remain the same but there would now be more emissions upwind of the population and, therefore, more damage.[3]

The problem is similar to the one we encountered under the effluent tax policy; in effect each firm is differently situated relative to the damage area, so the emissions of each will have a different impact on ambient quality in that area.[4] If the program were simply to allow trading of permits among all sources on a one-for-one basis, it could easily come to pass that a firm or group of firms with higher transfer coefficients, whose emissions therefore have a greater impact on ambient quality, could accumulate larger numbers of permits. One way to avoid this would be to adjust the trading to take into account the impacts of individual sources. Suppose the emissions from Source A were twice as damaging as the emissions of Source B simply because of the location of the two sources. Then the administrators of the program might set a rule that if Source A is buying permits from Source B, it must buy two permits to get one.

If we extend this into a situation with many sources, things can quickly get very complicated. Authorities would have to determine, for each source, how many permits would have to be purchased from each other source in order for the purchasing source to be credited with one new permit. If there were five sources, the agency would have to figure out only 10 such trading ratios, but if there were 20 different sources, it would have to estimate 190 of these ratios.[5] One way around this would be to use a zoned system, analogous to the zoned effluent charge we talked about earlier. Authorities would designate a series of zones, each of which would contain sources that were relatively similar in terms of their location and the impact of their emissions on ambient quality. Four such zones are shown in Figure 13-3. We could then do one of two things: allow trading by firms only with other firms in the same zone, or make adjustments for all trades across zone boundaries similar to the technique discussed above. Thus, for example, if sources in Zone A were judged to have transfer coefficients twice the size, on average, as sources in Zone B, any trade between sources in these two zones would be adjusted by that same factor of two: Any firm in Zone A buying permits from any firm in Zone B would have to buy two permits in order to get credit for one new one; any source in Zone B would have to buy only half a permit from a firm in Zone A to get credit for one new permit.

---

[3] This is sometimes called the "hot spot" problem.

[4] For example, one of the first trades of SO_2 permits under the 1990 Clean Air Act was a sale of permits from a Wisconsin power company to the Tennessee Valley Authority.

[5] In general, if there were n sources, there would have to be $[n(n-1)]/2$ trading ratios established.

TDPs and Problems of Competition

The question of allowing trading across zone boundaries or, on the contrary, restricting it to within zones has a much wider importance than might first appear. TDP programs work through a trading process, where buyers and sellers interact to transfer title to valuable property rights. Markets work best when there is substantial competition among buyers and among sellers; they work much less well if there are so few buyers or sellers that competitive pressures are weak or absent. In cases where there are few traders, one of them, or perhaps a small group, may be able to exercise control over the market, colluding on prices, perhaps charging different prices to different people, using the control of discharge permits to gain economic control in its industry, etc. From the standpoint of fostering competition, therefore, we would like to set our trading zones as widely as possible, to include large numbers of potential buyers and sellers.

But this may work against the ecological facts. In many cases there may be meteorological or hydrological reasons for limiting the trading area to a relatively narrow geographical area. If we are interested in controlling airborne emissions affecting a particular city, for example, we would probably not want to allow firms located there to trade permits with firms in another city. Or if our concern is controlling emissions into a particular lake or river, we could not allow sources located there to trade permits with sources located on some entirely different body of water. Thus, for environmental reasons we may want to have trading areas restricted,[6] while for economic reasons we would want to have trading areas defined broadly. There is no magic rule to tell us exactly how these two factors should be balanced in all cases. We can only look at specific cases as they come up and weigh the particularities of the environmental features with the subtleties of the competitive conditions in the industries where trading will occur.

TDP Programs and Enforcement

The directly controlling aspect of a TDP program is that sources are constrained to keep their emissions at a level no greater than the total number of discharge permits in their possession. Thus an administering agency would essentially have to keep track of two things: the number of permits in the possession of each source and the quantity of emissions from each source. Since the initial permit distribution will be well known, the agency must have some way of keeping track of permit transactions among market participants. Trades could, in fact, become complicated with multiple buyers and sellers, and with different types of transactions like temporary rentals and long-term leases in addition to permanent transfers. Since permit buyers (or renters) would have a strong incentive to have

---

[6] Though not always; we will discuss below the national trading market in lead permits used in the introduction of leaded gasoline into the U.S. economy.

their purchases revealed to the agency, and since all purchases imply sellers, a system of self-reporting, coupled with modern means of information transfer, may be sufficient to provide reliable information on which sources have the permits.

As regards monitoring, the administrative agency must be able to monitor polluters to see whether emissions at each source exceed the number of permits it holds. If permits are expressed in terms of total emissions over some period of time, a means has to be available to measure cumulative emissions at each source. This is the same requirement as with an effluent tax. If there were reasonable certainty that emissions were fairly even throughout the year, authorities could get a check on cumulative emissions by making spot checks of instantaneous rates. For most industrial sources of pollution, however, there is considerable daily, weekly, or seasonal variations in emissions, so more sophisticated monitoring would be required.

One desirable feature of TDP programs is that there may be an incentive for sources to monitor each other, at least informally. When, and if, some sources emit more than they have permits for, they are essentially cheating by not buying sufficient permits to cover all of their emissions. In effect this reduces the demand for permits below what it would otherwise be. And this has the effect of lowering the market price of permits. This clearly works against the interest of any firm holding large numbers of permits, which gives it an incentive to see that other firms don't cheat on emissions.

TDPs and the Incentive for R&D

One of our main criteria for judging an environmental policy is whether or not it creates strong incentives for firms to seek better ways of reducing emissions. Emission standards were weak in this regard, while emission taxes were much stronger. TDP programs in this respect are identical to the emissions tax, at least in theory. Consider the firm in Figure 13-4. Suppose that at present the firm's marginal abatement cost function is MAC_1. Emission permits sell for p each, and let us assume that this price is not expected to change. The firm has adjusted its holdings so that it currently owns e_1 permits.[7] Its emissions are therefore e_1 and its total abatement costs are $(a + b)$. The incentive to do R&D is to find a less costly way of controlling emissions, so the firm can cut emissions and sell the surplus permits. How much would it be worth to get marginal abatement costs shifted to MAC_2? With MAC_2, the firm would shift to an emissions level of e_2. Its total abatement costs here would be $(b + d)$, but it would be able to sell $(e_1 - e_2)$ permits for a revenue of $p(e_1 - e_2) = (c + d)$. The change in its position would thus be:

---

[7] These marginal abatement cost functions apply to a year; i.e., they are the costs per year of changing emissions. The price p is therefore a one-year purchase (or sale) price, what it would cost to buy or sell a permit for just one year. If a firm is buying a permit to hold permanently, the price will be some multiple of the annual value, much as the purchase price of a rental house is some multiple of its annual rental income.

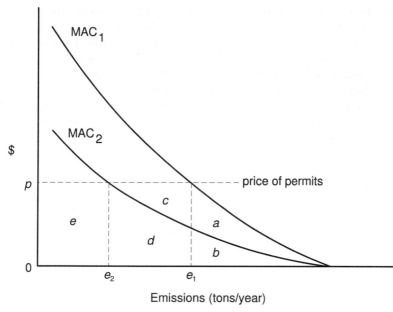

FIGURE 13-4
TDP and Technological Change.

$$\text{Total abatement costs} \atop \text{with } MAC_1 \quad - \quad {\text{Total abatement costs} \atop \text{with } MAC_2} \quad + \quad {\text{Receipts from} \atop \text{TDP sale}}$$

or $(a + b) - (d + b) + (c + d)$, which equals $(a + c)$. Check this with the savings under an effluent tax (above, pp. 238 to 239). It is exactly the same. The market price of the permit has the same incentive as a pollution tax; by not reducing their emissions, firms are forgoing the increased revenues they could have obtained by selling some of their permits.

SUMMARY

Programs of transferable discharge permits have started to become more popular among U.S. environmental policymakers in recent years. The Clean Air Act Amendments of 1990 contain a TDP program for SO_2 reduction among electric power producers; we will discuss it in Chapter 15. TDP programs have been proposed for control of solid waste and even for global CO_2 reduction. The spirit behind this approach, the transfer of emission rights from sources with low control costs to those with high costs, is also behind some recent developments in the control of nonpoint source waterborne emissions; we will discuss these later in the chapter on water pollution. There is the expectation that this approach could give us pollution control at a substantially lower cost than the current system of technology-based effluent standards, and also a sense that, politically, they would be more acceptable than emission taxes.

But TDP programs come with their own set of problems. Most especially, TDP programs take some of the burden of pollution control out of the hands of engineers and place it under the operation of a market. How that market operates is obviously critical to whether this type of policy will work. There is a host of important factors: who gets the permits at the beginning, the strength of their incentives to minimize costs, the degree of competition in the market, the transaction rules set by the administering public agency, the ability to monitor and enforce compliance, and so on. Nevertheless, the transferable discharge permit system seems to be an idea whose time has come, at least in the U.S.

Both transferable discharge systems and emission tax systems seek to take the burden and responsibility of making technical pollution-control decisions out of the hands of central administrators and put them into the hands of polluters themselves. They are not, we should stress, aimed at putting pollution-control *objectives* themselves into the hands of the polluters. It is not the market that is going to determine the most efficient level of pollution control for society. Rather, they are means of enlisting the incentives of the polluters themselves in finding more effective ways of meeting the overall objective of reducing emissions.

QUESTIONS FOR FURTHER DISCUSSION

1 In discussing emission taxes we considered the "two-part tax," where sources would pay a low, or zero, tax on some initial quantity of emissions, and a higher tax on anything over this level. How might the same feature be designed into a program of transferable emission permits?

2 What are the pros and cons of letting *anybody* (banks, private citizens, environmental groups, government agencies, etc.) buy and sell transferable discharge permits, in addition to emission sources themselves?

3 How might you design a transferable discharge permit system for solid waste? For phasing out of use a certain type of plastic? For phasing in a program of using recycled newsprint in newspapers?

4 What would the effect on a TDP market be if it were subject to the oversight of a committee which frequently changed the rules governing trades?

5 What do you think the effect on a TDP market would be if a judge decided that purchasers of discharge rights could be held liable if the sources that sold them the rights did not reduce their emissions commensurate with the sale?

SELECTED READINGS

Brady, Gordon L: "Emissions Trading in the United States: An Overview and Technical Requirements," *Journal of Environmental Management*, 17(1), 1983, pp. 63–79.

Clark, Timothy B.: "A New Approach to Regulatory Reform — Letting the Market Do the Job," *National Journal*, 11(32), August 11, 1979, pp. 1316–1322.

Dales, John: *Pollution, Property and Prices*, University of Toronto Press, Toronto, 1968.

Hahn, Robert W.: "Economic Perspectives for Environmental Problems: How the Patient

Followed the Doctor's Orders," *Journal of Economic Perspectives*, 3(2), Spring 1989, pp. 95–114.

Hahn, Robert W.: *A Primer on Environmental Policy Design*, Harwood Academic Publishers, Chur, Switzerland, 1989.

Hahn, Robert W., and Gordon L. Hester: "Marketable Permits: Lessons for Theory and Practice," *Ecology Law Quarterly*, 16(1), Winter 1989, pp. 361–406.

Hahn, Robert W., and Roger G. Noll: "Designing a Market for Tradeable Emission Permits," in Wesley Magat (ed.), *Reform of Environmental Regulation*, Ballinger Publishing Company, Cambridge, Mass., 1982, pp.119–146.

Project 88—Round II Incentives for Action: Designing Market-Based Environmental Strategies: A Public Policy Study sponsored by Senators Timothy E. Wirth and John Heinz, Washington, D.C., May 1991.

Roberts, Marc J.: "Some Problems in Implementing Marketable Pollution Rights Schemes: The Case of the Clean Air Act," in Wesley A. Magat (ed.), *Reform of Environmental Regulation*, Ballinger Publishing Company, Cambridge, Mass., 1982, pp. 93–118.

Rose-Ackerman, Susan: "Market Models for Water Pollution Control: Their Strengths and Weaknesses," *Public Policy*, 25(3), Summer 1977, pp. 383–406.

Tietenberg, Tom H.: *Emissions Trading: An Exercise in Reforming Pollution Policy*, Resources for the Future, Washington, D.C., 1985.

Tripp, James T. B., and Daniel Dudek: "Institutional Guidelines for Designing Successful Transferable Rights Programs," *Yale Journal of Regulation*, 6(2), Summer 1989, pp. 369–392.

U.S. Environmental Protection Agency: *An Evaluation of Marketable Effluent Permit Systems* (EPA-600/5-74-030), Washington, D.C., 1974.

ENVIRONMENTAL POLICY
IN THE U.S.

Having looked at the principles of designing effective environmental policy we now turn to an examination of actual policies; most of the remainder of the book, in fact, consists of chapters about public policies that have been put in place to deal with environmental problems of various types. The present section contains four chapters on U.S. environmental policies. There are three chapters on federal policy, on problems of water, air, and hazardous materials. Then there is a chapter on environmental policies of the states. Each of these policy areas is extremely complex, with its own history, character, and vocabulary. What the chapters aim for is a summary of the main elements of each policy area, utilizing the ideas we have discussed in the preceding chapters.

CHAPTER 14

FEDERAL WATER POLLUTION-CONTROL POLICY

Water is biologically necessary for life but, beyond this, water resources play a vital and pervasive role in the health and welfare of a modern economy. Water for direct human consumption is a small but critical part of the domestic system, which also includes water used in food preparation, cleaning, and sewage disposal. Water is an essential element in many industrial and commercial production processes, again both as an input and as a medium of waste disposal. Large amounts of water are used by farmers for irrigation, especially in the western U.S. And in recent decades water-based sports and recreation, both freshwater and saltwater, have become very popular.

The water resource system itself consists of a vast array of interconnected components, from the grandiose to the tiny. The surface-water system includes the huge main-stem rivers and Great Lakes as well as the thousands of small neighborhood streams and ponds. Add to these the innumerable person-made components, from the mill ponds of the first industrial era to the vast reservoirs and canals of today. Swamps and wetlands abound, ranging from small local bogs to the huge Everglades in southern Florida. And then there is the vast, but unseen, system of groundwater aquifers, exceeding surface waters in terms of sheer quantity of water. Saltwater resources are also of vital importance. Marshes and coastal lowlands are critical for fish and wildlife resources; beaches and scenic coasts are important recreational resources; coastal waters provide transportation and pleasure boating services; and saltwater fisheries are a major source of food.

Efforts to protect these water resources have gone on for a long time but with increasing vigor in the last few decades. In this chapter we will look at federal water pollution-control policy. Our objective is to review the main elements of that policy with the economic concepts we have developed in preceding chapters. We will also look at some recent policy innovations that seek to make use of economic incentive to achieve improvements in water quality. Most states and localities also have active water pollution-control efforts, some of which are tied into the federal programs; we will consider these in a later chapter.

TYPES OF WATER POLLUTANTS

One way to categorize waterborne pollutants is by their chemical and physical nature.[1]

- Organic wastes: degradable wastes such as domestic sewage, residuals from pulp mills, food processing plants; chemicals such as pesticides, detergents, solvents, oil.
- Inorganic substances: chemicals such as toxic metals, salts, acids; plant nutrients such as nitrate and phosphorous compounds.
- Nonmaterial pollutants: radioactivity, heat.
- Infectious agents: bacteria, viruses.

Waterborne emissions include all the different types of discharges discussed in Chapter 2. *Point sources* include outfalls from industry and domestic wastewater treatment plants. *Nonpoint sources* include agricultural runoff of pesticides and fertilizers and the chemicals and oils that are flushed off urban streets by periodic rains. Many sources, especially point sources, have *continuous* emissions, related to the rate of operation of the industrial plant or the domestic sewer system. There are also many *episodic* emissions, such as accidental releases of toxic materials, oil-tanker accidents, or occasional planned releases of industrial pollutants.

In Chapter 2 we also spoke of cumulative and noncumulative pollutants. In water pollution control it is more common to speak of *persistent* and *degradable* pollutants. Degradable waterborne pollutants undergo a variety of biological, chemical, and physical processes that change their characteristics after emission. Especially important are the oxygen-using chemical processes that rely on the oxygen contained in receiving waters to degrade the wastes.[2] The reason for focusing on oxygen requirements is that oxygen plays a critical role in water quality. High levels of dissolved oxygen (DO) are usually associated with high-quality water, water that will support high-quality recreational uses, and that can be used in domestic water-supply systems.

Since DO is used up in the degradation process, one way of measuring the quantity of waste emitted is through "biochemical oxygen demand," or BOD, the amount of oxygen required to decompose the organic material under specified conditions of temperature and time.[3] A substantial proportion of the BOD load introduced into the water resources of the country comes from municipal waste-treatment plants. Much of this consists of wastewater from treated domestic waste, which contains a variety of degradable organic compounds. Industrial

---

[1] G. Tyler Miller, Jr., *Resource Conservation and Management*, Wadsworth Publishing Company, Belmont, Calif., 1990, p. 201.

[2] Degradable wastes also include a variety of infectious bacterial agents that can cause such diseases as typhoid, cholera, and dysentery. Waste heat is also a degradable pollutant; it comes mostly from large-scale industrial processes that use water for cooling purposes.

[3] For example, 10 pounds of BOD_{10} is a quantity of material requiring 10 pounds of oxygen in order to be completely converted to its constituent elements over a period of 10 days and at a temperature of 20°C.

sources also contribute large amounts of BOD, some stemming from the sanitary facilities within the plants, but more importantly from the great variety of water-using steps in the production processes, such as cleaning, product formation, waste removal, and product transport.

When a BOD load is put into a river or body of water, it produces a temporary reduction in the DO level of that water, as the oxygen is used up to degrade the waste. But over time, through natural aeration processes, the DO content of the water will normally recover. The DO "profile" would thus look like Figure 14-1 (where the discharge point is marked x). We could think of this as the average DO level at various distances downstream from the point at which a BOD load is introduced, or the DO level at various times after a BOD load has been introduced into a lake. This is called a DO "sag," and illustrates the degradation process by which the water body is assimilating the BOD load. The important thing to see is that the DO reduction is reversible. It is also noncumulative—if the BOD source were stopped, the DO sag would shortly disappear.

Early water pollution-control efforts were centered on conventional pollutants like BOD, suspended solids, etc., for which there are common water quality measures such as DO, turbidity, acidity, and coliform count. It soon became clear that many rivers and water bodies had problems of *toxic* pollutants; i.e., pollution by particular waste substances that could have substantial direct impacts on the health of water ecosystems as well as of people making use of them. Toxics include heavy metals, pesticides, polychlorinated biphenyls (PCBs), and other industrial chemicals. Toxicity is often a matter of concentration; substances that are toxic at high concentrations may not be at low concentrations. This implies that the diluting ability of water is a valuable quality in addition to its capacity to transform degradable substances.

Persistent water pollutants are those that remain for a long period of time, either because they are nondegradable or because the rate of degradation is very slow. This category includes thousands of inorganic and organic chemicals of

FIGURE 14-1
Dissolved Oxygen Profile in Water After a BOD Load Has Been Introduced.

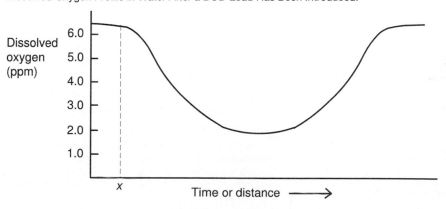

various descriptions, the wastes of a modern, chemical-based economy. Industrial wastes contain many such persistent pollutants. Wastes from mining operations can contain various metals as well as acid-mine drainage. Agriculture is the
source of a variety of pesticides, fertilizers, and soil runoff. The concept of
"persistent" does not mean permanent in a technical sense; many chemicals, oils,
solvents, etc., break down, but over a long period of time. In the process they
pose a persistent threat. Radioactive waste is physically degradable over very
long periods, but measured in terms of a human scale it is essentially a persistent
pollutant. Viruses are apparently also in this category.

FEDERAL POLICY: A BRIEF HISTORY

Prior to the twentieth century the only public policy initiatives taken toward
water pollution control were at the state level. In the "sanitary awakening" of
the mid-nineteenth century, the public began to appreciate the importance of
water quality for human health. Many states instituted public boards of health
in response.[4] The first federal law of any note covering water pollution control
was actually enacted at the very end of the nineteenth century (see Table 14-1).
This was the "1899 Refuse Act" empowering the U.S. Army Corps of Engineers
to grant permits to anyone desiring to put refuse of any kind into any navigable
waterway. The primary objective of this act was to ensure navigation, however—
not to control water pollution per se.

Very little happened, therefore, until after World War II. Then the Water
Pollution Control Act of 1948 was enacted, authorizing federal authorities to
assist the states in water pollution-control matters. Primary responsibility, however, was to remain at the state level. The 1948 Act also authorized a program
that over the years would become a major element of the federal effort: subsidies
to municipalities to construct waste treatment facilities. That act also sought to
develop new enforcement institutions, so-called enforcement conferences,
where federal, state, and local administrative authorities would come together
and hammer out water pollution-control policies. In 1965 came the Water Quality
Act, which, besides extending many provisions of past laws and refunding the
municipal waste-treatment subsidy program, sought to encourage the states to
develop *ambient standards* for water quality.

The early 1970s saw a rapid growth in the environmental movement and in
environmental advocacy in Washington, D.C. There was at the time a feeling
among environmental interest groups that past policy had not worked well
enough and quickly enough to respond to growing pollution problems. The
Environmental Protection Agency (EPA) had recently been formed (1970) and
this gave environmental issues more visibility and greater political representation. One result was the 1972 Water Pollution Control Act Amendments.
This Act did several things; it set a goal of zero discharges to be attained by 1985,

[4] The first such agency was in Massachusetts in 1869.

TABLE 14-1
MAJOR FEDERAL LEGISLATION ON WATER POLLUTION CONTROL

1899 Refuse Act
Required permit from the U.S. Army Corps of Engineers before refuse of any kind could be put into a navigable water. Primary purpose was to ensure navigability, but it had a brief, and not very successful, reincarnation in the 1960s as a water-quality measure.

1948 Water Pollution Control Act (WPCA)
Federal government was authorized to conduct investigations, research, and surveys; but no federal authority was established to enforce laws, set standards, or limit discharges; authorized federal government to make loans to municipalities to construct sewage treatment facilities.

1956 WPCA Amendments
Authorized the states to establish criteria for determining desirable levels of water quality; introduced the idea of an "enforcement conference," sponsored by federal agencies to bring together state and local interests to develop enforcement plans. Authorized federal government to make grants for municipal waste treatment facilities, with federal share up to 55 percent of construction costs.

1965 Water Quality Act
Required the states to develop *ambient quality standards* for interstate water bodies and implementation plans calling for effluent reductions from specific sources. State actions required federal approval, with a strengthened "enforcement conference" procedure.

1972 WPCA Amendments
Provided for a federally mandated system of *technology-based effluent standards,* with federal enforcement through the granting of discharge permits. Phase I (starting in 1977) permits were based on "Best Practicable Technology" (BPT); Phase II (starting in 1983) based on "Best Available Technology" (BAT); states could ultimately take over permitting process. Declared a goal of zero discharge to be attained by 1985. Made a large increase in the municipal treatment plant grant program, with federal share increased to 75 percent of construction costs. Mandated secondary treatment in municipal treatment plants.

1977 Clean Water Act
Established procedures for control of toxic effluent in addition to conventional effluent on which previous acts had focused; sources were required to meet "Best Conventional Technology" (BCT) for conventional pollutants and BAT for toxics, starting in 1984; increased authorization for treatment plant subsidies.

1981 Municipal Wastewater Treatment Construction Grant Amendments
Reduced federal share to 55 percent and substantially decreased the authorized funding level.

1987 Water Quality Act
Postponed some of the deadlines for adopting *technology-based effluent standards;* changed the waste treatment subsidy program from federal grants to federal contributions to state revolving funds.

Sources: Allen V. Kneese and Charles L. Schultz, *Pollution, Prices and Public Policy,* Brookings Institution, Washington, D.C., 1973, p. 31; Tom H. Tietenberg, *Environmental and Natural Resource Economics,* 2nd ed., Scott, Foresman, Glenview, Ill., 1988, pp. 410–411; A. Myrick Freeman III, "Water Pollution Control," in Paul R. Portney (ed.), *Public Policies for Environmental Protection,* Resources for the Future, Washington, D.C., 1990, pp. 100–101.

and it substantially increased the amount of money for the municipal waste-treatment subsidy program. More importantly, however, it established a powerful new, direct federal role in water pollution control.

The frustration with existing approaches led policymakers to try something new and more direct. The primary approach before then was an ambient-based one. States were supposed to establish ambient water quality standards, then translate these into specific emission reductions by the many firms and treatment plants contributing to the problem. In order to enforce emission limitations on particular firms, for example, authorities had to show how their emissions led to degradation of water quality below the ambient standards established by the states. This was often very difficult to do. Without a great deal of physical and chemical modeling it is hard to distinguish the impact of particular polluters on ambient levels when many sources contribute to the same problem. So in 1972 water pollution-control policy was drastically changed.

The new approach was for federal authorities to set specific effluent standards for individual sources. To enforce these standards the law reached all the way back to the 1899 Refuse Act. There would be a system of federally issued discharge permits. Each source of waterborne emissions would require a permit specifying the time, place, and maximum quantity of emissions. To provide the basis for these permits, the EPA would promulgate what are called *technology-based effluent standards* for all sources discharging wastes into the nation's waters. As we will discuss in more detail below, these are essentially emission standards that are tied to particular types of pollution-control technology. Thus, the primary approach to water pollution control was changed from an ambient-based to a technology-based system.

The procedures specified in the 1972 Act continue to be the primary approach to point-source water pollution control in the U.S. A considerable administrative apparatus has grown up around the specification and promulgation of the technology-based effluent standards. It became clear soon after the 1972 law was enacted that the deadlines were impossibly short; they required the EPA to establish effluent limitations within one year of that act. But setting standards that would withstand court challenge took much longer than this. The 1977 Clean Water Act pushed the deadlines back a number of years and relaxed the basis for establishing standards for conventional, but not toxic, pollutants. In 1981 a law was enacted that substantially decreased the federal contribution to municipal waste-treatment plants. In the 1987 Water Quality Act this program was changed from one of federal grants to one of federal contributions to state revolving funds. The 1987 Act also pushed back the target deadlines for the adoption of technology-based effluent standards and gave some recognition to the growing concern about nonpoint-source water pollution.

Reduced to its essentials the basic federal program for water pollution control consists of three elements: (1) federally determined technology-based effluent standards, (2) a combined state/federal effort to enforce these standards, and (3) municipal waste-treatment plant subsidies. The last of these has recently been substantially changed. Besides this primary program the EPA, together with other federal agencies and the states, has initiated a number of special programs aimed at particular water-quality problems. This includes programs on non-point-source water pollutants, estuarine water quality, groundwater protection, protection of drinking water supplies, and a water quality program for the Great Lakes.

TECHNOLOGY-BASED EFFLUENT STANDARDS

A technology-based effluent standard (TBES)[5] is an effluent standard set at the level of emissions that a source would produce if it were employing a particular type of abatement technology. Firms emitting waste materials or energy usually face a choice among different technologies and methods for reducing emissions. From among the possibilities each source must choose one particular package, which may involve, for example, particular types of equipment, raw materials, internal operating procedures, recycling machinery, treatment processes, or effluent removal techniques. Different packages of technologies and operating procedures lead to different costs as well as a different level of emissions. To establish a TBES, the EPA studies the effluent abatement technologies and procedures available to a particular type of industrial operation; after having selected one technology from among the many available, it sets the emission standard at the level of emissions that are produced when that technology is used by firms in that industry.

It would require enormous effort to establish effluent standards for each and every individual source. Thus the EPA sets standards for categories of polluting sources. Suppose, for example, we are concerned with sugar-beet processing

---

[5] Pollution-control policy is rife with acronyms. Table 14-2 contains a list of acronyms used in this chapter. In the text I use acronyms fairly heavily, but have also occasionally included the complete phrase as a reminder.

TABLE 14-2
GLOSSARY OF ACRONYMS USED IN THIS CHAPTER

BAT	Best available technology
BMP	Best management practices
BOD	Biochemical oxygen demand
BPT	Best practicable technology
CEQ	Council on Environmental Quality
DO	Dissolved oxygen
EPA	Environmental Protection Agency
NPS	Nonpoint source
TBES	Technology-based effluent standard
TSS	Total suspended solids
WPCA	Water Pollution Control Act

plants.[6] This is a process that uses a large amount of water for cleaning purposes; thus, the wastewater may contain large amounts of suspended solids and BOD. Table 14-3 shows the costs and emissions performance of five different technology options for plants in this industry. These are not costs and emissions for any particular plant; they are anticipated costs and emissions for a "representative" plant of each type. Each technological option refers to a particular collection of treatment equipment, operating procedures, fuels, etc., that the plants might adopt. The EPA, after having developed these estimates,[7] must now choose a particular level of emissions for the standard.

Clearly, lower levels of emissions can be obtained with greater costs; in fact, emissions into water bodies could be reduced to zero at a very high cost. To pick one set of emission levels for the standard requires that the EPA use some sort of criterion. The Water Pollution Control Act of 1972 states that the EPA should initially set emission standards on the basis of the "best practicable technology" (BPT) currently available to the firms. This was Phase I, to be achieved by 1977. Then starting in 1983, firms would be subject to Phase II effluent standards, based on "best available technology" (BAT).

Thus, to set the Phase I emission standard for sugar-beet processing plants, EPA would have to determine which of the technologies displayed in the table represented the "best practicable" level of technology. Clearly, this is open to interpretation, since the notion of "practicable" is not precise by any means. "Practicable" apparently refers to technology that is reasonably well known

---

[6] Sugar-beet processing uses substantial quantities of water. Some is used simply to move the product around the plant, while some is used in actual processing. Hydrated lime is used as a purifying agent, which leaves a large amount of "lime mud" to dispose of. Emission control can be done with a variety of water recycling and recirculation, screening, settling, stabilization ponds, and land disposal.

[7] In fact, these numbers would more than likely have been provided by an engineering consulting firm hired by the EPA. An agency that regulates thousands of plants in dozens of different industries has to look outside for technical help.

TABLE 14-3
ESTIMATED TOTAL COSTS AND EMISSIONS FROM SUGAR-BEET PLANTS USING ALTERNATIVE EMISSION ABATEMENT TECHNOLOGY

	No control	Technological option				
		A	B	C	D	E
Emissions (kg/kkg of raw product processed)						
BOD*	5.8	3.6	2.2	1.05	.23	0.0
TSS†	10.2	5.7	2.5	1.02	.30	0.0
Total costs ($ mil/year)	0.0	8.0	14.4	23.40	36.50	78.8

*Biochemical oxygen demand.
†Total suspended solids.

and readily available without excessive costs. Suppose EPA decides that technology C, with an estimated cost of $23.4 million per year, represents the best practicable technology for this type of processing industry. Then it would set emission standards at 1.05 kg/kkg for BOD and 1.02 kg/kkg for total suspended solids. All sugar-beet processing plants would then be subject to this emission standard. In Phase II EPA would be called upon to select the "best available technology" (BAT) for this type of industry. BAT would appear to be a more stringent standard than BPT, since it includes all technologies that are available whether or not they are practicable. But the rules also specify that BAT has to be "economically achievable." On this basis, technology E in Table 14-3 might be regarded as the BAT for sugar-beet processing plants. On the other hand, some (especially those in the industry) might argue that that technology doesn't realistically exist, that it is too costly to be considered "available" in any economic sense, in which case EPA might select D as the BAT.

Setting technology-based effluent standards for an industry is obviously a time-consuming business. It requires large amounts of economic analysis and hinges on an agency judgment about what "available" and "practicable" mean when applied to pollution-control technology. It is also politically controversial, with industries ready to challenge in court when they feel the standards are too constraining. It is no wonder that the EPA made very slow progress in setting TBESs after the 1972 law was enacted. In the 1977 Clean Water Act the criteria for selecting emission standards were changed. After 1984 sources were to meet standards based on "best conventional technology" (BCT). The notion of "conventional" technology is different, and weaker, than the idea of "available" technology; it presumably allows more weight to be put on the costs of installing and operating the technology.[8] In some cases the EPA has set BCT equal to BPT. The EPA also sets TBESs, called "pretreatment standards," for firms discharging wastes into public sewer systems. Their role is to reduce the burden on public wastewater treatment plants.

Technology-based effluent standards to control water pollution stem from the desire—widespread in the twentieth century—to find a technological fix for pollution problems. The original notion behind the 1972 Act was that enlightened engineering studies by the EPA would identify preferred pollution-control technologies, and that since emission standards would be based on these technologies, there would be few practical obstacles in the way of their timely adoption by firms. In fact, the very ambiguity of words like "practicable" and "conventional" means that a great amount of discretion and judgment must be

---

[8] The ambiguities of using these criteria to choose specific technology options led the EPA at one time to establish a benchmark for BCT of $1.15 per pound of pollutant removed. Anything above this was considered too costly to be "conventional." See David Harrison, Jr., and Paul R. Portney, "Who Loses from Reform of Environmental Regulation?" in Wesley A. Magat (ed.), *Reform of Environmental Regulation*, Ballinger, Cambridge, Mass., 1982, pp. 147–179.

used by people developing the standards. Over the years EPA has struggled valiantly to clarify the role of discretion and judgment in setting the standards. Industrial firms also have had views about what these words mean, which has led through the years to vast amounts of conflict and litigation.

TBESs and Water Quality

The justification for emission standards is presumably that they will lead to better ambient levels of water quality. Prior to the 1972 law, efforts had been devoted to getting the states to set ambient water-quality standards and design programs to achieve them. The switch to federally mandated emission standards immediately brought up the question of how these emission standards would relate to desired levels of ambient water quality. The answer is, not necessarily very closely. Compliance with the technology-based effluent standards (TBES) promulgated by the EPA does not necessarily imply that certain levels of ambient water quality have been attained, because the standards are set by reference to available technology and not by reference to the ambient quality of receiving waters. Table 14-4 shows some data on water-quality changes over the decade 1978–1987. These are the results of a survey of water-quality measuring stations throughout the U.S., and show the trend in recorded quantities of seven specific water pollutants over that decade. While there was substantial improvement in phosphorus and considerable improvement in three others (suspended solids, oxygen deficit, and fecal coliform bacteria), there was substantial worsening of readings in dissolved solids and nitrogen.

Although the federal effort has hinged on the promulgation of technology-based effluent standards, regardless of water quality, considerable progress has also continued over the last several decades in developing procedures for setting ambient water-quality standards. In recent years emphasis is tending to shift back toward an ambient water-quality approach, with closer coordination be-

TABLE 14-4
TRENDS IN WATER POLLUTANTS IN U.S. STREAMS, 1978–1987

Pollutant	Percentage of water-quality measuring stations reporting:		
	Improvement	No change	Deterioration
Dissolved solids	6	72	22
Nitrogen	6	73	21
Chloride	8	75	17
Suspended solids	12	80	8
Oxygen deficit	12	84	4
Fecal coliform bacteria	13	81	6
Phosphorus	18	79	3

Source: Dennis P. Lettenmaier, Eric R. Hooper, Colin Wagoner, and Kathleen B. Faris, "Trends in Stream Water Quality in the Continental United States, 1978–1987," *Water Resources Research,* 27(3), March 1991, pp. 327–339.

tween the federal TBES system and state-level programs for achieving targeted levels of water quality in rivers and lakes.

Efficiency and Cost-Effectiveness of TBESs

For a policy to be efficient it must balance damages and control costs. The technology-based effluent standards are designed, however, to be applied on a national basis; the same standards for, say, leather processing plants, will be applied to all leather plants in the country, whether they are located on a river just upstream from a large urban area or on a river in some remote part of the country. This is the result of a totally technology-based approach to pollution control, where questions of economic efficiency have been excluded from consideration.

Cost-effectiveness, as we have discussed many times so far, is a question of whether we are getting the maximum effect, in terms of reduced emissions, for the money spent. The simple key to this question is whether the policy is designed so that when sources are in compliance they will have the same marginal abatement costs. There is nothing in the logic of the TBES process that moves water-pollution sources in the direction of meeting the equimarginal condition. The procedure leads instead to the application of the same standards to all firms within each subcategory. For example, all sugar-beet processing plants in the country are subject to the same effluent standards. These will be cost-effective only if all individual plants in each category have exactly the same marginal abatement costs. This is unlikely to be the case. The EPA has designated around 600 subcategories of water-polluting industries, for each of which TBESs have been promulgated. But there are tens of thousands of individual industrial water-pollution sources, so some of the subcategories must contain very large numbers of sources. There can be little doubt that the sources in most subcategories are heterogeneous in terms of the production technology they are using, so we would expect them to be heterogeneous in terms of their marginal emission abatement costs. Thus, applying the same emission standards to each firm cannot be cost-effective.

The cost *in*effectiveness of equal treatment–type programs like TBESs has been examined directly in a series of river basin studies carried out by teams of economists and environmental scientists. These use large-scale models of individual river basins, incorporating the different estimated marginal abatement costs of various sources of pollution, together with the main hydrological features of the basins' water resources. They compare the costs of water pollution-control programs in which all sources were treated alike to those where sources are controlled in accordance with relative marginal abatement costs.

The best-known of these studies is the Delaware estuary study, and although the results are now fairly old, they nevertheless continue to illustrate very well the issues involved. The lower Delaware River runs through the heavily industrialized sections around Philadelphia and southwestern New Jersey, then opens out into the broad and shallow Delaware Bay. Wastewater emissions contribute to serious water-quality problems in the estuary, both in the traditional measures

TABLE 14-5

SUMMARY OF RESULTS OF THE DELAWARE ESTUARY WATER-QUALITY CONTROL STUDY

DO objective	Uniform treatment program	Least-cost program	Effluent charge program	
			Single	Zoned
	Million Dollars per Year			
2 ppm	5.0	1.6	2.4	2.4
3–4 ppm	20.0	7.0	12.0	8.6

Source: Allen V. Kneese and Blair T. Bower, *Managing Water Quality: Economics, Technology, Institutions,* Johns Hopkins Press for Resources for the Future, Baltimore, Md., 1968, p. 162.

of dissolved oxygen (DO) and in other types of organic and inorganic wastes. Investigators used a water-quality model that predicted the effects of changing waste loads in any part of the estuary on water quality elsewhere in the estuary. Superimposed on this was a mathematical model showing the relationship of abatement costs at any of the large effluent outfalls on the estuary to emission levels at those outfalls. By operating these models together researchers could estimate the costs of meeting water-quality goals by controlling emissions at each of the various sources.

The main results are summarized in Table 14-5. These show the costs of reducing BOD emissions from sources on the Delaware estuary so as to achieve given target levels of DO in the waters of the estuary. The exact levels of costs are not as important as the comparison of different types of policy approaches. The table shows two alternative target levels, one at 2 parts per million (ppm) and a higher one at 3–4 ppm of DO. To meet the lower DO target with a uniform treatment approach—that is, a policy of reducing emissions at each source in the same proportion—would have cost $5 million per year, while the costs of an equal treatment program attaining DO levels of 3—4 ppm would have cost an estimated $20 million annually. We note immediately that we have increasing marginal abatement costs: To reach the higher water-quality levels requires substantially larger costs. But the same DO targets could be reached at much lower cost by reducing emissions in a cost-effective way. The costs of a program designed to meet the targets with a set of emission controls satisfying the equimarginal principle were $1.6 million for 2 ppm and $7.0 million for 3–4 ppm DO. Note that these costs are roughly *one-third* of the costs of the uniform treatment program or, to put it another way, the uniform treatment approach would cost about three times more than a fully cost-effective program.[9]

[9] Similar results have been obtained in other studies; for example, for the Willamette River (Kenneth D. Kerri, "An Economic Approach to Water Quality Control," *Journal of the Water Pollution Control Federation*, 38[12], December 1966, pp. 1883–1897), the Miami River in Ohio (M. W. Anderson, "Regional Water Quality Management in the Miami Basin," Ph.D. thesis, Carnegie Mellon University), and the Merrimack Valley of Massachusetts (Alvin S. Goodman and William Dobbins, "Mathematical Model for Water Pollution Control Studies," *Journal of the Sanitary Engineering Division, Proceedings ASCE*, 92[SA6], December 1966, pp. 1–9).

To impose a least-cost approach by specifying allowable emissions at each source would, of course, require an administering agency to have an enormous amount of knowledge about marginal abatement costs at each of the sources. Alternatively, authorities could achieve cost-effective emission reductions by imposing an effluent tax on emissions. Researchers investigated several approaches to emission taxes in the Delaware study. One was a single emissions tax (in this case a single tax on BOD emissions) levied on all sources throughout the estuary. The annual costs of this single tax approach were estimated at $2.4 million for the 2 ppm target and $12.0 million for the target of 3–4 ppm. Why aren't the costs of the single emissions tax as low as the least-cost program? The problem here is that sources are differently situated on the Delaware estuary, so the emissions of each source do not have the same impact on water-quality targets.[10] The single emission tax would lead all sources to reduce emissions to the point where all marginal abatement costs were fully equalized, but a single tax is not able to account for the fact that some sources are more important than others in causing water-quality problems. To respond fully to these locational factors an administering agency would have to charge a unique effluent tax to each source, taking into account both its marginal abatement costs *and* its location relative to other sources. Of course, this would be a totally unrealistic administrative burden, given the hundreds of different BOD sources on the Delaware estuary. There is a trade-off, in other words, between lower control costs on one side and administrative complexity on the other.

As we discussed in Chapter 12, one answer to this is to institute a zoned emission tax. Here the sources are grouped into zones, and all sources in the same zone are charged the same tax, while sources in different zones are taxed at different rates. In the Delaware estuary study, the zoned emission charge has the same annual costs as a single tax approach for the lower DO target, but is substantially less costly for the higher DO target of 3–4 ppm. What this shows in effect is that the larger the improvement we want to achieve in water quality the greater the difference it makes to have a cost-effective program. Applying this to our discussion of TBESs leads us to the following conclusion: This type of system, where all sources are required to meet the same standard and all are encouraged to adopt the same effluent control technology, may be reasonable in terms of cost if we are seeking only a modest improvement in water quality. But if we wish to have substantial improvements, the TBES approach will normally be a lot less cost-effective than better designed programs.

TBESs and Technological Improvements

We saw in Chapter 12 that emission standards lead to weaker incentives to innovate in pollution control than economic incentive–type policies. In the case of TBESs, incentives are made even weaker by linking the emission standards to

---

[10] Technically, they have different transfer coefficients with respect to the various points where water quality was measured.

particular control technologies. When polluters are faced with this type of technology-linked standard, compliance tends to become a matter of adopting the technology the authorities have used to set the standard. Since permanent emissions monitoring is quite costly, administering authorities can check compliance by making periodic inspections to ascertain whether sources are using approved emissions-control technology. In order to minimize the risk of being penalized for noncompliance, polluters have the incentive to adopt the particular technology that EPA used to establish the standard. The result is that although the TBESs are nominally just emission standards, they end up tending to dictate the particular effluent control technologies chosen by firms. This substantially undermines any incentives to search for other, cheaper ways to meet the standards.

There is another dimension to these incentive effects. We mentioned above the importance, in designing a pollution-control program, of placing the control on the right element in the total input–production–emission process. This goes for any program, whether it uses standards or an incentive approach. The technology-based effluent standards in water pollution control are normally expressed in terms of quantity of emissions per unit of raw material input used in production. For example, the BOD standards for tanneries are expressed in terms of kilograms (kg) of BOD emitted per thousand kilograms (kkg) of raw material used in production. As a result of the BAT decisions made by the EPA, these range from .23 kg/kkg to 1.90 kg/kkg over the seven subsectors of the tannery industry. But the real pollution control issue is the total quantity of emissions during a given time period. The connection between these two factors can be shown as follows:

$$\text{Total emissions} = \text{Output} \times \frac{\text{Input}}{\text{Output}} \times \frac{\text{Emissions}}{\text{Input}}$$

"Output" refers to what the firm produces, "input" to the productive inputs used in the production process. The EPA standard applies only to the last expression in this equation. Another way for a firm to reduce its total emissions, however, is to reduce raw product (input) per unit of output; for example, by installing more efficient production equipment or better operating procedures. Still another way of reducing total emissions is to reduce total output, the first term in the expression above. For example, electric power companies can reduce total emissions by promoting energy conservation among their customers. The current standards do not get at these other sources of emission reductions. This may seem like an obscure point, but look at the newspaper article shown in Exhibit 14-1. It focuses primarily on air pollution, but it illustrates exactly the same problems in water pollution control. First, it shows the bias of current standards toward "end-of-the-line" treatment techniques; in our terms, the emphasis of current standards on the last term in the equation above. Second, it shows the thinking by many plant operators that there are profitable ways of reducing residuals by changing the production system itself; in our terms, by reducing the use of materials inputs in production, the second term in the equation. Third, it points up the frustration at the fact that there is no consistent incentive system to encourage these kinds of deeper changes. The problem cannot be solved, however, by looking around for some new partial incentive wrinkle to add on to the current system.[11] The basic problem, as we can see from the formula, is that the incentive has to be put on the right thing. In this case, expressing the standard in terms simply of total emissions would at least provide incentives to make improvements in all the factors of the equation, not just the last one.

TBESs and Enforcement

Effluent standards are enforced through a system of discharge permits. In order to discharge wastes into a river or body of water a firm must have a permit issued through the relevant EPA-backed state permitting program. The permit specifies the allowable emissions the source may make, and is subject to enforcement by state authorities. Given the enormous number of discharge points and the difficulties of monitoring emissions, enforcement becomes a critical program element. One response has been to distinguish between major and minor emitters, using criteria like quantity, toxicity, conventional pollution load, and impact of emissions. In this way more enforcement resources can be devoted to the major sources, which account for the largest proportion of total emissions.

Lacking high-quality techniques for monitoring emissions, control authorities are forced back on some other means of ensuring compliance. When emission standards are tied to certain technologies, enforcing authorities can try to confirm compliance simply by checking to see if firms have put in place the criterion technology.[12] The problem here is that there is a difference between *initial* compliance and *continued* compliance. The fact that a firm has installed certain pollution-control equipment does not necessarily mean that this equipment will be operated efficiently in the years to come. If operating costs are substantial and if nobody is effectively monitoring emissions, the incentive will be to save on operating costs and let emissions increase. It's very difficult to get good information on these matters, but several studies indicate that this is probably a substantial problem. In 1983 the General Accounting Office (GAO) reported that there was widespread failure of sources to meet the conditions of their discharge permits.[13] Of the 531 large wastewater treatment plants surveyed, the GAO found that 31 percent had significantly exceeded the permitted levels of discharge.[14] The actual level of noncompliance may be higher than this because the

---

[11] One business executive in the article expresses the wish that EPA would subsidize R&D and innovative investment; everybody likes incentives in the form of subsidies.

[12] The word "simply" in this sentence may be misleading. Nothing is simple in the world of pollution control. Polluters have challenged virtually every part of the federal pollution-control program, including enforcement procedures. Thus, over the years, legal doctrine has developed regarding such things as the specific procedures for visiting sources to check for compliance.

[13] U.S. General Accounting Office, *Wastewater Dischargers Are Not Complying with EPA Pollution Control Permits*, Washington, D.C., 1983.

[14] Technically, their discharge levels were at least 50 percent above permitted levels of at least one quality parameter (e.g., BOD emissions) for at least four consecutive months.

EXHIBIT 14-1

INDUSTRIAL SWITCH
SOME COMPANIES CUT POLLUTION BY ALTERING PRODUCTION METHODS

"Clean" Manufacturing Avoids Many Problems at Source Rather Than Mopping Up.

By Amal Kumar Naj, Staff Reporter of
The Wall Street Journal

According to conventional wisdom, sweeping clean-air laws will burden U.S. industry with billions of dollars in pollution-control costs and raise prices for a slew of commodities and finished goods.

Not necessarily so, more and more manufacturers say.

Surprisingly, they are actually reducing some costs as they install new pollution-cutting technologies. But the benefits come from new manufacturing techniques—not the waste and emission treatment encouraged by much environmental legislation.

And the benefits could be huge. U.S. manufacturing wastes can be halved by using existing technologies, the congressional Office of Technology Assessment estimates. Eliminating another 25% would require research and development.

Moreover, American companies produce five times the waste per dollar of goods sold compared with Japanese companies and more than twice that of the Germans, according to Joel Hirschhorn, a former official of the Office of Technology Assessment who now heads an environmental-technologies consulting firm. "Waste reduction can have a staggering effect on the bottom lines of American companies" and can improve their world-wide competitiveness, he says.

Some Specific Savings

Here are some savings that companies are already achieving:

- Carrier Corp. spent $500,000 in 1988 to eliminate toxic lubricants from its manufacture of air conditioners—and slashed annual production costs by $1.2 million.
- American Telephone & Telegraph Co. recently cut about $3 million of annual costs by ridding its circuit-board manufacture of an ozone-depleting compound.
- Whyco Chromium Co. says a new alloy that it developed to eliminate harmful byproducts from its process for coating nuts and screws has trimmed the cost 25%.

GAO results used self-reported data from polluters, who no doubt have an incentive to understate their violations. Studies by environmental economists have also concluded that noncompliance is a significant problem.[15] New and better ways of emissions monitoring are being developed. Pollution-control efforts will be considerably enhanced when they become inexpensive and accurate.

Technology-based effluent standards have an aura of concreteness and directness. What better way to get pollution reduced than simply to require polluters

---

[15] Clifford S. Russell, Winston Harrington, and William J. Vaughan, *Enforcing Pollution Control Laws*, Resources for the Future, Washington, D.C., 1986.

- And 3M Corp. estimates that manufacturing changes to control pollution have saved it $41 million in the past three years.

Of course, not all environmental pollution can be suppressed by manufacturing changes alone. Some measure of pollution-control technologies will be required to treat sludge, municipal garbage, and emissions from automobiles and utilities.

Inhibited by Risks

But few companies seem willing to try "clean" technologies that address the very source of pollution because of up-front risks and research and development costs associated with untried approaches. Mr. Hirschhorn says, "It's easier for companies to resort to easy and low-risk waste-reduction projects. But that only adds costs."

Even at companies that must continue resorting to pollution treatment as well, the preventive approach can generate substantial savings. For example, 3M estimates that its 2,500 different manufacturing changes since 1975 have produced total net savings of $500 million while halving its toxic emissions.

Thomas Zosel, manager of 3M's pollution-prevention programs, argues that such savings call for flexible enforcement of the regulations. He suggests that the EPA could allow additional time for compliance for companies trying out innovative manufacturing technologies. "Regulations currently don't allow that," he says.

Whyco Chromium, which coats nuts and bolts and other automobile fasteners for corrosion resistance, would like to spend more time improving manufacturing methods than treating its effluents. Two years ago, the Thomaston, Conn., company developed an organic compound that required only two to three coats, half as many as the previous nickel-cadmium-copper compound. It reorganized its plant with new equipment, but most of the "several hundred thousand dollars in investment was in research and development," says Mark Hyner, president.

And research, he says, is something his small company can't afford under the pressure of compliance deadlines. "Most of our time and resources are spent dealing with regulations. I would love for somebody from the EPA to come in and say 'Let's see how we can do things differently' or for the government to offer tax incentives for innovative technologies," he says. Mr. Hyner says his company, whose 1989 sales totaled $13 million, spends $2 million annually on treating and hauling wastes and maintaining a staff that oversees environmental compliance.

---

to adopt certain types of pollution-control technology? But this engineering-based approach is far less effective than it appears. We have seen how, from an economic standpoint, it is likely to be seriously cost *in*effective; for the money that is being devoted to pollution control under this system, substantially greater improvements in water quality could be achieved with other policy approaches. The apparent technological definiteness of the approach ("best practicable technology," "best available technology," etc.) is, in fact, far less effective in practice. The EPA is required to make countless engineering decisions in order to develop these standards. Not only is this very difficult for an administrating agency, but each of these decisions is a place where political interests can focus influence. The apparent concreteness of technology-based effluent standards is also substantially undermined by the monitoring and enforcement problem. What looks like a straightforward technological fix becomes, in reality, a policy with a great deal of hidden flexibility.

THE MUNICIPAL WASTEWATER TREATMENT PLANT SUBSIDY PROGRAM

A large proportion of waterborne emissions into the nation's waterways comes not from private industries but from public bodies, especially from the public sewer systems of urbanized areas. Whereas in the case of industrial pollution federal authorities adopted a policy of having polluters themselves pay for reducing emissions, the response toward public-sector pollution has been different. Here the major approach has been *federal subsidies* to construct treatment plants. The inspiration for this type of approach probably comes from two sources, the normal public-works mentality of the Congress and the fact that it is better politics to "get tough" on industrial polluters than on cities and towns.

Treatment of domestic wastes uses both physical and biological processes and is fairly standardized. The different degrees of treatment are designated *primary*, *secondary*, and *tertiary*, according to the process used and the extent of treatment given to the wastes. Primary treatment is essentially a set of physical steps built around a basic sedimentation process; it can remove about 35 to 40 percent of the primary BOD in the original waste stream. Secondary treatment uses biological means (e.g., "activated sludge") to further treat the waste. Primary and secondary processes together can reduce BOD by between 85 and 90 percent. These processes, though quite effective in removing BOD, are less so in handling plant nutrients like nitrogen and phosphorus. So-called tertiary treatment, making use of a variety of chemical processes, can reduce waste loads even more. The sequence of primary, secondary, and tertiary processes is subject to increasing marginal abatement costs; the greater the reduction one wants in BOD or other pollutants in the waste stream, the higher the marginal cost of getting it.

The 1972 WPCA Amendments mandated that all municipal sewer systems have at least secondary treatment by 1983. To reach this goal Congress authorized a program of federal subsidies to local municipalities to cover the costs of designing and constructing public wastewater treatment plants. These grants had been authorized in the 1956 WPCA Amendments, but they increased markedly in the early 1970s. In the 1972 Act the federal share of construction costs was increased from 55 percent to 75 percent, and in these years large new sums were appropriated for the program. From 1960 to 1985, federal grants amounted to about $56 billion in real terms.[16] The figures in Table 14-6 seem to show the impact of the program. From 1960 to 1988 the percentage of public sewer systems discharging untreated waste declined from 63 percent to less than 1 percent, while the percentage having at least secondary treatment increased substantially.

It's tempting to attribute this improvement to the federal program but, as

---

[16] That is, adjusted for inflation; see the discussion of "real" versus "nominal" values in Chapter 6.

TABLE 14-6
PROGRESS IN PUBLIC WASTEWATER TREATMENT FACILITIES

	1960	1970	1980	1988
Total U.S. population (millions)	180	203	224	246
Percentage served by waste treatment systems	61	71	71	72
Percentage of served population with:				
No treatment	63	41	1	1
Primary treatment only	33	N/A	31	15
At least secondary	4	N/A	68	84

Source: Council on Environmental Quality, *Environmental Quality, 1990,* p. 309; and previous issues. Figures rounded to the nearest whole number.

always, we have to look below the surface to find out what really went on. Figure 14-2 shows federal and local capital expenditures for public wastewater treatment plants. Prior to the growth of the federal grant program, local capital expenditures on treatment plants was relatively high. But as federal expenditures increased under the 1972 law, local expenditures decreased. There is a very good lesson to be learned from these figures. The lesson is that if we add a new factor

FIGURE 14-2
Capital Outlays on Municipal Wastewater Treatment Facilities, 1960-1983. State expenditures not available before 1978. (Source: *Congressional Budget Office,* Efficient Investment in Wastewater Treatment Plants, *Washington, D.C., June 1985, p. 5.*)

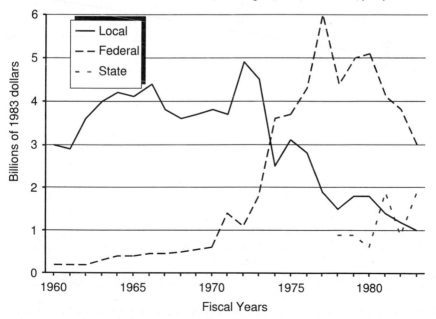

or a new program to an existing situation, we can't expect that what we will end up with is simply the old system plus the new feature. While the new federal subsidy program added large sums to construct municipal wastewater treatment plants, it was in reality accompanied by substantial reductions of funds for this purpose at the local level. When federal authorities increased funds for the program, local funds were diverted to other things. So although total capital spending for municipal treatment plants did increase during the 1970s, it did not increase by as much as would appear if one looks strictly at the history of the federal program.

There can be little question that the federal grant program for public treatment plant construction has produced results; there can be little doubt also that the program has cost much more than it should have. There are built-in sources of inefficiency that have substantially shaped the program. One is the allocation of the grant funds among municipalities. From an efficiency standpoint, one would want to allocate the funds to municipalities where treatment plant construction would have the maximum impact on water-quality improvement. The EPA has struggled to find a way of doing this in the face of overwhelming political pressures. Its approach has been to allocate grant funds on the basis of a "needs" survey. The needs survey was to take into account existing population, the pollution problem in different bodies of water, and the needs for preserving higher-quality water in these various bodies. The formula was open to interpretation and subject to judgment, especially political judgment. There have been strong pressures to allocate grant funds to states and municipalities more on the basis of their political significance than on water-quality improvement criteria.[17]

Any large subsidy program creates its own set of incentives; some may work toward the objectives of the program, and some probably will not. One problem with the waste treatment plant subsidies is that it created incentives for industrial polluters to solve their emission problems by connecting up to the subsidized public system. Municipalities might even use these subsidies to build really large plants that had excess capacity, then lure companies to locate in their area with the offer of cheap waste disposal. How can the federal government give municipalities a subsidy but keep them from passing it on to business polluters? The answer has been to adopt a set of emission standards called *"pretreatment standards."* These are standards applied to wastewater streams entering public sewer systems from private business sources. The objective is to get industrial polluters to undertake some treatment themselves before they put their wastes into the public sewer system.

Perhaps the biggest difficulty with the subsidy program has been the perverse incentives it has tended to create at the local level. When a substantial fraction of design and construction costs is picked up by somebody else, the incentives for

---

[17] U.S. Congressional Budget Office, *Efficient Investments in Wastewater Treatment Plants*, Washington, D.C., 1985.

grant recipients to seek out the most efficient approach and design for their wastewater treatment problem is substantially weakened. "A community that expects to pay only 5 cents to 25 cents on the dollar will have fewer incentives to control plant costs than if they had to pay the entire investment."[18] In many communities, plants costing tens of millions of dollars have been so heavily subsidized by the federal (and sometimes state) programs that local costs have been only a dollar or two per household. This substantially weakens local incentives to search energetically for the least-cost way of handling their municipal wastewater problem. Cities and towns were motivated instead to line up at the subsidy window and build large plants with "officially approved" treatment technology that qualified for large subsidies. The operating costs of these plants were not subsidized in the federal program; they had to be paid entirely by local groups. This sometimes led to situations where overly large treatment plants were not operated correctly because communities were trying to save costs.

In the 1987 Water Quality Act the treatment plant program was changed. The federal subsidy program was phased out and replaced with a state revolving fund program. From 1990 to 1994 federal payments are being made to build up these state funds. They will then be used to finance the construction of community wastewater treatment plants. The loans made from the funds are supposed to be largely paid back (this is why they are called "revolving funds"). This should substantially reshape local incentives, because local groups will now be responsible for covering the actual costs of constructing their treatment plants.

RECENT POLICY INNOVATIONS IN WATER POLLUTION CONTROL

The national system of technology-based effluent standards has been criticized from its beginnings, especially by economists, for its relative inflexibility and cost ineffectiveness. A nationally mandated program based on the premise that all sources should be subject to the same standards is bound to make water-quality improvements much more costly than they have to be. In recent years we have seen some innovative programs that try to build in flexibility and adaptability to local conditions. Most have been based on emission permit trading among sources on particular bodies of water. The localized scope of these new programs is appropriate. Most water pollution problems are local in nature; they center on the water-quality problems of particular rivers or lakes that result from the waste disposal activities of a geographically limited group of polluters. So it stands to reason that localized programs, on the level of a single river basin or lake or bay, can be designed to take advantage of local conditions in a way that a nationally mandated, technologically oriented policy cannot. As people gain more experience with these new types of programs, we will undoubtedly see a lot more of them, especially if the hoped-for cost savings materialize.

[18] Ibid., p. 10

Fox River (Wisconsin) Emission Permits

In 1981 the state of Wisconsin initiated a limited program of tradable BOD emission permits on the Fox River. This river is used for wastewater disposal by numerous groups, especially pulp mills and municipal treatment plants. Emissions to the river were already subject to control through the regular EPA technology-based effluent standards and emission permits. Allowable discharges vary over the year because variations in temperature and stream flow alter the river's BOD assimilative capacity. The goal of the trading program is to get the same level of water-quality improvement at a substantially reduced cost.

The trading scheme is aimed solely at BOD discharges. Initial distribution of emission rights was based on historic levels of emissions by the major polluters. The rights were distributed free and they are valid only for five years; after that they must be reissued by the administering agency. Traded emission permits also have a maximum life of five years.[19] The designers of the plan hoped that by allowing permits to be traded, firms or municipalities with relatively high marginal BOD abatement costs would buy permits from those with low marginal abatement costs. Some researchers had estimated that this would result in substantial cost savings in cleaning up the river.[20]

To date there have been relatively few trades of BOD emission permits among dischargers on the Fox River. A major difficulty with the Fox River program has been the relatively small number of potential participants. The pulp mills are few enough in number that they can potentially act as oligopolists instead of competitive bidders.[21] The municipalities are also relatively few in number, coupled with the fact that being publicly controlled wastewater treatment facilities, they don't necessarily have to make decisions on the basis of strict cost-minimization objectives. Municipal dischargers could also qualify for public subsidies, further undermining the incentives to minimize costs.

Another important factor working against trades was that the original permit allocations were too liberal. If polluters are to have incentives to trade, the quantity of permits initially allocated must be substantially less than current, or easily achievable, emission levels. In the Fox River case the number of permits given out did not imply a significant reduction of BOD emissions beyond what could be obtained by standard and easily available control techniques. In addition, municipal dischargers had historically been able to get waivers of emission limitations if they found them too costly to achieve. Also working against permit trades have been the rules that administrative authorities have established to govern transactions. In principle, trades should be allowed whenever market

---

[19] See Martin H. David and Erhard F. Joeres, "Is a Viable Implementation of TDP's Transferable?" in Erhard F. Joeres and Martin H. David (eds.), *Buying a Better Environment, Cost Effective Regulation Through Permit Trading*, University of Wisconsin Press, Madison, Wisc., 1983, pp. 233–248.

[20] William B. O'Neil, "The Regulation of Water Pollution Permit Trading Under Conditions of Varying Stream Flow and Temperature" in ibid., pp. 219–232.

[21] An "oligopoly" is an industry containing just a few firms. The auto and airline industries are oligopolies. In this example, although there may be many pulp mills nationwide, the Fox River TDP market included a relatively small number of them.

participants wish to make them; it is their cost calculations and objectives that should be allowed to govern their market participation. In the Fox River case, however, firms are required to justify the need for permits, and trades that "simply" reduce operating costs are not allowed.[22] This substantially limits the number of potential traders. In addition, the fact that the administering agency must reissue permits every five years creates uncertainty over whether purchased permits will be counted in a firm's new base when reauthorization occurs. All these factors have worked to reduce the number of trades that might otherwise have occurred. We can perhaps look at the Fox River case as providing a good laboratory for learning about designing and administering transferable discharge permit programs.

Point-Source/Nonpoint Source Emission Trading

Nonpoint source (NPS) emissions account for a substantial amount of the water pollution in the U.S. More than half of the BOD, suspended solids and in some regions phosphorus and nitrogen come from nonpoint sources. Similarly, nonpoint sources contribute large amounts of toxic pollutants to the country's water resources. Major nonpoint sources are agricultural runoff, urban street runoff, and activities related to land clearance and building construction. The EPA has initiated, in cooperation with the states, a National Estuaries Program to develop better pollution-control efforts in the major estuaries and bays of the coastal U.S. One result of water-quality studies done under this program is to demonstrate how much of the remaining water-quality problems in these areas is related to nonpoint-source pollutants. The fact that NPS emissions are diffuse and not concentrated into specific outfalls has made them very difficult to control. NPS pollutants are also normally very weather related, which makes the runoff patterns more difficult to monitor. Traditional approaches like emission standards are problematic because it is difficult to measure emissions accurately. Emissions taxes would run into the same problem. This means that the locus of control will normally have to be pushed back directly onto the practices and technologies that typically lead to substantial nonpoint-source runoff.

This suggests what we earlier called "design standards." These are standards that require certain techniques or practices to be used by sources whose activities lead to nonpoint-source emissions. Standards that rule out agricultural cultivation on steep, easily eroded land, standards specifying the design of urban storm sewers, and standards requiring home builders to take certain steps to control construction site runoff are types of design standards. The 1987 Water Quality Act, for example, establishes a program of federal subsidies for farmers to adopt "best management practices" (BMPs) to control agricultural pollution. While design standards may be necessary in the case of NPS emissions, we should keep in mind the difficulties inherent in their use. They require administrative deter-

[22] Robert W. Hahn, *A Primer on Environmental Policy Design*, Harwood Academic Publishers, Chur, Switzerland, 1989, p. 34.

mination of what particular technologies and techniques will be allowed in different circumstances. The danger is that they will undermine the incentives among polluters to find new and better ways of reducing NPS emissions.

Another method of controlling NPS emissions is to tax those activities or materials that lead to the emissions, rather than the emissions themselves, if possible. Taxes might be put on fertilizer used by farmers, for example, or on lawn chemicals used by suburban dwellers. The objective in this case is to induce a reduction in the use of materials that may ultimately end up in rivers, lakes, or groundwater aquifers.

Difficulties of control explain why NPS pollution has not been addressed as vigorously as point source emissions, despite their importance. Early federal water-quality laws directed state agencies to consider nonpoint-source pollution in their water-quality programs, but did not require that specific steps be taken. The 1987 law gives it somewhat more prominence and authorizes federal money to subsidize local efforts to control NPS pollution. In fact, there is a major contrast between the national, uniform policy that has been followed to control point-source emissions and the policy for nonpoint-source pollution. In the latter case federal authorities have essentially thrown the problem into the hands of the states. Their reasoning is that ". . . the application of uniform technological controls . . . is not appropriate for the management of non-point sources. Site specific decisions must consider the nature of the watershed, the nature of the water body, . . . and the range of management practices available to control non-point source pollution."[23] So in this case there is a recognition that a uniform national program is not appropriate.

There are many areas of the country where point sources and nonpoint sources exist in close proximity, essentially contributing to the same water-quality problems. The equimarginal principle would say in this case that the control of point and nonpoint sources should be balanced so that the marginal emission reduction costs are the same in the two cases. Historically, however, point sources have been controlled much more vigorously than nonpoint sources. What this means is that there may be many regions of the country where shifting more of the burden onto nonpoint sources would be an effective way of lowering the costs of water-quality improvements. One way of doing this is the trading of emission reduction credits between point sources and nonpoint sources, a program that is being tried in several parts of the country.

The best-developed trading program is that involving Dillon Reservoir in Colorado. The large impoundment is a major water source for Denver. In the early 1980s it was recognized that phosphorous loadings in the reservoir were causing water-quality problems. While some of the phosphorus was of natural origin, about half was from human activity. Somewhat more than half of this was from nonpoint sources—urban runoff, golf courses, construction sites, septic tanks, etc. The rest was from four municipal waste treatment facilities. Re-

---

[23] U.S. Environmental Protection Agency, *Non-Point Source Pollution in the U.S., Report to Congress*, Washington, D.C., 1984, pp. xiii–xiv.

searchers determined that point source control by itself would not be sufficient to avoid water-quality problems; even if municipal phosphorous emissions were reduced to zero, there would still be enough phosphorus to cause eutrophication in the reservoir.[24] Besides the very high direct abatement costs it would require, this would severely constrain future population growth in the county, which in the 1970s was the fastest growing county in the country.

The answer has been to initiate a phosphorus trading program between point and nonpoint sources of phosphorus. The program allocated baseline phosphorous loads to different polluters and then allowed phosphorous emission permits to be traded. The intention is to allow point sources, especially the municipal treatment plants, to buy phosphorous emission permits from nonpoint-source polluters whose marginal phosphorous abatement costs are lower. Those responsible for nonpoint-source emissions have a variety of means available to reduce their phosphorous loadings, such as sewering housing developments that are now using septic tanks, routing underground storm sewers through a series of storage tanks, and detention basins. Of course, the trading program requires that administrative authorities be able to monitor the nonpoint-source emissions at reasonable cost. To date (1991) several trades have been made, under the management of the Summit Water Quality Committee, composed of representatives from towns in the region as well as other public agencies. If the full trading potential is realized, it has been estimated that the trading program will allow the participants to solve the phosphorous problem in the reservoir at a cost savings of more than $1 million a year. Similar point/nonpoint-source trading programs have been initiated in the Cherry Creek reservoir of Colorado and the Tar-Pamlico basin of North Carolina. The idea is also being explored in other regions.[25]

SUMMARY

Current federal water pollution-control policy centers on the promulgation and enforcement of "technology-based effluent standards" (TBESs). These are emission standards stemming from the EPA's findings as to the "best available technology," or "best practicable technology," for specific industries. These technology-based standards, though appealing as "technological fixes," have a number of drawbacks. They are likely to give far less pollution control for the money spent than alternative approaches, because they normally violate the equimarginal principle. They also have negative impacts through reducing the long-run incentives polluters might have to find better ways of controlling waterborne emissions.

[24] Lane Wyatt, "A Basinwide Approach to NPS Management," Northwest Colorado Council of Governments, n.d. "Eutrophication" refers to the buildup of plant nutrients, leading to excess growth in underwater plants and algae.
[25] David Letson, "Point/Non-Point Source Pollution Reduction Trading: An Interpretive Survey," *Natural Resources Journal*, 32(2), Spring 1992, pp. 219–232.

We also discussed in the chapter the federal program of subsidies for munici-pal waste treatment facilities. Over the last several decades the proportion of the U.S. population being served by advanced (secondary or tertiary) treatment facilities has been substantially increased. Again, however, because of the per-verse incentives built into the program, substantially greater progress could have been made with the money spent.

As of this writing, federal authorities are considering a major new revision of federal water pollution-control policy. One objective will be to try and find greater opportunities for using incentive-based strategies to combat water pol-lution. The basic problem with emissions trading approaches is that they require relatively larger numbers of participants if competitive permit markets are to develop. But most water pollution problems are local, or at most regional, in nature. Thus, the potential number of traders is likely to be too small for effective trading. This perhaps implies that more emphasis should be put on the use of emission taxes as a means of attaining cost-effective water pollution-control programs.

QUESTIONS FOR FURTHER DISCUSSION

1 Most technology-based effluent standards have focused on "end-of-the-pipe" treat-ment technology. What is the reason for this, and what has been the likely impact?
2 Can you think of a way of designing a water pollution-control policy that combines a media-based approach with a technology-based approach?
3 Suppose your community could get a large subsidy to build a wastewater treatment plant. Suppose also that you were very anxious to attract new industries into your area to encourage economic development. What might this tempt you to do?
4 Controlling the residuals from the production of bleached tissue paper is about five times costlier than controlling the residuals from unbleached tissue paper. Analyze this difference with our standard pollution-control model. What does it suggest in terms of public policy toward water pollution control?
5 Recent federal-level efforts in water pollution control have focused on nonpoint source emissions. How might the different types of pollution-control policy be employed in the case of nonpoint source emissions?

SELECTED READINGS

Feenberg, Daniel, and Edwin S. Mills: *Measuring the Benefits of Water Pollution Abatement*, Academic Press, New York, 1980.
Freeman, A. Myrick, III: "Technology-Based Effluent Standards: The U.S. Case," *Water Resources Research*, 16(1), February 1980, pp. 21–27.
Freeman, A. Myrick, III: "Water Pollution Policy," in Paul R. Portney (ed.), *Public Policies for Environmental Protection*, Resources for the Future, Washington, D.C., 1990, pp. 97–149.
Harrington, Winston, Alan J. Krupnick, and Henry M. Peskin: "Policies for Nonpoint-Source Water Pollution Control," *Journal of Soil and Water Conservation*, 40(1), January–February 1985, pp. 27–32.

Kneese, Allen V., and Blair T. Bower: *Managing Water Quality: Economics, Technology, and Institutions*, Johns Hopkins Press for Resources for the Future, Baltimore, Md., 1968.

Luken, Ralph A.: *Efficiency in Environmental Legislation: A Benefit–Cost Analysis of Alternative Approaches*, Kluwer Academic Publishers, Boston, 1990.

Magat, Wesley A., Alan J. Krupnick, and Winston Harrington: *Rules in the Making: A Statistical Analysis of Regulatory Agency Behavior*, Resources for the Future, Washington, D.C., 1986.

McGarity, Thomas O.: "Media-Quality, Technology, and Cost–Benefit Balancing Strategies for Health and Environmental Regulation," *Law and Contemporary Problems*, 46(3), Summer 1983, pp. 159–233.

CHAPTER 15

FEDERAL AIR POLLUTION-CONTROL POLICY

As it travels through space, planet earth takes along with itself an enveloping, but relatively thin, layer of gases, without which it would be a cinder. That layer of atmospheric gases provides two critical services: direct life support for living organisms on the earth's surface and control over the radiation exchange between earth and space. Both of these services can be upset by human activity.

For human beings and other living organisms the air is what water is for fish. Unless you wear a gas mask, there is no escaping what the air has to offer. The surface air (the "troposphere") normally contains about 78 percent nitrogen, 21 percent oxygen, small amounts of other gases, and varying amounts of water vapor. It may also have many, many other things put there through special acts of nature and the activities of human beings. The upper layers of the earth's atmosphere (the "stratosphere") contain only about 5 percent of the planet's air, but it has a critical role to play in making it habitable. Trace gases in the stratosphere, particularly ozone, filter out about 99 percent of incoming ultraviolet radiation, acting like a giant sun block, without which we would be exposed to damaging levels of radiation. Other trace gases in the stratosphere provide greenhouse services; they trap some of the infrared radiation that is reflected back from the earth's surface, warming it and making it more hospitable to living organisms. As we have recently found out, both of these vital phenomena can be disrupted by human activity.

Human disruptions of the atmosphere are not new; instances of local smoke pollution have occurred for centuries. But in the last few decades the potential severity of air pollution problems has grown more acute, owing to the sheer scale of airborne residuals released and the exotic nature of some of the emitted substances. There are thousands of potential air pollutants—e.g., oxides of carbon, nitrogen and sulfur, volatile organic compounds, suspended particulate matter, photochemical oxidants, radioactivity, heat, and noise. These pollutants cause a diverse set of damages. Perhaps the most important are human health impacts. Prolonged exposure to airborne substances can lead to lung cancer, bronchitis, emphysema, and asthma; accidental releases can have acute impacts. Air pollution also causes damage to plants, as in, for example, the destruction of forests and reduced crop yields stemming from acid deposition. Air pollution can lead to severe damage of exposed materials, such as the surface erosion and discoloration of stone and concrete work and the corrosion of metals. Stratospheric ozone depletion and enhanced global warming have significant implications for humans and the earth's ecosystem. Not all air pollution is outdoors; in fact, indoor air pollution is a critical problem in many homes, factories, mines, and farms.

Many airborne pollutants are emitted on a continuous basis. The sulfur dioxide (SO_2) emissions from power plants, for example, are continuously produced as long as the plants are in operation. For individual motor vehicles, emissions start and stop with their operation, although for an entire urban area, auto and truck emissions vary continuously throughout the days and seasons according to the rhythms of economic activity. Episodic, especially accidental, emissions have been the cause of severe air pollution incidents; for example, the Bhopal disaster in India and, to a much lesser degree, the numerous transportation accidents that occur in many countries. The links between emissions and ambient air-quality levels can be complicated because of the complexities of meteorological phenomena. The best-known example of this is the creation of local weather conditions that trap air pollutants, sometimes for extended periods of time. The infamous "temperature inversions" over urban areas are well known.

Annual expenditures in the U.S. for air pollution control have about doubled since the early 1970s.[1] Has this had an impact? Table 15-1 shows aggregate U.S. emissions for major air pollutants in 1940, 1975, and 1989. These are divided into emissions from stationary sources and emissions from mobile sources. SO_2 emissions are largely from stationary sources; these emissions are currently higher than they were in 1940, but lower than in 1975. Nitrogen oxides from stationary sources, however, are higher today than in 1975 for stationary sources, but not for mobile sources. Some improvement has occurred in mobile-source volatile organic compounds (VOCs), stationary-source particulates, and mobile-source carbon monoxide (CO). The biggest success story is in lead emissions, with a vast decrease in emissions from both mobile and stationary sources. Table 15-2 shows some aggregated figures for ambient levels of various pollutants over the last several decades. A clear success story is shown in the lead figures; ambient levels of lead have been cut to a small fraction of what they were in the early 1970s, primarily because of the shift to no-lead gas. The other pollutants also show declines, but at more modest rates. We can conclude that air quality has improved in the U.S. over the last few decades, and no doubt this is related to the various air pollution-control programs we have put in place. What needs to be asked, however, is whether the sums of money the nation has put into air pollution control have bought as much improvement in air quality as they could have and should have. To answer this we have to look more closely at the policies themselves.

---

[1] In 1972 they were $14.6 billion and in 1988 they were $29.3 billion. See: Council on Environmental Quality, *Environmental Quality, 1990*, Washington, D.C., 1991, p. 272.

TABLE 15-1

STATIONARY- AND MOBILE-SOURCE EMISSIONS OF CRITERIA POLLUTANTS IN U.S., 1940, 1975, AND 1989*

	Annual emissions (million metric tons)		
	1940	1975	1989
Sulfur dioxide			
Stationary	14.7	25.0	19.1
Mobile	2.9	0.6	1.0
Nitrogen oxides			
Stationary	4.6	10.3	12.0
Mobile	2.2	8.9	7.9
Volatile organic compounds			
Stationary	13.4	12.5	12.1
Mobile	5.2	10.3	6.4
Particulates			
Stationary	20.4	9.2	5.7
Mobile	2.7	1.4	1.5
Carbon monoxide			
Stationary	52.3	19.1	20.9
Mobile	29.3	65.0	40.0
Lead			
Stationary	N/A	24.4	5.0
Mobile	N/A	122.6	2.2

*"Criteria pollutants" are discussed in the section on the history of federal air pollution policy.

Source: Council on Environmental Quality, *Environmental Quality, 1990,* Washington, D.C., 1991, pp. 320–322.

TABLE 15-2

CRITERIA AIR POLLUTANTS: NATIONAL MEAN AMBIENT CONCENTRATIONS AND ACTUAL EMISSIONS AS PERCENTAGE OF EMISSIONS WITHOUT CONTROL PROGRAMS

	Sulfur dioxide (ppm)	Carbon monoxide (ppm)	Ozone (ppm)	Nitrogen dioxide (ppm)	TSP $(\mu g/m^3)$	Lead (mg/m^3)
			Ambient Concentrations			
1975	.0154	11.96	.153	.029	61.9	1.04
1980	.0109	8.52	.136	.025	64.2	.61
1985	.0088	7.03	.123	.024	48.8	.23
1988	.0084	6.56	.136	.024	50.5	.08
			Emissions (%)			
1984	33	71	82	60	56	19
1988	30	58	72	58	43	3

Notes: *Ambient Levels:* "Criteria" air pollutants: see discussion of federal air-control policy; ppm = parts per million; $\mu g/m^3$ = micrograms per cubic meter; mg/m^3 = milligrams per cubic meter; TSP = total suspended particulates; sulfur dioxide and nitrogen dioxide records are arithmetic means; carbon monoxide and ozone records are second maximum readings over 8- and 24-hour periods, respectively; TSP records are geometric means; lead records are maximum quarterly recordings; data represent composite averages from all sites in the nationwide monitoring network.

Sources: Ambient Concentrations: U.S. Council on Environmental Quality, *Environmental Quality, 1990,* Washington, D.C., 1991, p. 323; *Emissions:* U.S. Environmental Protection Agency, *Environmental Investments: The Costs of a Clean Environment, A Summary,* Washington, D.C., December 1990, p. 5-2.

FEDERAL AIR POLLUTION-CONTROL LAWS: A BRIEF SKETCH

Like the case of water pollution, there was little federal concern or statutory activity in air pollution matters prior to the late 1960s. Air pollution was regarded as primarily a local concern, to be dealt with under local nuisance laws. Federal laws dealt mainly with providing funds for research and for state grants to train personnel and obtain technical assistance. However, in the 1967 Air Quality Act the Department of Health, Education and Welfare was charged with establishing criteria through which ambient air-quality standards could be set for six common air pollutants: sulfur dioxide (SO_2), nitrogen oxides (NO_x), ozone, particulate matter, carbon monoxide, and lead. These became known as the "criteria" pollutants, and ambient standards for these six were to be set by the states. By the end of the 1960s, however, frustration was widespread over the perceived weakness of this federal/state approach. The Clean Air Act Amendments of 1970 represented a much more aggressive assertion of federal power into air pollution matters. It established the basic contours of air pollution policy that persist to the present: uniform national ambient air-quality standards, a variety of technology-based emission standards, and stricter emission standards for automobiles.

In the Clean Air Act Amendments of 1977 federal legislators addressed some of the problems created by the uniform ambient standards of the 1970 Act. Air quality was worse in some cities than others, and better in rural areas. There was widespread concern after the 1970 law that cities in areas with air quality already better than the national ambient standard could compete unfairly for new industrial development. New firms might be attracted to these areas by the promise of less strict emissions controls than firms would face in areas where air quality was already worse than the standards. The 1977 CAA amendments differentiated "PSD" areas (PSD stands for "prevention of serious deterioration"—for a list of acronyms used in this chapter, see Table 15-3) and "nonattainment" areas. Stricter technology-based effluent standards would apply to PSD regions, where air quality was already better than the standard, than to nonattainment regions.[2]

After the 1977 Act there were no new federal air pollution statutes until 1990, a reflection of the Reagan administration's desire to reduce the "burden" of regulations on the U.S. economy. There were, however, some significant policy innovations that occurred during this period within the existing laws. These were the "bubble" and "offset" programs for air pollution control, which we will discuss in some detail below.

In 1990, after many years of negotiation and political conflict, Congress passed, and the president signed, the Clean Air Act Amendments of 1990. This statute contains five main sections, dealing with: (1) motor vehicles and fuels, (2) acid rain, (3) urban air quality, (4) air toxics, and (5) stratospheric ozone prob-

---

[2] The PSD regions were differentiated into three classes; see the detail in Table 15-4.

TABLE 15-3
GLOSSARY OF ACRONYMS USED IN THIS CHAPTER

AQCR	Air-quality control regions
BACT	Best available control technology
Btu	British thermal unit
CAA	Clean Air Act
CFC	Chlorofluorocarbon
CO_2	Carbon dioxide
ERC	Emission reduction credit
I&M	Inspection and maintenance
LAER	Lowest achievable emission rate
MACT	Maximum achievable control technology
NAAQS	National ambient air-quality standards
NO_x	Nitrogen oxides
NSPS	New-source performance standards
NSR	New-source review
PSD	Prevention of serious deterioration
RACT	Reasonably available control technology
SIP	State implementation plan
SO_2	Sulfur dioxide
TSP	Total suspended particulates
VOC	Volatile organic compounds

lems. The law is notable for including an innovative transferable discharge permit system for SO_2 emissions; apart from this it continues the typical command-and-control approaches that have characterized federal programs to date.

The continued problem of motor-vehicle pollution was addressed by a further tightening of new car emission standards and expansion of state inspection and maintenance (I&M) programs. In addition, the law mandates many new technologies, such as reformulated fuel, fume-catching nozzles at gas stations, and the development of a generation of clean cars. The law also attempts to deal more directly with toxic air pollutants. In earlier laws, the EPA had been directed to address the problem of airborne toxics, but over the years they had made relatively little progress. The 1990 Act specifically lists 189 toxic materials that are to be controlled, and requires that the EPA establish technology-based effluent standards to apply to sources emitting more than 10 tons/year of a single toxic or 25 tons/year of any combination of toxic compounds. The standard is to be the "maximum achievable control technology" (MACT), defined as technology based on the "best control technologies that have already been demonstrated"[3] in the designated industrial categories. The EPA has become aware over the years of some of the negative side effects of specifying too closely the technologies that polluters must use to reduce emissions; it claims that in the case of these MACT standards, it will aim at ". . . setting standards the industry must

---

[3] *EPA Journal*, 17(1), January/February 1991, p. 32.

TABLE 15-4
MAJOR FEDERAL AIR POLLUTION LAWS

Air Pollution Control Act (APCA) of 1955

Authorized the Secretary of Health, Education and Welfare to spend up to $5 million a year to do research and to help the states in training and technical assistance on matters of air pollution. Extended in 1959 and 1962.

Motor Vehicle Exhaust Study Act of 1960

Directed the Secretary of HEW to do a study on "Motor Vehicles, Air Pollution and Health" within 2 years.

Clean Air Act (CAA) of 1963

Authorized federal grants to states to develop state and local air pollution-control programs; established a conference system to deal with problems of interstate air pollution; extended authorization for federal research on air pollution.

Motor Vehicle Air Pollution Control Act of 1965

Authorized the Secretary of HEW to set *emission standards* for new cars (but no deadline was established); dealt with international air pollution and called for more research.

CAA Extension of 1966

Extended the CAA of 1963, and added authority to make grants to states to support air pollution-control programs.

Air Quality Act (AQA) of 1967

Provided for additional grants to states to plan air pollution-control programs; provided for interstate air pollution-control agencies, expanded research on fuels and vehicles; required HEW to establish air-quality regions of the country, publish air-quality criteria and control technology reports for the common pollutants; required states to establish ambient air-quality standards for the "criteria" pollutants and develop attainment programs; authorized HEW to give financial assistance to states to establish motor-vehicle inspection programs.

CAA Amendments of 1970

Established *national* ambient air-quality standards (NAAQSs) for criteria pollutants; required the establishment of new-car emission standards along with certification programs; EPA was to establish emission standards for major toxic or hazardous pollutants; EPA to establish technology-based emission standards for all *new sources* (NSPS) of the common air pollutants; required state implementation plans (SIPs) to control existing stationary sources of air pollutants.

CAA Amendments of 1977

Established the goal of "prevention of serious deterioration" (PSD) in areas already cleaner than the national standards; established three classes of already clean areas:

Class I areas: no additional air-quality deterioration permitted (includes national parks, etc.).
Class II areas: some air-quality deterioration to be permitted (includes most PSD regions).
Class III areas: air quality to be allowed to deteriorate to level of NAAQSs.

Established a technology standard "lowest achievable emission rate" (LAER) for new sources in nonattainment areas, and "best available control technologies" (BACT) for new sources in PSD regions.

CAA Amendments of 1990

Established tougher tailpipe standards for new cars, with longer warranty period; mandated pilot program of "clean" cars in some cities; reformulated fuels in some cities; Phase II pumps at gas stations; on-board fume canisters on cars; streamlined stationary-source permitting procedures; provided for reduction of 189 toxic airborne emissions through TBES ("maximum achievable control technology," MACT); provided for stricter local plans to reduce ozone, carbon monoxide, and particulates in the worst cities; further rules for phasing out of CFCs; provided for a system of transferable discharge permits among power plants to reduce sulfur dioxide emissions.

Sources: Arthur C. Stern, "History of Air Pollution Legislation in the United States," *Journal of Air Pollution Control Association,* 32(1), January 1982, pp. 44–61; Paul R. Portney, "Air Pollution Policy," in Paul R. Portney (ed.), *Public Policies for Environmental Protection,* Resources for the Future, 1990, Chapter 3; *EPA Journal,* January/February 1991, pp. 8–9.

achieve, rather than dictating equipment that industry must install."[4] Only time will tell if this more flexible regulatory approach will bear fruit.

Regarding criteria pollutants, the 1990 Act seeks to come to grips with the continuing nonattainment problem. In the 1977 law the metropolitan areas of the country had been given until 1987 to come into compliance with ambient standards. Although some progress had been made, many cities still failed to meet the standards at the end of the 1980s. Previous laws treated all these regions alike, but in 1990 an effort was made to recognize degrees of nonattainment. A system was established in the law to classify cities in terms of the severity of their air pollution problems. The law specifies five classifications for ozone, two for carbon monoxide, and two for particulate matter. Control programs of increasing severity are specified for cities in increasingly serious nonattainment categories. For example, emissions of volatile organic compounds and nitrogen oxides produce ground-level ozone, which, in turn, is instrumental in producing urban smog. In 1990, 96 cities failed to meet the national air-quality standard for ozone. The 1990 Act places these cities into five categories according to the severity of their ozone levels. The categories are "marginal," "moderate," "serious," "severe," and "extreme." Only one city—Los Angeles—is in the extreme category. The law then specifies increasingly stringent control techniques for cities according to which category they are in. These techniques are based primarily on the enforcement of technology-based effluent standards and the outright specification of technologies that must be adopted in the various regions.

Current federal air pollution statutes are long and complex, but they can be boiled down to the following:

- National ambient air-quality standards for criteria pollutants, with pollution-control programs of varying stringency in different urban areas based on the severity of the air pollution.
- Technology-based effluent standards for stationary sources of airborne emissions on: (1) all new sources, (2) existing sources in nonattainment regions, and (3) sources of toxic emissions.
- Emission standards for new cars, with inspection and maintenance programs (I&M) in some states.
- A variety of new technology specifications for automobile pollution ("clean cars," reformulated fuel, on-board vapor-catching devices, etc.).
- An emissions permit trading program for power plants in the Midwest.
- The phaseout of CFCs.

In the next few sections we will look more closely at these major parts of the air pollution-control program (the discussion of the CFC phaseout will be postponed until a later chapter).

---

[4] Ibid.

NATIONAL AMBIENT AIR-QUALITY STANDARDS

Before 1970 the states were encouraged to set their own ambient air-quality standards, using criteria and information provided by the federal government. This would have permitted different states to set different standards and, of course, to adopt different programs for their attainment. In 1970, however, Congress opted to shift to a system of *national* ambient air-quality standards (NAAQS), a single set of standards that would be imposed uniformly on all parts of the country. In 1977 this was altered somewhat through the recognition of PSD regions, in which efforts would be made to prevent any significant deterioration from current levels. But over the rest of the country the same ambient standards prevail.

In Chapter 11 we discussed the question of uniformity in standards. Unless marginal damage and marginal abatement costs happen to be the same in all regions, uniform national standards will not be efficient. They will be overly stringent where marginal damages are relatively low and/or marginal abatement costs relatively high; or not stringent enough where marginal damages are relatively high and/or marginal abatement costs relatively low. Thus, standards cannot in general be efficient unless they are established with an eye toward both marginal benefits and marginal control costs. The 1970 CAA, however, expressly forbade the EPA from taking abatement costs into account in setting the ambient standards. The 1970 law mandated that the EPA set "primary" and "secondary" standards for criteria pollutants *strictly on the basis of damages.*

- *Primary standards* are set to protect human health;
- *Secondary standards*, more restrictive than the primary standards, are set "to protect the public welfare from any known or anticipated adverse effects."

The current primary and secondary criteria air pollutant standards are shown in Table 15-5. Only one unique secondary standard has been created, that for sulfur dioxide. The standards as set imply that the damage functions associated with these criteria pollutants have *thresholds*, below which damages are minimal or nonexistent. When the standards were set, relatively little was known about the damage functions. Even today we are unsure if these thresholds exist. Recent results suggest that they may not, that in fact damages may occur even at very low levels of these pollutants, especially among particularly sensitive individuals in the population. But the costs of achieving zero levels of these pollutants would be enormous.

The implication of this is that in setting the national standards some informal recognition was undoubtedly given to abatement costs. Implicit concern with abatement costs has also occurred in enforcement. Despite the unambiguous nature of the standards, there are many urban areas of the country where ambient air quality is still worse than the standards, two decades after their establishment. Strict enforcement of the standards in a short period of time would simply have cost too much. Enforcement has involved an implicit trade-off of marginal

TABLE 15-5
NATIONAL PRIMARY AND SECONDARY AMBIENT AIR-QUALITY STANDARDS AS OF 1989

Pollutant	Primary standard (μg/m^3)*	Secondary standard
Particulate matter	50 (annual mean)[†]	Same as primary
	100 (24-hour mean)	
Sulfur dioxide	80 (annual mean)	1300 μg/m^3 (3-hour mean)
	365 (24-hour mean)	
Carbon monoxide	10 (8-hour mean)	None
	40 (1-hour mean)	
Nitrogen dioxide	100 (annual mean)	Same as primary
Ozone	235 (daily mean)	Same as primary
Lead	1.5 (quarterly mean)	Same as primary

*Micrograms per cubic meter.
[†]The standards are established over certain averaging times. In other words, they are expressed in terms of maximum average concentrations of the pollutants over some time period; for three of the criteria pollutants two such maximums are expressed in the standard.

Source: U.S. Environmental Protection Agency, *National Air Quality and Emissions Trend Report*, 1989 (EPA/450/4-91/003), Washington, D.C., February 1991.

damages and marginal abatement costs, according to the particularities of the different urban areas, the appearance of new abatement technology, and the willingness to pay for air pollution control, as manifested primarily in the ongoing political struggle in local areas.

STATIONARY-SOURCE CONTROL

Federal policy toward stationary-source air pollution control is intertwined with policy actions and administration by the states. The 1970 Clean Air Act Amendments require the EPA to establish national ambient standards and states to develop *state implementation plans* (SIPs), which, when enforced by the states, will decrease emissions enough to meet the standards. These SIPs are to be specified for designated geographical areas called *Air Quality Control Regions* (AQCRs). In those states where for one reason or another no SIP is developed, the EPA is authorized to administer the air pollution-control program through its regional office. The SIP plans are subject to approval by the EPA. To be approved, the SIPs must include a set of *technology-based effluent standards* (TBESs) to be applied to firms in various industrial categories and subcategories.

Technology-Based Effluent Standards

The stationary-source program contains several different types of TBESs, as shown in Table 15-6. The standards differ between existing and new sources and between nonattainment and PSD regions. Distinctions between existing and new sources are a prominent feature in environmental control programs. New

TABLE 15-6
TECHNOLOGY-BASED EFFLUENT STANDARDS (TBES) FOR
CONTROL OF LARGE STATIONARY SOURCES OF AIR POLLUTANTS

Nonattainment Regions	
Existing Sources:	RACT: "Reasonably Available Control Technology"
New Sources:	LAER: "Lowest Achievable Emission Rate"
Prevention of Significant Deterioration (PSD) Regions	
Existing Sources:	None
New Sources:	BACT: "Best Available Control Technology"

sources, or existing sources that are modified in some major way, are usually held to stricter standards than existing, established sources. In the air-quality program, new sources in nonattainment areas are subject to a LAER (lowest achievable emission rate) standard,[5] which is meant to be more restrictive than the RACT (reasonably available control technology) standard applied to existing sources in those areas. In PSD regions new sources are held to standards based on BACT (best available control technology), while existing sources are in effect not subject to any standard.[6]

The case for holding new sources to stricter standards (a *new-source bias*) than those applied to existing sources is usually made on the basis of cost; it normally costs more to retrofit existing plants with pollution-control equipment than to incorporate the equipment into new plants when they are being built. In effect the argument is that the marginal abatement costs of existing plants are normally higher than those of new plants, so cost-effectiveness justifies more restrictive emission standards for the former than for the latter. To a large extent, this is probably an economic argument being used to justify a course of action that is politically expedient. It is easier to put stricter limits on new sources than on existing ones because, by definition, the former will have less political clout than the latter. And existing firms may not be so opposed to applying stricter controls that make it relatively costly for new competitors to get into business. From an administrative standpoint a new-source bias is also easy to understand. In any given year there are many times more existing sources than there are new or modified sources, so more administrative resources may be concentrated on the latter. A focus on new sources also implies a gradualist approach, since it means that stricter standards will gradually spread through the various industries as old capital is replaced with new.

But the price paid for holding new sources to stricter standards may be high.

---

[5] LAER is defined as the lowest emission rate specified in any state implementation plan, whether or not any source is currently achieving that rate.

[6] In giving the states the primary responsibility to set TBESs, there was some fear among federal policymakers that economic competition among them would motivate some to set less restrictive standards to attract business. Thus, the EPA is empowered to set a floor level for standards applying to new or modified stationary sources. These are called new-source performance standards (NSPS).

The problem is that a new-source bias creates incentives to hold on to existing plants because they will be subject to less strict environmental standards than new or modernized plants. So in trying to ease the transition to lower pollution levels through a new-source bias, we may inadvertently slow up the rate of adoption of pollution-withholding technology. This is no doubt one of the main reasons so many urban regions of the U.S. continue to suffer from substantial air pollution problems many years after the beginning of the federal program.

Virtually all of the observations we made about technology-based effluent standards in water pollution control are also applicable to air pollution-control policy. It is an approach that tends to put the initiative and responsibility for pollution control in the hands of administrative agencies rather than the polluters themselves. Too much of the energy and creativity of polluting firms is devoted to finding ways of avoiding compliance rather than devising better means of controlling emissions. The incentives for R&D to develop new techniques of pollution control or to reach back into the production process to reduce residuals in the first place are weakened. But most importantly, TBESs have the effect of encouraging uniform compliance measures among sources. In a world where marginal abatement costs differ substantially across sources, this cannot be a cost-effective policy.

Numerous studies have been done by environmental economists to estimate excess costs of the command-and-control approach to air pollution control inherent in technology-based effluent standards. These studies involve complex models that incorporate economic factors, such as control costs at each source, with emission and meteorological factors that show how ambient air quality is affected by various patterns of emissions. The models can be run to determine the costs and ambient quality levels achieved with the CAC approach, then run again without the TBESs to see what the total control cost would be of a program that achieved the same ambient air quality but with a cost-effective distribution of emission reductions among firms. Table 15-7 summarizes the main results of some of the studies. The last column shows the ratio of the CAC program costs, incorporating various technology-based effluent standards, as indicated, to least-cost programs that would provide the same improvement in air quality. If the actual programs were also cost-effective, these ratios would be at or near 1.0. In fact, they vary from 1.07 to 22.0.

Four of the studies show CAC/least-cost ratios between 1.0 and 2.0. These are CAC programs that also come close to achieving minimum costs. The most likely explanation for this is that these cases involve multiple sources that have relatively small differences in marginal abatement costs. Most of the other ratios, however, are around 4.0 to 6.0, meaning that the actual programs involving TBESs were four to six times more costly than they would have been had they been designed to be cost-effective. The problem with this is not just that we are paying much more than is necessary to get the improvements in air quality, though this is certainly a serious shortcoming. The real problem is that since the actual control programs are so much more costly than they need be, we are in fact working with an aggregate marginal abatement cost function that is much

TABLE 15-7
COMPARISON OF CAC CONTROL COST WITH LEAST-COST PROGRAMS IN AIR POLLUTION CONTROL

Study	CAC benchmark	Ratio of CAC costs to least cost
1 Particulates, St. Louis (1974)	SIP regulations	6.00
2 Sulfur dioxide, four corners region (Utah, Colorado, Arizona, and New Mexico) (1981)	SIP regulations	4.25
3 Sulfates, Los Angeles (1982)	Applicable Clean Air Act emission standards	1.07
4 Nitrogen dioxide, Baltimore (1983)	RACT regulations	5.96
5 Nitrogen dioxide, Chicago (1983)	RACT regulations	14.40
6 Particulates, Baltimore (1984)	SIP regulations	4.18
7 Sulfur dioxide, Delaware Valley (1984)	Uniform percentage reduction	1.78
8 Particulates, Delaware Valley (1984)	Uniform percentage reduction	22.00
9 Airport noise, U.S. (1983)	Mandatory retrofit	1.72
10 Hydrocarbons, all domestic Du Pont plants (1984)	Uniform percentage reduction	4.15
11 CFC emissions, U.S. (nonaerosol) (1980)	Proposed emission standards	1.96

Source: Adapted from T. H. Tietenberg, *Emissions Trading: An Exercise in Reforming Pollution Control,* Resources for the Future, Washington, D.C., 1985, pp. 42–43. Individual studies are as follows: **1** Scott E. Atkinson and Donald H. Lewis, "A Cost-Effective Analysis of Alternative Air Quality Control Strategies," *Journal of Environmental Economics and Management,* 1(3), November 1974, pp. 237–250; **2** Fred Roach et al., "Alternative Air Quality Policy Options in the Four Corners Region," *Southwestern Review,* 1(2), Summer 1981, pp. 44–45; **3** Robert W. Hahn and Roger G. Noll, "Designing a Market for Tradeable Emission Permits," in Wesley A. Magat (ed.), *Reform of Environmental Regulation,* Ballinger, Cambridge, Mass., 1982, pp. 132–133; **4** Alan J. Krupnick, "Costs of Alternative Policies for the Control of NO_2 in the Baltimore Region," Resources for the Future, Washington, D.C., 1983, p. 22; **5** Eugene P. Seskin, Robert J. Anderson, Jr., and Robert O. Reid, "An Empirical Analysis of Economic Strategies for Controlling Air Pollution," *Journal of Environmental Economics and Management,* 10(2), June 1983, pp. 117–120; **6** Albert M. McGartland, "Marketable Permit Systems for Air Pollution Control: An Empirical Study," Ph.D. dissertation, University of Maryland, 1984, p. 67a; **7** Walter O. Spofford, Jr., "Efficiency Properties of Alternative Source Control Policies for Meeting Ambient Air Quality Standards: An Empirical Application to the Lower Delaware Valley," Resources for the Future, Washington, D.C., 1984, p. 77; **8** Ibid.; **9** David Harrison, Jr., "Case Study 1: The Regulation of Aircraft Noise," in Thomas C. Schelling (ed.), *Incentives for Environmental Protection,* MIT Press, Cambridge, Mass., pp. 81–96; **10** Michael T. Maloney and Bruce Yandle, "Estimation of the Cost of Air Pollution Control Regulation," *Journal of Environmental Economics and Management,* 11(3), September 1984, pp. 244–264; **11** Adele R. Palmer et al., *Economic Implications of Regulating Chlorofluorocarbon Emissions from Nonaerosol Applications,* Rand Corporation, Report No. R-2524-EPA, June 1980, p. 225.

higher than it need be, and therefore we are probably settling for smaller improvements in ambient quality than we might achieve if control programs were fully cost-effective.

New Directions in Stationary-Source Control

It was recognized very early that the CAC types of policies favored by current laws would produce far less improvement in ambient quality for the money spent than we would get with more efficient policies. In the mid-1970s the EPA began to experiment with alternatives that might be more flexible and cost-effective in meeting air-quality goals. The 1977 Clean Air Act authorized a limited type of emission permit trading, and several other approaches were developed on the initiative of EPA. These plans were, and are, meant to be strictly secondary to the primary approach based on technology-based emission standards. More recently, the interest in market-incentive approaches to pollution control, together with their acceptance by a number of the large environmental advocacy groups, led to the 1990 Clean Air Act Amendments, which specifically incorporates a new permit trading scheme for the control of airborne SO_2 emissions.

The earlier programs allow the trading of what are called "emission reduction credits" (ERCs). An ERC is essentially the same as what we have called a transferable discharge permit. Sources obtain ERCs by reducing their emissions below a given baseline level specified by administrative authorities. In order for an ERC to be tradable, the EPA rules require that it be "surplus," "enforceable," "quantifiable," and "permanent."[7] This does not mean that all trades must be permanent, only that the emission reductions giving rise to the ERC be permanent. There are four subprograms of the ERC trading program: offsets, bubbles, banking, and netting.

Offsets   This is a system designed to apply to nonattainment regions in order to accommodate economic growth while still making progress on cleaning up the air. It allows new sources, or major modifications of existing sources, to begin operations in a nonattainment area if the new emissions they will produce are offset by decreases in emissions among existing sources of the same pollutant in that area. The way this is done is for the new source to purchase ERCs from existing sources. In effect, the new sources help to finance existing sources to reduce their emissions below their baseline levels. In order to qualify for the right to buy ERCs, new sources must conform to the LAER standards set by EPA; that is, they must have emissions that do not exceed this standard. Offset transactions can occur among sources within the same firm or among different firms. If offsets are traded one for one, there will be no net change in total emissions as trades are made. Offset trading can also be used to "rachet down" the total quantity of emissions. This can be done by requiring buyers to obtain more than one offset for each unit of added emissions. Thus, for example, purchasers might be required to buy 1.5 ERCs for each unit increase in emissions.[8]

Bubbles   The bubble system is primarily meant for *intra*firm transactions. Suppose one firm has multiple sources of an air pollutant. This is common among

[7] Arlene R. Borowsky and Howard M. Ellis, "Summary of Final Federal Emissions Trading Policy Statement," *Journal of Air Pollution Control Administration*, 37(7), July 1987, pp. 789–790.

[8] In the 1990 Clean Air Act Amendments a system of "exchange rates" is adopted for some offset trades; for "moderate" areas in terms of ambient ozone, new sources must obtain 1.15 ERCs for each additional unit of VOCs it expects to emit; for "extreme" areas this ratio is 1.5 to 1, and the ratio varies between these limits for areas in the intermediate categories.

large industrial operations like refineries, whose plants often spread over a relatively large area. Instead of holding each source at the plant to the applicable TBES, the entire plant is treated as a single source, and an effluent standard is applied to this single consolidated source. This allows the firm to rearrange emission reductions among their various sources in accordance with the equimarginal principle.

Banking In 1979 the EPA gave states the right to create ERC banks, making it possible for sources to bank and save for future use any ERCs they had produced by reducing their emissions. States are required to develop a system where ERCs can be deposited and to develop procedures for transferring ERCs into and out of the appropriate bank accounts. Banked ERCs can be used for future offset and netting transactions.

Netting Netting transactions, like most bubble arrangements, are *intra*firm transactions applying to the modification of existing sources. They arise when existing firms are considering an expansion of their operations that would increase emissions enough to trigger a new source review (NSR). These NSRs are relatively involved, time consuming, and costly. Firms may be able to avoid NSRs if the increase in emissions in the part of the plant that is to be expanded can be offset by reductions elsewhere in the plant, so that the *net* increase in total emissions falls below the NSR-triggering level. The new source must still meet NSPS, but with netting the firm may be able to avoid certain requirements like having to find external offsets to cover their increased emissions.

These emission permit transfer programs were developed by the EPA in the 1970s and refined over the next decade. The "final" guidelines in trading rules were published in 1986, and they apply both to criteria pollutants and to listed hazardous air pollutants. There was reasonably widespread enthusiasm for their development, especially among environmental economists,[9] and an expectation that they would be useful in making the air pollution-control program more cost-effective. The actual results are more ambivalent. While there has been a relatively large number of transactions, there are many who feel that their full potential has not yet been reached.

Table 15-8 shows the number of ERC transactions that took place from the time the various systems were initiated until 1986, and the estimated cost savings they have made possible. Cost savings are the difference between control costs using the transfer programs and what costs would have been had these programs not been available. Several things stand out from these figures. The most obvious is that virtually all transactions have been internal, where individual firms have adjusted emissions among the several sources at their plants to lower compliance costs. This has made it possible for individual firms to move toward more cost-effective emission reduction. On the other hand, firms have not taken the

---

[9] But not among many environmental advocates, who inclined toward the position that permit trading would weaken the effort to control emissions in nonattainment areas.

TABLE 15-8

EMISSIONS TRADING ACTIVITY FROM INCEPTION OF PROGRAMS TO 1986

Type of trade	Estimated number of transactions		Estimated cost savings (millions)
	Internal	External	
Offsets	1800	200	Probably large, but difficult to measure
Bubbles	129	2	$435
Banking	< 100	< 20	Small
Netting	5,000 to 12,000	0	$25 to $300 in permitting costs; $500 to $12,000 in control costs

Source: Robert W. Hahn and Gordon L. Hester, "Where Did All the Markets Go? An Analysis of EPA's Emission Trading Program," Yale Journal of Regulation, 6(1), Winter 1989, p. 138.

opportunity to obtain cost savings that *interfirm* trading could bring about. The economists who estimated these numbers concluded that the uncertainties about the legal status of the ERCs and the costs of finding outside demanders and suppliers of credits led most firms to rely mostly on intrafirm trades.

A contributing factor was that few firms engaged in ERC banking, and those that did chose to bank their credits in internal accounts rather than at a central depository. Again, the uncertainty about the property-right status of the ERCs and the fear that banked credits might be confiscated by administrative authorities under pressure to reduce air pollution may have led them to avoid depositing excess credits in a central account. A more visible bank of excess emission credits might have contributed to the development of a more active external market for credits, with more information about present and expected future prices. This, in turn, would have fostered more external market transactions.

We should note also the great popularity of netting transactions compared to bubble arrangements. The explanation for this is that netting involves modified sources while bubbles apply to existing sources. When firms modify one of their sources, they may trigger the costly and lengthy permitting procedures that apply to new sources of emissions, procedures that do not apply to existing sources. Netting has become a reasonably popular way of trying to avoid this; a firm searches for sources elsewhere in its operations where it can cut back emissions so that the net increase in emissions will be small enough to avoid the need for a new or modified-source approach.

These emission reduction credit trading procedures have become a permanent part of the stationary-source air pollution-control program in the U.S. For a time there will be a built-in conflict between administrative needs to change rules so that markets may work more effectively and the needs of market users, for whom stability and certainty about future rules and accepted procedures are paramount. We would expect firms increasingly to take advantage of them as these administrative uncertainties are reduced.

THE TDP PROGRAM OF THE 1990 CAA

The 1990 Clean Air Act contains a program that is, from the perspective of historical pollution-control laws in the U.S., a considerable innovation. It is a transferable emission permit plan for controlling SO_2 emissions from U.S. power plants. The SO_2 coming from these plants is a major source of the acid rain that falls in the northeastern part of the U.S. and Canada. The EPA is to issue a quantity of emission permits to designated power plants. Each permit will allow the release of 1 ton of sulfur dioxide from that plant; thus, if, for example, operators of a particular plant have 20,000 permits, this plant would be allowed to emit a maximum of 20,000 tons of sulfur per year. The permits may be traded at prices agreed upon between buyer and seller. As we discussed in detail in Chapter 13, the purpose of a TDP program like this is to achieve a reduction in total SO_2 emissions at much lower cost than if all plants were required to meet the same proportionate reductions or if all firms were held to the same TBESs. The law calls initially for a reduction of approximately 20 percent from estimated total sulfur emissions of 1980, and a further 20 percent reduction in later years. The program represents a very substantial departure from the "command-and-control" approaches of the past. If it works according to expectations, at least the expectations of many environmental economists, it should save considerable amounts of money and give a big boost to the application of incentive-type measures to other environmental problems.

Initial Permit Distribution

The program has two phases. The first will run from 1995 to 2000 and will be limited to 110 electric utility plants located in 21 eastern and midwestern states. The plants involved are large coal-burning plants that currently emit more than 2.5 pounds of SO_2 per Btu of fuel used. Each of these plants will be allocated a prescribed number of permits (or "allowances," as they are called by the EPA). These allocations were calculated with the following formula:

$$\frac{\text{Number of}}{\text{permits}} = \frac{\text{Average Btus of fuel used}}{\text{1985–1987 (in millions)}} \times \frac{\text{2.5 pounds of } SO_2}{\text{per million Btus}}$$

The formula gives more permits to larger plants, as measured by the average quantity of fuel used during the base period 1985–1987. It is not exactly an equiproportionate system, but it moves in that direction by using a common sulfur conversion factor—2.5 pounds of SO_2 per million Btus of fuel—to calculate initial allowances. Two plants burning the same amount of fuel end up with the same permit allocation, even though one of them may have put more effort than the other into reducing SO_2 emissions. But since the plants are all large coal-burning plants, the formula in effect treats them roughly the same.

This initial allocation totals 5,489,335 permits. About 57 percent of these will go to power plants in five states: Ohio, Indiana, Georgia, Pennsylvania, and West Virginia. An additional special Phase I allocation of permits will be given to power plants in Illinois, Ohio, and Indiana.[10] The EPA will also hold back large quantities of permits. It will have a "bonus reserve" of up to 3.5 million permits, which can be used to allow certain states to accommodate growth in their electricity producing sectors or to provide temporary delays to power plants that wish to install scrubbers[11] to reduce SO_2 emissions. It also may auction off a number of permits, as well as sell a certain number at a fixed (real) price of $1,500/permit. The EPA will have an additional reserve of permits that it may allocate to utility firms that undertake approved programs in energy conservation or renewable energy development.

In Phase II, starting in 2000, the program is to be expanded to cover power plants throughout the country. At this point it is expected to cover about 1,000 power plants burning coal, oil, or natural gas. The formula for allocating permits will be much the same as in Phase I except that the SO_2 index will be lowered to 1.2 pounds of SO_2 per million Btus of fuel used. Furthermore, in Phase II there is to be an overall cap of 8.95 million permits given out by the EPA.

Trading Rules

Emission permits are tradable. Managers of an individual plant may do one of three things. They may simply hold on to the permits they were originally allocated and reduce their sulfur emissions to or below that level.[12] They could reduce their emissions below their permit holdings and sell the surplus permits. Or they could reduce their emissions to something more than their initial permit holdings and buy extra permits to cover the overage. Thus, market participants —buyers and sellers—will consist of these 110 utility plants adjusting their permit holdings to match their emission rates. But other participants may buy and sell permits. Other utilities that might wish to expand their electricity output, but are held in check by SO_2 emission limitations, may buy additional permits, as may new plants starting operations after the program is put into effect. The law also allows permits to be traded and held by private citizens, brokers, speculators, environmental groups, other types of business enterprises, etc. As an environmental group, you might wish to buy permits simply to try and get total SO_2 emissions reduced. As a manufacturer of pollution-control equipment, you might wish to buy a stock of permits that you could lend to your customers while they were installing your equipment. As a speculator, you might want to buy and hold permits because you think their price is going to rise.

---

[10] The initial allocation of permits was probably the most controversial issue when the law was being hammered out because it determines how the overall cost burden of SO_2 reduction will be distributed among plants, states, and regions. The extra allocation to the three midwestern states was simply a way to help get their political support for the program.

[11] A "scrubber" is a device for treating stack gases; it can remove up to 95 percent of the sulfur in the gas.

[12] They might reduce emissions below their permit holdings in order to have a reserve of surplus permits in hand for future contingencies.

The Role of the EPA

The role of the EPA is designed to be much more modest than in typical command-and-control type pollution control programs. It is to keep track of permit trades so that it knows at all times how many emission permits are held by each plant. It must also monitor emissions to ensure that no plant emits more than it is entitled to by the number of permits it holds. The law specifies that each source is to install and maintain continuous monitoring devices. In theory the EPA will be concerned only with whether emissions exceed allowances, its only direct control over technology choices is to approve for each plant ". . . a compliance plan that specifies the company's choice of one or more of the compliance methods authorized under the act."[13] Penalties for plants emitting more than they have permits to cover are set at $2,000/ton/year of excess emissions.

Will It Work?

Will the program run smoothly and produce reductions in SO_2 emissions at a substantial cost savings over a CAC-type program? The program is too new to know exactly how successful it will be. Much depends on the role that the EPA chooses to play over the years, and whether the inevitable adjustments that will have to be made in market rules are made with an eye toward increasing efficiency or toward giving one group of participants an additional advantage over others. A key is for the EPA to refrain from trying to dictate technology choices made by utilities to reduce their SO_2 emissions. The market will work best if utilities are allowed to use whatever means they find the cheapest (within reason) to reduce SO_2 emissions and then take advantage of this flexibility by buying or selling emission permits.[14]

One problematic factor in this program is that the main participants, electric utilities, may not have the "correct" economic incentives. Programs of transferable discharge permits are based on the assumption that polluters will be rational cost minimizers, and this is reasonably assured if they are operating in competitive industries. But the electric power industry in the U.S. is not a competitive industry. Electric utilities are instead regulated monopolies, individual plants with no competitors that are regulated by public utilities commissions. So, in fact, the public utility commissions in the various states will have a lot to say about how their power plants respond to the opportunities of the program, and we do not yet know how public utility commissioners will behave toward the program.

Despite these possible problems, the program represents a considerable innovation in U.S. pollution-control policies. It is the first large-scale example of a

---

[13] *EPA Journal*, 17(1), January/February 1991, p. 23.

[14] As the quote in the previous paragraph makes clear, however, some control over choices may be necessary. We have to remember the materials balances principle. If some utilities use stack-gas scrubbers to reduce their SO_2 emissions, they will end up with large quantities of sulfur sludge. This must be disposed of in a socially efficient way.

system of transferable discharge permits tried in the country and, in that sense, represents a kind of laboratory for environmental economists, who have been talking for many years about the advantages of moving to economic incentive programs to combat pollution.[15]

MOBILE-SOURCE AIR POLLUTION CONTROL

The other major part of the federal air-quality program is control of mobile-source emissions. While there are thousands of stationary sources of air pollution, there are many millions of mobile sources. Furthermore, the political fundamentals of mobile-source control are totally different from stationary-source emissions. It is often good politics to be seen chastising the polluting behavior of the businesses, especially corporations, responsible for stationary sources. It is quite different to take an aggressive stance against the millions of people whose cars cause the pollution, but who also vote. So the spirit of the mobile-source program has been to reduce emissions, but in a way that avoids placing an obvious burden on individual drivers. The EPA counts it as a benefit of the mobile-source provisions of the 1990 Act that "Most car owners probably will not be aware of the many vehicle and fuel changes that auto and oil companies make in response to the Clean Air Act."[16]

To examine the mobile-source program, it will help to set the stage. We can express the total quantity of mobile-source emissions in a given period in the following way:

$$\frac{\text{Total quantity}}{\text{of emissions}} = \frac{\text{Number of}}{\text{vehicles}} \times \frac{\text{Average miles}}{\text{traveled}} \times \frac{\text{Emissions}}{\text{per mile}}$$

If we were devising a cost-effective way of reducing the total quantity of emissions, we would want to balance the three factors on the right side of this equation according to the equimarginal principle. In fact, the federal mobile-source pollution-control program has focused almost completely on the last of these factors. And a major reason air pollution is still a serious problem in many regions is that although we have been diligently trying to produce cars with ever smaller emissions per mile, the first two factors in the equation have continued to grow relentlessly and virtually without control.

The federal mobile-source pollution-control program consists of the following major elements:

- At the manufacturing level, a "new-car certification" program that essentially sets emission standards on new cars, together with a warranty program that is meant to ensure the continued emissions performance of automobiles after they have left the plant.

---

[15]As of this date (April 1993), several trades have been made and others are pending. The trades are generating some public controversy. See, for example, "Lilco's Emissions Sale Spurs Acid Rain Concern,"*New York Times*, March 18, 1993.

[16] *EPA Journal*, 17(1), January/February 1991, p. 17.

- At the state level, inspection and maintenance (I&M) programs aimed at ensuring that the emissions performance of automobiles does not deteriorate as they are used.
- In nonattainment areas, a variety of technological specifications dealing with vehicles, fuels, and other components of the transportation system.

New-Car Emission Standards

The main emissions from mobile sources are hydrocarbons (sometimes called "volatile organic compounds" or VOCs), nitrogen oxides (NO_x), carbon monoxide (CO), and particulate matter. Lead used to be a major mobile-source pollutant but, since the advent of lead-free gas, this is no longer the case.[17] The first two of these (VOCs and NO_x) are smog precursors; that is, after they are emitted, they react with sunlight and among themselves to form the smog and elevated ozone levels that characterize so many urban areas.

The primary federal approach to controlling mobile-source emissions was set in the 1970 Clean Air Act. It consists of a "new-car certification program"—essentially a program of mandated emission standards on new cars. Manufacturers are required to certify that the emissions of new cars do not violate the legally mandated standards. Violations may lead to a variety of penalties, up to and including shutting down the assembly lines that produce the offending vehicles. Table 15-9 shows the emission standards established in federal laws over the last several decades. The first row shows emissions for a typical car of around 1970, based on average performance and gas mileage data. As of 1990 the mandated emission standards were quite small relative to these early performance data. The 1990 standard for VOCs, for example, was only about 5 percent of the actual emissions of two decades earlier. The CO and NO_x percentages are, respectively, 4 percent and 29 percent. What these numbers show are the very substantial reductions in new-car emissions (with the exception perhaps of NO_x) that have

TABLE 15-9
AUTOMOBILE EMISSION STANDARDS ESTABLISHED IN FEDERAL LAW, 1974–1994

		VOC	CO	NO_x
		Grams per mile		
Uncontrolled emissions:	(c. 1970)	8.7	87.0	3.5
Federal standards:	1974	3.0	28.0	3.1
	1978	1.5	15.0	2.0
	1980	0.41	7.0	2.0
	1990	0.41	3.4	1.0
	1994*	0.25	3.4	0.4

*To be met by 40 percent of all light vehicles manufactured in 1994, 80 percent in 1995, and 100 percent in 1996 and beyond.

[17] We will discuss the lead-reduction program later.

been achieved over the last 20 years. The Clean Air Act Amendments of 1990 have mandated a further drop in emission standards, beginning in the 1994 model year.

These reductions in standards have been controversial. Critics, especially automobile companies, maintained that they were unrealistic when they were enacted. But advocates held that unrealistic standards were useful because they provided the incentive for car companies to search for new control technologies. This approach goes under the name of "technology forcing." Technology forcing is one of those things, of which there are many others, that are good in moderation but perhaps counterproductive if used in excess. The very stringent emission standards written into the 1970 clean-air legislation were in fact not met; rather, they were postponed and not finally achieved until the early 1980s. We do not know whether more realistically timed emission standards might have led the automobile companies to spend more money on research and less on political efforts to get the standards postponed.

Although the emission standards have been progressively lowered through time, this trend actually overstates the reduction in emissions performance by cars in actual operation. The problem is that emissions performance of cars progressively deteriorates as the cars age and accumulate mileage. The federal program attempts to attack this problem in two ways. First it requires pollution-control equipment on automobiles to be long-lived enough to ensure that emissions standards will continue to be met for a given number of miles (the "warranty" program). In addition, it mandates that states with severe air-pollution problems initiate inspection and maintenance (I&M) programs, whereby individual cars can be checked for emissions. Owners whose cars exceed emission standards can then be held liable for repairs to bring them into compliance.

Lead Trading and the Switch to Lead-Free Gas

In the 1950s the practice of adding lead to fuel to augment its performance became common among gasoline refiners. As leaded gas became popular, the lead content of urban air began to show an alarming increase and concern mounted over the resulting health effects. In addition, lead in gasoline interfered with catalytic converters, the technology of choice for reducing other emissions. The federal response was to establish a timetable for the elimination of lead in gasoline. The program included a trading system to help reduce the overall cost of a transition to lead-free gasoline. In order to decrease the lead content of gas but maintain normal octane ratings, refineries had to install new equipment and operating procedures. But conversion costs differed among refineries, especially between large and small operations. Some could switch to lead-free gas quickly and at reasonably low cost, while for others conversion would take longer and be more costly. A proportional cutback program would have required each refinery to reduce the lead content of its gas according to a common timetable. Instead, a lead trading program was introduced to allow more flexibility and lower costs in the conversion process. Lead credits were earned by refineries reducing the lead content of their output in advance of the EPA timetable.[18] In 1982, for example, the EPA standard was 1.1 grams of lead per gallon of gasoline produced. Suppose a refinery instead produced 10,000,000 gallons of gas in that year containing an average of 0.9 grams of lead per gallon.[19] Then it would have 10,000,000 × (1.1 − .9) =2,000,000 grams of lead credits that it could sell to somebody else. Who would buy the credits? Other refineries who, because of their higher conversion costs, were moving more slowly in changing over their operations to low-lead gas.

This might sound like it was giving some refineries a chance to drag their feet in converting to low-lead gas, but the times involved were small. In fact, the lead trading had to be balanced out each quarter. That is, at the end of each quarter every refinery had to have a nonnegative balance of lead permits. So if a refinery did buy lead permits at some point in time, it still had to convert enough of its capacity to low-lead gas to account for those purchased lead rights. Thus, a refinery could gain only a few weeks, at most several months, of flexibility by purchasing lead rights. In 1985 banking was allowed. Firms after that could bank credits produced in a certain quarter, then use or sell them in a later quarter.

Despite what might look like limited trading possibilities, the lead market, which was national in scope, was widely used in the transition to low-lead gas. The national transition was essentially completed in 1988, and EPA estimates that it probably saved several hundreds of millions of dollars in total transition costs. Its success has been chalked up to two main points: initial widespread agreement on the overall goal of phasing out leaded gas and the ease of monitoring the amount of lead in gas.

While the lead trading program was a success in easing the lead "phase-down," getting lead out of gas was not achieved without compensating environmental costs. People wanted less lead, but they also still wanted high engine performance. Thus, the octane rating of gasolines was to some extent maintained by substituting other compounds for lead. Some of these, like benzene, toluene, and the xylenes, are known carcinogens in their own right, and have also increased the aromatic qualities of gasoline, which increases VOC emissions.

The 1990 Clean Air Act

Despite the apparent progress in lowering new-car emissions over the years, many urban areas of the country continue to exceed ambient standards, particularly for NO_x and VOCs. The reason is that the number of cars and the total mileage driven in these areas continue to increase unrelentingly. In the 1970s there had been for a short time an effort to introduce direct transportation controls in some urban areas. At that time, states were supposed to develop state

---

[18] For a good discussion of this program, see Robert W. Hahn and Gordon L. Hester, "Marketable Permits: Lessons for Theory and Practice," *Ecology Law Quarterly*, 16(1), Winter 1989, pp. 361–406.

[19] This discussion draws on Robert W. Hahn, *A Primer on Environmental Policy Design*, Harwood Academic Publishers, Chur, Switzerland, 1989, pp. 41–44.

implementation plans (SIPs) incorporating such things as parking restrictions, exclusive bus and car pool lanes, road user charges, etc., that would control car use. But, with few exceptions, states were never able to develop these transportation plans. Owing to very strong political forces behind the idea of free car use, mileage has continued to increase unabated throughout the last few decades.

The 1990 Clean Air Act, besides tightening emission standards, also incorporates a large number of federally mandated technology standards that are supposed to allow nonattainment areas to move toward attainment even without any direct controls on the overall number of cars. These standards include:

• "Reformulated" fuels: less volatile gas, oxygenated fuels, etc.
• Alternative fuels: requiring vehicles that run on methanol, natural gas, etc.
• Clean cars: zero-emission (electric) vehicles.
• VOC capturing equipment: installed on cars, with analogous equipment at filling stations.

Elaborate rules have been specified for the conditions and means by which these technologies are supposed to be phased into use in nonattainment areas. In addition, I&M programs are to be put into place in areas where they do not exist, and "enhanced" in areas that do have them. In some of the worst areas attention is also to be given to increased transportation planning so as to combat the VMT (vehicle miles traveled) problem.

Though the mobile-source parts of the 1990 law are a veritable jungle of technological specifications and CAC methods, several small incentive programs did manage to creep into the law. The Act requires that oxygenated fuels be used in certain nonattainment areas. Oxygenated fuels are fuels containing more than 2.7 percent oxygen by weight. The Act provides that credits may be earned for gasolines that exceed the minimum oxygen threshold. These credits may then be traded to other fuel suppliers within the same nonattainment area for the purpose of complying with the reformulated gasoline requirement. The Act also permits fleet owners, who are subject to minimum numbers of clean-fuel vehicles, to obtain tradable credits by purchasing more than the minimum number of these vehicles. These credits may then be sold to other sources, where they may be used to demonstrate compliance under the program in the same nonattainment area.

Incentive-Based Mobile-Source Programs

The mobile-source pollution-control program is a "have your cake and eat it too" program. We are trying to solve a massive air pollution problem through a series of technological fixes while doing little to address the basic attachment to the multiple-car family, high-performance vehicles, and the fully mobile life style. The technological fixes are meant to be as invisible as possible, in order not to disrupt these life-style factors. Some people have long-run visions of a complete conversion to electric vehicles, so that we might continue to accumulate cars and VMTs, but without emissions. This is a will-o'-the-wisp. Uncontrolled growth in the numbers of vehicles will lead to increasingly congested urban highways. In addition, the switch to electric cars means simply that much of the airborne emissions will move to the power stations that are required to generate the added electricity. The basic fact is that mobile-source air emissions are linked not only to the technical characteristics of cars and the fuel system, but also to the millions of decisions that individuals make about where, when, and how to travel. Without reshaping these decisions in the urban areas where air quality is seriously degraded, significant long-run improvements will be impossible.

This argues for more direct incentive-based approaches to mobile-source emissions. One approach that has been suggested is to levy a significantly higher tax on gasoline. With gasoline more expensive, motorists would have the incentive to think more about their driving habits, organize their driving more coherently, reduce total miles traveled, shift to more fuel-efficient vehicles, use mass transit to a greater extent, etc. The effects of the higher fuel price would filter throughout the transportation system and lead people to shift their behavior in places where the marginal costs of doing so are lowest, much as they did in the energy "crisis" of the 1970s. A substantial gas tax was discussed to a limited extent in the election campaign of 1992, but there are powerful political forces against it.

Another suggestion is to place a tax directly on vehicle emissions. As part of the state I&M programs, inspectors could record each year the total mileage that a vehicle had been driven. This total mileage could be multiplied by the emissions per mile, also measured at the time of inspection, to yield an estimate of total emissions in the preceding year. A tax could then be levied on these emissions. Unlike a fuel tax, which would have no direct incentive for drivers to worry about emissions, a tax on emissions would create an incentive to look at all the ways of lowering them, including reducing total miles driven, driving low-polluting vehicles, and so on. One attractive aspect of this approach is that the tax could be varied among regions to match the severity of regional air-quality problems.

SUMMARY

The federal effort to control airborne emissions has had several main elements. National ambient air-quality standards have been established, not on the basis of efficiency considerations as we have discussed them, but "to protect the public health," with an "adequate margin of safety," irrespective of the costs. In fact, the essential trade-offs between costs and benefits were left for administrators to work out behind the scenes. A distinction is made between nonattainment areas, where ambient standards are not met, and PSD regions, where they are. To meet the ambient standards, primary reliance is placed on technology-based emission standards. These TBESs are based on a number of different concepts, such as lowest achievable emission rate (LAER) for new sources in nonattainment areas and maximum achievable control technology (MACT) for hazardous emissions. Most economic studies of these TBESs in air pollution control show that for the total amount of money spent on pollution control, they achieve only a fraction of the emission reduction that a fully cost-effective program would attain.

The 1990 CAA contains an innovative national program of transferable emission permits, in this case applied to SO_2 emissions from large power plants. Emission permits are to be allocated to existing power plants; these permits may then be traded. The objective is to achieve a roughly 50 percent reduction in total SO_2 emissions in a cost-effective way. Substantial uncertainties surround this new market for discharge permits, and additional regulatory oversight and legal evolution will determine how well the system succeeds.

Mobile-source emission reductions have been sought almost entirely through establishing emission standards for new cars, and then trying to ensure that emissions do not increase as the cars are being used. The 1990 Clean Air Act attempts to mandate a number of technological changes, such as reformulated fuel and low-polluting vehicles. Little attention has been given to the important problem of reducing total vehicle miles in urban areas with seriously degraded air quality.

QUESTIONS FOR FURTHER DISCUSSION

1 How might one design a system of transferable discharge permits to control emissions from automobiles?
2 The federal mobile-source air pollution program means that new cars sold in rural regions meet the same emissions standards as cars sold in urban areas. Since there are a lot fewer cars in rural areas, this means that air quality will be a lot better there than in the cities. Is this efficient? Is it equitable?
3 What are the advantages and disadvantages of a "new-source" bias in stationary-source air pollution control? Consider especially its impacts on the incentives of the operators of existing sources.
4 Most of the firms included in the SO_2 emission permit trading program of the 1990 CAA Amendments are public utilities rather than profit-maximizing firms in the conventional sense. What effects might this have on the operation of the trading program?
5 What are the advantages and disadvantages of dealing with mobile-source emissions by instituting a substantial tax on gasoline?

SELECTED READINGS

Crandall, Robert W., Howard K. Gruenspecht, Theodore E. Keeler, and Lester B. Lave: *Regulating the Automobile*, Brookings Institution, Washington, D.C., 1986.

Downing, Paul B., and William D. Watson, Jr.: "Cost Effective Enforcement of Environmental Standards," *Journal of the Air Pollution Control Association*, 25(7), July 1975, pp. 705–710.

Hahn, Robert W., and Gordon L. Hester: "Where Did All the Markets Go? An Analysis of EPA's Emission Trading Program," *Yale Journal of Regulation*, 6(1), Winter 1989, pp. 109–153.

Hahn, Robert W., and Roger G. Noll: "Barriers to Implementing Tradeable Air Pollution

Permits: Problems of Regulatory Interactions," *Yale Journal on Regulation*, 1(1), 1983, pp. 63–91.

Harrison, David, Jr.: *Who Pays for Clean Air: The Cost and Benefit Distribution of Federal Automobile Emissions Standards*, Ballinger, Cambridge, Mass., 1975.

Krupnick, Alan J., and Paul R. Portney: "Controlling Urban Air Pollution: A Benefit–Cost Assessment," *Science*, 252, April 26, 1991, pp. 522–528.

Liroff, Richard: *Reforming Air Pollution Regulation*, Conservation Foundation, Washington, D.C., 1986.

Merrifield, John: "A Critical Review of the Evolutionary Approach to Air Pollution Abatement Policy," *Journal of Policy Analysis and Management*, 9(3), 1990, pp. 367–380.

National Research Council: *Rethinking the Ozone Problem in Urban and Regional Air Pollution*, National Academy Press, Washington, D.C., 1991.

Portney, Paul R.: "Air Pollution Policy," in Paul R. Portney (ed.), *Public Policies for Environmental Protection*, Resources for the Future, Washington, D.C., 1990, pp. 27–96.

Tietenberg, Tom H.: *Emissions Trading, An Exercise in Reforming Pollution Policy*, Resources for the Future, Washington, D.C., 1985.

U.S. Environmental Protection Agency: *National Air Pollutant Emission Estimates, 1940–1988* (EPA-450/4-90-001), Washington, D.C., 1990.

Wolozen, Harold, (ed.): *The Economics of Air Pollution*, W. W. Norton, New York, 1966.

CHAPTER 16

FEDERAL POLICY ON TOXIC AND HAZARDOUS SUBSTANCES

Within the general domain of environmental analysis and policy there is a class of pollutants that have come to be called "toxic" substances and "hazardous" materials. While all pollutants are damaging to some extent, these have been singled out for their special short- or long-run potency. Most are chemicals, the person-made organic and inorganic compounds that are now ubiquitous throughout all industrialized economies, and even widespread in developing countries. Figure 16-1 shows the rise of that industry in the U.S. From virtually nothing 70 years ago, it has grown in exponential fashion, and today chemicals and chemical products have permeated into every corner of the economy. In product improvements, new materials, food safety, health innovations, and many other dimensions, chemicals have enriched the lives of almost everyone. There is, however, a downside. A large number of these substances may cause human and ecosystem damages, certainly from exposure to concentrated doses, but also from long-run exposure to the trace amounts that show up virtually everywhere in workplaces, consumer products, and the environment.

The call to arms on chemicals in the environment was made by Rachel Carson in her book *Silent Spring*. She documented the ecosystem damage caused by the popular pesticide DDT and was largely responsible for getting it banned in the U.S. Other events have multiplied concern. Health damages to workers exposed to chemicals in the workplace, such as vinyl chloride and certain potent agricultural chemicals, have occurred with disconcerting frequency. In 1978, in the celebrated case of Love Canal, people found chemicals oozing into their houses built on top of an abandoned hazardous waste disposal site. Accidental releases of chemicals have become a growing problem, from the large-scale episodes like those in Milan, Italy, in 1976 and Bhopal, India, in 1984, to innumerable smaller airborne and waterborne accidents. There is rising concern about the damages from long-term exposure to chemical residues in food, clothing, and other consumer products.

The primary concern is the impact of chemicals on human health. The EPA, for example, has developed a rough estimate of 2,000 excess cancer deaths a year in the U.S. from toxic airborne pollutants (compared to total annual cancer deaths

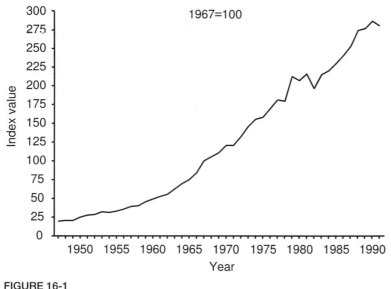

FIGURE 16-1
Chemical Production Index, United States, 1947–1990. (*Source:* U.S. Federal
Reserve Bulletin, *Washington, D.C., annual issues.*)

of about half a million).[1] Health damages from accidental releases and workplace
exposure are relatively easy to identify. Those from long-run exposure to trace
amounts of chemicals in water, air, and soil are much harder to measure.
Ecosystem damages are also important. Accidental waterborne chemical releases
have wreaked havoc among fish and other organisms in enclosed bodies of
water. Agricultural and industrial runoff has substantially damaged many rivers
and estuaries around the world.

Hazardous and toxic materials have characteristics that present unique problems for monitoring and control.

1 They are ubiquitous in the modern economy; each year sees the development
   of new chemicals. This makes it difficult even knowing what substances are
   being used and in what quantities. It accounts for the fact that much public
   policy has been directed at simply getting better information about quantities
   of hazardous and toxic materials at various places in the system.
2 With the thousands of substances in use, each with different chemical and
   physical properties, it is virtually impossible to be fully informed about the
   levels of danger that each one poses to humans and other parts of the ecosystem.
3 In many cases the quantities used are relatively small, as are the quantities that
   end up as effluent. This substantially increases monitoring problems. It also

[1] U.S. Council on Environmental Quality, *Environmental Quality, 1984,* Washington, D.C., 1985,
p. 58.

makes it easier for users to carry out surreptitious disposal. It is easy to see the plume of smoke coming out of the stack of an industrial plant; it is harder to track the much smaller quantities of chemicals used in production.

4 The damages caused by exposure to hazardous materials can often take many years, even decades, to show up. And whenever there is a long time gap between cause and effect, there is a tendency to downgrade the overall seriousness of the problem.

In the next few sections we will consider federal policy on hazardous and toxic substances and some of the major economic issues in the management of these materials. The policy world governing these materials is a jungle. There are numerous major and minor laws at the federal level, each applying to a piece of the total picture. Many federal agencies are involved, with territories staked out and objectives pursued in ways that are often inconsistent. Then there are public agencies at state and local levels that are actively pursuing efforts to come to grips with these types of pollutants. And all of this is within a setting where thousands of different substances are in use, hundreds more introduced each year, massive uncertainties about the human and nonhuman effects of most of them, and public concerns that flare up and die down in unpredictable ways.

To help sort out these complexities we will organize the following discussion into three sections: (1) laws governing the use of chemicals in industrial and agricultural production processes and in consumer goods; (2) laws governing airborne and waterborne emissions of toxic materials; and (3) laws governing the handling, treatment, and disposal of hazardous wastes. Table 16-1 lists the major federal laws in each category. We don't have the space or time to deal with each law in detail, so in the following sections we will give short sketches of the most important of the laws in each category, then discuss some of the major economic issues they present.[2]

FEDERAL LAWS GOVERNING CHEMICALS IN PRODUCTION AND CONSUMER PRODUCTS

At issue here is the management of chemicals in consumer products and in the workplace, with the objective of ensuring that these products and workplaces are "reasonably" safe. What "reasonably" means is a matter of public debate. Some might argue that these matters are not properly part of environmental economics. Household and work environments are not, properly speaking, parts of the *natural* environment and, in these cases, the relations of consumers to producers, and of workers to firm owners, are played out directly through markets. Nevertheless, environmental concerns have to some extent reached out

---

[2] For good discussions of toxic and hazardous substance laws see Mary Devine Worobec and Girard Ordway, *Toxic Substances Control Guide*, Bureau of National Affairs, Washington, D.C., 1989; Roger C. Dower, "Hazardous Wastes," and Michael Shapiro, "Toxic Substances Policy," in Paul R. Portney (ed.), *Public Policies for Environmental Protection*, Resources for the Future, Washington, D.C., 1990, chapters 5 and 6.

TABLE 16-1
FEDERAL LAWS DEALING WITH TOXIC AND HAZARDOUS SUBSTANCES

Policy and statute	Responsible agency	Coverage
A. Policies on Chemicals Used in Production and Consumer Products		
Federal Insecticide, Fungicide, and Rodenticide Act (1972)	EPA	Pesticides
Food, Drug, and Cosmetic Act (1938)	FDA	Basic coverage of food, drugs, cosmetics
Food additives amendment	FDA	Food additives
Color additives amendments	FDA	Color additives
New drug amendments	FDA	Drugs
New animal drug amendments	FDA	Animal drugs and feed additives
Medical device amendments	FDA	Medical devices
Section 346(a) of the Food, Drug, and Cosmetic Act	EPA	Tolerances for pesticide residues in human food and animal feeds
Fair Packaging and Labeling Act	FDA	Packaging and labeling of food and drugs for humans or animals, and of cosmetics and medical devices
Federal Hazardous Substances Act (1960)	CPSC	"Toxic" household products (equivalent to consumer products)
Consumer Product Safety Act (1972)	CPSC	Dangerous consumer products
Poison Prevention Packaging Act (1970)	CPSC	Packaging of dangerous children's products
Lead-Based Paint Poison Prevention Act	CPSC	Use of lead paint in federally assisted housing
Federal Meat Inspection Act	USDA	Food, feed, and color additives and pesticide residues in meat and poultry products
Poultry Products Inspection Act	USDA	Poultry products
Egg Products Inspection Act	USDA	Egg products
Federal Mine Safety and Health Act	MSHA	Coal mines or other mines
Toxic Substances Control Act (1976)	EPA	Requires premanufacture evaluation of all new chemicals (other than food, food additives, drugs, pesticides, alcohol, tobacco); allows EPA to regulate existing chemical hazards
Occupational Safety and Health Act (1970)	OSHA	Workplace toxic chemicals
B. Policies on Chemical Emissions		
Clean Air Act (amended 1970)	EPA	Hazardous air pollutants
Clean Water Act (amended 1972)	EPA	Toxic water pollutants
Safe Drinking Water Act (1974)	EPA	Drinking water contaminants

(Continued on Next Page)

TABLE 16-1
FEDERAL LAWS DEALING WITH TOXIC AND HAZARDOUS SUBSTANCES *(Continued)*

Policy and statute	Responsible agency	Coverage
C. Policies on Handling, Storage, Transportation, Treatment, and Disposal of Hazardous Wastes		
Resource Conservation and Recovery Act (1976)	EPA	Hazardous wastes
Maritime Protection, Research, and Sanctuaries Act	EPA	Ocean dumping
Comprehensive Environmental Response, Compensation, and Liability Act (1980)	EPA	Hazardous waste releases
Hazardous Materials Transportation Act (1975)	DOT	Transportation of toxic substances generally
Federal Railroad Safety Act	DOT	Railroad safety
Ports and Waterways Safety Act (1972)	DOT	Shipment of toxic materials by water
Dangerous Cargo Act	DOT	Shipment of toxic materials by water

EPA = Environmental Protection Agency; FDA = Food and Drug Administration; OSHA = Occupational Safety and Health Administration; CPSC = Consumer Product Safety Commission; DOT = Department of Transportation; USDA = Department of Agriculture; MSHA = Mine Safety and Health Administration.

Sources: Michael Shapiro, "Toxic Substances Policy," in Paul R. Portney (ed.), *Public Policies for Environmental Protection,* Resources for the Future, Washington, D.C., 1990, pp. 198–199; original sources are: Toxic Substances Strategy Committee, *Toxic Chemicals and Public Protection,* Washington, D.C., 1980, and Council of Environmental Quality, *Environmental Quality–1982,* Washington, D.C., 1982.

to subsume certain elements of the private environment as well as the world of nature properly speaking, so we follow that lead here. Homeowners exposed to formaldehyde leaking from insulation, a worker exposed to asbestos fibers in the workplace, are subject to the same kind of actual and potential damages as they are when exposed to toxic emissions coming from a neighborhood factory.

Consumer product safety is an issue that has been around for a long time. In the time of rapid industrial growth of the nineteenth and early twentieth centuries, the free-for-all business atmosphere led to many cases of intentional or inadvertent product adulteration, often with dire results. Then in the latter twentieth century the rise of the chemical economy produced markets so scientifically complex that they are beyond the powers of the average consumer. These developments have led to a number of federal laws, the most important of which are sketched out in the following sections.

Federal Insecticide, Fungicide, and Rodenticide Act (FIFRA)

There are about 48,000 different pesticide products available for use in the U.S., though these products contain only about 600 active chemical ingredients. A pesticide is a general term used to designate any substance meant to kill, repel, or control any nonhuman organism, from bacteria to bugs to oak trees. In fact, the law also covers certain noninsecticide products like growth hormones and new organisms developed through recombinant DNA research. The present act was first passed in 1947, but it has predecessors that go back to the early decades of this century.

FIFRA works through a straightforward command-and-control approach. In order for a pesticide to be used, it must be registered with the EPA. Thus, in setting registration requirements the agency can control the use of a pesticide. The EPA has established a complex registration procedure, with standards applying to evidence that must be presented by manufacturers seeking approvals. The registration of a particular pesticide must specify where and how it may be used. FIFRA also contains provisions for setting acceptable pesticide residue levels in foods. Normally these levels are nil, unless a tolerance level has been established or special exemption issued. To enforce the provisions of FIFRA, EPA may issue fines or criminal penalties, inspect facilities, seize products, or require product recalls. Enforcement of residue levels is also carried out by the Food and Drug Administration and the U.S. Department of Agriculture. FIFRA is a "balancing" law; that is, it allows the EPA to weigh both the benefits and the risks of a pesticide when considering whether to give it a registration. We will return to this below.

Food, Drug, and Cosmetic Act (FDCA)

While the previous law worked through a chemical registration technique, the FDCA works through legal prohibition of foods, drugs, or cosmetics that do not meet certain criteria. In effect, the law prohibits the sale of any food, drug, or cosmetic that is "adulterated" or "mislabeled." Foods or drugs are regarded as adulterated if they contain additives that are considered to be harmful. A drug is mislabeled if it is not considered to be safe and effective. A food additive may be several things. It may be a specific chemical, like a preservative or a coloring agent, added to food to give it some quality. It may be the residue from a pesticide used when the crop was in the field. It may be a chemical that migrated into the food from the packaging material in which it is enclosed. Naturally occurring substances are not included; thus, for example, peanuts are not banned although they naturally contain powerful carcinogenic chemicals called aflatoxins.

Additives and drugs not previously approved have to be tested in order to generate the scientific data that will determine whether the Food and Drug Administration (FDA) will grant approval for their use. In granting approval the FDA may specify the terms under which the chemical additive may be used, such as the amounts that may be used, the types of food with which they may be used, and any labeling requirements. A notable feature of the FDCA is the "Delaney Clause," which prohibits in food any additive that is shown to cause cancer in animals.

Toxic Substances Control Act (TSCA)

TSCA was intended to give federal authorities a comprehensive legal tool with which to control the manufacture and use of chemicals in the U.S., especially many industrial chemicals that could not be regulated effectively under other statutes. TSCA directs the EPA to carry out several functions:

- Complete an inventory of all chemicals produced or imported during the period 1975–1977, using information supplied by manufacturers and processors.
- Test existing chemicals for safety.
- Screen new chemicals.
- Regulate chemical use, for example, specifying conditions under which they may be used, setting labeling requirements, requiring additional testing, and so on.

Like FIFRA, TSCA is a "balancing" law; i.e., it says that EPA is to make decisions on any chemical by comparing the risks it may pose with the benefits it produces for firms and consumers.

Consumer Products Safety Act (CPSA)

The CPSA of 1972 established the Consumer Products Safety Commission, which is authorized to conduct safety studies of consumer products, promulgate mandatory safety standards for products, and ban products determined to be hazardous. These regulations apply to all characteristics of particular products, including any chemicals they may contain.

Occupational Safety and Health Act (OSHA)

The goal of this law is to ensure safe working conditions, and the technique used is setting *workplace standards*. These are of two types: health standards, which are supposed to protect workers against exposure to harmful agents in the workplace, and safety standards, which are supposed to protect workers from imminent physical harms, like falls, fires, or electrocution. Chemical exposure comes under the safety-standard rubric. Thus, under OSHA, the Occupational Health and Safety Administration (also called "O-SHA"), sets workplace exposure standards (called "permissible exposure levels," or PELs; see Table 16-2 for a list of acronyms used in this chapter) for specific chemicals that have been deemed dangerous. Since its enactment, for example, standards have been set for such chemicals as vinyl chloride, lead, benzene, cotton dust, and coke oven emissions. The standards are in the form of maximum ambient workplace concentrations of the chemical, and many of the standards also include "action levels" that trigger medical monitoring and surveillance of workers under certain conditions.

Another major part of OSHA is the system for informing workers of the

TABLE 16-2
ACRONYMS USED IN THIS CHAPTER*

BAT	Best available technology
HLW	High-level wastes
LLW	Low-level wastes
MACT	Maximum achievable control technology
MCL	Maximum contaminant levels
NCP	National contingency plan
NPL	National priorities list
PEL	Permissible exposure level
PRP	Potentially responsible party
TSDF	Treatment, storage, or disposal facility

*See Table 16-1 for the acronyms applying to the names of laws and regulatory agencies dealing with toxic and hazardous materials.

hazards posed by chemicals in the workplace. As we will discuss below, the way labor markets adapt to the presence of chemicals in the workplace and, thus, the need for various types of public policy depend critically on how much information is available to workers on the health risks associated with exposure to various chemicals. With this in mind, EPA promulgated under OSHA a "hazard communication standard" that requires chemical manufacturers and users to assess the hazards of chemicals they use and notify workers of these hazards in their work area. This is aimed at getting firms to develop chemical hazard assessment data and then make them available to workers.

ECONOMIC ISSUES IN CHEMICAL PRODUCTION AND EXPOSURE

The "Balancing" Issue

Perhaps the most important question in the use of chemicals is the criterion for determining acceptable levels of exposure or protection. In setting the benzene or cotton dust standards in workplaces or the formaldehyde regulations for building materials, what principle should regulating agencies follow in setting exposure standards? In discussing our general model of environmental pollution control in Chapter 5, we developed the idea of the efficient level of environmental pollution as being a trade-off between control costs and damages. Applying the same logic to the case of chemicals means that in setting chemical exposure levels we would try to determine the point where the benefits of reducing health or other risks are just balanced by the costs of decreasing the production and use of the chemical. This trade-off is pictured in Figure 16-2.

In very broad terms, FIFRA and TSCA permit a "balancing" approach when regulating a particular chemical, while OSHA and FDCA do not. Thus, in setting regulations for a given pesticide or a given industrial chemical, EPA may take

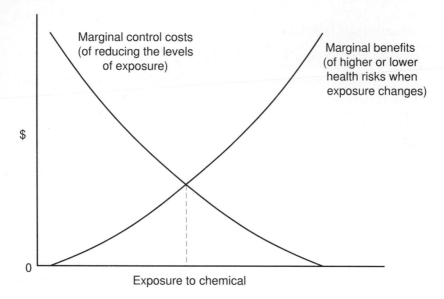

FIGURE 16-2
Cost–Benefit Balancing in Regulating Exposure to a Chemical.

into account both the health risks of using the chemicals and the costs to the economy if the chemicals are banned or regulated. The news clipping shown in Exhibit 16-1 reports the outcome of this procedure for a fungicide: ethylene bisdithiocarbamate, or EBDC.

Many objections have been made against a balancing approach in managing chemicals:[3] that scientific results are often too weak to show benefits and costs (especially costs) clearly; that matters of life and death are moral issues and ought to be treated as such; that it's the job of politicians, not economists, to determine the values that society ought to put on different outcomes; etc. We don't have the space to deal with all the issues here. They are basically the same questions that arose when we introduced the notion of the efficient level of emissions, or ambient quality, concepts we have used throughout the book.

There is no question that the data and analytical requirements of a balancing approach are high. This approach requires good dose-response information, exposure data, and estimates of the benefits of reducing risks to workers and consumers. Some would argue that sheer numbers make the balancing approach impossible. Can we ever expect to have enough information to permit an effective balancing approach to all the chemicals to which workers and consum-

---

[3] In recent years, the same kinds of questions have come to surround the results of the new science of biotechnology. Through genetic manipulation scientists can impart new qualities to existing organisms (a moth protein is put into potatoes so they won't bruise as easily; a viral gene is introduced into cucumbers to confer disease resistance, etc.). The current controversy is about whether these should be regulated in the same way as chemicals in food.

EXHIBIT 16-1

EPA IS LIKELY TO EASE CURBS ON A FUNGICIDE

Broad Use of a Popular, but Carcinogenic, Group of Fungicides Is Likely to Be Allowed to Resume Soon.

When the Environmental Protection Agency proposed a ban on most uses of ethylene bisdithiocarbamate fungicides in 1989, it offered industry a way out: If a survey of grocery shelves showed that the health risk from foods made from EBDC-treated crops fell within EPA guidelines, the ban wouldn't have to take effect. The agency's analysis, which had shown that the chemicals posed an unacceptably high risk of cancer, had been based on tests on crops in the fields.

Makers of the chemicals voluntarily halted most uses covered by the proposed ban as of Jan. 1, 1990. These included EBDC use on apples, pears, carrots, celery, cucumbers, squash and tobacco. Some uses—on crops such as grapes, peanuts and asparagus—weren't covered by the proposed ban or the voluntary withdrawal.

The four makers of the chemical—BASF, Du Pont, Elf Atochem and Rohm & Haas—have now completed the $10 million study, which looked at samples in hundreds of cities of groceries made from treated crops. Janet

Ollinger, a Rohm & Haas product-registration manager, says that "for the vast majority of samples, there was no measurable residue."

The EPA may announce its decision as early as this week. Officials say many of the uses covered by the proposed ban are likely to be allowed, so long as they don't result in a cancer risk of more than one in a million in the course of a lifetime. Ms. Ollinger says the industry is especially interested in resuming use of the chemical on apples, lettuce, peppers, watermelons, honeydew melon, cucumbers, broccoli, cabbage and dried beans.

Rick Hind, legislative director of Greenpeace's toxics campaign, charges that if the EPA allows these chemicals back on the market, it will "be using the population as guinea pigs. This is a very potent carcinogen."

---

ers may be exposed? The problem is compounded by the fact that to regulate one substance, we need more than just information on the risks and benefits of that one material. If a chemical is banned, either altogether or in particular uses, the full impact depends on what other substance might be used as a replacement. Thus, to assess a particular substance we have to know not only its own characteristics, but also what products would replace it if it were controlled, and what the full characteristics of these substitutes are.

One answer to this is that not all chemicals are of equal importance. It is possible to focus attention on substances that are in wide use or are used in relatively large quantities. Between 1975 and 1989, for example, the EPA reviewed 19 cancer-causing pesticides widely used in raising agricultural crops. Of the 245 registered food uses permitted with this group of pesticides, 96 were canceled as a result of the EPA review. According to the researchers who studied this EPA experience, "balancing" considerations played an important role in these decisions.[4] Not exclusively, however. The decisions were made partly in response to political activity ("lobbying") by environmental groups on one side and industry groups on the other.

The problem of testing a very large number of chemicals has focused attention on the deficiencies of current testing procedures and the risk estimates that arise from them. Results are hard to get from studies of humans, mainly because it is virtually impossible to get accurate exposure data. That means most risk information must come from laboratory experiments with animals, particularly mice and rats. The biggest problem here is one of extrapolating test results, from one organism to another with an entirely different metabolism, and from one dosage rate to another. A typical chemical in the human environment— for example, a pesticide residue in a certain type of food—might expose the average person to 1 or 2 μg of the substance each day. If mice were tested at this exposure level, an experimenter might need to test half a million mice to detect the one or two in a million probability of, say, getting cancer from the chemical. This is simply not practical, and to get around it researchers typically expose animals to much larger doses of the chemical under test. Though these exposure rates may be several thousand times higher than humans are typically subjected to, the results of the studies are nevertheless extrapolated to humans. In other words, animal experiments using massive doses are used to predict the effects on humans of exposure to tiny doses.

Chemical testing procedures have improved over the last several decades. The future will no doubt see further changes, and we may hope that at some point we will develop cheap, effective ways of testing a chemical for toxicity to humans. In the meantime, we must recognize that there is still a lot of uncertainty surrounding the average estimate of risk arising from using a particular chemical, and take that into account in making balancing decisions about its use.

As for letting the political process determine the trade-offs implicit in managing chemicals in the workplace and in consumer goods, this is clearly the way it should be. But not in the absence of the best available data from science, including economics. The political process responds to all kinds of real or imaginary influences, usually in the short run. Laws often get written in terms of absolutes; political representatives normally strive to avoid giving the impression that they are trading off human lives for anything else, especially economic values. Statutes written in absolute terms, or even in general qualitative terms,[5] essentially drive the balancing process underground, or into the administrative agencies,

---

[4] Maureen L. Cropper, William N. Evans, and Paul R. Portney, "An Analysis of EPA Pesticide Regulation," *Resources*, 102, Winter 1991, pp. 7–10.

[5] OSHA states that toxic materials in the workplace are to be controlled if they lead to ". . . material impairment of health or functional capacity. . . ." The Consumer Products Safety Act is aimed at products that constitute an "unreasonable risk of injury. . . ." The Comprehensive Environmental Response, Compensation and Liability Act (see later in this chapter) applies to hazardous substances in which there is "substantial danger to the public health . . .," etc. See John J. Cohrssen and Vincent T. Covello, *Risk Analysis: A Guide to Principles and Methods for Analyzing Health and Environmental Risks*, U.S. Council on Environmental Quality, Washington, D.C., 1989, pp. 13–15.

where trade-offs get made through implicit comparisons and unseen variations in enforcement. While the OSHA statute requires workplace standards to protect workers' health without regard to cost, it is in fact impossible to do this in practice. Rather, balancing takes place, without describing it as such, in the setting of the standards. Even more importantly, balancing occurs through enforcement; seemingly tough standards are promulgated but with weak enough enforcement that balancing is pursued in effect. Under these circumstances it may be better to follow an explicit balancing standard.

Uniform Standards

The problem of toxic materials in the workplace and in consumer products has been addressed largely by establishing standards of various types. This brings up several important issues. One is the issue of whether the standards should be uniform. Another is the issue of how markets ordinarily function to take account of risks present in workplaces and consumer products. We can illustrate these with a discussion of workplace standards, of the type that would be established by OSHA.

Consider Figure 16-3. It applies to a case of workplace exposure where workers are faced with the risk of accidental exposure to a chemical used in production. The horizontal axis shows the level of risk, starting at zero and increasing to the right. Higher risks are associated with increasing marginal damages, through the health effects of exposure to the chemical. There are two MC curves, each showing the marginal control costs of reducing workplace risk.

FIGURE 16-3
Management of Workplace Exposure.

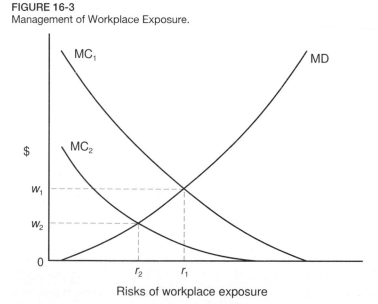

Risks of workplace exposure

Risk can be reduced through a variety of means: introducing safety equipment, rearranging the workplace, policing safe procedures, etc. But the costs of achieving reductions in risk vary from one situation to another. Because of different production technologies, workplaces differ, and the marginal costs of decreasing exposure risk also differ. We show two such marginal cost curves, MC_1 and MC_2. The former lies well above the latter, because we assume it represents a technology that is inherently riskier than the other, i.e., it is one where the marginal costs of reducing risk are relatively high.

Suppose a common standard for workplace exposure were set at r_1. In other words, a standard was established saying that all workplaces had to be arranged so that exposure risks were no higher than r_1. This standard is efficient for the workplace whose marginal control costs are MC_1. But it is not restrictive enough for the other one. Because of lower marginal control costs, the efficient level of risk for the latter is r_2. Enforcing a weaker standard in that workplace implies substantial efficiency loss.

There is a wider issue here. We note that if workplace exposure were managed efficiently in the two workplaces, marginal damages would be higher in one than in the other. For the riskier workplace, marginal damages would be w_1, while for the less risky workplace they would be w_2. We might expect, if the labor market works smoothly, that wages in Firm 1 would be higher than those in Firm 2; the higher wages would be necessary to attract workers into the riskier work situation of Firm 1. In other words, the normal working of the labor market may function in such a way as to produce higher wages in riskier situations. Then workers contemplating employment would face an array of wages and risks, and each could choose the combination that most closely matched her own preferences. Moreover, this would also produce an incentive for firms to find ways of reducing risks in the workplace, because they would gain through the savings in wages this would produce.

If the labor market worked smoothly like this, there would perhaps be no need for public efforts to set standards. To some extent it does, but there are always ways of making it work better. For the labor market to work smoothly, it must be reasonably competitive and, to be competitive, people on both sides of the market must have reasonably good alternatives. Often they do not. More importantly, competitive labor markets require that all participants know the risks involved in different job situations. This knowledge is often lacking. Very often workers are not fully aware of the chemical risks to which they are exposed, either because they do not know what chemicals are in the workplace, or more likely because they lack knowledge of the effects, especially long-run effects, of these substances. This suggests a strong role for public action, to see to it that workers are more fully informed about workplace risks.

Differentiated Control

We saw in water and air pollution policy—especially the latter— that the major laws have differentiated between "old" sources and "new" sources, regulating the latter more stringently than the former. We also discussed some of the problems this leads to. In toxics control the same thing exists, especially under TSCA. This act differentiates between existing chemicals and new chemicals and, in effect, sets more stringent testing requirements for the latter. This is likely to have the predicted effect: providing an incentive for chemical producers and users to hold on to older, more toxic chemicals, rather than develop replacements that are less toxic but which would have to go through more rigorous testing.

FEDERAL POLICY ON TOXIC EMISSIONS

Toxic emissions come in a great variety of forms, from small airborne releases of cleaning fluid from dry cleaning establishments to large-scale releases of toxics from substantial industrial plants. Also included are the concentrated accidental releases that have helped in the past to spur public concern about toxics in the environment. Not all toxics are chemicals; some, like heavy metals (mercury, cadmium, etc.), are by-products of various industrial and mining operations.

When emissions-control policies at the national level were first being hammered out, the main focus was on the management of conventional airborne and waterborne pollutants. For air this meant the criteria pollutants—SO_2, CO, O_3, NO_x, total suspended particulates, and lead—and for water it meant BOD, suspended solids, coliform count, etc. Even in these early days, however, it was known that there was a potentially serious class of toxic emissions stemming from industrial production operations, as well as from household sources. But the difficulties with even enumerating all of the possible substances involved, and of knowing what impacts each might have, essentially led to postponing coming to grips with the problem. In addition, the control of conventional pollutants has been effective to some extent in controlling toxics, since they are often closely associated. Indeed, the EPA estimated that, as of the mid-1980s, the criteria pollutant-control programs were responsible for a larger reduction in airborne toxics than specific toxic reduction programs were.[6] In recent years, however, more effort has gone into specific toxic emissions reduction programs.

Water Pollution-Control Laws

The 1972 Water Pollution Control Act Amendments, which established the major thrust of federal water pollution control, contained a section on toxic effluents. In keeping with the time, however, it was so utopian that it led to relatively little in the way of clear accomplishments. The law stated that, like conventional pollutants, toxic discharges were to be prohibited, and it gave the EPA just 15 months to come up with a list of toxic pollutants and the regulations that would govern their emissions. After that, polluters would have one year to come into compliance. In a situation so full of uncertainties, these deadlines were com-

[6] U.S. Council on Environmental Quality, *Environmental Quality 1984*, Washington, D.C., 1985, p. 58.

pletely unrealistic. It was another case where the public posture of looking tough on polluters was more important than the reality of achieving reductions in damaging emissions. In fact, relatively little progress was made in these early years. But another major toxic spill kept the issue in the public eye. A relatively small chemical plant in Virginia discharged quantities of the insecticide Kepone into the James River as well as into a nearby public wastewater treatment plant. It caused serious damage downstream and severely damaged the bacterial process in the municipal treatment plant. This helped to spur Congress to address toxic emissions more vigorously, which it sought to do in the 1977 Clean Water Act. This law identified 65 specific compounds and classes of compounds containing about 125 chemicals.[7] The EPA was directed to determine and promulgate technology-based effluent standards using the criterion of "best available technology" (BAT) for these toxic pollutants.

This is essentially where things stand today (1993). There were several toxic provisions in the 1987 Water Quality Act covering the identification of toxic "hot spots" in navigable waters[8] and the development of state plans to bring these waters up to applicable standards. The law also requires states, when developing their ambient water-quality standards, to set numerical criteria for certain priority toxic pollutants identified by the EPA.

Air Pollution-Control Laws

Airborne emissions of toxic compounds were also addressed in early environmental laws but, like the waterborne emissions, the pace of progress in actual control has been very slow. Section 112 of the 1970 Clean Air Act Amendments authorized the EPA to establish controls for any airborne emissions it felt were particularly dangerous. On the basis of EPA studies, that agency was first supposed to "list" a substance as hazardous, then develop technology-based emission standards, using BAT, for its control. Progress in listing hazardous pollutants was very slow; over the next two decades, the EPA was able to list and establish emission standards for only seven materials (arsenic, asbestos, benzene, beryllium, mercury, radionuclides, and vinyl chloride). The basic problem has been in getting unambiguous scientific results about the extent to which particular hazardous materials actually cause human health damages. In fact, in 1979 the EPA attempted to change the criterion so that it could use the results of animal (that is, nonhuman animal) studies to list hazardous materials. In 1985 the EPA announced its intention to list six more substances (1,3-butadiene, cadmium, ethylene dichloride, chloroform, ethylene oxide, and methylene chloride). But the 1990 Clean Air Act Amendments took the matter out of its hands. The law specifically mentions 189 toxic substances that are to be controlled, and

---

[7] These pollutants were actually identified in a prior court case where the Environmental Defense Fund had sued the EPA over its slow progress under the 1972 law. The settlement agreement of this case was incorporated into the 1977 law.

[8] A "hot spot" in this case is a section of water that does not meet specified ambient standards even when dischargers are brought under control.

the EPA is charged with determining technology-based emission standards, using a concept of "maximum achievable control technology" (MACT). The law establishes a timetable that EPA is supposed to meet in developing these standards. The act also contains plans for a program to prevent accidental releases of airborne toxics, the establishment of a National Urban Air Toxics Research Center, and numerous other sections.

Safe Drinking Water Act (SDWA)

This federal law was enacted in 1974 along strictly CAC lines. It directed the EPA to establish standards, in terms of "maximum contaminant levels" (MCLs) for any drinking water contaminant that was thought to pose a threat to human health. It was also given some powers in conjunction with the states to enforce the standards in public water supply systems, the primary targets of the law. By 1984, however, the EPA had promulgated only one MCL. Thus, in the SDWA Amendments of 1986, the EPA was specifically given three years to set MCLs for 83 drinking water contaminants. This law also included provisions for developing a drinking water monitoring program, more effective state/federal enforcement actions, and a public notice system whereby community residents can be notified if contaminant levels exceed MCLs. The act specifies a technology standard in terms of BAT (best available technology), especially for water treatment works, and has other provisions for programs to protect the quality of groundwater resources from which many communities take their drinking water.

ECONOMIC ISSUES IN TOXIC EMISSIONS

The early laws on hazardous waste were aimed at managing the flow of hazardous emissions coming from firms, in order to reduce potential impacts, especially on human health. In this respect it mirrored the approach taken in conventional pollutants. But toxic emissions are more difficult to manage. Smaller quantities make them much more difficult to monitor, even though in many cases small quantities can be quite damaging. This has led policymakers to attack the toxics problems by "moving back up the line"; i.e., by trying to reduce the amounts of material that are in need of disposal. This can be done in two ways: (1) by recycling residuals back into the production process and (2) by shifting technologies and operations so that the amount of residuals actually generated by firms is reduced. We will call these methods "waste reduction."[9]

Waste Reduction

The thought behind waste reduction is that by changing production processes and adopting new technologies and operating procedures, firms can substan-

---

[9] Some people prefer to distinguish between "waste reduction" and "recycling" as separate processes, but in our discussion we will lump them together.

tially reduce the quantities of hazardous waste they produce per unit of final product. For example, a firm might find a new way to operate a materials cleaning process to get the same effect but with less cleaning solvent. Or a firm might shift from using a process requiring a toxic material to one involving a nontoxic substance. Or an endproduct might be redesigned in a way that permits its fabrication using smaller quantities of hazardous materials. Waste reduction is obviously very complicated and firm-specific. Different processes lend themselves to different waste reduction procedures, and the costs of achieving significant waste reduction in one situation will be very different from the costs of other cases.[10] This is a setting where it is essentially impossible to achieve efficient controls by having a regulatory agency dictate particular technology choices for firms using toxic substances. The technical aspects of production processes and the situation of each firm are too heterogeneous for this approach. Instead, more effective means need to be found that will give firms themselves strong incentives to reduce toxic emissions in cost-effective ways.

How to give firms the appropriate incentives for waste reduction? Certain recent changes in hazardous-waste disposal laws have moved in this direction. With waste disposal more difficult, firms will be motivated to search for better ways of reducing the quantities of waste requiring disposal. A major flaw in this approach, however, is that the vast majority of hazardous waste is not subject to disposal regulations because it never leaves the premises of the firms where it is used. We will come back to this below.

To what extent might we rely on liability and compensation laws to provide the necessary incentives? We discussed the issue of liability conceptually in Chapter 10. By requiring polluters to compensate those whom they have damaged, these costs can become internalized, which would lead firms to take them into account in making their decisions. This could also operate through an insurance market, if premiums for hazardous waste damage policies could be set so as to reflect accurately the risks of damage associated with a firm's hazardous waste actions. The real problem is whether we know enough about risks to be able to rely on an efficient insurance market and compensation system. Although there are thousands of chemicals in use, we have very little hard information on exactly how much damage they may cause to humans; most of the dose-response information we have comes from studies on animals, especially mice. Under the circumstances, there is not enough information about risks and the damages to be able to establish consistent compensation awards or insurance premium rates that reflect true risks.

In the case of conventional pollutants we have discussed using incentive mechanisms like emission taxes. In applying this to toxics the biggest problem

---

[10] For some examples see Office of Technology Assessment, *Serious Reduction of Hazardous Waste*, Washington, D.C., 1986.

is accurate emissions monitoring. The widespread dispersion of these materials throughout the economic sector, together with the fact that many are emitted in nonpoint modes, makes widespread monitoring by third parties essentially impossible. Also, taxing emissions would provide a strong incentive for firms to dispose of toxics illegally, which would usually be difficult to detect because of the relatively small volumes involved. Taxes on waste disposal, however, may be somewhat more feasible, as we will discuss below. Another possibility is to levy a tax on the feedstocks used to manufacture chemicals, since these would be fewer in number and easier to measure than the chemicals themselves once they have moved into production channels. Still another possibility might be to institute deposit-refund systems for chemicals. Firms would pay a deposit along with the purchase price when the chemicals were bought. They could recover that deposit, or a portion of it, by documenting a reduction of emissions, that is, of the recovery of the chemical from the normal waste stream.

One way that incentives for waste reduction have been created in recent years is through making information more widely available about the presence and release of toxic materials. One reason hazardous wastes have been hard to manage is that with the relatively small quantities often involved, and with most disposal taking place in the same location where the materials were used, it has been difficult for the public to get accurate information on the quantities and qualities of hazardous materials present in the immediate area. This has been addressed in the Emergency Planning and Community Right-to-Know Act of 1986, which requires facilities with 10 or more employees that manufacture, process, or use chemicals in quantities above some threshold level to report their chemical emissions to EPA and state authorities. This is then published in a Toxic Release Inventory. Communities can then find out what hazardous materials are being used and discharged in their areas. As the news clip in Exhibit 16-2 shows, the negative publicity of this revelation has motivated many firms to seek ways of reducing their use of hazardous materials. As the article points out, however, the law is a fairly blunt tool; it provides no guidance on what actual damages may be coming from the hazardous materials releases and, in some cases, real damages and public concern may not be closely connected.

FEDERAL POLICIES ON THE MANAGEMENT OF HAZARDOUS WASTES

The control of airborne and waterborne toxic residuals does not address the major issue of the large quantities of hazardous materials that are left over after production (and recycling) is completed, and which must then be disposed of. This is the problem of hazardous wastes. Table 16-3 shows the massive amounts of hazardous waste generated in 1983 and the major industrial sectors where it originated. As one would expect, the largest part comes from the chemical industry.

EXHIBIT 16-2

RIGHT TO KNOW
A U.S. REPORT SPURS COMMUNITY ACTION REVEALING POLLUTERS

Northfield, Minn., and Others Are Shocked to Discover Who's Discharging What.

But Do the Numbers Mislead?

By Randolph B. Smith
Staff Reporter of The Wall Street Journal

NORTHFIELD, Minn.—Surrounded by clear skies, lush farmland and prime fishing lakes, this historic town is famed as a rural oasis. Its main street, where residents heroically foiled a bank robbery by Jesse James in 1876, attracts thousands of tourists. Its biggest industry is higher education and its tallest smokestack soars from the stately Gothic campus of Carleton College. Northfield's motto: "Cows, Colleges and Contentment."

But over the past 18 months, things have changed so much that an art supply store on the town's main street displayed a five-foot papier mache dead cow with its feet in the air and a sign: "Cows, Colleges and Carcinogens."

What happened? The uproar here was the result of a massive U.S. government data base called the Toxics Release Inventory. The dull-sounding report is raising Cain in communities throughout the U.S. for a simple reason: For the first time, the government is telling local communities who's causing pollution in their neighborhoods—and communities are shocked.

No Telltale Signs

Here, for instance, residents never suspected Sheldahl Inc., a maker of flexible electronic circuits for automobiles and computers. The clean, high-tech plant produces no telltale smoke or odors. "We always thought of Sheldahl as a good neighbor," says Joan Wolf, a poet and editor of a literary magazine. But then a newspaper reported that Sheldahl, the town's largest employer, was polluting the air with nearly 400 tons a year of methylene chloride, a widely used solvent classified as a "probable human carcinogen" although its emission into the air is unregulated. To defuse controversy, Sheldahl immediately volunteered to reduce the emissions 90% by 1993, but the issue has split the community.

In 1989, the federal government began disclosing the staggering quantity of toxic chemicals discharged annually from 20,000 plants across the nation. The Toxics Release Inventory lists plant-by-plant emissions of 320 chemicals believed to cause serious health effects—a total of nearly 5 billion pounds of emissions, mostly legal or simply unregulated. The report tells local citizens what poisons the neighborhood factory is putting out, how much and whether they're polluting the air, water or land. The government also reports what chemicals are being stored and whether any spills have occurred.

Significant Impact

The information is disclosed under the Emergency Planning and Community Right-to-Know Act, adopted in 1986 after the Bhopal disaster in India. "The law empowers citizens to act," says Charles Elkins, a top Environmental Protection Agency official. "You don't have to be a government expert to ask tough questions, such as why a plant pollutes twice as much as competitors in the same industry."

The first two annual reports on industry's toxic emissions have had significant impact. Dozens of Fortune 500 companies have announced voluntary reductions. Monsanto Corp., for example, has already reduced toxic air emissions 39% since 1987 and expects to meet its goal of 90% by 1992. Dow Chemical Co. plans to reduce overall emissions 50% by 1995. Du Pont Co. pledges to cut air emissions 60% by 1993 and cancer-causing components 90% by 2000. Chemical Manufacturers Association spokesman Owen Kean explains: "The public increasingly measures companies by their [emissions] numbers and what they are doing about them."

In California's Silicon Valley, 2,000 protesters marched against an International

Business Machines Corp. plant revealed in 1989 as the state's worst emitter of ozone-destroying chlorinated fluorocarbons. Right-to-know was a "significant factor" in IBM's decision to eliminate CFCs at all plants by end of 1993, a spokesman says.

Residents of Springfield, Mass., used the law to find out what dangers lurked in plants and warehouses adjacent to their homes. Companies had to "justify why they were using dangerous chemicals," says James Controvich, Springfield's emergency preparedness director. Monsanto, for example, agreed to move 1,000 drums of resins containing flammable solvents from a public warehouse to safer storage at its Springfield plant.

Right-to-know also generated public support for tougher laws. The report showed that air emissions, accounting for nearly 40% of all discharges, are "basically uncontrolled," says the EPA's Mr. Elkins. In October, Congress closed the loophole by mandating strict controls for 189 toxic chemicals under the revised Clean Air Act. In Louisiana, a state that resisted even minimal regulation, right-to-know prompted public outrage and legislative action: In 1989, it adopted its first comprehensive law aimed at cutting air emissions in half by 1995.

Some companies say emissions figures can be misleading. Hoffmann-La Roche Inc.'s Nutley, N.J., pharmaceuticals plant, for example, ranked among the state's top five polluters in reports released in 1989. But environmental groups failed to note that nearly three-quarters of the waste was sent to a sewage treatment plant and converted to harmless carbon dioxide and water, the company says. "You can't just look at emissions totals to measure risks," says Jack Kace, an assistant vice president.

The flap here started in June 1989, although it took more than the government's report alone to sound the alarm. The Toxics Release Inventory itself is so thick and obscure that it's difficult to compare plants or industries without a computer. Moreover, the report gives no indication of health risks. So environmental groups like the Natural Resources Defense Council pore through the data and release their findings. In 1989, the council listed the nation's biggest emitters of 11 known or probable cancer-causing chemicals—and Sheldahl was ranked 45. That was picked up by wire services and

published by the Minneapolis Star-Tribune, which is where the people of Northfield, population 14,000, first saw the news.

They were amazed. Sheldahl had been sending methylene chloride into the air for more than 25 years, but no one outside the plant knew it. Susan Lloyd, a special education teacher, tried to figure out what it meant. She called a dozen public officials to no avail, but she did glean crucial information: The state was about to renew Sheldahl's five-year emissions permit, which imposed no controls on methylene chloride. Citizens could demand a public hearing. She and friends collected 300 signatures on a petition forcing the state to delay the permit.

Sheldahl officials say the company has already spent nearly $5 million to phase out the solvent and can't afford expensive recovery equipment to stop emissions in the interim. James Donaghy, president and chief operating officer, says Sheldahl is moving "as quickly as we know how" without losing customers. "We are trying to balance all our constituencies," he says.

Residents quickly formed an organization, Clean Air Northfield, to investigate the health threat. Faculty at Carleton and St. Olaf College provided technical help.

The town became divided. Homemaker Sueanne Johansen points to the lush expanse of green grass between Sheldahl and the trailer park where she lives. "Our children play out there," she says. "Sheldahl tells us there are 'acceptable levels' of that stuff. Who are they kidding?" Yet her next-door neighbor, Patricia Srsen, has complete faith in Sheldahl, where she has worked 17 years as a data clerk. "It's the college professors blowing things out of proportion," she says. "They think manufacturing is a dirty word."

Whatever the outcome, though, remarkable progress has already been made in reducing methylene chloride risks for residents and workers alike, says Michael Pemrick, a Sheldahl maintenance worker. He says right-to-know provided the catalyst. "Once the community got involved," he says, there was tremendous pressure on Sheldahl to work much more expediently to reduce the risks.

Source: Wall Street Journal, January 2, 1991. Reprinted by permission of The Wall Street Journal, © 1991 Dow Jones & Company, Inc. All Rights Reserved Worldwide.

TABLE 16-3
ESTIMATED NATIONAL GENERATION OF INDUSTRIAL HAZARDOUS WASTES RANKED BY
MAJOR INDUSTRY GROUP, 1983 (in thousands of metric tons)

Major industry	Estimated quantity in 1983	Percentage of total
Chemicals and allied products	127,245	47.9
Primary metals	47,704	18.0
Petroleum and coal products	31,358	11.8
Fabricated metal products	25,364	9.6
Rubber and plastic products	14,600	5.5
Miscellaneous manufacturing	5,614	2.1
Nonelectrical machinery	4,859	1.8
Transportation equipment	2,977	1.1
Motor freight transportation	2,160	0.8
Electrical and electronic machinery	1,929	0.7
Wood preserving	1,739	0.7
Drum reconditioners	45	*
Total	265,595	100.0

*Less than .1 percent.

Source: Congressional Budget Office, *Hazardous Waste Management: Recent Changes and Policy Alternatives,*
Washington, D.C., 1985, p. 20.

Hazardous waste consists of a diverse set of materials. In liquid form there are waste oils, solvents, and liquids containing metals, acids, PCBs, and so on. There are hazardous wastes in solid form, such as metals dust, polyvinyls, and polyethylene materials. There are many materials between liquid and solid, called sludges, such as sulfur sludge, heavy metal, solvent and cyanide sludges, and dye and paint sludges. Then there are a variety of mixed substances such as pesticides, explosives, lab wastes, and the like. In legal terms, the EPA and various state environmental agencies have power to define what is considered a hazardous waste; in past years, the definitional net they have thrown over the full physical list of substances has left out some significant materials (like waste oil). Hazardous waste generation is not spread evenly over the U.S. The largest quantities of hazardous waste are produced in Texas, Ohio, California, Illinois, Louisiana, New Jersey, Michigan, and Tennessee. At the other end of the scale, Vermont, the Dakotas, Hawaii, Alaska, Maine, and Nevada produce relatively small amounts of hazardous waste.

Table 16-4 shows the results of a Congressional Budget Office (CBO) survey to find out how hazardous wastes were being disposed of in 1983. The greatest proportion was disposed of in injection wells, that is, deep wells driven into underground geologic formations (salt caverns and aquifers). From an industry standpoint this method is relatively cheap and flexible. Another substantial proportion of these wastes were discharged in wastewater, either directly into a stream or river or into a municipal waste treatment plant. Surface impoundment

TABLE 16-4
WASTE QUANTITIES MANAGED IN 1983, RANKED BY MAJOR TECHNOLOGY
(in millions of metric tons)

Technology	Description	Quantity managed	Percentage of total
Injection well	Injection of liquid wastes into wells or salt caverns	66.8	25
Sewer and direct discharge	Discharge of treated and untreated liquids to municipal sewage treatment plants, rivers, and streams	58.9	22
Surface impoundment	Placement of liquid wastes or sludges in pits, ponds, or lagoons	49.5	19
Hazardous waste landfill	Placement of liquid or solid wastes into lined disposal cells that are covered by soils	34.2	13
Sanitary landfill	Placement of wastes in unlined dump sites, which normally receive only inert, nonhazardous materials	26.7	10
Distillation	Recovery of solvent liquids from other waste contaminants through fractional distillation	10.9	4
Industrial boilers	Burning of wastes in industrial and commercial boilers as a fuel supplement	9.5	4
Oxidation	Chemical treatment of reactive wastes	3.0	1
Land treatment	Biodegradation of liquid wastes or sludges in soils	2.9	1
Incineration	Burning of wastes in advanced technology incinerators meeting stringent environment standards	2.7	1
Ion exchange	Recovery of metals in solution through membrane separative techniques	0.5	*

*Less than 1 percent.

Source: Congressional Budget Office, *Hazardous Waste Management: Recent Changes and Policy Alternatives,* Washington, D.C., 1985, p. 24.

and landfill disposal, into both hazardous waste (lined) landfills as well as unlined landfills, accounted for most of the remaining hazardous waste. Disposal of hazardous wastes through chemical treatment accounted for a relatively small proportion of the total. Although these numbers do not show it directly, about 96 percent of all hazardous waste generated in the U.S. is disposed of on-site; that is, at the site of the industrial plant where it was manufactured and/or used. Only 4 percent was transported to off-site disposal facilities.

The two major pathways leading to damage are through accidental releases and through releases stemming from improper handling, either at the site of use or at waste disposal facilities. Accidents have led to severe and obvious damages, to humans and to other parts of the ecosystem.[11] It has been less easy to document the damages coming from long-run exposure to small amounts of hazardous wastes. Ecosystems in the vicinity of industrial waste dumps are sometimes visibly affected. Human health effects have been harder to show, particularly when what is at issue is long-run exposure to small quantities of hazardous materials. Much more epidemiological and laboratory work remains to be done.

Federal policy has been directed at two types of problems: (1) developing a system to manage the storage, transportation, and disposal of current hazardous wastes and (2) cleaning up land disposal sites where large quantities of hazardous wastes were dumped in years past. The two major federal hazardous waste laws address these issues.

The Resource Conservation and Recovery Act of 1976 (RCRA)

There are four major parts to RCRA:

1 Definition of "hazardous wastes." In an ideal world, with free research resources, we would probably want to define "hazardous" in terms of the potential damages a substance might cause. But we don't live in this kind of world, so EPA has adopted a definition based on physical properties that apparently are capable of causing damage, in particular corrosivity, toxicity, reactivity, and explosivity. If a substance meets the criteria under any of these headings, it is deemed to be hazardous. Politics being what it is, however, certain well-known substances were expressly excluded in the act; in particular waste lubricating oil, wastes from oil and natural gas exploration, and radioactive wastes.
2 "Manifest" system. One of the fundamental problems of controlling hazardous waste emissions is simply knowing how much of the material has been produced and how and where it moves through the system to final disposal. The 1976 Act directed EPA to create a paper-trail system to track hazardous waste through the system. When material is generated, transported, stored, treated, or disposed of, it is supposed to be accompanied by a manifest stating the origin, quantities, and destination of the material. As it moves through the economic system, all waste is to be accompanied by its manifest. This would allow regulatory authorities to know the location of the waste at any point in time, which is fundamental to establishing any kind of control program.
3 Standards for treatment, storage, and disposal facilities. Performance and design standards are to be enforced on operators engaged in handling and disposing of hazardous materials. For example, a performance standard on hazardous waste incinerators is that they destroy 99.99 percent of the organic wastes in the incinerator feedstock. A design standard applied to hazardous

---

[11] In Chapter 7 we discussed current efforts to develop techniques to estimate ecosystem damages arising from hazardous waste releases.

waste landfill operators is that the landfills be constructed with approved liners to reduce the risk of contaminating nearby groundwater.

4 A permit system to enforce the standards. In order to stay in operation, hazardous waste transporters and disposers must obtain a permit from public authorities. The permit is supposed to be obtained only after all design and operating standards have been met.

At the present time there are about 500 licensed commercial treatment, storage, and disposal facilities in the U.S. We saw earlier that the vast majority of hazardous waste is actually used and disposed of at the site where it is generated; for this material the manifest system is obviously less useful, though the permit system still applies. There are currently about 2,500 generator-owned treatment, storage, and disposal facilities and 75,000 industrial landfills in the U.S.

In 1984 Congress enacted a significant set of amendments to RCRA. The growing efforts to control hazardous emissions under air and water pollution laws were pushing more of these materials toward land disposal. Simultaneously there was increasing concern about the safety of groundwater resources and possible contamination from hazardous waste disposal sites, even at sites that had supposedly been designed expressly to handle hazardous materials. The result was a law that severely restricts land disposal of hazardous wastes and directs the EPA to identify acceptable disposal means for various types of hazardous materials. It also extended control to hazardous waste sources not previously covered, such as underground storage tanks and small sources of hazardous waste (those producing between 100 and 1,000 kg of hazardous waste per month). The 1984 law continued and accelerated the trend in federal law in the direction of direct CAC-type controls: uniform technology and performance standards applied throughout the industry without regard to questions of cost-effectiveness or efficient risk reduction.

The Comprehensive Environmental Response, Compensation and Liability Act of 1980 (CERCLA)

The law is directed at cleaning up past hazardous waste disposal sites and has come to be called "Superfund," perhaps in reference to the massive sums of money involved. CERCLA was enacted in response to heightened public fears about the health impacts of past, and often forgotten, hazardous waste disposal sites. In some cases, as in the notorious Love Canal incident, people were exposed directly to hazardous materials that migrated through the soil; in other cases, the fear was, and is, of groundwater contamination from these old dump sites. CERCLA has several main features:

1 A financial fund, derived from a tax on chemical and petroleum feedstocks used by industry, and from private parties held to be responsible for past dumping. This fund is to be used to carry out site investigations and cleanups.

2 A method for selecting sites for cleanup actions. This is called the National Contingency Plan (NCP) and specifies procedures for identifying and investigating sites, determining cleanup plans, and deciding on who will pay for it. Part of the procedure involves a state–federal effort to create the list of sites that are in greatest need of action; this is called the National Priorities List (NPL), and it involves a hazard-ranking system taking into account the types and quantities of hazardous materials at the site and the possibility of human exposure.

3 Authority for the EPA to clean up sites itself, or to identify responsible private parties to clean up the sites.

4 A liability provision for natural resources damage. Besides cleanup liability, CERCLA has a provision for holding responsible parties liable for damages to natural resources stemming from spilled or released toxic materials. Thus, if a chemical is accidentally released into a river, the people causing the spill can be held liable for the damages this causes. Or, if an old landfill leaks toxic compounds, responsible parties may be held liable not only for cleaning up the site but also for damages to surrounding groundwater resources.

In 1986 Congress passed the Superfund Amendments and Reauthorization Act, or SARA. This act extended the fund and broadened the tax to include, along with the feedstock tax, an "environmental tax" on all corporations of .12 percent of their taxable income over $2 million.

The Superfund cleanup process is very long and complicated, starting with identifying the site and the "potentially responsible parties" (PRPs) who have used the site at some time in the past, then proceeding with cleaning up the site and delisting it from the NPL. Each step involves public authorities at all levels as well as numerous private parties. It is a process full of conflict, and the costs of the legal actions on a site can sometimes rival or even exceed the actual costs of cleaning up the hazardous material.

Radioactive Wastes

Radioactive wastes are governed by a separate set of statutes from all other types of hazardous wastes. There are two types of radioactive wastes: high-level wastes (HLW) and low-level wastes (LLW). HLW is made up primarily of spent fuel from nuclear power plants and wastes from government nuclear processing facilities. LLW comes from a variety of industrial and medical processes that utilize small amounts of radioactive material, and includes the material itself together with all manner of items that have become contaminated in normal production operations.

. The primary problem in HLW is to find a secure, *permanent* storage site, because the rate of radioactive decay is so slow that these wastes will be lethal essentially forever by human standards. The Nuclear Waste Policy Act of 1982 requires the Department of Energy (DOE) to find and develop a permanent underground depository for nuclear HLW. This has proved to be an immensely complicated task and one full of political conflict. The effort is funded by a tax of one-tenth of a cent per kilowatt-hour of electricity generated at all nuclear power plants. The standards for storage have been set by the EPA, in terms of the maximum allowable rate of release of radionuclides from the repository for the next 10,000 years! As of this writing (1992), a repository site has not yet been found. It is difficult, if not essentially impossible, to identify underground geological formations that are sure to be secure for the next 10,000 years. It is even more difficult to convince people living near candidate sites that no damage will come their way and that this is the best use of a portion of their landscape. Thus, the projected year of opening for the depository has been continuously set back, from 1998 at first to 2010 now, and this date will no doubt continue to slip.

Low-level radioactive wastes are disposed of for the most part in approved landfills. Prior to 1980, there were three landfill sites in the U.S. accepting low-level radioactive waste. These were in South Carolina, Washington, and Nevada. With the volume of these wastes climbing rapidly, these states began to raise objections to being its sole recipients. But there were negative incentives for other states to open their own sites, because of their fear that they would be forced to accept LLW from other states. The first result was a 1980 federal law, the Low Level Radioactive Waste Policy Act of 1980, which encouraged states to enter into interstate compacts to open sites that would accept all the waste from states in each compact. Very little happened over the next few years, however, because groups of states could not come to an agreement on these compacts. The law was therefore amended in 1985 to provide greater incentives for groups of states to enter into compacts to develop and operate LLW landfills. The primary incentive was a rapidly increasing surcharge per cubic feet of LLW that the sites in South Carolina, Washington, and Nevada would be authorized to charge, culminating in a complete cutoff of outside LLW after 1990.[12]

Transport Laws

While RCRA and CERCLA are the two main federal laws focused on handling hazardous wastes, we should also mention the Hazardous Materials Transportation Act (HMTA) of 1975, which gave the Department of Transportation authority to regulate the movement of hazardous materials when transported by air, water, highway, or rail. This is done by enforcing a set of packaging, labeling, and handling standards. Hazardous wastes shipped in bulk by sea are regulated by the Coast Guard under the Ports and Waterways Safety Act of 1972.

---

[12] The incentive for entering into interstate compacts was that they could then by law exclude waste from noncompact states. The compact system has not developed as Congress envisioned, and the full legal ramifications of the approach are still not settled. See L. David Condon, "The Never Ending Story: Low-Level Waste and the Exclusionary Authority of Noncompacting States," *Natural Resources Journal*, 30(1), Winter 1990, pp. 65–86.

ECONOMIC ISSUES IN MANAGING HAZARDOUS WASTE

The policy debate on hazardous waste management is fueled by the public fears and alarms that follow the highly publicized exposure incidents, like Love Canal, Times Beach, and similar events.[13] It is not hard to understand why public authorities have relied on conventional CAC-type operating standards to address these issues. It gives the impression that policymakers have established a system of positive control based on rational technical decisions. The CAC approach is certainly justified in some cases. If a landfill is to receive hazardous wastes, presumably it should be built to certain minimum technical specifications. This is especially true because of the difficulties of monitoring leaks from hazardous waste landfills. But this is a problem where economic incentive approaches can also be useful.

Waste-End Taxes

Taxes on hazardous wastes, levied at the place where they are generated or where they are disposed of, are a feasible way of providing the incentive for reducing the quantities produced, as well as directing the flow of wastes toward various channels. These have come to be called "waste-end taxes." The monitoring problem is much less a factor than with toxic emissions, since wastes are often in bulk form that lends itself to quantitative measurement. In fact, a tax of $2.13/ton of hazardous waste is currently charged at qualified disposal sites to support Superfund's Post-Closure Liability Trust Fund. Raising this tax would stimulate industry efforts at waste reduction. It would also lead to an increase in the prices of products that produce substantial quantities of waste in their manufacture. It has one unfortunate effect, however, in that it will also create an incentive to dispose of hazardous materials surreptitiously.

Deposit-Refund System

A major problem with many hazardous wastes is that they are in quantities that are difficult to monitor. This will continue to be the case even with the manifest system. Any kind of tax placed on hazardous material creates an incentive for disposers to conceal material discharged, perhaps by disposing of it on-site, into a public sewer system, or in some unapproved landfill. One way of turning these incentives around is to offer a subsidy for hazardous materials disposed of in approved ways. This, of course, would require a source of funds. A possibility would be to institute deposit-refund systems for hazardous materials. Firms would pay a deposit per unit of hazardous chemical at the time of purchase from a chemical supplier. They would then be paid a refund on materials when they were properly disposed of.[14]

---

[13] Times Beach is a community in Missouri that spread dioxin-contaminated oil on its roads. The federal government ended up buying all the houses in the community.

[14] For more on this idea see Clifford S. Russell, "Economic Incentives in the Management of Hazardous Wastes," *Columbia Journal of Environmental Law*, 13, Spring 1988, pp. 257–274.

Financing Hazardous Waste Site Cleanups

Cleaning up past hazardous waste sites is a lengthy and expensive process that involves complicated issues of liability, technical alternatives, and public risks. The EPA estimates that cleaning up the sites currently listed on the NPL will take more than $30 billion. This substantially exceeds the sums that will be raised under CERCLA through taxes on chemical feedstocks and the general corporate tax. A big question, therefore, is how to get greater resources from past or present dumpers, or their insurers, to help clean up the long list of sites currently on the NPL and new ones that may be listed. Several private insurers have suggested establishing large environmental trust funds, from mandatory or voluntary contributions, to be devoted to cleaning up hazardous waste sites. Others have suggested changing the current systems of financing and liability.

Ultimately the success in this effort may depend most critically on introducing changes that increase incentives for private firms to enter into cleanup agreements, among themselves and between themselves and the EPA. The courts have ruled that in pursuing PRPs to obtain cleanup funds, the EPA may use the doctrine of strict, joint, and several liability by responsible parties. What this means is that when more than one firm has dumped hazardous wastes into the site, the EPA may nevertheless sue and recover total cleanup costs from just one of the responsible parties. So, for example, a company that has dumped only a small portion of the wastes into a site can nevertheless be held responsible for the total cleanup costs at the site. The effect of this is to provide an incentive for this one firm to identify and recover costs from other parties that were responsible for dumping at the site. But there are also strong negative aspects to this approach. The doctrine can hold individual firms responsible for total cleanup costs of a site even though they may have dumped only a small proportion of total wastes at the site. This no doubt leads firms to hold back because the admission of even partial responsibility opens them up to the risk of having to pay total cleanup costs. This and other features make the process highly litigious, with firms spending enormous amounts of money suing one another, the EPA, municipalities, states, insurance companies, and so on. Exhibit 16-3 shows a news clip on this topic. The rules need to be changed so that energies spent this way can instead be devoted to cleaning up abandoned hazardous waste sites.

SUMMARY

The coming of the chemical society has led to new sources of environmental damage and opened up new requirements for managing toxic and hazardous materials. At the federal level a number of major laws deal with toxic and hazardous substances, and numerous federal agencies are responsible for their administration. For the most part the laws incorporate a variety of command-and-control measures to identify and monitor the use of toxic materials in workplaces and consumer products, to control toxic emissions from production, and to manage the complex process of disposing of hazardous materials.

EXHIBIT 16-3

THE REAL CLEANUP

Insurers' Superfund Focus: Hiring Lawyers.

By Michael Parrish, Times Staff Writer

Nearly 90% of the billions of dollars insurance companies have spent on Superfund toxic waste sites has been sunk into legal battles— mostly with their own policymakers, according to a RAND Corp. study released Thursday.

The money spent in court is enough, according to the study, to clean up 15 Superfund sites a year.

In contrast, the big industrial firms in the study have mostly gone ahead and paid for cleanups without fighting them in court, spending an average of just 21% of their Superfund money on legal costs.

Critics of the Superfund law, which is up for reauthorization by 1994, say the study supports their call for drastic reform.

"The only people cleaning up in Superfund are the lawyers," said Anne Ligon, assistant general counsel of the Superfund Action Coalition, a Washington lobbying group formed in January to represent companies faced with Superfund liabilities.

Insurers generally agreed.

But environmentalists, regulators and the RAND authors themselves found support for the current process in the study.

"It shows you the legal costs are not a big issue—except for the insurance companies," said Doug Wolf, an attorney with the Natural Resources Defense Council. "And I don't think we should let them dictate our policy for cleaning up abandoned waste sites."

The EPA spends about $1.5 billion a year in taxpayer dollars on Superfund cleanups. It has recovered $295 million from responsible parties since 1987 and is seeking $1 billion more.

While no one knows how much these parties have paid out for cleanups, their insurers are spending about $500 million annually in costs associated with the Superfund law.

The RAND researchers found that fully 88% of that $500 million is spent on lawsuits, with 47% of that sum being used to contest the claims of the insurance companies' own customers. Another 42% goes to defending policyholders against the EPA or other parties.

The RAND authors and others predict that some legal expenditures are bound to occur as state case law, which controls many of the legal battles, is sorted out.

And they see some evidence that the system is creating incentives for private companies to undertake cleanups before being forced to by the EPA: The study estimates that fully 10% of all cleanups costing a company more than $100,000 are being done without government involvement.

The large companies "have been willing to step forward and pay remedial costs, which many had doubted at the beginning of the program," noted Lloyd S. Dixon of RAND's Institute for Civil Justice, one of the study's authors.

The insurance companies and such groups as the Superfund Action Coalition want to replace the existing system with one using taxpayer funds to finance a public-works cleanup, much as billions of federal dollars have been spent in recent years to build new sewage treatment plants around the country.

"It's clear as a bell that Superfund's incredibly harsh and inequitable liability scheme has created and is going to continue to create considerable controversies," said Karl S. Lytz, an attorney at Latham & Watkins. He represents Montrose Chemical Corp. of California at one of the first Superfund sites listed in the nation—the Stringfellow acid pits in Riverside County.

Relations between companies such as Montrose and their insurers have grown "only more litigious over recent years," Lytz said. "And that level of fighting will continue."

But environmentalists, particularly, remain opposed to shifting to a public-works scheme.

"This report highlights [the insurance companies'] self-interest in that proposal," said Wolf of the NRDC. "They would benefit more than anyone else."

Important points exist where the management of toxics could be substantially improved. One of these is to improve the procedures for "balancing" the costs and benefits of using chemicals in particular products and processes. We also discussed the new emphasis on waste reduction, i.e., changes in production systems that lead to lower quantities of hazardous waste requiring disposal. Finally, we discussed the federal laws governing the handling and disposal of hazardous waste and the cleaning up of past dump sites.

QUESTIONS FOR FURTHER DISCUSSION

1 Handlers of hazardous wastes—i.e., firms that accept hazardous materials and transport them for disposal—sometimes dispose of the materials illegally or in unapproved landfills. How might a deposit-refund system be designed to provide incentives to dispose of hazardous materials in approved ways?
2 What are the advantages and disadvantages of using a limited liability approach to cleaning up hazardous waste sites; i.e., an approach whereby firms that dumped material in a site are held liable only for their own wastes?
3 "The EPA has estimated that the chemical residues on a certain food most likely contribute to 14 excess deaths in the U.S. population each year. Thus, if use of the chemical is banned we can expect the number of excess deaths to decrease by this number." Comment.
4 If workers have adequate information about the chemical (and other) risks in different workplaces, they can make informed decisions about work and wages. Can we expect the employment market normally to generate the efficient amount of information about risks?
5 It has frequently been suggested that taxes be placed on toxic materials at point of production; these would be easier to administer (as compared to taxes in intermediate-use stages) and would discourage overall use of the chemicals taxed. What are the efficiency implications of this approach?

SELECTED READINGS

Dorfman, Robert: "The Lessons of Pesticide Regulation," in Wesley A. Magat (ed.), *Reform of Environmental Regulation*, Ballinger, Cambridge, Mass., 1982, chapter 2.
Florio, James J.: "Congress as Reluctant Regulator: Hazardous Waste Policy in the 1980's," *Yale Journal on Regulation*, 3(2), Spring 1986, pp. 251–382.
Graham, John D., Laura C. Green, and Marc J. Roberts: *In Search of Safety: Chemicals and Cancer Risk*, Harvard University Press, Cambridge, Mass., 1988.
Grigalunas, Thomas A., and James L. Opaluch: "Assessing Liability for Damages Under CERCLA: A New Approach for Providing Incentives for Pollution Avoidance," *Natural Resources Journal*, 28(3), Summer 1988, pp. 509–533.
Harris, Christopher, William L. Want, and Morris A. Ward: *Hazardous Waste, Confronting the Challenge*, Quorum Books, New York, 1987.
Hird, John A.: "Superfund Expenditures and Cleanup Priorities: Distributive Politics and the Public Interest," *Journal of Policy Analysis and Management*, 9(4), Fall 1990, pp. 455–483.

Hirschhorn, Joel S., and Kirsten U. Oldenburg: *Prosperity Without Pollution: The Prevention Strategy for Industry and Consumers*, Van Nostrand Reinhold, New York, 1991.

Macauley, Molly K., Michael D. Bowes, and Karen L. Palmer: *Using Economic Incentives to Regulate Toxic Substances*, Resources for the Future, Washington, D.C., 1993.

Mendeloff, John: *The Dilemma of Toxic Substance Regulation*, MIT Press, Cambridge, Mass., 1988.

Quarles, John: *Federal Regulation of Hazardous Wastes, A Guide to RCRA*, Environmental Law Institute, Washington, D.C., 1982.

U.S. Congressional Budget Office: *Hazardous Waste Management: Recent Changes and Policy Alternatives*, Washington, D.C., 1985.

U.S. Environmental Protection Agency: *Waste Minimization—Issues and Options*, Vols. I, II, and III (EPA/530/SW-86/041, 042, 043), Washington, D.C., 1986.

U.S. Environmental Protection Agency: *Toxics in the Community, National and Local Perspectives, The 1989 Toxics Release Inventory National Report*, Washington, D.C., 1991.

U.S. Office of Technology Assessment: *Technologies and Strategies for Hazardous Waste Control*, Washington, D.C., 1983.

CHAPTER 17

STATE AND LOCAL
ENVIRONMENTAL ISSUES

In the 1950s and 1960s there was no strong federal presence in U.S. environmental policy; what initiative there was lay mostly at the state level. In the 1970s this changed dramatically, as strong federal laws were written that essentially shifted the policy center of gravity toward Washington. But in more recent years nonfederal involvement in environmental policy issues has grown rapidly. States and communities are playing three primary roles:

- Contributing to federal laws; most federal policies permit, require, or encourage some type of contributing state action, especially in enforcement.
- Adopting companion policies that express the particular environmental values, goals, or circumstances of individual states; these have often been a source of innovative policy ideas.
- Dealing with certain major issues that have been left for the most part to the states.

In this chapter we will take a look at some of these state and local issues. Given the diversity among the states, we cannot do a survey of the environmental policies being pursued in each one. After an introductory section in which we deal with general issues, we will take up three problems that have historically been left to the states: solid waste, land-use controls, and groundwater protection.

GENERAL ISSUES

The states vary widely in terms of their commitments to environmental quality, the severity of their environmental problems, and the progress they have made in environmental policy matters. Table 17-1 shows state rankings by total environmental expenditures, expenditures per capita, and environmental expenditures as a percentage of total expenditures for 1986. These numbers should be treated with caution, however. The nature and severity of environmental problems vary substantially among states. Air pollution is much more severe in some

TABLE 17-1
STATE ENVIRONMENTAL EXPENDITURES, 1986

Ranked by total environmental expenditures		Ranked by per-capita expenditures		Ranked by % state environmental expenditures of total state expenditures	
1. California	$1,199,938,000	Alaska	$326.00	Wyoming	15.00
2. Pennsylvania	332,549,763	Wyoming	135.33	Oregon	4.44
3. Wisconsin	260,289,169	South Dakota	75.90	South Dakota	4.31
4. New York	227,274,090	Montana	69.55	California	3.53
5. New Jersey	200,750,000	Wisconsin	55.31	Idaho	3.49
6. Illinois	181,897,000	Idaho	51.97	Montana	3.46
7. Michigan	173,007,900	California	50.70	Alaska	3.00
8. Florida	171,267,941	Oregon	49.01	New Hampshire	2.89
9. Washington	160,334,318	Delaware	47.74	Wisconsin	2.79
10. Alaska	130,973,900	Vermont	42.94	Pennsylvania	2.71
11. Oregon	129,052,806	Washington	38.80	Vermont	2.39
12. Missouri	123,279,074	New Hampshire	32.41	Missouri	1.96
13. Massachusetts	122,313,035	North Dakota	31.08	Washington	1.91
14. Texas	100,921,072	Pennsylvania	28.03	Mississippi	1.83
15. Ohio	92,169,500	New Jersey	27.25	North Dakota	1.82
16. Kentucky	88,448,194	Rhode Island	26.16	West Virginia	1.60
17. Virginia	87,316,466	Missouri	25.07	Delaware	1.57
18. Maryland	85,748,214	Utah	24.60	Kentucky	1.51
19. North Carolina	77,193,938	New Mexico	24.59	Nevada	1.41
20. Minnesota	73,482,950	Mississippi	24.38	New Jersey	1.39
21. Louisiana	73,079,329	Kentucky	24.16	Utah	1.36
22. Tennessee	70,911,499	West Virginia	23.68	Massachusetts	1.32
23. Georgia	68,986,592	Maine	22.31	Colorado	1.30
24. Colorado	64,319,886	Colorado	22.26	Michigan	1.25
25. Wyoming	63,604,967	Nevada	21.77	New Mexico	1.25
26. Mississippi	61,453,623	Massachusetts	21.32	Rhode Island	1.23
27. Alabama	60,252,564	Maryland	20.33	Maine	1.21
28. Montana	54,739,315	Hawaii	19.21	Tennessee	1.18
29. South Dakota	52,450,000	Michigan	18.68	Illinois	1.14
30. South Carolina	50,018,484	Minnesota	18.03	Louisiana	1.12
31. Idaho	49,063,734	Florida	17.57	Nebraska	1.09
32. Iowa	47,090,046	Louisiana	17.38	Iowa	1.07
33. Indiana	46,551,743	Virginia	16.33	Maryland	1.06
34. West Virginia	46,183,752	Iowa	16.16	Virginia	1.04
35. Oklahoma	43,892,933	South Carolina	16.02	North Carolina	1.04
36. Arizona	41,287,553	Illinois	15.92	Alabama	0.99
37. Connecticut	38,666,000	Alabama	15.47	Florida	0.98
38. Utah	35,947,156	Tennessee	15.45	South Carolina	0.97
39. New Mexico	32,046,123	Arizona	15.19	Arizona	0.95
40. Kansas	30,445,137	North Carolina	14.62	Connecticut	0.89
41. Arkansas	30,372,330	Oklahoma	14.51	Arkansas	0.88

TABLE 17-1
STATE ENVIRONMENTAL EXPENDITURES, 1986

Ranked by total environmental expenditures		Ranked by per-capita expenditures		Ranked by % state environmental expenditures of total state expenditures	
42. New Hampshire	29,850,570	Nebraska	13.32	Minnesota	0.88
43. Delaware	28,359,508	Arkansas	13.29	Kansas	0.87
44. Maine	25,096,481	New York	12.94	Oklahoma	0.85
45. Rhode Island	24,767,942	Kansas	12.88	Georgia	0.83
46. Vermont	21,944,786	Georgia	12.63	Hawaii	0.72
47. Nebraska	20,918,705	Connecticut	12.44	Indiana	0.69
48. North Dakota	20,293,798	Ohio	8.54	Ohio	0.60
49. Hawaii	18,540,533	Indiana	8.48	Texas	0.55
50. Nevada	17,413,195	Texas	7.09	New York	0.54

Source: R. Steven Brown and E. Garner, *Resource Guide to State Environmental Management,* The Council of State Governments, Lexington, Ky., 1988.

states than others. Hazardous-waste releases, while occurring in every state, are nevertheless concentrated in certain ones, particularly Texas and Louisiana. Florida has special water-quality problems because of the Everglades and because of its reliance on groundwater. Coastal states have special problems in managing their coastal resources. Mining regulation is a particular problem for some states, as is agricultural runoff in others. Given these great variations, equal expenditures in several states can mean quite different things in terms of achieved results in environmental quality.

Constitutional and Policy Issues

The U.S. Constitution governs the division of powers between the federal government and the states. In cases where valid (i.e., constitutional) environmental laws have been enacted at the federal level, these normally preempt state action. Thus, for example, federal laws to control coastal tanker traffic so as to reduce the threat of oil spills will usually preempt any state actions aimed at the same result. In cases where the federal government has not acted, states may do so provided they do not exceed constitutional limits. The most important of these is that states may not pass laws that discriminate against interstate commerce. In environmental matters, this has been held to bar states from passing laws restricting the importation of solid waste from other states. But virtually all state environmental actions will have some impact on interstate commerce, so the federal courts have become the arena for ongoing determination about the legitimacy of state environmental actions.

In addition to constitutional issues, there are important policy dimensions to the federal–state balance in environmental law. When environmental issues are truly local—contamination of a groundwater aquifer, for example—state action may be more appropriate because the balancing that is required involves strictly local interests; presumably the unique characteristics of the situation are best served by local political bodies. But when interstate environmental externalities are involved, federal action is called for to manage the conflicting claims of the different states. Another situation making state-level environmental actions problematic is that states usually feel that they are in competition among themselves for business growth, which may make them reluctant to pursue vigorous environmental programs. In recent years many states have moved to pull together the disparate environmental programs under their jurisdictions into single, EPA-like environmental agencies. These organizations should be able, at least theoretically, to develop greater expertise and make more coordinated and effective environmental decisions than was possible in the past.

Virtually all federal programs have provisions for substantial state and local participation. Federal water pollution law (incorporating technology-based effluent standards) works through a permitting system; sources must obtain permits for waterborne emissions and are supposed to operate in accordance with the terms specified in the permits. For the most part, it is the states that actually operate the permit system, though there are a few (e.g., New Hampshire and Oklahoma) where federal authorities are still responsible. Federal water law also requires the states to establish ambient water-quality standards in the various bodies of water within their boundaries. Traditionally these standards have been expressed in terms of the functions that particular water-quality levels would allow; e.g., standards for fishable–swimmable water and standards for drinkable water. In recent laws states have also been given the responsibility of setting ambient standards for waterborne toxics.

The states have permitting authority also under federal clean air act legislation. The 1990 Act allows them to operate fee systems for these permits, similar to the water program. Permit fees may be charged, *and these may be based on emission levels*; but fees are only supposed to be high enough to cover the costs of running the permit program. They may not be used, in other words, as full incentive-changing emission taxes like those we have discussed in previous chapters. In recent years, this type of "dedicated funding" system is being increasingly relied upon by states to fund their environmental programs. Rather than fund these efforts from general state revenues, they are turning to using sources in particular programs—permit fees, fines, trust funds, etc.—to get the money to run these programs. "Car owners pay for air-pollution control programs with a portion of their license-tag fees, factories pay for water quality efforts with fees for permits to discharge wastewater, recycling programs are funded by special levies on items like motor oil and batteries, and the fines forked over by violators of environmental rules pay for enforcement efforts."[1]

States may also regulate hazardous wastes but, according to RCRA, the state regulations must be at least as strict as applicable federal regulations. Many states

---

[1] *Environment Reporter*, Bureau of National Affairs, Washington, D.C., March 30, 1992, p. 2580.

have done this in various areas: definition of hazardous wastes, standards for incinerators, requirements for the manifest system, location requirements for hazardous waste disposal sites, insurance requirements for hazardous waste facility operators, and so on. State hazardous waste regulations are almost exclusively performance and technology standards. New Jersey's laws on incinerating hazardous wastes, for example, specify such details as minimum operating temperatures allowed and staffing requirements. Arkansas mandates the disposal method for different types of hazardous wastes. California statutes specify detailed design standards for hazardous waste landfills that are more stringent than federal standards. Many states have enacted their own "superfund" laws to supplement the federal law. Many of these are designed in the image of CERCLA, with a response fund, a site priority list, and various action criteria.[2] States also have taken varying degrees of responsibility for actions at some of the NPL sites.

Policy Innovations at the State Level

Over the last few decades, the states have been the source of some innovative environmental policy initiatives. This is especially true of California, which has been the source of several policy initiatives that have later spread to other states and the federal level. Chief among these has been mobile-source pollution control. The Los Angeles area was the first in the nation to experience smog, and the California response in the early 1960s was to require technological improvements in cars to reduce emissions. Since that time, vehicles sold in California have had to meet more stringent emission standards. The standards have not been legally preempted by federal emission limits, and in recent years a number of other states have considered adopting the California standards as a way of dealing with increasingly severe urban air pollution.

California is also helping to pioneer the use of tradable emission permits to control airborne emissions. The South Coast Air Quality Management District, a regional organization whose objective is to manage air pollution reductions in the Los Angeles basin, has recently designed a tradable permit program to apply to an estimated 2,000 large sources of reactive organic gases and nitrogen oxides. These sources would be assigned an initial holding of permits equal to their baseline emissions and would be allowed to trade the permits. The total emission cap for each source would be decreased by 5.8 percent per year for reactive organic gases and 8 percent a year for nitrogen oxides. The District estimates that cost savings of using the tradable permit approach, rather than a conventional command-and-control policy, will be nearly a billion dollars over the next decade.[3]

---

[2] See U.S. Environmental Protection Agency, *An Analysis of State Superfund Programs: 50-State Study, 1990 Update* (EPA/540/8-89/011), Washington, D.C., 1990.

[3] Laura Mahoney, "Emission Trading Program for Southern California Promises Air Quality Improvements, Big Savings for Industry," *Environment Reporter*, Bureau of National Affairs, Washington, D.C., February 21, 1992, pp. 2423–2424.

Many other environmental programs that have become law at the federal level were initially developed by one or more of the states. DDT was first banned by Wisconsin; this later became a national effort. The Federal Strip Mining Control and Reclamation Act of 1977 was substantially modeled after the Pennsylvania strip mining reclamation law. The federal toxics release inventory program is an idea that originated with programs in New Jersey and Maryland.

MUNICIPAL SOLID WASTE

In the rest of this chapter we will deal in some detail with several important environmental problems that traditionally have been left to states and localities. The first of these is solid waste, the disposal of which has emerged as a leading problem in many cities and towns across the country, especially in the East and along the West Coast. Landfilling, for a long time the preferred disposal method for urban solid waste, has come up hard against rising land shortages in many places, leading some localities to ship their solid wastes long distances for disposal, while others are moving into incineration. Additionally, rising fears of groundwater contamination from landfills and of air pollutants from incineration have turned what once was a disposal activity to which nobody gave a second thought into a prime environmental concern.

The Nature of the Problem

The municipal solid waste (MSW) stream is actually a trickle at the end of a long and very large flow of materials used in the U.S. economy. The EPA estimates that the total quantity of materials generated per person per day is about 304 pounds. Of this, approximately 190 pounds are industrial solid wastes, about 71 pounds are oil and gas wastes, about 35 pounds are mining wastes, and about 4 pounds are hazardous wastes. Thus, municipal solid waste amounts to approximately 3 to 4 pounds per person per day.[4] This is composed of a very diverse set of materials—everything from lawn clippings to moldy bread to automobile batteries to used refrigerators to construction debris. Table 17-2 shows some estimates of MSW generated per capita in the 1980s for the U.S. and several selected cities, and for several other countries. U.S. generation rates are higher than those for other countries, but Japan is not far behind. European countries seem to have generation rates that are approximately 70–80 percent of the U.S. rate. Within the U.S. rates vary substantially among cities, as the data indicate. The MSW problem is not equally acute everywhere. In localities with large populations and/or constrained landfill space the problem is one of immediate concern; in areas with the opposite characteristics it is much less so.

---

[4] These figures are quoted from Waste Management, Inc., and Piper and Marbury, *Waste Reduction: Policy and Practice*, Executive Enterprises Publications, New York, 1990, pp. 2–3.

TABLE 17-2
ESTIMATED MUNICIPAL SOLID WASTE
GENERATED, POUNDS PER CAPITA PER DAY

U.S. (1986)	3.2[†]
Albuquerque*	4.3
Boston	5.0
Chattanooga, Tennessee	9.4
New York	5.8
Philadelphia	5.8
San Francisco	7.2
Seattle	7.7
San Jose, California	4.8
Somerville, Massachusetts	2.2
Other Countries[†]	
West Germany (1984/1985)	2.6
Sweden (1980s)	2.4
Switzerland (n.d.)	2.2
Japan (1987)	3.0

*City data refer to 1988–1989.
[†]Net discards; i.e., material remaining after recycling but prior to energy recovery.

Source: U.S. Office of Technology Assessment, *Facing America's Trash, What Next for Municipal Solid Waste?* Washington, D.C., 1989, pp. 77, 79.

Technical Options for Reducing MSW

We define the following terms: TM is total materials used, by a firm or industry or economy, in a period of time; VM is virgin materials used; and RM is recycled materials used. Then it must be true that for any time period:

$$TM = VM + RM.$$

Materials-balance considerations[5] tell us that all materials inputs taken into an economic system must eventually end up back in the environment in some fashion. The form may change, as when solid materials are burned to yield energy and waste products. The time span can differ; some materials do not lend themselves to reuse and so are discarded almost immediately, while others can be recycled, perhaps many times. But recycling can never be perfect, because of conversion losses, wastage in consumption, etc. This means we should focus on the quantity of virgin materials used. Rearranging the above expression gives:

$$VM = TM - RM, \quad \text{or}$$
$$= TM(1 - r),$$

[5] See Chapter 2.

where r is the rate of reuse, or RM/TM. There are essentially two ways to reduce the use of virgin materials: reduce the overall quantity of materials (TM), and/or increase the reuse rate r; in other words, waste reduction and recycling.

Total materials use can be reduced in two ways: by reducing the rate of economic activity or by reducing the materials intensity of that activity. By "materials intensity" we mean the quantity of materials used per unit of production or consumption. And this in turn can be done in two ways: (1) by rearranging the composition of output and consumption away from products that use relatively large amounts of materials and toward those that use less; for example, a shift away from tangible goods toward services, and (2) by decreasing the materials intensity of particular products; for example, reducing the amount of packaging material in consumer electronics or food products.

The other alternative is recycling. This means reaching into the waste stream to extract materials that may be reused. Some may be reused directly, as when consumers reuse old boxes. But most require some reprocessing. Of course, the separation, transportation, and reprocessing technologies that are available critically affect the costs of recycled materials, and thus their ability to displace virgin materials.

Current Policy

The present policy picture is very complicated, as you would expect from the nature of the physical problem, the large number of materials involved, and the thousands of municipalities, small and large, searching for solutions. Table 17-3 lists some of the various measures that are, or have been, pursued in various states. For the most part these focus on some facet of recycling. When MSW first became an issue, it was regarded primarily as a disposal issue—people were taking to the landfill materials and products that could be recycled. Thus, the initial response of most communities was to think about materials recovery and recycling. Voluntary recycling programs began in the 1970s (the first was in Oregon). In some communities recycling has become mandatory for items that are recyclable. Recent figures show that about 13 percent of MSW is currently recycled. As Table 17-4 shows, the recycling rate for different materials varies from a high of 33 percent for aluminum to zero for wood. Of the material discarded, about 84 percent is landfilled and most of the remainder is incinerated.

THE ECONOMICS OF RECYCLING

In the recycling process there are two types of exchanges of interest: that of material from producers-suppliers to consumers-demanders; and that of recycled material from consumers-suppliers to producers-demanders. As in any economic transaction, the size and composition of the two flows of materials depend on the information sent from demanders to suppliers. This information stems from the countless decisions producers and consumers make that have

TABLE 17-3
MSW REDUCTION AND RECYCLING ACTIONS UNDERTAKEN IN STATES AND COMMUNITIES

Product bans: plastic nondegradable plastic bags, plastic-coated paper, polystyrene containers, disposable diapers, plastic six-pack rings, cans containing both plastic and metal, plastic bag purchases by state or local agencies, and so on.

Returnable disposal fees: fee on newsprint that is returned for recycling, returnable deposits on tires and car batteries.

Taxes on virgin materials content.

Consumer fees on MSW: fees per bag or can of unsorted MSW.

Prohibitions on landfilling certain products, like yard clippings, metal, and tires.

Bottle deposits.

Voluntary or mandatory material separation and curbside recycling.

Recycled or recyclable labels on products.

Technical assistance for recycling programs.

Grants and loans to municipalities for recycling programs.

Public construction of waste separation and reprocessing plants.

Public construction of waste-to-energy plants.

Tax credits and exemptions for recycling equipment and other investments by private businesses.

TABLE 17-4
MUNICIPAL SOLID WASTE GENERATED AND RECYCLED IN THE U.S., 1986 (million tons)

Materials	Gross discards		Amount recycled		Remaining trash	
Paper and paperboard	72	(40%)	18	(25%)	54	(35%)
Yard wastes	32	(18%)	0.5	(2%)	31	(20%)
Plastics	14	(8%)	0.2	(1%)	14	(9%)
Glass	13	(7%)	2	(15%)	11	(7%)
Food wastes	13	(7%)	0	(0%)	13	(8%)
Ferrous metals	12	(7%)	1	(8%)	11	(7%)
Wood	7	(4%)	0	(0%)	7	(4%)
Rubber and leather	5	(3%)	0.1	(2%)	5	(3%)
Textiles	4	(2%)	0	(0%)	4	(3%)
Aluminum	3	(2%)	1	(33%)	2	(1%)
Other	5	(3%)	1	(20%)	4	(3%)
Total	180	(100%)	24	(13%)	156	(100%)

Source: Waste Management, Inc., and Piper and Marbury, Waste Reduction: Policy and Practice, Executive Enterprises Publications, New York, 1990, p. 18; the data are adapted from U.S. Environmental Protection Agency, Characterization of Municipal Solid Waste in the United States: 1990 Update (EPA/530-SW-90-042A), Washington, D.C., 1990.

repercussions for materials use. Producers design products and the materials used with them; they make decisions on the total quantities of materials used and the amounts of virgin and recycled feedstocks they will use. Consumers choose products that contain different types and amounts of materials; they also decide how to dispose of the various materials that are left after the products have been "consumed."

Solid waste is a problem because of defects in the pricing systems that govern these transactions. Discarded solid waste produces a variety of environmental damages. For social efficiency these have to be reflected in disposal costs of people who make disposal decisions; namely, consumers. The harvesting of virgin materials leads to a variety of environmental costs. For full efficiency these costs have to be reflected in the prices paid by producers. On the consumer side, solid waste disposal is paid for almost everywhere by flat fees levied to cover the costs of collection and disposal. These fees can go up or down to reflect overall disposal costs (fees are going up in many areas because of increasing scarcity of landfill space), but the per-family fees do not vary according to the quantities of material discarded per family. Thus, there is no incentive for consumers to be very concerned about the amounts of solid waste they discard, nor any reason for them to be concerned about the amount of "excess" materials that accompany their purchases.[6]

Harvesting of virgin materials also leads to a variety of environmental costs. In many cases these costs are external to the harvesting firms, making the prices of virgin materials too low from the standpoint of social efficiency.[7] This, together with technological changes that have increased the cost of recycled materials (e.g., the advent of the large trash-compacting collection truck) have led to a substantial reduction in the proportion of materials recovered from the waste stream. In the next two sections we will look at these producer and consumer sides of the solid waste phenomenon.

Producer Use of Recycled Material

Figure 17-1 is an analysis of the producer side. The demand curve applies to a firm or industry; it shows the quantity demanded of a particular type of material in a given period, like a year. There are two sources of this material, virgin and recycled. We assume that this firm or industry is small relative to the total use of this material; thus, it can obtain virgin material feedstocks in whatever quantity it wishes at a constant price. This price is marked p_v and is shown as a horizontal line intersecting the demand curve at a quantity level q_0. But this material may also be obtained from recycled sources. Here, however, the procurement cost picture is more complicated. Reaching into the waste stream for recycled materials involves a number of special costs—of collection, separation, transportation,

---

[6] But remember the very first example discussed in Chapter 1, the "pay per throw" system being instituted by many communities in the last few years.

[7] A variety of public programs also have the effect of lowering the costs of virgin materials.

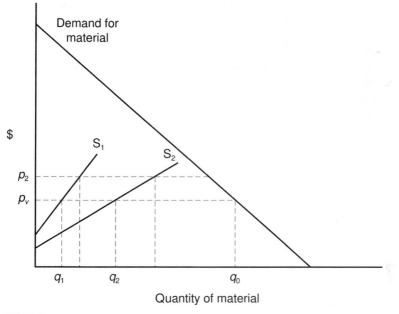

FIGURE 17-1
Use of Recycled Materials in Production.

reprocessing, etc. We assume that these costs increase with the amount of recycled material used. The supply curve of recycled material to this firm or industry is therefore an increasing function like S_1 or S_2. These two supply curves refer to situations with different recycling technology.[8] For S_1, costs go up relatively rapidly; S_2 increases much less rapidly. Consider for the moment the recycled material supply curve labeled S_1. If this is the one faced by this firm or industry, it will end up using q_1 of recycled materials. In other words, the producer will use recycled materials up to the point where its cost is equal to the price of virgin materials. Since the total materials use is q_0, the difference $(q_0 - q_1)$ consists of virgin materials.

The reuse ratio, the proportion of total materials coming from recycled feed-stock, is q_1/q_0. We can increase this ratio in three ways; increase q_1 while holding q_0 constant, decrease q_0 while holding q_1 constant, or both. Most community efforts at recycling are aimed at the first of these. For example, public curbside sorting and collection programs are ultimately aimed at making the supply of recycled material more abundant and, hence, less costly to producers. In terms of the model of Figure 17-1 these programs have aimed at shifting the recycled supply curve downward; say, from S_1 to S_2. If this is done, recycled materials use increases to q_2 and the recycling rate increases to q_2/q_0.

[8] In recent decades there have been rapid changes in the technologies of collecting, sorting, sifting, and reprocessing of various types of solid waste.

Another way of increasing the recycling ratio is to reduce the demand for materials in general, while holding constant the use of recycled materials. Diagrammatically this means shifting the whole materials demand curve back. This might be done, for example, by finding ways of producing output using fewer materials. It also might simply happen as consumers shift away from materials-intensive products to products that are less so. Finally, there is one way of simultaneously reducing total materials used and increasing recycled materials: Increase the price of virgin materials. If on Figure 17-1 we lift the virgin materials price to, say, p_2 through a tax, this will lead both to a move up the recycling supply curve and up the materials demand curve. This means an increase in the quantity of recycled materials and a decrease in the quantity demanded of materials in total. Raising the price on virgin materials with a tax thus has a double effect on the reuse ratio, since it works at both ends of the problem.

We can use this simple model to examine recent proposals for recycled-content standards in materials-using industries. Early enthusiasm for community recycling efforts led to situations in which the amounts of collected material outstripped technical ability to turn it into useful raw material, and in the absence of demand large quantities of sorted and collected material actually ends up in landfills. Thus, recent policy efforts have turned toward trying to increase the strength of demand for the recycled material. A number of states have thought to try this by introducing minimum-content standards for materials-using production processes. Minimum content standards require that all materials-using products manufactured or sold within a given state contain some specified percentage of recycled material.

We have talked many times of the cost-ineffectiveness of uniform standards in the face of heterogeneous emissions withholding costs. In the case of uniform content standards for materials, the same principle applies, but here the important factor is heterogeneity across materials-using firms in terms of the costs of obtaining and using recycled materials. For a truly cost-effective approach to the problem we would want to achieve equality across industries and materials in terms of *marginal recycling costs*. What this implies is having higher rates of recycled materials use by industries whose recycling costs are relatively low and lower rates for industries with relatively high recycling costs. One way to achieve this is to apply a tax on virgin materials. As we mentioned above, a tax of, say, $p_2 - p_v$ per unit of virgin materials, charged to all firms, would lead each to increase its recycling ratio in a way that satisfied the equimarginal principle. Another way would be to initiate a tradable permit system in the recycling market. A regulatory agency or statute would set an overall recycling objective for an industry, expressed in terms of the desired recycling rate. Each individual firm would then have three choices: (1) Increase its own recycling rate to the industry standard; (2) increase to a rate higher than the standard, and sell "excess" recycling permits; or (3) increase to less than the industry standard, buying however many permits are necessary to make up the difference.

In the real world, of course, things are a lot more complicated than they appear in our simple model. For example, one underlying assumption built into Figure 17-1 is that recycled material and virgin material are physically interchangeable. This is hardly ever true in practice. Although newspaper can be produced largely from recycled newspaper, some virgin newsprint is usually necessary to achieve minimum quality levels. The same is true of many recycled metals. It is also true that the recycling market, like any economic market, is very dynamic, whereas the model displayed in Figure 17-1 is essentially static; i.e., it is limited to events happening in a single time period. But producers normally look well into the future when making decisions. For example, even though current virgin materials prices are low, producers may nevertheless invest today in recycling and reprocessing works, if they *anticipate* that prices will increase in the future. But the simple model offers insight into basic recycling economics.

Consumer Recycling Decisions

It is sometimes easy to get the impression that in matters of solid waste the basic decision facing consumers is whether or not to recycle. But there are some prior decisions that are equally as important, decisions having to do with which particular goods to buy, and in what quantity. These decisions critically affect the total quantity of the solid waste stream and its composition. Subsequent recycling decisions determine how much of that waste stream ends up in the landfill.

To examine these choices we will use some illustrative benefit and cost numbers pertaining to two goods. Assume there are two similar products, but perhaps with different packaging, like bulk cereal and cereal in boxes, or drinks in plastic and drinks in glass containers. The data are in Table 17-5, and they apply to the situation of a single consumer. Goods A and B each sells for the same price, but one, because of handling convenience, has a higher value to this consumer. Of course for other consumers the numbers pertaining to "value to consumer" could be different. For this consumer the net value before disposal of these two goods is in favor of Good B.

Disposal Costs   We now introduce the disposal costs of materials coming with the product. We consider first the costs of disposal in the conventional way—in the community landfill. Disposal costs are in two parts, private and social. The private costs refer to the consumer's costs of handling and discarding the materials, while the social costs refer to the environmental damages caused by the material when disposed of in the community's landfill. The private disposal costs of the two containers are the same—the time it takes to bag up the trash and set it on the curb is the same no matter which product the consumer is dealing with. But the environmental costs for Good B are substantially above those of Good A, for example, because there is much more material involved, or because it uses a different type of material. We can now calculate the net benefits of the two goods for the consumer and for the community. Remember that the full social costs contain the costs borne by the individual consumer plus the other

TABLE 17-5
INDIVIDUAL AND COMMUNITY BENEFITS AND COSTS IN PRODUCT CHOICE AND
RECYCLING (numbers are assumed to be in cents)

	Product A	Product B
Purchase price	100	100
Value to consumer	140	160
Net value	40	60
Conventional (Landfill) Disposal Alternative		
Disposal costs		
Private	10	10
Social	10	40
Net benefits		
Private	30	50
Social	20	10
Recycling Alternative		
Disposal costs		
Private	10	40
Community transport	(cannot be recycled)	10
Environmental damage	10	0
Value of recovered material	0	20
Net benefits		
Private	30	20
Social	20	30

damage costs. Here we arrive at the nub of the problem, because from the individual's standpoint Good B is the preferred choice, while for the community Good A is the preferred choice. The environmental costs stemming from conventional disposal are essentially external costs; if consumers do not take them into account when making purchasing decisions, they will make choices that are best from their standpoint but not best from the perspective of the community.

Recycling   Let us now introduce recycling. The products are different in this respect. Product A cannot be recycled for technical reasons; thus, it will continue to be disposed of in the landfill. But Product B may be recycled, and the costs of doing so rest partly on consumers and partly on the community. There are private costs coming from the need to separate trash and handle the recycled goods in the home. The community also faces a transport cost, but offsetting this is the fact that the recycled material has a market value. These costs are shown in Table 17-5. With the items as indicated, we can calculate the benefits of the two goods in the presence of the recycling program. The net benefit of Product A stays the same, since it cannot be recycled. The net benefit of Product B is now substantially higher than it was before the recycling program, primarily because of the avoided environmental damage and the market value of the recycled material.

The Consumer's Choice   The consumer now has three alternatives: (a) Buy Product A, disposing of it in the community landfill; (b) buy Product B, recycling the associated material; and (c) buy Product B, but disposing of it in the landfill. We can tabulate the net benefits to individual and community as follows:

	Net benefits	
Option	Individual	Community
(a) Buy A	30	20
(b) Buy B, recycle	20	30
(c) Buy B, landfill	50	10

The individual's preferred choice is Product B without recycling, the community's preferred choice is B *with* recycling. The fundamental question is, What can we do to provide the incentive for the individual consumer to adopt the recycling alternative?

Consider one alternative that has been tried by many communities: mandatory recycling. We pass a local regulation making it illegal not to recycle the material from B if that product has in fact been purchased. That is, the ordinance requires that all purchased recyclable products must in fact be recycled. What this does, if it is enforced, is to take away option (c) from the consumer. So the consumer falls back on the next best alternative: buying the nonrecyclable Product A. This simple problem illustrates an important point: The recycling process starts back at the choice of purchase made by the consumer, and we have to look at the impacts of recycling ordinances on this purchase decision as well as on recycling decisions themselves. In the present case the mandatory recycling law has the effect of causing the consumer to shift purchasing away from recyclable products to nonrecyclable ones, thus substantially undermining the intent of the law.

Disposal Charges   A basic principle in environmental economics is that emission taxes can provide the incentive for polluters to adopt socially efficient rates of emissions. In the present situation the counterpart of emission taxes is consumer disposal charges. A completely efficient set of disposal charges would involve a charge on each item at a level equal to the social costs of disposal. A unit of Good A produces damages of 10¢, so its tax would be that much. The tax on a nonrecycled unit of Good B would be 40¢. For a recycled unit of B the tax is a little more complicated. If B is recycled, there is no environmental cost, but there is a community transportation cost of 10¢. But this is more than offset by the fact that the item has a 20¢ market value. Thus, the net tax is actually 10¢ − 20¢, or −10¢. The tax is actually a 10¢ payment to the consumer. If we levy these taxes on these products at the point of disposal, the net benefits of the various options to the individual consumer would now become: (a) 20¢, (b) 30¢, (c) 10¢, which are the same as the social net benefits of the previous tabulation. Now the consumer will choose (b), the recycling option. In effect, *these taxes have changed the pattern of private net benefits so that they are the same as community net benefits*. When this is done a consumer will have the incentive to (1) choose the product and (2) make the recycling decision, in ways that are efficient from the standpoint of the community.

In fact, a charge based on the social costs of disposal for each item is not going to be feasible in the real world; it would require authorities to evaluate the waste stream of each individual and charge according to the different items identified. What many communities are doing, rather, is to establish a single charge, per bag or can, of undifferentiated waste, and collecting separated and recyclable materials free. In this case the charge on nonseparated trash ought to be some average of the disposal costs of the various items in the waste stream. In our example, the social costs (in terms of environmental damages) of a unit of A are 10¢, and of a unit of B if not recycled, 40¢. If the authorities took an intermediate value, setting a charge of 25¢ per container thrown away, the private net benefits of the different alternatives would be: (a) 5¢, (b) 30¢, (c) 25¢. So in this case the tax would be sufficient to lead the consumer to buy B and recycle.[9] A tax much lower than this, however, would lead the consumer to buy B and dispose of it in the landfill, owing to the relatively high private costs of recycling.

A Deposit Program   We can look also at the effect of a *deposit program* on recyclable items. If a 40¢ deposit were put on item B, reflecting the damages done if it were thrown away rather than recycled, the array of net benefits for the individual would now be: (a) 30¢, (b) 20¢, (c) 10¢. The consumer refrains from throwing out the recyclable item, but also shifts back to (a), the nonrecyclable good. This is the same effect we saw earlier with mandatory recycling; the bottle bill leads this particular consumer to choose nonrecyclable items when shopping. One way around this is to have a deposit on *all* materials, equal to their disposal costs. For Good A, the nonrecyclable item, this essentially acts as a tax, and gives a result similar to the "perfect" tax discussed above.

We need to stress that these results depend on the particular numbers shown in Table 17-5. Some of these, like environmental damage costs and purchase price, would be the same for all consumers, but others, like private disposal costs, depend on the individual's own subjective valuation of the burdens of handling different types of products. These could differ among consumers and this could obviously lead to differences in response to various solid-waste policies. It is also quite true that many people obtain a certain amount of civic satisfaction from engaging in behavior that is efficient from the community's standpoint. But to get as much benefit as we can from recycling decisions made by consumers, we have to consider the benefits and costs of these decisions through their eyes.

[9] This is the essence of the "pay per throw" system that we discussed at the beginning of the book.

LAND-USE CONTROL POLICIES

Land-use issues, and the public control over land-use decisions, are also matters that historically have been left to the individual states and communities of the U.S. While in recent years we have seen certain federal initiatives, especially on the matter of wetlands preservation, the dominant perspective is still that land-use issues are primarily local issues and therefore require local policy responses. The environmental issues we have talked about heretofore have been about the management of flows of production and consumption residuals. We have discussed the various policy tools, standards, emission fees, TDPs, etc., to affect these residual flows. When it comes to land, the problem is somewhat different. The land surface of the earth is fixed in quantity, and human beings spread themselves around on it in accordance with varying incentive patterns and with varying impacts. The key problem, then, is how decisions are arrived at to devote particular pieces of land to particular human and nonhuman uses.

Since almost all environmental externalities have a spatial dimension, it might be tempting to think of all pollution as essentially a land-use issue. But while many of the large cases of air and water pollution are indeed spatial, they do not lend themselves to solutions through altered land-use patterns. The acid rain problem is not a land-use problem, for example. Certain local cases of environmental externalities, however, may be more closely related to decisions on land use. Local air pollution problems may be the result of transportation patterns produced by sprawling housing development. A community faced with noise pollution from a local airport may be able to manage it through land-use controls in the vicinity of the airport.

But many contemporary land-use issues are not pollution related; rather, they are about the human use of land that substantially reduces or destroys its environmental value. Within any localized region there are usually lands that have special environmental value, because of strategic ecological linkages or aesthetic values, or both. Some cases of this are:

- Wetlands, which provide important environments for plants and animals and are linked into other components of the ground and surface water system.
- Coastal lands, where scenic and recreational qualities are important.
- Critical habitats, where land-use patterns affect the health or survival of plant and animal species.
- Scenic and open land, where people may find vistas and experiences that have spiritual significance and recreational value.

To examine the economic logic of public and private land-use decisions let us focus on an example involving one particular piece of land. All land parcels are essentially unique and will have varying values in different uses, but we can use illustrative numbers to demonstrate the essence of the problem. The parcel is currently in open space, with all environmental values intact, and it is owned by a single individual. Suppose there are three mutually exclusive options for the parcel: (a) It may be developed without public restraints, (b) it may be preserved

TABLE 17-6
RETURNS AND COSTS OF VARIOUS LAND-USE OPTIONS

	Land use		
	Develop (a)	Preserve (b)	Develop with restrictions (c)
Returns			
Private	100	—	90
Public	—	50	—
Total	100	50	90
Costs			
Private	80	20	80
Public	50	—	10
Total	130	20	90
Net return			
Private	20	−20	10
Public	−30	30	0

in its current state, or (c) it may be developed but with certain restrictions set by the local environmental agency. The illustrative numbers in Table 17-6 show the returns and costs of these different courses of action. Naturally, when land-use decisions of this type are made, there is actually a stream of returns and costs off into the future, so the numbers in Table 17-6 in effect represent the *present values* of these streams of returns and costs.[10]

Let us first consider options (a) and (b). If the owner were to develop the land, he or she would realize a gross return of 100 and have construction costs of 80. But developing the land would have serious environmental costs; namely, the destruction of its ecological value, which we set at 50. We assume, and this is critical, that this lost ecological value is a loss to society but not a loss to the individual. There is no way for the landowner to package and sell this value, as it were. Thus, since there is no way for the owner to realize the ecological value of the land, the individual's decisions about using the land will be predicated on its private development value. The private net return is 20, while the full social return of developing the land is −30. In the absence of any public land-use policy the land would presumably be developed even though it represents a net loss to society.

It is instructive to look at it from the reverse perspective, the returns and costs of option (b): preservation. In this case private returns are nil, but public returns from the preserved ecological values of the land are 50. The cost in this case is

[10] For a discussion of the present-value concept see Chapter 6.

the forgone net return from developing the land, or 20. Thus, the net social returns from preservation are $50 - 20 = 30$.

We may now consider certain policy options. The most common local land-use tool is outright prohibition of certain land uses that are thought to have low or negative social returns, even though they may have positive private returns. This is done through the exercise of the *police power*, which is a power that communities have of prohibiting private activities that are detrimental to the wider public. The most common technique is *zoning*, in which communities rule out certain types of land uses where they would be destructive to the surrounding land values; e.g., factories in residential areas. Environmental restrictions on development also come under this heading, since these contribute to the health and welfare of the community. Thus, a police power approach to our problem would be simply to develop a zoning law or environmental preservation law that rules out option (a).

A major problem with a police power approach like this is that, although it may legally prohibit certain land uses like option (a), it does not change any of the numbers in the table, so it does not change any of the underlying incentives of the situation. An owner whose land has been subject to a development restriction by public authorities has much to gain by getting the authorities to relax the restraint. In fact it would make sense for the landowner in Table 17-6 to spend some portion of the expected net returns to try and get the authorities to reverse themselves.

Instead of outright prohibition the police power may be used to place conditions on development. For example, a developer might be required to leave a certain amount of open space, to avoid certain ecologically sensitive areas, or to install a public sewer system. This approach is sometimes called "incentive zoning." Table 17-6 depicts a third alternative, called "develop with restrictions," to capture this type of option. The owner is allowed to develop, but certain constraints are placed on this process, which have the effect of avoiding some of the ecological costs. Since the restrictions lower the developed value, the private net return is now only $90 - 80 = 10$. The social net return is now $90 - 90 = 0$, because all but 10 of the ecological costs have been avoided by the development restrictions.

The "Taking" Issue

One of the most contested issues in using local land-use controls for environmental protection purposes is the "taking" problem. The Fourteenth Amendment to the U.S. Constitution asserts that persons may not be deprived of their property without "due process of law." This requirement serves to restrict the exercise of the police power by local governments. A community may not simply invoke the police power to do anything it wishes. The police power may in general be exercised only when it is reasonable, clearly enhances public welfare, and is not arbitrary or discriminatory. The problem is in knowing when these conditions are met. In the example of Table 17-6, a local restriction that ruled out option (a) but permitted option (c) would lower the net private return from 20 to 10, thus lowering the private value of the land by that amount. Is this a valid exercise of the policy power?

A well-known recent case that went all the way up to the U.S. Supreme Court involved a coastal community. The community had put restrictions on the development of certain shoreline property, on the grounds that it was subject to flooding by the high water from ocean storms. The landowner sued, saying that the flood danger was exaggerated and that the regulations deprived him of the value obtainable by developing the property. The Supreme Court upheld the landowner.

A major difficulty with cases like this is that although private revenues and costs of land-use restrictions are usually known with accuracy, the same cannot be said about environmental values. In the example of Table 17-6, we assumed we knew exactly how much the environmental attributes were worth, but usually this is not true. So the courts have to try to balance known private values with unknown public environmental values. From the standpoint of public health, there may be little difficulty barring development in sensitive wetlands, on the grounds that these are linked into the hydrological systems on which many people depend for water supply.

But when public health is not so directly involved, things can be much less clear. Suppose that I own a particular farm in a community and that over time the people of the community have come to value the scenic qualities of my land. Clearly the land has environmental (scenic) value, but may the town pass a regulation saying that I can't develop it for that reason? In doing this, the town is essentially putting on me the entire burden of providing these scenic values.

One way around the taking issue is compensation to the landowner. A straightforward way of doing this is for a public agency or a private environmental group to purchase "in fee simple" the land in question. In the case of Table 17-6 a purchase price of 20 would just compensate the landowner for the lost development opportunities. The land is then taken out of the private market and its environmental values are preserved. This requires that the community or some private group have substantial financial resources. The Nature Conservancy, for example, is a private group, funded largely through contributions, that preserves sensitive land by outright purchase. But this option may be too expensive for many local communities faced with development pressures in their region. A less costly approach is to purchase just certain partial rights in the land, not the land in its entirety. In the case of Table 17-6, for example, the community might buy from the landowner just the right to undertake option (a), but not the right to pursue option (c). The value of this one right would be 10, the difference in net returns between the two options. This purchase of just the development right would preserve some, though not all, of the land's environmental values, but it may be a desirable course of action for a community faced with a shortage of resources.

GROUNDWATER PROTECTION

Groundwater supplies about a quarter of all water used in the U.S. Most of it is used in agriculture, but it is also a significant source of drinking water for many communities, especially those in rural areas. In recent years the quality of groundwater resources has been increasingly threatened from a variety of sources—agricultural runoff, industrial waste disposal, landfill leakage, underground storage tanks, etc. Groundwater resources are substantially different from surface water in terms of their regenerative capacity; once contaminated, groundwater aquifers are likely to be lost to use for a long time because of the very slow rate at which they are replenished.

Most groundwater pollutants stem from nonpoint-source emissions. As we have discussed many times, this essentially rules out any type of emission control policy that requires direct monitoring of emissions. Thus, groundwater pollution-control programs must focus on controlling the various practices and behaviors of sources that normally could be expected to threaten groundwater resources. To do this there is the full array of emission control policies, both CAC types and economic incentive strategies. Among the latter, for example, would be taxes on nitrogen fertilizers used by farmers, leading to lower rates of fertilizer use and therefore less nitrate runoff. Among the former are various types of technology specifications for underground waste disposal to reduce the probabilities of groundwater contamination. Among the states a wide array of protection programs have been undertaken, including performance standards for handling wastes in sensitive aquifer recharge areas; permit programs to govern large-scale wastewater absorption systems, spray irrigation systems, or land spreading of sewage sludge; regulations on bulk storage and waste transport facilities; and regulations on agricultural activities, particularly the use of fertilizers and chemicals.

Many states are moving in the direction of greater reliance on land-use zoning as a way of protecting groundwater aquifers. By ruling out, or regulating, various uses in the recharge areas, risks of contamination can be lowered. Florida has pioneered this effort, which is not surprising given the heavy reliance on groundwater of the large population in the southeastern part of that state. Nassau and Suffolk counties in New York have also adopted hydrologic zoning to protect critical groundwater resources.[11]

SUMMARY

In recent years state and local efforts have become more important in environmental policy matters. As greater attention shifts to problems of enforcing environmental policies and regulations, state-level efforts in this respect have become more critical. States have also served as the source of innovation in many

[11] Peter S. Tell, "Groundwater Protection Zones: United States and European Experiences," *International Environment Reporter*, March 1990, pp. 123–132.

areas of environmental policies, spurring federal efforts and trying out new ideas in the control of emissions. The leading role of California in fostering more aggressive air pollution control is especially notable.

States and localities have had the primary responsibility for solid-waste management, land-use controls, and the protection of groundwater resources. Community efforts at recycling are a major part of the effort to address solid-waste issues. We saw how recycling decisions depend on complex incentive situations facing consumers in their buying and disposal decisions and producers whose demands for recycled materials may lead them to reach into the solid-waste stream for sources of raw materials. Strong incentive situations also face local authorities when making land-use control decisions. Here the major issue is the change in land values produced by land-use regulations and the fine line between what may be considered a legitimate exercise of the police power and what is an unconstitutional "taking" of private property. These matters continue to evolve in the courts.

QUESTIONS FOR FURTHER DISCUSSION

1 Many communities have been successful in collecting recyclable material, but have been unable to find buyers for the recovered materials. How do you interpret this in terms of the concepts shown in Figure 17-1?
2 Another way of increasing the use of recycled material by industry is to subsidize its purchase of materials taken from the waste stream. How would you analyze this in terms of Figure 17-1?
3 How might the ideas used to reduce the costs of making the transition to lead-free gas (see Chapter 15) be adapted to the transition toward a situation in which a substantially larger proportion of the solid waste stream is recovered and recycled?
4 We alluded in this chapter to some of the advantages and disadvantages of pursuing environmental policy at the state level rather than the federal level. Do the same ideas apply when comparing state-level and community-level action? Consider this in the context of the municipal solid waste problem.
5 Many communities are instituting a "pay as you throw" system for solid waste. Discuss the equity implications of this type of system.

SELECTED READINGS

Black, Edward G.: "California's Community Right-to-Know," *Ecology Law Quarterly*, 16(4), 1989, pp. 1021–1064.
Conservation Foundation: *Groundwater Protection*, Washington, D.C., 1987.
Findley, Roger W., and Daniel A. Farber: *Environmental Law*, 2nd ed., West Publishing Company, San Francisco, 1988.
Fischel, William: *The Economics of Zoning Laws*, Johns Hopkins Press, Baltimore, Md., 1985.
Jaffe, Martin, and Frank DiNovo: *Local Groundwater Protection*, American Planning Association, Washington, D.C., 1987.
Jessup, Deborah Hitchcock: *Guide to State Environmental Programs*, Bureau of National Affairs, Inc., Washington, D.C., 1988.

Lennett, David J., and Linda E. Greer: "State Regulation of Hazardous Waste," *Ecology Law Quarterly*, 12(2), 1985, pp. 183–270.

Lester, James P., and Emmett N. Lombard: "The Comparative Analysis of State Environmental Policy," *Natural Resources Journal*, 30(2), Spring 1990, pp. 301–319.

Malone, Linda A.: *Environmental Regulation of Land Use*, Clark Boardman, New York, 1990.

Menell, Peter S.: "Beyond the Throwaway Society: An Incentive Approach to Regulating Municipal Solid Waste," *Ecology Law Quarterly*, 17(4), 1990, pp. 655–740.

Regens, James L., and Margaret A. Reams: "State Strategies for Regulating Groundwater Quality," *Social Science Quarterly*, 69(1), March 1988, pp. 53–69.

Ringquist, Evan J.: *Environmental Protection at the State Level*, Island Press, Washington, D.C., 1993.

U.S. Environmental Protection Agency: *Economic Incentives for Land Use Control* (EPA-600/5-77-001), Washington, D.C., 1977.

U.S. Office of Technology Assessment: *Facing America's Trash: What Next for Municipal Solid Waste?* Washington, D.C., 1989.

INTERNATIONAL ENVIRONMENTAL ISSUES

The prospects for the twenty-first century are for the world to continue to shrink and nations to become increasingly interconnected. These interactions will grow in environmental matters. Regional and global problems will demand greater levels of cooperation and more effective international institutions. As demonstrated by the 1992 "earth summit," problems of environmental degradation in developing countries and the relationships of growth and environmental values will become more important. As all countries struggle, to a greater or lesser extent, to manage their own environmental problems, greater value will attach to the exchange of information, technology, and policy experience. A look at this international experience can substantially deepen our perspectives on the nature of environmental issues and the way people have thought to address them.

We will first review some of the environmental policy efforts being made in other industrialized countries and in developing countries. We will then discuss several global environmental problems: stratospheric ozone depletion and the greenhouse effect. Finally, we will offer some perspective on the economics of international environmental agreements.

CHAPTER 18

ENVIRONMENTAL POLICIES IN OTHER INDUSTRIALIZED COUNTRIES

We begin by looking at experience in other industrialized countries of the East and the West. In the U.S. we have seen that there was a great burst of political energy in the early 1970s that launched many of the environmental initiatives at the federal level. Much the same took place in other countries; their primary environmental policies date from around the same time.

INTERNATIONAL COMPARISONS OF ENVIRONMENTAL QUALITY

Perhaps the best place to start is to look at several comparisons among countries in terms of environmental achievements. Good comparative data are not easy to obtain because the monitoring efforts of the countries have not been established with the primary goal of facilitating international comparisons. Each country collects and publishes its own data, using whatever bases, indices, and systems it finds most useful for its purposes. Thus, comparability is a problem. Efforts are slowly under way, especially among the European countries, to achieve some degree of uniformity in monitoring and data reporting. It is also the case that within any country environmental quality varies substantially among regions. In the U.S. southern California and other urban areas have severe air problems. In Germany there is the heavily industrial Ruhr Valley. Japan has the Tokyo–Osaka corridor. This means that international comparisons have to be made with care and confined to situations that are reasonably similar.

The most cogent comparisons are in terms of achieved levels of ambient quality. Table 18-1 shows comparative ambient SO_2 levels for six large cities around the world over the decade 1975–1985. At the beginning of this period Montreal had the lowest concentration, followed closely by New York. The figures for New York show a slight improvement over the decade, on the order of about 10 percent. Paris and London began the decade with much higher ambient levels of SO_2, but showed much larger improvement—roughly 50 percent. Berlin appears to fall into the same pattern. Perhaps the greatest success story is Tokyo, which started somewhat higher than North American

TABLE 18-1
AMBIENT LEVELS OF SO_2 FOR SIX MAJOR WORLD CITIES (annual average concentration, in $\mu g/m^3$)

	U.S. New York	France Paris	Germany Berlin	U.K. London	Japan Tokyo	Canada Montreal
1975	43.7	114.8	N/A	118.7	60.0	40.6
1980	38.0	89.0	90.0	69.0	48.0	41.0
1981	39.5	71.2	77.4	71.8	N/A	N/A
1982	39.1	67.6	81.9	57.3	42.2	N/A
1983	36.1	61.4	66.6	49.0	29.3	N/A
1984	38.4	57.0	N/A	46.2	26.9	N/A
1985	N/A	54.3	N/A	40.7	N/A	N/A

Source: U.S. Environmental Protection Agency, *International Comparison of Air Pollution Control,* Washington, D.C., 1988, pp. 11–12; as presented in Raymond J. Kopp, Paul R. Portney, and Diane E. DeWitt, *International Comparisons of Environmental Regulation,* Resources for the Future, Washington, D.C., 1990, p. 11.

cities but ended the decade with by far the lowest ambient concentrations of all the cities.

Table 18-2 shows some comparative data on various environmental measures for selected OECD (Organization for Economic Cooperation and Development) countries. The first two columns pertain to water pollution measures. Per-capita expenditures on water pollution control in the mid-1980s varied from a low of $31 in Canada to a high of $71 in West Germany. The percentage of population served by at least secondary treatment facilities varied from 37 percent in Norway to 94 percent in Sweden. These are substantial differences among countries. We defer until the next section a discussion of how to interpret these differences.

The third column of Table 18-2 shows data on fertilizer application in some of the countries. Application of fertilizer is associated with fertilizer runoff and consequent water pollution. But since this is a nonpoint-source emission, it is basically impossible to measure accurately the quantity of pollutant runoff. Thus, the next best thing is to look at the comparative rates of fertilizer application. Note the particularly high rates of use in European countries (Netherlands, U.K., and "West" Germany) and the relatively low rates in Canada and the U.S. These differences clearly relate to differences in population pressure and the amounts of cultivable land in the various countries. Finally, the last column in the table shows data on noise pollution. You can clearly see why concern about noise pollution has been much higher in Europe than in the U.S.

Table 18-3 contains some revealing data on emissions in a variety of European countries. It shows emissions per $1,000 of gross domestic product for individual countries in Eastern Europe, the former USSR, and the European Economic Community as a whole. The interest in these numbers stems from the comparison of emissions performance in Western Europe with that of the former Socialist countries of Eastern Europe. The EEC performance is markedly better in SO_2 and

TABLE 18-2

SELECTED ENVIRONMENTAL DATA, OECD COUNTRIES

Country	Per-capita expenditures for water pollution control[a]	Percentage of population served by secondary or tertiary water treatment facilities[b]	Tons of fertilizer applied per square kilometer of agricultural land	Percentage of population exposed to noise greater than 65 dB from road traffic[c]
Canada	31	66	2.6	7
Denmark	66	90	—	—
France	44	—[d]	13.3	16
Germany[e]	71	88	20.6	13
Italy	—	—	7.6	18
Japan	60	—	13.7	30
Netherlands	59	82	46.7	—
Norway	48	37	—	—
Spain	—	—	5.5	—
Sweden	52	94	7.6	—
United Kingdom	39	78	20.9	11
United States	54	74	5.1	7

[a]Mid-1980s, in U.S. dollars, at 1980 prices and exchange rates.
[b]Applies to late 1980s.
[c]Average sound level over a given period, normally 6 A.M. to 10 P.M.
[d]Dashes indicate data are not available.
[e]"West" Germany only.

Source: Organization for Economic Cooperation and Development, *The State of the Environment,* Paris, 1991, pp. 58–59, 180, 217, and 241.

TABLE 18-3

ENVIRONMENTAL EMISSIONS IN EASTERN EUROPE, USSR, AND EEC

Country	Emissions per $1,000 of GDP				
	Sewage (km^3)	PM[a] (kg)	Gases (m^3)	Solid waste (kg)	SO$_2$ (kg)
Bulgaria	195	—	17.4[b]	—	20
Czechoslovakia	54	17.6	54.1	—	38
GDR	39	13.3	47.4	158	29
Hungary	27	17.7	65.3	93	37
Poland	86	23.3	65.0	1,251	30
Romania	—	—	30.0[b]	—	33
Former USSR	145	—	52.4[c]	—	20
EEC[f]	—	1.4[d]	25.5[e]	249[e]	7

[a]Particulate matter.
[b]1982, SO$_2$ only.
[c]1981, includes gases and particulate matter.
[d]Excluding Ireland and U.K.
[e]Excluding Ireland.
[f]European Economic Community.

Source: Zbigniew Bochniarz, Statement in "U.S. Environmental Initiatives in Eastern Europe," hearings before the Subcommittee on Transportation and Hazardous Materials of the Committee on Energy and Commerce, U.S. Congress, House of Representatives, 101st Congress, 2nd Session, April 23, 1990, pp. 62–63.

particulate emissions and somewhat better in emissions of "gases." Its solid-waste "emissions," on the other hand, are higher than those for the GDR and Hungary, though nowhere near as high as those shown for Poland. In fact, the number for Poland is hard to believe.[1]

Interpreting Differences in Environmental Performance

We must take care in interpreting these comparative environmental data.[2] The first reaction might be to interpret different environmental indices as indicating the effort each country has put into pollution control. But a moment's reflection shows that this is not necessarily the case. Differences in ambient environmental quality between different countries can be explained in essentially two ways: (1) as differences in the efficient, or desired, levels of ambient quality and/or (2) as differences in the extent to which each country, through policy and its enforcement, have achieved these efficient levels.

These are depicted in Figure 18-1, which shows three familiar marginal damage/marginal abatement cost diagrams, with ambient quality indexed on the horizontal axes. Suppose that in comparing ambient quality levels in two countries, you find two points like e_1 and e_2 indicated on each diagram in the figure. Panel (a) shows that this could be the result of differences between the two countries in terms of their marginal abatement costs, given the same preferences for environmental quality in the two countries. In the short run this could be the result of different technological means for pollution control available in the two countries. But in the long run this factor would be less important, since pollution-control technology is mobile; whatever is available in one country can be made available in the other. Of course, the difference in marginal abatement cost functions could arise also because one country has adopted more cost-effective environmental control policies than the other. Other factors may also be at work. As we have stated many times, ambient conditions are the result of emissions *and* the assimilative capacity of the environment. So a country that has achieved low emissions may still suffer relatively high ambient concentrations because of the way its environment works: Similar emissions in Mexico City and New York will produce much dirtier air in the former because of its prevailing meteorological patterns. By the same token, similar ambient levels do not imply that countries have made similar efforts to control emissions, because in one the assimilative capacity of the environment may be greater.[3] Another real possibil-

---

[1] Solid-waste data are notoriously difficult to interpret and compare because different reporting entities, even different cities within the same country, will often define the term differently.

[2] The same might be said about comparisons among different regions of the same country.

[3] For example, there has been a running dispute between Great Britain and the other members of the European Commission (EC) over the basis of water pollution control. It stems from the fact that rivers in Great Britain tend to be short and have very substantial assimilative capacity, while those on the continent are longer, with less capacity. Thus, Great Britain has been in favor of an ambient standard approach to water-quality improvement within the EC, while other member states have leaned toward emission standards.

FIGURE 18.1
Interpreting International Differences in Ambient Pollution Levels.

ity is that there are differences in economic circumstances of the two countries—one relatively rich and the other relatively poor—so that the opportunity cost of pollution control in terms of forgone conventional income is higher in one than in the other. Note that the country with the highest ambient concentration may actually have spent more in total on abatement costs than the country with the lower concentration. We will have more to say on this point in Chapter 19 on the relationship of environmental quality to economic development.

Panel (b) depicts the case where the difference between e_1 and e_2 is explained by differences in the damages flowing from ambient pollution loads in the two countries. This could stem, for example, from real differences in willingness to pay for pollution control by people in similar economic and social circumstances—i.e., environmental quality as a matter of tastes and preferences—or from the fact that the two countries give a different priority to environmental quality. As an example of the former, consider the following case, which actually applies to the siting of an industrial plant that has some small but nonzero probability of catastrophic accident:

> Recently California and the United Kingdom have approved sites for Liquefied Energy Gas (LEG) terminals. In this, and perhaps this alone, they are the same. After a long drawn-out process in which it proved impossible to approve any of the proposed sites, California finally, with the help of a new statute passed expressly for the purpose, was able to give approval for an LEG facility at the remotest of all the sites on the list of possibles: Point Conception. Scotland has a longer coastline than California and most of the country is very sparsely populated (less than 25 persons to the square mile) and yet the approved site, at Mossmorran and Braefoot Bay on the Firth of Forth, lies within the most densely populated part of the entire country (with a population density of between 250 and 500 persons per square mile). Moreover, laden tankers will pass within a mile or so of Burntisland (an industrial town) and sometimes within four miles of Edinburgh—the capital city of Scotland! If the California siting criteria (explicit in Statute 1081) were to be applied to the Scottish case it would be quite impossible to approve the Mossmorran/Braefoot Bay site, and if the United Kingdom criteria (implicit in the Mossmorran/Braefoot Bay approval) were to be applied to the California case, any of the suggested sites could be approved, which means that the terminal would go to the first site to be suggested—Los Angeles harbor.[4]

Finally, panel (c) depicts the situation of different enforcement efforts. While both have the same desired level of ambient quality, one country has devoted more resources to enforcement and thus its actual level is lower. Throughout this book we have talked about the importance of enforcement. Most developed countries have significant antipollution laws on the books; most also have significant enforcement problems, as is illustrated in the following comments:

---

[4] Michael Thompson, "A Cultural Basis for Comparison," in Howard Kunreuthen and Joanne Linnerooth (eds.), *Risk Analysis and Decision Process, The Siting of Liquefied Energy Facilities in Four Countries*, Springer, Berlin, 1983, p. 233.

Some people here say the problem is that there is not an adequate body of environmental law in Ireland. But that is not true. There are 55 or so laws that affect what private industry can do to the environment. They are just not enforced. You can take it for granted that every single law is not being adequately enforced. Local authorities and corporations, too, actually have a pretty good record for responding to citizen complaints about pollution, since by then it is a political matter. But what you very rarely find is a local authority playing watchdog, checking up to see if regulations are being followed.[5]

In Spain, we have beautiful laws to protect the environment, but nobody is really complying with them. Industry knows that the chances are not very great that the government is going to suddenly crack down and begin enforcing the laws. They say they will gradually get tougher, but in my opinion it would be better to have fewer and simpler regulations and get a better record of compliance from the very beginning.[6]

Of course, when making comparisons among countries all three factors will normally come into play: abatement costs, damages, and enforcement efforts.

ENVIRONMENTAL POLICY IN OTHER COUNTRIES

Regardless of where one lives, there is much to learn through comparing one's own experience with that of others. The rest of this chapter examines some of the distinguishing environmental policy efforts of developed countries other than the U.S. It is not intended to try and offer a catalogue of events in each country; this would be impossible in the space we have, and also because environmental issues and responses are changing so rapidly that a catalogue of this type would quickly be out of date. Instead, we will try to single out particularly noteworthy policies or trends that characterize environmental policy in particular countries or groups of countries.

General Considerations

It is accurate to say that all countries rely heavily on "command and control" as the primary approach to pollution control. This means administrative determinations of such things as what technologies are to be installed, what emissions are to be, where firms may locate, how buildings and equipment should be designed, what fuels and inputs may be used, how certain substances are to be handled, etc. The institutions set up to do this, and the degree of participation encouraged and allowed by other groups, vary greatly from country to country. In most countries, some concept has been adopted to establish the technological

---

[5] Interview with Irish water-quality official, quoted in H. Jeffrey Leonard, *Pollution and the Struggle for World Product*, Cambridge University Press, Cambridge, England, 1988, p. 211.

[6] Interview with a private company manager for energy conservation and environmental affairs, quoted in Ibid.

level(s) on which to base command-and-control decisions. In Great Britain it is "best practicable means," which refers to "reasonably practicable and technically possible to prevent the emission of gases and render these discharges harmless."[7] Germany relies on the basic idea that pollution-control programs must involve "state-of-the-art" technology. In Sweden the underlying decision criterion is to choose ". . . what is technically feasible using the most effective technical devices and methods that are available in the area in question."[8] Italy has a standard calling for emissions reductions to ". . . the lowest level possible through available technologies."[9] As we have mentioned several times in previous chapters, this approach actually allows regulators to make implicit trade-offs between damage reduction and technical and economic feasibility.

National Political Styles in Environmental Policy

From our discussion of the different policy options available in environmental policy, one might get the impression that policy matters are primarily technical exercises in picking the right approach to match the environmental problem being addressed. But a number of studies have shown that environmental policies in different countries are also a reflection of their unique political cultures and institutions. In one study of air pollution policy in Sweden and the U.S., the author characterized the differences between the two countries as the difference between the hare and the tortoise.[10] The U.S. was the hare, with bursts of speed followed by pauses and rests, while Sweden was the tortoise, with slower but steadier progress. His side-by-side comparison of U.S. and Swedish policy approaches is the following:

U.S.	Sweden
1. Statutory ambient standards.	1. Nonstatutory emission guidelines.
2. Strict timetables for compliance.	2. Compliance timetables set on basis of economic feasibility.
3. Technology-forcing emission standards.	3. Adjustments of standards to technological developments.

In general, the U.S. style, at least during the 1970s covered in this study, emphasized formal and sharply defined objectives written into public laws, after much political wrangling, with later administrative compromises and delays to

---

[7] Roy Gregory, *The Price of Amenity: Five Studies in Conservation and Government*, Macmillan, London, 1971, p. 12.

[8] Göran A. Persson, "Sweden," in Edward J. Kormondy (ed.), *International Handbook of Pollution Control*, Greenwood Press, Westport, Conn., 1989, pp. 219–232.

[9] Giancarlo Pinchera, Silvia Brini, and Mario Cirillo, "Italy," in *European Environmental Yearbook*, 4th ed., Doc Ter, Institute for Environmental Studies, Milan, 1990, p. 415.

[10] Lennart J. Lundquist, *The Hare and the Tortoise: Clean Air Policies in the United States and Sweden*, University of Michigan Press, Ann Arbor, 1980.

accommodate reality. The Swedish approach was to set policy with far less public fanfare, negotiating voluntary agreements that were based on technical and economic feasibility. Despite these differences, the changes through time in ambient air quality were quite similar between the two countries. He concludes: "At this point, the overall result seems very much to be a dead heat. Neither of the two countries seems to have been remarkably more successful than the other in relieving its citizens from the blight of air pollution."[11]

Another interesting study has been done on the introduction of vinyl-chloride (VC) standards into industrial workplaces. VC is used to make polyvinyl chloride (PVC), which in turn is shaped into thousands of products—piping, flooring, food wrapping, credit cards, baby pacifiers, shoes, medical devices, etc. High levels of VC exposure in the workplace were identified in the early 1970s as a cause of serious health conditions among workers, particularly cancer. So, around this time many countries addressed the task of reducing VC exposure in plants producing PVC. The study was a comparison of the way the policy process worked in five countries: France, Great Britain, Japan, the U.S., and West Germany.[12] The basic contrast is between the adversarial style of the U.S. and the cooperative negotiating style of the others. The author characterizes the U.S. effort in the following way:

> . . . the key decisions in the adversarial case were made by agency officials and judges on the basis of virtually secret deliberations. Industry and labor did not cooperate but instead took steps to impede and discredit each other. Industry and government behaved similarly. Lawyers were active from start to finish, and no intermediaries acted as buffers among the parties. The various parties had only an indirect influence on the major decisions, and this was largely confined to public, highly publicized, courtlike hearings. Basic information was communicated through documents, and cost/benefit considerations were not an explicit part of the agency's decision process. In the end, OSHA issued its final regulations and required that industry achieve—under penalty of law—a very strict standard, one which exceeded the industry's technical capability at the time it was promulgated.[13]

By contrast, the cooperative styles of standard setting are characterized in the following way:

> . . . the parties involved directly influenced the critical decisions and actually made many of them. They achieved consensus through negotiations and discussions among middle-level officials over a period of several years. There were important intermediaries, and very few lawyers, involved in the process. Representatives of the major parties developed personal relationships in small working groups. Meetings were held in private—informally, and without rigid timetables. The working parties explicitly discussed cost and benefit. In the end, the decisions that emerged from these multipar-

---

[11] Ibid., p. 194.
[12] Joseph L. Badaracco, Jr., *Loading the Dice, A Five-Country Study of Vinyl Chloride Regulation*, Harvard Business School Press, Boston, 1985.
[13] Ibid., pp. 124–125.

tite discussions were less formal, they followed technology, and they included flexible open-ended recommendations that companies should seek to achieve the lowest feasible levels of VC exposure.[14]

Having established these two styles, however, the results show that the ambient workplace exposure standards arrived at in the adversarial process (the U.S.) were stricter than those established through the cooperative process.

A more recent comparative work looked at the environmental policy process in the U.S. and Great Britain. The author concludes that U.S. policy is based on formal rules and strict enforcement, while in Great Britain there is more emphasis on voluntary compliance. But, he concludes, these two approaches led to "roughly" similar environmental outcomes.[15] The British approach, along with similar styles in other European countries, is likely to shift over time more toward formal pollution-control directives and enforcement as a part of the European Commission's efforts to harmonize the pollution-control laws in the various member countries.

The U.S. approach also contrasts with that of Japan. Japanese environmental policy is based on a series of ambient standards that represent objectives, together with specific emission standards to move toward those objectives. National, generic emission standards are set, but at the local, or prefecture, level, particular emission standards are worked out on a source-by-source basis. This approach involves two characteristics that are specific to the Japanese experience. One is a high degree of negotiation between local pollution-control authorities and polluting sources, the results of which are to produce emission standards that are to some extent specific to each source. The other feature is the large amount of "administrative guidance." According to the basic national water pollution-control law, any operating unit that is the source of water-based emissions must submit a detailed plan showing the location, timing, type, etc., of emissions, and the methods and technologies to be used to control these emissions. Local pollution-control authorities then become heavily involved in the administrative guidance of these plans, along with the regular plant operators. The Japanese experience includes much more discretion at the local level. Pollution-control agreements may be struck between local authorities and firms. At first,

. . . many contracts were simply "gentlemen's agreements" (shinshi kyotei). For example, many early agreements declared that a company had an abstract duty to prevent pollution, to supply information, or to cooperate with local officials in a factory inspection. The company simply promised to take feasible and "appropriate" measures to prevent pollution. Such contracts in most cases did not contain provisions to handle violations.[16]

---

[14] Ibid., p. 124.
[15] David Vogel, *National Styles of Regulation, Environmental Policy in Great Britain and the United States*, Cornell University Press, Ithaca, N.Y., 1986.
[16] Julian Gresser, Koichiro Fujikura, and Aiko Morishima, *Environmental Law in Japan*, MIT Press, Cambridge, Mass., 1981, p. 248.

But more recently, local agreements have started to be

> . . . drafted more precisely, and are richer in content. For example, many agreements require companies to meet emission or effluent standards stricter than national standards; others stipulate that a factory use special low sulfur fuel; some require the use of the most advanced pollution prevention technology, contain stipulations on factory operations, or provide for inspection of the factory. In some cases these contracts also authorize drastic enforcement measures like stop-work orders, emergency enforcement by proxy, strict liability for damages, fines, cancellation of a contract (where a sale of land between local government and a factory is involved), and as previously mentioned, interruption of the municipal water supply upon notice of violation.[17]

It needs to be stressed that these differences in style and institutions, though they may sound significant, may not have significant impacts on the levels of ambient quality actually achieved. They should not be interpreted as better or worse styles from among which a country may choose. Each national style is unique, stemming from a country's own political culture, and the effectiveness of policy has to be considered within the context of these particular styles.

Statutory Laws for Compensating Victims of Pollution

Many countries have common law systems whereby individuals who have been injured by the pollution of some other individual can sue for damages. The fact-finding and award of compensation are then worked out in courts of law. In recent years also various statutory provisions have been enacted to make hazardous waste dumpers, or oil spillers, liable for damage they cause. But in several countries explicit statutes allow for individuals who have been damaged by pollution to collect compensation.

In Japan the compensation statute enacted in 1973 is called *The Law for the Compensation of Pollution-Related Health Injury*. The law establishes an administrative structure and a health certification procedure, whereby victims living in designated parts of the country can be compensated for medical expenses and lost earnings from specific, officially designated, pollution-related diseases. These diseases are minamata (mercury poisoning), itai-itai (cadmium poisoning), chronic arsenic poisoning, emphysema, chronic bronchitis, asthma, and asthmatic bronchitis. The effect of this law is to replace what in many countries would be a piecemeal process of individual court cases with an overall, centrally directed system for compensating those damaged by pollution. Although it is probably much less expensive than a case-by-case court approach, it still has many of the same problems; for example, determining whether health cases are in fact pollution related, establishing fair compensation levels, and so on.

The incentive effects of this approach may also be questioned. In a system where victims are free to sue particular companies for compensation of pollution-related disease, there is presumably a direct incentive for polluters to take

---

[17] Ibid.

steps to reduce their potential liability. But this incentive may be quite weak if a firm is just one among many that contribute to a particular case of pollution, because here the public-good nature of pollution works against individual responsibility. In the Japanese system the direct link between the behavior of individual firms and its compensation payments is broken. The fund from which victims are compensated is derived from taxes on polluters, especially on SO_2 emissions. The tax rate varies by regions, but is the same for all sources within the same region. The tax is not set, however, at a level equal to full marginal damages from emissions, and thus does not have the emissions-reducing incentive of a tax, as we have discussed earlier. The tax is established as a revenue source to get sufficient funds to cover compensation payments. Theoretically, this would be a reasonably efficient tax if compensation covered all damages. But the law specifies that only medical costs and lost wages may be compensated, which probably understates total damages by a substantial margin. The part of the law dealing with compensation for air pollution damages was terminated in 1988 as a result of pressure from industry and finance interests. Their view was that since ambient standards were then being met, there was no further need for compensation.[18]

A law of compensation for pollution damage also exists in the Netherlands. The compensation is paid from a special fund at whose expense ". . . any person suffering damage which is due to air pollution occurring above the territory of the Netherlands, and which for reasons of equity shall not be borne by that person, may be granted, on application, compensation."[19]

Guiding Principles of Pollution Control

In various countries around the world authorities have sought to adopt governing principles for the design of pollution-control policies. In Japan pollution-control efforts were initially developed under the principle of "harmonization," which was essentially a requirement that pollution-control laws be "harmonized" with the requirements of economic growth. In China, new industrial construction is supposed to be pursued within the principle of "three at the same time." Each new construction plan is supposed to contain a special section on environmental protection showing how pollution-control methods will be designed, installed, and operated.[20]

Countries of the Organization for Economic Cooperation and Development (OECD) have sought to pledge their allegiance to what is called the "polluter

[18] Ken'ichi Miyamoto, "Japan" in *European Environmental Yearbook*, 4th ed., Doc Ter, Institute for Environmental Studies, Milan, 1990.

[19] Alfred Rest, "Responsibility and Liability for Transboundary Air Pollution Damage," in Cees Flinterman, Barbara Kwiatkowska, and Johan G. Lammers (eds.), *Transboundary Air Pollution, International Legal Aspects of the Co-operation of States*, Martinus Nijhoff Publishers, Dordrecht, Holland, 1986, p. 324.

[20] Rui Lin Jin and Wen Liu, "Environmental Policy and Legislation in China," in *Proceedings of the Sino-American Conference on Environmental Law*, Natural Resource Law Center, University of Colorado School of Law, Boulder, Colo., 1989, p. 173.

pays principle" (PPP). This principle states that it is the polluters themselves who should bear the cost of measures to reduce pollution to levels specified by public authorities. While this may sound like a rule based on ethical considerations, it is really grounded in political economics. It is meant to rule out situations where governments subsidize pollution-control expenditures of firms or industries in order to give them an economic advantage over competitors who must pay their own compliance costs. This is regarded as especially important among the closely competing firms and industries of the countries of Europe. There are exceptions allowed to the PPP in certain cases of undue economic hardship, short-term transition periods, and cases that have no significant impacts on international trade and investment. Since most countries, in OECD as elsewhere, subsidize pollution reduction to a greater or lesser degree, it has been necessary for political diplomats to find ways of reconciling principle and reality. In general, this has been done by defining the PPP abstractly enough that it can be held compatible with a wide number of arrangements.

Emission Charges

In some countries emission charges have been widely used for many years. This is especially the case in Europe. In recent years many governments in Europe have been moving toward a greater use of charges. Our discussion of emission taxes in Chapter 12 focused on taxes as a means of bringing about cost-effective emission reductions. These might be called "incentive" taxes or, as they are sometimes called in Europe, "balancing" taxes. The emission taxes employed in Europe are not incentive taxes of this type. Rather, they are employed primarily to raise money that can then be used to subsidize pollution-control activities of public and private organizations.

This is depicted in Figure 18-2, which shows the marginal abatement cost of a single polluter. The initial emission level is e_1, and the authorities set a maximum target of e^* for the firm. An emission tax rate of t^* would provide the incentive needed to bring about a reduction of emissions to e^*. But this would entail a substantial tax obligation for the firm. Instead, the authorities establish a charge at a rather low level; for example, t_1. This has very modest incentive effects; it leads the firm to reduce emissions from e_1 to e_2. But it provides a tax revenue to the regional agency equal to the cross-hatched area. This amount, together with the sums from other water polluters who are taxed in the same fashion, is used to subsidize the installation of water pollution-control efforts among these and other sources. The tax is justified because it is a good source of funds needed for the subsidy program, not because it provides incentives for polluters to reduce their emissions.[21]

Although this is a tax program, the real incentive effects, if there are any, are

---

[21] The emphasis on revenue raising is so primary that emissions to be taxed are often estimated rather than measured exactly. But this is not as controversial as it might be because the tax rates are low and because the tax revenues are recycled back into the industry or region from which the taxes were collected.

FIGURE 18-2
Emission Charges in Europe.

in the subsidies. We saw earlier that subsidies, if they were given out at a common rate per unit of emissions reduced, would meet the criterion of cost-effectiveness. There is no evidence that this is actually the way the European programs work, however. Rather, regional pollution-control authorities, such as the Agences Financieres de Bassin in France and the Genossenschaften in Germany, establish budgets each year that include the various projects and programs to be supported, then set the tax at whatever level is needed to raise enough money to cover these plans.

In recent years many European countries have moved even more strongly in the direction of revenue-raising emission taxes. Germany is planning a tax on hazardous wastes. France has recently enacted a tax on SO_2 and NO_x from power plants and other industrial firms. Italy has a plastic bag tax, 90 percent of which is waived if the bags are biodegradable. Denmark has instituted a tax on building materials (e.g., sand and gravel) to encourage recycling. Spain is planning taxes on waterborne emissions. But perhaps the most important new source of revenue will be carbon, or CO_2, taxes, which many European countries are contemplating. These are justified on the basis of the global-warming problem, though it has to be remembered that these are primarily revenue-raising rather than incentive taxes.

Environmental Analysis

Although the U.S. is probably the leader in developing techniques for measuring the social benefits of environmental improvements, significant progress is also being made in Europe. The control of air and water pollution there is complicated by the presence of many international boundaries in a relatively small geographical area. Efforts at harmonizing environmental laws, spearheaded by the European Economic Commission, can be helped along by the accumulation of results of benefit-measurement studies.

German scholars have sought to measure losses in agricultural and forest outputs resulting from decreased yields caused by air pollution. Air pollution damages have also been measured through increased expenditures for maintenance, replacement, and cleaning of buildings and windows in high emissions areas.[22] European environmental economists have been interested in measuring the damages of noise pollution. A study in Switzerland sought to measure these damages by looking at the negative effects of traffic noise on house prices. A study in the Netherlands looked at rent levels. In that country renters of houses and apartments may sometimes obtain reductions in their monthly rent payments if they are exposed to high noise levels. The value of these rent reductions indicates the extent of damages. Travel cost methods have also been used to estimate the recreational value of environmental resources. In France, for example, this approach was used to estimate damages caused by the grounding of the tanker Amoco Cadiz in 1978.[23]

European environmental economists are turning increasingly to contingent valuation (CV) methods to assess the benefits of improvements in environmental quality, although these results are not as widely accepted among policy administrators as they are beginning to be in the U.S.[24] Residents of Berlin were asked how much they would be willing to pay for better air quality, as specified in several alternative possibilities—e.g., the avoidance of more severe air pollution, or an improvement that would make air quality on normal days as good as it currently was on holidays. In Norway, researchers have used CV methods to investigate the benefits produced when the level of acidity was reduced in certain lakes heavily used for fishing.[25] In Sweden, a CV study was done to estimate the visual benefits people get from a scenic agricultural landscape.[26]

ENVIRONMENTAL POLICY IN SOCIALIST COUNTRIES

It may be tempting to think that Socialist economic systems would be better than market economies in managing environmental quality issues because they in-

[22] O. J. Kuik, F. H. Oosterhuis, H. M. A. Jansen, K. Holm, and H.-J. Ewers, *Assessment of Benefits of Environmental Measures*, Graham and Trotman for the Commission of the European Communities, London, 1992, pp. 37–88.

[23] F. Bonnieux and P. Rainelli, *Catastrophe écologique et dommages économiques*, Institut national de la recherche agronomique, Paris, 1991.

[24] O. J. Kuik et al., *Assessment of Benefits of Environmental Measures*, p. 29.

[25] S. Navrud, "Estimating Social Benefits of Environmental Improvements from Reduced Acid Deposition: A Contingent Valuation Survey," in H. Folmer and E. van Ierland (eds.), *Valuation Methods and Policy Making in Environmental Economics*, Elsevier, Amsterdam, 1989, pp. 69–102.

[26] L. Drake, *The Nonmarket Value of the Swedish Agricultural Landscape*, Swedish University of Agricultural Sciences, Department of Economics, Uppsala, 1987.

volve pervasive central direction over all economic decisions, Administrative agencies, apparently with control over all the important variables, could make sure that all "externalities" were properly accounted for in production planning, and plant managers would be directed to pursue courses of action that ensured efficient levels of emissions and ambient environmental quality.

It has not worked out this way, however. Not only have centrally planned economies failed miserably in environmental matters, but their failures even in basic economic planning and administration have led their citizens to move toward market systems. With the opening up of the former Soviet Union and the countries of Eastern Europe, it has become apparent that the state systems have produced extreme environmental damages in many regions. Large environmental assets have been seriously degraded, and in many places ambient air and water quality was allowed to get bad enough to have severe repercussions on human health.

To some extent this is because of the basic philosophy of the political leaders, coupled with a closed political system, and to some extent it relates to the perverse incentives built into the concept of planning. Central economic planning requires that economic power and political power be merged in the same institutions and authorities. Thus, economic decisions—how and where resources are to be used—are made by reference to what their implications are for the continuation and consolidation of political power. Economic production is needed to buttress political power. Efforts to regulate that production have the potential to reduce that power. Thus, in the choice between economy and environment, the winner will normally be production.

One aspect of this power relationship has been the lack of avenues for local groups to protest environmental damages and bring about changes in production plans. This hinged importantly on the lack of public information on environmental matters. Communist regimes were reluctant to collect, tabulate, and publish data on the state of environmental problems in their countries. Thus, it was impossible for groups to monitor environmental damages and "lobby" for change.[27] Instead, environmental issues were "buried under mountains of paper and streams of declarations and statements."[28]

Incentive problems also are important. In a centrally planned economy, each enterprise and industry is programmed into the plan and is assigned certain output and input targets. Once the plan is adopted, it imparts great inflexibility to the economic system. For pollution-control equipment to be installed in a firm, for example, the entire plan had to be reworked, with new input and output targets. In a market economy, the market would adjust to the new pollution-control costs; prices would adjust in related markets, and inputs and outputs would be adjusted in response. This flexibility simply was not possible in centrally planned economies. Only if the environmental problem constitutes a dire emergency is there likely to be any response. In the former USSR, for example, the

---

[27] Cynthia B. Schultz and Tamara Raye Crockett, "Economic Development, Democratization, and Environmental Protection in Eastern Europe," *Environmental Affairs*, 18(1), Fall 1990, pp. 53–84.
[28] Ibid., p. 63.

environmental oversight units created within the various enterprises had little authority to interfere with the smooth running of production. This rigidity and inability to enforce regulations that might upset the grand production plan has been commented on also in China.[29]

The other element is the incentive structure at the industry and factory levels. Plant managers were supposed to meet the planned output and input targets for their enterprises. In the USSR, plan fulfillment led to the managers receiving a bonus. But this has perverse incentives because plant managers are led to do all they can to reduce plan targets as much as possible, so that they will be easy to fulfill. In 1978 a law:

> . . . required that bonuses and rewards for workers and managements be made contingent upon a plant's fulfillment of all sections of its plan, including the environmental section, not just the production norms. The resolutions assign the individual enterprise a large number of environment "rights." These include the right to plan its environmental targets, to create environmental sections, to improve its environmental technology, to undertake capital construction in the area of environmental protection, to design a bonus and reward system to stimulate the observance of environmental norms, to provide environmental education, and to account to the responsible ministry for the fulfillment of its environmental norms.[30]

But what happens to production targets can easily happen to environmental targets. If a firm is given the power to develop its own environmental targets, then rewarded for meeting them, it is certain that the targets will be extremely modest.

In this there is an important lesson for pollution-control policy in market economies. Tying environmental target fulfillment to the bonus system ensures that the targets will be set as low as managers can get them, and that firms will do the minimum necessary to achieve them. The same can be said of standard setting in market economies. If firms are required to meet certain standards, they have the incentive to try to get them set as low as possible and to do no more than is necessary to meet the standard. There is no incentive to look for better ways of pollution control and to reduce emissions even beyond the standard if that is efficient. It is only through incorporating economic incentives into the pollution-control policy that these stronger incentives can be brought into play.

Another public policy failing pointed up especially clearly by the experience in Socialist countries is the environmental damages resulting from what might be called the "grandiose project" syndrome. With all economic planning and policy strictly centralized, authorities often begin to devote their efforts to large-scale projects meant to have very substantial impacts on economic growth in various sectors and regions. The possible local environmental impacts of such projects can often be overlooked because the decision process does not permit

---

[29] Yan Liu, "The General Policy of Controlling the Environment Comprehensively to Make the Chinese Economy and Environment Gradually Develop in Harmony," in *Proceedings of the Sino-American Conference on Environmental Law*, Natural Resources Law Center, University of Colorado School of Law, Boulder, Colo., 1989, pp. 195–201.

[30] Barbara Jancar, *Environmental Management in the Soviet Union and Yugoslavia*, Duke University Press, Durham, N.C., 1987, p. 131.

effective representation by people who will experience these damages. Exhibit 18-1 recounts a particularly egregious case, the destruction of the Aral Sea in the former Soviet Union by a grandiose scheme to produce irrigated cotton.

This discussion should not be taken to imply that nothing was ever done in

---

EXHIBIT 18-1

THE ARAL SEA: LESSONS FROM AN ECOLOGICAL DISASTER

The Aral Sea is dying. Because of the huge diversions of water that have taken place during the past thirty years, particularly for irrigation, the volume of the sea has been reduced by two-thirds. The sea's surface has been sharply diminished, the water in the sea and in surrounding aquifers has become increasingly saline, and the water supplies and health of almost 50 million people in the Aral Sea basin are threatened. Vast areas of salty flatlands have been exposed as the sea has receded, and salt from these areas is being blown across the plains onto neighboring cropland and pastures, causing ecological damage. The frost-free period in the delta of the Amu Darya River, which feeds the Aral Sea, has fallen to less than 180 days—below the minimum required for growing cotton, the region's main cash crop. The changes in the sea have effectively killed a substantial fishing industry, and the variety of fauna in the region has declined drastically. If current trends continued unchecked, the sea would eventually shrink to a saline lake one-sixth of its 1960 size.

This ecological disaster is the consequence of excessive abstraction of water for irrigation purposes from the Amu Darya and Syr Darya rivers, which feed the Aral Sea. Total river runoff into the sea fell from an average 55 cubic kilometers a year in the 1950s to zero in the early 1980s. The irrigation schemes have been a mixed blessing for the populations of the Central Asian republics—Kazakhstan, Kyrghyzstan, Tajikistan, Turkmenistan, and Uzbekistan—which they serve. The diversion of water has provided livelihoods for the region's farmers, but at considerable environmental cost. Soils have been poisoned with salt, overwatering has turned pastureland into bogs, water supplies have become polluted by pesticide and fertilizer residues, and the deteriorating quality of drinking water and sanitation is taking a heavy toll on human health. While it is easy to see how the problem of the Aral Sea might have been avoided, solutions are difficult. A combination of better technical management and appropriate incentives is clearly essential: charging for water or allocating it to the most valuable uses could prompt shifts in cropping patterns and make more water available to industry and households.

But the changes needed are vast, and there is little room for maneuver. The Central Asian republics (excluding Kazakhstan) are poor: their incomes are 65 percent of the average in the former U.S.S.R. In the past, transfers from the central government exceeded 20 percent of national income in Kyrghyzstan and Tajikistan and 12 percent in Uzbekistan. These transfers are no longer available. The regional population of 35 million is growing rapidly, at 2.7 percent a year, and infant mortality is high. The states have become dependent on a specialized but unsustainable pattern of agriculture. Irrigated production of cotton, grapes, fruit, and vegetables accounts for the bulk of export earnings. Any rapid reduction in the use of irrigation water will reduce living standards still further unless these economies receive assistance to help them diversify away from irrigated agriculture. Meanwhile, salinization and dust storms erode the existing land under irrigation. This is one of the starkest examples of the need to combine development with sound environmental policy.

Source: World Bank, *World Development Report 1992, Development and the Environment*, Washington, D.C., 1992, p. 38. Reprinted by permission.

Socialist countries to protect the environment. It would be just as false to give the impression that market economies always automatically adjust to give the efficient levels of ambient environmental quality. Any economic system, if it is intent on putting its entire emphasis on material development, will downplay the impacts of this on the natural environment. Exhibit 18-2 shows a case of this in a market economy. Lack of regulatory oversight in the markets of a developing Chilean economy have led to environmental chaos. The story points up another vital factor: To get the necessary regulatory intervention it is vital to have open, responsive political systems where those who suffer environmental damage can seek redress.

DEVELOPMENTS IN ENVIRONMENTAL ACCOUNTING[31]

A number of countries have begun to take steps to either alter or augment their national income accounts to take into account the effects of economic growth on natural resource and environmental assets. National income accounting was developed around 50 years ago by governments who felt the need for a way of knowing how the overall economy was doing from year to year. Familiar measures like gross domestic product, net domestic product, and the rate of unemployment are meant to give us a summary of the total amount of economic activity in a year's time and of the status of certain aggregate variables that affect overall economic welfare. But in recent years conventional national income accounting has been criticized because it does not adequately deal with the resource and environmental implications of economic growth. Consider the standard production possibilities curve in Figure 18-3, showing marketed economic output on the vertical axis and environmental quality on the horizontal axis. Aggregate economic activity as reported in the conventional accounts consists only of measured marketed output. Thus, for example, a move from m_1 to m_2 would be regarded as an improvement in economic welfare. But this improvement has been accompanied by a reduction in environmental quality from e_1 to e_2. To get a complete picture of changes in social welfare we need to take into account both the increase in marketed output and the reduction in environmental quality.

Researchers and public authorities in different countries are approaching this problem in several ways. The basic question is how to measure and treat the "quantity" $e_1 - e_2$ in Figure 18-3. A number of countries, the U.S. included, have sought simply to measure annual total costs of pollution-control expenditures. The next logical step is perhaps to deduct these costs from measured output, on the grounds that they do not represent a true increase in economic welfare but expenditures necessary to protect ourselves from pollution. This procedure has been undertaken in France and Japan.

[31] The discussion in this section relies heavily on Henry M. Peskin and Ernst Lutz, "A Survey of Resource and Environmental Accounting in Industrialized Countries," World Bank Environment Department, Working Paper No. 37, Washington, D.C., August 1990.

EXHIBIT 18-2

THE GREENING OF SANTIAGO

Chile Tries to Clean Up Pinochet's Polluted Legacy.

Brook Larmer *in Santiago*

Remember when the fall of dictators in Eastern Europe unveiled an environmental nightmare? Commentators called it the natural fruit of the Communist system. But take a look at Chile, Latin America's shining example of pure free-market economics. Two years after the exit of Gen. Augusto Pinochet, Chileans are starting to see the dark side of unregulated capitalist growth. Loggers have plundered the country's native forests. Fishermen have depleted the stocks of mollusks and fish. And the vital mining industry has destroyed entire valleys and river basins. The most palpable sign of trouble, however, is the blanket of noxious haze that suffocates Santiago, making it one of the world's smoggiest cities. Says Patricio Rodrigo, who helped draft a new environmental-protection law: "Chile is 15 to 20 years behind the rest of the world on this issue."

Make that 17 years. From 1973 to 1990, Pinochet ruled with absolute authority, routing the leftist opposition and rousing a dormant economy with privatization and deregulation. Growth has averaged 6 percent per year since 1985 with low inflation, Latin America's best record. But to regain Chile's edge in the global marketplace, Pinochet let industries pollute and exploit natural resources with virtually no limits. Environmentalists were seen as antigrowth troublemakers: "Scratch a green, find a red," went the motto. Finance Minister Hernán Büchi lured investors by lauding the lack of restrictions as part of Chile's "low production costs." Some 700 laws and 2,000 regulations were on the books, but only one official had the job of enforcing them. "There was an excess of faith in the market as a regulator," says Juan Escudero, general secretary of Santiago's Decontamination Commission. "It was chaos."

Both blessed and cursed by Chile's growth, President Patricio Aylwin now faces a daunting task: protect the environment without sacrificing the economy. Nowhere can the challenge be seen more clearly than in Santiago—if anything can be seen clearly these days. A thick layer of contaminants settles almost daily over the city, trapped by cold air and mountains on all sides. The causes of the filth: haphazard development and an out-of-control bus system that Pinochet began deregulating in 1975. Two thirds of the smog's harmful elements come from the 11,000 privately owned buses that spew diesel fumes through the city. The government bought out 2,600 of the worst offenders. But pollution still reached lethal levels for two days in July, forcing the government to shut schools and factories and to warn parents to keep their children indoors. The government now hopes to put the brakes on the bus mess by selling routes, favoring operators with newer buses and lower fares.

The smog not only obscures the view of the majestic snowcapped Andes, it threatens to fog up Chile's economic future. A recent U.S. government report warned that Chile's lack of environmental standards and regulations could hurt its long-desired free-trade agreement with the United States. Partly in response, Aylwin's government has gone green: proposing new measures requiring all new vehicles to use catalytic converters, charging cars for driving downtown, creating a "pollution bourse" in which companies buy and sell the right to pollute. A broad environmental-protection bill is moving through the legislature, albeit as slow as sludge. But after 17 years of neglect, it signals a change in the atmosphere.

FIGURE 18-3
National Income Accounting and the Neglect of Environmental Quality.

But the method of deducting pollution-control expenditures does not get directly at measuring the values of environmental quality change as represented by the distance $e_1 - e_2$ in the figure. The first step in doing this is to measure the *physical* quantities of environmental resources and changes in these quantities over time. Attempts to measure physical changes in the total resource endowments of a nation are being undertaken in several countries, notably France and Norway. The French are trying to develop a complete environmental accounting system: Les Comptes du Patrimoine Natural (natural endowment accounts), which can be used to measure physical changes in natural and environmental resources resulting from economic production and consumption.

To put the quantity $e_1 - e_2$ in value terms, however, requires taking the next step—to place values on the physical changes in environmental resources. Major work on this is being done in the Netherlands. The objective is to put monetary values on the various dimensions of environmental degradation, including the reduced value of resources and the damages from pollution. A valuation approach like this is also being undertaken by the United Nations.

We are just at the beginning of efforts to incorporate environmental values into national income accounts. The conceptual and measurement problems are very difficult, and it will be some time before acceptable procedures can be developed and believable numbers estimated. But if it is successful this work could have a profound impact on public policy decisions.

SUMMARY

In many other industrialized countries major pollution-control efforts started in the decade of the 1970s, as they did in the U.S. Policy in different countries is pursued through means that are congenial to the political culture and institutional history of each one. For the most part, pollution-control efforts have relied on various command-and-control approaches involving standards of various types. In many European countries, emission taxes have been widely used, but historically these have been primarily to raise revenues, which can then be used to subsidize pollution-control efforts. In the future, these could perhaps easily be transformed into incentive taxes with a primary pollution-control objective.

Environmental standards may be set at the national level (as in, e.g., Germany, Italy, and the U.S.) or at the local level (as in France and England). But their *enforcement* tends to be very local, involving "bargaining" between emitters and local officials—not bargaining in the formal sense, but give-and-take between these parties as to what courses of action are to be undertaken by different sources to control emissions.

The large-scale environmental degradation of the ex-Socialist countries bears an instructive lesson for pollution control in all countries. The initial reaction to environmental pollution is to think that it comes about because authorities lack the necessary means of control to bring about emission reductions. But in the ex-Socialist countries, authorities presumably had total control and environmental damages have still been massive. This points up the importance of having open political systems, readily available information on what the state of the environment really is, and incentive systems that lead polluters to internalize the damages their emissions produce.

QUESTIONS FOR FURTHER DISCUSSION

1 How would the "polluter pays principle" apply to the case of mobile-source air pollution?
2 Suppose a law is enacted in which everyone is compensated fully for whatever environmental damage he or she suffers. What would the incentive effects of such a law be?
3 Consider the "European" approach to emission taxes. For a single source, is it possible that a low emissions tax could produce enough revenues to pay for all of the abatement costs required to reduce this source's emissions to an efficient level? What factors affect this? (Hint: You will want to explore this with the help of our standard emission-control model.)
4 What factors determine whether it would be more effective to proceed against polluters by hammering them in court or by sitting down with them to try to work things out on a "reasonable" basis?

5 "The U.S. is no longer number one in pollution-control expenditures; other countries are spending more per capita than we are on environmental quality programs!" One often sees statements like this, especially in newspaper stories. How do you react to the statement?

SELECTED READINGS

Barde, Jean-Philippe, and David W. Pearce (eds.): *Valuing the Environment, Six Case Studies*, Earthscan Publications, London, 1991.

Bower, Blair T., Rémi Barré, Jochen Kühner, and Clifford S. Russell: *Incentives in Water Quality Management, France and the Ruhr Area*, Resources for the Future, Washington, D.C., 1981.

Brown, Gardner M., Jr., and Ralph W. Johnson: "Pollution Control by Effluent Charges: It Works in the Federal Republic of Germany: Why Not in the U.S.?" *Natural Resources Journal*, 24(4), October 1984, pp. 929–966.

Downing, Paul B., and Kenneth Hanf (eds.): *International Comparisons in Implementing Pollution Laws*, Kluwer Nijhoff Publishing, Boston, 1983.

Folmer, Henk, and Charles Howe: "Environmental Problems and Policy in the Single European Market," *Environmental and Resource Economics*, 1(1), 1991, pp. 22–45.

Gresser, Julian, Koichiro Fujikura, and Akio Morishima: *Environmental Law in Japan*, MIT Press, Cambridge, Mass., 1981.

Huppes, Gjalt, and Robert A. Kagan: "Market-Oriented Regulation of Environmental Problems in the Netherlands," *Law and Policy*, 11(2), April 1989, pp. 215–239.

Johnson, Ralph W., and Gardner M. Brown, Jr.: *Cleaning Up Europe's Waters*, Praeger, New York, 1976.

Johnson, Stanley P., and Guy Corcelle: *The Environmental Policy of the European Community*, Graham and Trotman, London, 1989.

Kormondy, Edward J.: *International Handbook of Pollution Control*, Greenwood Press, Westport, Conn., 1989.

Lutz, Ernst, ed., *Toward Improved Accounting for the Environment*, The World Bank, Washington, D.C., 1993.

Park, Chris P. (ed.): *Environmental Policies: An International Review*, Croom Helm, London, 1986.

Peskin, Henry M., and Ernst Lutz: "A Survey of Resource and Environmental Accounting in Industrialized Countries," World Bank, Environment Department Working Paper No. 37, Washington, D.C., August 1990.

Reese, Craig E.: *Deregulation and Environmental Quality*, Quorum Books, Westport, Conn., 1983.

Russell, Clifford S.: "Monitoring and Enforcement of Pollution Control Laws in Europe and the United States," in Rüdiger Pethig (ed.), *Conflicts and Cooperation in Managing Environmental Resources*, Springer-Verlag, Berlin, 1992, pp. 195–213.

Wilczynski, Piotr: *Environmental Management in Centrally-Planned Non-Market Economies of Eastern Europe*, Environment Working Paper No. 35, World Bank, Washington, D.C., July 1990.

CHAPTER 19

ECONOMIC DEVELOPMENT AND THE ENVIRONMENT

There was a time, several decades ago, when problems of environmental quality were widely regarded as being unique to developed, industrial economies. Industrial development was associated with air and water pollution, overreliance on chemicals, visual blight, etc. Developing countries, on the other hand, were thought to have fewer environmental problems because their preindustrial technology was more environmentally benign, and because they had not yet committed themselves to a materialistic style of life, with the negative trade-offs many feel that this implies.

Ideas have changed in recent years, however. For one thing, it has become clear that massive environmental degradation has in fact occurred in the developing world. Rural areas have seen large-scale soil erosion and water-quality deterioration, deforestation, and declining soil productivity. Urban areas have experienced seriously diminished air and water quality. Furthermore, this environmental deterioration in developing countries was not just a matter of aesthetics or quality of life, but rather a more serious issue involving the diminishment of economic productivity and the acceleration of social dislocation. Out of this realization grew the idea of "sustainability" as a guide to decisions affecting the natural resource system.

In this chapter we will explore the interrelationship of economic development and the environment among the nonindustrialized countries of the world. In keeping with the distinction made back in Chapter 2, we will approach it on two levels: the positive and the normative. From the positive standpoint we want to understand how development and environmental degradation are reciprocally related, and what factors account for this interrelationship. From a normative standpoint we will take up questions about the types of public policies that are best under these circumstances.

GENERAL CONSIDERATIONS

It is common to distinguish between economic *growth* and economic *development*. There is a simple, as well as a more complicated, way of distinguishing between these concepts. In simple terms, growth refers to increases in the aggregate level of output, while development means increases in per-capita output. Thus, a country could grow, but not develop, if its population growth exceeded its rate of economic growth. The more complicated way is to say that economic growth refers to increases in economic activity without any underlying change in the fundamental economic structure and institutions of a country, while development also includes a wider set of technological, institutional, and social transformations. Changes in such things as education, health, population, transportation infrastructure, and legal institutions are all part of the development process. This should alert us to the fact that when talking about environmental issues in developing countries we will usually be talking about situations where the social and technological milieu can be very different from that in industrialized countries. At the same time it implies that in environmental policy matters, a wider set of choices may be available because of the more thoroughgoing institutional transformations taking place in many developing countries.

In speaking of these issues, there is the tendency to divide the world into just two parts: developed and developing, or "first" world and "third" world.[1] Of course, any brief classification like this is an enormous oversimplification of the real world. At the very least we should think not of a simple categorization like this but of a continuum, running from the poorest to the richest, or along any other dimension of interest. The countries of the world are spread along that continuum, though not necessarily evenly. It's also true that national aggregates can tend to obscure some important development problems *within* particular countries. Many countries that look reasonably good on the basis of national macrodata have pockets of poverty and underdevelopment that would be sufficient to put these regions in the less developed ranks if national political boundaries were drawn differently.

ENVIRONMENTAL DEGRADATION IN DEVELOPING ECONOMIES

Many people in the developed world have been brought to a realization of the existence of environmental problems in the developing world through recent global concerns, such as global warming and the rapid pace of species extinction. A disproportionately high number of the world's endangered species are residents of developing countries, so efforts to preserve the habitats of these species have brought people to focus on the development–environment linkages in nonindustrialized countries. Similarly, the developed world's concern about global warming has heightened concern about deforestation, because forests act to absorb atmospheric CO_2. In many developing countries the harvesting of fuel wood and timber and the conversion of forested lands to agricultural uses have

---

[1] In the argot of international political economics, the "first" world is used to refer to the developed industrial market economies, while the "third" world refers to the group of developing economies. The "second" world referred at one time to the Socialist economies.

led to high rates of deforestation. Thus, large-scale deforestation has the potential to worsen the global greenhouse effect.

But from the standpoint of the developing countries themselves, their worst environmental problems are probably the water and air pollution they suffer, especially in their expanding urban areas. In the developed world, the chemical treatment of water supplies, together with the treatment of wastewater, have largely neutralized the water system as a source of human disease; continued water pollution control is justified on recreational and aesthetic grounds. This is not the case in many developing countries, where water pollution is still responsible for vast amounts of disease and death. Lack of treatment facilities leads to widespread exposure to disease-bearing human wastes. In places where there has been an expansion of industry, mining, and the use of agricultural chemicals, rivers have become contaminated with toxic chemicals and with heavy metals. Seepage of hazardous materials from industrial sites and waste dumps is increasingly threatening the groundwater resources toward which many countries are turning as surface waters become more heavily contaminated.

In a recent review of studies by the U.S. Agency for International Development (USAID) and the World Health Organization (WHO), the World Bank concluded that providing access to safer water and adequate sanitation to those who currently lack it would have the following effects:

- 2 million fewer deaths from diarrhea each year among children under five years of age
- 200 million fewer episodes of diarrheal illness annually
- 300 million fewer people with roundworm infection
- 150 million fewer people with schistosomiasis
- 2 million fewer people infected with guinea worm.[2]

Air pollution is also a significant problem in developing countries. Data from the United Nations Global Environment Monitoring System (GEMS) indicates that in the mid-1980s about 1.3 billion people around the world were exposed to levels of particulate matter that exceeded WHO standards; most of these were in developing countries. In many countries gasoline is still virtually all leaded, leading to serious damages from airborne lead pollution. Indoor air pollution is also a more serious problem than in developed countries, owing to the continued heavy reliance on biomass fuels for cooking and heating.

ECONOMY AND ENVIRONMENT

While the concern about environmental problems has been of more recent origin, issues related to economic growth in the less-developed world have been uppermost for many years; indeed, historically they have been the defining focus of this group of countries. This emphasis on economic development will continue

---

[2] World Bank, *World Development Report 1992, Development and the Environment,* Oxford University Press for the World Bank, New York, 1992, p. 49.

as they strive to close the economic gap with the developed economies. What we need to look at, therefore, is the relationship between economic development and environmental quality.

A Static View

Probably the most frequently mentioned viewpoint on these matters is that developing countries simply cannot afford high levels of environmental quality. According to this view, the situation of these countries, in comparison to developed economies, can be pictured by the production possibilities curves (PPCs) of Figure 19-1. "Marketed output" refers to the conventional types of goods and services produced and distributed through economic markets. The PPC labeled A is for a typical developed country, while B refers to a developing nation. Because of past resource exploitation, or population pressures, or less sophisticated technology, B lies entirely within A. Thus, to achieve higher levels of marketed income, which it must if it is to develop, it must be willing to put up with lower levels of environmental quality. For example, for the developing country to reach a level of marketed output of c_1 it must trade off environmental quality back to the level e_2. The developed country, because of the factors mentioned above, can have c_1 of marketed output with a much higher level of environmental quality—e_1 instead of only e_2. As one economist has put it:

> . . . the poorer countries of the world confront tragic choices. They cannot afford drinking water standards as high as those the industrial countries are accustomed to.

FIGURE 19-1
Production Possibilities Curves of Developed and Developing Countries.

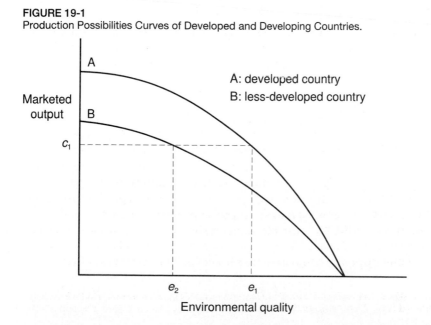

They cannot afford to close their pristine areas to polluting industries that would introduce technical know how and productive capital and that would earn urgently needed foreign exchange. They cannot afford to bar mining companies from their unexploited regions. Nor can they afford to impose antipollution requirements on these companies that are as strict and expensive as those in richer industrial countries. They should always realize that environmental protection measures are financed out of the stomachs of their own people; the multinationals cannot be made to pay for them.[3]

Developing countries, according to this view, cannot afford the high levels of environmental quality sought in the developed world because this would mean lower monetary incomes and a lessened capacity to support their populations.

There is another side to this argument, however. The production possibilities curve approach sees marketed output and environmental quality as substitutes; more effort devoted to reducing environmental impacts must necessarily lead to lower monetary incomes. But in the developing world there are clear cases where environmental quality and measured GDP are complementary. Most developing countries depend proportionately more on primary industries than do developed ones. For example, they usually have a greater proportion of their population involved in agriculture. Thus, degradation of environmental resources has the potential for being more highly destructive of productive assets in developing countries. In industrial countries, environmental quality issues hinge primarily on matters of human health and the aesthetic quality of the environment. Furthermore, technological developments have decoupled, to a considerable extent, the resource-using sector from the rest of the economy. In developing countries, on the other hand, environmental issues are related to human health and productivity and also to the degradation of the future productivity of the natural resource base on which many people are directly dependent. According to this argument, the environment and the economy are not so much substitutes as they are complements.

Sustainability

But these are essentially static arguments, and the essence of economic development is long-run change. So the relevant question is: How is long-run economic development likely to affect environmental quality? The normal expectation is that development would shift the production possibility curve of Figure 19-1 outward. As economies change, becoming less tied to natural resources, and as less polluting technologies are adopted, this outward shift would improve the potential trade-offs between marketed output and environmental quality. Developing countries could then devote more resources to improving environmental quality.

Sometimes the opposite has happened, however; the short-run effort to in-

---

[3] Robert Dorfman, "An Economist's View of Natural Resources and Environmental Problems," in Robert Repetto (ed.), *The Global Possible*, Yale University Press, New Haven, Conn., 1985, pp. 67–76.

crease or maintain marketed incomes, in effect, tended to shift the PPC curve to the left and worsen the available choices. This has occurred when the search for short-run economic growth has led to irreversible reductions in the productivity of some part of a country's environmental assets. Here we consider "environmental assets" very broadly, to include such things as soil fertility and forestry resources along with urban air and water pollution. The concept that has become widely used to talk of this phenomenon is *sustainability*. A practice is sustainable if it does not reduce the long-run productivity of the natural resource assets on which a country's income and development depend.[4]

Sustainability is fundamentally a matter of renewable resources. When non-renewable resources are used, they automatically become unavailable to future generations. The rule to follow here is to use them at the correct rate—neither too fast nor too slow—and to see to it that the natural wealth that they represent is converted into long-lived human-made wealth as they are used. Thus, for example, the petroleum resources of many developing countries must be converted to long-term productive capital, both private and public, if they are to contribute to the long-run economic development of the extracting country. By productive capital we mean not only physical capital (roads, factories, etc.), but also human capital (education, skills) and what we might call "institutional capital" (an efficient legal system, effective public agencies, etc.).

Long-Run Relationships

It is widely anticipated that over the next few decades, developing countries will experience relatively rapid rates of economic growth. The World Bank, for example, estimates that collectively they will grow at a rate of 4–5 percent a year.[5] With long-run growth rates of this type, what impacts can we expect on environmental quality in these countries? If all technological factors were to stay the same over this period, environmental impacts and damages would increase along with this economic growth. But these factors are unlikely to remain constant. Economic development brings with it many changes. The most obvious is an increase in per-capita incomes and, as people's income goes up, so does their willingness to sacrifice for improved environmental quality. Developing economies usually also experience a variety of structural changes, often in the direction of replacing relatively high-polluting industries with those that pollute less.

Studies have been done to investigate the relationship between various environmental quality indices and the income levels attained in different countries.

---

[4] The concept of "sustainability" received its major impetus in the influential report put out by the World Commission on Environment and Development: *Our Common Future*, Oxford University Press, Oxford, England, 1987. This report is popularly called "The Brundtland Report" because the Commission, created by the United Nations in 1983, was headed by Mrs. Gro Harlem Brundtland, prime minister of Norway.

[5] World Bank, *World Development Report 1992, Development and the Environment*, Oxford University Press for the World Bank, New York, 1992, p. 9.

The objective is to see if as income levels change, there are systematic changes also in environmental quality variables. Several of the leading results are shown in Figure 19-2. These are based on "cross-section" analyses of income levels and environmental quality. This involves looking at the environmental characteristics of a large number of countries, with widely varying income levels, and then using statistical methods to discover the underlying relationships, if indeed there are any. In fact, studies show clear relationships between income levels and a variety of environmental quality indices. In Figure 19-2, note that there are essentially three types of relationships:

1 Those showing steady declines as incomes increase. This applies to access to safe water and sanitation facilities, which countries can presumably more easily afford as incomes rise, but which also are normal goods in the sense that as incomes increase people are willing to pay larger amounts for them.
2 Those that first increase but then decrease with income, which applies to ambient amounts of particulates and SO_2. This pattern is probably due to the fact that in its early stages industrial development leads to greater air pollution, while with continued development there is a shift in industry type toward cleaner industries, as well as a rising public demand in more well-to-do countries for pollution control.
3 Those showing a steady increase with income gains; this applies to municipal solid wastes and CO_2 emissions per capita. The first is a reflection of the growth in material standards of living as incomes increase, while the second results from the increasing demand for fossil-based energy that normally accompanies development.

These relationships as pictured are not inevitable. They can be taken as general tendencies, which may be different in particular countries, depending on technology choices adopted as well as the preferences of their citizens. It points out that for many environmental problems the situation is likely to get better as development occurs; indeed, economic development may be seen as a way of combating these problems—which is why continued efforts need to be directed at encouraging equitable growth and open political processes in the developing world.

THE POLLUTION-HAVEN HYPOTHESIS

In recent years we have heard much of the idea of developing countries being "pollution havens," places where firms can move and operate without the strict environmental controls of the developed countries. The idea essentially has two parts:

• That stringent environmental standards in industrialized countries are causing some firms, especially "pollution-intensive" ones, to flee to countries with less stringent standards,
• That some developing countries have tried, with some success, to attract

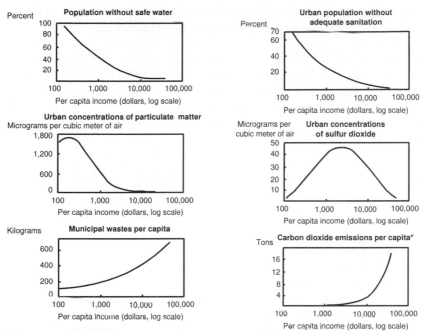

*Emissions are from fossil fuels.

Note: Estimates are based on cross-country analysis of data from the 1980s.

FIGURE 19-2
Environmental Indicators in Relation to Country Income Levels. *(Sources: World Bank, World Development Report 1992, Development and the Environment, Oxford University Press for the World Bank, New York, 1992, p. 11, based on a paper by Nemat Shafik and Sushenjit Bandyopadhyay, "Economic Growth and Environmental Quality: Time Series and Cross-Section Evidence"; Gene Grossman and Alan B. Kreuger, "Environmental Impacts of a North American Free Trade Agreement," Discussion Paper No. 158, Woodrow Wilson School, Princeton University, 1991.)*

pollution-intensive firms with the promise of lower pollution-control standards, in the hopes of bolstering their rates of economic growth.

Sometimes these ideas are wrapped into the issue of the "multinationals," that
is, firms owned in one country but operating establishments in others.

It is surprisingly difficult to get conclusive data on this matter. Most opinions
are formed on the basis of anecdotal, or episodic, events like the Bhopal disaster
in India. But these are not good sources from which to draw conclusions about
general trends. Nor is it possible to approach this question by looking at different
environmental regulations in the various countries. Almost all countries, developing and developed, have regulations on the books that appear to place emissions under reasonably strict controls, but that are not usually followed in
practice because of weak enforcement. Ideally, we would like to have data on
the emissions performance of firms, or groups of firms, before and after they have
moved from developed to developing countries. But data like these are not
available. Thus, the way we have to proceed is to identify "dirty" industries and
look at how they have grown or declined in different countries, developed and
developing. "Dirty" industries are simply those industries that normally emit
relatively large amounts of pollutants, while "clean" industries are all the rest.

The problem with this approach, of course, is that many factors besides
environmental regulations could cause dirty industries to migrate among countries—e.g., labor costs, raw materials availability, infrastructure availability, and
especially the state of the product cycle. By the last we mean the fact that during
the process of growth of any economy certain industries will tend to expand and
decline at different times. Certain basic manufacturing industries, which may be
"dirty," will often expand early in a country's development and decline later as
incomes increase. So these industries might be moving around from one country
to another (not literally moving, but rather expanding in some countries and
declining in others) in response to where those countries are in the product cycle,
rather than because of environmental regulations.

To date a number of studies have been done on this issue. Figure 19-3 shows
some data like those used in this work. It shows the capital investments made in
developing countries by affiliates of U.S. corporations between 1971 and 1986.
For "all manufacturing," the trend is very modestly increasing over this time.
Two "dirty" sectors are identified, metals and chemicals. The data for chemicals
also show a modest increase in the 1970s, but the 1980s show a modest decline.
The data for the metals industry are very volatile, with large spikes in 1976–1977
and 1982–1983; overall, however, the trend seems to be modestly increasing. On
the basis of results like this, the conclusion seems warranted that there has been
no large-scale flight of industrial corporations to pollution havens in developing
countries. As one of them concluded:

> Most individual industries have responded to environmental regulations with tech-
> nological innovations, changes in production processes or raw materials, more efficient
> process controls, and other adaptations that in the United States have proved more
> economical and less drastic than flight abroad. Even when these adaptations have not

FIGURE 19-3
Capital Expenditures In Developing Countries Made by Affiliates of U.S.
Corporations, 1971–1986. *(Source:* Survey of Current Business, *52–62(10), October
1972–October 1982; 63–66(3), March 1983–March 1986.)*

reduced regulatory burdens, the environmental problems have generally not been substantial enough to offset more traditional factors—market considerations, transportation, availability of raw materials, labor costs, political stability—that determine how most firms select overseas locations for branch-plant construction.[6]

Several more recent studies are less clear, however. One group of researchers took a look at the relative rates of growth of toxic-intensive industries in developed and developing countries. A toxic-intensive industry is one that releases relatively large amounts of toxic chemicals per unit of output produced. They conclude that the poorest economies have the highest rate of growth in toxic-intensive industries, a result that is consistent with the pollution-haven hypothesis.[7] Other researchers have also obtained results that are consistent with the hypothesis.[8] But at this point in time it is impossible to rule out other competing explanations, as mentioned above. Further studies are needed.

---

[6] H. Jeffrey Leonard, *Pollution and the Struggle for the World Product,* Cambridge University Press, Cambridge, England, 1988, p. 113. Other studies include Charles Pearson, *Multinational Corporations, Environment and the Third World,* Duke University Press, Durham, N.C., 1987; and C. Duerksen and H. J. Leonard, "Environmental Regulations and the Location of Industries: An International Perspective," Columbia Journal of World Business, 15, Summer 1980, pp. 52–68.

[7] Robert F. B. Lucas, David Wheeler, and Hemamala Hettige, "Economic Development, Environmental Regulation and the International Migration of Toxic Industrial Pollution, 1960–1988," in Patrick Low (ed.), *International Trade and the Environment,* World Bank Discussion Paper No. 159, Washington, D.C., 1992, pp. 67–86.

[8] Patrick Low and Alexander Yeats, "Do 'Dirty' Industries Migrate?" in ibid., pp. 89–104.

ENVIRONMENTAL POLICY CHOICES IN DEVELOPING COUNTRIES

While it may be true that development can help to alleviate some environmental problems, there is nothing automatic about this; appropriate public policies are still called for. This is especially true for those factors, like CO_2 emissions and solid waste, that get worse with development. Most discussions of the strengths and weaknesses of alternative policies have been directed toward developed countries. There is an important question about how much the lessons learned in this context apply also to developing countries. While the environmental problems are in principle the same, involving externalities, common-property resources, public goods, etc., the sociopolitical situations are markedly different from those in most developed countries.

Benefit–Cost Analysis

The basis of effective policy is in the analysis of the benefits and costs of different courses of action. Much more than in developed countries, damages in developing countries affect economic productivity through impacts on human health, soil fertility, resource depletion, and the like. Thus, there is a critical need for estimates of environmental damages in developing countries. In recent years, a number of international agencies have sponsored a series of "country environmental studies" (CESs) in various developing countries. But so far these have been aimed primarily at taking inventories of the physical dimensions of environmental problems. They have not dealt with policy issues to any great extent, nor have they gotten to the point of trying to value the damages caused by environmental deterioration.[9] These studies would be especially important to pursue in those countries because they would show more clearly the extent of pollution-related damages and provide support for more active public policies.

There are several important issues regarding the use of standard benefit–cost approaches in developing countries. One is the emphasis on willingness to pay as a measure of the benefits of pollution reduction. Willingness to pay reflects not only tastes and preferences, but also ability to pay. In many developing economies poverty is widespread, so a standard willingness-to-pay approach to valuing environmental damages may yield only modest estimates of these damages. In the face of enormous poverty, willingness-to-pay estimates may be quite small despite what look to be high rates of environmental degradation. Thus, if willingness-to-pay approaches are used, they must be used with frank recognition that the distribution of income is heavily skewed, and value judgments are called for in making decisions on environmental quality programs. This argues also for putting more emphasis on lost productivity, particularly in the long run, in assessing the damages of environmental degradation.

---

[9] Walter Arensberg, "Country Environmental Studies, A Framework for Action," in Denizhan Eröcal (ed.), *Environmental Management in Developing Countries*, Organization for Economic Cooperation and Development, Paris, 1991, pp. 279–295.

Another special difficulty in applying benefit–cost analysis of environmental programs to developing countries is discounting. In developed economies, discounting is a relatively benign procedure that helps make choices among programs with different time profiles of benefits and costs. But in developing countries the focus is more on long-run development, and here the role of discounting is less clear. It's often asserted that people in developing countries, especially those with lower incomes, discount the future very highly, preferring to emphasize actions that will pay off in the short run because of their immediate need for income. Thus, environmental improvement programs, if they deliver the bulk of their benefits only in the long run, may take lower priority than economic development projects that pay off more quickly. High rates of discount can also lead people to overlook negative environmental impacts that occur far off into the future. The present value of even severe long-run environmental damage can be quite low when it is evaluated with a positive discount rate. [10] For some people these arguments imply using a very low, perhaps even zero, discount rate in evaluating environmental and developmental projects in developing countries. But this would make it impossible to coordinate public policies and development projects with decisions being made in the private sector, and would treat a dollar of net benefits 10 years from now as equivalent to a dollar of net benefits today. It is perhaps better to utilize a normal discount rate in evaluating programs, but to augment the typical benefit–cost study in developing countries with an analysis of the impacts of the program on long-run sustainability. [11]

Reducing Environmental Disincentives of Current Policies

We normally view environmental policy as requiring activist intervention to remedy the problems of uncontrolled externalities, the undersupply of public environmental goods, etc. But many times environmental improvements can be had by altering current policies that have negative environmental impacts. In many cases these policies have been put in place in the belief that they will spur economic growth. But their impact is to create distortions in local economies that lead both to lower growth rates and to environmental degradation.

A good example of this is the practice many governments have of subsidizing pesticide use by farmers. In many cases these subsidies were undertaken in the belief that they would spur farmers to adopt new crop varieties and intensive methods of cultivation. But the subsidies often continue well after their useful-

[10] We are not talking here about unpredictable consequences; rather, those that are predictable but far into the future. When CFCs were introduced as refrigerants in the early twentieth century, nobody predicted the impacts they would have on the global atmosphere. Likewise, nobody foresaw the negative effects of DDT. At the time these substances were introduced, science was not well enough advanced to have predicted these outcomes. There is a difference, however, between consequences that are not predictable and those that are predictable but far enough in the future to be neglected in today's decision making

[11] David Pearce, Edward Barbier, and Anil Markandya, *Sustainable Development, Economics and Environment in the Third World*, Edward Elgar Publishing, Aldershot, England, 1990.

ness in this regard has ceased. Table 19-1 shows the estimated annual rate of pesticide subsidies offered to farmers in eight developing countries. The range is from 19 percent to 89 percent of the retail cost of the pesticide. The result of these subsidies is predictable: the overuse of agricultural chemicals and the damages that result. These include heavy pesticide exposure of farm workers, contamination of nearby surface and groundwater resources, and the rapid development of immunity by target pests. Throughout the developing world, the subsidies involve hundreds of millions of dollars that could better be spent in other ways, or simply left in the private sector.

Other agricultural subsidies—for example, on irrigation water and fertilizer—have similar effects. In recent years much attention has focused on overly rapid rates of deforestation in developing countries. In many cases this happens because of government policies. Policies that underprice the value of timber concessions offered to logging companies increase the incentive to harvest timber at a high rate. Uncontrolled private access to communal forest resources reduces the incentive to conserve timber stocks. Misguided public road building can open up large areas to timber harvesting. In some cases land grants to individuals cannot become permanent unless and until the land is cleared and put into agricultural production, which obviously creates the incentive to get rid of the trees as soon as possible. The result of these policies is timber harvest that is higher than it should be, pursued in places it should not be, with the resulting impacts in soil loss, polluted water, reduction in the global CO_2 sink, and so on.

We should not think, however, that distorting public policies with negative environmental impacts are features solely of the developing world. In fact, the developed world also has many such policies. In the U.S., agricultural price supports coupled with land-use restrictions have led to excessive rates of pesti-

TABLE 19-1
ESTIMATED AVERAGE RATE AND VALUE OF PESTICIDE SUBSIDIES IN EIGHT DEVELOPING COUNTRIES

Country	Percentage of full retail costs	Total value ($ million)
China	19	285
Colombia	44	69
Ecuador	41	14
Egypt	83	207
Ghana	67	20
Honduras	29	12
Indonesia	82	128
Senegal	89	4

Source: Robert Repetto, "Economic Incentives for Sustainable Production," in Gunter Schramm and Jeremy J. Warford (eds.), *Environmental Management and Economic Development,* Johns Hopkins Press for the World Bank, Baltimore, Md. 1989, p. 72.

cide use in certain crops. Publicly subsidized flood insurance has led people to develop shoreline property that might best be left undisturbed.

Institutional Policy: Property Rights

Economic development usually implies wide-ranging economic and political transformations. An important part of this is developing modern economic institutions which can provide the appropriate incentive structures to shape the decisions that will lead toward development. Inappropriate property rights institutions have often been singled out for having environmentally destructive consequences. Thus, one major avenue for policy to protect environmental resources is to alter property rights institutions.

In a recent study of resource depletion in Ethiopia, the author lists a series of stages through which a portion of the rural economy had evolved.[12]

Stage 1 Because of population pressure the average harvest of fuel wood begins to exceed the average rate of wood production.

Stage 2 Peasants begin to use straw and dung for fuel; thus, less of these are available for maintaining soil fertility.

Stage 3 Almost all tree cover is removed, all dung is sold for cash, and wheat yields begin a serious decline.

Stage 4 Soil erosion becomes dramatic because of reduced tree cover and declining fertility.

Stage 5 There is a total collapse of fertility; peasants abandon their land, swelling urban populations.

The basic question is: Why did this sequence of stages take place? It might be more instructive to ask this the opposite way: Why didn't something like the following scenario happen? Fuel wood harvest increases because of increasing demand, this increases the price of fuel wood because of increased scarcity. Peasants see the increasing incomes to be made by growing and selling fuel wood, so they devote portions of their land to growing fuel wood and act to conserve the remaining supplies in the face of its increasing value. Finally, a substantial fuel wood harvest and market appear, with a considerable proportion of the land devoted to fuel wood production. Why, in other words, did the rising market price of fuel wood lead to wiping out the forest? Why did not the peasants act to make themselves better off by conserving and even increasing the production of an increasingly valuable resource?

One part of the answer is property rights. Most of the forested land was not owned by individuals or small groups, but was essentially an open-access resource. Anyone who wanted to harvest wood from these lands had the right to do so. In Chapter 4 we examined a simple model of an open-access resource

---

[12] Kenneth J. Newcombe, "An Economic Justification for Rural Afforestation: The Case of Ethiopia," in Gunter Schramm and Jeremy J. Warford (eds.), *Environmental Management and Economic Development*, Johns Hopkins Press for the World Bank, Baltimore, Md., 1989, pp. 117–138.

showing that individuals making decisions on the basis of benefits and costs to themselves will overlook common-property externalities they inflict on others. A resource of this type often will be overexploited. Viewed from another angle, when there is open access to a resource, the incentive that any individual might have to reduce the rate of use and conserve the resource is totally undermined. If someone reduces his or her harvest, others will simply take what has been left. Open-access resources promote a "use it or lose it" situation.

Thus, one of the root causes of the deforestation, which began the whole unraveling process in the example, was an institutional one, a property rights system that created incentives for wiping out the resource even though rising scarcity was making it socially desirable to conserve it. This problem has oc-curred with great regularity in developing countries, especially with land and forest resources. The most straightforward response would seem to be to change the property rights system so that the normal incentives for conservation can operate. This means instituting a system of individual or small-group property rights.

We have to keep in mind that like any single policy recommendation, this one is no panacea for all of the environmental problems of developing countries. It will work in some situations and not in others. Overuse of resources, such as the deforestation mentioned above, can occur on "private" lands if the owners cannot effectively defend their boundaries and keep out would-be encroachers. This means, among other things, that there have to be effective and equitable legal institutions to settle land-use conflicts. Establishing private property rights in developing countries also means facing the demographic realities. In places with great population pressure, private property rights would hardly be feasible if that cut off a substantial proportion of the population from resources they need in order to subsist. Even in places without noticeable population pressure, essentially the same problem could occur if the property rights are distributed inequitably in the first place.

There are many other dimensions to the property rights issue. It is a topic of great controversy, and the debate is often carried out in overly simplistic terms. It is clear, however, that a wide range of resource and environmental problems in developing countries have been made much worse by ill-defined property rights and the open-access externalities to which these give rise. In those situations, innovations in property rights institutions can be extremely effective.

Population Policy as Environmental Policy

Many people feel that the only effective way to control environmental destruction in developing countries is to control the number of people in those countries. In the simplest possible terms, the total impact of a group of people on their environmental resources can be expressed in the following way:

$$\text{Total environmental impact} = \text{Environmental impact per person} \times \text{Number of people.}$$

It is clear that total environmental impact can increase as a result of increases in either or both of these factors. The contrary is also true: Decreases in total impact can result from decreases in either or both of the factors. More complicated scenarios are possible: Changes in technology, economic structure, etc., that lower the per-capita environmental impacts in a country can be more than offset by population increases. But two factors are involved. Population declines, or declines in the rate of population increase, may be very helpful, but they are not sufficient in themselves to ensure a reduction in aggregate environmental degradation.

The world population is generally expected to increase from the current 5 billion to perhaps 15 to 20 billion over the next century, with two-thirds of this increase occurring in the developing world. Whether the increase is at the high end of this range or substantially lower depends in large part on the long-run behavior of fertility rates in these development countries. [13] While fertility rates in developing countries are sometimes very high, many have started to decline in recent years. To some extent this is a reflection of rising incomes, because increasing incomes are almost always associated with lowered fertility rates. Other important causal factors are a reduction in infant mortality, increased availability of family planning services, and (especially) increases in educational opportunities for women. Continued emphasis on these factors is in the best interest of people in the developing world, not solely for environmental reasons, but also to reduce poverty directly and to make it easier to institute developmental changes.

However, while reductions in population growth rates can certainly help to reduce the overall impacts any group of people has on its environmental resources, it is no substitute for undertaking environmental policies in their own right. For one thing, diminished population growth rates do not necessarily automatically imply diminished environmental damages. Even with comparatively lower populations, for example, it is anticipated that developing countries will experience marked increases in urbanization in the next half century, and probably beyond. Unless confronted directly, this will lead to more severe air and water pollution in these burgeoning urban areas. As another example, decreases in agricultural populations may not be accompanied by reduced resource damages if, simultaneously, a shift to chemical agriculture occurs without proper safeguards against water pollution and increased pest resistance. In other words, although population policies may facilitate reduced environmental damages, they are no substitute for direct environmental policy itself.

Command-and-Control or Market Incentives?

We come, therefore, to the important question of the types of environmental policies that are most appropriate for developing economies. We have stated

---

[13] The fertility rate is the average number of children born per woman over their lifetimes; a rate of 2.0 implies zero population growth. Some developed countries have fertility rates of less than 2.0. In the developing world, fertility rates currently average about 3.8.

several times, in the context of developed economies, that no single policy approach will be the best for all environmental problems; certain problems call for one approach, others call for something else. The same is true of developing countries. But beyond this, we must ask if anything characterizing the developing world might cause us to lean more heavily in one direction or another. In particular, should policymakers in these countries rely relatively more on command and control, through standards of various types, or would it be better to emphasize economic incentive types of policies?

One especially relevant factor is that developing countries can ill afford, given the resource requirements of economic development, to devote more resources to environmental quality improvement than is necessary. This is an argument for making sure that the pollution-control policies adopted are cost-effective, and this in turn is an argument in favor of incentive policies. We have seen repeatedly throughout this book that incentive-type policies, in situations where monitoring emissions is possible and where materials-balance problems are addressed, can be expected to be substantially more cost-effective than command-and-control strategies. They make it possible to take advantage of different abatement costs across sources, and also provide long-run incentives for firms to search for cheaper ways of reducing emissions.

Tradition is strong, however, and to date developing countries have been following in the early footsteps of the developed economies; that is, they have relied primarily on command-and-control policies. There are some exceptions. Singapore has instituted a program to charge drivers for using urban roads during heavily congested peak-use times of the day. The primary element of the program is the requirement that drivers using the central city at peak hours purchase daily or monthly licenses. Substantial improvements in air quality have resulted.[14]

Nevertheless, command and control is still the dominant trend in environmental policy in most developing countries. This may be the result of relatively weak policy institutions. It is a common observation that the capacities and performance of public regulatory agencies are relatively weak in many third-world countries. This problem, of course, is not unique to them; administrative deficiencies in developed countries account for part of the large gap between the laws and their enforcement. But most observers agree that this is a particularly thorny problem for developing countries. It is not solely a matter of professionalism and lack of political clout. It is also a fact that centralized public bureaucracies in many developed countries have grown so large that they have become not only unproductive but actually predatory.

For some observers, this institutional weakness implies that developing countries ought to move away from command-and-control measures toward

---

[14] Theodore Panayotou, "Economic Incentives in Environmental Management and Their Relevance to Developing Countries," in Denizhan Eröcal (ed.), *Environmental Management in Developing Countries*, Organization for Economic Cooperation and Development, Paris, 1991, pp. 83–132.

economic incentive policies. For others, who perhaps are impressed that developed countries themselves are only beginning to place greater reliance on incentive measures, these institutional shortcomings imply that environmental regulations in developing countries are best kept relatively simple and direct— in other words, simple command-and-control strategies through uniform standards. The Brundtland Commission itself concluded that in developing countries, ". . . regulations imposing uniform performance standards are essential to ensure that industry makes the investments necessary to reduce pollution."[15]

The resolution of this question rests on recognizing that the category "developing countries" actually includes a wide range of experience. At one end of the spectrum are countries that are still almost totally agricultural, substantially uniform technologically, and with only the beginnings of a modern economic sector. At the other end of the spectrum are countries that have developed relatively large industrial, financial, and transportation sectors, important economic links to the rest of the world, and, most importantly, comparatively sophisticated political institutions. In the former countries, simple command-and-control approaches are likely to be best: a prohibition on a certain pesticide, for example, or limits on a certain irrigation practice. These may be enforced without sophisticated monitoring, and technical uniformity among producers means that these steps will be reasonably cost-effective. But in more advanced developing countries, incentive-based policies have much more to recommend them. Here the necessary political institutions may have been put in place, technological complexity makes it much more difficult to achieve acceptable levels of cost-effectiveness with command-and-control approaches, and strong long-run incentives for continued technical innovation in pollution control are of paramount importance.

THE ROLE OF THE DEVELOPED COUNTRIES

Developing countries are struggling with a wide array of economic, political, and social problems that stand in the way of lasting economic modernization. To graft environmental concerns onto the process puts an added burden on everyone in these countries, whatever their position. The developed countries have an important role to play in helping the third world to make this transition, not just for humanitarian reasons but also because many environmental problems are becoming increasingly international in scope. As these countries catch up to the developed economies, their technical choices and emission-control efforts will have a direct bearing on important global problems, such as CO_2 emissions and the global greenhouse effect, toxic chemical releases, nuclear radiation emissions, and so on.

[15] World Commission on Environment and Development, *Our Common Future*, Oxford University Press, New York, 1987, p. 220.

Technology Transfer

By "technology transfer" we refer to the transfer, from developed to developing countries, of technologies and skills that can provide the impetus for economic development with lower environmental impacts than could be attained without the transfer. The focus is not on direct investment,[16] per se, but on the transfer of knowledge that citizens of developing countries themselves can adapt to their own needs and styles of operation. Technology transfer has been an important concept in economic development efforts for decades. But it has taken on new urgency in the context of recent environmental problems. It has become evident that if the rest of the world goes through the same high-pollution course of development as the developed countries have done, the drain on world resources will be enormous and the impact on the global environment potentially disastrous. Thus, technology transfer is essential to convert developing countries more quickly to environment-friendly techniques without having to go through intermediate developmental stages.

Concrete provisions for the transfer of technology have been written into some recent international environmental treaties. The 1989 Basel Convention on Hazardous Waste obligates the signatories to provide technical assistance to developing countries in the implementation of the treaty. The 1990 amendments to the Montreal Protocol on protection of the ozone layer has a requirement that developed countries make available to developing countries, on reasonable terms, new reduced-CFC technology; it also establishes a fund to help developing countries meet the requirements for reduced emissions.[17] In 1990 the five Nordic countries formed the Nordic Environment Finance Corporation to provide help for environmentally sound investment in Eastern and Central Europe.

Technology transfer has two important parts. The first is the initial development of new technologies and procedures. These are a product of innovation in industries searching for ways of reducing emissions and in the pollution-control industry itself. Thus, one element in technology transfer is the provision of incentives for a brisk level of innovation in the originating countries. This implies pollution-control policies that provide these incentives, about which we have said a lot in earlier chapters. In particular, we have discussed the positive incentives for innovation provided by economic-incentive types of policies, and the negative effects provided by technology-based standards.

The second element of environmental technology transfer is getting the ideas, technical means, and necessary training effectively into the receiving countries. The word "effectively" is important because history is full of cases in which

---

[16] "Direct investment" is when a foreign company, usually a "multinational," builds and operates an enterprise in a developing country. "Indirect" or "portfolio" investment is where a foreign firm invests money in a domestic enterprise. For example, if Browning-Ferris Industries (a big Houston company in waste management and pollution control) starts its own company in, say South Korea, this is direct investment. If it chooses instead to get into that market by investing in an existing South Korean waste management firm, this is indirect investment.

[17] Chapter 21 contains a discussion of international environmental treaties in general, while Chapter 20 discusses the specific provisions of the Montreal Protocol.

transferred techniques have failed to work as anticipated. It is much more than just moving a machine from one location to another; a tremendous array of problems must be worked out to bridge the informational, cultural, commercial, and political gaps that separate people in different countries. At the end of the process, which normally will involve many different business, trade, political, and environmental groups, the objective is to transfer technology that is compatible with local skills and labor availabilities.

Just as the policy environment in the originating countries has much to do with rates of innovation there, so the policy environment in receiving countries plays a strong role in providing the incentives for local firms to search for, and be receptive to, new pollution-control technologies. Exhibit 19-1 contains a story about the leather industry in Kenya. It illustrates several things—e.g., the role of a research institute funded by foreign donors and a local policy environment that will provide leather tanning companies with a sufficient "regulatory push" to improve their environmental performance.

Debt-for-Nature Swaps

Suppose you and I are neighbors and I owe you $100 on a past loan. Suppose further that I keep a very untidy yard, never mowing the grass and keeping several junk cars next to my garage. You offer to wipe out the $100 debt if I will agree to clean up my yard. That is a debt-for-nature swap. Many developing countries owe large sums to lenders in developed countries, particularly commercial banks. These loans have been made for a variety of purposes, primarily to support investment and consumption in the developing countries. In many cases the debtor nations have found it difficult to pay back the loans. Debt-for-nature swaps are where environmental groups in the developed world buy portions of this debt and retire it in return for environmental preservation efforts by the developing country that owes the debt.

The first debt-for-nature swap was in 1987. Conservation International, a private group, bought $650,000 of Bolivia's commercial debt from the Citicorp Investment Bank for $100,000. In return for retiring this debt, the government of Bolivia agreed to place a 4-million acre piece of tropical rain forest in protected status and create a fund for the management of the area. Debt-for-nature swaps have since been concluded with numerous other countries, including Ecuador, Costa Rica, the Philippines, Madagascar, and the Dominican Republic.[18]

How effective debt-for-nature swaps can be is a difficult question. As a debt-retiring device, the approach can have little impact because of the vast amount of debt outstanding. As an environmental tool, it can be more effective, even though the scope of the overall problem is huge in comparison to the means. Perhaps their primary use will be to target very specific instances where critical environmental links are threatened, or where they can be used to get a larger

---

[18] Catherine A. O'Neill and Cass R. Sunstein, "Economics and the Environment: Trading Debt and Technology for Nature," *Columbia Journal of Environmental Law*, 17, Winter 1992, pp. 93–151.

EXHIBIT 19-1

ISSUES IN THE TRANSFER OF ENVIRONMENTAL TECHNOLOGY TO DEVELOPING COUNTRIES

Making leather has traditionally been a dirty and often unsociable exercise. Tanneries have been located outside towns, downwind and downstream to carry away noxious smells and wastes. Today, leather production still involves considerable use of water and generation of wastes. On average, one metric ton of raw hide yields only 200 kilograms of leather. The by-products include 50 cubic meters of wastewater, containing a range of chemicals, and half a metric ton each of wet sludge and solid wastes.

Increasingly, however, industrialists and researchers are finding ways both to reduce the generation of pollution and waste and to upgrade the efficiency of the production process. A wide range of techniques and approaches can be applied, from simple low-cost housekeeping improvements through the substitution of less damaging chemicals to the introduction of intrinsically cleaner production technologies. Innovative ways of using tanning wastes as raw materials for glue, fertilizer, and animal fodder are also being developed.

The challenge of diffusing "best practice" has been increased by the relocation of leathermaking during the last 30 years from the industrial to the developing world, where pollution control regimes are often weaker and where resources for environmental protection are scarce. In many developing countries, the leather industry has played a central role during industrialization; it is agro-based, labor-intensive, and adaptable to small-scale, low-technology production.

There is no such thing as a standard tannery; processes differ widely depending on location, sophistication, and the market for the final product. International best practice has to be translated into the local context; pilot projects are often needed to demonstrate the feasibility of change. Research institutes and trade associations together play a vital role in this process. In Kenya, the lead agency for the tanning industry is the Leather Development Centre (LDC) at the Kenya Industrial Research and Development Institute (KIRDI).

A weak institutional and legislative frame-

program started. Even in these cases, however, significant problems remain. One of the most difficult is something we have talked about throughout this book: enforcement. Once a private group has bought and retired a certain amount of debt, it may be hard to ensure that the country with which they have made the agreement will continue to abide by the deal.

Environmental Values in International Aid Institutions

Some of the most egregious cases of environmental damage in developing countries have actually stemmed from projects initiated and funded by international aid organizations, whose objectives are primarily to help these countries develop economically. A well-publicized example is the project funded partly by the World Bank to build roads and encourage colonization in the northwestern part of Brazil. The building of the roads attracted many more migrants into the area than was anticipated, ". . . making already underfunded public agencies work has meant that Kenyan industry has to date not received a sufficient regulatory push for improved environmental performance. In addition, lack of information and financial resources has limited the ability of local companies to assess and install cleaner technologies from abroad. An expert working at the Leather Development Centre sums up the challenge thus: "It is common among Kenyan tanneries to rely on traditional methods of processing leather, resulting in heavy production and discharge of pollution in the wastewater."

Collective efforts led by research institutes and/or industry associations can help spread the costs of improvement while minimizing the inherent risks of innovation. This is the role that the Leather Development Centre plays. It has been developed in phases over 10 years with technical and financial assistance from the United Nations Industrial Development Organization (UNIDO) and the Federal Republic of Germany. The center's aim is to provide advice and support to local companies on two interconnected issues: identifying and developing enhanced process and product technologies, which will boost the industry's domestic and export

potential, and developing and diffusing better ways of reducing the environmental hazards from leather production. The LDC has established a pilot tannery plant, a leather design and production unit, a quality control laboratory, and a wastewater demonstration unit at its facilities in Nairobi. Although most of its funding comes from domestic and external government sources, a nominal fee is charged for the centre's services.

The first step toward sustainable development for the leather industry is the creation of awareness among industrialists of the need for change. Once awareness has been raised, the center can provide tools to help companies overcome pollution problems. It uses its pilot production and treatment plants as models for training and demonstration purposes during seminars and workshops. This is coupled with regular visits to the tanneries themselves by LDC experts, and targeted assistance programs.

even less capable of controlling large-scale deforestation."[19] Many international donors have leaned toward the big project: dams, power stations, infrastructure, etc. These have often been pursued in ways that were not sensitive to environmental impacts because the donors, together with governments in recipient countries, have been so focused on spurring economic growth.

What this problem calls for is a more complete adoption of the general benefit–cost approach, interpreted broadly to mean the accounting for, and comparison of, all benefits and costs, whether or not they can be monetized in a formal framework. In particular, more attention must be given to working out the environmental impacts of these development projects. In recent years many international lending organizations have begun to take the environmental issues of developing countries more seriously. For example, the World Bank has created a new Environmental Department and changed its proce-

[19] World Bank, *World Development Report 1992, Development and Environment*, Oxford University Press, New York, 1992, p. 80.

dures so that the environmental implications of proposed projects will be taken into account in making lending decisions. Bank policy now requires complete environmental assessments for all projects that have significant impacts on the environment.

SUMMARY

Environmental problems in developing countries have become increasingly critical in the last few decades. While the appearance of global issues has helped people to see that all countries are inextricably linked in the global environment, more attention has also been directed at traditional air and water pollution problems of developing countries. The issue of long-run sustainability of the natural resource and environmental assets of these countries has become a policy focus point.

Analysis of past trends shows that development tends to make some environmental problems worse and others better. Some phenomena, such as SO_2 pollution, seem to get worse as countries initially begin to develop rapidly and then improve as development leads to higher per-capita incomes. There is some evidence, though it is not particularly strong, that "dirty" industries in developed countries have been migrating to developing ones, but the reasons for this are still not clear. The "pollution-haven" hypothesis does not receive strong support in the data.

Policy institutions in developing countries have historically been relatively weak, but this is changing. Most environmental policy in these countries has followed the lead of the developed world, in terms of being based on command-and-control principles. Some have suggested that developing countries should emphasize incentive-based policies so as to achieve higher levels of cost-effectiveness. Population control has frequently been recommended as a means of lessening environmental impacts. While lower rates of population growth may facilitate environmental improvements, they are not sufficient for attaining improvements in environmental quality.

Finally, the developed world can play a substantial role in helping third-world countries develop without large-scale environmental destruction. The primary mechanism for this is through technology transfer, understood broadly to include the transfer of skills and technological capabilities that are culturally sound, and not solely the transfer of Western capital goods.

QUESTIONS FOR FURTHER DISCUSSION

1 How does the notion of "sustainability" square with the fact that developing countries must usually draw heavily on their natural resource base if they are to develop economically?
2 Do the imperatives of "sustainability" imply that benefit–cost analysis applied to programs in developing countries should be different from benefit–cost analysis as it is applied in developed countries?

3 When a multinational business firm from the developed world opens operations in a developing nation, should it be held to the environmental standards of its country of origin or to those of the country in which it is operating?

4 Suppose we introduce a new criterion, "administrative feasibility," for evaluating environmental policies in developing countries. How might this affect choices among different types of policies?

5 We have spent a great deal of time in this book discussing the importance of having strong incentives for firms to engage in R&D to find improved means of pollution control. Apply this idea to the notion of "technology transfer."

SELECTED READINGS

Baker, Doug S., and Daniel B. Tunstall (eds.): *1990 Directory of Country Environmental Studies: An Annotated Bibliography of Environmental and Natural Resource Profiles and Assessments,* World Resources Institute, Washington, D.C., 1990.

Binswanger, Hans P.: "Brazilian Policies that Encourage Deforestation in the Amazon," *World Development,* 19(7), July 1991, pp. 821–829.

Bojo, Jan, Karl-Goran Maler, and Lena Unemo (eds.): *Environment and Development: An Economic Approach,* Kluwer Academic Publishers, Boston, 1992.

Eröcal, Denizhan (ed.): *Environmental Management in Developing Countries,* Organization for Economic Cooperation and Development, Paris, August 1991.

Eskeland, Gunnar, and Emmanuel Jimenez: "Choosing Among Policy Instruments in Pollution Control: A Review," Country Economics Department, World Bank, Washington, D.C., June 20, 1990.

Eskeland, Gunnar S., and Emmanuel Jimenez: "Curbing Pollution in Developing Countries," *Finance and Development,* 28(1), March 1991, pp. 15–18.

Logan, Bernard I.: "An Assessment of the Environmental and Economic Implications of Toxic-Waste Disposal in Sub-Saharan Africa," *Journal of World Trade,* 25(1), February 1991, pp. 61–76.

Lyon, Randolph M.: "Transferable Discharge Permit Systems and Environmental Management in Developing Countries," *World Development,* 17(8), August 1989, pp. 1299–1312.

Mayda, Jaro: "Environmental Legislation in Developing Countries: Some Parameters and Constraints," *Ecology Law Quarterly,* 12(4), 1985, pp. 997–1023.

Pearce, David, Edward Barbier, and Anil Markandya: *Sustainable Development, Economics and Environment in the Third World,* Earthscan Publications, London, 1990.

Pearce, David, Edward Barbier, Anil Markandya, Scott Barrett, R. Kerry Turner, and Timothy Swanson: *Blueprint 2: Greening the World Economy,* Earthscan Publications, London, 1991.

Ramakrishna, Kilaparti: "The Emergence of Environmental Law in the Developing Countries: A Case Study of India," *Ecology Law Quarterly,* 12(4), 1985, pp. 907–935.

Ross, Lester: *Environmental Policy in China,* Indiana University Press, Bloomington, Ind., 1988.

Walter, Ingo: "Environmentally Induced Industrial Relocation to Developing Countries" in Seymour Rubin and Thomas Graham (eds.), *Environment and Trade,* Osmon Allanheld, Totowa, N.J., 1982, pp. 67–101.

CHAPTER 20

THE GLOBAL ENVIRONMENT

People all around the world are struggling to come to grips with local environmental problems and improve their immediate surroundings. But over the last few decades, we have had to broaden our outlook, for we have started to become aware of problems in which the "environment" is that of the entire world. For all of history, one of the ways humans have reacted to local environmental destruction is migration. But at the planetary level this option is not available. There is no escape if we inadvertently make the planet less habitable.

Complementing the daunting physical facts are the sobering political/economic facts that have made it virtually impossible for the world's nations to act collectively. We seem to be in a race between the accumulating scientific data that scientists, still with great uncertainty, are straining to interpret, and the growing efforts to develop international institutions and perspectives that will make concerted action possible.

In this chapter we will look at several of these global environmental problems. We will consider first the problems of the global atmosphere and its degradation—specifically stratospheric ozone depletion and the global greenhouse effect. We will then look at the issue of diminishing biological diversity which, though it is occurring at different rates in various parts of the world, nevertheless has truly global significance. Each of these issues is very complicated scientifically and politically, and we can only touch on their most important elements. We will focus on their economic aspects.

OZONE DEPLETION

The Physical Problem

At sea level ozone is a pollutant produced when emissions of hydrocarbons and nitrogen oxides interact in the presence of sunlight. A variety of health problems and agricultural crop damages have been traced to elevated levels of surface ozone. But most of the ozone in the earth's atmosphere is located in the stratosphere, a zone extending from about 10 km to about 50 km in altitude. This stratospheric ozone is critical in maintaining the earth's radiation balance. The atmosphere surrounding the earth essentially acts as a filter for incoming electromagnetic radiation. The atmospheric gas responsible for this is ozone, which blocks a large percentage of incoming low-wavelength, or ultraviolet, radiation.

Several decades ago scientific evidence began to appear that the ozone content of the atmosphere was showing signs of diminishing. In the late 1970s a large hole appeared in the ozone layer over Antarctica. More recently, significant ozone reduction has been found throughout the entire stratosphere, including those areas over the more populated parts of the world. In the 1970s scientists discovered the cause of this phenomenon. It had been known for some time that the chemical content of the atmosphere has been changing at a rapid rate and on a global scale. Atmospheric concentrations of CO_2, CH_4, N_2O, and various chlorinated gases are estimated to be increasing at a rate of 0.2 percent to 5.0 percent per year.[1] Ozone disappearance was linked to the accumulation of chlorine in the stratosphere. Chlorine was found to insert itself into what was normally a balanced process of ozone production and destruction, vastly increasing the rate of destruction. And the source of the chlorine turned out to be a variety of manufactured chemicals which, released at ground level, slowly migrated up to higher altitudes. The culprits are substances called halocarbons, chemicals composed of carbon atoms in combination with atoms of chlorine, fluorine, iodine, and bromine. The primary halocarbons are called chlorofluorocarbons (CFCs), which have molecules consisting of combinations of carbon, fluorine, and chlorine atoms. Another subgroup is the halons, composed of these elements plus bromine atoms; bromine, in fact, acts similarly to chlorine in breaking down ozone molecules. Carbon tetrachloride and methyl chloroform are also implicated in ozone destruction.

CFCs were developed in the 1930s as a replacement for the refrigerants in use at the time. Unlike those they replaced, CFCs are extremely stable, nontoxic, and inert relative to the electrical and mechanical machinery in which they are used. Thus their use spread quickly as refrigerants and also as propellants for aerosols (hair sprays, deodorants, insecticides), industrial agents for making polyurethane and polystyrene foams, and industrial cleaning agents and solvents. Halons are widely used as fire suppressors. When these substances were introduced attention was exclusively on their benefits; there was no evidence that they could have long-run impacts on the atmosphere. The very stable nature of these gases allows them to migrate very slowly in the atmosphere. After surface release, they drift up through the troposphere into the stratosphere, where they begin a long process of ozone destruction.

[1] Robert T. Watson, "Atmospheric Ozone," in James G. Titus (ed.), *Effects of Changes in Stratospheric Ozone and Global Climate, Volume 1, Overview,* U.S. Environmental Protection Agency, Washington, D.C., 1986, p. 69.

Damages from Ultraviolet Radiation

Several years ago it was thought that ozone depletion might confine itself to small parts of the stratosphere, in which case damages from the increasing surface flux of ultraviolet radiation would be limited. But recently strong evidence has appeared that significant ozone depletion is occurring over large portions of the world's highly populated regions. Thus, damages are likely to be much more widespread. It is generally believed that each 1 percent drop in stratospheric ozone will produce a 2 to 3 percent increase in ultraviolet radiation at the earth's surface.[2] On this basis, radiation increases over the next century are expected to be at least 3–4 percent at the tropics and 10–12 percent at the higher latitudes.

Current research indicates that there are two main sources of damage to humans: health impacts and agricultural crop losses. Health damages are related to the increased incidence of skin cancers and eye disease. The dose-response relationships developed by the EPA indicate that for each 1 percent increase in UV_B radiation, basal-cell and squamous-cell cancer cases would increase by 1 percent and 2 percent, respectively, while melanoma skin cancers would increase by less than 1 percent, and cataracts by about .2 percent.[3] Increased UV_B radiation can also be expected to increase food production costs because of the physical damages it produces in growing plants. Damages are also expected in other parts of the earth's physical ecosystem.

Policy Responses[4]

The potential seriousness of the ozone-depletion problem has concentrated peoples' minds and led to some relatively vigorous policy responses. Initially several countries took unilateral actions. In 1978 the U.S. and several other countries (Canada, Sweden, Norway, Denmark) banned CFCs in aerosol cans, but not as a refrigerant. In the 1980s the continued scientific evidence of ozone depletion led to international action. Under the auspices of the United Nations, 24 nations signed in 1987 the *Montreal Protocol on Substances That Deplete the Ozone Layer*. It committed the high CFC-using signatories to a phasedown of CFCs and halons to 50 percent of their 1986 levels, to be achieved by 1998. Signatory countries currently using low levels of CFCs were given a 10-year grace period: Starting in 1999 they were to cut back to 1995–1997 levels, as shown in Table 20-1.

Soon after the Montreal agreement it became clear that this reduction was not enough, partly because continuing research showed that the problem was getting worse, and partly because some large CFC-producing countries had not

---

[2] Alphonse Forziati, "The Chlorofluorocarbon Problem," in John H. Cumberland, James R. Hibbs, and Irving Hoch (eds.), *The Economics of Managing Chlorofluorocarbons*, Resources for the Future, Washington, D.C., 1982, p. 54.

[3] U.S. Environmental Protection Agency, *Regulatory Impact Analysis: Protection of Stratospheric Ozone*, Vol. II, Appendix E, Washington, D.C., 1987, pp. E3–E4.

[4] For a good discussion of the issues in this section see Peter M. Morrisette, "The Evolution of Policy Responses to Stratospheric Ozone Depletion," *Natural Resources Journal*, 29(3), Summer 1989, pp. 793–820.

TABLE 20-1
SUMMARY OF THE TERMS OF THE MONTREAL PROTOCOL FOR OZONE-DESTROYING
CHEMICALS

Original 1987 Agreement

Substances controlled: CFCs-11, -12, -113, -114, -115, halons 1211, 1301, 2402.

High-CFC-using countries:
  Reduce production and consumption to 50% of 1986 levels by 1998.
  As of 1992, halon production to be held at or below 1986 levels.

Low-CFC-using countries:
  As of 1999, cut back to 50% of 1995–1997 levels over the next 10 years.

1990 Agreement

Regulates 10 additional substances, including CCl_4.

High-using countries (consumption greater than 0.3 kg/person):
  20% reduction in production and consumption from 1986 levels by 1993.
  50% reduction in production and consumption from 1986 levels by 1997.
  100% reduction in production and consumption from 1986 levels by 2000.

Halons frozen at 1986 levels by 1992, then phased out by 2000, except for certain "essential" uses.

CH_4 to be phased out by 2005.

Low-CFC-using countries: 10-year grace period on phaseout schedules, no export of CFCs.

Multilateral fund to aid developing countries with phaseout problems and to foster technology transfer.

No imports or exports of controlled substances with nonparties after 1990.

Source: Office of Technology Assessment, *Changing by Degrees: Steps to Reduce Greenhouse Gases,* Washington, D.C., 1991, pp. 67–68.

signed the original agreement. Thus, in 1990 the Montreal Protocol countries agreed to phase out the production of CFCs completely by the year 2000, to add carbon tetrachloride and methyl chloroform to the list, and to introduce a longer-run schedule for phasing out HCFCs. It also instituted a fund, created from contributions of developed countries, to be used to help finance CFC-reducing technological changes in developing countries. Additional countries signed the agreement in subsequent years. In the 1991 meeting, China finally agreed to sign the Protocol, leaving only India as the major CFC-using nation still outside the agreement.

The Montreal Protocol has been a success in many ways. It has found wide agreement among nations of the world. It very effectively focused attention on the burgeoning body of scientific evidence of ozone depletion, using it to motivate political agreement. And it created conditions where both developed and developing countries could find agreement. It remains to be seen whether it will provide a model for future international agreements. What is unique in the CFC agreement is that we are dealing essentially with a restricted set of substances. In all producing countries, the CFC-producing industry is composed of a few large chemical companies. So international policy has been driven not only by scientific results, but also by international competition in this industry. U.S. firms have been leaders in developing substitutes for CFCs, and they, therefore, have led the charge for a CFC phaseout. Other international environmental agreements in the future may not have the same kind of economic realities behind them.

It is too early to tell whether the phaseout schedule specified in the Montreal Protocol will be achieved by the signatory states. There are no direct enforcement steps that may be undertaken by international authorities, in this or in any other agreement. Each country must, therefore, enforce its own cutbacks as it sees fit. If they do not do so with sufficient vigor, the available sanctions are international embarrassment or trade sanctions, with uncertain results.[5]

The Economics of CFC Controls

In economic terms we have a problem here similar to the phasing out of leaded gasoline. The objective is reasonably clear and widely shared; the basic problem is how to bring it about in different countries. In advanced economies the main focus has been put on developing substitute chemicals that will perform the same tasks as CFCs—as refrigerants, cleaning agents, etc.—but have little or no ozone-depleting impact. Table 20-2 shows the major CFCs and some of the substances chemists are looking at as substitutes. CFC-11, -12, and -113 are the most common substances in use, but these have very long atmospheric lifetimes and rather high ozone depletion potentials (ODPs). The halons have even higher ODPs. Research has emphasized the development of a variety of hydrochlorofluorocarbons (HCFCs) and hydrofluorocarbons (HFCs) that have both shorter atmospheric lifetimes and much lower, or zero, ODPs. So what is essentially driving the rate of CFC phaseout in advanced economies is the cost of developing these substitutes, together with the costs of changeover from the old to the new chemicals. Some substances may be simply "drop-in" substitutes, while others will require getting rid of old capital equipment (refrigerators, air conditioners, etc.) and installing new equipment.

To meet the phaseout timetables agreed upon[6] under the Montreal Protocol each country will have to adopt some explicit control policy on production, imports, and exports of the targeted substances. In the U.S., the approach has been for the EPA to allocate transferable production quotas among the five domestic CFC producers. Each of these firms is required to reduce its CFC production in stages to meet the mandated phaseout schedule. A major problem with setting production ceilings in this way is that it can lead to unwarranted increases in profits for current manufacturers of CFCs. In effect it gives firms in

---

[5] In the meeting at which the Protocol was adopted, the parties voted to postpone taking up enforcement issues until their next meeting. At the next meeting, enforcement issues were again postponed.

[6] Some countries have acted on their own to move up the phaseout of CFCs. The U.S., for example, has committed itself to a complete phaseout of CFCs by December 31, 1995.

TABLE 20-2
MAJOR OZONE-DEPLETING CHEMICALS

		Atmospheric lifetime (years)	Estimated ozone-depletion potential*
Chlorofluorocarbons			
CFC-11	CCl_3F	40–80	1.0
CFC-12	CCl_2F_2	80–150	1.0
CFC-113	$C_2F_3Cl_3$	100	0.8
CFC-114	$C_2F_4Cl_2$	270	1.0
CFC-115	C_2F_5Cl	600	0.6
Halons			
H-1211	CF_2B_RCl	15	3.0
H-1301	CF_3B_R	110	10.0
H-2402	$C_2F_4B_{r_2}$		6.0
Carbon tetrachloride	CCl_4	60	1.06
Methyl chloroform	$C_2H_3Cl_3$	6	0.1
Hydrochlorofluorocarbons			
HCFC-22	$CHClF_2$	20	0.05
HCFC-123	CF_3CHCl_2	2	0.02
HCFC-124	$CHClFCF_3$	4	0.02
HCFC-141b	CCl_2FCH_3	10	0.1
HCFC-142b	CH_3CClF_2	22	0.06
Hydrofluorocarbons			
HFC-125	CHF_2CF_3	15	0.0
HFC-134a	CH_2FCF_3	5	0.0
HFC-143a	CH_3CF_3	40	0.0
HFC-152a	CH_3CHF_2	2	0.0

*The ozone-depletion potential (ODP) of a compound is defined as the estimated ozone depletion of a unit mass of the compound divided by the ozone depletion of a unit mass of CFC-11.

Source: U.S. Congress, House Committee on Energy and Commerce, Subcommittee on Oversight and Investigations, *Ozone Layer Depletion,* Hearings, 101st Congress, 1st Session, May 15, 1989.

the industry, who may have been operating as rivals, a way of acting like monopolists. Figure 20-1 illustrates this with a simple market model. It shows a typical downward sloping demand curve for CFCs, together with a flat marginal cost curve. Left to itself, competitive forces would lead to a production level of q_1 and a price that equals marginal production costs. But if public authorities limit production to q_2, the price will now increase to p_2, which is substantially above production costs. Thus, an amount equal to area a becomes potential excess profits earned in the industry because of the output restrictions.

When tighter CFC controls and faster phaseouts of CFCs were being discussed by the U.S. Congress in the late 1980s, there was widespread feeling that at least some of these excess profits should accrue to the public. Several means were discussed. One was to auction off CFC production rights to the various chemical-producing companies. The bidding process, if it worked well, would transfer

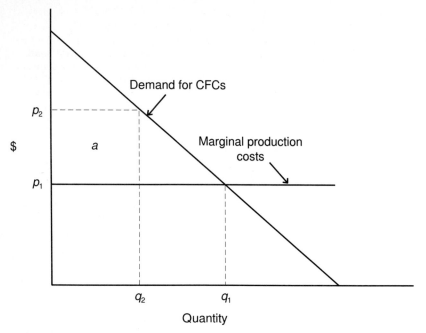

FIGURE 20-1
Government-Imposed Production Limitations Lead to Monopoly Profits.

some portion of the excess profits to the public. The other approach, which was finally adopted, was to tax the production of CFCs. In theory, a tax equal to ($p_2 - p_1$) would transfer all of the excess profits to the public. It could then be used for any number of purposes, perhaps put into general revenues or used specifically to help the CFC conversion process. The system adopted establishes a base tax rate, then sets different taxes on the various ozone-depleting chemicals according to the expression:

$$\text{Tax rate} = \text{Base rate} \times \text{Ozone-depleting potential.}$$

The base rate was initially $1.37 per pound, to increase to $1.67 in 1992, to $2.65 in 1993, and finally to $3.10 in 1995. Thus, the initial tax on, e.g., CFC-113 was $1.096 ($1.37 × .8).[7]

The 1990 Clean Air Act Amendments contained a number of other parts on ozone depletion. It established a phaseout program for HCFCs, with production to be eliminated by 2030. It established a national recycling program for CFCs used in refrigerators and air conditioners, and it introduced prohibitions on the venting of CFCs from equipment currently containing these substances.

---

[7] Because of the insistence of halon makers and users, the tax on halons was set at $.25 per pound.

In an earlier chapter we talked about how lead trading was used to reduce the overall cost of switching to no-lead gas. The Montreal Protocol contains the same type of approach for switching out of the production plus consumption[8] of substances controlled by the agreement. This is the trading of emission reduction credits among countries. Thus, if a country fails to meet its required production cutback because of the needs of "industrial rationalization," it is supposed to offset the excess emissions by getting comparable reductions in other countries.

GLOBAL WARMING

The Physical Problem

Another major global problem is the threat of a long-run increase in the surface temperature of the earth. This goes under the name of "global warming," or sometimes the "greenhouse effect." The principle of a greenhouse is that the enclosing glass (or nowadays plastic) allows the passage of incoming sunlight, but traps a portion of the reflected infrared radiation, which warms the interior of the greenhouse above the outside temperature. Greenhouse gases in the earth's atmosphere play a similar role; they serve to raise the temperature of the earth's surface and make it habitable. With no greenhouse gases at all, the surface of the earth would be about 30°C cooler than it is today, making human life impossible.

Under "normal" (i.e., preindustrial) conditions, trace amounts of greenhouse gases were in global balance. They were given off by decaying plant and animal materials and absorbed by forests and oceans. Into this rough balance came human beings and one of their greatest cultural accomplishments: the industrial revolution. That event was basically a revolution in energy use, involving a vast increase in the extraction of energy from fossil fuels—first coal, and later petroleum and natural gas. Combustion of fossil fuels, together with deforestation and a few other activities, has led to an increase in the CO_2 content of the atmosphere by about 20 percent from the beginning of the industrial revolution. In the last three decades alone it has increased 8 percent, and many scientists predict an approximate doubling by the middle of the next century. The main greenhouse gases, their approximate proportionate contribution to global warming, and their major sources are shown in Table 20-3.

If the global climate changes as many have predicted, we will be moving into a world very different from the one we now know. Widespread scientific opinion today suggests that the accumulation of greenhouse gases will lead sometime in the next century to a rise in surface temperature of 1.5–4.5°C.[9] The rate of heating is put at about 0.3°C per decade. This may not sound like a very rapid change,

[8] "Production plus consumption" is defined as production plus imports minus exports.
[9] James G. Titus and Stephen R. Seidel, "Overview of the Effects of Changing the Atmosphere," in James G. Titus (ed.), *Effects of Changes in Stratospheric Ozone and Global Climate, Volume 1, Overview,* U.S. Environmental Protection Agency, 1986, pp. 3–19.

TABLE 20-3
MAJOR GREENHOUSE GASES AND THEIR PRIMARY SOURCES

Gas	Proportionate effect (%)	Major source
CO_2	49	Fossil fuel combustion, deforestation, cement production
CH_4 (methane)	18	Landfills, agriculture, termites
N_2O (nitrous oxide)	6	Fertilizers, land clearing, biomass burning, fossil fuel combustion
Other (CO, NO_x, . . .)	13	Various

but historical studies have shown that in past episodes of warming and cooling, during which agricultural societies of the time suffered major dislocations, climate change occurred at a rate of only about .05°C per decade. Today's rate of change, in other words, is expected to be very much faster than those faced by humans in the past.

Global warming is expected to bring about a general rise in sea level because of the expansion of sea water, the melting of glaciers, and perhaps eventually the breaking up of polar ice sheets. Although this will be a general rise, it will have different local impacts on tidal and current patterns. Changes in meteorological patterns will also vary widely among regions. In the northern hemisphere, polar regions will warm faster than equatorial zones; on the continental landmasses the centers will become drier than the peripheries, etc. Our ability to predict these changes will improve as the global climate models of atmospheric scientists are better developed.

Human and Ecosystem Impacts

Although this is a problem of the global environment, its impacts on humans and ecosystem will vary greatly from one country and region to another. A sea-level rise would have devastating impacts in certain societies, like those of the Pacific islands, or those concentrated in low river deltas. Impacts will be relatively less in countries where development may be redirected toward interior regions. The drowning of coastal wetlands throughout the world could have important impacts on fisheries and, thus, on societies that rely heavily on marine resources. There will be very substantial impacts on ecosystems and individual species of plants and animals, not just because of the amount of change but also because the rate of change will be fast by evolutionary standards. In ice ages of the past, weather changes have happened slowly enough to allow species of plants and animals to migrate and survive. The rapid pace of change expected in the greenhouse phenomenon may be too quick for many organisms to adjust to changing habitats. It will also put a severe strain on species that occupy narrow ecological niches because relatively small changes in weather patterns can destroy the habitats on which they depend.

Perhaps the biggest impacts on humans will be through the effects of changed climate patterns on agriculture and forestry. Here the story gets very complicated, not only because weather patterns will be differently affected throughout the world, but also because crops, and the systems of cultivation adopted by farmers, vary a lot in terms of their ability to withstand changes in temperature and water availability. A recent study commissioned by the EPA concludes that the agricultural impacts of atmospheric warming will hit developing nations harder than developed countries. As the news clip in Exhibit 20-1 indicates, it is expected that African nations will be impacted the most. Previous studies had tended to conclude that agriculture could be adapted to future climate changes through crop development and technical changes. The new study casts some doubt on the ability of many developing countries to do this, because many of their crops are already closer to the limits of tolerance for warmer temperatures. Research on the impacts of the greenhouse effect will challenge scientists for many years to come.

Scientific Uncertainties and Human Choice

The discussion in the last few paragraphs may represent widespread thinking among scientists, but we must recognize that the predictions about global warming remain uncertain. The results come from highly complex models of the earth's atmosphere, which require enormous amounts of meteorological and socioeconomic data and incorporate large numbers of interrelationships and feedbacks. Small changes in the models can greatly change the conclusions. Unforeseen events can upset the phenomenon, as the recent eruption of Mount Pinatubo seems to have done. Other person-made factors can intervene; for example, it now appears that accumulated SO_2 in the lower atmosphere reflects sunlight, thus working against the greenhouse phenomenon. The same may be true of CFCs in the upper atmosphere. Small wonder, then, that there are still differences among scientists about the seriousness of the problem. The news clip shown in Exhibit 20-1 depicts some of these differences.

What are we to do in the face of these uncertainties? Some have argued that we should do little until clear evidence of greenhouse warming actually occurs, then adapt to it if and when it does. The problem with this is that the results could be devastating for countries that cannot easily adapt. Equity considerations suggest that we ought to take action now rather than wait. But even without the equity issue, action is still called for. In Chapter 6 we introduced a few concepts to help in analyzing situations involving risk. We talked in particular about risk aversion in cases involving small probabilities of very large losses. There is scientific uncertainty about the extent of global warming in the future, but the potential negative consequences are so great that it behooves us to be risk averse. In plain terms: better to be safe than sorry. All of which suggests strongly that we undertake steps today to reduce the probability of serious global warming in

---

EXHIBIT 20-1

THE DIFFERENTIAL IMPACT OF THE GREENHOUSE EFFECT

Warming Will Hurt Poor Nations Most.

The name implies a place where plants thrive, but don't let words fool you. The expected greenhouse warming will likely harm agriculture in many countries, particularly the poorer ones, warns the first international study on this topic.

"Our main conclusion is that the developing countries are most vulnerable to climate change in terms of agriculture," says Cynthia Rosenzweig, an agronomist at Columbia University and NASA's Goddard Institute for Space Studies in New York City. Rosenzweig led the agriculture study with Martin Parry of the University of Oxford in England.

Conducted by scientists in 25 countries, the study indicates that the global warming from greenhouse gas pollution will enhance agricultural disparity between rich and poor nations. In temperate zones, where developed nations reside, global warming may increase crop yields; but a warming will probably diminish yields in tropical areas, where many developing nations are located.

Agriculture in mid-latitude and high-latitude countries may benefit from global warming because it will help plants currently limited by the colder temperatures of these regions. Conversely, countries nearer the equator will suffer because conditions there already lie close to the limit of temperature tolerance for many crops. Warmer temperatures will stress these plants even more, Rosenzweig says.

According to the study, decreased crop yields and increased food prices could significantly swell the ranks of people suffering from hunger. By the year 2060, the number of people at risk of hunger could rise 10 to 50 percent above the level projected with no climate change, a number estimated at 640 million people for that year. The hunger threat will hit African nations hardest, the study finds.

In the real world, farmers continually alter their methods to suit the weather, so Rosenzweig and Parry tested the impact of modest adaptation strategies, such as altering planting dates, changing the crop varieties, or stepping up irrigation efforts in areas where it is already practiced. Such methods could offset most negative aspects of climate

---

the future. We have to recognize, however, that we are still in a trade-off situation. We are trading off the cost of measures taken today against benefits in terms of reduced future risk. This means we need to pay close attention to the cost-effectiveness of different policies.

Technical Responses to the Greenhouse Effect

The greenhouse effect results from an increase in the production of greenhouse gases relative to the ability of the earth's ecosystems to absorb them. So the primary means of reducing the warming lies in reducing the output of greenhouse gases and/or augmenting the CO_2-absorbing capacity of the natural world. Since CO_2 is the main greenhouse gas, we will focus on the issue of reducing global CO_2 emissions.

change in developed countries, but the developing world would benefit little from these minimal strategies, the researchers report.

Even extreme adaptations—such as installing irrigation systems or developing new crop varieties —would not erase the negative impacts of climate change in the developing world, the study suggests. However, slowing population growth could offset the increase in hunger caused by even severe climate change.

To make the agricultural projections, Rosenzweig and her colleagues started with three different climate forecasts provided by separate general-circulation models, which simulated how a doubling of greenhouse gases will alter climate. The scientists plugged the climate forecasts into models that estimate crop growth, taking into account how increasing carbon dioxide will fertilize plants. The crop-growth results then went into a model that simulates world food trade.

In the past, scientists lacked a clear view of how climate change might affect tropical regions—in part, says Rosenzweig, because projections suggest that temperatures would increase less dramatically in tropical areas than in mid-latitude and polar zones. Prior to the new study, researchers could argue that enhanced crop growth from higher carbon dioxide levels would balance the relatively small temperature rise expected in the tropics, she says.

The agriculture study, commissioned by the U.S. Environmental Protection Agency, is the first to take a detailed global look at the agricultural impacts of climate change. In doing so, it offers a bleaker picture than previous reports.

Gary Evans, head of the Agriculture Department's global change office, says the study's disturbing conclusions don't square with observations about agricultural trends in the United States.

"Technological capabilities in agriculture have proven for the last 50 to 75 years to be able to keep up with any shifts and changes that have taken place," he says, suggesting that similar developments around the world may be able to cut the losses from climate change in developing nations. Pointing to the current famine in Somalia, Evans speculates that war and other problems will cause greater food shortages than will climate change.

Source: Science News, 142(8), August 22, 1992, p. 142. Reprinted by permission from Science News, the weekly Newsmagazine of Science, copyright 1992 by Science Service, Inc.

To get an overall view of the current world production rate of CO_2 and how it may be altered, consider the following equation:

$$\text{Total } CO_2 \text{ production} = \text{Population} \times \frac{GDP^{10}}{\text{Person}} \times \frac{\text{Energy}}{GDP} \times \frac{CO_2}{\text{Energy}}$$

			Rates of change		
Global	1.7	1.7	1.0	−0.6	−0.4
India	4.5	2.0	1.2	1.2	0.1
U.S.	3.7	0.9	3.8	−1.0	0.0

[10] Gross domestic product.

The quantity of CO_2 emissions depends on the interaction of four factors. The first is population. Other things remaining equal, larger populations will use more energy and therefore emit larger amounts of CO_2. The second term is GDP per capita, a measure of the domestic output of goods and services per capita. We normally associate increases in this factor with economic growth. Neither of these first two factors can be considered likely candidates for reducing CO_2 emissions in the short run. Deliberate population control measures are unlikely to be effective, and no country is likely to be willing to reduce its rate of economic development. In the long run, however, the interaction of these two factors will be important, as history seems to show that lower population growth rates can be achieved by substantial improvements in economic welfare.

This means that significant near-term CO_2 reductions will have to come from the last two terms in the expression. The third is what we mean by "energy efficiency," the amount of energy used per dollar (or per franc or rupee or cedi) of output. The key here is to move toward technologies of production, distribution, and consumption that require relatively smaller quantities of energy. The last term is CO_2 produced per unit of energy used. Since different energy forms have markedly different CO_2 outputs per unit, reductions in CO_2 can be achieved by switching to less CO_2-intensive fuels.

The table under the equation shows how these four factors have been changing in recent years. The first row shows the annual growth rate in global CO_2 output, which is the sum of the global growth rates of the factors comprising the formula. Note that, worldwide, although energy efficiency and CO_2 intensity are declining, these are being more than offset by high growth rates in population and GDP per capita. But growth rates in the underlying factors differ a great deal among countries. In the table we compare those of India and the U.S. for illustrative purposes. In India, increases in all factors, especially population, have contributed to a very rapid rate of growth in CO_2 emissions. In the U.S., lower population growth rates, together with increases in energy efficiency (decreases in energy per GDP) have moderated the growth rate of CO_2 emissions. It is differences among countries in these contributing factors that complicate the adoption of effective worldwide agreements to limit CO_2 emissions. We will come back to this point below.

In the short run, i.e., over the next few decades, we will have to fight the greenhouse effect chiefly with increases in energy conservation and efficiency, a switch to low-carbon fuels, and a reduction in the use of chemicals with high greenhouse impacts. Table 20-4 lists the major types of changes that could be made in different economic sectors. There is no single source that we could call on to get drastic reductions in CO_2 production. Instead, significant changes could be made in hundreds of different places—transportation, industry, households, and agriculture. These changes are both technical— as, for example, the switch to more energy-efficient equipment and low-CO_2 fuels—and behavioral—for example, changing driving habits and adopting less energy-intensive life styles. Two primary questions have to be asked about these changes: First, what are they likely to cost and, second, how can we best bring them about?

TABLE 20-4
MEANS OF REDUCING GREENHOUSE GASES

Energy production
Reduce demand for electricity (see Households).
Switch to nonfossil fuels (solar, biomass, nuclear, hydroelectric).
Switch from high-carbon (coal) to low-carbon (gas) fossil fuels.
Reduce energy transmission losses.
Remove carbon from fuel and emissions.

Households
Reduce demand for energy (less heating, air conditioning, . . .).
Switch to less energy-intensive products.
Switch to more energy-efficient technologies (solar heaters, insulation, . . .).
Switch out of CFCs in car air conditioners. . . .

Industry
Increase energy efficiency of production processes.
Switch to low- or no-carbon fuels.
Increase energy efficiency in buildings, lighting, . . .
Switch out of CFCs and other greenhouse gases.

Transportation
Reduce miles driven and travel speeds.
Increase fuel efficiency of vehicles.
Switch to mass transit systems.

Agriculture and food system
Reduce methane production from livestock production and rice paddies.
Improve energy efficiency in farming.
Reduce CFC use in refrigeration.
Reduce energy use in transportation.
Increase land uses that lead to greater carbon storage.

Forestry
Reduce rates of deforestation.
Increase rates of reforestation.

Source: From material in U.S. Office of Technology Assessment, *Changing by Degrees,*
Steps to Reduce Greenhouse Gases, Washington, D.C., 1991.

Costs of CO_2 Emission Reductions

How costly would it be for different countries to reduce substantially their
emissions of greenhouse gases over the next several decades? We can be sure
that the marginal costs of CO_2 reduction are increasing; the greater the reduction,
the more it will cost. But how steeply they increase is a matter of great complexity.
Any meaningful CO_2 reduction is going to take many years, probably decades,
to bring about, because it means shifting the major technological and fossil fuel
biases that have been built into contemporary economies over a long period.
Thus, to cost out any control program, it's necessary to predict technological and
economic changes well into the future. In a world that is as technically and
politically dynamic as the one we live in today, this is very hard to do.

One way to estimate costs, called a "bottoms-up" analysis, is to put together technical information from specific economic sectors to construct a generalized picture of CO_2 reduction costs for the entire economy. One result of an analysis like this is estimates of CO_2 control costs for different technological options. Table 20-5 shows some cost-effectiveness results obtained in a large study by the U.S. Office of Technology Assessment (OTA). They show the estimated costs per ton of reducing CO_2 emissions in the U.S. by adopting different technical alternatives. The estimates are relatively short run, in the sense that the OTA was looking at things that could be accomplished over the next 25 years. Several options have negative CO_2 reduction costs. These are approaches that would pay for themselves without even considering CO_2 removal, primarily through savings in energy. Several things stand out in these numbers. Many are in the general range of $100–$300 per ton of CO_2 removed. Considering that the total quantity of CO_2 emissions in the U.S. today is about 5 billion tons per year, one can get a rough idea of the costs of decreasing these emissions by a substantial fraction. These are also marginal costs; that is, they are costs of reducing CO_2 emissions starting with where we are today. If we ever succeed in moving to a much more energy-efficient economy, the costs of making further reductions in CO_2 emissions will no doubt increase, probably a lot.

Some cost figures that stand out are the low estimates for afforestation, as essentially an add-on to the current conservation reserve program, and the high costs of CO_2 removal through shifting to mass transit. Afforestation looks like a good buy for CO_2 removal, but the other side of the coin is that because of the relatively small numbers of acres involved, the total amount of CO_2 that could be removed through this means in the U.S. is relatively modest. As far as the high

TABLE 20-5
COST-EFFECTIVENESS OF ALTERNATIVE MEANS OF REDUCING CO_2, U.S.

Means	Costs per ton of CO_2 ($)
Co-firing boilers with natural gas	510
Early retirement of coal plants, replaced with nonfossil fuels	280
Increased energy efficiency in homes	175 to 300
Increased energy in commercial buildings	−190 to 75
Cogeneration—commercial	85 to 210
Increased fuel efficiency in cars	−220 to −110
Increased fuel efficiency in light trucks	−510 to −410
Mass transit	1,150 to 2,300
Cogeneration—industry	55 to 120
Urban tree planting	180
Afforestation with CRP*	35
Increased CO_2-absorbing capacity through management of existing forests	150 to 200

*CRP stands for Conservation Reserve Program, a program to help farmers reduce production on marginal lands. The program would emphasize tree planting on these acreages.

Source: U.S. Office of Technology Assessment, Changing by Degrees, Steps to Reduce Greenhouse Gases, Washington, D.C., 1991, Appendix A.

cost estimates for rapid transit, these numbers show the effects of the long-run growth patterns in the economy. The trends in population dispersion and transportation technology over the last century have left us with a situation that is not amenable to mass transit to reduce transportation energy requirements. This is a strong reminder, if one is needed, of how decisions taken at one point in time can have consequences much later, when conditions have totally changed.

The other approach to estimating the cost of CO_2 control is a "top-down" analysis, where one studies national economies as single units, factoring in assumed rates of technical change and measuring other critical parameters like how the use of different fuels has responded to changes in their relative prices. A common approach is to measure the effects of CO_2 emission reductions on rates of economic growth. One way of summarizing the results is to estimate the extent to which GDP, at the end of the study period, would be reduced from the level it would have attained if there had been no program of CO_2 reduction. Table 20-6 summarizes some of the results of these studies, expressed as "end-year GDP as percentage of baseline." Note that the estimates vary a lot; they range from a low of – 0.2 percent to –15.0 percent. Even the estimates for the U.S. vary greatly among the different studies. To a large extent this is because of different research approaches—different assumptions, data, and the like. But it also reflects the inherent difficulty and uncertainty of doing studies that try to

TABLE 20-6
RESULTS OF STUDIES ON THE COSTS OF CO_2 REDUCTIONS

Study	Emission reduction from baseline (end year)	End-year GDP as percentage of baseline
Mann-Richels		
U.S.	−20 (2030)	−3.3
Other OECD	−20 (2030)	−1.2
Russia, Eastern Europe	−20 (2030)	−4.5
China	−20 (2030)	−5.0
Rest of world	−20 (2030)	−1.0
Congressional Budget Office (U.S.)	−36 (2000)	−0.6
Jorgenson/Wilcoxen (U.S.)	−36 (2060)	−1.1
Blitzer et al. (Egypt)	−35 (2002)	−15.0
Glomered et al. (Norway)	−26 (2010)	−2.7
NEPP (Netherlands)	−25 (2010)	−4.2
Bergman (Sweden)	−51 (2000)	−5.6
Dixon et al. (Australia)	−47 (2005)	−0.2

Sources: The studies were summarized in P. Hoeller, A. Dean, and J. Nicolaisen, "A Survey of Studies of the Costs of Reducing Greenhouse Gas Emissions," Working Paper No. 89, Organization for Economic Cooperation and Development, Department of Economics and Statistics, Paris, 1990; and Joel Darmstadter, "The Economic Cost of CO_2 Mitigation: A Review of Estimates for Selected World Regions," Discussion Paper ENR91-06, Resources for the Future, Washington, D.C., 1991.

extrapolate well into the future. This is especially true when we make assumptions about rates of technological change that are likely to occur in the future, in situations with and without the constraints on CO_2 emissions.

Policy Responses

Identifying possible CO_2-reducing technical and behavioral changes is one thing; adopting policies that can motivate their widespread adoption is another. Possible policy approaches for greenhouse gases fall into the same two categories we have discussed before: (1) standards, either emission or technology standards, and (2) incentive-based strategies. In thinking about policies on global warming, there are two levels to consider, the international and the domestic. At the international level, steps must be undertaken to obtain reductions in the aggregate CO_2 emissions from each country. At the national level, total emission reductions must be obtained through domestic policies. Policies at the two levels could be a complex mix of command-and-control (CAC) and incentive-based strategies.

We have no international agreement for CO_2 reduction as of yet (1993). But the precedent for one may have been established in other agreements, especially the CFC treaty. The Montreal Protocol divided the world's countries into two groups, then prescribed essentially equiproportionate reductions for the countries in each group. Similarly, the various SO_2- and NO_x-reducing provisions in present transboundary air pollution agreements call for equiproportionate reductions in emissions. These are, therefore, essentially CAC types of approaches, and they have the same built-in perverse incentives we have talked about earlier: They reward those who have been profligate in the past and penalize those who have been frugal. Countries like the U.S., where relatively little emphasis has been placed on fuel efficiency, will have an easier time meeting such standards for CO_2 reduction than countries like France, where carbon output per dollar of GDP is one-half that of the U.S.

We can be sure that the assignment of CO_2 limits to the many countries of the world will be especially controversial. What formula might be followed in setting these allocations? Consider the following possibilities:

- Equiproportionate reduction in emissions.
- Ability to pay. Base emission reductions/transfer payments on current per-capita income levels.
- "Polluter pays" principle. Base emission reductions/transfer payments on current or past contributions to the problem.
- Equal per-capita consumption. Base emission reductions on the idea that all per-capita consumption levels should be the same.

These rules would have substantially different implications for different countries of the world. The data in Table 20-7 show population, income, and CO_2 emissions data for a selected group of countries. The countries were selected to illustrate the differential impacts of the rules, not because they are in any way

TABLE 20-7
ECONOMIC AND CARBON EMISSIONS DATA FOR SELECTED COUNTRIES, 1987

Country	Population (millions)	GDP per capita ($)	Total emissions (mil tons)	Emissions per capita (tons)	Emissions per dollar GDP (grams)	Emissions (% of total)
China	1,031.9	320*	578	0.56	2,024	9.6
France	54.3	16,234	92	1.70	133	1.5
India	685.2	371	130	0.19	655	2.2
U.S.	226.5	18,506	1,139	5.03	276	18.9
World (average or total)			6,030	1.08	327	—

*1989.

Source: Emissions per capita and total emissions taken from John Walley, "The Interface Between Environmental and Trade Policies," *The Economic Journal,* 101(405), March 1991, p. 103. Population and income data are from United Nations, *1987 Demographic Yearbook,* New York, 1989, pp. 173–175.

more significant than others. If the cutback were based on total emissions, the largest reduction would be allocated to the U.S., followed by China, then India, and France. But if it were based on emissions per capita, the order would be U.S., France, China, and India. If emissions reductions were based on energy efficiency, the largest cutbacks would actually be allocated to China and India because, although their emissions per capita are low, incomes are even lower, giving them relatively high numbers for emissions per dollar of GDP. Finally, if we were to allocate emission reductions on the basis of proportionate share of total CO_2 emissions, the U.S. would have the largest cutback, followed by China, India, and France.

One important item these data do not include is the costs to the various countries of doing nothing; i.e., simply adapting to global warming. These costs are likely to place limits on the extent to which any particular country will readily accept CO_2 emission reduction requirements, since it is unlikely to be interested in spending more in control costs than the cost of accommodating to the change. For cooler countries in higher latitudes, with relatively little critical shoreline, adaptation costs may be fairly "modest." Countries in the opposite situation will have very high costs of adapting to higher temperatures and rising sea levels. Countries differ also in terms of agricultural adaptability, the ability to shift crops, varieties, cultivation methods, and so on, to maintain production in the face of climate changes. So countries are likely to have very different perceptions about how they will be affected by global warming. The obstacles to an effective international agreement on CO_2 reduction are many, and the need for creative treaty diplomacy is great.

We have talked many times in this book about the cost-ineffectiveness of proportionate cutbacks in emissions from different sources. The same principles are at work here, where by "sources" we mean countries. To have a CO_2 program that is *globally* cost-effective, some economists have suggested that we institute a system of transferable discharge permits at the international level. Countries would be allocated CO_2 emission permits equal to their permitted base-level emissions, as determined by some formula such as one of those discussed above. These permits would then be tradable among countries. The marginal costs of CO_2 reduction could be expected to differ substantially among countries, on the basis of such factors as wealth and economic growth rates, fossil fuel availabilities, and energy technologies. Thus trading opportunities exist that could substantially reduce the overall global costs of reducing CO_2 emissions. Another salutary feature of global carbon TDPs is that they could easily be used to address questions of international equity. The current belief is that it will cost developing countries more, relative to their current wealth, to reduce CO_2 emissions than developed economies. Thus the direction of transfers would in general go from less to more developed countries. On top of this, developing countries might be given proportionately larger numbers of permits in the initial distribution. In buying these extra permits developed nations would be transferring extra amounts of wealth to the developing countries, which they could use to switch to low-carbon development paths. However, the political practicability of this approach is open to serious question.

But a CO_2 treaty might be reached in which countries committed themselves to cutbacks of various amounts. To achieve such a cutback a country would have numerous policy options. Technology and emission standards are possibilities. In some cases governments may be able effectively to dictate certain economy-wide technology choices; e.g., the widespread adoption of nuclear power in France. Or a country might adopt performance or emission standards; e.g., the corporate average-fuel economy (CAFE) standards in the U.S. These require that car manufacturers meet minimum average mileage standards among all models made in a given year. But the enormous number and variety of different fuel-using technologies would work against using technology or performance standards as the primary policy approach to CO_2 reduction.

This kind of situation would lend itself well to the use of carbon taxes to provide the incentive to reduce fuel consumption and to shift to lower carbon forms of energy. These would be charges on the carbon content of fuels consumed. In a recent study of carbon taxes in the U.S., the Congressional Budget Office estimated that charges starting at \$10/ton of carbon in 1991 and rising to \$100/ton by 2000 would result in reductions in CO_2 emissions of 8–16 percent in 2000 below what they would have been without the tax.[11] Naturally the coal industry and heavy energy-using industries would be the hardest hit by such a tax. In recent years many countries have considered the adoption of carbon taxes.[12]

---

[11] U.S. Congressional Budget Office, *Carbon Charges as a Response to Global Warming: The Effects of Taxing Fossil Fuels,* Washington, D.C., August 1990.

[12] These countries are Australia, Austria, Canada, Denmark, France, Germany, Japan, The Netherlands, New Zealand, Norway, Sweden, and the United Kingdom. See Peter M. Morrisette and Andrew J. Plantinga, "The Global Warming Issue. Viewpoints of Different Countries," *Resources,* 103, Resources for the Future, Spring 1991, p. 3.

Suggestions have been made for a worldwide CO_2 emissions tax, a single tax that would apply to all sources in all countries. This would achieve cost-effectiveness at both the intercountry level and intersource level within each country, provided governments did nothing to thwart the uniform application of the tax domestically. Economic studies of this approach have been neatly summarized by Nordhaus. Figure 20-2 shows the relationship between different levels of carbon tax and the percentage of reduction in CO_2 emissions. The points shown in the graph are the results of the different studies reviewed by Nordhaus. The studies differed in terms of the countries and exact circumstances to which they applied, but they do seem to tell a reasonably consistent story. The curved line drawn through the points, representing what the author feels is the best summary of the studies. In effect the curve shows the marginal costs of reducing CO_2 emissions. To get a worldwide reduction of 20 percent in CO_2 emissions would require a tax of about \$45/ton of carbon. A 50 percent CO_2 reduction would need a \$140 tax, and the curvature of the graph shows that deeper CO_2 cutbacks would require progressively larger taxes.

Whether any significant international effort can be mounted to establish a worldwide carbon tax is highly problematic. A tax high enough to produce significant CO_2 reductions would be especially burdensome in developing countries. Support might be encouraged if the proceeds of the tax could be shared out among countries so as to reduce the overall impact on poorer nations. Along with these equity matters, real questions exist about the difficulties of monitoring and enforcing the tax. Self-monitoring by the individual countries is likely to be the

FIGURE 20-2
Estimates of the Reductions of CO_2 Emissions Produced at Different Tax Rates. *(Source: Based on William D. Nordhaus," A Survey of Estimates of the Cost of Reduction of Greenhouse Gas Emissions," paper prepared for the National Academy of Science, Committee on Science, Engineering, and Public Policy, February 1990.)*

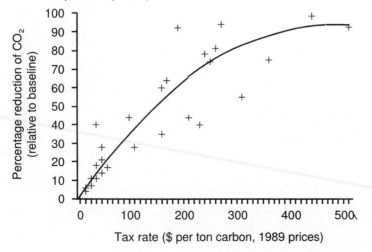

only practical solution to this issue, since it is unlikely that countries would willingly permit international monitoring efforts. Sanctioning countries that exceed their TDP quotas or fail to pay taxes would be difficult. The United Nations lacks executive power to enforce international environmental agreements. The International Court of Justice (ICJ) acts chiefly as a place for discussing disputes and lacks mechanisms to enforce rulings. This leaves enforcement up to a combination of moral pressure and whatever unilateral actions states might take, like trade sanctions.

The U.S., the country with the largest greenhouse-gas emissions, has so far not committed itself to specific CO_2 emission reductions. For many years the U.S. has opted for what is called a "no-regrets" policy. This means that it will adopt policies with desirable greenhouse effects only if they also have more immediate environmental impacts (including CFC reduction and energy consumption), so that if the greenhouse problem later turns out not to be serious, there will be "no regrets" for having adopted the policy.[13]

BIOLOGICAL DIVERSITY

Another problem that we have begun to appreciate in recent years is the world-wide reduction in diversity among the elements of the biological system. This can be discussed at several levels: diversity in the stock of genetic material, species diversity, or diversity among ecosystems. But the long-run health of the whole system requires that there be diversity among its parts. Biological uniformity produces inflexibility and weakened ability to respond to new circumstances; diversity gives a system the means to adapt to change.

The human population cannot maintain itself without cultivating certain species of animals and plants. But the continued vigor of this relationship actually depends also on the stock of wild species. About 25 percent of the prescription drugs in the developed societies are derived from plants.[14] Diseases are not static; they evolve in response to efforts made to eradicate them. Thus, wild species of plants constitute a vital source of raw material needed for future medicines. Wild species are also critical for agriculture. Through traditional plant and animal breeding, and even more through modern methods of biotechnology, genetic material and the qualities they entail may be transferred from wild species into cultivated ones. In 1979 a species of wild maize resistant to an important crop virus was discovered in a remote corner of Mexico. When transferred to species of domestic corn, this characteristic substantially enhanced the agricultural value of that crop.

The stock of species at any particular time is a result of two processes: the

---

[13] C. Boyden Gray and David B. Rivkin, Jr., "A No-Regrets Environmental Policy," *Foreign Policy*, 83, Summer 1991, pp. 47–65.

[14] U.S. Office of Technology Assessment, *Technologies to Sustain Tropical Forest Resources and Biological Diversity*, Washington, D.C., May 1992, p. 60.

random mutations that create new species of organisms and the forces that determine rates of extinction among existing species. Scientists currently estimate the number of extant species at between 5 and 10 million, of which about 1.4 million have been described. When a species goes extinct, we lose forever whatever valuable qualities that organism may have had. The normal, long-run rate of species extinction has been estimated at about 9 percent per million years, or .000009 percent per year.[15] Thus, this is the normal rate at which the information contained in the species stock vanishes. At several times in the geological past, the rate of extinctions has been very much higher. One of these times was the period, millions of years ago, during which the dinosaurs died off. Another is today. But while the earlier period was the result of natural causes, today's rapid destruction of the stock of species is due primarily to the actions of human beings.

Some species go extinct because they are overexploited. But the vast majority are under pressure because of habitat destruction. This comes primarily from commercial pressures to exploit other features of the land—logging off the trees for timber or wood, converting the land to agricultural uses, clearing the land for urban expansion, etc. This has been a particular problem in many third-world countries, which contain a disproportionately large share of the world's wild species, but which are also under great pressure to pursue modern economic development.

The information contained in the global stock of genetic capital has consistently been undervalued. This is partly because we do not know what is there or what portions of it may turn out to be important in the future. It is also because, almost by definition, it is impossible to know the value of the genes in a species that has gone extinct; we cannot miss something we never realized we had. But primarily the undervaluation of the stock of wild germ plasm is a function of the institutional structures governing the management of wild species. Whereas the market values of conventional products ensure that their production will be pursued with vigor, there are normally no comparable market values for the information contained in the wild gene pool.

In the U.S. the Endangered Species Act (ESA) of 1973 was enacted to help preserve individual species. When a species is listed as either "endangered" or "threatened," steps may be undertaken toward its preservation. This includes prohibitions on the "taking" (killing or wounding) of any individual of that species, and a requirement that actions authorized or funded by any federal agency not put in jeopardy the continued existence of the species. This ESA type of approach is pursued also in a number of other federal laws (such as the Bald Eagle Protection Act of 1940, the Marine Mammal Protection Act of 1972, and the Salmon and Steelhead Conservation and Enhancement Act of 1980). Each state also has its own endangered species laws. But while these laws have had some

---

[15] Edward O. Wilson (ed.), *Biodiversity*, National Academy Press, Washington, D.C., 1986.

success in preserving individual species, they are relatively ineffective at preserving diversity, which is not a matter of a single species but of a relationship among a large number of species.

The effective maintenance of biodiversity depends on the maintenance of habitats in amounts big enough that species may preserve themselves in complex biological equilibria. This involves first identifying valuable habitats and then protecting them from development pressures that are incompatible with preserving the resident species. In the U.S., a large network of reserved lands has been preserved in the public domain, in national parks, wilderness areas, wildlife refuges, and the like. The fact of the matter is, however, that the world's primary areas of genetic and species abundance and diversity are in developing countries in Central and South America, Africa, and Southeast Asia.[16]

Efforts have been made in some of these countries, sometimes vigorously and sometimes not, to protect areas of high biological value by putting them into some sort of protected status—sanctuaries, reserves, parks, etc. But here the situation is usually much more complicated by high population pressures. People who are struggling to get enough resources to achieve some degree of economic security may feel that something called biological diversity is not particularly relevant. Land reservation for species preservation is essentially a zoning approach, and it suffers the same fundamental flaw of that policy: It does not reshape the underlying incentives that are leading to population pressure on the habitats.

One suggestion that has been made to change this is to create a more complete system of property rights over genetic resources. At the present time, property rights are recognized for special breeder stock, genetically engineered organisms, and newly developed medicines. This provides a strong incentive for research on new drugs and the development of improved crops. But this incentive does not extend backward to the protection of wild gene plasm, especially in developing countries. Thus, the suggestion is to clarify property rights in wild species and let countries themselves exercise these property rights in world markets for genetic information.[17] By allowing them to sell the rights to parts of the genetic stock countries would have a way of realizing the values inherent in these stocks and so would be motivated to devote more effort and resources to their protection. Countries would also have stronger incentives to inventory and describe species that are still unknown.

In fact, events may be moving in this direction already. A contract was recently signed between Merck and Company, a U.S. pharmaceutical firm, and the Instituto Nacional de Biodiversidad of Costa Rica. The contract calls for an up-front payment of $1 million, plus royalties on discoveries of commercial value, while the Costa Rican agency will undertake steps to catalogue and

---

[16] The countries especially recognized for biological diversity are Mexico, Columbia, Brazil, Zaire, Madagascar, and Indonesia.

[17] See the discussion in Roger A. Sedjo, "Property Rights for Plants," *Resources*, 97, Resources for the Future, Washington, D.C., Fall 1989, pp. 1–4.

preserve biological resources in that country. The American Cancer Institute has negotiated contracts with Zimbabwe, Madagascar, and the Philippines for access to genetic resources in these countries. A British firm named Biotics is functioning as a broker between potential suppliers and buyers of genetic resources.[18]

Especially important is how this type of approach would filter down to affect individuals who are actually using the land. It is highly doubtful if substantial amounts of land could be put off limits to any type of development if population pressure continues high. So attention needs to be directed also at developing modes of commercial agriculture that are compatible with genetic and species preservation.[19] Production based on retaining natural habitat requires two things: that cultivators have secure property rights and that there be strong markets for the types of "crops" produced in this kind of system.

SUMMARY

In recent years we have seen the rise of truly global environmental problems, especially those dealing with the disruption of the global atmosphere. In these cases it is as if all the nations of the world were homeowners living around a small lake, each one dependent on the lake for water supply, but each one also using the lake for waste disposal.

Depletion of the earth's protective ozone layer has been a result of the widespread use of chlorofluorocarbons for refrigerants, solvents, and other uses. What once were regarded as miracle chemicals now have turned out to be life threatening. The increased ultraviolet radiation this will produce at the earth's surface is expected to increase skin cancers and eye cataracts, and have a substantial impact on agricultural production. In recent years chemical companies have had success in developing substitutes for CFCs. This greatly facilitated the signing of the Montreal Protocol, an international agreement among most of the nations of the world that will lead to a phaseout of the production and consumption of CFCs over the next few decades.

The global greenhouse effect will be more difficult to deal with. Burning fossil fuels has increased the CO_2 content of the atmosphere, affecting the earth's radiation balance and leading to an increase in mean global temperatures. Substantial impacts are expected on weather patterns around the globe. These are expected to disrupt agricultural operations in significant ways. A rise in the sea level will have profound impacts on coastal communities. A substantial attack on the phenomenon will require cutting back on the use of fossil fuels. Virtually all countries are dependent to a greater or lesser extent on fossil fuels to power their economies. Thus, we must emphasize cost-effective policies to improve energy efficiency and to switch to fuels that emit less CO_2. It is likely to

[18] R. David Simpson and Roger A. Sedjo, "Contracts for Transferring Rights to Indigenous Genetic Resources," *Resources*, 109, Fall 1992, Resources for the Future, Washington, D.C., pp. 1–5.

[19] Tim Swanson, "Conserving Biological Diversity," in David Pearce (ed.), *Blueprint 2: Greening the World Economy*, Earthscan Press, London, 1991, pp. 181–208.

be many years before a meaningful international agreement can be reached on this problem.

The destruction of biological diversity is a subtler global problem, but it may be just as costly in the long run. Dealing with this problem will require greater efforts to preserve habitat and develop agriculture that is compatible with species preservation. Effective action will mean doing something about the incentives that currently lead to species destruction.

QUESTIONS FOR FURTHER DISCUSSION

1 Many countries are adopting a "wait and see" strategy on CO_2 emissions and atmospheric warming. What would a rational "wait and see" strategy look like?

2 When CFCs were first introduced 50 years ago, their benefits were obvious, and nobody appreciated the long-run impacts they might have. How do we guard ourselves against unforeseen long-run effects like this?

3 In the absence of a worldwide agreement to reduce CO_2 through a carbon tax, how effective might it be if just one, or a small number, of countries instituted a tax unilaterally?

4 Rather than placing a tax on fuels or the carbon content of fuels, taxes might be put on fuel-using items, such as "gas-guzzling" cars, less efficient appliances, or houses with poor insulation. Which type of tax would be more efficient?

5 Global warming is predicted to affect countries differently, which is one reason it is difficult to get all countries to agree on a global CO_2 treaty. Do you think it will be easier to get agreement *after* the results start showing up in different countries?

6 How many different formulas can you think of for allocating a reduction in global CO_2 among the nations of the world? Compare and contrast these in terms of efficiency and equity.

SELECTED READINGS

Benedick, Richard: *Ozone Diplomacy*, Harvard University Press, Cambridge, Mass., 1991.

Binswanger, Hans: "Brazilian Policies that Encourage Deforestation in the Amazon," *World Development*, 19(7), 1991, pp. 821–829.

Broome, John: *Counting the Cost of Global Warming*, White Horse Press, Isle of Harris, U.K., 1992.

Chandler, William U. (ed.): *Carbon Emission Strategies: Case Studies in International Cooperation*, World Wildlife Fund and the Conservation Foundation, Washington, D.C., 1990.

Chapman, Duane, and Thomas Drennen: "Equity and Effectiveness of Possible CO_2 Treaty Proposals," *Contemporary Policy Issues*, 8(3), July 1990, pp. 16–25.

Cline, William R.: *Global Warming: Estimating the Economic Benefits of Abatement*, Organization for Economic Cooperation and Development, Paris, 1992.

Dixon, John A., and Paul B. Sherman: *Economics of Protected Areas: A New Look at Benefits and Costs*, Island Press, Washington, D.C., 1990.

Donaldson, D. M., and G. F. Betteridge: "The Relative Cost Effectiveness of Various Measures to Ameliorate Global Warming," *Energy Policy*, 18(6), July/August 1990, pp. 563–571.

Dudek, Daniel J., and Alice LeBlanc: "Offsetting New CO_2 Emissions: A Rational First Greenhouse Policy Step," *Contemporary Policy Issues*, 8(3), July 1990, pp. 29–42.

Firor, John: "The Straight Story About the Greenhouse Effect," *Contemporary Policy Issues*, 8(3), July 1990, pp. 3–15.

Lashof, Daniel A., and Dennis A. Tirpak: *Policy Options for Stabilizing Global Climate*, Hemisphere Publishing Company, New York, 1990.

Manne, Alan S., and Richard G. Richels: *Buying Greenhouse Insurance, The Economic Cost of CO_2 Emission Limits*, MIT Press, Cambridge, Mass., 1992.

Marchant, Gary E.: "Freezing Carbon Dioxide Emissions: An Offset Policy for Slowing Global Warming," *Environmental Law*, 22(2), 1992, pp. 623–683.

Marland, G.: *The Prospects of Solving the CO_2 Problem Through Global Reforestation*, U.S. Department of Energy, DOE/NBB-0082, Washington, D.C., 1988.

McNeely, Jeffrey: *Economic and Biological Diversity, Developing and Using Economic Incentives to Conserve Biological Resources*, Columbia University Press, New York, 1989.

Nordhaus, William D.: "The Costs of Slowing Climate Change: A Survey," *The Energy Journal*, 12(1), 1991, pp. 37–65.

Victor, David G.: "Limits of Market-Based Strategies for Slowing Global Warming: The Case of Tradable Permits," *Policy Science*, 24(2), May 1991, pp. 199–222.

CHAPTER 21

INTERNATIONAL
ENVIRONMENTAL
AGREEMENTS

In the last chapter we discussed several global environmental issues. In one of these—stratospheric ozone depletion—nations of the world have signed an international agreement to reduce emissions of the main chemicals causing the problem. Today many nations are urging a treaty on global warming. As countries continue to grow, more and more environmental problems will spill beyond national borders—not just these global cases, but also a rising number of environmental externalities inflicted by people in one country on those of another. So while environmental policies continue to evolve within individual countries, there will be a growing need to develop multicountry attacks on environmental problems.[1] In the final chapter of this book, therefore, we will take a look at some of the economic issues involved in the creation of international environmental agreements.

International environmental policy has a distinctly different character from national policies. The most salient difference is that on the international level there are no effective enforcement institutions. Within any country authoritative regulatory authorities can be called upon to enforce whatever laws are passed, though this does not imply by any means that all environmental laws will be adequately enforced. But on the international level enforcement authorities do not exist. Thus, environmental policy at this level consists essentially of international agreements among sovereign states, where each country pledges to follow certain specified courses of action as regards emissions reductions or other steps for environmental protection. Enforcement then has to be carried out either through voluntary means like moral suasion, or else through retaliation by whatever pressure a country or group of countries may be able to exert on recalcitrant countries.

In this chapter we review some of the main features of international environ-

---

[1] The international scope of many environmental problems was first highlighted by the 1972 United Nations Conference on the Human Environment (the "Stockholm Conference" or first "earth summit"), which led to the United Nations Environment Program (UNEP) and the 1992 global environmental conference in Brazil.

mental agreements, focusing especially on the incentive situations facing countries that are considering an agreement. We begin with a brief descriptive section that will show the great variety of international environmental agreements that have been concluded to date. We then discuss cases that involve just two countries, followed by the case of multiple-country agreements. We will end with a discussion of an issue that will become increasingly important as national economies continue to grow: the environmental quality implications of international trade.

GENERAL ISSUES

The history of international agreements on natural resource matters goes back many centuries, to the time when countries sought to agree on navigation rules to cover ocean passages. In the twentieth century international treaties have proliferated as a result of the rapidly expanding list of environmental problems involving multiple countries. Table 21-1 shows a partial list of current multilateral agreements pertaining to natural and environmental resources. Numerous treaties have been concluded on marine pollution, beginning with oil-pollution agreements and later extending to more general pollution-control measures. Although much attention has been given recently to the issue of protecting the resources of biological diversity, the first international treaties on flora and fauna were actually made decades ago. By now there are many such treaties, including the important 1973 convention on international trade in endangered species.[2]

The agreements listed in Table 21-1 are all multilateral treaties, involving anywhere between 3 and 161 countries. Note the difference in almost all cases between the year of adoption and the year of entry into force. An agreement once "adopted" does not come into force, i.e., does not become binding, until it has been signed by the appropriate political authorities of a certain proportion of the participating countries. Thus, some agreements, including the comprehensive convention on the "Law of the Sea," have never come into force. A standard international agreement will contain provisions specifying the actions to be undertaken by each signatory country, as well as numerous institutional and logistical matters, such as what kind of governing agency is to be established, how its work is to be funded, what information is to be shared, and so on.

Many of the multilateral treaties are actually regional in scope. This includes, for example, the water and air pollution-control treaties among the countries of Europe. The United Nations has sponsored a number of regional agreements involving countries bordering particular seas (Mediterranean, Red Sea, southeastern Pacific, western African coastal waters, Caribbean, etc.). Besides the multilateral treaties there are hundreds of bilateral treaties, addressing the

---

[2] A "treaty" is an agreement in which all the details have presumably been worked out and expressed in the document to which each signing country agrees. A "convention" is an agreement in which parties agree on a general framework that is expected to be supplemented in the future by one or more "protocols" that work out the details.

TABLE 21-1

SELECTED INTERNATIONAL ENVIRONMENTAL AGREEMENTS

Name of agreement	Date of adoption	Date of entry into force	Number of signatories
Marine Pollution			
International Convention for the Prevention of Pollution of the Sea by Oil (as amended 11/4/62 and 10/21/69)	1954	1958	71*
Agreement for Cooperation in Dealing with Pollution of the North Sea by Oil	1969	1969	8
International Convention on Civil Liability for Oil Pollution Damage (as amended)	1969	1975	63
International Convention Relating to Intervention on the High Seas in Cases of Oil Pollution Casualties	1969	1975	54
Convention on the Prevention of Marine Pollution by Dumping of Wastes and Other Matter ("London Dumping")	1972	1975	
International Convention for the Prevention of Pollution from Ships, 1973	1973	—	19
Convention on the Prevention of Marine Pollution from Land-Based Sources	1974	1978	13
Convention for the Protection of the Mediterranean Sea Against Pollution	1976	1978	18
International Rivers			
Protocol Concerning the Constitution of an International Commission for the Protection of the Moselle Against Pollution	1961	1962	3
Agreement Concerning the International Commission for the Protection of the Rhine Against Pollution	1963	1965	6
Convention on the Protection of the Rhine Against Chemical Pollution	1976	1979	6
Convention Creating the Niger Basin Authority and Protocol Relating to the Development Fund of the Niger Basin	1980	1982	8
Flora and Fauna			
European Treaty on the Conservation of Birds Useful to Agriculture	1902	1902	11
Convention Relative to the Preservation of Fauna and Flora in Their Natural State	1933	1936	54
Convention of Nature Protection and Wildlife Preservation in the Western Hemisphere	1940	1942	19

*Four countries have renounced the Convention.

TABLE 21-1
SELECTED INTERNATIONAL ENVIRONMENTAL AGREEMENTS *(Continued)*

Name of agreement	Date of adoption	Date of entry into force	Number of signatories
Flora and Fauna			
International Convention for the Regulation of Whaling (as amended)	1946	1948	43[†]
International Convention for the Protection of Birds	1950	1963	10
International Plant Protection Convention	1951	1952	92
International Convention for the High Seas Fisheries of the North Pacific Ocean (as amended)	1952	1953	3
Convention on Fishing and Conservation of the Living Resources of the High Seas	1958	1966	35
International Convention for the Protection of New Varieties of Plants (as amended)	1961	1968	17
Convention on the African Migratory Locust	1962	1963	16
African Convention on the Conservation of Nature and Natural Resources	1968	1969	29
European Convention for the Protection of Animals During International Transport	1968	1971	20
Benelux Convention on the Hunting and Protection of Birds (as amended)	1970	1972	3
Convention on Wetlands of International Importance Especially as Waterfowl Habitat	1971	1975	50
Convention for Conservation of Antarctic Seals	1972	1978	12
Convention on International Trade in Endangered Species of Wild Fauna and Flora	1973	1975	96
Agreement on Conservation of Polar Bears	1973	1976	5
Convention on Conservation of Nature in the South Pacific	1976	—	3
Nuclear			
Convention on Third Party Liability in the Field of Nuclear Energy (as amended)	1960	1968	14
Vienna Convention of Civil Liability for Nuclear Damage	1963	1977	10
Treaty Banning Nuclear Weapon Tests in the Atmosphere, in Outer Space and Under Water	1963	1963	117
Treaty on the Prohibition of the Emplacement of Nuclear Weapons and Other Weapons of Mass Destruction on the Sea-Bed and the Ocean Floor and in the Subsoil Thereof	1971	1972	79
Convention on Early Notification of a Nuclear Accident	1986	1986	31

[1]Three withdrawals

TABLE 21-1
SELECTED INTERNATIONAL ENVIRONMENTAL AGREEMENTS *(Continued)*

Name of agreement	Date of adoption	Date of entry into force	Number of signatories
Air Pollution			
Convention on Long-Range Transboundary Air Pollution	1979	1983	30
Protocol to the 1979 Convention on Long-Range Transboundary Air Pollution on Long-Term Financing of the Co-operative Programme for Monitoring and Evaluation of the Long-Range Transmission of Air Pollutants in Europe (EMEP)	1984	1988	27
Protocol to the 1979 Convention on Long-Range Transboundary Air Pollution on the Reduction of Sulphur Emissions or Their Transboundary Fluxes by at Least 30 Percent	1985	1987	18
Protocol to the 1979 Convention on Long-Range Transboundary Air Pollution Concerning the Control of Emissions of Nitrogen Oxides or Their Transboundary Fluxes	1988	—	24
Vienna Convention for the Protection of the Ozone Layer	1985	1988	36
Montreal Protocol on Substances that Deplete the Ozone Layer	1987	1989	43
Miscellaneous			
The Antarctic Treaty	1959	1961	32
European Convention on the Protection of the Archaeological Heritage	1969	1970	17
Convention on the Prohibition of the Development, Production and Stockpiling or Bacteriological (Biological) and Toxin Weapons, and on Their Destruction	1972	1975	101
Convention Concerning the Protection of the World Cultural and Natural Heritage	1972	1975	98
Treaty for Amazonian Co-operation	1978	1980	8
Convention on the Conservation of Antarctic Marine Living Resources	1980	1982	21
Convention Concerning Occupational Safety and Health and the Working Environment	1981	1983	9
United Nations Convention on the Law of the Sea	1982	—	161
Convention on the Regulation of Antarctic Mineral Resource Activities	1988	—	6
Basel Convention on the Control of the Transboundary Movements of Hazardous Wastes and Their Disposal	1989	—	116

Source: Scott Barrett, "Economic Analysis of International Environmental Agreements: Lessons for a Global-Warming Treaty," in Organization for Economic Cooperation and Development, *Responding to Climate Change, Selected Economic Issues,* Paris, 1991.

environmental problems of just two countries. The U.S. and Canada have concluded a number of bilateral agreements, including those dealing with acid rain and with the management of the Great Lakes. The U.S. and Mexico have also worked out several environmental agreements dealing with hazardous waste shipments, the use of the Colorado and Rio Grande rivers, and other matters.

THE ECONOMICS OF INTERNATIONAL AGREEMENTS

When international agreements are being negotiated, the focus is usually on political issues. This is natural, since what is going on are complex negotiations among sovereign states. But underlying the political interactions—national sovereignty, political assertiveness, creative diplomacy, etc.—lie many bedrock economic factors that affect the perceived benefits and costs accruing to the different participants and the incentives they have for entering into environmental agreements. In the next few sections we will discuss some of these issues.

Bilateral Agreements

Let us first consider the case of just two countries—call them Country A and Country B. B is downwind from A, so SO_2 emissions from A contribute to acid rain both at home and in B. In B, SO_2 emissions contribute to acid rain only in that country; because of prevailing wind patterns, there is no reciprocal acid rain externality inflicted by B upon A. This situation is pictured in Figure 21-1. It shows the marginal abatement costs in A (MAC) and the marginal damage functions associated with the emissions of that country. Marginal damages arising in A itself are shown as MD_A, while MD_T are aggregate marginal damages for both A and B. The marginal damages in B from A's emissions, in other words, are $MD_T - MD_A$. If A were managing its emissions without regard to the externalities produced in B, it would regard point e_1 as the efficient level of emissions.

But for emissions in A to be internationally efficient, it is necessary to take into account the effects on B. The "globally efficient" level of emissions is e_2. The added attainment costs in A to achieve this further reduction in emissions is an amount equal to the area $(d + f)$. But this is more than offset by a reduction in damages totaling $(c + d + f)$, of which f represents damage reduction in A, while $(d + c)$ is damage reduction in B.

We saw in Chapter 10 that negotiations between polluters and those damaged can result in efficient emission levels, given that property rights are clearly defined and that transactions costs are minimal. On the international level, direct negotiations between private parties involved are essentially ruled out, because under international law private citizens of one country do not have the right to sue private citizens in another country. Instead, negotiations must be carried out among political authorities of the two countries. This is where diplomacy comes in because, in the example above, the reduction in A's emissions from e_1 to e_2 involves negative net benefits *in that country*—added costs of $(d + f)$ and reduced

Emissions of Country A

FIGURE 21-1
Bilateral Transboundary Pollution and the Economics of Reaching an
Agreement.

damages of only *f*. So, in effect, authorities would be asking people in Country
A to make a sacrifice to benefit people in another country. This kind of thing
happens all the time within individual countries. But across countries the institutions of policy are weaker, depending essentially on diplomatic skills and
whatever international sanctioning can be carried out through moral, economic,
or political means.

According to the precedents in international law, cases like this are supposed
to be covered by a polluter pays principle (PPP). The Trail Smelter case of 1935
is an important source of that precedent. Trail Smelter was a metal refinery in
British Columbia whose SO_2 discharges damaged farm crops across the border
in the U.S. The tribunal finding in favor of the farmers stated that under the
principles of international law "... no State has the right to use or permit the use
of its territory in such a manner as to cause injury by fumes in or to the territory
of another."[3] This declaration was embodied in the Declaration of the 1972
United Nations Conference on the Human Environment (the first "earth summit"), which covered all types of transboundary pollution. Most international
agreements seek to incorporate the polluter pays principle.

---

[3] Quoted in William A. Nitze, "Acid-Rain: A United States Perspective," in Daniel Barstow
Magraw (ed.), *International Law and Pollution*, University of Pennsylvania Press, Philadelphia, 1991,
p. 346.

But since international agreements are voluntary, we may suppose that individual countries will never sign any agreement that makes them worse off. In other words, each prospective signatory must regard the agreement as leaving them at least as well off as they would be without it. In our example, this means that we may have to shift partially to a "victim pays principle" (VPP). The net loss to A in going from e_1 to e_2 would have to be compensated by Country B. A has added abatement costs of $(d + f)$ in going from e_1 to e_2, but it also experiences added benefits (reduced damages) of f, so its extra costs are equal to d. Since B's damage reduction totals $(c + d)$, it could compensate A for these costs and still be ahead by an amount equal to c.

There are many issues that come up in international bargaining about environmental externalities of this type. Bargaining depends critically on the perceptions by each country of its own marginal damages and marginal abatement costs, as well as on how convincing it can be in expressing these views to other countries. In the case of Figure 21-1, for example, A has an interest in convincing B that the added abatement costs of going from e_1 to e_2 are very high, while its own domestic benefits from this move are quite low. B, on the other hand, has an interest in convincing A that it would experience real reductions in damages from a reduction in emissions, but not so high that it could afford very large compensation payments. Countries engaged in negotiations of this type will usually be involved at the same time in negotiations on other problems, as well as with negotiations with other countries. Thus, they will be concerned with the net outcome of all these negotiations, and this could dictate a position on this one issue quite different from what one would expect solely on the basis of the merits of this particular case. John Krutilla's study of the agreement between the U.S. and Canada over use of the Columbia River, for example, indicates that the distribution of costs in the treaty was primarily related to the desire of the U.S. to stimulate economic development in Canada.[4]

Multilateral Agreements

Let us now consider a situation where a number of countries all contribute to an environmental problem that affects all of them. Examples are acid rain pollution stemming from SO_2 emissions, pollution of a regional sea by riparian countries, stratospheric ozone depletion through emissions of CFCs, and the greenhouse effect stemming from CO_2 emissions. In these cases the damages suffered by each country are related to the level of total emissions, present and probably past, of all the countries. From an economic standpoint there are both efficiency and equity issues in these types of international agreements. There is the basic efficiency question of balancing overall benefits and costs. For most international agreements, especially the truly global ones, there are enormous difficulties in

---

[4] John V. Krutilla, *The Columbia River Treaty: A Study of the Economics of International River Basin Development*, Johns Hopkins Press, Baltimore, Md., 1968.

the way of estimating total global benefits with any accuracy. The impacts are too massive, and there are extraordinarily difficult problems of trying to compare benefits across countries that are in very different economic circumstances. So on the benefit side we usually settle for an enumeration of the physical impacts of various environmental changes and some idea of how these impacts might be distributed among countries. This means that most of the emphasis is likely to be placed on abatement costs and their distribution.

There are two major issues related to cost: (1) what methods to adopt in various countries to meet the performance required by the agreements and (2) how to share the overall costs among the participating countries. Of course, the questions are related because cost-effective measures undertaken by signatory countries can substantially reduce the costs of the overall program that must be shared. The importance of cost distribution arises because these global emission control agreements supply global public goods. The benefits accruing to any particular country from, say, a 20 percent cut in CO_2 will be the same no matter where, and by whom, the CO_2 is reduced.[5] Thus, each country has some incentive to get other countries to bear as much of the total global abatement costs as they can. The costs accruing to each country can be affected in two ways:

- Through the choice of the rule by which overall emission reductions will be distributed among countries, and
- By payments going from some countries to others to help offset control costs among the recipients. These are transfer payments, sometimes called, in the jargon of economics, "side payments."

We will analyze this situation with a simple application of "game theory." Game theory is not specifically about games, like baseball or poker, although it can be applied to them. It is about making decisions when the outcomes of the decisions depend in part on the actions undertaken by intelligent opponents. More generally, game theory is about making choices in situations where the payoffs from the choices depend on the choices made by other people. A farmer trying to decide when to harvest a crop is not facing a game situation. Nature is not on the other side trying to make decisions that will improve its position relative to the farmer; nature just is. But a farmer trying to decide when to sell her or his crop is involved in a game because many other farmers are trying to make the same decision, and the outcome of one of them, in terms of, say, the price received, will depend in part on the decisions made by the other farmers as well as her or his own decision. The reason it is applicable here is that when one country acts, its impact on the regional or global environment will depend on how other nations also act.

Suppose several countries are contributing to acid deposition in a particular

---

[5] This does not mean that the benefits will be the same for all countries. We know this is not true because of the way the global meteorological system works. Only that the effects on any particular country are invariant to the source of the reduction.

region. Acid deposition comes largely from emissions of sulfur dioxides, which in the atmosphere are oxidized into sulfates, and which then are removed, sometimes well downwind, by rainfall in the form of acid rain, or by dry deposition on plants or the land surface. To keep things extremely simple so we can get to the essence of the problem, suppose there are just two countries emitting SO_2 in this region.[6] Each is damaged by the resulting acid deposition, and each would benefit from a cutback in SO_2 emissions. But the benefits obtained by each country depend not only on their own SO_2 reductions but also on those made by the other country.

Let us assume, for purposes of simplicity, that each country has two available strategies: (1) to emit at current levels and (2) to reduce emissions by some substantial amount. The top panel of Figure 21-2 shows the (gross) benefits that would accrue to each country from these two options. Since each country has two alternatives, there are four possible outcomes, so the results can be depicted in a 2 × 2 matrix as shown. On the axes of the matrix appear the two strategies available to each country, while in the interior of the matrix appear the benefits accruing to each, expressed, say, in millions of dollars per year. The first number in each cell represents the benefit accruing to Country A, while the second is the benefit to B, of the combination of strategies chosen. Thus, for example, if A chooses to emit at the uncontrolled level, while B chooses to reduce emissions, benefits to A and B will be, respectively, 2 and 1. If they were both emitted in an uncontrolled fashion (i.e., high emissions for both), "benefits" would be −1 to each country.

If we consider only these gross benefits, the best strategy for each is to reduce its emissions; the payoff would be 4 to A and 8 to B, and neither could improve its position by doing otherwise. But this reckons without control costs. Suppose that to reduce emissions it costs A $3 million per year and B $6 million per year. We must now deduct these control costs from the gross benefit figures. Doing so gives the results shown in panel (b) of Figure 21-2. We have now a set of net payoffs that have a very interesting pattern, characteristic of many international environmental problems. They show a situation where individual countries, each choosing strategies that are best for themselves, can bring about a situation that is worse for everybody.

Suppose Country A is trying to decide whether to devote the resources to reducing emissions. It must do this without knowing with certainty what Country B will choose to do. But in this case it will not make any difference. Suppose B were to choose to control its emissions. In this case A would get the highest net benefits by choosing not to control its emissions (net benefits of $2 million rather than $1 million). On the other hand, suppose B did not control its emissions. Here

---

[6] It may seem odd to analyze a case of multinational agreements using a two-country example, but since the discussion has to do with the incentives a country faces in trying to decide whether or not to conclude an agreement, this is in fact not a drawback. One good way to think of it is for A to represent a single country and for B to represent all other countries as a whole.

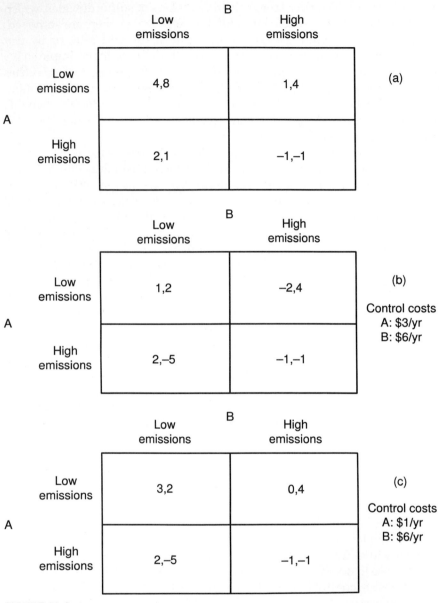

FIGURE 21-2
Payoffs Received by Two Countries Considering an International Environmental Agreement.

again, A is better off choosing the no-control option (losses of –$1 million rather than –$2 million). Thus, regardless of B's choice, A's best choice is not to control emissions. You can examine B's choices in the same way, with the same result: Regardless of A's choice, B will be better off by choosing to continue with high emissions. Thus, neither country will reduce emissions, which will result in both of them realizing lower net benefits than if they were both to reduce their emissions.

This is a paradoxical result. Both countries, acting individually, choose strategies leading to a situation having total benefits of –$2 million, whereas if both had controlled emissions, total global net benefits would have been $3 million. The reason for the paradox is the following: Although both countries would be better off if they both reduced emissions, compared to both emitting at the high level, each would be still better off if they could be in a situation where the other country controls emissions while they do not. You can see this most clearly by starting from a position of low emissions for each country. Under these circumstances B would be getting benefits of $2 million per year. But if A is reducing its emissions, B could do even better by *not* reducing emissions. Although total emissions would go up, savings in control costs would allow it to reap net benefits of $4 million per year. What it is doing is essentially taking a free ride on A's emission-control efforts. But, of course, with each country trying to free ride on the other's control efforts, neither country will end up reducing emissions, so we end up in the lower right of the figure, with everybody worse off.

The main job of any environmental agreement is to get countries to agree to reduce their emissions and to resist the temptation to try and garner even larger net benefits by free riding on the control efforts of others.[7]

Of course things can change over time, making it easier or harder to bring about agreement. Suppose that technological change in Country A results in a lowering of control costs there from $3 per year to only $1 per year. Now the payoff matrix changes to the one shown in panel (c) of Figure 21-2. And here we have a substantial change in incentives. Because of the reduced control costs, it now is rational for Country A to reduce emissions, regardless of what B does. If B controls emissions, A's net benefits would go from $2 to $3, while if B does not control emissions, A's net benefits go from –$1 to $0. This is a situation where it is efficient for one country to engage in emission reduction on its own even if other countries do not follow suit. Note that in panel (c) it is still individually rational for B not to control emissions, implying that the two countries, in the absence of any agreement, would end up in the northeastern corner of the payoff matrix, with A at the lower emission level and B with uncontrolled emissions.

The two countries may try to develop an agreement whereby B also commits to reducing emissions. This would certainly be of benefit to A, but it nevertheless remains that B will be individually better off by refusing to reduce emissions. This, of course, is where international diplomacy comes in—convincing Country B that it should reduce emissions even though it may see its interests lying elsewhere. One approach that may be useful is moral suasion; Country B could be branded an opportunist in taking advantage of others' efforts to clean up the

---

[7] Back in Chapter 4 we introduced the notions of public goods and common-property resources, and indicated how the temptation to free ride would lead to market failure in these kinds of situations. Here we are simply applying the same ideas to international environmental agreements.

global commons. Other possibilities suggest themselves. With A already committed to reducing emissions, B's net benefits are $2 higher when it persists with high emissions rather than reduces emissions. Country A may have a way of otherwise retaliating on B, perhaps by placing restrictions on exports from B to A, in order to drive up the cost to B of continuing at the high emission level. If the total benefits of this option can be brought below $2 through trade sanctions, Country B would find it in its interest to reduce its emissions.

Another approach might be for Country A to offer financial incentives, or some other side payments, to B to get it to reduce emissions. If B reduces emissions, A would gain by $3 per year, while B would have a reduction in net benefits of $2. A payment of, say, $2.5 from A to B to reduce emissions would make both countries better off. Exhibit 21-1 shows a news clip that is relevant to this situation. It is not a negotiation between two countries but between two groups of countries, the third-world nations (the "group of 77") and the developed countries. The negotiations at the 1992 Rio conference focused on aid that the developed nations (the "north") would give to third-world countries (the "south") to finance environmentally sound economic development. The comments of one negotiator are comments that Country B might make to Country A in the example: The north (Country A) cannot achieve the full set of environmental goals by itself, and if it wishes to have greater participation by the south (Country B) it must treat the south "more generously."

Another possibility might be technology transfer. Suppose that by transferring pollution-control technology from A to B, the emission abatement costs of the latter could be reduced from $6 to $2. Recalculating the payoffs in the game matrix shows that if A reduces its emissions, it is now efficient for B also to reduce emissions. Of course, in actuality, international environmental agreements normally involve more than two countries. The reason for limiting the analysis to just two was to be able to show in simple fashion the nature of the underlying incentive situation. When multiple countries are involved, the same incentives are involved but it becomes more complicated to analyze them clearly. In this case, each country is in a game with all the other countries, and what is usually involved is trying to get a big enough subset of them to agree on a common course of action.[8] Thus, each country must assess its net gains from joining an agreement along with some number of other countries and compare them with their net gains if they stay out of the agreement. With each country facing different benefits and abatement costs, the overall results may be hard to discern. It's also true that when multiple countries are involved, the patterns of negotiating technology transfers, bribes, sanctions, etc., that will motivate individual coun-

---

[8] When negotiations are taking place among a large number of countries, it often happens that subsets will form agreements among themselves to act jointly with respect to the others. For example, in working up to the Montreal Protocol, a group of four countries formed the "Toronto Group" (that's where they had their first meeting) which developed a unified position and encouraged the rest to act.

EXHIBIT 21-1

NEGOTIATORS IN RIO AGREE TO INCREASE AID TO THIRD WORLD VITAL TO GLOBAL CLEANUP

Non-Industrialized Lands Drop Demand for Vow to Double the Funds by Year 2000.

By Paul Lewis
Special to The New York Times

RIO DE JANEIRO, June 13 — Less than 24 hours before the end of the Earth Summit, North and South finally compromised today on principles that encourage richer countries to increase aid to the third world, clearing the way for approval of the global cleanup plan that is the centerpiece of the conference.

After 13 days of negotiations, third-world countries finally abandoned an attempt to obtain a specific commitment from the industrialized world to nearly double aid to poorer countries by the year 2000. The money would pay for the plan to guarantee that the third world's development is environmentally sound.

Instead, the third-world countries accepted that the United States is unwilling to be bound by a longstanding United Nations goal of raising aid levels to 0.7 percent of its economic output and that Britain, Japan, Germany and several other big aid donors refused to commit themselves to achieve that target by any particular date.

Third-World Leverage

But in this unusual North-South exchange, in which the third world almost for the first time enjoys genuine leverage, the industrialized Northern countries have committed themselves to reach that target "as soon as possible" and pledged themselves to see the environmental goals set forth in the plan, known as Agenda 21, are fully met. That implies they must find more money for the third world.

In addition, the North agreed to highlight in a statement adopted today that a new international body created to monitor compliance with environmental targets accepted at the talks will also enforce the promises they have made to give the third world more assistance.

On Sunday, during the summit talks' concluding session, Pakistan, the current chairman of the Group of 77, as the third-world countries are known at United Nations meetings, will express those nations' disappointment at the financial offers the North has made so far.

And Pakistan will implicitly remind the North that it cannot significantly improve the environment without Southern cooperation. Their statement will warn that without the additional assistance it has been promised, the developing South will be unable to develop in an environmentally sound manner.

"We are saying we cannot generate the new resources needed to start up Agenda 21 without new help, so if the North wants us to meet those goals they must treat us more generously," Pakistan's United Nations representative, Jamsheed A. Marker, commented after the meeting.

Third-world countries say they think that they are owed that assistance because the developed northern nations are responsible for most of the damage industrialization has inflicted on ecological systems so far. Third-world countries say the North should be willing to pay for the limits it has put on the development of poorer countries.

The compromise on financing Agenda 21 was finally hammered out by a small group of developed and developing countries today and awaits approval by a wider plenary meeting of all the 178 nations attending.

According to the compromise declaration, industrial countries that have not met the 0.7 percent aid target "agree to augment their aid programs in order to reach that target as soon as possible and to endure a prompt and effective implementation of Agenda 21."

tries to join an agreement become much more complicated than with just two countries.

International Agreements in Practice

The game theory matrices and payoff structures discussed in the last section are useful to depict the incentives facing individual countries that might be considering an international environmental agreement. But it's impossible to use them to predict the results of such agreements because international negotiations on environmental treaties are only one dimension of the full set of international interactions among countries. How an individual country behaves in bargaining over, e.g., a treaty reducing CO_2 emissions depends not only on the merits of that particular problem but on the whole gamut of international relationships in which it is involved. If it is involved simultaneously in negotiations on other matters, it may be more concerned with the total outcome and be willing to compromise in some areas in return for concessions in others. In addition, when countries are involved in many negotiations they may be concerned particularly with shoring up their reputations as hard bargainers, which may lead them to behave in certain cases in ways that look to be inconsistent with their self-interest. The outcomes of treaty negotiations depend on context and the strategic possibilities that the times have made available, which is another reason we use the simple models of the previous section for depicting the underlying economic logic of international agreements, and not for actually predicting events.

Cost-Effectiveness in Multinational Agreements

The discussion above was couched in terms of an international agreement to secure certain emission reductions from each of the participating countries. This is the way most international agreements are shaped; there is a strong bias toward treating each country in the same way by applying the same reduction goals to each. Only in the recent CFC-reduction treaty (the Montreal Protocol) has there been a differentiation among countries, and here it was a simple distinction between developed countries as a group and developing ones as another group. Within each broad group the CFC-reducing targets are the same for each country.

We have discussed the efficiency aspects of this approach many times throughout the preceding chapters. The main problem is that it does not take advantage of differences in marginal abatement costs among sources, meaning countries in this case. To accomplish this would require larger cutbacks from nations with relatively low marginal abatement costs and less reduction from those with higher costs. But these nonuniform reductions appear to run counter to the principle of treating everybody alike. Suppose each of two countries would benefit the same amount from cutbacks in emissions, but have different marginal abatement cost functions. These are pictured in Figure 21-3. The marginal abatement costs of Country A rise much more steeply than those of Country B. Current

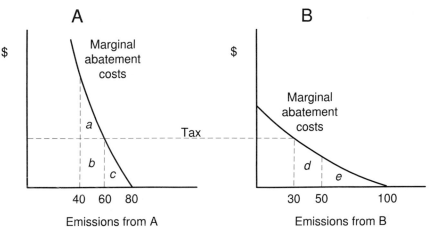

FIGURE 21-3
Cost-Effectiveness in International Agreements.

emissions are 100 from A and 80 from Country B. An agreement requiring a uniform 50 percent reduction would put A at 40 and B at 50. But the costs of achieving this would be much higher for A ($a + b + c$) than for B ($d + e$). Country A might very well fail to agree with uniform reductions when there would be such a large discrepancy in total abatement costs. If it were desired nonetheless to specify a treaty in terms of specific cutbacks from each, they could perhaps be set so that the total abatement costs of each country were the same (assuming each country had reliable information about the other country's abatement costs), but this would violate the uniform emission reduction principle; nor would it be cost-effective.

When abatement costs differ among countries, in other words, it will be difficult to achieve cost-effectiveness if there is strong allegiance to the same type of equiproportionate rule. One possible way of doing this would be to institute a global transferable discharge permit system (TDP), whereby the number of permits given out in the initial distribution met some equiproportionate reduction principle, with trading then moving the distribution of permits toward one that more nearly satisfied the equimarginal rule. Whether this is even remotely feasible in today's international political climate is highly doubtful.

INTERNATIONAL TRADE AND THE ENVIRONMENT

Another connection between international affairs and the environment is through patterns of international trade. Profound changes are occurring in the world economy and in the economic interactions among the 200 or so countries that make it up. It once appeared simple: Industrialized countries produced manufactured goods, some of which they traded among themselves, and some of which they exported to developing countries in return for primary products.

But in the latter part of the twentieth century things are changing dramatically through the rise of the multinational company, owing allegiance to customers and suppliers, not to particular countries; the development of a truly global, integrated, financial market; the appearance of briskly expanding industrial countries from among the previously less developed group; the development of huge new regional trading blocs, southeast Asia, North America, the European Community; and the massive change in the old Socialist bloc and its reintegration into the world economy.

The full range of environmental implications of these changes will be hard to sort out. We can summarize the general issues as follows:

- The reciprocal interaction of trade flows and environmental protection. How will increased trade affect environmental damages in trading countries, and how will national efforts to protect the environment impact on international trade? These issues can be looked at from the standpoint of just two trading countries, or from that of more comprehensive trading networks.
- The question of whether, and under what conditions, an individual country may legitimately put restrictions on its trade, by restricting either imports or exports, in the name of preserving environmental quality.
- The circumstances under which the world community as a whole can effectively improve the world environment by placing restrictions on international trade.

Free Trade vs. Environmental Trade Restrictions

Over the last four decades or so the countries of the world have made special efforts to foster free and unhindered trade. This has been done in the name of improved economic welfare. Free trade allows countries to prosper by giving them expanded markets for things on which they have a comparative advantage in production, and gives them greater opportunities to procure goods for which they have a comparative disadvantage. The prosperity of many countries, both developed and developing, depends critically on international trade. The problem is whether the emphasis on moving toward free trade may make it more difficult for countries to protect the environmental resources that they value.

The main international institution governing trade is the General Agreement on Tariffs and Trade (GATT), which came into being in the late 1940s. Its purpose is to set out a list of rules and procedures to be followed by nations in their international trade relationships. It is especially aimed at reducing the barriers to trade, to get nations to refrain from putting tariffs and quotas on imports or subsidies on exports, and in general to move toward conditions of free trade among the world's nations, almost all of whom are GATT signatories. One section of the GATT agreement also outlaws what are called nontariff barriers such as excessive inspection requirements, excessive product specifications, and the like. But there is a very broad list of conditions that are exceptions to GATT rules; for example, governments are allowed to set restrictions in order to achieve the "protection of human, animal or plant life or health," and the "conserving of natural resources."

Consider the analysis of Figure 21-4. It shows the behavior of producers and consumers of a product in a particular country that also relies upon imports for a large part of its supply. The demand curve (D) is domestic demand for the product, while S is the domestic supply curve; i.e., the supply curve of domestic producers. Without imports, price and quantity would settle at the intersection of these two curves. But let us introduce an import supply curve, labeled I. This supply curve is actually horizontal because we assume that a relatively large amount of this item is produced in the world, so this importing country could import larger or smaller quantities without affecting the world price. With the addition of imports, this country now ends up with a total consumption at q_0. Domestic production, meanwhile, is q_1. The difference, $(q_0 - q_1)$, is imported. The domestic price is also equal to the world price.

The GATT rules allow governments to set import restrictions on products that have direct health implications, as long as it is done in a nondiscriminatory way. Suppose the good in question is automobiles, the use of which causes air pollution. Setting tight emission standards increases the production costs for automobiles and therefore their prices. The importing country may require imported cars to meet strict emission standards, which would have the effect of lifting the import supply curve to I'. This is nondiscriminatory as long as domestic producers are held to the same standards, in effect shifting the domestic

FIGURE 21-4
Effects of Environmental Regulations on Domestic Production and Imports.

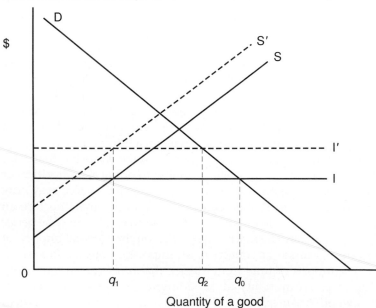

supply curve up to S'. The result of this is first to lower the total quantity of cars purchased by people in this country, from q_0 to q_2. Second, assuming that the emission standards increase the costs of domestic supply as much as they do imports, the pollution control applied to both domestically produced cars and imports will leave domestic production unchanged but reduce imports, from ($q_0 - q_1$) to ($q_2 - q_1$).

In this case the purpose of the strict emission standards was to protect human health. When it is not a matter of human health but, say, one of environmental aesthetics, the case may be less clear. In recent years Denmark placed a ban on the use of nonrefillable drink containers. This was presumably done in the name of reducing litter. It also proceeded to ban the importation of nonrefillable containers from neighboring European countries. These countries objected, saying that the ban was really just a way of protecting Danish drink producers from competition. But in this case the European court ruled in favor of Denmark.

Things become decidedly less clear when it is not the consumption of a good that causes pollution but its production. Suppose that a country produces a product, in the process also causing a certain amount of air pollution. Suppose further that it adopts an air pollution program to curb emissions from this industry. Suppose even further that the item is produced in other countries and imported, but that the countries from which it is imported do not undertake any type of pollution-control efforts. The producers of the importing country are now at somewhat of a cost disadvantage because they have to operate under environmental constraints and their competitors don't. Can this country legally (i.e., within the GATT rules) put a tariff on the importation of this item to equalize the cost burden? One might argue that this would tend to protect people in other producing countries who are exposed to air pollution from the firms making this item, but GATT rules presumably allow countries to take action only to protect their own citizens, not those in other countries. And a tariff against the good may have no impact on lessening air pollution in other countries; the only way that could be done would be through explicit pollution-control programs in those countries, and there is certainly no way for the first country to enforce such programs.

The interrelationship of environmental issues and trade problems has recently raised the possibility that environmental standards will be co-opted by those whose interest is primarily to protect themselves against international competition. It is a familiar sight to see representatives of some industry that feels threatened by producers in other countries appealing to political authorities for a tariff or some other barrier against imports. Environmental factors may now give them added ammunition. If they can plausibly argue that the foreign competitors are causing damage to environmental resources, they may be better able to justify the trade barrier. The key is whether the environmental impacts of foreign producers are legitimately a concern of the importing country. In a recent case, the U.S. barred imports of tuna from Mexico that had been caught using methods that cause excessive mortality among dolphins. The question that needs to be sorted out is whether Americans really do have a substantial willingness to pay for protecting dolphins, wherever they may be, or whether this was just being used as an excuse by U.S. tuna companies to shield themselves from foreign competition.

Trade Restrictions to Advance International Environmental Goals

In some cases international environmental agreements involve trade agreements.

Montreal Protocol   As part of the international effort to reduce ozone-depleting chemicals, the Montreal Protocol prohibits exports of controlled substances (basically CFCs) from any signatory nation to any state not a party to the Protocol. Furthermore, signatory countries may not import any controlled substance from any nonsignatory state. The purpose of these trade regulations is to ensure that production of CFCs and other ozone-depleting chemicals does not simply migrate to nonsigning countries.

London Guidelines on Chemicals   As we have discussed many times throughout this book, one major obstacle to controlling environmental pollutants is lack of information—information on pollutant emissions, damages, control costs, etc. On the international level the problem is even more severe than it is domestically because of the different ways countries have approached pollution-control problems and the vastly different information requirements and availabilities among them. In 1989, 74 countries agreed to adopt the "London Guidelines for the Exchange of Information on Chemicals in International Trade," under the auspices of the United Nations Environment Program (UNEP). The guidelines require that any country banning or severely restricting a particular chemical notify all other countries of its actions, so that the latter can assess the risks and take whatever action they deem appropriate. The guidelines also encourage "technology transfer," stating that states with more advanced chemical testing and management technology should share their experience with countries in need of approved systems.

Basel Convention on Transboundary Movements of Hazardous Wastes This 1989 agreement is aimed at the issue of international trade in hazardous wastes. It does not prohibit this trade but does put requirements on it, especially information requirements. It puts an obligation on countries to prohibit any export of hazardous wastes unless appropriate authorities in the receiving country have consented in writing to the import and unless it has assurances that the waste will be properly disposed of. It also has provisions on notification, cooperation on liability matters, transmission of essential information, and so on.

Convention on International Trade in Endangered Species of Wild Fauna and Flora (CITES)   There is currently a large international trade in flora and fauna, dead and alive: roughly 500,000 live parrots, 10 million reptile skins, 10 million cactus plants, 350 million ornamental fish, 50 million furs, etc., each year.[9] CITES came into force in 1975. Under it, each country is supposed to establish its own permit system to control the movement of wildlife exports and imports. It is also supposed to designate a management body to handle the permit system and a scientific body to determine whether trade is likely to be detrimental to the survival of the species. Species are separated into three classes: I—species threatened with extinction, in which commercial trade is banned and noncommercial trade regulated; II—species that may become threatened if trade is not held to levels consistent with biological processes, for which commercial trade is allowed with conditions; and III—species that are not currently threatened but for which international cooperation is appropriate, for which trade requires permits.

The endangered species trade is considered by many to be a qualified success, though much more remains to be done, especially in improving national permit processes. There are some simple lessons to be derived from considering this type of trade restriction, which we will pursue by looking at an international supply-and-demand model of an endangered species. The same conclusions can apply to other cases; e.g., export restrictions on logs to protect rain forests. Consider the market model of Figure 21-5. This shows the world, or aggregate, supply and export-demand conditions for a species of wildlife. The supply function is based on the costs of hunting, transporting, processing, recordkeeping, etc., necessary to bring the wildlife to the point of export. It is an aggregate supply function made up of the supply function of the various countries in which that species grows. The demand function shows the quantities that the export market will take at alternative prices. The intersection of the two functions shows the market price and quantity of this type of wildlife that will be traded in a year's time.

Two types of trade constraints could be used to reduce the quantity of this species moving in international trade: export controls and import controls. Each will reduce the quantity traded, but they will have very different impacts on price. Export controls work by essentially making exporting more costly, which has the effect in Figure 21-5 of shifting the supply function upward from supply curve S_0 to supply curve S_1. The result of this is a reduction in quantity traded, in this case to q_1. The amount that quantity falls depends on the extent to which the supply curve shifts up and also on the slope of the demand function; the steeper this slope the less will quantity contract. But this approach to trade reduction also leads to an increase in price, from the original price p_0 to p_1. This price increase could have several impacts, depending essentially on property rights. Imagine a case where the endangered species is subject to private ownership, either by individuals or by small, well-defined groups. Perhaps the habitat of the species is under private ownership, for example. The higher price for the

[9] Laura H. Kosloff and Mark C. Trexler, "The Convention on International Trade in Endangered Species: Enforcement Theory and Practice in the United States," *Boston University International Law Journal*, 5, Fall 1987, pp. 327–361.

Quantity of trade in an endangered species

FIGURE 21-5
Effects of Trade Policy on the International Market in an Endangered Species.

species now becomes a signal for its owners to be more concerned about its safety and welfare because, in this circumstance, efforts at conservation will have a direct market payoff.

The added price will have the opposite effect, however, when property rights in the endangered species are ill-defined or completely absent, which is the usual case. Most of the habitats for the world's endangered species are common property, in the sense that either everybody has the right to enter and harvest the animal or plant, or that, as in public parks, authorities are unable to keep people from taking the species "illegally." We saw, in Chapter 4, the problem to which common-property resources are prone: Since other users cannot be kept out, nobody has an incentive to conserve the resource. It's either use it or lose it to some other harvester. The increased price for the endangered species in this case will work against conservation. It will encourage higher rates of extraction, higher rates of poaching on common-property habitats, and thus higher pressure on the endangered species.

Controlling imports, on the other hand, drives the price downward. Import controls have the effect of reducing the demand for the imported species. In Figure 21-5 this leads to a backward shift in demand, from D_0 to D_1. This has been drawn so as to give the same quantity reduction as before. But in this case the price drops to p_2. The effect of this price decrease is to decrease the incentives discussed in the previous paragraphs. In particular, where endangered species are subject to common-property exploitation, the lower price would lead to reduced pressure to harvest and less rapid population decline. Something of this sort has happened recently as a result of an international ban on ivory imports. The ban has led to a substantial drop in the world price of ivory, which has reduced the pressure of poachers on the elephant in many parts of Africa.

SUMMARY

With environmental issues becoming more international in scope and significance, there will be increasing interest among countries to address these issues with international agreements. International agreements are much more problematic than domestic policies because enforcement is much weaker on the international level. International externalities are essentially of two types. In the first, one country's pollution causes damage in another country. Here the problem of who pays (polluter or victim) when agreements are negotiated is of primary relevance. In the second, each country's emissions affect all countries, including itself. Here the basic problem is how to get individual countries to forgo attempts to free ride on the control efforts of others. The strength of the incentive to free ride depends on a country's perceived benefits and costs of an international agreement, together with whatever "side payments," money subsidies, technology transfers, etc., are part of the agreement.

In recent years serious issues have arisen over the relationship of environmental damage and international trade. Some people see free international trade as being environmentally destructive and are in favor of placing restrictions on trade in the name of environmental values. In these cases there is a problem in sorting out legitimate and justified concern for elements of the environment, especially in another country, from purely commercial interests that are seeking shelter from international competition.

QUESTIONS FOR FURTHER DISCUSSION

1 The game theory presentation in Figure 21-2 shows each country with only two options: high emissions or low emissions. How different does the game become when what is at issue is not whether to cut back or not, but how much to cut back?
2 In panel (b) of Figure 21-2 each country has an incentive to free ride on the other's emission reductions. Suppose we institute a deposit-refund system to enforce emission reductions. At the beginning of the year they both pay a deposit, which they get back at the end of the year if their emissions are still low. If there can be only one deposit amount for both countries, what should it be?
3 We talked about "side payments" in the form of technology transfers, given to developing countries to lower the costs to them of joining international environmental agreements. What other types of side payments might be effective in this regard?
4 Suppose Country A imports a product from Country B, and that Country B lacks environmental laws governing the production of the item. Under what conditions might Country A be justified in putting a tariff on the imported item?

5 If all countries adopted the same emission standards in similar industries, would this tend to equalize production costs and put each country on the same footing with respect to environmental matters?

6 "International environmental agreements are very much shaped by the fact that enforcement on the international level is difficult, if not impossible." Discuss.

7 In a recent case, the U.S. attempted to put restrictions on the importation of tuna from Mexico because Mexican fishers used methods that destroyed relatively large numbers of dolphin when catching the tuna. These fishing methods are illegal for U.S. tuna fishers. Is this trade restriction efficient? Is it equitable?

SELECTED READINGS

Andresen, Steinar, and Willy Ostreng: *International Resource Management, The Role of Science and Politics*, Belhaven Press, London, 1989.

Barrett, Scott: "Economic Analysis of International Environmental Agreements: Lessons for a Global Warming Treaty," in Organization for Economic Cooperation and Development, *Responding to Climate Change: Selected Economic Issues*, Paris, 1991, Chapter 3.

Barrett, Scott: "The Problem of Global Environmental Protection," *Oxford Review of Economic Policy*, 6(1), Spring 1990, pp. 68–79.

Charnovitz, Steve: "Trade Negotiations and the Environment," in *International Environment Reporter*, Bureau of National Affairs, Washington, D.C., March 11, 1992, pp. 144–148.

d'Arge, Ralph C., and Allen V. Kneese: "State Liability for International Environmental Degradation: An Economic Perspective," *Natural Resource Journal*, 20(3), July 1980, pp. 427–450.

Flinterman, Cees, Barbara Kwiatkowska, and Johan G. Lammers: *Transboundary Air Pollution, International Legal Aspects of the Co-operation of States*, Martinus Nijhoff Publishers, Dordrecht, Holland, 1986.

Low, Patrick (ed.): *International Trade and the Environment*, Discussion Paper No. 159, World Bank, Washington, D.C., 1992.

Mäler, Karl-Göran: "International Environmental Problems," in Dieter Helm (ed.), *Economic Policy Toward the Environment*, Blackwells, Oxford, England, 1991, pp. 156–201.

Organization for Economic Cooperation and Development: *Economics of Transfrontier Pollution*, Paris, 1976.

Rubin, Seymour J., and Thomas R. Graham (eds.): *Environment and Trade, The Relation of International Trade and Environmental Policy*, Allanheld, Osmun Publishers, Totowa, N.J., 1982.

INDEX OF NAMES

INDEX OF SUBJECTS